MEMORY AND NATION

Yr Athro Huw Pryce

MEMORY AND NATION

Writing the History of Wales

EDITED BY
REBECCA THOMAS, SADIE JARRETT
AND KATHARINE OLSON

UNIVERSITY OF WALES PRESS
2025

© The Contributors, 2025

Reprinted 2025

All rights reserved. No part of this book may be reproduced in any material form (including photocopying or storing it in any medium by electronic means and whether or not transiently or incidentally to some other use of this publication) without the written permission of the copyright owner except in accordance with the provisions of the Copyright, Designs and Patents Act. Applications for the copyright owner's written permission to reproduce any part of this publication should be addressed to the University of Wales Press, University Registry, King Edward VII Avenue, Cardiff CF10 3NS.

www.uwp.co.uk

British Library Cataloguing-in-Publication Data
A catalogue record for this book is available from the British Library.

ISBN 978-1-83772-234-1
eISBN 978-1-83772-235-8

The rights of the Contributors to be identified as authors of this work have been asserted in accordance with sections 77 and 79 of the Copyright, Designs and Patents Act 1988.

For GPSR enquiries please contact:
Easy Access System Europe Oü, 16879218. Mustamäe tee 50, 10621, Tallinn, Estonia. *gpsr.requests@easproject.com*

Printed and bound by CPI Group (UK) Ltd,
Croydon, CR0 4YY

Typeset by Marie Doherty

CONTENTS

Acknowledgements ⁚ Diolchiadau — vii
List of Figures and Tables ⁚ Rhestr o Ffigyrau a Thablau — ix
Abbreviations ⁚ Byrfoddau — xi
Notes on Contributors ⁚ Bywgraffiadau Cyfranwyr — xiii

Introduction ⁚ Rhagymadrodd — 1

PART I: TEXTS AND THEIR HISTORIES
RHAN I: TESTUNAU A'U HANES

1. How did Medieval Welsh Chroniclers Find their Information? — 13
   David Stephenson

2. The Reception of Gerald of Wales in Welsh Historical Texts — 36
   Georgia Henley

3. Trioedd Ynys Prydein fel Testunau Hanes — 56
   Nia Wyn Jones

4. From Llandaf to Liber A: Welsh Charters and Diplomatics in Long Perspective — 92
   Charles Insley

5. The Development of Old Welsh Boundary Clauses — 118
   Ben Guy

PART II: HISTORY AND IDENTITY
RHAN II: HANES A HUNANIAETH

6. Naming and National Identity: The Monastic Orders in Late Medieval Ireland and Wales Compared — 149
   David E. Thornton

7. Gwystlon yn *De gestis Britonum* a *Brut y Brenhinedd* — 172
   Rebecca Thomas

8. The Context of *Laudabiliter* in the Works of Gerald of Wales — 194
   Thomas M. Charles-Edwards

9	The Medieval Bishops of Bangor and the Writing of Welsh History *Shaun McGuinness*	203
10	'Pinnacles of Preaching' and Men of 'Bold Learning'?: Protestant Reforms, the History of Wales, and the Elizabethan Bishops of Bangor – A Case Study of Nicholas Robinson (*c*.1530–1585) *Katharine Olson*	232

PART III: MEMORY AND NATION
RHAN III: COF CENEDL

11	Antiquarianism, Ancestry and 'Ancient Britons': Welsh Historical Consciousness, Cultural Patronage and the Identity of the Gentry, *c*.1800–1920 *Shaun Evans*	271
12	'Th'enlighten'd crowd with grateful raptures glow': History, Setting Norms and Victorian Modernity in Eisteddfod Competitions, 1815–1855 *Marion Löffler*	299
13	'Ireland Raids Wales': Pageants and the Performance of History in the 1920s *Paul O'Leary*	329
14	Tattooing Owain Glyndŵr? The Body, Memory and Interpretations of Welsh History *Mari Elin Wiliam with the assistance of Owen Hurcum*	352
15	'Time Present and Time Past': Narrating Nation and Society in Welsh Historical Writing, 1970–2010 *Neil Evans*	379
16	Llyfryddiaeth o Weithiau Cyhoeddedig Huw Pryce ⁝ A Bibliography of the Published Works of Huw Pryce (hyd 2023 ⁝ to 2023) *Rhidian Griffiths*	404

Manuscripts Cited ⁝ Rhestr o Lawysgrifau	423
Selected Bibliography ⁝ Llyfryddiaeth Ddethol	425
Index ⁝ Mynegai	461

ACKNOWLEDGEMENTS : DIOLCHIADAU

We would like to take the opportunity here to acknowledge the generous support received by those involved in the production of this volume. It has been a pleasure working with the whole team at University of Wales Press. We are grateful for their enthusiastic support for the project, advice and assistance throughout the process. We would also like to thank the anonymous reviewer for their helpful feedback. Finally, we owe a great debt of gratitude to Professor Nancy Edwards for her assistance during the early stages of this volume's development.

Hoffem gymryd y cyfle hwn i gydnabod cefnogaeth hael y sawl sydd wedi bod ynghlwm â chynhyrchu'r gyfrol hon. Mae wedi bod yn bleser gweithio gyda thîm Gwasg Prifysgol Cymru. Rydym yn ddiolchgar am eu cefnogaeth brwdfrydig i'r prosiect, ac am bob cyngor a chymorth. Hoffem ddiolch hefyd i'r darllenydd di-enw am eu sylwadau defnyddiol. Yn olaf, mae arnom ddyled arbennig i'r Athro Nancy Edwards am ei chymorth yn ystod camau cynnar datblygu'r gyfrol.

LIST OF FIGURES AND TABLES ⁝ RHESTR O FFIGYRAU A THABLAU

Figures ⁝ Ffigyrau

Chapter 12
Figure 1	Title page of *Seren Gomer* (1823)	301
Figure 2	The bardic frame made by Thomas Price 'Carnhuanawc'	308

Chapter 14
Figure 1	Tattoo of Conwy Castle on Glennydd	359
Figure 2	Owain Glyndŵr traditional tattoo	361
Figure 3	Welsh pin-up girl	367
Figure 4	'Sexy St David's Pinup'	368
Figure 5	Bearded Welsh lady	369

Tables ⁝ Tablau

Chapter 2
Table 1	Contents and structure of London, British Library, Cotton Julius D. x	37
Table 2	Contents and structure of London, British Library, Harley 3725	47

Chapter 5
Table 1	Definite articles preceding consonants in the boundaries of the Book of Llandaf	138

Chapter 6
Table 1	Welsh names of Augustinian canons	159
Table 2	Irish names of Augustinian canons	162

ABBREVIATIONS : BYRFODDAU

AWR	Huw Pryce with Charles Insley (ed.), *Acts of Welsh Rulers 1100–1283* (Cardiff, 2005)
BBCS	*Bulletin of the Board of Celtic Studies : Bwletin y Bwrdd Gwybodau Celtaidd*
ByT (RB) : *ByT* (LlC)	*Brut y Tywysogyon*, Red Book of Hergest version, ed. and trans. Thomas Jones (Cardiff, 1955)
ByT (P20)	*Brut y Tywysogyon*, Peniarth 20 version, ed. Thomas Jones (Cardiff, 1941); trans. Thomas Jones (Cardiff, 1952)
CBT	Cyfres Beirdd y Tywysogion
CMCS	*Cambridge Medieval Celtic Studies*, 1–25 (1981– summer 1993); *Cambrian Medieval Celtic Studies*, 26– (winter 1993–)
DGB	*De gestis Britonum*, ed. and trans. Michael D. Reeve and Neil Wright, *Geoffrey of Monmouth, the History of the Kings of Britain: an Edition and Translation of De gestis Britonum [Historia Regum Britanniae]* (Woodbridge, 2007)
GPC	*Geiriadur Prifysgol Cymru*
NLWJ	*National Library of Wales Journal*
ODNB	*Oxford Dictionary of National Biography*
RSTC	Revised Short Title Catalogue
STC	Short Title Catalogue
TRHS	*Transactions of the Royal Historical Society*
WHR	*Welsh History Review : Cylchgrawn Hanes Cymru*

NOTES ON CONTRIBUTORS :
BYWGRAFFIADAU CYFRANWYR

Professor **Thomas Charles-Edwards** is Emeritus Professor of Celtic at Oxford University. His books include *Early Irish and Welsh Kinship* (Oxford, 1993), *Early Christian Ireland* (Cambridge, 2000) and *Wales and the Britons, 350–1064* (Oxford, 2012).

Mae'r Athro **Thomas Charles-Edwards** yn Athro Celtaidd Emeritws ym Mhrifysgol Rhydychen. Mae ei lyfrau yn cynnwys *Early Irish and Welsh Kinship* (Rhydychen, 1993), *Early Christian Ireland* (Caer-grawnt, 2000) a *Wales and the Britons, 350–1064* (Rhydychen, 2012).

Dr **Shaun Evans** is Lecturer in Welsh and Early Modern History at Bangor University and Director of the Institute for the Study of Welsh Estates. His research focuses on gentry culture, tenant-landowner relations, estate landscapes and the country house in Wales *c.*1500–1900.

Mae Dr **Shaun Evans** yn Ddarlithydd mewn Hanes Modern Cynnar a Hanes Cymru ym Mhrifysgol Bangor ac yn Gyfarwyddwr Sefydliad Ymchwil Ystadau Cymru. Canolbwyntia ei ymchwil ar ddiwylliant bonedd, y berthynas rhwng tirfeddianwyr a thenantiaid, tirweddau ystadol a phlastai yng Nghymru *c.*1500–1900.

Dr **Neil Evans** has published widely on a variety of topics in modern Welsh and British history. He is an honorary research fellow at Bangor University, a Fellow of the Royal Historical Society and a vice-president of *Llafur*. With Prof. Huw Pryce, he edited *Writing a Small Nation's Past: Wales in Comparative Perspective, 1850–1950* (London, 2013) and is currently editing the University of Wales Press book series Race, Ethnicity: Wales and the World jointly with Prof. Charlotte Williams.

Mae Dr **Neil Evans** wedi cyhoeddi yn eang ar bynciau amrywiol yn hanes y Gymru a Phrydain fodern. Mae'n gymrawd ymchwil er anrhydedd ym Mhrifysgol Bangor, yn Gymrawd o'r Gymdeithas Hanes

Frenhinol ac yn is-lywydd *Llafur*. Gyda'r Athro Huw Pryce, golygodd *Writing a Small Nation's Past: Wales in Comparative Perspective, 1850–1950* (Llundain, 2013) ac mae'n cyd-olygu cyfres Gwasg Prifysgol Cymru 'Race, Ethnicity: Wales and the World' gyda'r Athro Charlotte Williams.

Dr **Ben Guy** is Assistant Professor in Celtic in the Department of Anglo-Saxon, Norse and Celtic at the University of Cambridge. His work ranges across the history, language and literature of medieval Wales. He is the author of *Medieval Welsh Genealogy: An Introduction and Textual Study* (Woodbridge, 2020).

Mae Dr **Ben Guy** yn Athro Cynorthwyol mewn Celteg yn yr Adran Eingl-Saesneg, Llychlyneg a Chelteg, Prifysgol Caer-grawnt. Mae wedi gweithio ar hanes, iaith a llenyddiaeth y Gymru ganoloesol. Efe yw awdur *Medieval Welsh Genealogy: An Introduction and Textual Study* (Woodbridge, 2020).

Dr **Georgia Henley** is Associate Professor of English at Saint Anselm College in Manchester, New Hampshire. Her work concerns the literary history and manuscript cultures of medieval Wales and the March of Wales. She is the author of *Reimagining the Past in the Borderlands of Medieval England and Wales* (Oxford, 2024) and the co-editor, with Dr Joey McMullen, of *Gerald of Wales: New Perspectives on a Medieval Writer and Critic* (Cardiff, 2018).

Mae Dr **Georgia Henley** yn Athro Cysylltiol mewn Saesneg yng Ngholeg Sant Anselm ym Manceinion, New Hampshire. Mae ei gwaith yn canolbwyntio ar hanes llenyddiaeth a diwylliant llawysgrifol Cymru a'r Gororau yn yr Oesoedd Canol. Hi yw awdur *Reimagining the Past in the Borderlands of Medieval England and Wales* (Rhydychen, 2024), a chyd-olygodd, gyda Dr Joey McMullen, *Gerald of Wales: New Perspectives on a Medieval Writer and Critic* (Caerdydd, 2018).

Dr **Charles Insley** is Senior Lecturer in Medieval History at the University of Manchester. Recent publications include '"Between the Ribble and the Mersey": Lancashire before Lancashire and the Irish Sea World', *Anglo-Norman Studies*, 44 (2021); 'Boundaries of Language and Languages of Boundaries in Cornish Charters of the Tenth and Eleventh

Centuries', in R. Gallagher, E. Roberts and F. Tinti (eds), *The Languages of Early Medieval Charters: Latin, Germanic Vernaculars and the Written Word* (Leiden, 2020). Between 1995 and 1997 he was Prof. Huw Pryce's research assistant on the *Acts of Welsh Rulers* project.

Mae Dr **Charles Insley** yn Uwch-ddarlithydd mewn Hanes Canoloesol ym Mhrifysgol Manceinion. Ymhlith ei gyhoeddiadau diweddar mae '"Between the Ribble and the Mersey": Lancashire before Lancashire and the Irish Sea World', *Anglo-Norman Studies*, 44 (2021); 'Boundaries of Language and Languages of Boundaries in Cornish Charters of the Tenth and Eleventh Centuries', yn R. Gallagher, E. Roberts a F. Tinti (goln), *The Languages of Early Medieval Charters: Latin, Germanic Vernaculars and the Written Word* (Leiden, 2020). Rhwng 1995 a 1997 bu'n ymchwilydd cynorthwyol ar brosiect *Acts of Welsh Rulers* yr Athro Huw Pryce.

Dr **Sadie Jarrett** is a historian specialising in early modern Wales. Most recently, she was a career development fellow at The Queen's College, Oxford.

Mae Dr **Sadie Jarrett** yn hanesydd sy'n arbenigo ar Gymru'r cyfnod modern cynnar. Yn ddiweddar, bu'n gymrawd datblygu gyrfa yng Ngholeg y Frenhines, Rhydychen.

Dr **Nia Wyn Jones** lectures in History at Bangor University, where she completed her thesis on historical writing in medieval Wales. Before that, she studied at the universities of Oxford and Cambridge.

Mae Dr **Nia Wyn Jones** yn darlithio mewn Hanes ym Mhrifysgol Bangor, lle cwblhaodd ei doethuriaeth ar ysgrifennu hanes yn y Gymru ganoloesol. Cyn hynny, astudiodd ym mhrifysgolion Rhydychen a Chaer-grawnt.

Dr **Rhidian Griffiths** was Keeper of Printed Books and then Director of Public Services at the National Library of Wales. He has published on the history of music in Wales, as well as the Middle Ages.

Bu Dr **Rhidian Griffiths** yn Geidwad Llyfrau Printiedig ac yna yn Gyfarwyddwr Gwasanaethau Cyhoeddus yn Llyfrgell Genedlaethol

Cymru. Mae wedi cyhoeddi ar hanes cerddoriaeth yng Nghymru yn ogystal â'r Oesoedd Canol.

Dr **Marion Löffler** is Reader in Welsh History and History at Cardiff University, where she researches and teaches the history of eighteenth- and nineteenth-century Wales in its British, empire and global contexts, focusing on cultural and political exchanges and influences. She has published widely on the nineteenth-century reverberations of the French Revolution of 1789 in Wales. Her monographs are *The Literary and Historical Legacy of Iolo Morganwg* (Cardiff, 2007), *Welsh Responses to the French Revolution: Press and Public Discourse* (Cardiff, 2012) and *Political Pamphlets and Sermons from Wales* (Cardiff, 2014).

Mae Dr **Marion Löffler** yn Ddarllenydd mewn Hanes Cymru a Hanes ym Mhrifysgol Caerdydd, lle mae'n ymchwilio a dysgu hanes Cymru yn y ddeunawfed ganrif a'r bedwaredd ar bymtheg yn ei gyd-destun Prydeinig, ymerodraethol a byd-eang, gan ganolbwyntio ar gyfnewid a dylanwadau diwylliannol a gwleidyddol. Mae wedi cyhoeddi'n eang ar atseiniau Chwyldro Ffrengig 1789 yng Nghymru. *The Literary and Historical Legacy of Iolo Morganwg* (Caerdydd, 2007), *Welsh Responses to the French Revolution: Press and Public Discourse* (Caerdydd, 2007) a *Political Pamphlets and Sermons from Wales* (Caerdydd, 2014) yw ei monograffau.

Dr **Shaun McGuinness** is an Honorary Research Associate at Bangor University. His PhD thesis, entitled 'The Bishops of Bangor and their *Acta*, 1092–1306', includes a first edition of Bangor episcopal *acta* which has been published by the Canterbury and York Society: *Bangor Episcopal Acta, 1092–1306* (Woodbridge, 2025).

Mae Dr **Shaun McGuinness** yn Gymrawd Ymchwil er Anrhydedd ym Mhrifysgol Bangor. Mae ei ddoethuriaeth, 'The Bishops of Bangor and their *Acta*, 1092–1306', yn cynnwys y golygiad cyntaf o *acta* esgobaethol Bangor a gyhoeddwyd gan Gymdeithas Caer-gaint ac Efrog yn 2025: *Bangor Episcopal Acta, 1092–1306* (Woodbridge, 2025).

Professor **Paul O'Leary** is Emeritus Professor at Aberystwyth University and was co-editor of the *Welsh History Review*. Among his publications is *Claiming the Streets: Processions and Urban Culture in South Wales,*

c. *1830–1880* (Cardiff, 2012). He is co-editor, with Dr Neil Evans and Prof. Charlotte Williams, of *A Tolerant Nation? Revisiting Ethnic Diversity in a Devolved Wales* (Cardiff, 2015) and, with Dr Beth Jenkins and Dr Stephanie Ward, of *Gender in Modern Welsh History: Perspectives on Masculinity and Femininity in Wales from 1750 to 2000* (Cardiff, 2023).

Mae'r Athro **Paul O'Leary** yn Athro Emeritws ym Mhrifysgol Aberystwyth a bu'n cyd-olygu *Cylchgrawn Hanes Cymru*. Mae ei gyhoeddiadau yn cynnwys *Claiming the Streets: Processions and Urban Culture in South Wales, c.1830–1880* (Caerdydd, 2012). Cyd-olygodd, gyda Dr Neil Evans a'r Athro Charlotte Williams, *A Tolerant Nation? Revisiting Ethnic Diversity in a Devolved Wales* (Caerdydd, 2015), a, gyda Dr Beth Jenkins a Dr Stephanie Ward, *Gender in Modern Welsh History: Perspectives on Masculinity and Femininity in Wales from 1750 to 2000* (Caerdydd, 2023).

Dr **Katharine Olson** is Associate Professor of History at San Jose State University and an Honorary Research Associate at Bangor University. She has published on medieval and early modern Britain and Ireland and is an expert in the history, literature, and culture of medieval and early modern Wales and the Marches. Her work focuses on religion, society, culture, the history of the book, and the Reformation.

Mae Dr **Katharine Olson** yn Athro Cysylltiol mewn Hanes ym Mhrifysgol San Jose State ac yn Gymrawd Ymchwil er Anrhydedd ym Mhrifysgol Bangor. Mae wedi cyhoeddi ar Brydain ac Iwerddon yr Oesoedd Canol a'r cyfnod modern cynnar ac mae'n arbenigo ar hanes, llenyddiaeth, a diwylliant y Gymru ganoloesol a modern cynnar a'r Gororau. Canolbwyntia ei gwaith ar grefydd, cymdeithas, diwylliant, hanes y llyfr, a'r Diwygiad.

Dr **David Stephenson**'s early academic career focused on the study of medieval Wales, on which he wrote his DPhil thesis, published as *The Governance of Gwynedd*, and used his tenure of the Sir Maurice Bowra Research Fellowship of Wadham College, Oxford to lay the foundations for future work on medieval Powys. His *Medieval Powys* was awarded the inaugural Francis Jones Prize for Welsh History in 2017, and he has published extensively on the medieval Welsh chronicles, as well as wider aspects of the subject in volumes such as *Medieval Wales c.1050–1332* (Cardiff, 2019) and *Patronage and Power in the Medieval Welsh March* (Cardiff, 2021).

Ar gychwyn ei yrfa academaidd, canolbwyntiodd Dr **David Stephenson** ar ymchwilio i'r Gymru ganoloesol. Cyhoeddwyd ei draethawd DPhil fel *The Governance of Gwynedd* yn 1984, a defnyddiodd ei gyfnod fel Cymrawd Ymchwil Syr Maurice Bowra yng Ngholeg Wadham, Rhydychen, i osod y seiliau ar gyfer gwaith ar y Bowys ganoloesol. Enillodd ei *Medieval Powys* Wobr Francis Jones am Hanes Cymru yn 2017, ac mae wedi cyhoeddi'n helaeth ar groniclau canoloesol Cymreig ac agweddau eraill o hanes Cymru mewn cyfrolau megis *Medieval Wales c.1050–1332* (Caerdydd, 2019) a *Patronage and Power in the Medieval Welsh March* (Caerdydd, 2021).

Dr **Rebecca Thomas** is a Senior Lecturer in Medieval History at Cardiff University, and an expert in the history, culture and literature of medieval Wales. She is author of *History and Identity in Early Medieval Wales* (Cambridge, 2022).

Mae Dr **Rebecca Thomas** yn Uwch-ddarlithydd mewn Hanes Canoloesol ym Mhrifysgol Caerdydd, ac yn arbenigo ar hanes, diwylliant a llenyddiaeth y Gymru ganoloesol. Hi yw awdur *History and Identity in Early Medieval Wales* (Caer-grawnt, 2022).

Dr **David E. Thornton** is Assistant Professor of European History at Bilkent University, Turkey. He has a PhD from the department of Anglo-Saxon, Norse and Celtic, Cambridge, and a MA in Welsh History from the University of Bangor (when it was still the University College of North Wales). His current research interests focus on the prosopography of monastic orders in late medieval Britain and Ireland.

Mae Dr **David E. Thornton** yn Athro Cysylltiol mewn Hanes Ewropeaidd ym Mhrifysgol Bilkent, Twrci. Mae ganddo ddoethuriaeth o'r Adran Eingl-Saesneg, Llychlyneg a Chelteg, Prifysgol Caer-grawnt, a gradd feistr mewn Hanes Cymru o Brifysgol Bangor (pan yn Goleg Prifysgol Gogledd Cymru). Canolbwyntia ei ymchwil gyfredol ar brosograffeg urddau mynachaidd Prydain ac Iwerddon yn yr Oesoedd Canol diweddar.

Notes on Contributors ⁝ *Bywgraffiadau Cyfranwyr*

Dr **Mari Elin Wiliam** is Lecturer in Modern History and Welsh History at Bangor University. Her two main research interests are national identities in the twentieth century and the histories of everyday life. She has published on the history of devolution, the monarchy and the nuclear industry in Wales, and she has a particular interest in the cultures of north-east Wales.

Mae Dr **Mari Elin Wiliam** yn Ddarlithydd mewn Hanes Modern a Hanes Cymru ym Mhrifysgol Bangor. Ei dau brif ddiddordeb ymchwil yw hunaniaethau cenedlaethol yn yr ugeinfed ganrif a hanesion bywyd bob dydd. Mae wedi cyhoeddi ar hanes datganoli, y frenhiniaeth a'r diwydiant niwclear yng Nghymru ac mae ganddi ddiddordeb penodol yn niwylliannau gogledd-ddwyrain Cymru.

INTRODUCTION : RHAGYMADRODD

Rebecca Thomas, Sadie Jarrett and Katharine Olson

The idea behind this volume was to offer a response to the work of Professor Huw Pryce, through bringing together contributions by colleagues, collaborators and friends. It quickly became apparent that this would have to be a wide-ranging volume due to the wide-ranging nature of Professor Pryce's own work. His career has been marked by numerous seminal contributions to the field of medieval Welsh history, not least the *The Acts of Welsh Rulers 1120–1283* (Cardiff, 2005). This volume represents the first edition of charters and other documents issued by rulers of Wales in the twelfth and thirteenth centuries, thus making this material accessible and facilitating new lines of historical enquiry. Alongside several publications on Anglo-Welsh relations and Welsh identity, Professor Pryce has also worked extensively on Welsh law and the medieval church. An interest in medieval historical writing is evident in a series of contributions on Gerald of Wales and chronicle writing. However, this interest also extended beyond the Middle Ages, from Humphrey Llwyd to the Victorians and a monograph on J. E. Lloyd (Cardiff, 2011) uncovered how his academic forebear at Bangor shaped the writing of Welsh history in the twentieth century. Professor Pryce's exploration of historical writing reached its pinnacle in his monumental *Writing Welsh History*, published by Oxford University Press in 2022. As the first volume to investigate how Welsh history has been written from the sixth century to the twenty-first, it sets the benchmark for all future work on historical writing.

The sheer breadth of Professor Pryce's expertise is evident in his bibliography, compiled at the end of this volume by Dr Rhidian Griffiths. It would be too ambitious for a single edited volume to attempt to cover the same ground. Instead, this volume uses one of Professor Pryce's broad interests – the writing of Welsh history – as a springboard.

What follows, then, are fifteen chapters all tackling different aspects of how Welsh history has been written or otherwise constructed, from the medieval period to the twenty-first century. Despite what appears to be a focus on a single strand of Professor Pryce's work, many of these chapters speak to his broader interests too – including charters, names and identity construction, the medieval church and Anglo-Welsh political relations.

This volume is divided into three overlapping sections. The chapters in Part I, 'Texts and their Histories', investigate how different texts were constructed in the Middle Ages, ranging from studies of chronicles and charters to the Welsh triads. David Stephenson questions from where medieval Welsh chroniclers might have extracted their information, whilst Nia Wyn Jones approaches the Welsh Triads as a coherent text and examines how it envisaged the history of the island of Britain. In Stephenson's case, much of the investigation focuses on non-textual connections – in other words, where the chronicle narratives reveal possible oral sources or the potential for encounters with eyewitness accounts. For Jones, intertextuality is crucial to understanding the Welsh Triads, and attention is drawn to the links with the Latin history of the Britons *Historia Brittonum* and the poetry of the Gogynfeirdd. This intertextuality, which lies at the heart of Professor Pryce's discussion of medieval and early modern texts in his *Writing Welsh History*, rears its head too in Georgia Henley's chapter. Henley investigates the influence of Gerald of Wales on a cluster of texts composed at Llanthony Priory. Whilst these texts draw directly on Gerald's works on Wales, his influence can also be seen on their thematic preoccupations and conceptualisation of history. Henley's chapter reminds us, then, that intertextuality can be measured not simply through direct quotations, but also through the transmission of ideas. These chapters also follow the interdisciplinary approach that can be seen often Professor Pryce's work – his article in *English Historical Review*, 468 (2001) a notable example – that seeks to draw on both historical records and literary texts such as poetry to tackle key themes in medieval history.

Part I finishes with two complementary chapters that examine a key source base for any historian of medieval Wales: charters. Charles Insley's chapter places *The Acts of Welsh Rulers* at its centre, but also zooms out to consider these documents in the broader context of evidence for charter writing across the period *c*.500–1283 – in Wales, and beyond. Insley further explores how Welsh rulers used charters to express political power – and the role played by the past in that context. Ben Guy's chapter places the charters in the Book of Llandaf at its centre and illustrates how this material can be used to tell a much broader story, namely the development of boundary clauses from the seventh century to the twelfth. Guy's chapter investigates how the form of these boundary clauses developed, together with the language (Latin and vernacular) used. In so doing, this chapter shows the value of this early material for understanding documentary culture in the twelfth and thirteenth centuries.

In Part II, five chapters tackle the theme of 'history and identity' in different ways. Taking its cue from Professor Pryce's 2001 *English Historical Review* article, David Thornton's chapter presents and analyses the names of regular canons at six Augustinian monasteries in Wales and Ireland. Thornton argues that this prosopographical data is revealing of the ethnic composition of individual houses – and can provide valuable insight into a particular house's history. How identity is constructed is also the subject of Rebecca Thomas's chapter; where Thornton focused on monks, Thomas investigates hostages. Historical writing and identity construction go hand in hand in this chapter, through the examination of how Geoffrey of Monmouth and his Middle Welsh translators depicted this group. Thornton's chapter examined individual names as indicators of identity, whereas Thomas turns to how individuals are described, including examining the terminology of hostageship in both Latin and Welsh.

When writing about 'history and identity' in medieval Wales, it would be remiss not to mention Gerald of Wales, a writer who has loomed large in Professor Pryce's work. We have already encountered Gerald, or his influence at least, in Georgia Henley's chapter, but we meet the prolific writer once more in Thomas Charles-Edwards's contribution. Charles-Edwards investigates how Gerald presented *Laudabiliter* – the alleged papal privilege to Henry II, blessing the invasion of Ireland – across three of his works. Through closely analysing the context in which *Laudabiliter* is placed in these texts, Charles-Edwards illuminates Gerald's own evolving attitude towards the invasion of Ireland. How ecclesiasts wrote history is a key theme that continues through the final chapters in this section. For Shaun McGuinness's chapter, the ecclesiasts in question are the bishops of Bangor in the later eleventh, twelfth and thirteenth centuries. McGuinness examines how these bishops contributed to historical writing – whether through writing history themselves or through influencing those who did. Gerald again lurks in the background here, through his relationship with Bishop Rotoland. The final chapter in this part turns to the sixteenth century. Katharine Olson explores the cultural and religious contributions of the Elizabethan bishops of Bangor, with a particular focus on Nicholas Robinson. She examines Robinson's endeavours to play an active religious role in his diocese as well as his scholarly (for example, historical and antiquarian) pursuits, including the writing of National Library of Wales Peniarth 383, considering these within the wider context of the changing expectations for the role of the bishop in Reformation Wales.

As already observed, Professor Huw Pryce's interests ranged far beyond the medieval. The chapters in Part III follow his interest in historical writing into the modern era, with a special focus on interaction with the medieval past. Thus, Shaun Evans's chapter examines how the Welsh gentry engaged with the past in the nineteenth and twentieth centuries, and the role this engagement played in shaping their Welsh identity. This wide-ranging chapter includes consideration of the establishing of societies for the preservation of manuscripts, the editing and publishing of early texts, and local history writing. Evans also draws attention to the participation of the gentry in eisteddfodau, which is the focus of Marion Löffler's chapter. Löffler investigates especially the development of historical competitions at the eisteddfod – how these were written and judged, by whom, and to what end. Löffler's discussion illuminates attitudes towards the practice of history and the purpose it served in constructing nationhood in the nineteenth century.

These chapters speak to a broad interest in and engagement with the Middle Ages in the modern era – an engagement that is not solely confined to what is written on the page. Indeed, in *Writing Welsh History* Professor Pryce observes that academic writing is only one part of the story.[1] We see this clearly in other chapters in this section too. Thus, Paul O'Leary investigates the pageants that were held at Harlech Castle in the 1920s. O'Leary's chapter examines the involvement of historians in these pageants, and the blurring of the boundary between professional and public history that such involvement entailed. This chapter reveals much too about the interplay between writing and performing history. How history might be visually constructed is the subject of Mari Elin Wiliam's chapter, which focuses on how narratives of Welsh history can be found in tattoos in the twenty-first century. Wiliam's investigation delves into the significance of historical tattoos and how and why certain individuals – such as Owain Glyndŵr – are celebrated in this way. Through the prism of tattoos, Wiliam is able to tackle fundamental questions about individual interaction with history and its role in the construction of national identities. The final chapter in this volume returns to the writing of Welsh history by historians. Neil Evans takes as his subject four historians of twentieth- and twenty-first-century Wales: A. H. Dodd, Glanmor Williams, Gwyn A. Williams and John Davies. Evans's chapter explores how these historians set about writing the history of Wales and delves into the context that shaped their writing.

Taken together, these chapters address a wide range of aspects of the writing or construction of Welsh history. In so doing, they each illustrate how far this field has come, whilst also pointing to new directions for research and historical writing. In 2022, *Writing Welsh History* set the agenda for future work on the subject. This volume hopes to show how that work might look.

Much of this introduction has focused on Professor Pryce's research interests and how his publications have shaped the direction of this volume. However, something must also be said about his broader contribution to the field of Welsh history. Many of the contributors to this volume were doctoral students at Bangor or had the privilege of collaborating with Professor Pryce in another capacity, as post-doctoral researchers, colleagues or on research projects. For many of us, the Bangor Colloquium on Medieval Wales was a regular welcome fixture of the academic calendar, and *Welsh History Review* and Boydell's Studies in Celtic History series invaluable publication venues. Professor Pryce's generous support and encouragement has shaped, and continues to shape, the careers of many. This sort of impact is largely unquantifiable. Yet it is hoped that this volume says something about Professor Huw Pryce's contribution, and how much it is appreciated. *Diolch o galon.*

• • •

Syniad y gyfrol hon oedd cynnig ymateb i waith yr Athro Huw Pryce trwy gyfres o gyfraniadau gan gyd-weithwyr, cyfoedion a ffrindiau. Daeth i'r amlwg yn weddol sydyn y byddai'n rhaid i'r gyfrol fod yn un eang, a hynny oherwydd ehangder gwaith yr Athro Pryce ei hun. Nodweddir ei yrfa gan sawl cyfraniad arloesol i faes hanes y Gymru ganoloesol, gan gynnwys *The Acts of Welsh Rulers 1120–1283* (Caerdydd, 2005). Dyma'r golygiad cyntaf o siarteri a dogfennau eraill arweinwyr Cymru'r ddeuddegfed ganrif a'r drydedd ar ddeg, ac yma gwneir y deunydd hwn yn hygyrch am y tro cyntaf gan hwyluso ymchwil newydd. Ynghyd â sawl cyhoeddiad ar berthynas y Cymry a'r Saeson a hunaniaeth Gymreig a Chymraeg, mae'r Athro Pryce wedi gweithio'n estynedig ar y gyfraith a'r eglwys ganoloesol. Daw ei ddiddordeb mewn ysgrifennu hanesyddol i'r amlwg mewn cyfres o gyfraniadau ar Gerallt Gymro a chroniclau. Fodd bynnag, mae'r diddordeb hwn hefyd yn ymestyn y tu hwnt i'r Oesoedd Canol; o Humphrey Llwyd i Oes Victoria, ac yn ei lyfr ar J. E. Lloyd (Caerdydd, 2011) taflodd oleuni ar ddylanwad ei gyndaid academaidd ym Mangor ar hanesyddiaeth Cymru yn yr ugeinfed ganrif. Daeth uchafbwynt gwaith yr Athro Pryce ar hanesyddiaeth gyda'i gyfrol nodedig *Writing Welsh History*, a gyhoeddwyd gan Wasg Prifysgol Rhydychen yn 2022. Dyma'r ymgais cyntaf i archwilio'r broses o ysgrifennu hanes y Cymry o'r chweched ganrif hyd yr unfed ar hugain, ac mae'r gyfrol yn gosod y safon ar gyfer pob gwaith pellach yn y maes.

Ceir blas ar ehangder arbenigedd yr Athro Pryce yn ei lyfryddiaeth, wedi ei lunio i'w gynnwys ar ddiwedd y gyfrol hon gan Rhidian Griffiths. Amcan rhy uchelgeisiol fyddai i un gyfrol olygiedig gwmpasu ystod mor eang o bynciau. Bwriad y gyfrol hon yn hytrach yw defnyddio un o ddiddordebau'r Athro Pryce – hanesyddiaeth Cymru – fel sbringfwrdd. Yr hyn sy'n dilyn, felly, yw pymtheg pennod, pob un yn ymwneud â rhyw agwedd ar lunio hanes Cymru, o'r Oesoedd Canol hyd yr unfed ganrif ar hugain. Er mai syniad y gyfrol yw canolbwyntio ar un agwedd o waith yr Athro Pryce, mewn gwirionedd mae sawl un o'r penodau yn cyffwrdd â'i ddiddordebau ehangach – gan gynnwys siarteri, enwau a chreu hunaniaethau, yr eglwys ganoloesol, a chysylltiadau gwleidyddol rhwng y Cymry a'r Saeson.

Rhennir y gyfrol yn dair rhan sydd yn gorgyffwrdd â'i gilydd. Yn Rhan I, 'Testunau a'u Hanes', ceir penodau yn archwilio sut y lluniwyd testunau amrywiol yn yr Oesoedd Canol – o groniclau a siarteri i'r Trioedd. Mae David Stephenson yn holi o ble y cafodd croniclwyr eu gwybodaeth, tra bo Nia Wyn Jones yn trin y Trioedd fel testun cydlynol ac yn archwilio'i weledigaeth ynghylch hanes ynys Prydain. Yn achos Stephenson, canolbwyntia'r astudiaeth i raddau helaeth ar gysylltiadau nad ydynt yn destunol – hynny yw, lle y ceir awgrym yn y croniclau o ddefnydd o ffynonellau llafar neu'r posibilrwydd o ddod ar draws adroddiad gan lygad-dyst. I Jones, mae rhyngdestunoldeb yn allweddol er mwyn deall y Trioedd, a rhoddir sylw i gysylltiadau testunol gyda hanes Lladin y Brythoniaid *Historia Brittonum* a cherddi'r Gogynfeirdd. Gwelir y rhyngdestunoldeb hyn, sydd mor ganolog i drafodaeth yr Athro Pryce o destunau canoloesol a modern cynnar yn ei *Writing Welsh History*, hefyd ym mhennod Georgia Henley. Archwilia Henley ddylanwad Gerallt Gymro ar glwstwr o destunau a gyfansoddwyd ym Mhriordy Llanddewi Nant Honddu. Tra bo'r testunau hyn yn tynnu'n uniongyrchol ar weithiau Gerallt ar Gymru, gwelwn ei ddylanwad hefyd yn y themâu sydd o ddiddordeb iddynt ynghyd â'u cysyniad o hanes. Mae cyfraniad Henley yn ein hatgoffa, felly, bod modd mesur rhyngdestunoldeb trwy drosglwyddiad syniadau gymaint â dyfyniadau uniongyrchol. Mae'r penodau hyn hefyd yn dilyn y dull rhyngddisgyblaethol a welir yn aml yng ngwaith yr Athro Pryce – mae ei erthygl yn *English Historical Review*, 468 (2001) yn enghraifft nodedig – sydd yn tynnu ar gofnodion hanesyddol a thestunau llenyddol megis barddoniaeth er mwyn ymgiprys â themâu allweddol mewn hanes canoloesol.

Gorffenna Rhan I gyda dwy bennod gyflenwol sy'n archwilio math allweddol o ffynhonnell i unrhyw hanesydd y Gymru ganoloesol: siarteri. *The Acts of Welsh Rulers* yw man cychwyn a chanolbwynt pennod Charles Insley, ond mae hefyd yn ehangu ei drafodaeth i ystyried y dogfennau hyn yng nghyd-destun y dystiolaeth dros lunio siarteri yn y cyfnod *c*.500–1283 – yng Nghymru a thu hwnt. Archwilia Insley sut y defnyddiwyd siarteri gan arweinwyr y Cymry i fynegi pŵer gwleidyddol – a'r rôl oedd gan y gorffennol i'w chwarae yn y cyd-destun hwnnw. Siarteri Llyfr Llandaf sy'n ganolbwynt i bennod Ben Guy, ac mae'n amlinellu sut y mae modd defnyddio'r deunydd hwn i adrodd stori ehangach, sef datblygiad cymalau ffiniau o'r seithfed ganrif hyd y ddeuddegfed. Archwilia pennod Guy sut y datblygodd ffurf y cymalau hyn, ynghyd â'r iaith a ddefnyddiwyd (Lladin a Chymraeg). Wrth wneud, dengys y bennod bwysigrwydd y deunydd cynnar er mwyn deall diwylliant dogfennol y ddeuddegfed ganrif a'r drydedd ar ddeg.

Yn Rhan II, mae pum pennod yn trin a thrafod y thema 'Hanes a Hunaniaeth'. Gan ddefnyddio erthygl 2001 *English Historical Review* yr Athro Pryce fel dechreubwynt, â David Thornton ati i gyflwyno a dadansoddi enwau canoniaid rheolaidd mewn chwe mynachdy Awstinaidd yng Nghymru ac Iwerddon. Dadleua Thornton bod y data prosograffegol hyn yn datgelu rhywbeth am gyfansoddiad ethnig y tai unigol – ac yn cynnig mewnwelediad i'w hanes. Creu hunaniaeth yw pwnc pennod Rebecca Thomas hefyd: tra bo Thornton yn canolbwyntio ar fynachod, archwilia Thomas hithau wystlon. Â ysgrifennu hanes a chreu hunaniaeth law yn llaw yn y bennod hon, trwy ystyriaeth o sut y cafodd y grŵp hwn eu cyflwyno gan Sieffre o Fynwy a'r sawl a gyfieithodd ei waith i'r Gymraeg. Archwilia Thornton arwyddocâd enwau unigol fel ffordd o fesur hunaniaeth, tra bo Thomas yn edrych ar sut y caiff unigolion eu disgrifio, gan gynnwys archwilio terminoleg gwystlo yn Lladin ac yn Gymraeg.

Wrth fyfyrio ar 'hanes a hunaniaeth' yn y Gymru ganoloesol, cam fyddai peidio â sôn am Gerallt Gymro, awdur sydd wedi ymddangos droeon yng ngwaith yr Athro Pryce. Rydyn ni wedi dod ar draws Gerallt – ei ddylanwad, o leiaf – unwaith yn barod, ym mhennod Georgia Henley, ond gwelwn yr awdur toreithiog hwn eto yng nghyfraniad Thomas Charles-Edwards. Archwilia Charles-Edwards sut y cyflwynodd Gerallt *Laudabiliter* – y fraint Pabyddol honedig i Harri'r II, yn cysegru ei ymosodiad ar Iwerddon – mewn tri o'i weithiau. Trwy ddadansoddi cyd-destun *Laudabiliter* ym mhob un o'r gweithiau, mae Charles-Edwards yn taflu goleuni ar y datblygiad yn agwedd Gerallt tuag at yr ymosodiad ar Iwerddon. Mae dulliau eglwyswyr o ysgrifennu hanes yn thema sy'n parhau ym mhenodau olaf y rhan hon. Yn achos pennod Shaun McGuinness, esgobion Bangor yn yr unfed ganrif ar ddeg, y ddeuddegfed a'r drydedd ar ddeg yw'r eglwyswyr dan sylw. Archwilia McGuinness sut y cyfrannodd yr esgobion hyn at ysgrifennu hanes – boed trwy ysgrifennu hanes eu hunain neu drwy ddylanwadu ar y rhai hynny a wnaeth. Unwaith eto mae Gerallt yn llechu yn y cefndir yma, trwy ei berthynas â'r esgob Rotoland. Mae'r bennod olaf yn y rhan hon yn troi i'r unfed ganrif ar bymtheg. Mae Katharine Olson yn ystyried cyfraniadau diwylliannol a chrefyddol esgobion Bangor yn ystod Oes Elizabeth, gyda chanolbwynt arbennig ar Nicholas Robinson. Archwilia ymdrechion Robinson i chwarae rôl grefyddol weithredol yn ei esgobaeth yn ogystal â'i weithgarwch ysgolheigaidd (hanesyddol a hynafiaethol, er enghraifft), gan gynnwys ysgrifennu Llawysgrif Llyfrgell Genedlaethol Cymru Peniarth 383. Gosodir gyrfa Robinson yn y cyd-destun ehangach o newid disgwyliadau ynghylch rôl yr esgob yng Nghymru'r Diwygiad.

Fel y nodwyd eisoes, ymestynna diddordebau'r Athro Pryce tu hwnt i'r Oesoedd Canol. Mae'r penodau yn Rhan III ('Cof Cenedl') yn dilyn y diddordeb hwn mewn hanesyddiaeth i'r cyfnod modern, gyda chanolbwynt arbennig ar ymwneud â'r gorffennol canoloesol. Felly, archwilia pennod Shaun Evans berthynas uchelwyr y bedwaredd ganrif ar bymtheg a'r ugeinfed â'r gorffennol, a sut y cyfrannodd y berthynas honno at greu hunaniaeth Gymreig. Mae'r bennod eang hon yn cynnwys ystyriaeth o sefydlu cymdeithasau i warchod llawysgrifau, golygu a chyhoeddi testunau cynnar, ac ysgrifennu hanes lleol. Mae Evans hefyd yn tynnu sylw at sut y cymerodd yr uchelwyr ran mewn eisteddfodau, sef canolbwynt pennod Marion Löffler. Archwilia Löffler yn benodol ddatblygiad cystadlaethau hanesyddol yn yr eisteddfod – sut y'u hysgrifennwyd a'u beirniadu, gan bwy ac i ba bwrpas. Mae trafodaeth Löffler yn taflu goleuni ar agweddau tuag at hanes fel crefft a'i bwrpas wrth lunio cenedligrwydd yn y bedwaredd ganrif ar bymtheg.

Mae'r penodau hyn yn arddangos diddordeb ac ymwneud eang â'r Oesoedd Canol yn y cyfnod modern – ymwneud sy'n mynd tu hwnt i'r hyn gaiff ei ysgrifennu ar y dudalen. Yn wir, yn *Writing Welsh History*, noda'r Athro Pryce mai un rhan yn unig o'r stori yw gwaith academaidd.[2] Gwelwn hyn yn glir mewn penodau eraill yn y rhan hon hefyd. Felly, mae Paul O'Leary yn archwilio'r pasiantau a gynhaliwyd yn Castell Harlech yn yr 1920au. Dadansodda pennod O'Leary rôl haneswyr yn y pasiantau, a goblygiadau eu hymrwymiad ar gyfer deall y ffin rhwng hanes proffesiynol a hanes cyhoeddus. Mae'r bennod hon hefyd yn ymwneud â'r berthynas rhwng ysgrifennu a pherfformio hanes. Ffyrdd o lunio hanes yn weledol yw pwnc pennod Mari Elin Wiliam, sydd yn canolbwyntio ar yr adroddiadau o hanes Cymru a welir mewn tatŵau yn yr unfed ganrif ar hugain. Â Wiliam ati i archwilio arwyddocâd tatŵau hanesyddol a sut a pham bod unigolion penodol – megis Owain Glyndŵr – yn cael eu dathlu yn y ffordd hon. Trwy brism tatŵau, mae Wiliam yn mynd i'r afael â chwestiynau sylfaenol ynghylch rhyngweithiad personol â hanes a'i rôl wrth lunio hunaniaethau cenedlaethol. Dychwela pennod olaf y gyfrol hon i ysgrifennu hanes Cymru gan haneswyr. Canolbwyntia Neil Evans ar bedwar hanesydd o Gymru'r ugeinfed ganrif a'r unfed ar hugain: A. H. Dodd, Glanmor Williams, Gwyn A. Williams a John Davies. Mae pennod Evans yn ystyried sut yr aeth yr haneswyr hyn ati i ysgrifennu hanes Cymru ac yn ymchwilio i'r cyd-destun a ddylanwadodd ar eu gwaith.

Gyda'i gilydd, mae'r penodau hyn yn ymdrin ag ystod eang o agweddau ar ysgrifennu neu lunio hanes Cymru. Wrth wneud hyn, dangosant pa mor bell y mae'r maes wedi dod, tra hefyd yn awgrymu cyfeiriadau newydd. Yn 2022, gosododd *Writing Welsh History* yr agenda ar gyfer gwaith pellach ar y pwnc. Â'r gyfrol hon ati i ddangos sut y gallai'r gwaith hwnnw edrych.

Mae'r rhan fwyaf o'r rhagymadrodd hwn wedi canolbwyntio ar ddiddordebau ymchwil yr Athro Pryce a sut y maent wedi siapio cyfeiriad y gyfrol hon. Fodd bynnag, rhaid sôn hefyd am ei gyfraniad ehangach i faes hanes Cymru. Bu sawl un o'r cyfranwyr i'r gyfrol hon yn fyfyrwyr doethurol ym Mangor; tra bo eraill wedi cael y fraint o gyd-weithio gyda'r Athro Pryce mewn ffyrdd eraill, fel ymchwilwyr ôl-ddoethurol, cyd-weithwyr neu ar brosiectau ymchwil. I nifer helaeth ohonom, roedd i Golocwiwm Bangor ar Gymru'r Oesoedd Canol le pwysig yn y calendr academaidd, a *Cylchgrawn Hanes Cymru* a chyfres Studies in Celtic History Gwasg Boydell yn cynnig cyfleon cyhoeddi amhrisiadwy. Mae cefnogaeth hael ac anogaeth yr Athro Pryce wedi siapio, ac yn parhau i siapio, gyrfaoedd nifer ohonom. Anodd yw mesur y math hwn o gyfraniad. Ond rydym yn gobeithio bod y gyfrol hon yn dweud rhywbeth am gyfraniad yr Athro Huw Pryce, a chymaint y gwerthfawrogir y cyfraniad hwnnw. Diolch.

Notes

1 Huw Pryce, *Writing Welsh History* (Oxford, 2022), p. 299.
2 Huw Pryce, *Writing Welsh History* (Oxford, 2022), t. 299.

PART I : RHAN I
TEXTS AND THEIR HISTORIES : TESTUNAU A'U HANES

1

How did Medieval Welsh Chroniclers Find their Information?

David Stephenson

Many medieval Welsh chroniclers incorporated in their writings material derived from earlier annals or chronicles. Much has been done in relatively recent scholarship to elucidate the stages by which chronicles in the form in which we have them were often constructed by fusing together several earlier sources, while significant effort has been directed at tracing 'axes of textual transmission' within and beyond Wales and the March.[1] But most chronicles were much more than compilations from earlier annals. The core of much medieval chronicling was the gathering of materials from original, often unwritten, sources rather than existing chronicles. There follows an analysis of such unwritten sources, or in some cases written materials which had not passed through earlier chronicles, together with an examination of how an awareness of the nature of such material may help to resolve some otherwise puzzling episodes recorded in Welsh chronicles.

We can sometimes identify information sought out by a chronicler based in, say, a specific church or religious house. In such a case the relevant section of a chronicle or set of annals may have a significantly local focus, consisting of information to which the chronicler had ready access. Very good examples of this are to be found in the material gathered by Daniel ap Sulien, who has been identified as the author of *Brut y Tywysogyon* for the period 1100–27. He was active initially at Llanbadarn Fawr and then after 1116 at, probably, the clas church of Meifod until his death in 1127.[2] A successor seems to have worked in Arwystli, almost certainly at Llandinam in the period 1128–32, and members of Daniel's following, probably including his son Cedifor, appear to have returned to Llanbadarn Fawr in the 1130s, and continued to write the chronicle there until the 1170s, after which chronicling activity was largely taken over by the Cistercian house of Strata Florida.[3] There are further examples of chroniclers working at identifiable Welsh religious centres including, but not limited to, St Davids, Whitland, Cwm-hir, Aberconwy and Abergavenny.[4]

A very similar category of information is that brought to the chronicler by an external reporter or reporters – for example, it has been suggested that information provided by Gerald of Wales may form the basis for some of the text of the B-text of *Annales Cambriae* in the period *c*.1190–1203.[5] Indeed, Gerald makes it clear that travellers visited Welsh monasteries in significant numbers in the twelfth and thirteenth centuries; we can assume that they were often the sources of stories which were incorporated into the works of monastic chroniclers.[6] Further, it has been argued that in the early decades of the fourteenth century the role of informant to a chronicler in the lordship of Bromfield and Yale was assumed by the significant figure of Madog ap Llywelyn.[7]

It is likely that some entries in chronicles originated as materials provided as memories by the elders of a region. An example from *Brut y Tywysogyon* is perhaps the clearest example of a 'folk-memory' entering a chronicle. This entry is for 1022, but was likely composed in the late eleventh century:[8]

> Ac yna y dechymygawd nebun Yscot yn gelwyd y vot yn vab y Veredud vrenhin ac y mynawd y alw ehun yn vrenhin. Ac y kymerth gwyr y Deheu ef yn arglwyd ar y teyrnas; a'e henw vu Rein. Ac yn y erbyn y ryfelawd Llywelyn ap Seisyll, goruchaf vrenhin Gwyned a phenaf a chlotuorussaf vrenhin o'r holl Vrytanyeit. Yn y amser ef y gnotae henafyeit y teyrnas dywedut bot y gyuoeth ef o'r mor py gilyd yn gyflawn o amylder da a dynyon, hyt na thybygit bot na thlawt nac eissiwedic yn y holl wladoed, na thref wac na chyfle diffyc.[9]

> And then a certain Irishman falsely pretended that he was son to king Maredudd and he desired to have himself called king. And the men of the South received him as lord over their kingdom; and his name was Rhain. And Llywelyn ap Seisyll, supreme king of Gwynedd and foremost and most praiseworthy king of all the Britons, warred against him. In his time the old men of the kingdom were wont to say that his territory from the one sea to

the other was replete with an abundance of wealth and men, so that it could not be imagined that there was a man either poor or needy in all his lands nor an empty township nor a place of want.

No other single passage in the Welsh chronicles captures so clearly the influence of a memory passed down to a chronicler's time by elders. But there is no shortage of possible examples of material derived from instances of community memory. Thus, under 1153, the Red Book *Brut y Tywysogyon* reports that 'eilweith y diffeithawd Rys Gyfeilawc drwy y vudugolyaeth' ('a second time Rhys ravaged Cyfeiliog victoriously').[10] However, there is no mention in the chronicle of a 'first' ravaging of Cyfeiliog by Rhys. This 1153 reference may therefore represent a memory of an event which had gone unrecorded in the annals.

There are of course other categories of information on which Welsh chroniclers sometimes drew. First amongst these is evidence inserted in chronicle texts from written record sources – frequent in English chronicles but less obvious in Welsh ones, perhaps suggesting production in a culture in which the written element was less prominent than it was in England.[11] It has been suggested that there is a clear example in the *Annales Cambriae* B-text report of a truce negotiated between Henry III and Llywelyn ap Gruffudd in 1260, which seems to reflect precise details of proposals put forward by the prince.[12] Another possible instance of such a reference to a record source or sources may be *Brut y Tywysogyon*'s account of the Treaty of Montgomery: points are not given in the order in which they appear in the treaty, but it does look as though the chronicler has emphasised the parts of the treaty which seemed particularly important. Thus, we have references in the *Brut* to the subordination of all Welsh rulers to Llywelyn, his recognition as prince of Wales, and the financial costs of this to the prince, points which reflect specific clauses of the treaty.[13]

Of particular interest are examples of a specific category of source material represented by reports from numerous observers of a specific event, which may have a firm foundation in fact, but may also represent rumours, or apparently factual reports which are based to a significant degree on assumptions. Close examination often reveals that there are regional tendencies to regard events in different ways. In other words, different audiences or observers may hear or see what seems significant to them, rather than the totality of a narrative. And audiences in different areas or regions may hear only part of a story so that the account emerges as substantially different from region to region. We can examine two case studies of different chronicles presenting contrasting narratives as a result of regional variations in the information being picked up by their chroniclers.

Why was William de Braose hanged in 1230?

The first is constituted by the account in chronicles of the background to the execution of William de Braose the Younger in Gwynedd in 1230. The bulk of the chronicle accounts, both English and Welsh, are clear that de Braose was executed because he had been conducting an affair with Joan, Llywelyn's wife. A selection of the chronicles shows this clearly.

The Annals of Tewkesbury, s.a. 1230:

> Lewelinus princeps Norwallie retinuit Willelmum de Breuse filium Reginaldi post Pascha; eo quod ipsum ut dicitur zelotiparet, occidit et suspendi fecit.[14]

> Llywelyn prince of North Wales detained William de Braose son of Reginald after Easter, because he (William) as it is reported, had cuckolded him; he then killed him, by hanging him.

Brut y Tywysogyon (RB), s.a. 1230:

> Y ulwydyn honno y croget Gwilym Brewys Jeuanc y gann Lywelin ap Ioruerth, wedy y dala yn ystauell y tywyssawc gyt a merch Jeuan vrenhin, gwreic y tywyssawc.

> That year William de Braose the younger, was hanged by Llywelyn ap Iorwerth after he had been caught in the prince's chamber with king John's daughter, the prince's wife.[15]

Annals of Chester:

> Item Willelmus de Breaus inculpatus est a Lewelino principe Wallie de uxore sua, et suspenditur. Et mulier carcerata custodia diu.[16]

William de Braose was accused by Llywelyn prince of Wales regarding his wife, and he was hanged. The woman was held in prison for a long time.

Though they are rather different in emphasis,[17] the chronicles quoted above (with the exception of the very brief and uninformative reference in the Cardiff chronicle) all indicate that the relationship between Joan and William de Braose was the cause of the latter's execution. But in contrast, one set of annals has a different emphasis in its account of the execution. These are the Margam Annals, the relevant portion of which is set out below:

> Eodem anno Lewelinus proditorie, ut dicebatur, nocte cepit Willelmum de Breusa juniorem in domo sua cum esset Paschalis festivitas, eo quod haberet eum suspectum de uxore sua secundum quosdam; re autem vera secundum alios, ex veteri odio progenitorum suorum, scilicet Willelmi de Brewsa senioris, et Matildis de Sancto Walerico uxoris suae, qui multos Walenses tam nobiles et potentes, quam alios fecerant occidi. Cumque eundem Willelmum et milites qui cum eo venerant, et familiam suam, aliquanto tempore vinctos in carcere tenuisset, illum quidem fecit suspendi; garciones abire permisit, et quosdam alios redemptos pecunia liberos dimisit. Cuius suspendio divulgato, insultantes Walenses exclamaverunt 'Nunc vindicatus est sanguis Walensium quem Willelmus de Breusa et sui effuderunt super terram.'[18]

In that year, as it was said, Llywelyn treacherously captured William de Braose the Younger by night in his residence during the Easter festivity, because according to some he suspected his relationship with his [Llywelyn's] wife. According to others the truth was the old hatred against William's ancestors, that is William de Braose senior and his wife Matilda de Saint-Valerie, who had had many Welsh people killed, both nobles and magnates as well as others. When he [Llywelyn] had held William and the knights who had accompanied him and his entourage in prison for some time, he had William hanged; he allowed the servants to leave, and he set the others free when they were ransomed for money. When the news of the hanging got out, the Welsh exultantly exclaimed 'Now the blood of the Welsh that William de Braose and his men shed upon the ground has been avenged!'

At this point it is helpful to examine the abbot of Vaudey's letter to the bishop of Chichester which mentions the episode, and the light it sheds on the Margam Annals for 1230.[19] After explaining that it had needed much diplomacy to establish a suitable place for a meeting between the bishop and Llywelyn, the abbot turned to the topic of William de Braose:

> De domino W. de Braus quicquid dicatur sciatis pro certo quod in crastino apostolorum Philippi et Jacobi apud quoddam manerium quod dicitur Crokein factus est Crokin, id est suspensus in arbore quodam nec idem clam aut de nocte sed palam et plena die coram octingentis viris et eo amplius covocatis ad hoc miserablile et lamentabile spectaculum, et summonitis viris pluribus, et illis maxime quibus dominus W de Braus senior et eius filii propter progenitorum suorum necem aut alterius modi illatam molestiam, erant infesti.[20]

> Whatever is said about William de Braose you should know for certain that on the morrow of the feast of Philip and James [2 May], at a certain manor called Crokein [Crogen] he was made Crokin that is hanged from a tree, not secretly or by night, but publicly, in broad daylight, in the presence of more than eight hundred persons, called together for this wretched and lamentable spectacle, and especially those whose forebears had been killed or injured by William de Braose senior and his sons.

When we compare this letter with the account in the Margam Annals, it seems that the annalist has focused on the assembling of people who hated the de Braose family and made that into the primary reason for the execution of William. The Margam annalist has noted the suspicion of an affair, but as simply one alternative factor in William's fate. Clearly there were more people in the region from which the Margam annalist was gathering information who saw the execution as revenge for the atrocities against the Welsh committed by the de Braose family. It was these people who had made the journey to see revenge being exacted by the execution of William the Younger. The alleged affair of William and Joan made less of an impact in south Wales, and thus received less attention in the Margam Annals. In a somewhat similar development, the Cardiff chronicle recorded Llywelyn's killing of William, but did not explain why this had been done.[21]

The three deaths of Hywel Sais ab yr Arglwydd Rhys

The sort of circumstances envisaged in the case of the detention and execution of William de Braose the Younger, where we appear to find reports emanating from people who were present at, or who heard from those claiming knowledge of, a part rather than the entirety of an incident, may help to shed light on the curious matter of the reports of the death of Hywel Sais ab yr Arglwydd Rhys. This is one of the rare examples of several chronicles – *Brut y Tywysogyon*, the *Annales Cambriae* B-text, the *Cronicon de Wallia* and the genealogical tract contained in *Cronicon de Wallia* – presenting different accounts of the same episode which are in specific particulars contradictory.[22] The relevant parts of these sources are as follows:

Brut y Tywysogyon (RB), s.a. 1204:[23]

> Y vlwydyn racwyneb y brathwyt Hwel Seis ap yr Arglwyd Rys yg Kemeis drwy dwyll y gan wyr Maelgwn, y vrawt; ac o'r brath hwnw y bu varw, ac y cladwyt yn Ystrat Flur yn vn ved a Gruffud y vrawt, wedy kymryt abit crefyd ymdanaw.

> The following year Hywel Sais, son of the Lord Rhys, was wounded in Cemaes through treachery by the men of Maelgwn, his brother; and of that wound he died, and he was buried at Strata Florida, in the same grave as Gruffudd, his brother, after he had assumed the habit of the Order.

Cronicon de Wallia (Text I), s.a. 1204:[24]

> Howelus filius Resi Magni, iuuenis egregious, spes suorum, horror hostium, dolo apud Kemmeys ab hominibus Mailgonis

uulnere letali est transfixus. Hic itaque sumpto religionis habitu Griffini fratris sui convectus sepulcro apud Stratflour honorifice est sepultus.[25]

Hywel son of Rhys the Great, an outstanding young man, the hope of his people, the terror of his enemies, was fatally wounded by trickery on the part of Maelgwn's men. Clad in the monastic habit, he was carried to the tomb of his brother Gruffudd at Strata Florida, where he was honourably buried.

A genealogical tract relating to children of the Lord Rhys amongst the materials in *Cronicon de Wallia* (Text II) (with no specific date but possibly *c*.1277) recounts the story as follows:

Hoel cognomine Seys, cuius porcio hereditaria fuit in Demecia … [places in Dyfed listed] … Hic etiam semper regi Anglie fuit fidelis et in rediendo de parliamento apud Stugul infirmabatur et ibidem est mortuus et apud Taleleche est sepultus …[26]

Hywel, known as 'Sais', whose hereditary share [of his father's lands] was in Dyfed … [places in Dyfed listed] … was consistently faithful to the king of England and returning from a negotiation he fell ill at Chepstow and died there and was buried at Talley …

Annales Cambriae B-text, s.a. 1199:

Houelus seys Resi filius erga pascha curiam regis Iohannes adiuit et in reditu suo apud striguil egritudine coreptus · obiit uel ut alii uolunt a francis occisus est qui omnes Wallie duces largitate precellabat.[27]

Hywel Sais, son of Rhys went to King John's court around Easter, and on his return he was stricken with an illness at Chepstow and died, or, as others would have it, he was killed by the French. He excelled all other Welsh leaders in generosity.

It should be noted that the account in the *Annales Cambriae* B-text seems to have been misdated by some years. As other entries under 1199 in the same chronicle text are correct or very nearly so, it looks as though the entry relating to Hywel's death has been added, incorrectly, at a later stage in the construction of the B-text. The compiler of the B-text has preserved two versions of Hywel's death, with one emphasising sickness, and the other violence. As to which version is to be preferred, the only serious consideration so far given to Hywel's date and circumstances of death is that of J. E. Lloyd.[28] He, like others who have looked at the case, concluded that the *Brut* version was preferable, namely that the death occurred in 1204, that Hywel was killed by men of his brother Maelgwn and that he was buried in Strata Florida. This is the most detailed version, with a precise place of burial. In what follows it will be treated as probably the most accurate version of Hywel's death.

We can now move to consideration of the process of composition. We can clearly trace three quite different views of the events which led to Hywel Sais's death. The three different accounts of Hywel's death are as follows:

1. He died at Chepstow as the result of an illness. A somewhat similar account adds that he was buried at Talley abbey.
2. He was killed by the 'French'.
3. Hywel was killed in Cemais by men of his brother Maelgwn, and he was buried at Strata Florida in the tomb of his brother Gruffudd.

Now let us try to reconstruct a process of dissemination of ideas concerning Hywel's death, in such a way as to establish why they were all at some points thought credible. It is possible that some of the different accounts involve a complete misidentification, though that seems unlikely in the case of someone as eminent as Hywel Sais. In fact, it seems probable that a single narrative may lie behind all three accounts. We may suggest the following sequence: returning from a meeting in England, Hywel contracted an illness which became severe at Chepstow. This became known. When it was subsequently learned that he had died, it was assumed by some that he had died at Chepstow. Some people, however, learnt that he had been buried at a place much further west, and assumed that he was taken for burial to Talley, a relatively recent foundation by the Lord Rhys. It subsequently became known that Hywel had died by violence, and it was assumed that this was inflicted by 'the French' – in other words French speakers, probably Marchers. This account, recorded in an unknown source, or preserved in popular memory, was added into *Cronicon de Wallia* Text II at a late date, possibly *c*.1276/7.

A quite different account, probably emanating from west Wales and probably relating events after Hywel's illness, told of Hywel being killed by men of Maelgwn, his brother, and being buried at Strata Florida. As the most precise and detailed of the accounts, it is most likely to be the most accurate. It is this version that appears in *Cronicon de Wallia* Text I, and in *Brut y Tywysogyon*. There was no need to mention an illness at Chepstow, because the source of this version of events had the final story of death at the hands of Maelgwn's men and the precise details of Hywel's burial.

As in the case of the accounts of the execution of William de Braose, we are dealing here with a sequence of different stories, some of which seem to be based on rumour or assumptions, albeit with a possibly true initial narrative element (the illness at Chepstow) amplified by conjecture. However, only the 'final' story that appears in *Cronicon de Wallia* Text I and in the *Brut* is likely largely accurate.

Cistercian networks

A further source of information is the evidence provided by 'professional networks': poets, decanal chapters, Cistercian newsletters. This category of sources of chronicle materials can be very important. It includes, as well as newsletters which were used by the Cistercians to disseminate information between a number of houses, the mortuary letters and rolls that sometimes come to view. Julian Harrison refers to these in his important but sometimes overlooked work on Cistercian chronicling in the British Isles.[29] Harrison notes that visitors were very useful for those confined to the cloister – but we need to remember that many were not so confined. Chroniclers had ample opportunity to contact people outside the cloister – for example when monks and *conversi* were present at a grant to a monastery, with lay witnesses, some of whom were certain to be knowledgeable – as well as rulers, and monks from other houses. This was especially important in the later twelfth century and the earlier thirteenth century, the period which saw a large number of endowments of religious houses.[30]

It has been suggested that the Cistercian granges may have been important as 'listening posts' which picked up information from their locality.[31] A good example is the case of events in Abermule in mid Wales. This was close to the Cistercian house of Cwm-hir, but was in fact a grange of Strata Florida. Events there in the 1260s were recorded in the *Brut*, fairly clearly a chronicle being constructed at Strata Florida, but were not included in the annals being written at Cwm-hir.[32] This suggests that granges may have been expected to have a role in the recording of events in their vicinity, perhaps by oral transmission between the granges and the parent monastery, perhaps via the *magister conversorum*, while those events might not be mentioned in annals written at another house even if it was located nearby.

In the specific case of Cistercian chronicling, Julian Harrison has made a number of helpful observations which can be applied to the situation in Wales, particularly that relating to the chronicle text or texts underlying *Brut y Tywysogyon*. Of particular value are his comments that some annalistic works 'testify to the circulation of newsletters' and that 'it is … likely that some Cistercian chroniclers learnt of the deaths of important clerics from mortuary briefs and mortuary rolls, or were indebted to the bearers of those documents for the transmission of other recent news'.[33] A situation of this sort becomes apparent in the text of the *Brutiau* in the late twelfth and early thirteenth centuries, when a distinct pattern emerges. The deaths of abbots of other Cistercian houses beyond Strata Florida, where the chronicle was being assembled, those of bishops of St Davids, within which diocese Strata Florida lay, or important burials in Cistercian abbeys, are recorded in terse form, often at the start or the end of an annal. Examples include, but are not limited to, the following, all but the last taken from the Red Book version.[34]

1176 [start of annal]:

> Y ulwydyn racwynep y bu uarw Kynan, abat y Ty Gwynn, a Dauid, escop Mynyw.

> The following year died Cynan, abbot of Whitland, and David bishop of Menevia.

1184 [the entire annal]:

> Y ulwydyn racwyneb y bu farw Ryderch, abat y Ty Gwynn, a Meuryc, abat y Cwm Hir.

> The following year died Rhydderch, abbot of Whitland; and Meurig, abbot of Cwm-hir.

1187 [start of the annal]:

> Yn y ulwydyn honno y bu uarw Ithel, abat Ystrat Marchell.

> In that year died Ithel, abbot of Strata Marcella.

1196 [final entry in the annal]:

> Y vlwydyn hono y bu varw Gruffud, abat Ystrat Marchell.

> That year died Gruffudd, abbot of Strata Marcella.

1198 [last entry in the annal]:

> Y vlwydyn hono y bu varw Pyrs, esgob Myniw.

> That year died Peter, bishop of Menevia.

1200 [start of the annal]:

> Deucant mlyned a mil oed oet Crist pan vu varw Gruffud ap Kynan ap Ywein yn Aber Conwy, wedy kymryt abit crefyd ymdanaw.

> One thousand and two hundred was the year of Christ, when Gruffudd ap Cynan ab Owain died at Aberconwy after having assumed the habit of the Order.

1211 [end of annal, only in *ByT* (P20)]:

> Yny vlwydyn hono ybu varw Gruffud vab juor a Maredud vab karadawc

In that year died Gruffudd ab Ifor and Maredudd ap Caradog.[35]

An important point that emerges from the above survey of apparent notifications of deaths of prominent persons related to Cistercian houses beyond Strata Florida is that, in some cases, the terse notification is supplemented by material in the body of the annal relating to the region of the house mentioned in the notification. This applies to regions to which little reference is made for the period under review in the chronicle as a whole. This in turn possibly suggests that we may be dealing with material passed on to the Strata Florida chronicler by the person(s) responsible for bringing the death-notification to the latter abbey. A case in point is the account of the killing of Owain ap Madog, lord of Mechain, in 1187. Immediately after the notice of the death of Ithel, abbot of Strata Marcella comes the following:

> Ac yna y llas Ywein ap Madoc, gwr mawr y uolyant – kanys cadarn oed a thec a charedic a hael ac adurn o voesseu da – y gann deu vab Ywein Kyfeilawc, nyt amgen, Gwenwynwyn a Chadwallon.

> And then Owain ap Madog, a man of great praise – for he was strong and comely and beloved and generous and an ornament of good manners – was slain by the two sons of Owain Cyfeiliog, namely, Gwenwynwyn and Cadwallon.[36]

However, a more significant and problematic example comes in the decade following the notice of the death of Owain ap Madog, and concerns Pool castle.

Events at Pool castle, 1196–8

The chronicle record of events in 1196 seems to provide an even more illuminating case of the way in which a notice of the death of a prominent member of a Cistercian house could be accompanied by details of events close to that house which might not normally have been included in *Brut y Tywysogyon*. Focussing on the connection between the notification of a death and a record of other events nearby may also shed light on an apparent clash of chronicle and record evidence.

In that year we have an annal which closes with the brief record of the death of abbot Gruffudd of Strata Marcella. Strata Marcella of course lay within the polity of Powys, and was founded by Owain Cyfeiliog, lord of that land, and father of the prince of Powys, Gwenwynwyn. In the body of the annal for 1196 there is reference to the attack on Gwenwynwyn's territory, launched by Hubert Walter and an English force. The attack concentrated on Gwenwynwyn's castle of Pool (today's Powis Castle), and we are told in the *Brut* that sappers had tunnelled under the castle and forced its surrender, only for Gwenwynwyn to recover possession of it within a short time:

Ac odyna, kyn diwed y vlwydyn hono y kynullawd Gwenwynwyn y wyr y gyt ac yd ymladawd yn wrawl a'r dywededic gastell, ac y kymhellawd y ymrodi idaw drwy amot hefyt rodi rydit y'r castellwyr y vynet yn iach a'e dillat a'e harueu gantunt.

And thereupon, before the end of that year, Gwenwynwyn gathered his men together, and he manfully laid siege to the said castle and forced it to surrender to him, on condition, too, that the garrison be given liberty to depart to safety and their raiment and arms with them.[37]

It should be noted that the account of Gwenwynwyn's recovery of the castle by the close of the year is substantially corroborated by the Annals of Chester, which appear to be reporting independently of the *Brut*.[38]

There is however a major and as yet unresolved problem about the account of Gwenwynwyn's recapture of his castle of Pool: it appears to be flatly contradicted by the evidence of the Pipe Rolls. For the year ending at Michaelmas 1197 these inform us that John Lestrange had received ten marks for custody of Pool castle;[39] and for Michaelmas 1198 record that John Lestrange was paid one hundred marks for provisioning/equipping Pool castle and for its custody, and for removing therefrom the siege of the Welsh.[40] It would seem that Lestrange was keeping the castle from a date (unknown) in the year to Michaelmas 1197, and that he was very fully occupied in defending it from a siege by Gwenwynwyn's forces in the year to Michaelmas 1198. Nothing further is heard of the castle as being in English hands, and we have to assume that in the period before 29 September 1198 it was finally retaken by Gwenwynwyn.

The problem is to reconcile the date for the recapture of the castle by Welsh forces given in the chronicles, with that implied by the Pipe Rolls. A satisfactory solution has so far proved elusive. But if we focus on the way in which the *Brut* was compiled it may be possible to make some progress. Let us assume that the entries in the Pipe Rolls are basically correct. We therefore have to turn to the entry in the *Brut*, in the light of the conjectured reconstruction of how it was put together for the year 1196 (probably ending in March 1197 by our reckoning). We may have to assume that the references to the two sieges in one year may be correct, but also that they may not represent a complete account of everything that happened to Pool castle in the period 1196–8, particularly if the account in the *Brut* under 1196 is to be seen as information supplied by the person(s) who brought the news of the death of the abbot of Strata Marcella to Strata Florida. There may have been no follow-up to the story in the annal for 1197, in which the chronicler's energy, information and interest was largely dominated by the focus on the death of the Lord Rhys. If the annal for 1198 does not begin until March 1198 by our reckoning, the focus of the chronicler had probably shifted to the campaign instigated by Gwenwynwyn in 1198 against Painscastle.[41] So the chronicler may have had no information about events at Pool castle in 1197–8. He will therefore have recorded only part of the story, introducing an apparent contradiction between his account and that of the Pipe Rolls, whereas the two types of sources may have been recording different elements in a sequence of events.[42] The full sequence may remain somewhat elusive, but a conjectural reconstruction may run as follows. There was a first siege of Pool castle in 1196 by English forces, involving its surrender and occupation by those forces; this was followed in 1196 by a siege undertaken by Gwenwynwyn, which was marked by his recovery of the castle. Subsequently, probably in 1197 the castle may have been occupied for a second time by English forces led by John Lestrange, who held it until a date in 1198, when it finally fell again into the hands of Gwenwynwyn. Most of this can be recovered from the Pipe Rolls, the account in which is not included in the *Brut*. It is probable that no report of developments at Pool castle after 1196 reached the chronicling centre at Strata Florida as no event had taken place at Strata Marcella which might have triggered an account of events near to that abbey. Thus consideration of the way in which information reached the chronicler may hold the key to the apparent clash between chronicle and record sources.

A chronicler's sudden enthusiasm for Caerleon

A further example of the importance of Cistercian networks in chronicle construction is provided by the material in *Brut y Tywysogyon* relating to the abbey of Llantarnam (Caerleon). References in the *Brut* to Caerleon and its rulers are few. The Peniarth 20 version contains only a handful of references, which occur for the following years: 1158; 1171; 1172; 1173; 1175; 1179; 1217; 1231. The most obvious point about these references is their chronological distribution. They show a marked concentration in the 1170s, and it is on this period that we need to focus. The references to developments in that decade are as follows:

1171: Henry II journeys through south Wales,

> Ac yn yr hynt hono ar auon wysc yduc ef gaerllion ar wisc y ar Jor ap ywein ap karadawc ap Gruffud ac or achaws hono jor ay deuuab ywein a hywel ... allawer orei ereill adystriwassant gaer llion oll hyt ytwr ac adiffeithassant oll hayach y wlat.

> And on that journey, on the river Usk, he took Caerleon-on-Usk from Iorwerth ab Owain ap Caradog ap Gruffudd. And for that reason Iorwerth and his two sons, Owain and Hywel ... and many others destroyed all Caerleon to the tower, and ravaged nearly all the land.[43]

1172: the annal describes Henry II's meeting with Iorwerth ab Owain and Henry's grant of a truce to Iorwerth, followed by the killing of the latter's son Owain, described as 'gwasjeuag adwyn' ('an excellent young man') by men of the earl *Bristaw* ('of Bristol'), as a result of which Iorwerth ab Owain and his son Hywel ravaged lands around Gloucester and Hereford.[44]

1173: After recording the clash between Henry II and Henry the younger, the chronicle continues:

> Ac val yr oed y brenhined velly yn ymrysson ytu draw yrmor Jor ap ywein o gaerllion adechreuawd ymlad achaerllion duw

> merchyr ypymthecvet dyd o galan awst ac ef ay kafas y dreis sadyrngweith wedy daly duw gwener kyn no hyny pawb or a oed yn amdiffyn ybayli athros y rei hyny y rodet y kastell dranoeth.

> And whilst the kings were thus contending beyond the sea, Iorwerth ab Owain of Caerleon began to lay siege to Caerleon on Wednesday the fifteenth day from the Calends of August. And he took it by force on a Saturday, having captured, on the Friday before that, all who were defending the bailey. And for those the castle was surrendered on the following day.[45]

The chronicle then describes how Hywel ab Iorwerth took Gwent Is Coed, except for the castles, and was given hostages by the leading men of that land.

1175:

> Blwydyn wedy hyny y delis Hywel vab Jor o gaerllion heb wybot yw y dat ywein penkarn y ewythyr ac y tynawd ylygeit oy ben ac y dispadawd ef rac geni ohonaw ettiued avei vedyanus ar gaer llion. aduw sadwrn rac wyneb ygorysgynawd yfreing kaer llion wedi gyrru jor ahywel y vab ymeith ohonei.

> A year after that, Hywel ap Iorwerth of Caerleon, unknown to his father, seized Owain Pencarn, his uncle; and he gouged his eyes out of his head and castrated him, lest he should beget issue who might hold authority over Caerleon. And on the following Saturday the French gained possession of Caerleon, having driven Iorwerth and Hywel, his son, out of it.[46]

The *Brut* subsequently records that Iorwerth ab Owain of Caerleon was one of those Welsh lords who had incurred the king's displeasure who went with the Lord Rhys to attend Henry II's council at Gloucester. All then returned to their lands, 'gan rodi kaerllion y jor vab ywein' ('yielding Caerleon to Iorwerth ab Owain').[47]

1179:

Y gossodet kouent ynant thirnon yn emyl kerllion yr hon a elwir dewma.

A [Cistercian] community was set up at Nant-teyrnon near Caerleon, which is called Dewma.[48]

In brief, the account of the 1170s in the *Brut* tells of the confiscation of Caerleon by Henry II in 1171 from Iorwerth ab Owain, and the struggle by Iorwerth and his son Hywel to re-establish themselves there. It also notes Hywel's violent deed to ensure that he, rather than his uncle, should succeed Iorwerth. The sequence ends with the foundation of the monastery of Caerleon, later Llantarnam, by Hywel ab Iorwerth, probably acting for his father.[49] The *Brut* references to Caerleon, Iorwerth and Hywel in the 1170s seem, from the exact (and correct) dates employed, to have been made by someone very close to the events described.[50] There can be little doubt that they emanate from somewhere in or near to Caerleon itself, and from someone who, in all probability, knew some of the principal figures involved.[51] It is possible that they existed in the form of notes which were taken over by the newly founded Cistercian house, and that their purposes may have included recording the deeds of the members of the Welsh dynasty who became the patrons of the abbey, and also of justifying that foundation as a way of reducing the turbulence of the region. It was part, in other words, of the materials put together to support the creation of a new Cistercian house, and as such it is understandable that the account of Llantarnam's origin should pass to that abbey's mother house, Strata Florida, which was also the place to which in the 1170s the writing of the chronicle material underlying the *Brut* was being entrusted. Once the new abbey at Caerleon had been founded, it appears to have passed largely out of the sphere of interest of the chroniclers of Strata Florida.[52]

Conclusion

The issue of where and from whom the chroniclers found their information is thus a topic eminently worthy of further consideration. In the first place it reminds us that if we can understand the processes of gathering information we may have the key to some apparent puzzles in the statements of chroniclers, a point illustrated in the first two case studies set out above. A further point to emerge from this study is the importance of networks, not just of textual transmission but of reporting of events, current or historic, which helped those who were responsible for chronicling to add to or to refine their accounts of developments. And even more significantly we may realise that at least as important as the scribe who constructed a chronicle in whole or in part were the informants of various types who brought to the chronicler the information on which his work was based.[53]

Notes

1 Notable examples of this approach include J. Beverley Smith, 'Historical writing in medieval Wales: the composition of *Brenhinedd y Saesson*', *Studia Celtica*, 42 (2008), 55–86; Georgia Henley, 'The Cardiff chronicle in London, British Library, MS Royal 6 B XI', in Ben Guy, Georgia Henley, Nia Wyn Jones [published as O. W. Jones] and Rebecca Thomas (eds), *The Chronicles of Medieval Wales and the March* (Turnhout, 2020), pp. 231–87; Georgia Henley, 'Networks of Chronicle Writing in Western Britain: The Case of Worcester and Wales', in Francesca Tinti and D. A. Woodman (eds), *Constructing History across the Norman Conquest* (Woodbridge, 2022), pp. 227–70. A typically very clear discussion of the complex borrowings between chronicles is provided by Huw Pryce: 'Chronicling and its contexts in medieval Wales', in Guy et al. (eds), *Chronicles of Medieval Wales*, pp. 1–32.

2 This comment is based on what seems to me to be an evident break in the *Brut* text in c.1116, *pace* Nia Wyn Jones [published as O. W. Jones], 'Brut y Tywysogion: the History of the Princes, and Twelfth-Century Cambro-Latin Historical Writing', *Haskins Society Journal*, 26 (2014), 209–27 (pp. 218–24), where the whole period 1100–27 is seen as 'the Llanbadarn History'.

3 Pryce, 'Chronicling and its contexts', pp. 12–14.

4 Thus the C-text of *Annales Cambriae* is fairly clearly a product of St Davids: see Kathleen Hughes, 'The Welsh Latin chronicles: Annales Cambriae and related texts', in Kathleen Hughes, *Celtic Britain in the Early Middle Ages: Studies in Welsh and Scottish Sources by the Late Kathleen Hughes*, ed. David Dumville (Woodbridge, 1980), pp. 67–85 (p. 73), and Henry Gough-Cooper, 'Meet the ancestors? Evidence for antecedent texts in the late thirteenth-century Welsh Latin chronicles', in Guy et al. (eds), *Chronicles of Medieval Wales and the March*, pp. 107–37. For chroniclers working at Whitland and Cwm-hir, see David Stephenson, 'The chronicler at Cwm-hir abbey 1257–63', in R. A.

Griffiths and Phillipp R. Schofield (eds), *Wales and the Welsh in the Middle Ages* (Cardiff, 2011), pp. 29–45; David Stephenson, 'In search of a Welsh chronicler: the *Annales Cambriae* B-text for 1204-30', *CMCS*, 72 (2016), 73–85. For writing at Aberconwy abbey, see Nia Wyn Jones [published as O. W. Jones], '*O Oes Gwrtheyrn*: A Medieval Welsh Chronicle', in Guy et al. (eds), *Chronicles of Medieval Wales and the March*, pp. 169–229, and for Abergavenny, David Stephenson, 'The Continuation of *Brut y Tywysogyon* in NLW, MS Peniarth 20 Revisited', in Guy et al. (eds), *Chronicles of Medieval Wales and the March*, pp. 155–68 (pp. 157–61).

5   David Stephenson, 'Gerald of Wales and Annales Cambriae', *CMCS*, 60 (2010), 23–37.

6   See Gerald of Wales's account of the throng of visitors at Strata Florida, when he objected to the shameful way in which he had been treated at that house, by being denied the privileges appropriate to a bishop-elect and an archdeacon, being instead 'harboured in the public hall among the common guests and the noise of the people' ('tantum in aula publica inter hospites communes et strepitum popularem locaretur'): *Giraldi Cambrensis Opera*, ed. J. S. Brewer, James F. Dimock and George F. Warner, 8 vols (London, 1861–91), III, 202; H. E. Butler (ed.), *The Autobiography of Gerald of Wales* (Woodbridge, 2005), p. 226.

7   Stephenson, 'The Continuation', pp. 163–8. This is perhaps a reminder that in some cases it is an informant rather than a scribe who is the key figure in the development of a chronicle text, and that the concept of authorship is sometimes a complex one.

8   I have argued that this passage is probably an entry made in the 1090s, based on the memories of 'the old men' or elders, probably told to the chronicler some two decades earlier: David Stephenson, *Medieval Powys: Kingdom, Principality and Lordships, 1132–1293* (Woodbridge, 2016), pp. 27–8.

9   *ByT* (RB), s.a. 1022 (ed. and trans. Jones, pp. 20–1).

10 *ByT* (RB), s.a. 1153 (ed. and trans. Jones, pp. 132–3). The Peniarth 20 version notes that Rhys ap Gruffudd ravaged Cyfeiliog in 1153, but does not mention that this was for the second time: *ByT* (P20), s.a. 1153 (trans. Jones, p. 58).

11 For just a few examples of the importance of contemporary record sources in English chronicles of the twelfth and thirteenth centuries see Antonia Gransden, *Historical Writing in England* (London, 1984), pp. 198 (Henry of Huntingdon (d. 1155), who used many official documents in his work, and had planned to insert 'decrees of councils and other documents in a separate book'); 270–1 (references to the use of documents in many of the local chronicles of the twelfth century); 361 (the 'omnivorous appetite for documents' of Matthew Paris at St Albans, many of which were gathered in his *Liber Additamentorum*).

12 Stephenson, 'The chronicler at Cwm-hir abbey', pp. 36–7.
13 *ByT* (RB), s.a. 1267 (ed. and trans. Jones, pp. 256–9); for the record of the treaty see *AWR*, p. 363. The relevant clauses of the treaty are 16 (and 10), for sums owed and to be owed by Llywelyn to the king; in clause 10 the granting of the fealty and homage of the Welsh barons to Llywelyn; in clause 9 the grant to Llywelyn of the principality of Wales, with the provision that he and his heirs shall be called and shall be princes of Wales.
14 Henry Richards Luard (ed.), 'Annales de Theokesberia', in Henry Richards Luard (ed.), *Annales Monastici*, 5 vols (London, 1864–9), I (1864), 43–180 (p. 74).
15 *ByT* (RB), s.a. 1230 (ed. and trans. Jones, pp. 228–9).
16 Richard Copley Christie (ed.), *Annales Cestrienses or Chronicle of the Abbey of S. Werburg at Chester* (London, 1887), pp. 56–7. The Cardiff chronicle has only a cursory reference to the killing of William de Braose by Llywelyn ab Iorwerth: 'Lewelinus princeps Northwallie interfecit Willelmum de Breuse' (ed. Henley, 'The Cardiff chronicle', p. 261).
17 The Tewkesbury and Chester accounts are vague compared to that in *Brut y Tywysogyon*. This may suggest that stories of what had happened reached Tewkesbury and Chester in only summary form, or that the chroniclers in those centres were less interested in the details.
18 Henry Richards Luard (ed.), 'Annales de Margan', in Luard (ed.), *Annales Monastici*, I, 3–40 (p. 38). I am grateful to Andrew Shell for discussion of this episode.
19 The letter is fairly clearly to be dated to the period soon after 18 May 1230.
20 W. W. Waddington (ed.), *Royal and other Historical Letters illustrative of the Reign of Henry III, Volume I, 1216–1235* (London, 1862), pp. 366–7; see also J. G. Edwards (ed.), *Calendar of Ancient Correspondence concerning Wales* (Cardiff, 1935), p. 37.
21 See n. 16 above.
22 This is noted by J. E. Lloyd, *A History of Wales from the Earliest Times to the Edwardian Conquest*, 2 vols (3rd edn, London, 1939), II, 618 n. 37, as 'one of the few cases in which there is an irreconcilable divergence between *AC* and *BT*'. We might add that the divergence, as set out below, extends further than *AC (B)* and *ByT*.
23 *ByT* (RB), s.a. 1204 (ed. and trans. Jones, pp. 186–7). The Peniarth 20 and Red Book versions are in substantial agreement: see *ByT* (P20) (trans. Jones, p. 82).
24 References to Text I and below to Text II are to the numbers applied to the text in the edition of Thomas Jones, '"Cronica de Wallia" and other documents from Exeter Cathedral Library MS 3514', *BBCS*, XII (November 1946), 27–44, and in a separate print.

25 Jones, '"Cronica de Wallia" and other documents', 32.
26 Jones, '"Cronica de Wallia" and other documents', 41.
27 Taken from the edition by Henry Gough-Cooper, 'Annales Cambriae. The B Text. From London, National Archives, MS E164/1, pp. 2–26' (2015), online at *http://croniclau.bangor.ac.uk/documents/AC%20B%20first%20edition.pdf* (accessed 15 August 2022), p. 69 (b1221.2).
28 Lloyd, *History of Wales*, II, 618 n. 37. See also *AWR*, p. 9, which notes that '[i]n 1204 Hywel Sais ap Rhys, an ally of Gruffudd [ap Rhys] died, probably from wounds inflicted by Maelgwn's men in Cemais'.
29 Julian Harrison, 'Cistercian Chronicling in the British Isles', in Dauvit Broun and Julian Harrison (eds), *The Chronicle of Melrose Abbey. A stratigraphic edition. Volume I: Introduction and facsimile edition* (Woodbridge, 2007), pp. 13–28 (pp. 25–6), which notices Cistercian newsletters, the circulation of mortuary rolls and the passage of information by those carrying such documents.
30 A good example of such a gathering to witness a grant is provided by a charter (*AWR*, no. 9, pp. 150–1) of Cadwallon ap Hywel of Arwystli to Strata Marcella, issued in 1206 at far-off Llandovery, and witnessed by the prior of Cwm-hir, a monk of Whitland, a monk of Strata Florida, a monk and several *conversi* of Strata Marcella, and a number of secular clergy and laymen, some at least of whom were from the Llandovery region.
31 Stephenson, 'The chronicler at Cwm-hir abbey', p. 34.
32 Stephenson, 'The chronicler at Cwm-hir abbey', p. 35.
33 Harrison, 'Cistercian chronicling', pp. 25–6.
34 For the following, see *ByT* (RB) (ed. and trans. Jones, pp. 166–7, 168–9, 170–1, 176–7, 182–3).
35 *ByT* (P20) (ed. Jones p. 157; trans. Jones, p. 86). Gruffudd ab Ifor, lord of Senghennydd, was a benefactor to Margam abbey: see *AWR*, p. 46 and nos 616–17; Maredudd ap Caradog, lord of Meisgyn, was also a benefactor of Margam: see *AWR*, p. 19, no. 150, and cf. no. 121.
36 *ByT* (RB), s.a. 1187 (ed. and trans. Jones, pp. 170–1). The name of Gwenwynwyn's brother was Caswallon rather than Cadwallon: see Stephenson, *Medieval Powys*, pp. 71, 79–80.
37 *ByT* (RB), s.a. 1196 (ed. and trans. Jones, pp. 176–7).
38 Christie (ed.), *Annales Cestrienses*, pp. 44–5.
39 Doris M. Stenton (ed.), *The Great Roll of the Pipe for the ninth year of the reign of King Richard the First* (London, printed for the Pipe Roll Society, 1931), p. 156.
40 Doris M. Stenton (ed.), *The Great Roll of the Pipe for the tenth year of the reign of King Richard the First* (London, printed for the Pipe Roll Society, 1932), p. 172.
41 Stephenson, *Medieval Powys*, p. 85.

42 The Annals of Chester may well have followed a similar course, assuming that Gwenwynwyn's recapture of his castle in 1196 was the end of the story. It may be that John Lestrange met with little resistance in his re-entry into the castle at some point (probably) in 1197; the castle must have been damaged to the point of being nearly useless after the initial English undermining exercise. It would appear from the Pipe Roll payments to Lestrange that he had a limited garrison in a largely ruinous castle in 1197, but that he put considerable work into re-establishing the castle in the year ending Michaelmas 1198, work which provoked a second siege by Gwenwynwyn. But by that point attention had switched to events at Painscastle.
43 *ByT* (P20) (ed. Jones, pp. 117–18; trans. Jones, p. 66). The Red Book text (*ByT* (RB), s.a. 1171, pp. 154–5) appears to be inaccurate at this point.
44 *ByT* (P20) (ed. Jones, pp. 121–2; trans. Jones, p. 68). Cf. *ByT* (RB), s.a. 1172 (ed. and trans. Jones, pp. 158–9).
45 *ByT* (P20) (ed. Jones, p. 124; trans. Jones, p. 70). Cf. *ByT* (RB), s.a. 1173 (ed. and trans. Jones, pp. 162–3).
46 *ByT* (P20) (ed. Jones, p. 125; trans. Jones, p. 70). Cf. *ByT* (RB), s.a. 1175 (ed. and trans. Jones, pp. 162–3).
47 *ByT* (P20) (ed. Jones, pp. 126–7; trans. Jones, p. 71). Cf. *ByT* (RB), s.a. 1175 (ed. and trans. Jones, pp. 164–5).
48 *ByT* (P20) (ed. Jones, p. 129; trans. Jones, p. 72). Cf. *ByT* (RB), s.a. 1179 (ed. and trans. Jones, pp. 168–9).
49 A charter issued by Hywel ab Iorwerth 'almost certainly no earlier than 1179' (*AWR*, quote at p. 35, charter edited as no. 467) records Hywel as having established Llantarnam. Hywel's father did not die until *c*.1184 but may have been incapacitated for some time before that date, with Hywel acting for him.
50 That is not to say that the giving of exact dates for events was a characteristic only of the references to Caerleon: it is a general characteristic of the *Brut* in general in this period and appears to reflect the move of the chronicle to Strata Florida.
51 This is suggested by the interjected comment about Owain, son of Iorwerth ab Owain, that he was 'an excellent young man': see above, n. 44.
52 It may be that Llantarnam developed its own chronicle, now lost. For possible evidence of subsequent chronicling activity at Llantarnam see Diana Luft, 'The NLW Peniarth 32 Latin Chronicle', *Studia Celtica*, 44 (2010), 47–70.
53 I should like to thank Rebecca Thomas for numerous helpful observations and suggestions in the final stages of this paper. I am solely responsible for the inadequacies that remain.

2

The Reception of Gerald of Wales in Welsh Historical Texts

Georgia Henley

This chapter surveys three historical texts from medieval Wales that are related to the twelfth-century cleric Gerald of Wales (*c*.1146–1223) and his writings. Two of these, the mid-thirteenth-century *Genealogy of the Lords of Brecknock* and the fifteenth-century *Register and Chronicle of the Abbey of Aberconwy*, use Gerald's Welsh works (*Itinerarium Kambriae* and *Descriptio Kambriae*) as sources, both directly and indirectly, while another, the twelfth-century *History of Llanthony Priory*, may have been written by Gerald himself, as Robert Bartlett has recently shown.[1] This discussion is inspired by the fact that the only two monastic histories surviving from medieval Wales (for Llanthony Priory and Aberconwy Abbey) are linked to Gerald in some way, and by the fact that the dedicatee of this volume, Huw Pryce, has contributed significantly to our understanding of Gerald of Wales and his use of Welsh history.[2] This chapter is, therefore, interested in Welsh history's use of Gerald. In the pages below, I outline each text and its links to Gerald, demonstrating how he shaped the writing of histories of these monastic houses, and how ties to Gerald are displayed not only in textual correspondences, but in thematic interests. This chapter shows overall that while Gerald's works on Wales – the *Itinerarium* and *Descriptio Kambriae*, and perhaps now the *History of Llanthony Priory* – had a very limited reception in medieval Wales (and were not, to our knowledge, translated into Middle Welsh), his influence is nevertheless seen indirectly in the writing of Welsh history in both Latin and French.[3] I begin by discussing the *History of Llanthony Priory*, which sets out some of Gerald's major preoccupations in the vein of Welsh monastic history, before following these threads of interest in the *Genealogy of the Lords of Brecknock* and the *Register and Chronicle of the Abbey of Aberconwy*.

History of Llanthony Priory

The *History of Llanthony Priory* was only very recently identified by Robert Bartlett as a work of Gerald of Wales, and therefore benefits from new scholarship placing it in the context of the rest of Gerald's considerable output. Though the authorship of the *History of Llanthony Priory* cannot be verified with perfect certainty, this chapter accepts Bartlett's argument that it is Gerald's work. In any case, the *History* repeats a significant amount of information about Llanthony from Gerald's *Speculum ecclesiae* and reflects Gerald's considerable interest in Llanthony Priory in the *Itinerarium Kambriae*.[4]

The *History of Llanthony Priory* is extant in London, British Library, Cotton Julius D. x, ff. 31r–53v, a manuscript from the second half of the thirteenth century that is thought to originate at Llanthony Prima or perhaps Llanthony Secunda Priory. The text is preceded in the manuscript by the Life of Robert of Béthune, bishop of Hereford (1131–48) by William Wycombe, prior of Llanthony Secunda,[5] written in Latin, and the *Genealogy of the Lords of Brecknock*, written in French, and discussed below.

Table 1: Contents and structure of London, British Library, Cotton Julius D. x

Part	Quire	Foliation	Text	Hand
i	1	2–9	Life of Robert of Béthune	1
	2	10–17	Life of Robert of Béthune	1
	3	18–25	Life of Robert of Béthune	1
	4	26–29	Life of Robert of Béthune (ends 28r); *Genealogy of the Lords of Brecknock* narrative genealogy (28r–29v)	1
ii	5	30–43	*Genealogy of the Lords of Brecknock* genealogical diagram (30r) in Hand 1; *History of Llanthony Priory* (31r–43v) in Hand 2	1, 2
	6	44–53	*History of Llanthony Priory* (change to Hand 3 on 50v)	2, 3

Diana Tyson has argued that the manuscript was formed of two parts (see Table 1). Concerning the combining of the two parts, she writes, the hand starting the second part [Hand 2] *could* be marginally earlier than the one preceding it [Hand 1], which raises the question of the assembling of the codex. I tentatively suggest two possibilities for this: either the first part was made to fit the already executed second part, or the whole was written in the order as it stands with the scribe starting the second part using a rather old fashioned script.[6]

I would think the former scenario is more likely. Bartlett, following the observations of Tessa Webber, records two hands in part ii, and cites a 'later-thirteenth-century' date for Hand 2 and a 'turn of the thirteenth/fourteenth centuries' date for Hand 3.[7] In any case, the two parts, formed of the Life of Robert of Béthune and the *History of Llanthony Priory*, were bound together at an early date, because all the hands are roughly contemporary; at which time, *Genealogy of the Lords of Brecknock*, written in the same hand as the Life and straddling parts i and ii, was added to empty pages at the end of quire 4 and the beginning of quire 5.

Bartlett has suggested that the manuscript is from Llanthony, probably Prima, since the *History* is notably critical of Secunda, while others think it is from Secunda.[8] The texts work together to present the history of both priories of Llanthony as intertwined in the interests of the noble families of the area, particularly the lords of Brecon and earls of Hereford. John Spence has argued that the *Genealogy of the Lords of Brecknock* may have been written in the mid-thirteenth century for Eleanor and Humphrey V de Bohun (d. 1265) or for their children.[9]

The *History of Llanthony Priory* places the history of Llanthony Prima and Secunda in the context of a series of noble patrons, whose generous endowments reflect their piety and the virtues of the monastic community, and encourage further generosity by future patrons. To give a brief summary: the *History* explains how Llanthony Prima began life as a place of refuge in the Vale of Ewyas in Wales for William, an exceedingly pious attendant of the Norman baron Hugh de Lacy (n.d.).[10] The valley of Ewyas is beautiful, fruitful and unappreciated by the local (Welsh) inhabitants: 'The neighbouring people are fierce, untilled by the plough of God's word, nomadic, untrustworthy, loving to live by plunder, unfamiliar with fixed residences, "carried in as a guest wherever the storm drives them"' ('Gens uicina fera, uomere uerbi Dei inculta, uaga, inconstans, rapina uiuere gaudens, certarum sedium ignara, "quocumque eam rapit tempestas, hospita fertur'").[11] William the hermit is joined in 1103 by Ernisius, former chaplain of Queen Matilda (1080–1118) and a hermit in his own right. Together they found a church with the blessings of Urban, bishop of Llandaf (d. 1134), and Ramelinus [Reinhelm], bishop of Hereford (d. 1115), and dedicate it in 1108 to St John the Baptist. Llanthony Prima's first patron is Hugh de Lacy (d. 1186), who is praised highly for his cultivation of the priory:

> [H]orum patrocinium et temporalis solacii curam gerendam innato religionis amore, suscepit Hugo de Laci, prefati loci tunc aduocatus, uir quidem genere nobilis, sed nobilior moribus, inter primos regni principes nominatissimus, pauperum et oppressorum misertor benignissimus. Hic, ne in aliquo paterne religionis degener argueretur, liberalitatis et deuocionis insignia, que traxit et stipite, felicibus indiciis in flores fructusque salubres produxit.

> Hugh de Lacy, at that time advocate of the place, a man indeed noble by descent but more noble in his conduct, most renowned among the chief barons of the kingdom, most kindly and compassionate towards the poor and oppressed, undertook their protection and the care of all their temporal needs, from his innate love of the religious way of life. So that he might not be deemed to have declined in any way from the religious way of life of his father, he developed into health-bringing flowers and fruit the marks of liberality and devotion that he had drawn from his stock, as was shown by happy signs.[12]

This passage reflects an overall theme of the text: the importance of the nobility's support of the church. Hugh is praised in the context of his family's previous devotion: the *History* continues with further discussion of his father (Gilbert de Lacy, 1133–63), who also built and provided for a monastery (presumably St Peter's, Hereford); his brother, who became a monk and abbot at St Peter's, Gloucester; and his nephew, who joined the Knights Templar. The *History* establishes Llanthony's land rights and its relationship with this family through extensive praise, as if encouraging Hugh (and perhaps other descendants who were reading the work) to continue in the tradition of Hugh's father in patronising the priory. It continues:

Hic ergo Hugo, ne tantarum uirtutum laudibus, que in totam generis sui successionem naturali quadam innate religionis linea ineuitabiliter defluxerunt, aliquatenus priuaretur, non minus ceteris circa prenominatos fratres extitit in largiendo munificus, in colloquendo affabilis, in prouidendo sollicitus, nam eis donaria multa et predia ampla contulit.

So this Hugh, lest he should be deprived somewhat of the praises for such great virtues which had flowed inevitably by a kind of natural line of innate religiosity in the whole succession of his family, showed himself to be, no less than the others, generous in giving to the brethren, affable in his speech with them, thoughtful in providing for them, for he conferred upon them many gifts and wide estates.[13]

With these gifts, the two hermits are able to expand into a monastic community. They choose the Augustinian order and are joined by brethren from London and Colchester. As their good reputation spreads, Henry I (1068/9–1135), Queen Matilda and other barons also endow the monastery with generous gifts, which are refused by the monks because of their great humility and poverty. Gifts from patrons simultaneously elevate the monastery's status and highlight the monks' rejection of worldly goods. The contrast between Hugh's piety and the fierce, nomadic wildness of the local Welsh population accords with Gerald of Wales's sentiments about the Welsh elsewhere.[14] It also accords with his praise of the monks of Llanthony in the *Itinerarium Kambriae*, which he combines with criticism of monastic orders (particularly the Cluniacs) who violate their vows of poverty and grow wealthy from greed.[15]

The *History* goes on to account for the acrimonious circumstances of the creation of Llanthony Secunda, after the monks of Llanthony Prima are persecuted by wild Welsh people and flee the premises to Gloucester. The author is critical of the behaviour of the monks of Llanthony Secunda, who sack their mother-house for its possessions. The *History* further praises Walter Constable (d. *c*.1126) who adopts the monastic habit at the end of his life and grants the monks of Llanthony a new site in Gloucester:[16]

Conuenit super hoc Milonem Constabularium comitem Herefordie, exponens ei fratrum necessitates, ad memoriam reducens deuocionem patris sui Walteri, qui apud eos eciam humatus quiescit. Dedit ergo eis prefatus Milo locum quondam extra urbem Gloucesterie.

[The bishop] went to Miles the constable, earl of Hereford, about this, explaining to him the brethren's needs, recalling to memory the devotion of Walter his father, who lay buried among them. So this Miles gave them a place outside the city of Gloucester.[17]

The text also details the tenures of the succession of abbots of Llanthony Secunda. These passages, overall, demonstrate a keen focus on the relationship between aristocracy and church, showing through positive example how pious lordly patronage should work. The text praises the patrons who have been generous to the church – just as, in contrast, the Giraldian section of the *Genealogy of the Lords of Brecknock* shows how nobility who abuse the church are punished by God. The *History* also contains the familiar theme of grievance in its discussion of the moral superiority of Llanthony Prima in the face of the monks' shameful exit to Gloucester. These are themes that are characteristic of Gerald's writings.

The Genealogy of the Lords of Brecknock

The mid-thirteenth-century *Genealogy of the Lords of Brecknock* is extant in London, British Library Cotton Julius D. x, the same manuscript as the *History of Llanthony Priory* discussed above, and complements some of the themes just outlined. This text, written in French, describes the history of the marcher lordship of Brecon from its origins in the 1090s, when Bernard de Neufmarché (d. 1121×5?) conquered Brycheiniog from Rhys ap Tewdwr (d. 1093), to the 1240s, when the lordship was in the hands of the Bohun family. The text describes the inheritance of the lordship, passing from Bernard de Neufmarché to Miles fitz Walter (d. 1143) through his marriage to Sibyl (n.d.), daughter of Bernard, then to Miles's son Roger (d. 1155), and then to the Braose family through the marriage of Miles's daughter Bertha (n.d.) to William (II) de Braose (n.d.). Finally, the lordship passes to the Bohun family through the marriage of Eleanor de Braose (n.d.) to Humphrey (V) de Bohun (d. 1265). The narrative genealogy (Cotton Julius D. x, ff. 28r–29v) is accompanied by a family tree diagram that visualises the lineage described in the narrative genealogy (f. 30r).[18] A mid-thirteenth-century composition date is probable for both items, given that the last individuals mentioned are Eleanor de Braose, her husband Humphrey (V) de Bohun and their children; it may be that they were intended patrons of the genealogy or perhaps the manuscript as a whole.[19]

The text is important to the present discussion because its first section (describing the deeds of Bernard de Neufmarché, Miles fitz Walter, Miles's children, and their relationship to the lordship of Brecon) is substantially a translation into French of Gerald of Wales's *Itinerarium Kambriae* i. 2, the only known translation of Gerald's writings into French. This section of the text contains typical Giraldian intrigue, family strife and themes of justice for wrongs committed against family members. As it occurs in the same manuscript, in a contemporary hand, as the *History of Llanthony Priory*, a work now thought to be written by Gerald, it is striking that it uses the *Itinerarium Kambriae* as a substantial source. One speculates that the scribe who wrote the *Genealogy* into the pages preceding the *History* recognised the connection.

In the first paragraph of the narrative genealogy, Bernard and Nest's son Mahel is disinherited after Mahel beats his mother's lover, and his mother Nest takes revenge by denying that Mahel is Bernard's son. For this reason, the lordship passes to Mahel's sister Sibyl and her husband Miles fitz Walter. The text is as follows:

> Sa mere Neste sus son baron ama un chivalir, e a partir de sa mere le baty e ledement le defela, dunt sa mere grevement a ly se corusa; e apres la mort Bernard de Nefmarche, son baron, a la curt Henry le veyl s'en ala e devant le roy e tut son baronage apertement iura qe ceti Mael n'estoy pas le fiz Bernard de Nefmarche mes de un autre chivalir, qe ele pro ama, le aueyt consu ...

> The mother Nest loved a knight more than her husband, and upon the knight's departure from his mother, [Mahel] beat him and wounded him horribly, for which reason his mother became grievously angry with him. And after the death of her husband Bernard de Neufmarché, she went to Henry [the elder]'s court, and in the presence of the king and all his nobility she publicly

swore an oath that this Mahel was not the son of Bernard de Neufmarché, but that she had conceived him by another knight, whom she loved very much ...[20]

This passage is a translation of Gerald of Wales's *Itinerarium Kambriae* i. 2:

> Mater ejusdem, contra jugale vinculum, adulterinis amplexibus militem quemdam adamavit. Quo comperto, militem noctu a matre redeuntem filius offendens, flagellatum graviter mutilatumque cum dedecore remisit magno. Mater vero, mira facti confusione percussa, muliebrique dolore anxie concussa, totum in vindictam virus evomuit. Accedens igitur ad Anglorum regem Henricum primum, assertione vindice magis quam vera proposuit, et coram curia publice sacramento corporaliter praestito confirmavit, filium suum Mahelem non a Bernardo, sed ab alio quodam, quem secretis et illicitis adamaverat amplexibus, fuisse progenitum.

> His mother, against the bonds of matrimony, fell in love with a certain knight in adulterous embraces. When this was discovered, her son, encountering the knight returning from his mother one night, beat him severely, mutilated him, and sent him away in great disgrace. The mother, shocked by the extraordinary shame of what had happened, and in her anxiety shaken by feminine grief, vomited forth all of that poison into revenge. Therefore, going to Henry I, king of the English, she reported a claim that was more vindictive than true, and publicly confirmed at court with an oath in person that her son Mahel had been fathered not by Bernard, but by a certain other man, with whom she had fallen in love in secret and illicit embraces.[21]

Both the *Genealogy* and its Latin source go on to explain that this vengeful act of perjury led to King Henry giving the lordship of Brecon to Sibyl, the daughter of Nest and Bernard, who married Miles fitz Walter. In other words, the incident explains why the lordship was inherited by a daughter instead of a son. It is characterised by the typically Giraldian irony of a woman, accused of adultery, using that claim of adultery against her accuser (who happens to be her son).²² The episode also exhibits the misogyny that runs through Gerald's works: he viewed women as irrational, vindictive causes of temptation for men.²³ At the same time, the episode represents a theme that runs through the *Genealogy*: the inheritance of the lordship through women, whose marriages and children determine its wayward course through the marcher families of the region. The overall impression is that women are important for perpetuating family dynasties and therefore hold some degree of power in a system of primogeniture, but are warned not to overstep that role by doing something rash like refuting claims to paternity.

A generation later, another act of vengeance occurs, this time divine. Miles and Sibyl's son William wrongfully persecutes David fitz Gerald, bishop of St Davids (1148–76), who happens to be Gerald of Wales's uncle, and is punished by slowly dying of a head injury after an accident at Bronllys Castle. The *Genealogy* states:

> Le dreyn de ces sink, Willame le conestable, estoyt le plus felons des autres, e pursuit tant le eueske de Seynt Dauid, Dauid le secund, qui nul repos pur ly auer ne pout en sa euesche, mes s'enfui en Engletere la ou il pout de luy en luy. Eschey endementirz qe l'euantdit Willame estoyt herbege a Bientles ou Sire Watir de Clifford au chastel, e par mesaventure arderent les mesons de meme cely chastel. Si chey une pire de la haute tour sur la teste Willame, le auantdit seygnur de Brekenoch, e greuement le estona.

> The last of the five, William Constable, was the most wicked of all of them, and so severely persecuted the Bishop of St Davids, David the second, that he had no respite for his possessions and could not be in his bishopric, but was exiled in England, where he could go from place to place. It came about that the aforementioned William was staying at the dwelling of Bronllys with Walter de Clifford in the castle, and through misfortune they burned the buildings of that castle. A stone fell from the high tower onto the head of William, the aforementioned lord of Brecon, and gravely injured him.²⁴

This passage is a translation of Gerald of Wales's *Itinerarium Kambriae* i. 2:

Praedictorum autem fratrum quinque, et filiorum comitis Milonis, penultimus ille, et postremus hereditatis possessor, inhumana prae ceteris crudelitate notabilis, adeo in Menevensem episcopum David secundum, suasque tam possessiones, quam terras et homines, desaevire statuerat, ut a finibus de Brecheniauc non praesul jam, sed tanquam exul existens, tam Angliam quam alias diocesis suae partes frequentaret. Contigit autem interea ut in castro de Broynles cum Waltero de Cliffordia Mahel hospitio susceptus, aedibus casuali incendio consumptis, lapide a principali turre deorsum cadente percussus in capite letaliter obrueretur.

Moreover, Mahel, the second youngest of these five brothers, all sons of Earl Miles, the last in the line of inheritance and even more noteworthy than the others for his heartless cruelty, was so determined to rage against David II, bishop of St David's, and his possessions and his lands and his men, that David was forced from the territory of Brycheiniog, where he is not now bishop, but living in exile, he went to England and to other parts of his diocese. It happened meanwhile, moreover, that after Mahel had been received as a guest by Walter de Clifford in the castle of Bronllys, the buildings were burned down by an unintentional fire, and Mahel was struck on the head by a stone that fell from the main tower and mortally wounded.[25]

Mahel (William in the *Genealogy of the Lords of Brecknock*) then recognises the error in his ways and sends a note to Bishop David acknowledging that his injury is an act of divine retribution; he dies of the wound eventually.[26] Like the previous episode, this story illustrates an important theme for Gerald: sinful acts will be revenged, one way or another.

These initial portions of the *Genealogy of the Lords of Brecknock* represent a direct translation of Gerald's *Itinerarium Kambriae*, albeit with an error in the name of Miles's son in the above episode, with no other texts incorporated. The translation reflects stylistic choices that have been made by the translator: the French text is often less verbose, simpler and more to the point than the *Itinerarium*, as if the translator was lifting facts from the source text while leaving behind the rhetorical flourishes that Gerald relished.

The *Genealogy* then departs from this source: in the *Itinerarium*, Gerald goes on to discuss the legend of Brychan Brycheiniog, which the *Genealogy* does not include.[27] Instead, it looks forward, continuing to discuss the heirs of the lordship in chronological order. Its main aim appears to be to explain how the lordship came to be in the hands of the Bohuns, not to discuss the early history of Brycheiniog and its foundation by Brychan. In its focus on the post-Norman-Conquest history of the lordship (beginning not with Brychan, but with Bernard de Neufmarché), the *Genealogy* is rather less 'Welsh' in its focus than Gerald's account of the history of Brecon in the *Itinerarium*.

In sum, Gerald seems to have been a useful source for the early history of the lordship of Brecon, and his information about the lordship brought characteristically Giraldian themes: the importance of loyalty to the family over the individual, dedication to the church, obedience to church leadership, and justified punishment of behaviour when these norms are violated. Though Gerald is a source for just the first two episodes in the text, he leaves an indelible mark, as the story of the inheritance of the lordship of Brecon is then framed by these themes. The following text, *History of Llanthony Priory*, further highlights these themes. The scribe who wrote the *Genealogy* into the blank pages immediately preceding the *History of Llanthony Priory* may have seen resonances and similarities across these texts and made a decision to pair them together. The history of the lordship and the history of the priories are intertwined.

The Register and Chronicle of the Abbey of Aberconwy

The final text under discussion here is the *Register and Chronicle of the Abbey of Aberconwy*, extant in a late fifteenth-century manuscript (London, British Library, Harley 3725, ff. 40v–65v).[28] It is preceded in the manuscript by a chronicle of Hailes Abbey, a Cistercian abbey in Gloucestershire. This is a composite manuscript consisting of two parts. Part i contains the chronicle of Hailes Abbey in a single hand, while part ii contains Esechias's *Liber de annis* (a prognostication note about 1 January), the *Register and Chronicle of the Abbey of Aberconwy* and an English translation of *Somnia Danielis* (a manual for interpreting dreams), also in a single hand. Both hands are fifteenth century. The British Library cataloguer suggests that parts i and ii were produced separately, but with part ii created as an intentional supplement to part i, as it carefully imitates the layout of part i. The cataloguer suggests further that David Winchcombe, a brother of Hailes Abbey who became abbot of Aberconwy in 1482, brought part i with him from Hailes to Aberconwy, a Cistercian abbey in Gwynedd, where part ii was added.[29] Daniel Huws disagrees, stating that 'the two parts of the codex have neither signatures, early foliation, script, annotation nor indeed anything in common to suggest that their association is medieval in origin'.[30] On this observation, David Stephenson writes:

> it seems clear therefore that the juxtaposition of Hailes and Aberconwy texts in London, British Library MS Harley 3725 should not lead us to assume a common origin for the two texts. This is not quite the same as proving that there is accordingly no link between the two.[31]

Stephenson refers to the association between Hailes and Aberconwy that developed in the late fifteenth century as part of the reform of the Welsh Cistercian houses.[32] He argues that the chronicle was compiled by someone with an interest in Welsh Cistercians at Hailes Abbey, perhaps in aid of David Winchcombe's impending move to Aberconwy.[33]

Table 2: Contents and structure of London, British Library, Harley 3725

Part	Quire	Foliation	Text	Hand
i	1	2–13	Hailes Abbey chronicle	1
	2	14–25	Hailes Abbey chronicle	1
	3	26–37	Hailes Abbey chronicle (ends 31v); 32r blank; 32v scribbled note; *Nota de modo et tempore fundatoris abathie de Hayles* (33r–37v)	1
ii	4	38–43	Esechias, *Liber de annis* (ends 40v); *Registrum Aberconway* (begins 40v)	2
	5[34]	44–51	*Registrum Aberconway*	2
	6[35]	52–57	*Registrum Aberconway*	2
	7	58–65	*Registrum Aberconway*; later notes added to 65v	2
	8	66–73	*Somnia Danielis* (in English)	2
	9	74–81	*Somnia Danielis* (in English)	2

Aberconwy was founded in 1186 by monks from Strata Florida, a Cistercian house in Ceredigion. It was patronised by princes of Gwynedd, including Gruffudd ap Cynan (d. 1200), Hywel ap Gruffudd (d. 1216), Llywelyn ab Iorwerth (*c*.1173–1240) and Dafydd ap Llywelyn (*c*.1215–46), all of whom are buried there. The abbey was relocated by Edward I to Maenan a few miles away *c*.1283–4. The *Register and Chronicle of the Abbey of Aberconwy* discusses the abbey's foundation in the context of Welsh history, with material taken from Geoffrey of Monmouth's *De gestis Britonum* Book XII and Gerald of Wales's *Descriptio Kambriae*, as David Stephenson has noted.[36] It also includes various grants to the abbey, including a charter to Aberconwy by Gruffudd ap Cynan, a list of the abbey's possessions and annals detailing thirteenth-century Welsh history.[37]

The *Register and Chronicle*'s use of Geoffrey and Gerald as sources is indirect, rather than direct, as these sections of the *Register and Chronicle* are sourced from an adaptation of Geoffrey *Epitome historiae Britanniae*, a late fourteenth-century Latin chronicle originally from the diocese of Llandaf.[38] The relevant section of the *Register and Chronicle*, ultimately taken from the *Epitome*, reads:

> [P]ost Kadwalladrum, reliquie Britonum perdiderunt nomen suum et regnum. Iam non uocantur Britones, sed Wallenses. Tantam inquietationem patiebantur per barbaricos Saxones quod non potuerunt eis amplius resistere. Et sic debilitati, petierunt Cambriam, modo Walliam. Et ibi per multa tempora regebantur per principes generis sui. Regebantur enim omnes per unum principem solum usque ad tempus Rothri vawr .i. Rodrici magni. Iste Rodricus magnus regebat totam Walliam tempore suo. **Post cuius mortem .iii. filii eius, videlicet Merwynus, Anaraud, et Cadell, diuiserunt inter se totam Walliam in iii. partes. Merthwin principatum Gwyneth .i. Northwalliam. Anaraud principatum Powysie. Cadell principatum de Henparth .i. Sowthwalliam.** Unusquisque istorum cum posteris suis regebat partem suam ut princeps post multos annos. Et postquam multi anni essent euoluti, iste due partes, videlicet Powysia et Sowthwallia, perdiderunt nomen principis sui et principatus.[39] Princeps uero Northwallie reassumpsit nomen integrum tocius principatus Wallie quo gaudebat usque cum posteris suis usque ad Lewelinum Principem. Wap gruff' Wap ll. Wap Ierwarth

Droyndon. Post cuius mortem, nullum hucusque habuerunt principem de genere suo, sicut manifeste sequentibus declarabitur.

After Kadwalladrus, the remaining Britons lost their name and their kingdom. Now they are not called Britons, but Welsh. They suffered so much harassment by the barbarous Saxons that they were not able to resist them anymore. And thus weakened, they made for Cambria, now Wales. And there they were ruled for a long time by the princes of their race. They were all ruled by one prince alone up to the time of Rhodri Mawr, that is, Rodricus the Great. This Rodricus the Great ruled over all Wales in his time. **After his death, his three sons, namely Merthwynus, Anaraud, and Cadell, divided Wales among themselves into three parts. To Merthwynus went the principality of Gwynedd, that is, North Wales; to Anaraud, the principality of Powys; to Cadell, the principality of Henparth, that is, South Wales.** Each one of them with his descendants ruled his part as prince for many years, And after many years had passed, these two parts, that is, Powys and South Wales, lost their name of 'prince' and 'principality'. The prince of North Wales regained the entire name of the whole principality of Wales, for which he rejoiced, with his descendants up to Prince Llywelyn ap Gruffudd ap Llywelyn ab Iorwerth Drwyndwn. After his death, none of his race had the title 'prince', as will be shown clearly in the following.[40]

Stephenson has noted that the information about the division of Wales among the three sons of Rhodri Mawr, which led to three major kingdoms of Wales ruled by Rhodri's descendants, and represented in bold type above, is a detail that originates with Gerald of Wales's *Descriptio Kambriae* i. 2.[41] It is known as the 'Rhodri Mawr origin story'. Rhodri Mawr (d. 878) was a king of Gwynedd who brought Ceredigion and Powys under his control, and an important ancestor in the genealogies of medieval Welsh princes. Though these particular paragraphs are taken from the *Epitome historiae Britanniae*, the story of the tripartite division is ultimately from Gerald.[42] It does not occur in Geoffrey of Monmouth's *De gestis Britonum*. The relevant section of Gerald's *Descriptio Kambriae* reads:

Divisa est antiquitus Wallia totalis in tres partes tanquam aequales; plus equivalentiae tamen, quam justae quantitatis et proportionis habita consideratione; Venedotiam scilicet, quae nunc Nortwallia, id est, Borealis Wallia dicitur; Sudwalliam, id est Australem Walliam, quae Kambrice Deheubarth, id est, Dextralis pars dicitur; cujus etiam portio septem cantaredis est conserta Demetia, et Powisiam, quasi mediam et orientalem.

 Divisionis autem hujus haec causa suberat. Rothericus magnus, qui Britannice Rotheri Maur dicebatur, totique Walliae praesidebat, tres filios habuerat, Mervinunm, Anaraut, et Cadelh. Hi tres totam inter se Walliam diviserunt. Mervino cessit Nortwallia, Anaraut Powisia, Cadelh vero, cum populi totius et fratrum benedictione, Sudwallia.

From time immemorial Wales has been divided into three more or less equal parts, more equal in value than in size and proportion, namely, Gwynedd, which is now called Nortwallia, that is, North Wales; Sudwallia, which is South Wales, called Deheubarth in Welsh, i.e. 'the right-hand part', a sub-section of which, containing seven cantrefs, is called Demetia; and Powys, the middle and eastern part.

 The reason for this division was as follows. Roderick the Great, who in British is called Rhodri Mawr and who ruled over all Wales, had three sons, Merfyn, Anarawd and Cadell. These three divided all of Wales between them. To Merfyn was given North Wales, to Anarawd Powys, and to Cadell South Wales, with the blessing of all the people and his brothers.[43]

Gerald's account differs from earlier Welsh historical texts that note a division into two parts (north and south Wales) at the time of Maelgwn Gwynedd (d. 547/549), with Powys absent from the explanation (reflecting historical reality). In the twelfth century, by contrast, when Powys was a major kingdom during the rule of Madog ap Maredudd (d. 1160), it made sense to include Powys. Ben Guy argues that this story was created retrospectively to 'legitimise' the descendants of Rhodri who had formed three kingdoms by the mid-twelfth century.[44] Even if anachronistic, the story reflected a contemporary understanding of Welsh political geography. Stephenson notes that Gerald is probably the ultimate source for the tripartite division information appearing in the *Register and Chronicle* because it repeats a significant mistake made by Gerald: in later Welsh genealogies, Anarawd's descendants are kings of Gwynedd, and Merfyn's descendants are kings of Powys, not the other way around.[45] It is remarkable that this information is ultimately from Gerald, even if mediated through the *Epitome*, as it shows the far reach of his work on the writing of history in medieval Wales.

In the *Register and Chronicle*, this information, appearing as a preface to the history of Aberconwy, focuses on Gwynedd over the other kingdoms. It cuts some information about the kings of south Wales, shifting the south Wales focus of the original source text, the *Epitome* (which was probably written in the diocese of Llandaf) to north Wales. Nevertheless, here again Gerald's writings have an influence on how the Welsh past is portrayed. Placing the history of Aberconwy in the context of the history of Welsh princes strengthens a cultural link between nobility and church that runs through all three of the texts discussed here.[46] In the case of the *Genealogy of the Lords of Brecknock*, this theme appears in the context of a lesson about respect for church administrators learned by William Constable; in the *Register and Chronicle*, the text takes pains to record the identities of founders and benefactors of Aberconwy, honouring them as worthy patrons.

Overall, the framework of the tripartite division of Wales places the abbey of Aberconwy in the context of Welsh political history, with a focus on the kingdom of Gwynedd. That it accomplishes this from an English chronicling perspective is remarkable: David Stephenson has shown that the Gwynedd events described between 1190 and 1241 are ridden with errors, and that the chronicle appears to rely on English chronicle sources, like the Annals of Tewkesbury, the Annals of Worcester and the Hailes Abbey chronicle in London, British Library, Cotton Cleopatra D, iii (ff. 1–72, s. xiv), rather than any source from north-west Wales.[47] He suggests Hailes Abbey as a point of origin for the *Register and Chronicle*.[48] This shows a considerable degree of interest in Welsh history on the part of chronicle compilers and readers who may have been English and/or working in England, who functioned primarily outside a circle of influence that would have included chronicle sources from the local Aberconwy area, and whose chronicle sources were primarily English. The reform of the Welsh Cistercian houses in the 1480s, if this was indeed the impetus for compiling the material in the chronicle, as Stephenson has argued, led to a substantial degree of reading about, and reworking, the history of Wales on the part of a house in the borderlands charged with a programme of reform.

Conclusion

In conclusion, these three texts share broad trends that fall outside the typical themes of historical writing in the Welsh vernacular. These themes are linked both directly and indirectly to Gerald's substantial interests in Welsh ecclesiastical and secular history, and they include the intertwined histories of lordships, noble patrons and individual monasteries; the importance of a close relationship between aristocracy and church; and the contextualisation of monastic foundations in the early history of the Norman presence in Wales (in the *History of Llanthony Priory*, the story begins with Hugh de Lacy's squire, and in the *Genealogy* with Bernard de Neufmarché). Overall, these three relatively unknown texts, all with the imprint of Gerald's writings on them in different ways, show that Gerald had a farther reach in Welsh monasteries' understanding of history than previously realised. Even though his influence on Welsh history is not shown, for example, in Welsh-language historical writing from medieval Wales, nor in any extant translations of his works into Middle Welsh, we can see that his Latin works were being read and received in both Latin and French in Wales. Gerald therefore shaped the understanding of Welsh church history to a greater degree than previously realised.

Notes

1   *The History of Llanthony Priory*, ed. and trans. Robert Bartlett (Oxford, 2022); see also Robert Bartlett, 'Gerald of Wales and the *History of Llanthony Priory*', in Georgia Henley and A. Joseph McMullen (eds), *Gerald of Wales: New Perspectives on a Medieval Writer and Critic* (Cardiff, 2018), pp. 81–96.

2   Huw Pryce, 'Gerald of Wales and the Welsh Past', in Henley and McMullen (eds), *Gerald of Wales: New Perspectives*, pp. 19–45; see also Huw Pryce, 'Gerald of Wales: Medieval Ethnographer of the Welsh', in W. John Morgan and Fiona Bowie (eds), *Social Anthropologies of the Welsh: Past and Present* (Canon Pyon, 2021), pp. 41–55; Huw Pryce, 'Giraldus and the Geraldines', in Peter Crooks and Seán Duffy (eds), *The Geraldines and Medieval Ireland: The Making of a Myth* (Dublin, 2016), pp. 53–68; Huw Pryce, 'Gerald of Wales, Gildas and the *Descriptio Kambriae*', in Fiona Edmonds and Paul Russell (eds), *Tome:*

Studies in Medieval Celtic History and Law in Honour of Thomas Charles-Edwards (Woodbridge, 2011), pp. 115–24.

3   For Gerald's reception in Wales, see Georgia Henley, 'Gerald's Circulation and Reception in Wales: The Case of *Claddedigaeth Arthur*', in Henley and McMullen (eds), *Gerald of Wales: New Perspectives*, pp. 223–42.

4   See discussion in *History of Llanthony Priory*, ed. and trans. Bartlett, pp. xxvii–xxviii.

5   This work is titled *Speculum vite Roberti Herefordensis episcopi* and it is edited by Henry Wharton (ed.), *Anglia Sacra Pars Secunda* (London, 1691), pp. 295–321.

6   Diana B. Tyson, 'A Medieval Genealogy of the Lords of Brecknock', *Nottingham Medieval Studies*, 48 (2004), 1–14 (p. 4).

7   *History of Llanthony Priory*, ed. and trans. Bartlett, p. xiii.

8   *History of Llanthony Priory*, ed. and trans. Bartlett, p. xii; John Spence, 'Genealogies of Noble Families in Anglo-Norman', in Raluca L. Radulescu and Edward Donald Kennedy (eds), *Broken Lines: Genealogical Literature in Medieval Britain and France*, Medieval Texts and Cultures of Northern Europe, 16 (Turnhout, 2008), pp. 63–78 (p. 66); Neil R. Ker, *Medieval Libraries of Great Britain: A List of Surviving Books* (2nd edn, London, 1964), p. 108.

9   John Spence, *Reimagining History in Anglo-Norman Prose Chronicles* (Woodbridge and Rochester, 2013), p. 28; see also discussion in Georgia Henley, *Reimagining the Past in the Borderlands of Medieval England and Wales* (Oxford, 2024), pp. 120–35 (p. 130).

10 Hugh de Lacy is a son of the Norman baron Walter de Lacy (d. 1085) who came to Britain in the Norman Conquest and took over lands in Gloucestershire and Herefordshire.

11 *History of Llanthony Priory*, ed. and trans. Bartlett, pp. 10–11. This is a section that parallels what Gerald says about Llanthony in his *Itinerarium Kambriae* i. 3.

12 *History of Llanthony Priory* 1.4, ed. and trans. Bartlett, pp. 24–5. Gerald of Wales discusses this Hugh de Lacy's activities in Ireland in the *Expugnatio Hibernica*.

13 *History of Llanthony Priory* 1.4, ed. and trans. Bartlett, pp. 24–7.

14 I am grateful to the editors of this volume for noting this contrast. See R. R. Davies, *The First English Empire: Power and Identities in the British Isles 1093–1343* (Oxford, 2000), pp. 117–37.

15 Gerald of Wales, *Itinerarium Kambriae* i. 3 (ed. James F. Dimock, *Giraldi Cambrensis Opera Volume 6* (London, 1868), pp. 37–47).

16 He is the father of Miles fitz Walter (d. 1143), discussed further below in the *Genealogy*.

17 *History of Llanthony Priory* 2.2, ed. and trans. Bartlett, pp. 56–7.

18 For further discussion, see Henley, *Reimagining the Past*, pp. 120–35.

19 Spence, *Reimagining History*, p. 28.

20 London, British Library Cotton Julius D. x, ff. 28r–v; see also Tyson, 'Medieval Genealogy', 8–9.
21 Gerald of Wales, *Itinerarium Kambriae* i. 2 (ed. Dimock, p. 29; trans. Lewis Thorpe, *Gerald of Wales: The Journey through Wales and the Description of Wales* (London, 1978), p. 89). Translations of Gerald's *Itinerarium Kambriae* and *Descriptio Kambriae*, here and elsewhere, are adapted from Thorpe with the aid of forthcoming work by The Writings of Gerald of Wales project, undertaken by Thomas Charles-Edwards, Paul Russell and Jacob Currie. I am grateful to the project investigators for allowing me to see excerpts of their texts and translations in advance of publication. Any errors are my own.
22 For Gerald and irony, see Simon Meecham-Jones, 'Style, Truth and Irony: Listening to the Voice of Gerald of Wales's Writings', in Henley and McMullen (eds), *Gerald of Wales: New Perspectives*, pp. 127–43.
23 Examples of Gerald's misogynistic views are too many to numerate here; for discussion of Gerald's views of women and inheritance, see Susan M. Johns, *Gender, Nation and Conquest in the High Middle Ages: Nest of Deheubarth* (Manchester, 2016), pp. 49–82.
24 London, British Library Cotton Julius D. x, f. 28v; see also Tyson, 'Medieval Genealogy', 9.
25 Gerald of Wales, *Itinerarium Kambriae* i. 2 (ed. Dimock, pp. 30–1; trans. Thorpe, *Gerald of Wales*, pp. 90–1). Translation adapted from Thorpe with the aid of forthcoming text and translation from The Writings of Gerald of Wales project.
26 This discrepancy in the names of the sons is noted by Tyson, 'Medieval Genealogy', 9 n. 37. Both William and Mahel were sons of Miles fitz Walter, but the *Genealogy of the Lords of Brecknock* misidentifies which son was involved in the accident at Bronllys Castle.
27 For Brychan Brycheiniog and associated genealogical tracts, see Ben Guy, *Medieval Welsh Genealogy: An Introduction and Textual Study* (Woodbridge, 2020), pp. 130–6.
28 It is edited in the *Register and Chronicle of Aberconway from the Harleian MS. 3725*, ed. Henry Ellis (London, 1847), and discussed by David Stephenson, *The Aberconwy Chronicle*, Kathleen Hughes Memorial Lectures on Mediaeval Welsh History, 2 (Cambridge, 2002); Daniel Huws, *Medieval Welsh Manuscripts* (Aberystwyth, 2000), pp. 276–7; Daniel Huws, *A Repertory of Welsh Manuscripts and Scribes, c.800–c.1800*, 3 vols (Aberystwyth, 2022), I, 684.
29 Stephenson refutes the suggestion that the *Register and Chronicle* was compiled at Aberconwy, due to a lack of use of north Welsh sources in the chronicle, some serious errors in dates and facts relating to Gwynedd, and a heavy use of English chronicling sources: *Aberconwy Chronicle*, pp. 6–15.
30 Huws, *Medieval Welsh Manuscripts*, p. 277 n. 29.

31 Stephenson, *Aberconwy Chronicle*, p. 2.
32 Stephenson, *Aberconwy Chronicle*, p. 15; David Williams, *The Welsh Cistercians*, 2 vols (Caldey Island, 1984), I, 81. The abbots of Louth Park, Woburn and Hailes were ordered to visit Welsh Cistercian houses in the 1480s as part of a programme of reform.
33 Stephenson, *Aberconwy Chronicle*, pp. 6, 15–16.
34 Quire 5 is marked as quire 6 on f. 44r.
35 Quire 6 has no quire mark.
36 Stephenson, *Aberconwy Chronicle*, pp. 2–3.
37 Stephenson argues that these annals rely on the chronicle of Hailes Abbey in London, British Library, Cotton Cleopatra D. iii (ff. 1–72, s. xiv¹); Stephenson, *Aberconwy Chronicle*, pp. 13–15.
38 I discuss this chronicle at length in *Reimagining the Past*, ch. 1.
39 Here, the *Register and Chronicle* skips a section of text in the *Epitome* explaining that the descendants of Cadell ruled over Deheubarth until the time of Rhys ap Gruffudd, and it lists Rhys's lineage back to Rhodri Mawr. It makes sense that an audience interested in Aberconwy, a north Wales foundation, was not interested in the kings of south Wales, and so this information was left out.
40 *Register and Chronicle of Aberconwy*, p. 6; London, British Library Harley 3725, ff. 42r–v, with modern punctuation and capitalisation added. My translation.
41 He notes further that the epithet Iorwerth Drwyndwn to refer to Llywelyn ab Iorwerth's father may also be a detail taken from Gerald: Stephenson, *Aberconwy Chronicle*, p. 10.
42 Stephenson, *Aberconwy Chronicle*, pp. 3–4; see also discussion in Guy, *Medieval Welsh Genealogy*, pp. 118–21.
43 Gerald of Wales, *Descriptio Kambriae* i. 2 (ed. Dimock, p. 166; trans. Thorpe, p. 221). Translation adapted from Thorpe with the aid of forthcoming text and translation from The Writings of Gerald of Wales project.
44 Guy, *Medieval Welsh Genealogy*, p. 119.
45 Stephenson, *Aberconwy Chronicle*, p. 3; for further discussion, see Guy, *Medieval Welsh Genealogy*, pp. 118–21.
46 It also gives greater emphasis to the charter of Gruffudd ap Cynan, whose lineage could be traced back to the origin legend of the earlier sections. I am grateful to Rebecca Thomas for this point.
47 Stephenson, *Aberconwy Chronicle*, pp. 6–13.
48 Stephenson, *Aberconwy Chronicle*, p. 15.

3

Trioedd Ynys Prydein fel Testunau Hanes

Nia Wyn Jones

Cyfres o osodiadau cwta, yn trafod hen hanes y Cymry a'u teyrnas, drwy restru tri pheth, yw Trioedd Ynys Prydein.[1] Mae pynciau'r Trioedd yn cynnwys unigolion, grwpiau a digwyddiadau: y 'Tri Gwyndeyrn', neu brenhinoedd bendigaid; y 'Tri Chyfor [byddin] a aeth o'r Ynys hon'; y 'Tair Anfad Gyflafan'.[2] Mae eu hyd hefyd yn amrywio: o deitlau cryno a thri enw syml i ambell un sy'n cynnig tair stori fer mewn brawddegau llawn – mae triawd y Tri Chyfor dros ddau gant o eiriau o hyd.[3]

Pwrpas y bennod hon yw trafod y Trioedd fel gweithiau hanes. O ystyried taw eu pwrpas yw amlinellu, trwy restru ar sail thema, hanes y Cymry, mae'n nodedig cyn lleied o drafodaeth sydd wedi bod ohonynt fel testunau hanesyddol. Efallai bod golygiad meistrolgar Rachel Bromwich wedi cyfrannu i'r ffaith yma i raddau – hawdd yw meddwl am gyfrol mor addysglawn a chynhwysol fel y gair olaf ar bwnc. Ond mae modd cynyddu ein dealltwriaeth o'r Trioedd yn eu cyd-destun canoloesol, yn enwedig o ystyried y datblygiadau yn ein dealltwriaeth o'r Gymru ganoloesol ers cyhoeddiad cyntaf golygiad Bromwich yn 1961.[4]

I ddechrau, trafodaf y Trioedd yn gyffredinol ac, yn fwy penodol, 'Cyfres Gynnar' y Trioedd, y testun sy'n cynnig ffocws i'r bennod hon. Bydd trafodaeth o gysylltiadau'r Gyfres Gynnar â thestunau eraill yn arwain at y casgliad bod Clynnog Fawr yn Arfon yn ganolfan bwysig i gyfansoddiad y gyfres hon. Â'r bennod ymlaen i ddehongli Trioedd Ynys Prydein fel testun hanes, a bydd y trioedd llawnach sy'n terfynu Cyfres Gynnar y Trioedd yn cynnig strwythur ar gyfer y drafodaeth fanylach hon. Bydd hefyd drafodaeth o'r berthynas rhwng testun y Trioedd a barddoniaeth llys beirdd y tywysogion yn cynnig modd i fesur sut yr oedd testunau o'r fath yn cael eu defnyddio a'u dehongli, ac yn cynnig casgliadau am bwysigrwydd gwleidyddol ac ymarferol hanes yng Nghymru'r Oesoedd Canol.

Mae diffinio 'Trioedd Ynys Prydein' yn gymhleth. Mae golygiad Bromwich yn cyfuno nifer o lawysgrifau gwahanol i gyfres gydlynol o drioedd, i greu testun hollgynhwysol ond artiffisial. Cynigir blaenoriaeth i destun llawysgrif Peniarth 16, sef y 'Gyfres Gynnar' (*'Early Version'* Bromwich).[5] Mae dadl Bromwich bod y fersiwn hwn o'r Trioedd yn gynharach na'r fersiwn llawnach a geir yn Llyfr Gwyn Rhydderch a Llyfr Coch Hergest yn cael ei lled-dderbyn yma.[6] Derbynnir hefyd bod trefn y testun yn y llawysgrif hon, a'r fersiwn tebyg ond llai cynhwysfawr yn llawysgrif Peniarth 45, yn cynrychioli testun cyflawn.[7] Fel mae'r drafodaeth isod yn amlygu, ni allwn hawlio taw'r Gyfres Gynnar yw'r dystiolaeth gynharaf o Trioedd Ynys Prydein fel testun – mae cyfeiriadau beirdd llys y ddeuddegfed ganrif at drioedd unigol yn sicr yn dystiolaeth o drioedd unigol sy'n rhagddyddio'r Gyfres Gynnar. Ond fel y testun cyflawn cynharaf sy'n goroesi o'r Trioedd y caiff y Gyfres Gynnar ei thrafod yma.

Y Gyfres Gynnar

Mae'n rhaid cyfiawnhau y tybiaethau hyn i raddau. Mae llawysgrifau canoloesol Trioedd Ynys Prydein yn eu cynnwys mewn nifer o drefniadau gwahanol, ac yn cynnwys detholiad gwahanol o drioedd.[8] Y llawysgrif gynharaf i gynnwys y testun yw Peniarth 16, rhan iv, darn yn wreiddiol o lawysgrif lawnach Aberystwyth, Llyfrgell Genedlaethol Cymru 5266B. Llawysgrif o ail hanner y drydedd ganrif ar ddeg yw hon, o ogledd Cymru.[9] Mae'r fersiwn hwn o'r Trioedd hefyd yn bresennol yn llawysgrif Peniarth 45, llawysgrif sy'n dyddio o hanner cyntaf y bedwaredd ganrif ar ddeg, efallai i'w chysylltu ag ardal Brycheiniog.[10] Mae'n ymddangos nad yw fersiwn Peniarth 45 o'r Trioedd yn deillio o Peniarth 16 yn uniongyrchol – yn hytrach maent ill dau yn tarddu o gopi cynharach.[11] Serch hyn, mae'r ddwy lawysgrif yn cynnwys yr un tri thestun (*Brut y Brenhinedd* yn fersiwn Dingestow; cyfres gynnar Trioedd Ynys Prydein; Bonedd y Saint), sy'n awgrymu bod y rhain hefyd yn y llawysgrif wreiddiol mae'r fersiynau yma yn deillio ohoni.[12]

Mae trefn y trioedd unigol yn y ddwy lawysgrif yn sylweddol gyfath, a dim ond tri thriawd wedi eu neilltuo o Beniarth 45 yn ymddangos yn Peniarth 16, a dim byd sylweddol unigryw yn Peniarth 45.[13] Mae'r drefn, heblaw am y neilltuadau hyn, yn union yr un fath. Gan amlaf mae'r cyfresi llawnach o drioedd mewn llawysgrifau eraill yn wahanol iawn o ran trefn nid yn unig i Beniarth 16 a 45, ond hefyd i'w gilydd.[14]

Sail y drafodaeth hon yw 37 triawd y Gyfres Gynnar, yn seiliedig ar lawysgrif Peniarth 16 – gyda chymhariaeth â thestun Peniarth 45, fel y'i cyflwynwyd yng ngolygiad Bromwich.[15] Derbyniaf hwn fel testun sefydledig, cydlynol ac mae'r sylwadau a chasgliadau sy'n dilyn am Trioedd Ynys Prydain fel gwaith hanesyddol o fewn ei gyd-destun wedi eu seilio yn bennaf ar y testun hwn fel cyfanwaith. Rhaid hefyd cynnig sylw ynghylch Trioedd y Meirch, sydd i'w gweld yn llawysgrifau Peniarth 16 a Peniarth 45 ill dwy. Er bod y trioedd hyn yn wreiddiol bresennol yn y ddwy lawysgrif, mae eu harwahanrwydd o ran pwnc, y gwahaniaethu rhyngddynt a'r Trioedd yn y ddwy lawysgrif, a'r ffaith eu bod yn ymddangos yn annibynnol yn *Llyfr Du Caerfyrddin* yn cyfiawnhau'r penderfyniad i drin y gyfres o Trioedd Ynys Prydain 1–37 fel testun ar wahân i Drioedd y Meirch.[16] Rhaid, serch hyn, cydnabod bod cysylltiad cryf rhwng y ddau destun, a bydd Trioedd y Meirch yn allweddol i unrhyw astudiaeth ehangach o Trioedd Ynys Prydain.

Rhaid hefyd ystyried cwestiynau sylfaenol dyddiad ac awduraeth y 'Gyfres Gynnar' o Trioedd Ynys Prydein. Mae'r llawysgrif hynaf, Peniarth 16, wedi ei dyddio i ail hanner y drydedd ganrif ar ddeg, sy'n cynnig *terminus ante quem*.[17] O ran dyddiad y testun ei hun, roedd Rachel Bromwich yn gweld Trioedd Ynys Prydain fel datblygiad graddol dros gyfnod estynedig ac mae gwaith pellach i'w wneud ar y datblygiad hwn.[18] Mae tystiolaeth gadarn ym marddoniaeth llys y ddeuddegfed ganrif bod rhai trioedd unigol yn hŷn o beth amser na'r Gyfres Gynnar – mae'n annhebygol, felly, taw'r Gyfres Gynnar fel y mae oedd y casgliad cynharaf o Trioedd Ynys Prydain a gofnodwyd.[19] Yn hytrach na ffocysu ar y posibilrwydd o ddatblygiad cynharach y testun, mae'r drafodaeth hon yn pwysleisio bodolaeth y Gyfres Gynnar fel cyfanwaith cydlynol a phwrpasol. O'r pwynt yma ymlaen, bydd unrhyw gyfeiriad diamodol at 'y trioedd' neu 'Trioedd Ynys Prydain' yn cyfeirio at y Gyfres Gynnar, trioedd 1–37.

O ran y Gyfres Gynnar, rhaid nodi bod arwyddion amlwg na all y testun ddyddio o gyfnod cynharach na tua chanol y ddeuddegfed ganrif. Mae'r triawd sy'n agor y gyfres, *Teir Lleithiclwyth*, yn awgrymu'n gryf dylanwad gwleidyddiaeth eglwysig y ddeuddegfed ganrif. Mae'r sôn am ffigyrau o ddechrau'r ddeuddegfed ganrif yn nhrioedd 30 a 24 hefyd yn awgrymu'r fath ddyddiad. Mae triawd 24 yn cyfeirio at Gilbert mab Catgyffro, efallai'r Gilbert de Clare (m. 1117) a feddiannodd Ceredigion yn gynnar yn y ddeuddegfed ganrif, neu o bosib ei fab.[20] Yn sicr, mae'r enw Gilbert yn awgrymu cyfnod ar ôl i'r enw hwn ddod yn adnabyddus yng Nghymru'r ddeuddegfed ganrif trwy'r teulu de Clare.[21] Mwy sicr yw'r cyfeiriad yn nhriawd 30 at Alan Fyrgan, neu Alan Fergant, dug Llydaw (m. 1119).[22] Awgrymog hefyd yw'r cyfeiriad at Gwasgwyn yn nhriawd 35, sy'n debygol o ddyddio o gyfnod wedi priodas Harri II gydag Eleanor o Aquitaine yn 1152, pan ddaeth yr ardal yn amlycach i bobl Ynys Prydain.[23]

Mae cynnwys y ffigyrau hyn yn arddangos un agwedd o amrediad cronolegol eang cyfres gynnar y trioedd. Mae'r trioedd yn cynnwys ffigyrau'r ddeuddegfed ganrif, a hefyd o'r gorffennol cyn-Rufeinig, ffigyrau o'r Mabinogi a'r cyfnod canoloesol cynnar. Ynys Prydain oll yw byd y Trioedd, gyda diddordeb mwy penodol yng Nghymru, Cernyw a'r Hen Ogledd.

Trioedd Ynys Prydein

Mae'r triawd agoriadol, y Tair Lleithiclwyth (y llwythau a eisteddant ar leithig, mainc neu orsedd), yn crisialu'r pwyslais daearyddol triphlyg yma, gyda thri phrif lys yr Ynys: Mynyw (Tyddewi) yng Nghymru; Celli Wig yng Nghernyw; Pen Rhionydd yn y gogledd.[24] Dyma'r tiriogaethau a barhaent i siarad ieithoedd Brythoneg i'r ail fileniwm wedi Crist, a dyma gynfas yr hanesion a gatalogiwyd yn y trioedd yma. Mae'r dirwedd ddelfrydol yma yn un sy'n cael ei dominyddu gan y Brenin Arthur, *pen teyrnedd* ym mhob un o'r tri *lleithig*:

Teir Lleithicl6 yth Ynys Prydein:

Arthur yn Pen Teyrned ym Mynyw, a Dewi yn Pen Esgyb, a Maelgwn Gwyned yn Pen Hyneif;
Arthur yn Pen Teyrned yg Kelli Wic yg Kernyw, a Bytwini Esgob yn Ben Esgyb, a Charadawc Vreichuras yn Ben Henyf;
Arthur yn Ben Teyrned ym Penn Ryonyd yn y Gogled, a Gwerthmul Wledic yn Benn Hyneif, a Chyndeyrn Garthwys yn Benn Esgyb.[25]

Fel y nodwyd eisoes, mae'r olygfa yma o'r gorffennol pell yn un sy'n perthyn i'r ddeuddegfed ganrif neu'r drydedd ar ddeg. Ymgyrchoedd Tyddewi dros ddominyddiaeth esgobol o Gymru sy'n gyfrifol am leoliad prif lys Arthur yng Nghymru.[26] Yn y gogledd, hefyd, er gwaethaf pwysigrwydd yr ardal hon i'r Hengerdd, mae ôl gwleidyddiaeth eglwysig y ganrif hon ar bersonau llys Arthur. Cyndeyrn oedd nawddsant eglwys Glasgow, a oedd hefyd yn ymladd dros annibyniaeth i'w hesgobaeth drwy ddyrchafu'r sant yma – rheswm cyfoes i awdur y Trioedd weld Cyndeyrn fel archdeip archesgob yr Hen Ogledd.[27]

Mae'r elfennau yma o driawd 1 yn arddangos gwybodaeth ar ran yr awdur o wleidyddiaeth eglwysig y ddeuddegfed ganrif. Gellid dadlau ar yr ochr seciwlar bod amlygrwydd y brenin Arthur yn y triawd yn adlewyrchiad o ddiwylliant llysoedd brenhinol y cyfnod. Crybwyllwyd Arthur a'i ddilynwyr yn aml yn y Gyfres Gynnar, fel yma, yn nhriawd 21:

Tri Thaleithya6c Cat Enys Prydein:

Drystan mab Tallwch, a Hueil mab Caw, a Chei mab Kenyr Keinuarua6c.
    Ac 6n oed taleithya6c arnadunt wynteu ell tri: Bedwyr mab Bedra6c oed h6nn6.[28]

Mae'n amlwg o driawd 26 fod awdur y Gyfres Gynnar yn gweld chwedl Trystan fel un oedd yn cynnwys Arthur.[29] Hueil fab Caw oedd brawd yr hanesydd Gildas, ac yn ôl Caradog o Lancarfan yn ei fuchedd o Gildas, lladdwyd Hueil gan Arthur ei hun.[30] Awgrymwyd y ffaith yma hefyd yn *Culhwch ac Olwen*, testun oedd efallai yn gyfarwydd i awdur Cyfres Gynnar y Trioedd.[31] Mae'n drawiadol, felly, mor gyson yw delwedd y gyfres gynnar yma o'r chwedl Arthuraidd ag un chwedl Gymraeg *Culhwch* ynghyd â bucheddau Lladin Caradog o Lancarfan.

Mae blaenoriaeth – yn wir, dominyddiaeth – Arthur a'i lys felly'n agwedd amlwg. Dwysáu y mae'r sefyllfa yma yng nghyfresi diweddarach y trioedd, gyda'r fformiwla safonol o 'tri *x* Ynys Prydain' yn newid i 'tri *x* llys Arthur'.[32] Gwelwn gymeriadau rhamant Arthuraidd diweddarach hefyd yn cael eu cynnwys ym mydolwg y trioedd diweddarach yma.[33] Ond mae'r tueddiad hwn hefyd yn amlwg yn y gyfres gynnar, gyda'r ymadrodd 'tri *x* llys Arthur' yn ymddangos gyntaf yn nhriawd 9, *Tri 6nben Llys Arthur*.[34] Mae'n ymddangos felly bod y trioedd, wrth iddynt ddatblygu, yn destunau oedd yn defnyddio ac addasu i destunau chwedlau newydd – ond ymddengys y benthyciadau a'r berthynas rhyng-destunol yma yn sylfaenol hefyd i Gyfres Gynnar y Trioedd.

Rhaid nodi nad oes arwydd uniongyrchol o ddylanwad *De gestis Britonum* (*DGB*) Sieffre o Fynwy ar y Gyfres Gynnar. Ond nid yw hwn o reidrwydd yn arwydd bod delwedd y Gyfres Gynnar o'r gorffennol Arthuraidd, Frythonaidd yn symlach nac yn burach na darlun Sieffre, nac ychwaith bod y trioedd yn dyddio i'r cyfnod cyn cyfansoddi *DGB*, tua 1138. Dim ond yn raddol y daw dylanwad Sieffre yn amlwg yng Nghymru, ond erbyn blynyddoedd olaf y ddeuddegfed ganrif mae arwyddion digamsyniol o ddylanwad naratif Sieffre ar feirdd llys.[35] Fel y nodir isod, mae arwyddion yn y Gyfres Gynnar o ddylanwad chwedl *Breuddwyd Maxen Wledig*, testun sydd ei hun yn dangos dylanwad y cyfieithiadau Cymraeg o *DGB* Sieffre. Mae'r Gyfres Gynnar fel y mae, felly, yn sicr yn dyddio o'r cyfnod ar ôl i waith Sieffre fwynhau rhywfaint o ddylanwad. Mae'n amlwg felly, os oedd yr awdur yn ymwybodol o waith Sieffre, dewisodd beidio â'i ddefnyddio. Ond mae Trioedd Ynys Prydein llawn gymaint o strwythuriad ymwybodol o'r gorffennol pell ag yw gwaith Sieffre – nid catalog niwtral o straeon traddodiadol ydyw, ond amlinelliad cynhwysol o orffennol y Cymry.[36]

Tra bo'r awdur yn troi ei gefn ar waith Sieffre, nid oedd ychwaith yn ysgrifennu mewn gwagle testunol. Mae'r Trioedd yn waith rhyngdestunol – mae'n amlwg bod yr awdur yn ymwybodol o nifer o straeon, llawer ohonynt mewn fersiynau ysgrifenedig, am orffennol y Cymry, a hefyd yn creu straeon ar ei liwt ei hun.[37] Mae'r ymdriniaeth â'r Trioedd yn y gorffennol wedi ffocysu arnynt fel storfa ysgrifenedig o wybodaeth oedd, yn y bôn, yn draddodiad llafar.[38] Mae hyn yn sylfaenol i ymdriniaeth Bromwich o'r Trioedd:

> I hope to show in the following pages that the original nucleus of *Trioedd Ynys Prydein*, when separated from the late accretions which have been introduced from literary sources, consisted in an index to this body of orally preserved narrative.[39]

Ond mae campwaith trylwyr a threiddgar Bromwich hefyd yn amlinellu'r lliaws o groes-gyfeiriadau sydd rhwng y testun yma a'r chwedlau a cherddi a thestunau eraill sy'n goroesi o'r Gymru ganoloesol. Byddwn i yn pwysleisio'r ffaith bod y rhain yn gysylltiadau *testunol*, ac er gwaethaf pwysigrwydd sylfaenol traddodiad a pherfformiad llafar i nifer helaeth ein testunau Cymraeg Canol, mae gosod pwyslais ar y benthyca testunol yma yn cynnig casgliadau cadarnach na'r pwyslais ar draddodiad llafar.

Y chwedlau

Nodwyd yn aml y gorgyffwrdd rhwng y Trioedd a Phedair Cainc y Mabinogi.[40] Mae rhyngberthynas y testunau'n agos ac yn gymhleth i'w amlinellu. Mae'r Pedair Cainc yn cyfeirio'n uniongyrchol at ddeg triawd. Nid yw tri ohonynt yn bodoli mewn unrhyw destun o Trioedd Ynys Prydein sy'n goroesi.[41] O'r saith sy'n weddill, mae tri ohonynt yn perthyn i gyfres ehangach y llyfrau Gwyn a Choch yn hytrach na'r gyfres gynnar.[42] Mae'r gweddill yn cyfeirio at y Tri Chudd a'r Tri Datgudd (triawd 37, yn cael ei gyfrif fel dau driawd yn rhestr Ifor Williams), y Tri Lleddf Unben a'r Tri Aniwair Deulu. Ond cawn hefyd gyfeiriadau at themâu a chymeriadau'r Pedair Cainc yn y Trioedd mewn modd sy'n dangos gwybodaeth eang o bwnc y chwedlau – cyfeiriadau sydd o dro i dro yn trafod digwyddiadau sylfaenol debyg i straeon y Pedair Cainc ond sydd tamaid yn wahanol o ran manylion penodol.[43] Er enghraifft, mae triawd 26 yn nodi hanes Pryderi mab Pwyll Pen Annwn yn cadw moch Pendaran Dyfed yng Nglyn Cuch yn Emlyn. Cawn leoliad o'r gainc gyntaf, a chymeriadau sy'n bresennol trwy'r Mabinogi, a stori sy'n debyg i ran o'r bedwaredd gainc – ond mae'r gwahaniaethau pwysig yn dangos nad yw'r triawd yn tynnu'n uniongyrchol ar y Pedair Cainc fel y maent yn goroesi heddiw.[44]

Rhaid casglu bod y Trioedd a'r Pedair Cainc yn dylanwadu ar ei gilydd yn uniongyrchol, ond mewn ffyrdd sy'n gwneud mesur y berthynas destunol yn eglur yn anodd. Os gwelwn y Pedair Cainc fel testun sy'n datblygu yn bennaf yn ysgrifenedig, byddai hyn yn awgrymu proses weddol gymhleth, ond mae hefyd yn bosib bod y Trioedd a'r Pedair Cainc yn trefnu yr un defnydd storïol, llafar mewn ffyrdd braidd yn wahanol. O ystyried cysylltiadau posib y ddau destun gyda Chlynnog Fawr (trafodir isod), mae hefyd bosibilrwydd eu bod wedi dylanwadu ar ei gilydd wrth iddynt gael eu hailysgrifennu a'u golygu drwy fersiynau gwahanol. Er i Ifor Williams honni y gellid hepgor y cyfeiriadau at y Trioedd o destun y Pedair Cainc fel glosau ymylol, anghytuna Bromwich, gan ddadlau bod y Trioedd wedi dylanwadu yn sylfaenol ar strwythur y Pedair Cainc.[45] Rhaid casglu bod y berthynas yn un gymhleth, ac o ystyried y cysylltiad agos rhwng y Pedair Cainc a'r cyfresi llawnach o drioedd yn Llyfr Gwyn Rhydderch a Llyfr Coch Hergest, mae trafodaeth lawnach o'r cwestiwn hwn y tu hwnt i gwmpas y bennod hon.[46]

Mae'r berthynas rhwng *Culhwch ac Olwen* a'r Trioedd hefyd yn un agos. Mae nifer o'r unigolion a rennir rhwng y testunau yn gymeriadau gymharol anenwog.⁴⁷ Ymddengys rhai ohonynt yn rhestri hirfaith y chwedl yn unig, tra bod eraill, megis Menw mab Teirgwaedd neu Echel Vordwytwll, yn fwy creiddiol i'r stori.⁴⁸

Barn Bromwich ac Evans yw bod y rhestri yn chwedl *Culhwch* yn tynnu ar y Trioedd, er efallai Trioedd mewn ffurf mwy cyntefig nag sy'n goroesi yn y Gyfres Gynnar. Fy nheimlad i, wrth gymryd y Gyfres Gynnar fel cyfanwaith, yw bod chwedl *Culhwch* yn hytrach yn ffynhonnell i'r ddelwedd o'r llys Arthuraidd a gynigiwyd yn y Trioedd. Yn sicr, mae triawd 1, gyda'i ddelwedd o lys Arthur yng Nghelli Wig a Mynyw yn cynnwys elfennau sy'n gyson â delwedd *Culhwch* o lys Arthur.⁴⁹ Mae'r ffaith bod ambell driawd yn y Gyfres Gynnar yn adlewyrchu chwedl *Culhwch* yn fanylach nag eraill hefyd yn arwyddocaol, er enghraifft triawd 9:

Tri Vnben Llys Arthur: Gobrwy mab Echel Vordwytwll, a Chadrieith mab Porthavr Gadw, a Fleudur Flam.

Dyma'r unig un o'r gyfres gynnar i ddefnyddio'r fformiwla 'tri *x* Llys Arthur'. O'r tri enw, mae dau yn chwedl *Culhwch*.⁵⁰ Mae triawd 27, y tri *lledrithawg*, hefyd yn rhannu dau ffigwr â'r chwedl – Drych eil Cibddar, sydd yn ymddangos gyda'r un tadenw cymharol anarferol yn *Culhwch*, a hefyd Menw mab Teirgwaedd, un o brif gymeriadau'r chwedl, sydd yn defnyddio'r un term amdano ('lledrith').⁵¹ Mae'r trydydd ffigwr yn y triawd hwn, Coll fab Collfrewy, yn ymddangos yn y triawd blaenorol (26) fel *gwrdueichyat*, meichiad pwerus, un sy'n hela mochyn.⁵² Efallai bod awdur Cyfres Gynnar y Trioedd yn nhriawd 27 yn ystyried ffigyrau 'lledrithiog' o chwedl *Culhwch* (chwedl sydd yn disgrifio hela'r Twrch Trwyth), ac felly yn tynnu i mewn ffigwr amlwg o'r stori am foch yr oedd wedi manylu amdani yn y triawd blaenorol – Coll mab Collfrewy, sy'n hela'r hwch Henwen yn yr un modd.⁵³

Mae'r ddau destun yn tueddu rhestru ffigyrau amryliw o ystod eang o ffynonellau. Ceir yn y Trioedd ymgais i osod trefn ar orffennol Ynys Prydain trwy blethu cymeriadau a digwyddiadau o gyfnodau gwahanol ar sail tebygrwydd a thema – mae'r catalogio hollgynhwysol yma hefyd yn amlwg yn *Culhwch*, sy'n trefnu straeon a chymeriadau o gwmpas Arthur a'i lys fel yn y triawdau hwyrach sy'n lleoli arwyr yn *llys Arthur*. Mae'r ddau yn dystion i ymgeisiau Cymry'r cyfnod i gynhwyso defnydd amrywiol gorffennol eu pobl a'u hynys o fewn gweithiau ysgrifenedig cynhwysol. Gallwn hefyd gynnwys *DGB* o fewn y disgrifiad hwn. Cynnyrch Sieffre oedd hanes cydlynol, Lladin, mewn arddull ac ieithwedd a oedd yn gyfarwydd ac yn dderbyniol i'r llys Seisnig-Normanaidd ac ar draws Ewrop benbaladr. Cynnyrch awdur *Culhwch* oedd chwedl anhrefnus a diddorol. Y catalog thematig ac amrywiol dan sylw y bennod hon oedd cynnyrch yr un ymgais yn achos y Trioedd. Ond mae'r tri thestun gwahanol hyn yn esiamplau cymharol o allu Cymry'r Oesoedd Canol i gloddio i'w gorffennol, eu achau a'u chwedlau, ac ailstrwythuro'r defnydd crai mewn ffyrdd hynod o greadigol i greu hanesion newydd.[54] Nodwyd uchod hyblygrwydd creadigol awdur y Trioedd i ddefnyddio ffigyrau lled-gyfoes dechrau'r ddeuddegfed ganrif yn ei amlinelliad o orffennol Ynys Prydain – fel Alan Fergant (m. 1119) yn cael ei osod ym mrwydr Camlan. Tebyg o ran creadigedd digywilydd yw defnydd Sieffre o Fynwy o achau Harleaidd y ddegfed ganrif i boblogi ei ddarlun o lys Arthur yng Nghaerleon.[55] Tebyg hefyd yw parodrwydd awdur *Culhwch* i gynnwys holl orffennol y Cymry yn ei ddarlun o lys Arthur yng Nghelli Wig.[56]

Tarddiad y Trioedd

Gall rhai cysylltiadau testunol gynnig mewnwelediad cliriach i wneuthuriad Cyfres Gynnar y Trioedd. Mae'r gorgyffwrdd sylweddol rhwng Trioedd Ynys Prydein ac achau Bonedd y Saint yn arwyddocaol yma: cawn ffigyrau cymharol anenwog sy'n perthyn i draddodiad ysgrifenedig. Enghraifft dda yw 'Pryder mab Dolor Deiuyr a Brennych', un o'r tri *gwrddfaglawg* neu bugeiliaid nerthus yn ôl y Trioedd, a thad i Ddwyfael yn ôl Bonedd y Saint.[57] Mae'r ach hon yn perthyn i 'gynffon' testun gwreiddiol Bonedd y Saint, sy'n cynnwys defnydd ychwanegol, anhrefnus braidd yn ôl ei olygydd, Barry Lewis, sydd hefyd wedi nodi y tebygrwydd sylweddol rhwng Bonedd y Saint a Trioedd Ynys Prydein fel testunau.[58] Arwyddocaol hefyd yw'r ffaith i'r ddau destun ymddangos ynghyd yn eu llawysgrifau cynharaf.[59]

Clynnog Fawr yn Arfon yw man cyfansoddi tebygol Bonedd y Saint, ac felly gall y cysylltiadau testunol hyn awgrymu perthynas hefyd rhwng Clynnog Fawr a Chyfres Gynnar y Trioedd.[60] Dyma'r argraff sy'n dod hefyd o gysylltiadau testunol arall. Mae trioedd 10 a 32 ill dau yn trafod tri mab Disgyfdawd: Gall, Ysgafnell a Diffydell. Mae'r teulu yma'n weddol unigryw i'r Trioedd, ac mae'n debygol taw creadigrwydd llenyddol awdur Cyfres Gynnar y Trioedd a welwn fan yma. Ond mae ffurf ar yr enw Disgyfdawd hefyd yn bresennol yn Englynion y Beddau: 'Cicleu don drom dra thywawd am fedd Disgyrnin disgyffedawd'.[61] Daw'r englyn yma o'r gyfres (Cyfres III) sydd, yn ôl dadansoddiad cymhellgar Patrick Sims-Williams, yn deillio o Glynnog Fawr.[62] Mae'r gyfres yma o englynion yn ffurfio rhan o'i ddadl bod Pedwaredd Gainc y Mabinogi hefyd yn gysylltiedig â Chlynnog, a byddai cysylltiad Cyfres Gynnar y Trioedd â'r un eglwys hefyd yn gymorth i esbonio'r berthynas gymhleth, ddwyochrog rhwng y Trioedd a'r Pedair Cainc. Cawn efallai awgrym pellach o'r cysylltiad yma yn triawd 26, triawd manwl Coll fab Collfrewy a'r *gwrddfeichiaid*. Mae Henwen yr hwch, ar ei thaith gymhleth o Gernyw i'r Fenai, yn dod at 'Riw Kyuerthuch yn Eryri' – er gwaetha'r ffurf wahanol ar yr enw, mae'n bosib gweld hwn fel adlais neu ddwbl o Fryn Cyfergyr, lleoliad yr ymosodiadau rhwng Lleu Llawgyffes a Gronw Pebr yn y bedwaredd gainc.[63] Nodwyd uchod yr arwyddion o gefnogaeth i ymgyrchoedd Tyddewi i sefydlu archesgobaeth yn y ddeuddegfed ganrif sy'n bresennol yn nhriawd cyntaf y Gyfres Gynnar – perthnasol yn y cyswllt yma yw nodi pwysigrwydd yr archddiacon Symeon o Glynnog yn annog Owain Gwynedd i gefnogi ymgyrch yr esgob Bernard yng nghanol y ddeuddegfed ganrif.[64]

Mae awgrym pellach o'r cysylltiad ag Arfon yn yr un triawd: caiff cath-blentyn Henwen ei geni yn Llanfair yn Arfon, hynny yw Llanfair Isgaer, cyn cael ei thaflu i'r Fenai.[65] Roedd Llanfair Isgaer yn perthyn i Briordy Awstinaidd Beddgelert yn hytrach nag i Glynnog, ond mae'r cyfeiriad at 'y Maen Du yn Llanveir yn Aruon' yn awgrymu gwybodaeth leol.[66] Tra bod cysylltiad yn ymddangos rhwng y Trioedd a Chlynnog, felly, a bod mynachlogydd yn ganolfannau anochel i greadigaeth llawysgrifau a llythrennedd yn y cyfnod yma, rhaid gwarchod, efallai, rhag clymu testun fel y Trioedd yn rhy agos i'r fynachlog benodol hon. Testun hanesyddol a barddonol yw'r Trioedd yn y bôn, a rhaid cofio'r cysylltiadau rhwng testunau Cymraeg Canol ardal Clynnog a'r teulu o feirdd a chyfreithwyr uchelwrol a drigent gerllaw. Amlygwyd y cysylltiadau hyn gan waith y diweddar Dafydd Jenkins ar Iorwerth ap Madog a disgynyddion eraill Gwrydr ap Dyfnaint, ynghyd â gwaith Patrick Sims-Williams.[67] Amlygant cysylltiadau rhwng y llyfrau cyfreithiol, Iorwerth ap Madog a'i deulu, treflan Pennardd ger Clynnog a'r testunau a gysylltir â Chlynnog ei hun. O Iorwerth ap Madog y mae'r llyfr cyfraith *Llyfr Iorwerth* yn dwyn ei deitl, ac o'i berthynas Cyfnerth ap Morgenau y daw teitl *Llyfr Cyfnerth*, ac mae pwysigrwydd Pennardd, sydd i'w gysylltu â'r teulu hwn, yn amlwg yn y testunau cyfreithiol a Phedair Cainc y Mabinogi ill dau.

Roedd y teulu hwn yn cynnwys ynadon ac ysgolheigion cyfreithiol ynghyd â beirdd llys – Einion ap Madog ap Rahawd a ganodd i Ruffudd ap Llywelyn, a hefyd yr Ynad Coch a farwnadodd Llywelyn ap Gruffudd. Teulu a oedd yn gwasanaethu llys tywysogion Gwynedd fel cyfreithwyr, fel beirdd, a hefyd fel gweinyddwyr, gerllaw eglwys bwysig Clynnog.[68] Galwyd Pennardd yn *henaf kynghellaurdref* yn llyfr Damweiniau Colan a soniwyd amdano hefyd ym mhedwaredd gainc y Mabinogi.[69] Mae'r testunau cyfraith a gysylltir â Iorwerth ap Madog hefyd yn dangos parch amlwg at eglwysi Clynnog a Bangor.[70] Ond er gwaethaf agosatrwydd daearyddol Pennardd a'i theulu i Glynnog, rhaid hefyd nodi cysylltiad â Beddgelert. Roedd tir Pennardd yn eiddo i briordy Awstinaidd Beddgelert nes 1269, pan gymerodd tywysog Cymru, Llywelyn ap Gruffudd, feddiant o'r tiroedd yma trwy eu cyfnewid â thiroedd ei hun gerllaw Beddgelert.[71]

Yng Nghaernarfon, y llys tywysogol hynafol oedd yn sefyll rhwng Clynnog, Llanfair Isgaer a Beddgelert, y cytunwyd y cyfnewid tiroedd yma. Mae lleoliad y llys tywysogol yn Arfon rhwng y ddwy fynachlog, y cysylltiadau rhwng teulu Pennardd a llys tywysogion Gwynedd, a hefyd pwysigrwydd tebygol y llys fel cynulleidfa rhai o'r testunau a gysylltir â'r lleoliadau yma – y chwedlau, a'r Trioedd a'u cysylltiadau â'r farddoniaeth llys – yn cynnig darlun o fyd go-iawn y testunau a'u hawduron. Dyma gyd-destun addas i'r Trioedd – y gofod rhwng mynachlogydd Clynnog a Beddgelert, teuluoedd barddol a chyfreithiol Arfon, a llysoedd tywysogion Gwynedd lle'r oedd y teuluoedd hyn yn canu a gwasanaethu.

Tri Triawd: 1. Y Tri Cyfor

I ddychwelyd o'r cyd-destun i'r testun ei hun. Tra bod ymgais yn y Trioedd i gatalogio a threfnu, y mae hefyd themâu a chysondebau a all amlygu syniadau eu hawdur am y gorffennol. Mae'r agwedd hon amlycaf ar ddechrau a diwedd y testun. Mae'r ddelwedd driphlyg o Ynys Prydain yn y triawd cyntaf yn gosod cynfas ar gyfer y trioedd i ddod, y strwythur daearyddol ar gyfer y straeon sy'n cael eu crybwyll yng nghorff y gwaith. Mewn ffordd gymharol, mae'r tri triawd sy'n terfynu'r Gyfres Gynnar yn diffinio'r themâu pwysicaf yng ngweledigaeth yr awdur o hanes Ynys Prydain.[72] Trioedd gymharol hirfaith ydynt, ymhell tu hwnt i rhestri syml. Disgrifiant y tri *chyfor*, byddinoedd wnaeth adael yr Ynys heb ddychwelyd; y tair *gormes* neu orthrwm a ddaethant i'r Ynys heb adael; a thri chuddiad a thri datguddiad Ynys Prydain, cyrff neu fwystfilod a oedd yn gwarchod y deyrnas rhag ymosodiadau neu ormesoedd.

Tri Chyuor a aeth o'r Enys hon, ac ny doeth dracheuyn 6r un onadunt:

6n a aeth gan Elen Luyda6c a Chynan e bra6t;

Eil a aeth gan Yrp Lluyda6c yn oes Cadyal mab Eryn, a doeth eman y erchi kymorth; ac nyt archei o bob pryf gaer namyn deu kymeint ac a delei gantha6 idi. Ac ny doeth gantha6 y'r gaer gyntaf namyn ef a'e was. Ac ardustru 6u rodi hynny ida6. A h6nn6 eissyoes llwyrhaf llu a aeth o'r Enys hon. Ac ny doeth dracheuyn byth nep onadunt. Sef lle y trigws y gwyr hynny: yn dwy enys yn emyl Mor Groec. Sef yw y dwy enys hynny: Gals ac Auena.

Trydyd Kyuor a aeth gan Gaswalla6n mab Beli, a Gwenwynwyn a G6anar, meibyon Llia6s mab Nwy6re, ac Aryanrot merch 6eli eu mam. Ac o Arllechwed yd hanoed y gwyr hynny. Ac aethant y gyt a Chaswalla6n eu hewyt(h) yr drwy vor yn ol y Cesaryeit. Sef lle y mae y gwyr hynny yg Wasgwyn.

A sef eiryf a aeth ym pob 6n or lluoed hynny: 6n 6il ar ugeint. A'r rei hyny oed y Tri Aryanllu. Sef acha6s y gelwit y 6elly, 6rth vynet eur ac aryant yr Enys ganthunt. Ac eu dethol wynteu o oreu y oreu.

Wrth ddisgrifio'r *tri chyfor*, mae triawd 35 yn amlygu maint a chyfoeth anferth y lluoedd yma, yn pwysleisio na ddaeth yr un ohonynt yn ôl drachefn, a hefyd eu bod wedi eu dewis o goreuon yr ynys. Y fyddin gyntaf yw'r rhai a aeth gydag Elen *Luyddog* a'i brawd, Cynan, hynny yw byddin Macsen Wledig ar ei goncwest dybiedig o Rufain. Yn ôl *Breuddwyd Maxen Wledig*, ar ôl goresgyn Rhufain, mae'r fyddin hon yn trefedigaethu Llydaw.[73] Ni chaiff yr holl hanes yma ei adrodd yn y triawd, ond o ystyried y tebygrwydd amlwg rhyngddo a'r drydedd esiampl yn y triawd yma (gwladychu Llydaw a Gasgwyn), cawn dybio bod yr elfennau hyn o'r stori hefyd wrth feddwl yr awdur. Dyma, felly, ddiwedd oes y Rhufeiniaid yn llygaid y Cymry. Mae'r ail lu yn digwydd yng nghyfnod Cadial fab Eryn (unigolyn anhysbys fel arall) a phwysleisir bod ymadawiad llu mor fawr yn achos edifar. Aeth y trydydd llu i erlyn y *Cesaryeit*, hynny yw byddin Rufeinig Iŵl Cesar, dan arweinyddiaeth Caswallon. Mae dau o'r tri llu felly yn nodi dechrau a diwedd y cyfnod Rhufeinig ym Mhrydain, a'r llall yn un na allwn benodi dyddiad iddo.

Mae'r lluoedd yma yn diffinio agwedd bwysig ar hanes Ynys Prydain – bod cyrchoedd tramor, er gwaethaf eu llwyddiant, yn tueddu i ddiffrwytho'r ynys o'i phobl orau, ac yn arwain at newidiadau hanesyddol pwysig. Roedd hwn eisoes yn hen syniad i'r Cymry, yn bresennol yn *Historia Brittonum* y nawfed ganrif, sy'n nodi o effaith hynt Macsen Wledig, *Maximianus* yn y testun, ar Brydain:

> Hi sunt Brittones Armorici, et nunquam reversi sunt hucusque in hodiernum diem. Propter hoc Britannia occupata est ab extraneis gentibus et cives expulsi sunt, usque dum Deus auxilium dederit illis.[74]

> Rhain yw'r Brythoniaid Armoricanaidd, ac ni ddaethant fyth yn ôl drachefn, hyd at y dyddiau yma. Dyna pham y mae Prydain wedi ei feddiannu gan estroniaid, a'r dinasyddion wedi cael eu gyrru allan nes bod Duw yn cynnig cymorth iddynt.

Trafodwyd eisoes y deialog rhwng y Trioedd a chwedlau Cymraeg, ond yma mae yr un mor amlwg bod y Trioedd yn ymateb i, ac yn datblygu, themâu testunau hanes Lladin megis *Historia Brittonum*. O ystyried bod triawd 35 wedi ei osod yn union cyn trafodaeth o ymosodiadau tramor ymysg gormesoedd triawd 36, mae'n amlwg bod tebygrwydd sylweddol rhwng themâu a meddylfryd y ddau destun. Efallai taw adlewyrchiad anuniongyrchol yw hwn o ddylanwad *Historia Brittonum* ar syniadau ehangach o orffennol y Cymry. Ond gallwn hefyd ystyried dylanwad uniongyrchol – mewn un ffordd neu'r llall, mae *Historia Brittonum* wedi dylanwadu nid yn unig ar driawdau unigol ond ar strwythur a syniadaeth y Gyfres Gynnar. Fel yn yr hanes Ladin, mae ymgyrchoedd gogoneddus tramor yn gwanhau'r deyrnas ac yn galluogi gormesoedd tramor i dorri undod yr ynys. Mae'n bosib hefyd bod y ffaith i'r tri *Arianllu* borthi i ffwrdd aur ac arian yr Ynys yn ddatblygiad neu efelychiad pwrpasol o sylw *Historia Brittonum* bod lluoedd y Rhufeiniaid wedi cymryd aur ac arian yr Ynys.[75]

Cawn rai arwyddion pellach o ddylanwad *Historia Brittonum* ar sylwedd y Trioedd. Mae tystiolaeth yr hanes Ladin am gladdu Guorthemir mab Guorthigirn (Gwrthefyr mab Gwrtheyrn), ar yr arfordir i warchod Ynys Prydain rhag ymosodiadau tramor, yn llechu y tu ôl i'r tri chudd a'r tri datgudd yn nhriawd 37 a drafodir isod.[76] Mae'r cyfeiriad at Eda Glinvawr yn nhriawd 30 yn dangos yr un llysenw ag a roid i'r brenin hwn gan *Historia Brittonum*, *Eata Glinmaur*, yn ei achau o frenhinoedd Bryneich.[77]

Mae lle felly i ystyried y posibilrwydd fod gan awdur y Trioedd gopi o *Historia Brittonum*.[78] Efallai bod term fel 'Glinvawr' am frenin Bryneich yn adlewyrchiad o draddodiad llafar, neu draddodiad ysgrifenedig Gymraeg – mae'n sicr yn digwydd yn adran yr *Historia* sy'n arddangos y gorgyffwrdd mwyaf â thestunau Cymraeg, lle enwir Taliesin, Aneirin a chynfeirdd eraill llai hysbys.[79] Ond mae'n anodd darllen y Trioedd a'r *Historia* ochr wrth ochr heb ystyried cysylltiad o ryw fath. Yng ngoleuni cysylltiadau'r Trioedd gydag eglwysi hynafol Gwynedd, yn enwedig Clynnog, mae'n deg dadlau bod goroesiad *Historia Brittonum*, testun a gyfansoddwyd yng Ngwynedd yn y nawfed ganrif, mewn sefydliad o'r fath yn bosibilrwydd.[80] Mae siarter cadarnhad tiroedd Clynnog o'r bymthegfed ganrif yn awgrymu bod cofnod ysgrifenedig Clynnog Fawr yn yr Oesoedd Canol yn mynd yn ôl mor bell â dyddiau cynnar llinach y Merfynion, cyfnod cyfansoddi *Historia Brittonum*.[81] Cawn efallai nodi bod y berthynas agos rhwng syniadaeth hanesyddol Trioedd Ynys Prydein a *Historia Brittonum* yn awgrymu'r posibilrwydd ehangach bod traddodiad cynhenid yng Nghymru o ystyriaeth neu ehangiad ar waith Lladin Nennius, sydd i'w weld yn natblygiad themâu'r hanes Lladin i ffurf Gymraeg driawdol erbyn cyfansoddi'r Trioedd.[82] Efallai taw dyma sydd y tu ôl i'r gosodiad diddorol yn nhriawd 35 bod y Cymry a aethant gydag Yrp Luyddog yn trigo 'yn dwy ynys yn ymyl mor Groeg – Gals ac Avena'. Mae'n bosib bod perthynas rhwng y gosodiad yma a manylyn hynod yn *Historia Brittonum* – sef bod Belinus mab Minocan, sail trydydd cyfor triawd 35, ar ôl ymladd Iŵl Cesar wedi meddiannu holl ynysoedd *Tyrreni maris*. Mae'n bosib bod efelychiad, dehongliad neu adlewyrchiad o'r darn hwn o *Historia Brittonum* yn llechu y tu ôl i chwedl Yrp Luyddog yn y Trioedd.[83]

Mae amrediad triawd 35 o ran ei gyfuniad o straeon yn drawiadol. Ynghyd â gorgyffwrdd â'r *Historia Brittonum*, chwedl ddi-dyst Cadial ab Eryn, stori Elen Luyddog a Macsen, a'r ymgiprys rhwng Iŵl Cesar a Chaswallon oedd yn bwynt cychwyn y cyfnod Rhufeinig, mae'r triawd hefyd yn cyfeirio at Bedair Cainc y Mabinogi. Dyma un o'r unig esiamplau o destun sy'n croesi'r bwlch rhwng byd chwedlonol y Pedair Cainc a'r cyfnod hanesyddol mwy sefydledig.[84] Mae cymeriad Arianrhod yn y triawd yma yn cadarnhau rhywbeth na chaiff ond ei awgrymu yn y Pedair Cainc: bod digwyddiadau'r chwedlau hynny yn cael eu gweld fel rhai sy'n perthyn i'r cyfnod cyn dyfodiad y Rhufeiniaid i'r ynys. Mae ymddangosiad cymeriad Caswallon yn yr ail gainc yn awgrymu hyn, ond yn y triawd dyma Arianrhod ei hun fel chwaer y brenin sy'n maeddu cyrchoedd Iŵl Cesar a'i erlid o'r ynys.

Ifor Williams a gynigiodd bod modd amlinellu chwedl goll am Gaswallon ac Iŵl Cesar o gyfeiriadau'r Trioedd a'r Gogynfeirdd.[85] Mae amlinelliad y stori yma yn cynnwys cystadleuaeth bosib rhwng Cesar a Chaswallon dros gariad Fflur; gyrru Cesar allan o'r ynys gyda meibion Arianrhod; a rôl ddiddorol i geffyl Caswallon, Meinlas, fel rhan o'r cytundeb anffodus a ddaeth â'r Rhufeiniaid i'r Ynys.[86] Mae'r gorgyffwrdd â'r Pedair Cainc ym mherson Arianrhod yn codi cwestiwn pryfoclyd – os oedd ffurf brôs ysgrifenedig ar y chwedl yma, a fyddai wedi bod yn bosib ystyried hon yn bumed cainc y Mabinogi? Does dim diffiniad o nifer ceinciau'r Mabinogi yn ein tystiolaeth ganoloesol, ac mae'r straeon am Gaswallon a Chesar yn sicr yn gorgyffwrdd â'r Pedair Cainc o ran cymeriad ac, i raddau, o ran themâu – rôl ceffylau fel rhodd yn dechrau rhyfel, er enghraifft; cyrchoedd tramor costus yn arwain at newid mewn rheolaeth dros yr ynys; a rôl merch – Branwen, Fflur – yng nghanol hyn oll. Byddai hyn yn codi'r posibilrwydd o Iŵl Cesar fel un o gymeriadau'r Mabinogi – ochr yn ochr â ffigyrau sydd wedi eu gor-ddehongli fel duwiau a ddyneiddiwyd, cawn ffigwr hanesyddol a ddwyfolwyd gan ei gyfoedion.[87]

Trawiadol yn y cyswllt yma yw pa mor wahanol y mae'r hanes am gyrchoedd Iŵl Cesar, nid yn unig i'r ffynonellau Lladin clasurol, ond hefyd i naratif haneswyr eraill y ddeuddegfed ganrif, gan gynnwys Sieffre o Fynwy.[88] Nid yw'n hollol annibynnol ohonynt: mae'r chwedlau Cymraeg a hanes Sieffre ill dau yn rhannu'r un ffynonellau, gan gynnwys *Historia Brittonum*, ac, fel y nodir isod, mae olion sgil-effaith dylanwad straeon Sieffre ar y Trioedd.[89] Serch hyn, gwelwn ddatblygiad gwahanol yn y corff Cymraeg o dystiolaeth – efallai pwrpasol wahanol. Drwy nodi a threfnu naratif mor anghyffelyb o'r ymosodiadau Rhufeinig, roedd awdur y trioedd yn ymateb i'r naratifau Lladin blaenorol yma, mewn ffordd gymharol i sut mae chwedlau prôs fel *Lludd a Llefelys* a *Breuddwyd Maxen* yn ymateb i naratif Sieffre o Fynwy yn *DGB*.[90]

Mae'r gymhariaeth â *Breuddwyd Maxen* yn un bwysig. Er nad yw triawd 35 yn cyfeirio at Facsen Wledig yn uniongyrchol, mae presenoldeb Elen Luyddawg a'i brawd Cynan yn amlygu gwybodaeth yr awdur o'r stori, ynghyd â chyfeiriad diddorol at Owain fab Macsen yn nhriawd 13.[91] Mae'r ffurf ar yr enw Macsen a ddefnyddiwyd yn nhriawd 13 yn arddangos dylanwad gwaith Sieffre o Fynwy – trwy'r cyfieithiadau Cymraeg o'i waith y sefydlwyd y ffurf Maxen/Macsen yn hytrach na Maxim.[92] Mae'r enw yma yn y Trioedd felly yn dyddio ar ôl cyhoeddiad gwaith Sieffre yn 1138, ond cawn arwydd arall o ddylanwad penodol y cyfieithiadau Cymraeg yn y ffaith taw enw chwaer Cynan, sylfaenydd chwedlonol Llydaw, yw Elen – un o ddatblygiadau *Brut y Brenhinedd* yw rhoi'r enw hwn i chwaer Cynan, sydd heb enw yn hanes Lladin Sieffre.[93]

Mae llysenw Elen, Lluyddawg, yn debygol iawn o ddangos dylanwad chwedl *Breuddwyd Maxen*. Er i Elen ferch Coel, mam Cwstenin, ddwyn y llysenw hwn yn gynharach, chwedl *Breuddwyd Maxen* yw'r cyntaf i'w gysylltu ag Elen chwaer Cynan.[94] O ystyried cysylltiadau Cyfres Gynnar y Trioedd gyda Chlynnog ac Arfon, a gwybodaeth fanwl awdur *Breuddwyd Maxen* o Arfon, mae'n deg gweld y dylanwad hwn fel un uniongyrchol a bod y Trioedd yma yn dilyn testun *Breuddwyd Maxen*.[95] Does dim llawer o dystiolaeth bellach am ddylanwad testunol gwaith Sieffre ar y Trioedd, ac efallai dyma awgrym bod awdur y Gyfres Gynnar yn gwrthsefyll dylanwad hanes Sieffreaidd yn bwrpasol – yn y cyddestun yma, dylanwad *Breuddwyd Macsen* ar ffurf yr enwau a'r chwedl sydd fwy tebygol nag un *Brut y Brenhinedd*. Does dim rhaid derbyn yn llawn dadl Brynley Roberts am ddyddiad ysgrifennu chwedl Macsen ar ôl digwyddiadau 1215–17, sydd wedi'r cwbl yn dibynnu ar gyd-destun gwleidyddol tybiedig.[96] Ond os felly, byddai'r Gyfres Gynnar fel y mae yn dyddio i'r cyfnod wedi hyn.

Rhaid hefyd sylwi ymhellach ar ffigwr Owain fab Macsen. Nid yw Owain yn ymddangos yn chwedl *Breuddwyd Maxen*, a'r brif ffynhonnell gynharach ar ei gyfer yw achau Sant Cadog o Lancarfan, sydd ochr yn ochr â buchedd y sant hwn yn llawysgrif Cotton Vespasian A. xiv, rhan i.⁹⁷ Diddorol yn y cyswllt hwn yw nodi arwyddion eraill a all fod yn awgrymog o ddylanwad Llancarfan – tra bod Hueil fab Caw (triawd 26) yn ymddangos yn chwedl *Culhwch*, mae hefyd yn bresennol yng ngwaith Caradog o Lancarfan, *Buchedd Gildas*.⁹⁸ Os oes unrhyw gysylltiad â Llancarfan, rhaid cofio taw hon yn y ddeuddegfed ganrif oedd y ganolfan bwysicaf am ledaenu gwybodaeth am *Historia Brittonum*, sydd hefyd â'i gysgod ar y Trioedd – ni fyddai angen, felly, i *Historia Brittonum* fod wedi goroesi yng Nghlynnog, nac yng Ngwynedd.⁹⁹ Yn y cyfeiriad arall, rhaid nodi bod Owain fab Macsen yn dod yn gysylltiedig ag ardal Nant Gwynant erbyn y bymthegfed ganrif – ffaith diddorol o ystyried cysylltiadau Llanfair Isgaer a Pennardd â Beddgelert.¹⁰⁰ Ond amwys iawn yw'r cysylltiadau hyn oll.

Tri Triawd: 2. Gormesoedd

I ddychwelyd at yr ail o'r gyfres o dri thriawd cwmpasog sy'n terfynu'r Gyfres Gynnar o'r trioedd. Mae triawd 36, fel y nodwyd uchod, yn datblygu'r triawd blaenorol – ar ôl yr amlinelliad o gyrchoedd gogoneddus ond sy'n gwacáu'r ynys yn nhriawd 35, cawn yn y triawd olynol amlinelliad o'r *gormesoedd* (ymosodiadau anghyfiawn) a ddaeth i'r ynys wedyn. Y tair gormes yw: y Coraniaid yn oes Caswallon ap Beli; y Gwyddyl Ffichti neu'r Pictiaid; a'r Saeson dan Hengist a Horsa. Amlygwyd yn achos y ddau gyntaf o'r ymosodiadau yma 'nid aeth yr un ohonynt drachefn', ac yn achos yr olaf byddai'n ddigon amlwg bod y Saeson yn dal yn bresennol ar yr ynys.¹⁰¹ Ymosodiadau'r Pictiaid a'r Saeson a ddinistriodd reolaeth y Brythoniaid dros Ynys Prydain unedig, drwy chwalu eu rheolaeth dros ogledd yr ynys a Lloegr. Mae ffurf driphlyg ddelfrydol yr ynys dan deyrnasiad Arthur a amlygwyd yn y triawd cyntaf, felly, mewn cyferbyniad â'r gormesoedd yma – y Gwyddyl Ffichti a'r Saeson oedd prif elynion Arthur. Cawn yn y triawd yma dystiolaeth bellach o ddylanwad testunau Lladin, *Historia Britonum* Nennius a *DGB* Sieffre o Fynwy, ar y Trioedd.¹⁰² Mae'r ffaith bod gormes y Gwyddyl Ffichti yn aros ar yr Ynys yn awgrymu bod awdur y Trioedd yn ystyried yr ynys ddaearyddol fel ei gynfas, gan gynnwys yr Alban.¹⁰³

Mae lle'r Coraniaid yma yn fwy amwys. Roedd Bromwich yn awyddus i ddehongli'r term fel llygrad o *Cesarieid*, dilynwyr Iŵl Cesar yn nhriawd 35.¹⁰⁴ Efallai bod hwn yn berthnasol i greadigaeth y term

Coraniaid yn wreiddiol, a'u lleoli yn amser Caswallon ap Beli, neu ei frodyr honedig, Lludd a Llefelys, gan taw cyfnod sail hanesyddol y ffigyrau chwedlonol yma (Cassivelaunus) oedd cyfnod y cyfarfod cyntaf rhwng byddinoedd Rhufeiniaid a Brythoniaid mewn gwirionedd. Byddai hefyd yn awgrymu'r patrwm o ymgyrch milwrol tramor ac yna gormes wleidyddol. Ond mae problemau gyda dehongli'r Coraniaid fel Rhufeiniaid. Mae'r Gyfres Gynnar o'r Trioedd yn ei wneud yn amlwg nad oes dryswch rhwng Cesariaid a Choraniaid yn y testun ei hun – maent yn ymddangos y naill ochr i'r llall mewn trioedd cyfagos. Mae *Cyfranc Lludd a Llefelys* yn amlygu'r Coraniaid fel hil o gorachod goruwchnaturiol, ac mae ymddangosiad y chwedl yma o fewn cyfieithiadau Cymraeg o *DGB* yn ei wneud yn eglur bod y rhain yn cael eu gweld fel llwyth gwahanol i'r Rhufeiniaid.[105] Gallwn ychwanegu at hyn sylw triawd 36 na adawodd un o'r Coraniaid yr ynys fyth wedyn, tra bod y Cesariaid yn gadael, yn nhriawd 35, wedi eu herlid gan luoedd Caswallon.

Gwnaeth y Rhufeiniaid hefyd adael mewn ffaith hanesyddol, ond o ran dealltwriaeth awdur y Trioedd o'r berthynas rhwng Rhufain ag Ynys Prydain, mae'n debygol iddo weld hyn yn nhermau tebyg i naratif *Historia Britonum* (a ddatblygwyd ymhellach gan Sieffre o Fynwy) – hynny yw, perthynas hyd-braich o uwch-arglwyddiaeth a theyrnged.[106] Fel y dynodwyd yn adroddiad y trioedd o fuddugoliaeth Caswallon, roedd hon yn berthynas gyda nifer o wahanol naratifau o wrthdaro a chydweithio. Prin y gellid ei rhoi yn yr un categori â gormesoedd y Pictiaid a'r Saeson.

Y mae felly'n well deall Coraniaid triawd 36 yn debyg i'r hil oruwchnaturiol a ddisgrifiwyd yn *Lludd a Llefelys*. Un o gonglfeini'r cysyniad o *ormes* i'r Cymry canoloesol, ynghyd â'i gyfuniad o drosiadau cyfreithiol a gwleidyddol, yw'r syniad y gall y term fynegi naill ai gormes wleidyddol/ethnig *neu* ffenomen oruwchnaturiol. Mae'n debygol felly bod awdur y trioedd, yn ei gyfuniad o ormesoedd gwleidyddol y Saeson a'r Pictiaid gydag un lledrithiol y Coraniaid, yn bwrpasol amlygu y gwahanol ddefnyddiau posib o'r term 'gormes'.

Y Beirdd a'r Trioedd

Yn y bôn mae'r diddordeb yma mewn ystyr neilltuol geiriau a thermau, a'r ffyrdd y gellid eu diffinio yn hanesyddol, yn allweddol i strwythur a phwrpas Trioedd Ynys Prydein. Tra fy mod wedi pwysleisio yn y drafodaeth hyd yma weledigaeth hanesyddol yr awdur, mae cyfansoddiad llenyddol yr un mor hanfodol i'w waith – a hynny mewn ffyrdd mesuradwy. Gwnaed defnydd helaeth o'r Trioedd fel storfa cyfeiriadau hanesyddol a chwedlonol gan y beirdd llys, fel yng ngwaith Cynddelw a Llywarch ap Llywelyn – gwŷr llengar, ond hefyd swyddogion llys i dywysogion Powys, Gwynedd a'r Deheubarth.[107] Perfformiwyd eu cyfansoddiadau i'r tywysogion yma yn y llys brenhinol, o flaen gwesteion a swyddogion eraill. Roedd y fframwaith hanesyddol a amlygwyd yn y Trioedd yn cynnig ffordd i'r beirdd wreiddio eu noddwyr, arweinwyr gwleidyddol y Cymry cyfoes, yn hanes y Brythoniaid – hanes a oedd yn cael ei ail-ategu fel rhan o batrwm delfrydol, arwrol ymddygiad yr arweinwyr yma. Trwy eu gweithredoedd cyfoes, roedd tywysogion y Cymry, yng ngweledigaeth eu beirdd, yn adfer gweithredoedd Cadwallon, Owain ab Urien, ac arwyr eraill, mewn ffyrdd penodol.

Mae cerddi mawl y beirdd llys i Owain Gwynedd yn ei uniaethu gydag Owain ab Urien mewn nifer o ffyrdd – trwy adleisio geiriad cerddi hanesyddol Taliesin, trwy gyfeirio at ei elynion fel Deifyr a Bryneich, a hefyd – yng ngwaith Gwalchmai ap Meilyr – drwy gyfeirio ato fel *gwynndeyrn*, y term a ddefnyddiwyd am Owain ab Urien yn y Trioedd.[108] Mae'n amlwg o'r cyfeiriadau yma bod adleisiau'r farddoniaeth yn tynnu ar amrediad helaeth o destunau – hengerdd a chwedlau – yn hytrach nag ar restri llwm y Trioedd yn unig. Ond mae'r strwythur triawdol, eu cyfuniad o debygrwydd hanfodol ar draws amser, yn efelychiad o feddylfryd y bardd llys oedd yn gweld yn Owain Gwynedd ac Owain yr Hen Ogledd yr un gweithredoedd yn erbyn yr un hen elynion.

Yng ngwaith Llywarch ap Llywelyn gwelwn hefyd yr un awydd. Mae ei gyfres o englynion i Lywelyn ab Iorwerth yn cymharu Llywelyn â nifer o unigolion sy'n ymddangos yng nghyfres gynnar y trioedd – Arthur, Nudd Hael, Llŷr, Beli a Rhun – a hefyd rhai sydd ddim, Benlli a Godiar.[109] Ond cawn hefyd adlais o derminoleg y Trioedd – mae ymddangosiad y gair *trahawg* yn llinell 20 y gerdd yn awgrymu Triawd 23 y Gyfres Gynnar, y *Tri Trahawg*, sydd yn crybwyll Rhun ab Einion – efallai'r Rhun sy'n ymddangos yn llinell 46 y gerdd.[110] Cawn awgrym pellach o wybodaeth Llywarch ap Llywelyn o'r Trioedd mewn awdl i Llywelyn ab Iorwerth a gyfansoddwyd oddeutu 1216.[111] Er gwaethaf ffocws pendant y gerdd hon ar weithredoedd rhyfelgar diweddar Llywelyn yn erbyn ei elyn o Bowys, Gwenwynwyn, eto mae'r bardd yn cyflwyno'r gweithredoedd yma trwy eiriau Trioedd Ynys Prydein. Mae'r gerdd yn defnyddio dau derm, *aerfeddawg* (arweinydd mewn brwydr) a *rhuddfoawg* (anrheithydd neu ysbeiliwr coch), yn llinellau cyntaf y gerdd sydd hefyd yn deitlau i drioedd 20 a 25 y gyfres gynnar.[112] Dim ond yn y Trioedd, y gerdd hon ac mewn un gerdd arall gan Gynddelw y mae'r term *aerfeddawg* yn ymddangos.[113] Mae rhyfela ag ysbail Llywelyn ym Mhowys yn 1216 yn cael ei weld trwy dermau chwedloniaeth hanesyddol y Trioedd.

Mae amrediad cyfeiriadau'r trioedd yn gorgyffwrdd yn aml gyda'r Hengerdd, a barddoniaeth y Gogynfeirdd o'r ddeuddegfed ganrif ymlaen yn cyfeirio'n aml at ffigyrau o'r trioedd ac o dro i dro at driawdau penodol.[114] Mae'n ymddangos hefyd bod pwrpas nifer o'r trioedd yn fwy penodol na chlymu digwyddiadau hanesyddol yn thematig – ymhellach, y pwrpas oedd esbonio a chyd-destunoli termau hynafol neu dywyll, geiriau oedd yn cynnig sylwedd i farddoniaeth lys. Mae termau megis *deifiniawg, rhuddfoawg, gwyndeyrn*, teitlau triawdau penodol, yn ymddangos hefyd mewn cerddi beirdd llys fel Cynddelw, Prydydd y Moch, Gwalchmai ap Meilyr, ac eraill.[115] Roedd y Trioedd yn cynnig esboniad a rhestr o'r derminoleg ddyrys yma a'i defnydd at bwrpas moliant arwrol – roedd yr esiamplau o dri unigolyn neu ddigwyddiad yn arddangos y term penodol i'r darllenydd o fardd lawn cymaint ag yr oedd y term yn disgrifio'r straeon yr oedd yn eu cysylltu.

Cymaint yw'r gorgyffwrdd rhwng gwaith y beirdd a'r Trioedd, teg yw dychmygu awdur y Gyfres Gynnar fel aelod o'r dosbarth hwn. Nododd Rachel Bromwich bod nifer o esiamplau o ddyfynnu uniongyrchol o Trioedd Ynys Prydein yng ngwaith y Gogynfeirdd yn arddangos mwy o agosrwydd at fersiynau hwyrach y Trioedd o lawysgrifau'r bedwaredd ganrif ar ddeg nag at y Gyfres Gynnar sy'n sail i'r drafodaeth hon.[116] Mae'r drafodaeth uchod wedi dangos fod y Gyfres Gynnar, yn y ffurf fel y mae, yn debygol o fod yn gynnyrch degawdau cyntaf y drydedd ganrif ar ddeg, tra bod cyfeiriadau'r Gogynfeirdd yma yn dyddio i ail hanner y ddeuddegfed ganrif, y dystiolaeth farddol felly yn dangos bod rhai o drioedd cyfresi hwyrach o Trioedd Ynys Prydein yn hŷn na'r Gyfres Gynnar lawn. Mae hyn yn cefnogi dadl Bromwich bod y Trioedd fel corff o waith yn ddatblygiad graddol dros gyfnod hir, tra hefyd yn amlinellu'r angen am astudiaeth lawnach o ryngberthynas y testunau yma. Mae lle hefyd i ofyn os yw agosatrwydd y cyfresi hwyrach at waith y beirdd llys yn dangos dylanwad y beirdd eu hunain ar destun y Trioedd – hynny yw, bod nifer o'r trioedd ychwanegol a geir yng nghyfresi llawnach, hwyrach Trioedd Ynys Prydein wedi eu ysgrifennu gan y beirdd llys sy'n crybwyll y cymeriadau hyn yn eu cerddi.[117]

Tra bod y Trioedd yn frith o gyfeiriadau hanesyddol, mae natur y farddoniaeth lys yn gwneud cyd-destun byw yr hanes yma llawer mwy pendant: cyfansoddwyd y cerddi gan unigolion penodol o flaen arweinwyr penodol a'u llysoedd. Canwyd awdl gan Lywarch ap Llywelyn i Rhys Gryg, tywysog o Ddeheubarth, fel llysgenhadaeth ar ran Llywelyn Fawr o Wynedd – dadleua Rhian Andrews iddi gael ei chanu yn Hydref 1220, yn llys Rhys ei hun yng nghastell Dinefwr.[118] Mae'r gerdd yn cyfeirio'n uniongyrchol at driawd y *Tri Hael*, triawd 2 y Gyfres Gynnar, ond hefyd at ddau o'r trioedd a geir yn y llawysgrifau hwyrach yn unig.[119] Tra bod y gerdd ei hun yn foliant i Rhys, caiff Llywelyn ab Iorwerth, arglwydd Llywarch ac uwch-arglwydd Rhys Gryg, ei glodfori fel awdurdod uwch fyth – dyma le y crybwyllir Arthur, sydd i'w gymharu â Llywelyn yn hytrach na Rhys.[120] Fel y mae Arthur yn uwcharglwydd ar holl frenhinoedd Prydain yn nhriawd agoriadol y Gyfres Gynnar, mae Llywelyn yn uwcharglwydd dros Rys Gryg – a tra bod Rhys i'w gymharu â'r Tri Hael, mae rhai fersiynau o'r triawd yma yn amlygu bod un ffigwr yn goreuo ar y tri brenin hael yma, sef Arthur.[121]

Mae ambell gymhariaeth farddonol at y Trioedd mwy amwys – mae 'Marwnad Gruffudd ap Llywelyn' gan Dafydd Benfras yn cynnwys cymhariaeth i Gwanar:

> Gwanar gar, trimud far, trymrudd,
> Gwenwyn gwyn gennyf nid ymgudd.[122]

> Perthynas i Wanar, â llid cyflawn, o wedd drist,
> Nid yw'r gŵyn chwerw sydd arnaf yn ei chuddio'i hun

Tra bod y gerdd yn cyfeirio at gymeriadau eraill sy'n gyfarwydd o'r Trioedd, Llachau a Nudd Hael, mae'r cyfeiriad at Gwanar yn gyfyngedig i'r gerdd yma ac i driawd 35. Ar ben hyn, mae'r ymadrodd 'gwenwyn gwyn' yn y linell olynol yn dangos bod y bardd yn efelychu triawd 35 y Gyfres Gynnar, lle mae Gwenwynwyn a'i frawd Gwanar yn erlyn y *Cesaryeit* yng nghwmni Caswallon ap Beli. Mae Dafydd Benfras felly yn tynnu ar y Trioedd, a'u manylion am yr ymladd rhwng y Brythoniaid a'r Rhufeiniaid, wrth alaru am Ruffudd ap Llywelyn.[123]

Mae hyblygrwydd y gorffennol yn nhermau ei agosatrwydd at y presennol yn hanfodol i strwythur Trioedd Ynys Prydein: caiff tri pheth eu cyfuno at ei gilydd heb angen am unrhyw agosatrwydd cronolegol. Mae'r tri digwyddiad neu berson, er iddynt gael eu gwahanu gan ofod hirfaith o amser, yn cael eu cyfuno gan eu tebygrwydd o ran anian neu sefyllfa, yn yr un ffordd yn union yr oedd y bardd yn cysylltu ei noddwr ei hun gydag arwyr y gorffennol pell trwy gymharu eu hymddygiad.

Mae'r rhan fwyaf o'r trioedd, o safbwynt hanesyddol neu chwedlonol, yn rhwystredig o dalfyr o ran manylder. Maent yn nodi gair aneglur neu fwriadol rhyfedd, ac yna tri enw heb fanylu ymhellach – yr enwau sy'n esbonio'r gair, yn hytrach na'r gwrthwyneb. Ond dyma hefyd ran o bwrpas y testun, gan fod cerddi llys yn gofyn am drysorfa eang o eiriau, ac yr oedd yr eirfa arbenigol yma yn addurn i grefft bardd – fel y gwawdiwyd yn y chwedl *Breuddwyd Rhonabwy* drwy ffigwr bardd Arthur, Cadyrieith.[124] Cronfa o gyfeiriadaeth hanesyddol oedd y Trioedd, ond cronfa hefyd o eirfa barddonol, geirfa a ddiffiniwyd trwy ei berthynas â'r hanesion yma ond a allai hefyd wasanaethu meistri newydd yn y byd gwleidyddol gyfoes.

Gan taw pwrpas y cyfeiriadau a geiriau hanesyddol oedd i bortreadu gweithredoedd y noddwr fel rhai oedd yn gyson â brenhiniaeth iawnfryd a thraddodiadau'r Cymry, roedd dealltwriaeth gynhwysfawr o'r gorffennol yma yn agwedd hanfodol o farddoniaeth, a dyma pham ysgrifennwyd testunau fel y Trioedd. Caiff y defnydd canoloesol o'r gorffennol ei drafod yn aml yn nhermau defnyddioldeb gwleidyddol naratifau hanesyddol, ond mae'r gofod rhwng tudalen cronicl mynachol a busnes wleidyddol llys brenhinol yn aml yn eang, ac yn anodd i'w groesi. Yn achos barddoniaeth lys, mae'r bardd ei hun eisoes wedi croesi'r gofod rhwng y testun ysgrifenedig a'r llys gwleidyddol. Pa destunau eraill o Brydain yr oesoedd canol sydd mor ddefnyddiol, neu mor benodol, yn eu harddangosiad o'r defnydd gwleidyddol o hanes?

Tri Thriawd: 3. Cudd a Datgudd

I ddychwelyd unwaith eto at y trioedd sy'n cloi'r Gyfres Gynnar, mae celfyddyd lenyddol hefyd yn amlwg yn nhrefniant trioedd 35 a 36: mae triawd 35 yn trafod y tri llu a *aeth* o'r ynys heb ddychwelyd, tra bod triawd 36 yn enwi'r tair gormes a *ddaeth* i'r ynys heb adael. Mae'r rhyngberthynas rhwng achos ac effaith yn y digwyddiadau hanesyddol a bortreadwyd yma yn cyfochri'n gelfydd gyda symudiad cyferbyniol y ddwy naratif. Yn gryno a thaclus o ran mynegiant, fel sy'n briodol i destun beirdd llys, mae'r digwyddiadau a hefyd drefn trafod y digwyddiadau ill dau wedi eu gosod yn bendant ac yn grefftus.

Mae'r patrwm yma yn parhau yn yr olaf o driawdau'r Gyfres Gynnar, y trydydd o'r tri thriawd terfynol dan sylw manwl yma. Wrth i driawd 35 a 36 drafod cyrchoedd heb ddychwelyd ac ymosodiadau heb adael, mae'r triawd olaf yn trafod *cudd a datgudd*, cuddiad a datguddiad:

Tri Chud a Thri Datcud Enys Prydein:

Penn Bendigeituran mab Llyr, a gladwyt yn y G6yn6ryn yn Llundein. A hyt tra vei y Penn yn yr ansa6d yd oed yno, ny doy Ormes byth y'r Enys hon;

Eil, Esgyrn G6ertheuyr 6endigeit a gladwyt ym pryf byrth yr Enys hon;

Trydyd, y Dreigeu a gladwys Llud mab Beli yn Dinas Emreis yn Eryri.

Yma hefyd cawn symudiadau cyferbyniol yn y gorffennol, ac eto esiampl o thema sy'n sylfaenol i weledigaeth awdur y Trioedd o hanes Ynys Prydain. Tra bod cyrchoedd tramor yn gwanhau'r ynys a'i gadael yn agored i ormesoedd gwleidyddol neu oruwchnaturiol, mae datguddiad cyrff arwyr a dreigiau goruwchnaturiol yn gallu amddiffyn yr ynys. Amlinellwyd yma patrymau'r gorffennol, ond mae hefyd deimlad o beth *allai* fod wedi digwydd, o orffennol posib arall – pe cedwid pen Bendigiedfran ynghudd, ni ddeuai unrhyw ormes, a gan taw cyn teyrnasiad Caswallon ap Beli yr oedd Bendigeidfran yn llywodraethu (fel yr amlygwyd yn ail gainc y Mabinogi) roedd cuddiad ei ben yn rhagddyddio'r holl ormesoedd a restrwyd yn nhriawd 36. Eto saif y triawd yma yng nghanol brithwe o gyfeiriadau rhyngdestunol, i destunau Cymraeg a Lladin ill dau. Mae'r cuddiad cyntaf yn manylu digwyddiadau ail gainc y Mabinogi, sydd ei hun yn cyfeirio at y triawd yma. Mae'r ddau guddiad arall dan ddylanwad syniadau *Historia Brittonum*.[125]

Yn y fersiwn cynharaf o driawd 37, yma yn y Gyfres Gynnar, mae'r triawd yn cogio disgrifio'r cuddiadau *a'r* datguddiadau, ond mewn gwirionedd dim ond y cuddiadau a ddisgrifir. Mae'r gyfres ddiweddarach o drioedd yn Llyfr Coch Hergest yn datrys hyn, trwy ychwanegu manylion am ddatguddiad pen Bendigeidfran gan Arthur, datgladdu corff Gwrthefyr gan ei dad, Gwrtheyrn, a hefyd datguddiad yr un Gwrtheyrn o'r ddwy ddraig. Ond mae'n ymddangos yn annhebygol imi bod y Llyfr Coch yn copïo fersiwn hŷn a pherffeithiach o'r triawd, yn hytrach nag ychwanegu manylion i ffurf foelach y Gyfres Gynnar. Ar un cyfrif, byddai datguddiad Arthur o ben Bendigeidfran yn gwrthddweud digwyddiad tair gormes rhwng cyfnod claddu Bendigeidfran a datguddiad Arthur o'i ben.

Teimlaf bod penderfyniad awdur y Gyfres Gynnar i wrthod manylu ar y tri datgudd yn un pwrpasol. Darniol ac awgrymiadol yw'r testun yn gyffredinol, yn hytrach na chwmpasog a thrylwyr – cawn rai straeon a digwyddiadau yn weddol lawn, ond nid yn hollol fanwl, a'r awgrym trwy gydol y testun yw y *dylai*'r gynulleidfa wybod manylion llawnach y personau a'r digwyddiadau a grybwyllir. Mae'n rhaid bod elfen chwareus, heriol i orffen y testun ar y nodyn hwn – heriwyd gwybodaeth y darllenydd. Ond, fel yr awgrymiad o lwybrau nas cymerwyd yn hanes pen Bendigeidfran, mae hefyd yn gadael hanes Ynys Prydain yn agored, sydd efallai gydag ymhlygiadau gwleidyddol.

Yn y triawd blaenorol, triawd 36, amlygwyd am *ddwy* o'r Gormesoedd, y Coraniaid a'r Gwyddyl Ffichti, 'ni aeth un ohonynt yn ôl drachefn'. Ond nid yw hyn yn cael ei nodi am y Saeson, sy'n cadw'r drws yn agored i'r posibilrwydd y gall yr ormes yma gael ei datod, ei therfynu. Mae triawd 37 wedyn yn gorffen gyda chuddiad y ddwy ddraig yn Ninas Emrys, heb ddisgrifio eu datguddiad – ond byddai darllenydd gwybodus yn gyfarwydd â'r ffaith bod datguddiad y dreigiau yn *Historia Brittonum* (ynghyd â'i ailysgrifeniad gan Sieffre o Fynwy) yn cyd-fynd â phroffwydoliaeth Ambrosius neu Emrys y byddai'r Brythoniaid yn y pen draw yn gyrru'r Saeson o'r ynys.[126] Trwy adael y testun mor benagored, mae Cyfres Gynnar Trioedd Ynys Prydein yn arddangos y posibilrwydd o newid a datblygiad yn nyfodol gwleidyddol y Cymry.

Tra bod y testun hwn yn un darniol ac awgrymiadol, mae Cyfres Gynnar Trioedd Ynys Prydein yn haeddu cymhariaeth gydag ymgeisiadau mwy hirwyntog, naratifol i ddiffinio a threfnu gorffennol Ynys Prydain. Yn ei byrdra mae ei phŵer, ac y mae'r awdur yn sefydlu ei destun yn bwrpasog o fewn gwead eang o destunau eraill, rhai Cymraeg a Lladin. Mae'r Gyfres Gynnar yn cynnig dadansoddiad cydlynol o hanes Prydain a'r Cymry, yn enwedig yn y tri thriawd llawn ond dwys sy'n dod â'r testun i ben. Y mae hefyd yn awgrymog ynglŷn â dyfodol y

Cymry. Mae hyn i'w ddisgwyl mewn gwaith sydd mor agos i waith beirdd llys y cyfnod, a oedd efallai yn awduron cerddi darogan ynghyd â cherddi mawl politicaidd i dywysogion y wlad.[127] Mae agwedd thematig a chysylltiadol y testun tuag at y gorffennol, hyblygrwydd ei gysylltu rhwng digwyddiadau ac unigolion o gyfnodau cronolegol gwahanol iawn, yn adlewyrchu gallu ei ddarllenwyr a'i ddefnyddwyr o feirdd i edrych tuag at y gorffennol a'r dyfodol ill dau wrth iddynt foli eu noddwyr yn y presennol. Nid peth caeedig na therfynol oedd gorffennol Ynys Prydain i awdur y Trioedd yma na chwaith i'w gynulleidfa – roeddynt yn gweld eu hunain yn ei chanol, a gallent ffurfio dyfodol yr Ynys gyda'u dealltwriaeth o'i gorffennol fel arf.

. . .

The Triads of the Island of Britain as Historical Texts

Abstract

This chapter focuses primarily on the 'Early Series', the thirty-seven triads found in manuscript Peniarth 16, investigating its relationship with other vernacular and Latin texts and considering how it functioned as a historical text in medieval Wales. An introductory section outlines previous scholarly discussion of the composition and the scope of the Early Series, considering especially its focus on Arthurian characters together with the lack of Galfridian influence. This serves as a springboard for considering intertextuality more broadly. Attention is drawn to connections with the Four Branches of the Mabinogi, *Culhwch and Olwen* and the Bonedd y Saint genealogies. These connections lead to the conclusion that Clynnog Fawr in Arfon was an important centre for compiling the Early Series. There follows a more detailed discussion of the Triads of the Island of Britain as a historical text, framed around the three fuller triads found at the end of the Early Series (the three armies that left the island; the three oppressions that came to the island; the three concealments and three revelations). This discussion reveals how the triads develop the historical narrative present in the ninth-century Latin text *Historia Brittonum* and emphasises the importance of considering this text alongside fuller historical narratives. The discussion then turns to the relationship between the text of the Triads and the court poetry of the Poets of the Princes, as a means of assessing how such texts were used and interpreted. These texts were a storehouse of historical references upon which poets could draw and the historical framework of the Triads enabled poets to situate their patrons in the context of the heroic history of the Britons. The Triads illustrate how history was used in medieval Wales, and its political importance.

Nodiadau

1 Mae'r bennod yn gynnyrch prosiect ymchwil a ariannwyd gan yr AHRC, The Search for Parity: Rulers, Relationships and the Remote Past in Britain's Chronicles, *c*.1100–1300 – rhaid imi ddiolch i fy nghyd-ymchwilydd Emily Winkler am drafodaethau ar y pwnc, ac i Rebecca Thomas, Ben Guy a Barry Lewis am gynnig sylwadau ar ddrafftiau cynharach o'r bennod.
2 *Trioedd Ynys Prydein: The Triads of the Island of Britain*, gol. Rachel Bromwich (4ydd arg., Caerdydd, 2014), trioedd 3, 35, 33.
3 *Trioedd*, gol. Bromwich, trioedd 3, 35.
4 Ailolygwyd ac adnewyddwyd cyfrol Bromwich yn 1971, 2006 a 2014. Am ymdriniaethau ers 1961: Eric P. Hamp, 'On the Justification of Ordering in TYP', *Studia Celtica*, 16 (1981), 104–9; Rebecca Shercliff, 'Arthur in *Trioedd Ynys Prydain*', yn Ceridwen Lloyd Morgan ac Erich Poppe (goln), *Arthur in the Celtic Languages* (Caerdydd, 2019), tt. 173–86.
5 Aberystwyth, Llyfrgell Genedlaethol Cymru, llsgr. Peniarth 16, rhan iv.
6 Er hyn, fel nododd Bromwich, mae ambell driawd unigol yn y cyfresi hwyrach yn agosach i'r trioedd sydd yn cael eu crybwyll ym marddoniaeth y ddeuddegfed ganrif: 'Cyfeiriadau Traddodiadol a Chwedlonol y Gogynfeirdd', yn Morfydd E. Owen a Brynley F. Roberts (goln), *Beirdd a Thywysogion: Barddoniaeth Llys yng Nghymru, Iwerddon a'r Alban* (Caerdydd, 1996), tt. 201–18 (t. 206); *Trioedd*, gol. Bromwich, tt. 44, 71.
7 Aberystwyth, Llyfrgell Genedlaethol Cymru, llsgr. Peniarth 45. Am rhyngberthynas y fersiynau, gw. *Trioedd*, gol. Bromwich, tt. xi–xxxviii.
8 *Trioedd*, gol. Bromwich, tt. xiii–xv.
9 Daniel Huws, *Repertory of Welsh manuscripts and scribes c.800–c.1800*, 3 cyfrol (Aberystwyth, 2022), I, 211, 340–1; II, 213.
10 Huws, *Repertory*, I, 355–6; II, 214.
11 *Trioedd*, gol. Bromwich, tt. xix–xx.
12 Deillio o gynsail cyffredin y mae fersiwn LlGC 5266B a Peniarth 45 o *Brut Dingestow* hefyd, gyda llawysgrif arall rhwng Peniarth 45 a'r cynsail – yn gyson â rhyngberthynas fersiynau Peniarth 16 a Peniarth 45 o'r Trioedd. Brynley F. Roberts, 'Fersiwn Dingestow o *Brut y Brenhinedd*', *BBCS*, 27 (1976–8), 331–61 (yn enw. tt. 332, 341–4, 351).

13 *Trioedd*, gol. Bromwich, tt. xix–xx.
14 *Trioedd*, gol. Bromwich, tt. xiii–xv.
15 Sail adran gyntaf golygiad Bromwich, *Trioedd*, tt. 1–102. Ni chaiff unrhyw ddarnau o'r testun o fewn cromfachau, sydd yn ychwanegiadau o lawysgrifau eraill, a hefyd y fersiynau sylweddol amrywiol o drioedd a ychwanegwyd i'r testun o WR (Llyfr Gwyn Rhydderch a Llyfr Coch Hergest), eu cynnwys yn y testun o dan sylw yma.
16 Mae Peniarth 16 yn gadael gweddill llinell y testun gorffenedig o driawd 37 yn wag – newid sylweddol o ysgrifennu dwys y tudalennau blaenorol – ac yn cynnig lle (nas defnyddiwyd) ar gyfer priflythyren mawr i ddechrau Trioedd y Meirch. Mae'r brif lythyren goch sy'n marcio dechrau testun Trioedd y Meirch hefyd yn weladwy ar dudalen olaf Peniarth 45. *Llyfr Du Caerfyrddin*, gol. A. O. H. Jarman gydag E. D. Jones (Caerdydd, 1982), t. 12; *Trioedd*, gol. Bromwich, tt. xix, lxxx–lxxxvii; Rachel Bromwich, 'The Triads of the Horses', yn Sioned Davies a Nerys Ann Jones (goln), *The Horse in Celtic Culture: Medieval Welsh Perspectives* (Caerdydd, 1997), tt. 102–20.
17 Huws, *Repertory*, I, 211, 340–1.
18 Am weledigaeth Bromwich o ddatblygiad y testun, gw. *Trioedd*, gol. Bromwich, tt. lxxxvii–xcix; am ddatblygiadau hwyrach, tt. xvi–lii; Shercliff, 'Arthur in *Trioedd Ynys Prydain*'.
19 Gw. isod, tt. 73–7.
20 *Trioedd*, gol. Bromwich, triawd 27; Richard Mortimer, 'Clare, Gilbert de [Gilbert fitz Richard, Gilbert of Tonbridge] (d. 1117)', *ODNB*, https://doi.org/10.1093/ref:odnb/5436.
21 *Trioedd*, gol. Bromwich, tt. 360–1.
22 *Trioedd*, gol. Bromwich, triawd 30 a t. 277; Gwenno Piette, *Brittany: a Concise History* (Caerdydd, 2008), tt. 36–8; Elizabeth Hallam a Charles West, *Capetian France 987–1328* (3ydd arg., Abingdon, 2020), t. 64.
23 *Trioedd*, gol. Bromwich, t. 87.
24 Rhaid cymharu'r berthynas rhwng Arthur fel *pen teyrnedd* a'r lleill fel *pen henyf* yr ardaloedd yma i'r cyferbyniad rhwng un *regnum* Gwrtheyrn a *regiones* niferus eraill Ynys Prydain yn *Historia Brittonum*: Rebecca Thomas, *History and Identity in Early Medieval Wales* (Cambridge, 2022), tt. 42–7.
25 *Trioedd*, gol. Bromwich, triawd 1.
26 J. C. Davies, *Episcopal Acts and Cognate Documents Relating to Welsh Dioceses 1066–1272*, 2 gyfrol (Cardiff, 1944–6), I, 190–232. Nododd Bromwich: 'we can hardly doubt that the *Teir Lleithiclwyth* is an addition to the series made by a monastic scribe, working at a date between *circa* 1120–50' (Bromwich, *Trioedd*, t. xci) – ond byddwn yn pwysleisio pwysigrwydd y triawd yma fel agoriad y Gyfres Gynnar yn hytrach na'i wahanu o'r gweddill. Roedd statws archesgobol Tyddewi eto'n bwnc llosg oddeutu 1200.

27 Dauvit Broun, 'The Welsh identity of the kingdom of Strathclyde *c*.900–*c*.1200', *Innes Review*, 55 (2004), 111–80 (yn enwedig tt. 117–19, 140–3, 167–71); Richard Oram, *Domination and Lordship: Scotland 1070–1230* (Edinburgh, 2011), tt. 7, 57–8, 228–9, 336–46.

28 *Trioedd*, gol. Bromwich, t. 41.

29 *Trioedd*, gol. Bromwich, t. 50; Shercliff, 'Arthur in *Trioedd Ynys Prydain*', t. 176; Rachel Bromwich, 'The Tristan of the Welsh', yn Rachel Bromwich, A. O. H. Jarman a Brynley F. Roberts (goln), *The Arthur of the Welsh: the Arthurian Legend in Medieval Welsh Literature* (Cardiff, 1991), tt. 209–28.

30 *Trioedd*, gol. Bromwich, t. 400; Hugh Williams, *Gildas: De Excidio Britanniae*, 2 gyfrol (London, 1899), tt. 401–3.

31 *Culhwch ac Olwen: an Edition and Study of the Oldest Arthurian Tale*, gol. R. Bromwich a D. Simon Evans (Cardiff, 1992), t. 8 n. 78.

32 Shercliff, 'Arthur in *Trioedd Ynys Prydain*', tt. 175, 177, 181.

33 *Trioedd*, gol. Bromwich, trioedd 71, 72, 73, 80, 86, a hefyd 'Appendix IV'; Shercliff, 'Arthur in *Trioedd Ynys Prydain*', tt. 179–81.

34 *Trioedd*, gol. Bromwich, triawd 9.

35 Brynley F. Roberts, 'The Treatment of Personal Names in the Early Welsh Versions of *Historia regum Britanniae*', *BBCS*, 25 (1972–4), 274–90; Bromwich, 'Cyfeiriadau Traddodiadol a Chwedlonol', t. 204; am gyfeiriadau Arthuraidd: Barry Lewis, 'Arthurian References in Medieval Welsh Poetry, *c*.1100–*c*.1540', yn Ceridwen Lloyd Morgan ac Erich Poppe (goln), *Arthur in the Celtic Languages* (Cardiff, 2019), tt. 187–202. Mae Ben Guy yn amlinellu dylanwad gwaith Sieffre ar gerddi Cynddelw erbyn 1187: 'Constantine, Helena, Maximus: on the appropriation of Roman history in medieval Wales, *c*.800–1250', *Journal of Medieval History*, 44 (2018), 381–405 (tt. 400–1).

36 Am gymhariaeth rhwng Sieffre, y Trioedd ac achau'r saint: Barry Lewis, 'Approaching the Genealogies of the Welsh Saints', yn David N. Parsons a Paul Russell (goln), *Seintiau Cymru, Sancti Cambrenses: Astudiaethau ar Seintiau Cymru/Studies in the Saints of Wales* (Aberystwyth, 2022), tt. 65–100 (tt. 95–9).

37 Mae trioedd 10, 15 a 32 yn cynnig eu hun yn y cyswllt yma.

38 Fel amlinelliad o'r safbwynt yma, *Trioedd*, gol. Bromwich, t. liv.

39 *Trioedd*, gol. Bromwich, t. lv.

40 *Pedeir Keinc y Mabinogi allan o Lyfr Gwyn Rhydderch*, gol. Ifor Williams (Caerdydd, 1930), tt. xxiv–xxx [*PKM*]; *Trioedd*, gol. Bromwich, tt. lxxi–lxxv. Am drioedd y drydedd gainc: *Manawydan uab Llyr*, gol. Ian Hughes (Caerdydd, 2007), tt. xxiii, xxv–xxvi, xxx–xxxi, 17–18; y bedwaredd gainc: *Math uab Mathonwy: the Fourth Branch of the Mabinogi*, gol. Ian Hughes (Dublin, 2013), tt. xlv, xlix–l, lxii, lxviii–lxix, lxxix–lxxx, xc.

41 *PKM*, gol. Williams, t. xxv, rhifau 1, 2 ac 8; *Trioedd*, gol. Bromwich, t. lxxii.

42 *PKM*, gol. Williams, t. xxv, rhifau 5, 7 a 9; *Trioedd*, gol. Bromwich, trioedd 53, 67.
43 *Trioedd*, gol. Bromwich, trioedd 13 (Cynweissyat: Caradog ap Bran), 26 (Gwrdueichyat: Pryderi, Pwyll Pen Annwn a Phendaran Dyfed), 28 (Prif Hut: Math fab Mathonwy).
44 *Trioedd*, gol. Bromwich, tt. 50–1; *PKM*, gol. Williams, tt. 1, 26, 39, 46, 68–73.
45 *PKM*, gol. Williams, t. xxx; *Trioedd*, gol. Bromwich, tt. lxxi, lxxiv–lxxv.
46 *Trioedd*, gol. Bromwich, tt. lxxii–lxxiv; 54–5; trioedd 8, 26W, 53, 67.
47 *Culhwch ac Olwen* (1992), tt. xli–xlii; *Culhwch ac Olwen*, gol. Rachel Bromwich a D. Simon Evans (2il arg., Cardiff, 1997), tt. 7–13, ll. 7.182–3, 8.196, 8.194–5, 9.250–1; *Trioedd*, gol. Bromwich, tt. 353, 337, 381.
48 *Culhwch ac Olwen* (1997), tt. 8.199, 15.408, 16.426, 20.538, 36.1025, 40.1178, 40.1154; *Trioedd*, gol. Bromwich, trioedd 9, 27. Mae Gwythelin/ Gwdolwyn Gorr yn ymddangos yn y rhestr o ddilynwyr Arthur ynghyd ag yn yr anoethau, *Culhwch ac Olwen* (1997), tt. 13.364–5; 25.657.
49 *Trioedd*, gol. Bromwich, triawd 1; *Culhwch ac Olwen* (1997), t. 13.356. Mae'r esgob Bytwini yn y ddau destun, er nad yw Caradog Vreichfras yn ymddangos yn *Culhwch*.
50 *Trioedd*, gol. Bromwich, triawd 9; *Culhwch ac Olwen* (1997), tt. 7.182–3, 8.195–6. Am Cadrieith, sydd ddim yn *Culhwch*, gw. *Trioedd*, gol. Bromwich, tt. 297–8 a *Culhwch ac Olwen* (1997), t. 101.
51 *Culhwch ac Olwen* (1997), tt. 15.409 'lleturith', 16.428 'lletrith'.
52 *Trioedd*, gol. Bromwich, triawd 26.
53 Gwelwn hefyd ddylanwad o destun *Culhwch* ar Drioedd y Meirch a'r gyfres hwyrach yn y llyfrau Gwyn a Coch. *Trioedd*, gol. Bromwich, trioedd 44, 45, 46, 52, 92, 93 (efallai hefyd 53, 56).
54 Am Sieffre fel Cymro: Nia Wyn Jones [cyhoeddwyd fel O. W. Jones], 'The Most Excellent Princes: Geoffrey of Monmouth and Medieval Welsh Historical Writing', yn Joshua Byron Smith a Georgia Henley (goln), *A Companion to Geoffrey of Monmouth* (Leiden, 2020), tt. 257–90 (tt. 268–70); hefyd Joshua Byron Smith, 'Introduction and Biography', yn yr un gyfrol, tt. 1–28 (tt. 11–21).
55 Ben Guy, 'Geoffrey of Monmouth's Welsh Sources', yn Joshua Byron Smith a Georgia Henley (goln), *A Companion to Geoffrey of Monmouth* (Leiden, 2020), tt. 31–66 (tt. 52–8).
56 *Culhwch ac Olwen* (1992), tt. xxxvii–xlvi, 7–13.
57 Cyfeiriadau at *Trioedd*, gol. Bromwich, a 'Bonedd y Saint' [BS] yn P. C. Bartrum (gol.), *Early Welsh Genealogical Tracts* (Cardiff, 1966), tt. 51–67. Alan Fyrgan, triawd 30, BS 58 (Llonyaw Llawhir); Pryder mab Dolor Deifyr a Bryneich, triawd 16, BS 56 (Dwyuael); Pasgen ab Urien, triawd 23,

BS 55 (Nidan). Mae cyfeiriad hefyd at Eda Glinfawr, triawd 30, BS 71 (Eda Glynuawr), ond nid yw'r ach yma yng nghasgliad cynharaf Bonedd y Saint, ac yn debyg mae'n cael ei ychwanegu yng Nglyn-y-Groes. Mae un gorgyffyrddiad arall yn dyddio i'r cyfnod canoloesol diweddarach: Gwgon Gwron ap Peredur ab Eliffer Gosgorddfawr, triawd 8, BS 74.

58 Barry Lewis (gol.), *Bonedd y Saint: an Edition and Study of the Genealogies of the Welsh Saints* (Dublin, 2023); Lewis, 'Genealogies of the Welsh Saints', tt. 84–7, 94–9.
59 Lewis, 'Genealogies of the Welsh Saints', tt. 95, 98.
60 Lewis, 'Genealogies of the Welsh Saints', t. 85.
61 *Trioedd*, gol. Bromwich, triawd 26; Peniarth 98B; John K. Bollard (gol.), *Englynion y Beddau: the Stanzas of the Graves* (Llanrwst, 2015), P14, tt. 57, 105.
62 Patrick Sims-Williams, 'Clas Beuno and the Four Branches of the Mabinogi', yn Bernhard Maier, Stefan Zimmer a Christiane Batke (goln), *150 Jahre "Mabinogion" – Deutsch-Walisische Kulturbeziehungen* (Tübingen, 2001), tt. 111–27 (tt. 116–22).
63 *Math uab Mathonwy*, gol. Hughes, tt. 17, 96.
64 D. Simon Evans (gol.), *Historia Gruffud vab Kenan* (Caerdydd, 1977), tt. ccxlviii–ccxlix, 107; Paul Russell (gol.), *Vita Griffini filii Conani* (Cardiff, 2005), t. 46 a n. 144; Davies, *Episcopal Acts*, I, 265.
65 *Trioedd*, gol. Bromwich, triawd 26.
66 C. N. Johns, 'The Celtic Monasteries of North Wales', *Trafodion Cymdeithas Hanes Sir Gaernarfon*, 21 (1960), 14–43, map rhwng tt. 16 ac 17; John Caley a Jospeh Hunter (goln), *Valor Ecclesiasticus Temp. Henrici Viii*, 6 chyfrol (Llundain, 1810–34), IV (Llundain, 1821), 432; VI (Llundain, 1834), tt. xvi, xviii. Ailsefydlwyd priordy Beddgelert fel tŷ Awstinaidd oddeutu 1200×1220: Alan Bott a Margaret Dunn, *A Guide to the Priory and Parish Church of St Mary Beddgelert, Gwynedd* (Godalming, 2004), tt. 9–12, 77–8; 'Event detail for site: Beddgelert c.1200: Foundation', *https://www.monasticwales.org/event/193* (cyrchwyd 24 Ebrill 2023).
67 Dafydd Jenkins, 'A Family of Medieval Welsh Lawyers', yn Dafydd Jenkins (gol.), *Celtic Law Papers Introductory to Welsh Medieval Law and Government* (Brussels, 1973), tt. 121–33; Patrick Sims-Williams, 'Edward IV's Confirmation Charter for Clynnog Fawr', yn Colin Richmond ac Isobel Harvey (goln), *Recognitions: Essays Presented to Edmund Fryde* (Aberystwyth, 1996), tt. 229–42; adolygiad o'r bennod hon gan Dafydd Jenkins, *CMCS*, 35 (1998), 79; Sims-Williams, 'Clas Beuno', tt. 118–19, 121–2, 125. Am ach y teulu, Ben Guy, *Medieval Welsh Genealogy: an introduction and textual study* (Woodbridge, 2020), t. 310.
68 'Gwaith Einion ap Madog ap Rahawd', gol. Gruffydd Aled Williams, yn *Gwaith Dafydd Benfras ac Eraill o Feirdd Hanner Cyntaf y Drydedd Ganrif ar Ddeg*

(Caerdydd, 1995), t. 347. Mac'n bosib iawn taw Ystrwyth ap Gwrydr yw'r *Instructus* sy'n gwasanaethu Llywelyn Fawr, er taw tebygrwydd yr enw yw'r brif ddadl dros hyn: Jenkins, 'Medieval Welsh Lawyers', tt. 124, 130; David Stephenson, *The Governance of Gwynedd* (Cardiff, 1984), tt. 30–1, 224–5; Guy, *Medieval Welsh Genealogy*, t. 310 n.

69 Dafydd Jenkins (gol.), *Damweiniau Colan, Llyfr y Damweiniau yn ôl Llawysgrif Peniarth 30* (Aberystwyth, 1973), t. 19; *Math uab Mathonwy*, gol. Hughes, t. 110.

70 Morfydd Owen, 'Royal Propaganda: Stories from the Law-Texts', yn Morfydd Owen, Paul Russell a Thomas Charles-Edwards (goln), *The Welsh King and his Court* (Cardiff, 2000), tt. 224–54 (t. 240).

71 *AWR*, rhif 367. Am leoliad Pennardd: Stephenson, *Governance of Gwynedd*, t. 157. Rhoid tiroedd meibion Ithel ap Dafydd ym Mhennardd i Llywelyn, ond cadwyd cyfran Iorwerth Hagr (druan) o'r tiroedd yma yn nwylo priordy Beddgelert. Efallai ei fod hefyd yn berthnasol nodi bod cyfres III Englynion y Beddau yn cyfeirio at Ddinas Emrys (III.17), er rhaid pwysleisio bod cysylltiadau y testun yma ag ardal Pennardd a Chlynnog llawer amlycach: Sims-Williams, 'Clas Beuno', tt. 119–20.

72 *Trioedd*, gol. Bromwich, trioedd 35, 36, 37.

73 *Breudwyt Maxen Wledic*, gol. Brynley F. Roberts (Dublin, 2005), tt. 10–11.

74 *Historia Brittonum* [*HB*], pennod 27, yn J. Morris (gol.), *Nennius: British History and the Welsh Annals* (Chichester, 1980), t. 65. Cyfieithiad o'r fersiwn Saesneg yn yr uchod, tt. 24–5.

75 *HB*, pennod 30 (gol. Morris, t. 66); Thomas, *History and Identity*, tt. 114–17.

76 *HB*, pennod 44 (gol. Morris, tt. 72–3).

77 Cawn hefyd Edelflet/Ethelfrith, brenin Bryneich (593–617) yn triawd 32, ond dim ond yn fersiwn y Llyfr Gwyn o'r Trioedd (yn triawd 10) mae'r unigolyn yma yn derbyn y llysenw *Ffleissavc* a rhoid hefyd iddo yn *Historia Brittonum*. *HB*, pennod 57, 61 (gol. Morris, tt. 77, 78); *Trioedd*, gol. Bromwich, tt. 17, 30, 68, 337–8. Sylwa Rebecca Thomas am y llysenwau yma 'it is impossible to know if the *Historia* [*Brittonum*] stands at the head of that tradition or is simply the earliest extant attestation of it': *History and Identity*, t. 80.

78 Am wybodaeth y beirdd o *Historia Brittonum*: Bromwich, 'Cyfeiriadau Traddodiadol a Chwedlonol', tt. 203–4.

79 *HB*, pennod 57, 61–5 (gol. Morris, tt. 77–80).

80 Am gyd-destun yr *Historia Brittonum*: Ben Guy, 'The Origins of the Compilation of Welsh Historical Texts in Harley 3859', *Studia Celtica*, 49 (2015), 21–56; am safbwynt gwahanol, ond nid un y mae'r awdur presennol yn ei dderbyn: Keith J. Fitzpatrick-Matthews, 'Genealogia Brittonum: revisiting the textual tradition of the Historia Brittonum', *Studia Celtica*, 54 (2020), 45–73 (yn enw. tt. 66–7).

81 Er bod y teitl a roddir i Merfyn yn y ddogfen grynoëdig yma, *princeps*, yn codi amheuon, mae'r rhestr o roddion o gyfnod Rhodri Mawr a'i feibion yn arddangos cymhlethdod ac anghysondeb o ran teitlau sy'n fwy awgrymog o gofnodion dilys. *The Record of Caernarvon*, Record Commission (Llundain, 1838), tt. 257–8; Huw Pryce, 'The Church of Trefeglwys and the End of the "Celtic" Charter Tradition in Twelfth-century Wales', *CMCS*, 25 (1993), 15–54 (t. 49); Sims-Williams, 'Edward IV's Confirmation Charter'.
82 Rhaid imi ddiolch i Ben Guy am yr awgrym yma.
83 *HB*, pennod 19 (gol. Morris, tt. 63–4).
84 Am destun arall sy'n cyflawni'r un weithred: 'Llywelyn ab Iorwerth Genealogies', gol. Guy, *Medieval Welsh Genealogy*, tt. 349–89, yn enwedig §10, §27, ac ymhellach Guy, 'Constantine, Helena, Maximus', tt. 403–4. Mae'r gorgyffwrdd sylweddol rhwng y casgliad achyddol yma a'r Trioedd yn awgrymog iawn.
85 Ifor Williams, 'Hen Chwedlau', *Transactions of the Honourable Society of Cymmrodorion 1946–1947* (1948), 28–58 (tt. 41–3); *Trioedd*, gol. Bromwich, tt. 305–6, 354.
86 Rhaid nodi bod yr amlinelliad yma yn dibynnu ar gyfuniad o gyfeiriadau ar draws testunau *Trioedd Ynys Prydein*. *Trioedd*, gol. Bromwich, trioedd 35, 36, 38, 51, 59, 67, 71, 89.
87 Yr astudiaethau amlycaf yw rhai W. J. Gruffudd, *Math vab Mathonwy: an Inquiry into the Origins and Development of the Fourth Branch of the Mabinogi with a Text and a Translation* (Cardiff, 1928); W. J. Gruffudd, *Rhiannon: an Inquiry into the Origins of the First and Third Branches of the Mabinogi* (Cardiff, 1953), yn enw. tt. 109–12; hefyd Proinsais Mac Cana, *The Mabinogi* (2il arg., Cardiff, 1992), tt. 50–3. Am archwiliad diddorol o botensial straeon y Pedair Cainc i adlewyrchu gwirionedd hanes y cyfnod cyn-Rhufeinig: John T. Koch, 'A Welsh Window on the Iron Age: Manawydan, Mandubracios', *CMCS*, 14 (1987), 17–52.
88 *DGB*, IIII.54–69 (gol. a chyf. Reeve a Wright, tt. 69–85).
89 Am dystiolaeth sylweddol o'r defnydd gan Nennius o ffynonellau sy'n wahanol i unrhyw ddefnydd clasurol sy'n goroesi gw. Thomas, *History and Identity*, tt. 104–16.
90 Brynley F. Roberts (gol.), *Cyfranc Lludd a Llefelys* (Dublin, 1975), tt. xiii–xvii, xxvii–xxxii; *Breudwyt Maxen*, gol. Roberts, tt. lxi–lxxvi.
91 *Trioedd*, gol. Bromwich, trioedd 35, 13.
92 Guy, 'Constantine, Helena, Maximus', tt. 400–1; mae'r ffurf *Maxen* hefyd yng ngwaith Cynddelw Brydydd Mawr: Nerys Ann Jones ac Ann Parry Owen (goln), *Gwaith Cynddelw Brydydd Mawr I* (Caerdydd, 1991), 16.88 (t. 192).
93 *Breudwyt Macsen*, gol. Roberts, tt. lxiv–lxvii; Guy, 'Constantine, Helena, Maximus', tt. 401–3; Henry Lewis (gol.), *Brut Dingestow* (Caerdydd, 1942), t. 75.

94 *Breudwyt Macsen*, gol. Roberts, tt. lxiv–lxv; Guy, 'Constantine, Helena, Maximus', tt. 402–3.
95 Nodwyd gwybodaeth fanwl awdur *Breuddwyd Maxen* gan sylwebwyr eisoes. Mae lle i fanylu ymhellach ar y wybodaeth yma. Mae'r chwedl yn cyfeirio at ddau leoliad yng Nghaernarfon: un 'en aber er auon', 'caer Aber Seint', lle mae Macsen yn cwrdd ag Elen a'i theulu, a'r gaer mae ei gŵr wedyn yn adeiladu iddi, 'e gaer uchaf en Arvon'. *Breudwyt Macsen*, gol. Roberts, ll. 45–7, 171–2, 212, 228–9. Mae'n amlwg imi taw'r gaer gyntaf yw Henwalia, caer Rhufeinig hwyrach (neu efallai warws) sydd yn gwarchod aber yr Afon Seiont, a'i muriau dal yn hynod sylweddol a thrawiadol. Cyfeiriwyd ato fel 'Hengaer' yn 1823. Caer ehangach Segontiwm, yn uwch ar y bryn, fyddai felly y *Gaer Uchaf*, a'r ystyr yn un llythrennol. Elfen o chwedl *Breuddwyd Maxen*, felly, yw esboniad canoloesol hynafiaethol ar y ffaith bod dwy gaer Rhufeinig sylweddol i'w gweld yng Nghaernarfon, yn agos at ei gilydd. S. D. Boyle, 'Excavations at Hen Waliau, Caernarfon, 1952–1985', *BBCS*, 38 (1991), 191–212.
96 *Breudwyt Macsen*, gol. Roberts, tt. lxxvi–lxxxvi.
97 Guy, *Medieval Welsh Genealogy*, tt. 81, 85.
98 *Trioedd*, gol. Bromwich, t. 400; Williams, *Gildas*, tt. 401–3. Am y berthynas rhyngddynt, gw. *Culhwch ac Olwen* (1997), t. 78.
99 Guy, *Medieval Welsh Genealogy*, tt. 79–100.
100 Rhys Goch Eryri sydd â'r dystiolaeth gynharaf: Dylan Foster Evans (gol.), *Gwaith Rhys Goch Eryri* (Aberystwyth, 2007), 8.103, tt. 88, 206; *Trioedd*, gol. Bromwich, tt. 466–7; *The Cambrian Journal* (1859), trawsgrifiad gan Robert Williams o lythyr Edward Llwyd, 1693, tt. 209–10.
101 *Trioedd*, gol. Bromwich, triawd 36.
102 Er taw'r Saeson yw prif elynion Arthur yn *Historia Brittonum*, mae Sieffre yn cyfuno rhain gyda'r Pictiaid a'r Scotiaid – efallai'n ddylanwad ar *Gwyddyl Ffichi* (Pictiaid Gwyddelig) y Trioedd. Mae'r rhwyg yn undod Ynys Prydain a ddaeth o ddyfodiad y Pictiaid eisoes yn *Historia Brittonum*, ynghyd â'r gosodiad 'manent ibi usquem in hodiernum diem. Tertiam partem Brittaniae tenuerunt et tenent usque in hodiernum diem' ('maent yn byw yno hyd heddiw. Daliasant drydedd ran o Brydain ac maent yn ei dal hyd heddiw'). Mae'n bosib gweld cysgod y gosodiad yma tu ôl i 'nyt aeth ór un onadunt dracheuyn' y Trioedd. *HB*, pennod 12, 56 (gol. a chyf. Morris, tt. 20, 35, 61, 76); *DGB*, I.5.44–5 (gol. a chyf. Reeve a Wright, t. 7), 9.143–9.152 (gol. a chyf. Reeve a Wright, tt. 193–205); *Trioedd*, gol. Bromwich, t. 93; Brynley F. Roberts, 'Geoffrey of Monmouth, *Historia Regum Britanniae* and *Brut y Brenhinedd*', yn Rachel Bromwich, A. O. H. Jarman a Brynley F. Roberts (goln), *The Arthur of the Welsh: the Arthurian Legend in Medieval Welsh Literature* (Cardiff, 1991), tt. 97–119 (tt. 102–3).

103 Cymharer *Historia Brittonum*, y Pictiaid yn meddiannu *tertiam patrem Brittaniae* ('traean o Brydain'). Am drafodaeth: Thomas, *History and Identity*, tt. 25–6, 28.
104 *Trioedd*, gol. Bromwich, tt. 92–3.
105 John Jay Parry (gol.), *Brut y Brenhinedd, Cotton Cleopatra Version* (Cambridge, MA, 1937), tt. 64–71; *Lludd a Llefelys*, gol. Roberts, tt. xxxii–xxxiii.
106 Thomas, *History and Identitiy*, tt. 103–19; *HB*, pennod 19–31 (gol. Morris, tt. 63–7); *Breudwyt Macsen*, gol. Roberts, tt. xlvii–xlviii, lii–liii.
107 Tra bod golygiad Rachel Bromwich o'r Trioedd yn cynnig cyfeiriadau brith i waith y Gogynfeirdd, mae trafodaeth cynilach yn ei 'Cyfeiriadau Traddodiadol a Chwedlonol'.
108 Am yr adleisiau yng ngherddi Cynddelw Brydydd Mawr i Owain Gwynedd, D. Myrddin Lloyd, 'Barddoniaeth Cynddelw Brydydd Mawr II: Canu i Owain Gwynedd', *Y Llenor*, 13 (1934), 49–59; am Gwalchmai ap Meilyr, 'Gorhoffedd Gwalchmai': J. E. Caerwyn Williams a P. I. Lynch (goln), *Gwaith Meilyr Brydydd a'i Ddisgynyddion*, CBT I (Caerdydd, 1994), rhif 9, ll. 48 a t. 214 n. 48. Am drafodaeth Rachel Bromwich o'r adleisiau yma, *Trioedd*, t. lxiii.
109 Elin M. Jones a Nerys Ann Jones (goln), *Gwaith Llywarch ap Llywelyn, 'Prydydd y Moch'*, CBT V (Caerdydd, 1991), rhif 20, ll. 5, 19, 21, 36, 37, 46.
110 Mae'n aml anodd penderfynu pa Rhun a gyfeiriwyd ato yng ngwaith y Gogynfeirdd. *Trioedd*, gol. Bromwich, rhif 23, a tt. 490–3.
111 Jones a Jones (goln), *Gwaith Llywarch ap Llywelyn*, rhif 24.
112 Jones a Jones (goln), *Gwaith Llywarch ap Llywelyn*, rhif 24, ll. 3, 6.
113 *Trioedd*, gol. Bromwich, t. 48.
114 Dyma restr o gyfeiriadau (yn cynnwys cyfeiriadau posib neu ansicr) at ffigyrau'r Gyfres Gynnar yng Nghyfres Beirdd y Tywysogion. Rhoir ar ôl yr enw rhif y triawd penodol yng nghromfachau, wedyn am y farddoniaeth rhoir rhif y gyfrol, y gerdd a'r linell. Afan Ferddig (11), IV.6.268; Aneirin (33, 34), VI.25.5; Arthur (1, 12, 20, 26), I.6.8, II.22.27, III.9.16, IV.17.67, V.5.12, V.11.53, V.12.8, V.20.5, V.23.64, V.26.96, VI.20.83, VII.24.154, VII.46.24, VII 51.8,19, VII 54.30; Bedwyr mab Bedrawc (21), I.18.18; Beli Mawr (35, 36, 37), I.26.8, III.21.35, V.2.13, V.17.18, V.25.49, VI.20.90, VII.1.18, VII.24.39, VII.54.29; Bendigeidfran fab Llyr (37), III.7.17, IV.17.71, V.11.27, V.20.37, VII.51.5; Cadwaladr Fendigaid (17), I.6.22, VI.15.13, VII.36.11; Cadwallon ap Cadfan (12, 29), III.10.41, V.1.36, V.23.91, V.23.137, VI.20.72, VII.49.19; Cadyrieith (9), III.7.36; Cai mab Cynyr Ceinfarfog (21), I.18.18, IV.4.207; Caradog Freichfras (1, 18), IV.5.140; Caswallon ap Beli (35, 36), III.12.25, III.16.42, III.24.134, IV.3.22; Cynan (35), I.6.21; Cynfelyn Drwgsl (5), IV.5.33, V.19.8; Dreon ap Nudd (31), IV 9.79; Drystan mab Tallwch (19, 21, 26), VII.54.26; VII.56.9; Dunawt mab Pabo Post Prydein (5), VII.13.7, VII.25.5, VII.56.26; Eliffer Gosgorddfawr (8), VI.35.3; Geraint

mab Erbin (14), V.7.9, VII.51.31; Golydan Fardd (34), VI.15.11; Gwalchmai mab Gwyar (4), IV.4.182, VII.2.15; Gwanar mab Lliaws fab Nwyfre (35), VI.29.92; Gweir Gwrhydfawr (19), III.20.19, V.13.16, VI.4.27; Gwenddolau mab Ceidio (6, 29, 32), IV.9.202; Gwenwynwyn mab Lliaws fab Nwyfre (35), VI.29.93; Gwgawn Gwron mab Peredur mab Eliffer Osgorddfawr (8), III.26.36; IV.4.265; Llacheu mab Arthur (4), III.21.149, IV.6.47, IV.9.163, IV.11.16, VI.29.24, VII.24.125, VII.52.16; Lleu Llaw Gyffes (30), III.21.185; Lludd mab Beli (37), VI.7.4; Llyr Llediaith (8), III.13.34, IV.9.50, V.20.37, VII.53.28, VII.54.36; Llywarch Hen mab Elidir Lydanwyn (8), VI.18.68, VI.33.20; Maelgwn Gwynedd (1), I.16.28, I.8.54, I.9.154, III.20.2, IV.2.42, IV.4.271, IV.9.183, VI.14.19, VI.15.5; March mab Meirchion (14, 26), IV.3.12; Maxen Wledig (13), III.16.88; Mordaf Hael mab Serfan (2), I.17.48, II.2.4, III.21.129, V.2.30, V.11.55, V.26.105, VI.1.13, VI.18.94, VII.22.22, VII.50.24; Morfran eil Tegid (24), II.14.56, III.21.6; Morgant Mwynfawr (20), IV.4.22, IV.6.221, V.23.175; Nudd Hael mab Senyllt (2), III.26.57, V.2.30, V.11.55, V.26.105, V.20.35, VI.8.21, VI.18.89, VI.29.77, VI.29.126, VII.22.21, VII.25.40, VII.47.8, VII.49.8, VII.50.24; Owain mab Urien (3, 11), III.5.67, VII.52.32; Pryderi mab Pwyll Pen Annwfn (26), I.26.38, III.21.67, VII.23.18; Rahawd eil Morcant (12) IV.9.12; Rhufawn Befr mab Dewrarth Wledig (3), II.6.2; Rhun mab Beli (20), V.20.46, VI.35.54, VII.23.10; Rhun mab Maelgwn (3, 17), I.3.24, I.8.53, III.16.79, III.20.44, III.21.38, III.24.96, IV.1.14, IV.12.17, IV.4.86, IV.6.110, IV.13.32, V.20.46, V.23.166, V.23.200, VI.18.95; Rhydderch Hael ap Tudwal Tudglyd (2), V.2.30, V.11.55, V.26.105, VI.18.91, VII.53.27; Selyf mab Cynan Garwyn (25), III.11.9; Taliesin (7, 25, 33), I.17.18, III.24.154, V.25.3, VI.15.33, VI.25.37; Urien mab Cynfarch (6, 11, 25, 33), I.1.36, I.3.26, III.16.97, III.16.102; Uthr Bendragon (28), VII.10.3.

115 Bromwich, 'Cyfeiriadau Traddodiadol a Chwedlonol', tt. 208–9.
116 Yn enwedig Gwaith Cynddelw: Bromwich, 'Cyfeiriadau Traddodiadol a Chwedlonol', t. 206; Cynddelw Brydydd Mawr, 'Marwnad Rhirid Flaidd ac Arthen ei Frawd', Jones ac Owen (goln), *Gwaith Cynddelw I*, rhif 24, ll. 46; *Trioedd*, ed. Bromwich, triawd 22 a tt. 44, 71; Gruffudd Aled Williams, 'Owain Cyfeiliog: Bardd-dywysog?', yn *Beirdd a Thywysogion*, tt. 180–201.
117 Gw. hefyd awgrym Rachel Bromwich fod gan Cynddelw ei hun rôl yn '[gosod] sylfaen i'r casgliad o *Trioedd Ynys Prydain*': 'Cyfeiriadau Traddodiadol', t. 215.
118 Rhian M. Andrews, 'Y Bardd yn Llysgennad, Rhan 1: Llywarch Brydydd y Moch yn Neheubarth', *Dwned*, 20 (2014), 11–30 (tt. 29–30); Rhian M. Andrews, 'Y Bardd yn Llysgennad, Rhan 2: Bleddyn Fardd yn Neheubarth', *Dwned*, 21 (2015), 49–68; Jones a Jones (goln), *Gwaith Llywarch ap Llywelyn*, rhif 26.

119 Andrews, 'Bardd yn Llysgennad 1', 25; *Trioedd*, gol. Bromwich, trioedd 2, 47, 48.
120 Andrews, 'Bardd yn Llysgennad 1', 23; Jones a Jones (goln), *Gwaith Llywarch ap Llywelyn*, rhif 26, ll. 95–100.
121 *Trioedd*, gol. Bromwich, triawd 2. Dim ond yng nghyfres Peniarth 50 y mae Arthur yn un o'r Tri Hael, ond mae cyfeiriad Llywarch Prydydd y Moch ato yn y cyswllt yma yn awgrymu naill ai bod fersiwn felly o'r triawd ar gael erbyn 1220 (dyddiad y gerdd), neu bod triawd 2 wedi ei addasu yn ddiweddarach yng ngoleuni cerdd Prydydd y Moch: Jones a Jones (goln), *Gwaith Llywarch ap Llywelyn*, rhif 11, ll. 53–6. Mae'r tueddiad yma i bwysleisio Arthur fel pedwerydd cymal mewn triawd, yn uwch na'r tri a restrwyd, yn ymddangos hefyd yng nghyfresi'r llyfrau Gwyn a Choch. Shercliff, 'Arthur in *Trioedd Ynys Prydain*', tt. 180–1.
122 Gol. N. G. Costigan (Bosco) yn *Gwaith Dafydd Benfras ac eraill o feirdd hanner cyntaf y drydedd ganrif ar ddeg*, CBT VI (Caerdydd, 1995), rhif 29, ll. 93–4.
123 Gallwn gymharu y cyfeiriad mwy amwys yma at Wenwynwyn a Gwanar gydag effaith Cyfres Gynnar y Trioedd ar ddewis Einion ap Gwgon o'r gair *ysgymyt* (triawd 24) i ddisgrifio Llywelyn Fawr. Hamp, 'Justification of Ordering in TYP', 109; *Trioedd*, gol. Bromwich, triawd 23, 24; Einion ap Gwgon, 'Mawl Llywelyn ab Iorwerth', gol. R. Geraint Gruffudd yn *Gwaith Dafydd Benfras*, rhif 18.
124 'ac nyt oed dyn a adnapei y gerd honno, namyn Kadyrieith e hun': *Breudwyt Ronabwy Allan o'r Llyfr Coch o Hergest*, gol. Melville Richards (Caerdydd, 1948), t. 20; ymhellach ar Gadyrieith: *Trioedd*, gol. Bromwich, tt. 217–18; Bromwich, 'Cyfeiriadau Traddodiadol a Chwedlonol', tt. 213–15.
125 *HB*, pennod 42, 44 (gol. Morris, tt. 71–2).
126 *HB*, pennod 42 (gol. Morris, tt. 71–2); *DGB*, 115 (gol. a chyf. Reeve a Wright, t. 149), 205 (gol. a chyf. Reeve a Wright, t. 279).
127 Am awgrymiad o hyn: Marged Haycock (gol.), *Prophecies from the Book of Taliesin* (Aberystwyth, 2013), tt. 17–18.

4

From Llandaf to *Liber A*: Welsh Charters and Diplomatics in Long Perspective

Charles Insley

Introduction

One of the many contributions made by Huw Pryce to the study of Welsh medieval history has been in diplomatics. As well as a number of significant contributions in essay or article form, it is, above all, his monumental *Acts of Welsh Rulers*, published in 2005, that stands as a testament to the significance of his scholarship in this field. The edition represents the first consolidated treatment of all of the surviving *acta* issued by the native rulers of Wales between the early twelfth century and the Edwardian Conquest of Wales in 1283 and as such has been and will continue to be an absolutely indispensable research tool for those working on medieval Welsh history.[1] What follows is in part a reflection on what the material edited in *Acts of Welsh Rulers* tells us more broadly about Welsh medieval history, set in a wider consideration of the history of charter-writing and charter use during the period *c*.500–1283.

The term 'charters', of course, covers a multitude of documentary forms and while we might regard all documents recording the conveyance, conferring or sale of rights or property as 'charters', we are in reality looking at a range of distinct diplomatic forms. The second issue that immediately rears its head is the antiquity or otherwise of a 'charter' culture in Wales. The third point, and the focus of the following discussion is that much of the work on Welsh charters and diplomatics is explicitly not in long perspective. There is a very rich tradition in Welsh historiography of using charters as a tool for micro-history; for the deep exploration of a particular locality across a relatively short space of time, but rather less frequently does the Welsh diplomatist step back and think about what the body of Welsh diplomatic material as a corpus might reveal. There are, of course, some excellent examples of the latter approach. Without being remotely exhaustive, we might think of Wendy Davies's pioneering, in all senses of the word, work on the Llandaf material, John Reuben Davies's work, also on *Liber Landavensis*, as well as work over the last twenty or more years by Huw Pryce.[2] Generally, though, such synoptic approaches are the exception, rather than the norm in the way that Welsh charters are used by historians; and even then it might be noted (perhaps a little pedantically) that discussions of the Llandaf material are rather geographically limited, concerned as they are with south-east Wales. One might also point out, perhaps churlishly, that even *Acts of Welsh Rulers* concerns a relatively narrow period – the slightly less than 150 years between 1137 and 1283.

Terminology, form and function

'Charters' encompasses a diverse, if not large, range of documentary material for medieval Wales as well as a range of distinct albeit related diplomatic forms. In a wider context, diplomas appeared earlier in the Middle Ages and had their origins in the title deeds, public and private, used in the later Roman world.[3] They were in essence evidentiary; that is, they recorded something that had already happened, a gift or sale of lands or rights. They were not generally dispositive; that is, the document itself was not an active agent in the process of conveyance, merely a witness to it, generally drawn up after the fact.[4] The time elapsed between the grant being enacted and the diploma recording it being drawn up could vary significantly, from a matter of hours to years in some cases. These documents were almost always framed in the past tense, and in a Welsh context often in the third person: that is 'x gave to y so much land in this place'. These diplomas generally detailed the terms of the grant, whether for physical property or other rights or privileges, such as lordship rights. This detail may also have extended to a detailed physical description of the property including its boundaries. In turn, these boundary descriptions might be quite simple, or more detailed perambulations of the estate concerned. These documents also often included a list of witnesses who were allegedly present when the grant or sale was made. In some cases, the diploma also included a proem/*arenga* which often took the form of a description of the motivation behind the gift or sale. More occasionally the proem might involve less specific meditation on a particular religious theme, for instance the need to record such transactions lest they be lost to fallible human memory or the need to securely heavenly salvation through the use of earthly treasures.

From the middle of the twelfth century, a new type of charter distinct from the diploma emerges in Wales, strongly influenced by documentary practice in England and northern Europe more generally. What emerged in England in the early twelfth century in turn had its origins in the late Anglo-Saxon writ. Unlike the diploma, whose origins lay in late Antique property deeds, the writ's origins lay in epistolary forms: it was, in origin, a letter, instructing someone to do something.[5] By the early eleventh century, what some scholars have termed 'writ-charters' emerged into the surviving documentary record. These documents retained the epistolary phrasing of the writ – they were usually addressed to a group of individuals – but were now being used to convey lands or rights, functions that had hitherto been confined to diplomas.[6] Although an overlap of function between the diploma and the writ-charter can be seen, in terms of their relationship to property transactions, the writ-charter retained its active character; it generally instructed or notified a group of individuals to do something.[7] Property transactions therefore became framed in terms of notifying the officers of the shire court that land or rights had been granted to an individual. By the later eleventh century, the Anglo-Saxon diploma had all but vanished, and a new type of charter, which merged elements of diploma formulation with the epistolary framing of the writ-charter appears in the documentary record.[8] While some have continued to refer to these as writ-charters, they lacked the individual address of the writ and writ-charter, being addressed to all and sundry. The late Richard Sharpe called these documents charters, and it is these documents which became universal in the twelfth century as the means of granting and conveying property.[9] In Wales this newer form of conveyance rapidly seems to have supplanted the older diploma-type form in use, perhaps by the second half of the twelfth century.[10] Although their origins are distinct from those of the diploma, the charters of the twelfth century and beyond borrowed sometimes significant amounts of their formulation from their diploma predecessors. They also included lists of witnesses and a small, but significant number also included the same sort of boundary details recorded in earlier documents.

Survival

Unsurprisingly, perhaps, the majority of surviving Welsh charters and other documents date from the two centuries immediately before the Edwardian Conquest of 1283–4. Kari Maund and Huw Pryce identified 618 documents of all types connected with the leading dynasties in Wales from the period between 1100 and 1283; in comparison, fewer than 200 documents survive in any form from the period between *c.*600 and 1100.[11] Within this broad distribution towards the later part of the period up to 1283, some important patterns can be seen that require comment. About two-thirds of the surviving documents from between 1100 and 1283 date from the thirteenth century, which perhaps reflects both the increasing use of the written word in the administrative culture of native lords, but also an increasing level of engagement between Welsh rulers and the English Crown and thus a significant increase in the amount of documentary business.[12] Over half, some 346 documents, of what survives from the period after 1100 survive as copies in the archives of the medieval English state, now preserved in The National Archives at Kew.[13] This in large part also reflects the engagement of Welsh lords and Welsh religious institutions with an increasingly dominant and domineering English kingdom and its wider northern European territories, whose kings saw themselves as feudal overlords of Wales. This increasingly intense documentary engagement between the English and the Welsh culminated in the political crises of the later 1270s and ultimately the English conquest of native Wales in 1283–4.[14] This material includes direct correspondence between Welsh lords and the English state, but also material from the archives of religious houses within and without Wales.

The Edwardian conquest also ensured the survival of charters and documents from Wales. Welsh lords and Welsh religious houses needed, or were required, to have their possessions and rights confirmed by the new regime, so their charters were offered up for royal confirmation and those confirmations in turn preserved in the records of the English government. This means that more material than might otherwise have survived was indeed preserved, given the tendency for the archives of religious houses to have been dispersed during the religious upheavals of the sixteenth and seventeenth centuries. In this context it is important to note that only two significant collections of original documents, including charters as well as other memoranda, survive from the period after 1100: the charters of the Cistercian abbeys of Strata Marcella in Powys, and Margam in Glamorgan.[15] Both collections are now preserved in the National Library of Wales in Aberystwyth.[16] Almost everything else survives in later copies.

In terms of geographical spread, the surviving post-1100 material is drawn from all over Wales, albeit with a predominance of documents surviving from the kingdom and later principality of Gwynedd. This in part reflects the predominance of Gwynedd in Welsh politics after 1200, although we perhaps need to be aware of the dangers of circular reasoning here. Of our surviving 618 documents, around 250 were issued in the name of Llywelyn ab Iorwerth (r. c.1199–1240) and his successors alone. This is in striking contrast to the pre-1100 material, which is drawn almost entirely from south-east Wales, in Glamorgan and Gwent. This earlier pattern reflects that the vast majority of what survives does so in one place: the early twelfth-century collection of charters and historical narratives copied into *Liber Landavensis*.[17] Beyond the 159 charters in *Liber Landavensis*, there are six records of gifts and transactions, perhaps eighth and ninth century in date, entered as marginal memoranda in the Lichfield Gospels, and fourteen charters, possibly dating from the late seventh and eighth centuries, included in Lifris of Llancarfan's *Vita Cadoci* (*Life of St Cadog*), written in the 1080s.[18] These also relate to south-east Wales. In effect, we have no real witness to any charter culture in Wales outside the south-east before around 1100.

Origins

Mention of *Liber Landavensis* raises the issue of the origins of charters in medieval Wales. It is not impossible to think that the use of documentary forms to record property transactions may even have even been a late/sub-Roman survival.[19] Much of the discussion about the antiquity of charter-type documents in Wales, and the forms they might have taken in the earlier medieval period, has been tied up with debates about the antiquity of the material in *Liber Landavensis*. As it stands, *Liber Landavensis* dates from the first quarter of the twelfth century, and the charters contained within it need not necessarily date from much earlier. However, it is overwhelmingly likely that the charters do predate their inclusion in *Liber Landavensis*. It is much less clear by how much, although there is some agreement that they date back to at least the ninth century.[20] Some scholars, most notably Wendy Davies, have suggested that some of the charter texts may be contemporary with the dates they carry, and may therefore date back to the middle of the sixth century, significantly predating the appearance of charters in England in the mid- to late seventh century.[21] Others are more sceptical and suggest that given the scale of rewriting of the charters that seems to have taken place in the eleventh and twelfth centuries prior to and as part of the processes of including them in *Liber Landavensis*, it is impossible to say with any certainty from how much earlier they date.[22]

Ultimately, the question of the date and status of the charters in *Liber Landavensis* is still one that is open. The texts as they stand in *Liber Landavensis* have clearly been subject to editing and modifying, but by how much and over how long a period is less certain. It is safe to assume, though, that there are several layers of rewriting between what is in *Liber Landavensis* and the putative original texts; Davies suggests seven stages of editing and collation up to the 1120s.[23] As Ben Guy has shown with the Llandaf charters concerning Moccas, now in Herefordshire, it is likely that much of the rewriting concerned substituting the church of Llandaf for an original, earlier beneficiary and that the core of many of the charter texts incorporated into *Liber Landavensis* are substantially genuine.[24]

What may shed some light on the matter, however, is the extent to which a shared diplomatic culture can be identified across what we might in shorthand terms call the 'Celtic west', in particular Wales, Cornwall and Brittany.[25] The existence of a common or shared Latin charter tradition across these areas is not one universally accepted by historians, although Wendy Davies provides a persuasive case for seeing a distinct way of structuring the text of a charter across Wales and Brittany.[26] There are some significant similarities in formulation between early Welsh charters, early Breton charters and the one surviving early charter from Cornwall.[27] In Davies's words, a charter structure was 'determined by the consistent inclusion of three constituent parts; disposition, witness list and sanction and the almost universal use of the third person and the perfect tense'.[28] This was accompanied with a general absence of anything resembling an invocation and initial protocol or address of the sort that could be seen in diplomas from continental Europe.[29] Davies also notes the echoes of imperial rescripts in the formulae of some of the Welsh and Breton charter material, suggesting that, at some remove, perhaps, these charters ultimately had their origin in the sorts of documents used to record late Antique property transactions.[30] These similarities are enough to suggest, at least, the possibility that what we see in south-east Wales in *Liber Landavensis* and to a lesser extent in the Lichfield memoranda did ultimately have their origins, in some form at least, in the very early Middle Ages, that is the sixth and possibly even the fifth centuries.[31] Whether this can be said for Wales beyond the limited geographical reach of *Liber Landavensis*, the Lichfield memoranda or the texts in Lifris's *Vita Cadoci* is much less clear. It is in this context worth noting that some of the area covered by the Llandaf charters was in a part of Wales that had a significant number of villas itself and was close to the zone in the south-west of the English midlands characterised by lavish villas in the late Roman period.[32] This may, therefore, have been the sort of elite society that made use of documents to record property transactions, including the sort of property deeds that developed into the diplomas of the early medieval west.[33] Whether the same was true further north and west in Wales in the early Middle Ages is more difficult to say.

Whatever the case regarding the antiquity of the contents of *Liber Landavensis*, it is very clear that by the tenth century at the very latest, charters were an important means of recording land transactions, especially those involving the church, in south-east Wales. Welsh kings were also participants in the documentary culture of their neighbours to the east. The tenth century saw the emergence of a single English kingdom ruled by the family and descendants of Alfred the Great (r. 871–99).[34] Significantly, his grandsons Æthelstan (r. 924–39), Edmund (r. 939–46) and Eadred (r. 946–55) held large assemblies at which charters were produced and which were attended by the major Welsh kings of the day.[35] They would, presumably, have seen how their English neighbours did things, including using charters not just as means of recording and memorialising property transactions, but for articulating claims to power through the use of ambitious royal styles and the recording of large numbers of witnesses.[36]

The absence of surviving early Latin charters from much of wider Wales poses an important question: does the absence of evidence indicate evidence of absence? Does the almost total lack of surviving charter-type material from beyond south-east Wales before *c.*1100 indicate the absence of charters from those societies, or simply the absence of surviving evidence? This question is, to an extent, tied up with a broader question about the use of charters across the Insular world in the early Middle Ages where there is no surviving contemporary witness. This is the case not just for much of Wales, but also Ireland and Scotland, where the oldest contemporary charter survivals date from the early twelfth century. Indeed, Dauvit Broun would argue that charters were not used in these areas prior to the twelfth century.[37]

In part, this is a debate about semantics and what precisely constitutes a 'charter' in this context. Broun would draw a distinction between property records – effectively notices of gifts or sales, often in the vernacular – and charters, but this is potentially a blurred boundary, especially when the property records could be in Latin and incorporated some of the formulation observable in charters, such as address and dispositive clauses. One is tempted here to talk about 'notices in charter form'. Related to this is the question of whether texts that we regard as unambiguously as charters, that is, in Latin with all of the relevant structural elements in terms of formulation, but are preserved, like property notices, in religious books ever had an independent life as single-sheet parchment documents before being copied into the manuscript.[38] Dafydd Jenkins and Morfydd Owen raise this very question with some of the Lichfield Gospels memoranda.[39] In other words, distinctions that are drawn between 'charters' and 'property records' which hinge on formulation and whether the text existed as a single-sheet start to break down when the evidence is examined in detail. There is a very grey area where charters were set down in religious books rather than on single sheets, and records of property transactions could incorporate aspects of charter formulation.

This does not necessarily answer the question of whether Wales beyond the south-east was familiar with charters at an early date. It does, perhaps, allow for a more nuanced framing of the question, inasmuch as property transactions may have been recorded in forms that indicate some familiarity with charters as written records, even if single-sheet parchment documents were not ever produced. There are certainly small pieces of evidence that suggest that such familiarity, at the very least, extended beyond the areas covered by the Llandaf and Llandeilo charter material. There are the footprints of an early charter surviving from Clynnog Fawr, on the Llŷn peninsula in Gwynedd.[40] This charter, as Davies notes, survives in both Latin and Welsh versions, the former embedded in a fourteenth-century confirmation in the *Record of Caernarvon*, while the latter is in the fourteenth-century Life of St Beuno.[41] The diplomatic elements that survive in the Latin suggest parallels with the diplomatic in the Lichfield memoranda.[42]

Other evidence that Welsh society, beyond what might be thought of as the 'Llandaf/Lichfield charter space', was familiar with charters can be found in the presence of boundary clauses, which are a distinctive feature of Welsh charters right up until the later thirteenth century.[43] These are heterogeneous in form and, after 1100, occur in documents from much of *Pura Wallia*, with surviving examples from Gwynedd, Powys, Deheubarth, Ceredigion, Morgannwg and Gwynllŵg.[44] They are also a major presence in the collection of texts in *Liber Landavensis* and in some of the Lichfield memoranda.[45]

What might these boundaries indicate? Across the period up to 1284 they are heterogeneous in both form and language. Some are wholly in Welsh, some in a mixture of Welsh and Latin, some wholly in Latin. Some are what might be termed 'dimensional' boundaries; that is, a simple set of compass points. Some are perambulations or circuits of the sort that would be familiar to those who work on Anglo-Saxon diplomas with detailed topographical delineations of a particular estate or property or jurisdiction.[46] Within the Llandaf material there is a broad chronological progression across the sequence of charters with bounds, from simple dimensions to perambulations, and away from purely Latin descriptions, although this is not absolute.[47] Detailed work by Jon Coe also suggests that even some of those bounds which are predominantly or exclusively in forms of Old or Middle Welsh predate the early tenth century and extensive Anglo-Saxon involvement in the Herefordshire-Monmouth border area.[48] Elsewhere in the corpus of surviving Welsh charters, similar heterogeneity of practice regarding the incorporation and structuring of boundary clauses can be observed right up to the late thirteenth century, with perambulations alongside dimensional bounds and mixtures of Latin and Old/Middle Welsh.

Coe's conclusions about the dating of the Llandaf bounds are important. One might be tempted to see perambulations in Welsh charters as imitative of Anglo-Saxon practice, since vernacular perambulations emerge in West Saxon charters in the early to mid-ninth century. This might suggest, as Ben Guy does, shared innovation as part of the wider relationship between West Saxon kings and those of south-eastern Wales.[49] However, we should also not necessarily see this as simple imitation; that by the tenth century there was already a diversity of ways of delineating an estate in a charter is suggestive of antiquity rather than a practice imported *de novo* from across Offa's Dyke. More broadly, the diversity of boundary practice (in comparison to Old English practice which by *c*.925 was almost entirely dominated by the vernacular perambulation) across Wales might also be suggestive of antiquity outside the Llandaf/Lichfield charter space.

Practice around the drafting and inclusion of boundaries is one way of approaching the existence or otherwise of a 'charter culture' outside south-east Wales. Relics of older formulation might be another. Some of the charters that survive from the twelfth century seem to have strong parallels in terms of their formulation with the earlier Latin charter tradition identified by Davies.[50] In particular, the formulation of a charter granted by the mid-twelfth-century king of Powys, Madog ap Maredudd (1131–61), confirming a grant of land at Trefeglwys in Arwystli, conforms, as Huw Pryce showed, in almost all respects to the Latin charter model outlined by Davies.[51] It is possible that this is simply a twelfth-century Powysian borrowing of form and practice from further south, but it is at least equally likely to be a relic of an existing charter tradition in Powys that might have dated back a century or more.[52]

This possibility is also supported by the footprints of older 'diploma' type formulation that occurs in charters which in other respects conform to the norms (as far as there are any) of twelfth-century Welsh charter practice. By the mid-twelfth century, the vast majority of surviving Welsh charters did not depart from the basic address-notification-disposition-corroboration formulation that seems to have become well established across Britain. However, three Powysian charters have a verbal invocation and one of them, a grant by Owain Cyfeiliog to Strata Marcella dated 1191, also has a proem, as do three twelfth-century charters issued in the name of Llywelyn ab Iorwerth for, respectively, Cymer Abbey, Ynys Llannog priory and the Hospitallers of Dolgynwal.[53] Invocations and proems were common elements in diplomas, but seem largely absent from the writ-charter type of documents that predominate in Wales after 1100. The possibility is, therefore, that these are also relics of an older diplomatic practice and tradition. This is not clear cut, however: the Latin charter model identified by Davies and represented by Madog ap Maredudd's Trefeglwys charter did not generally utilise proems and Huw Pryce has suggested that in the case of Owain Cyfeiliog's 1191 charter, the presence of a proem might ultimately be based on a Burgundian exemplar from Strata Marcella's mother-house, Cîteaux.[54] The presence of proems in three Venedotian charters for different beneficiaries – two representative of new European orders but one for a much older foundation – may, however, be plausibly regarded as a relic of an older diplomatic tradition.

The terms in which ecclesiastical beneficiaries were introduced in twelfth- and thirteenth-century charters may also have been a relic of much older practice. In English charters, the norm was for such grants to be issued to a named individual – a bishop, or an abbot, generally – and then the church to which they belonged. However, in Welsh *acta*, a different formulation was used: the grant was made to 'God, Saint X and the church of Y'.[55] This way of framing things can be seen in the older Latin charter-writing tradition outlined by Davies and can also be seen in the one surviving pre-1000 charter from Cornwall.[56] Again, the likelihood is that this, too, represents the survival of older native Welsh diplomatic traditions. The evidence is ultimately too diffuse for any real certainty, but there is at least a strong likelihood that there was a set of distinct diplomatic traditions across native Wales beyond the south-east that significantly predated the eleventh century.

Documentary culture in Wales, *c*.1100–1284

By the second half of the twelfth century, charters survive from across the major Welsh polities. While a few of these charters, such as the Trefeglwys charter of Madog ap Maredudd already discussed, seem to echo the type of formulation we see in some of the Llandaf material, the majority look rather different, and conform to a new model of charter writing, that of the Anglo-Norman charter. These documents were often rather brief and, in the case of both letters and charters, opened with a general address clause; that is, the document was not addressed to named individuals, but to everyone present both now and in the future.[57] The subsequent formulation of both charters and letters followed standard forms used in English diplomatic and, from the later twelfth century, charters would include the sort of warranties that were appearing in contemporary English and Scottish documents. Welsh lords had also begun to append to their *acta* the same sort of seals with equestrian images used by English lords.[58]

This imitation by Welsh lords of the documentary practice of their neighbours in part simply represents the complex links and networks that straddled the Anglo-Welsh frontier. Like all medieval frontiers, this was not so much a hard and fast line on a map but a diffuse zone of interaction and connectivity, both before and after the eleventh century.[59] This is especially true in Gwent and Glamorgan, where areas that had fallen under Anglo-Norman rule at the end of the eleventh century were back under native Welsh rule by the later 1130s.[60] The same is also true for north-east Wales, roughly the modern county of Flint, which seems to have been under English lordship by the time of Domesday Book (1086), but was in Welsh hands for much of the twelfth and thirteenth centuries.[61] Although historians often cast the relationships around the Welsh frontier as largely hostile and antagonistic, warfare was only one of a range of interactions. For instance, Llywelyn ab Iorwerth (d. 1240) seems to have enjoyed a generally very amicable relationship with his immediate neighbours, the earls of Chester.[62]

It is also possible to fit the change in Welsh documentary culture across the twelfth and thirteenth centuries into a narrative of what Robert Bartlett has called 'Europeanisation'.[63] In brief, this is the expansion of the political and cultural norms of what Bartlett identified as the European heartland – largely France, the German-speaking lands and northern Italy – to its peripheries, in particular the Iberian Peninsula, Eastern Europe, the Baltic and Britain and Ireland. This was both a military and a cultural expansion, with the armoured knight and the castle at its vanguard, followed by the reformed monastic orders; in particular, but not exclusively, the Cistercians. In this context, it might be suggested that the increasing use by Welsh lords of the documentary forms associated with the Anglo-Norman and Angevin elite was part of this Europeanisation.

The relative wealth of surviving documentary material from the post-1100 period in Wales reflects, as we have already seen, the increasing engagement between Welsh lords and institutions and the English, but it is also witness to an increasing, if slow, bureaucratisation of Welsh political and administrative culture. Welsh princes and lords employed scribes to write their official documents and had officials who sealed them. It is likely, though, that for many lords these scribes were 'borrowed' from nearby monastic institutions and that what bureaucracy existed was very embryonic.[64] Even in Gwynedd, which by the thirteenth century seems to have had the most sophisticated documentary culture and administration in native Wales, it seems likely that its rulers relied to a significant extent on key religious foundations, in particular Aberconwy Abbey, for personnel to produce their *acta*.[65] In terms of charters, at least, this seems to be a world with a significant amount of 'beneficiary diplomatic', where the majority of surviving charters were written not by the donor/benefactor, but by or on behalf of the beneficiary, especially when the beneficiary was a church.[66] In large part this reflects the fact that the church had a significant, if not complete, monopoly of the technologies and expertise necessary for the production of documents. Nonetheless an increasing use of the written word for a whole range of purposes beyond the recording of property transactions is clearly evident in the surviving material, and this presupposes the presence of individuals within princely and lordly households whose business it was to write documents for their lord.[67] Such individuals might be represented by one of the witnesses to a grant made by Llywelyn ab Iorwerth to Ynys Lannog on Anglesey, described as 'John, our notary (*notario nostro*)', while 'David, clerk of Llywelyn (*cleric Lewelini*)' was among the witnesses to a marriage agreement between Llywelyn ab Iorwerth and Earl Ranulf III of Chester.[68]

The one Welsh polity of the period 1100–1283 that clearly stands out in the sophistication of its documentary culture was Gwynedd.[69] By the early thirteenth century, under the long rule of Llywelyn ab Iorwerth (*r. c.*1199–1240), Gwynedd had emerged as much the most powerful and organised Welsh principality.[70] The deaths of Madog ap Maredudd in 1161 and Rhys ap Gruffudd in 1197 were followed by the fragmentation of Powys and Deheubarth respectively.[71] By the middle decades of the thirteenth century, Gwynedd's rulers were, through a judicious mixture of submission and resistance, able to take advantage of tensions within the English political establishment and translate their ambitions into an English acknowledgement of their status as the most powerful rulers in Wales.[72]

Gwynedd's political dominance of Wales was reflected by, and in some sense was a product of, the sophistication of its rulers' administration and manipulation of documentary culture. It is unclear whether the rulers of Gwynedd had a 'chancery' as such, that is, an office staffed by clerks specifically entrusted with writing documents for the ruler, and perhaps fixating on terminology is not helpful here.[73] What is clear is that there was a high degree of standardisation and sophistication in the surviving *acta* issued in the name of the princes of Gwynedd by the early thirteenth century. There are also at least three surviving documents issued in the name of Llywelyn ab Iorwerth which make reference to a *notarius* and a further five witnessed by individuals bearing the title *cancellarius*.[74] The northern redaction of the laws of the Welsh laws make reference to an official called the *cynghellor* which is sometimes glossed by the Latin term *cancellarius* (chancellor).[75] None of this proves the existence of a princely chancery or writing office in Gwynedd, but it is clear that whoever produced the princes' official documents was closely supervised and that the princes were able to exert a high degree of control over the *acta* issued in their name.

This level of control can be observed in the formulation of their surviving *acta*. First, there is what appears to be a systematic imitation of contemporary practice in English royal and baronial diplomatic; secondly, the development of princely styles can be seen which clearly reflected the hegemonic ambitions of Gwynedd's rulers in the thirteenth century. This included the systematic and consistent use of titles, but also from around 1210 the use of the plural of majesty in the granting phrase. This use seems to have been pioneered in English royal *acta* in the 1190s, so its rapid adoption by Llywelyn ab Iorwerth and those drafting his charters and letters is impressive.[76] It is also likely to have been a conscious act of imitation on their behalf. In this respect, Llywelyn ab Iorwerth and his descendants seem to have been especially alive to the potential for using their *acta* to lay claim to a particularly exalted status within Wales.

This impression is reinforced by a consideration of the titles deployed in their *acta* during the thirteenth century. Clearly articulated and systematically used titles were relatively uncommon in Welsh *acta*, even those issued by members of the major dynasties. It is difficult to see anything like a systematic approach to *intitulationes* in the pre-1100 material, while after 1100 both Rhys ap Gruffudd, ruler of Deheubarth until his death in 1197 and Owain Gwynedd (1137–70), ruler of Gwynedd, occasionally used titles which laid claim to rule over all or part of Wales.[77] Elsewhere in Wales, titles were used much more sporadically and without any real consistency of formulation or titulature.[78] The vocabulary of power was eclectic and variable, with specific honorific titles such as 'king', 'prince' or 'lord' used very infrequently.

The exception was Gwynedd. Although Owain Gwynedd seems to have dropped the title of *Princeps Wallie* by his death in 1170, his son Dafydd used a modified form, *Princeps Norwallie* ('Prince of North Wales'), in his documents and his nephew Llywelyn ab Iorwerth initially adopted the same style following his acquisition of sole rule over Gwynedd in 1199 or 1200.[79] This style seems logical and, crucially, accessible to the political and clerical elite of the Angevin world with which Welsh rulers were increasingly engaged.[80] However, between *c.*1225 and 1230, Llywelyn's *acta* shifted to the use of an entirely new style, where he was described as 'Prince of Aberffraw and Lord of Snowdon' (*princeps de Aberfrau et dominus Snaudonie*).[81] This title needs some unpacking. The claim to be 'prince of Aberffraw' was rooted in the compilation and redaction of Welsh law texts in the twelfth and thirteenth centuries, in particular in Redactions B and C of the Laws, compiled in the second quarter of the thirteenth century.[82] These laws articulated the notion that the three paramount courts and political centres of ancient Wales were Dinefwr in the south, Pengwern in Powys and Aberffraw in Gwynedd. These 'courts' were clearly avatars for the twelfth-century principalities and by around 1200, Dinefwr (Deheubarth) and Pengwern (Powys) had effectively fallen by the wayside, leaving Aberffraw (Gwynedd), purportedly the senior of the three courts, in place. In Redactions B and C of the Laws it alone paid gold to the king of London, whereas the other courts paid gold to Aberffraw.[83] Llywelyn's adoption of this title was therefore a claim to superiority over the other two 'courts', that is, the rest of native Wales and was, in effect, a revival of his grandfather's claims to be 'prince of Wales'.[84] Although the specifics of this terminology may have been lost on the English clerks and officials with whom Llywelyn corresponded, it was rather less likely to have been lost on Llywelyn's Welsh contemporaries.

The second part of Llywelyn's title was also clearly deliberately chosen. If Aberffraw was a figurative and symbolic chief seat of Wales, Snowdonia was Gwynedd's heartland. Its difficult terrain made external attack challenging and it was protected by a series of castles erected in the late eleventh and twelfth centuries at locations such as Aberlleiniog on Anglesey, Degannwy at the mouth of the Conwy, Dolwyddelan further up the Conwy valley, Cricieth on Cardigan Bay and Dolbadarn between Llyn Padarn and Llyn Peris.

The titles used consistently by Llywelyn in his documents were, therefore, clearly and carefully developed to both reflect and lay claim to what Llywelyn saw as his authority over the rest of native Wales, but perhaps articulated in a way that would not attract the same sort of English royal anger that Owain Gwynedd's adoption of the title of *Princeps Wallie* had done in the 1160s. Llywelyn's death in 1240, and the struggle between his sons Gruffudd and Dafydd to secure control of Gwynedd seems to have led to a reversion to the older style of *princeps Norwallie* 'prince of North Wales'.[85] Indeed, in one of his small number of surviving charters, Dafydd, who ruled Gwynedd between 1240 and his death in 1246, was described as 'David, son of Llywelyn, **formerly** Prince of North Wales' ('Dauid filius Lewelini **quondam** princeps Norwallie'), as if his own status was rather precarious.[86] Although Llywelyn ap Gruffudd initially adopted the same style in his documents as his uncle and grandfather, *princeps Norwallie* 'prince of North Wales', by 1258 his *acta* proclaimed him *princeps Wallie* 'prince of Wales'.[87] This title was formally conceded to him by Henry III in the Treaty of Montgomery in 1267, a century after Owain Gwynedd's deployment of the same title had reportedly driven Henry II into fits of anger.[88]

Identity, independence and the wider world

Thus far we have seen that by the early thirteenth century, Welsh rulers had adopted the language and form of the official documents used in England and, more widely, across the Angevin world. In this respect, we might see Welsh documentary culture passively representing Bartlett's 'Europeanisation' in action, as the cultural norms and practices of English political culture inexorably spread across Britain and Ireland.[89] However, as Huw Pryce has noted, the official documents issued by Welsh rulers also show that they had significant agency in precisely how they engaged with the wider world. The adoption of English forms of documentation was not simply about imitation of a culturally more powerful neighbour, but can also be situated in the political discourses of Wales itself.[90] External exemplars were important not just because they were external, but because they could be used as levers by Welsh lords within Welsh politics.[91] This can be seen most clearly of all in how adept the rulers of Gwynedd were in the later twelfth and thirteenth centuries at turning the official documentary forms of their English neighbours into tools for their own hegemonic ambitions, both in terms of the quantity of documents they issued, and the political messages they conveyed.

In other ways, too, the documentary culture of twelfth- and thirteenth-century Wales shows a much more nuanced engagement between Welsh lords and the individuals and institutions that wrote their *acta* and the documentary forms of their English neighbours. Although the diplomatic forms used in Wales largely conformed to English practice, there were important variations. The survival of older elements of formulation that may have predated the twelfth century, discussed above, suggest that Welsh scribes were not simply content to imitate their neighbours, but to adapt and develop them to suit local need and circumstances.[92]

The Welsh *acta*, therefore, also show the extent to which the individuals drawing them up were prepared to experiment with the documentary forms they were using, and to mix older Welsh traditions with the new forms based on English practice. What is perhaps a little more surprising is that a significant number of these *acta* seem to have been produced in houses belonging to the Cistercian order. We might want to see the Cistercians, at the cutting edge of European monastic reform in the twelfth century, as a force for 'European' cultural imperialism in Wales, but in some ways the opposite seems to have been the case.[93] Cistercian houses such as Strata Marcella and Strata Florida seem to have been the houses where charter scribes, in particular, were most willing to experiment and to incorporate these elements of older Welsh diplomatic practice.[94] It is also worth noting that by the thirteenth century, the Cistercian abbey of Strata Florida in Ceredigion seems to have become the main locus of historical writing in Wales, supplanting the much older native foundation of Llanbadarn Fawr.[95]

The surviving documents issued by Welsh lords in the period after 1100 are also likely to represent an increasingly routine engagement between them and the wider northern European world. Welsh lords patronised religious foundations not just in native Wales, but in the March and, indeed, within England as well. Abbeys such as Haughmond in Shropshire, Margam in Glamorgan and Goldcliff priory in Gwent drew patronage from Welsh, English and Marcher benefactors.[96] Welsh religious institutions corresponded with each other, but also religious house across northern Europe, especially those belonging to the Cistercians. It is certainly possible to see the surviving documents as representing ever closer engagement between the Welsh and their neighbours. We need to be careful, however, not to overemphasise this engagement. Wales remained well beyond the Edwardian Conquest a relatively remote land. Unlike the kings of Scots and their magnates, Welsh princes, even those of Gwynedd, did not tend to attract foreigners into their service, either lay or ecclesiastical.[97] Conversely, few Welshmen sought service of any kind outside Wales before the later thirteenth century. Nonetheless, Wales, its lords and its churches were far from isolated in this period, and the rulers of Gwynedd, at least, invested heavily in relationships beyond Offa's Dyke.

As in other respects, this seems to be especially true of the rulers of Gwynedd, whose surviving correspondence reveals extensive engagement with the wider politics of the Angevin and Plantagenet worlds.[98] In the 1160s, Owain Gwynedd corresponded with and sought the friendship and support of Louis VII, likely trying to take advantage of the strained relationship between the French king and Henry II.[99] Nearly a century later, the surviving *acta* of his successor, Llywelyn ap Gruffudd, also shows the rulers of Gwynedd to have been fully engaged with the complexities of Plantagenet politics. Llywelyn clearly saw the baronial disruption and rebellion led by Simon de Montfort, earl of Leicester, as a significant opportunity.[100] Not only did Llywelyn ultimately marry de Montfort's daughter Eleanor, but also sought concessions, including acknowledgement of his status as de facto ruler of Wales, from the baronial party. In this respect, the so-called Treaty of Pipton (1262), agreed between Llywelyn and de Montfort, could be seen as a dress rehearsal of the agreement between Llywelyn and Henry made five years later at Montgomery.[101] The treaty of Montgomery acknowledged and formalised a title that Llywelyn had been claiming in his *acta* since 1258.[102] In that year, Llywelyn had concluded an alliance with a major political faction in Scottish politics, headed by Walter Comyn, earl of Menteith and Alexander Comyn, earl of Buchan, against English interference.[103] In this instance, Llywelyn seems to have been taking advantage of the relative weakness of the Comyn faction, de facto rulers of Scotland during the minority of Alexander III, and their need for support outside Scotland.[104]

Conclusions

The charters and letters that survive from medieval Wales are an immensely valuable body of source material for Welsh history and one which Huw Pryce has done much to illuminate. The charter material in *Liber Landavensis* provides evidence of early territorial organisation in south-east Wales as well as the extent to which early medieval Wales may have shared a documentary culture with other parts of the Atlantic Archipelago in the early post-Roman period. The material that survives from the period after 1100 shows not just Wales being increasingly drawn into an English political orbit, but also the extent to which Welsh rulers were active, rather than passive, agents in that process and were able to articulate sophisticated political agendas through their *acta*. In their relationships with religious houses outside Wales, their agreements with non-Welsh rulers and their deployment of equestrian seals on their *acta*, the surviving material paints a picture of a Welsh lay elite that looked increasingly like their counterparts in England and Scotland. The surviving *acta* are also witnesses to the development of the administrative structures and processes of Welsh lay and ecclesiastical individuals and communities up to the conquest of 1283–4 and the extent to which documents became an increasingly important part of the way in which they did business. At the same time, though, the surviving *acta*, especially that from the period after 1100, show a Welsh elite society that was also intensely aware of its own past. We can see Welsh society becoming more 'European' in some respects, as Bartlett might argue, but never losing a sense of its own history. The *acta* produced for and by Welsh lords and rulers were at the same time both forward looking, in the sense of reflecting contemporary documentary practice across the Angevin and Plantagenet worlds, but also deeply rooted in an awareness of the Welsh past.

Notes

1   I was involved in the *Acts of Welsh Rulers* project as a research assistant working for Huw Pryce between 1995 and 1997.

2   Wendy Davies, 'St Mary's Worcester and *Liber Landavensis*', *Journal of the Society of Archivists*, 4 (1972), 459–85 (repr. in her *Welsh History in the Early Middle Ages* (Farnham, 2009), no. I); Wendy Davies, *The Llandaff Charters* (Aberystwyth, 1979); Wendy Davies, *An Early Welsh Microcosm. Studies in the Llandaff Charters* (London, 1978); John Reuben Davies, *The Book of Llandaff and the Norman Church in Wales* (Woodbridge, 2002); Huw Pryce, 'The Church of Trefeglwys and the End of the "Celtic" Charter Tradition in Twelfth-century Wales', *CMCS*, 25 (1993), 15–54; Huw Pryce, 'Owain

Gwynedd and Louis VII: the Franco-Welsh Diplomacy of the First Prince of Wales', *WHR*, 19 (1998), 1–28; Huw Pryce, 'Culture, power and the charters of Welsh rulers', in Marie Therese Flanagan and Judith A. Green (eds), *Charters and Charter Scholarship in Britain and Ireland* (London, 2005), pp. 184–202; Huw Pryce, 'Welsh Rulers and European Change', in H. Pryce and J. Watts (eds), *Power and Identity in the Middle Ages: Essays in Memory of Sir Rees Davies* (Oxford, 2007), pp. 37–51.

3   Wendy Davies, 'The Latin charter-tradition in western Britain, Brittany and Ireland in the early mediaeval period', in D. Whitelock, R. McKitterick and D. Dumville (eds), *Ireland in Early Mediaeval Europe. Studies in Memory of Kathleen Hughes* (Cambridge, 1982), pp. 258–80 (p. 275), repr. in her *Welsh History in the Early Middle Ages*, no. XI; see below (pp. 97–8) for a discussion of the 'Celtic charter' tradition in a Welsh context.

4   Although see Geoffrey Koziol, *The Politics of Memory and Identity in Carolingian Royal Diplomas* (Turnhout, 2012), pp. 37–9, 296–9, for a view of diplomas as much more 'active' documents, where the drawing up of the diploma was 'to institute, publicize and memorialize crucial alterations to the political regime'; diplomas were 'memorials of struggles for power and were often fashioned as weapons in those struggles' (*Politics of Memory*, p. 37).

5   The best discussion of the evolution of the writ can be found in Richard Sharpe, 'The use of writs in the eleventh century', *Anglo-Saxon England*, 32 (2003), 247–91 (pp. 247–9); see also Florence E. Harmer, *Anglo-Saxon Writs* (Manchester, 1952), pp. 14–16; R. C. van Caenegem, *Royal Writs in England from the Conquest to Glanvill: Studies in the Early History of the Common Law* (London, 1959), pp. 108–10.

6   Sharpe, 'The use of writs', 248–52; see also Mark Hagger, 'The earliest Norman writs revisited', *Historical Research*, 82 (2009), 181–205 (pp. 183–5).

7   Sharpe, 'The use of writs', 251.

8   Sharpe, 'The use of writs', 249; Hagger, 'The earliest Norman writs revisited', 184–5.

9   Sharpe, 'The use of writs', 249.

10   *AWR*, pp. 47–142; David Bates, 'The earliest Norman writs', *English Historical Review*, 100 (1985), 266–84; see also Dauvit Broun, *The Charters of Gaelic Scotland and Ireland in the Early Middle Ages*, Quiggin Pamphlets on the Sources of Medieval Gaelic History 2 (Cambridge, 1995), p. 18.

11   *AWR*; Kari Maund, *A Handlist of the Acts of Welsh Rulers* (Cardiff, 1996).

12   Charles Insley, 'Imitation and Independence in Native Welsh Administrative Culture, *c.*1180–1280', in D. Crook and L. J. Wilkinson (eds), *The Growth of Royal Government under Henry III* (Woodbridge, 2015), pp. 104–20 (pp. 107–11).

13   Insley, 'Imitation and Independence', p. 107.

14 Huw Pryce, 'Anglo-Welsh Agreements, 1201–77', in R. A. Griffiths and P. Schofield (eds), *Wales and the Welsh in the Middle Ages: Essays Presented to J. B. Smith* (Cardiff, 2011), pp. 1–19; A. D. Carr, 'Anglo-Welsh Relations, 1066–1282', in M. Jones and M. Vale (eds), *England and her Neighbours, 1066–1453: Essays in Honour of Pierre Chaplais* (London, 1989), pp. 121–38.

15 Graham C. G. Thomas (ed.), *The Charters of the Abbey of Ystrad Marchell* (Aberystwyth, 1997); G. T. Clark (ed.), *Cartae et Alia Munimenta quae ad Dominium de Glamorgancia Pertinet*, 6 vols (Cardiff, 1910); Robert B. Patterson, *The Scriptorium of Margam Abbey and the Scribes of Early Angevin Glamorgan* (Woodbridge, 2002).

16 The Margam charters (both single sheets and enrolled copies) are preserved in the Penrice and Margam collection in the National Library of Wales, the Strata Marcella charters (single sheets) in the Wynnstay Estate Records.

17 The Book of Llandaf is preserved in the National Library of Wales (Aberystwyth, National Library of Wales, MS 17110E). Edited in J. G. Evans with J. Rhys, *The Text of the Book of Llan Dâv* (Oxford, 1893).

18 Lifris, 'Vita Sancti Cadoci', ed. and trans. A. W. Wade-Evans, *Vitae sanctorum Britanniae et Genealogiae* (Cardiff, 1944), pp. 24–141; Davies, 'Latin charter-tradition', pp. 260–1; Dafydd Jenkins and Morfydd E. Owen, 'The Welsh Marginalia in the Lichfield Gospels Part I', *CMCS*, 5 (1983), 37–66; Dafydd Jenkins and Morfydd E. Owen, 'The Welsh Marginalia in the Lichfield Gospels Part II: The "Surexit" Memorandum', *CMCS*, 7 (1984), 91–120.

19 See Wendy Davies, 'Roman Settlements and Post-Roman Estates in Southeast Wales', in P. J. Casey (ed.), *The End of Roman Britain. Papers arising from a Conference, Durham 1978*, B.A.R. British Series 71 (Oxford, 1978), pp. 153–73 (pp. 158–61) (repr. in her *Welsh History in the Early Middle Ages*, no. VII), for this possibility.

20 Patrick Sims-Williams, *The Book of Llandaf as a Historical Source* (Woodbridge, 2019), pp. 7–16.

21 Davies, *Early Welsh Microcosm*, pp. 7–22; Davies, 'St Mary's Worcester and Liber Landavensis'; Davies, *Llandaff Charters*, pp. 74–9.

22 Davies, *The Book of Llandaff and the Norman Church in Wales*, pp. 98–108. See now Sims-Williams, *The Book of Llandaf*, who describes his critique of Wendy Davies's work as 'constructive and appreciative but not uncritical' (p. 2).

23 Davies, *Early Welsh Microcosm*, pp. 12–14.

24 Ben Guy, 'The *Life* of St Dyfrig and the Lost Charters of Moccas (Mochros), Herefordshire', *CMCS*, 75 (2018), 1–37 (pp. 23–4).

25 See Davies, 'Latin charter-tradition'.

26 For a persuasive critique of the 'Celtic Latin charter' model as applied to Scotland and Ireland, see Broun, 'The charters of Gaelic Scotland and Ireland',

pp. 20–47 and Dauvit Broun, 'The Writing of Charters in Scotland and Ireland in the Twelfth Century', in Karl Heidecker (ed.), *Charters and Use of the Written Word in Medieval Society* (Turnhout, 2000), pp. 113–32 (esp. pp. 115–19).

27 Davies, 'Latin charter-tradition', p. 260; Oliver J. Padel, 'The Charter of Lanlawren (Cornwall)', in Katherine O'Brien O'Keeffe and Andy Orchard (eds), *Latin Learning and English Lore: Studies in Anglo-Saxon Literature for Michael Lapidge* (Toronto, 2005), pp. 74–85; Charles Insley, 'Languages of Boundaries and Boundaries of Language in Cornish Charters of the Tenth and Eleventh Centuries', in Robert Gallagher, Edward Roberts and Francesca Tinti (eds), *The Languages of Early Medieval Charters: Latin, Germanic Vernaculars and the Written Word* (Leiden, 2020), pp. 342–77 (pp. 357–8, 363–4).
28 Davies, 'Latin charter-tradition', p. 262.
29 Davies, 'Latin charter-tradition', p. 262.
30 David, 'Latin charter-tradition', pp. 275–6.
31 Davies, 'Latin charter-tradition', pp. 276–7.
32 Wendy Davies, 'Land and Power in Early Medieval Wales', *Past and Present*, 81 (1978), 3–23 (pp. 5–6) (repr. in her *Welsh History in the Early Middle Ages*, no. IX); see also Davies 'Roman Settlements and Post-Roman Estates', pp. 153–8.
33 Davies, 'Roman Settlements and Post-Roman Estates', p. 158.
34 Charles Insley, 'Southumbria', in Pauline Stafford (ed.), *A Companion to the Early Middle Ages: Britain and Ireland c.500–c.1100* (London, 2009), pp. 322–40 (pp. 322–4); George Molyneaux, *The Formation of the English Kingdom in the Tenth Century* (Oxford, 2015).
35 T. M. Charles-Edwards, *Wales and the Britons, 350–1064* (Oxford, 2013), pp. 510–19; Sarah Foot, *Æthelstan, First King of the English* (New Haven, 2012), p. 87; Simon D. Keynes, 'Welsh Kings at Anglo-Saxon Royal Assemblies (928–55)', *Haskins Society Journal*, 26 (2014), 69–122.
36 Charles-Edwards, *Wales and the Britons*, p. 515; D. P. Kirby, 'Hywel Dda: Anglophil?', *WHR*, 8 (1976), 1–13.
37 Broun, 'The Writing of Charters', pp. 114–19.
38 Sims-Williams (*The Book of Llandaf*, pp. 13–14) discusses the prevalence of charter material in religious books across the Atlantic archipelago, but also notes that there are no surviving examples earlier than the ninth century.
39 Jenkins and Owen, 'The Welsh Marginalia in the Lichfield Gospels Part I', 60–5.
40 Davies, 'Latin charter-tradition', p. 271; Sims-Williams, *The Book of Llandaf*, pp. 12–13.
41 Davies, 'Latin charter-tradition', p. 271; see also Patrick Sims-Williams, 'Edward IV's Confirmation Charter for Clynnog Fawr', in C. Richmond and

41 I. Harvey (eds), *Recognitions: Essays presented to Edmund Fryde* (Aberystwyth, 1996), pp. 229–41.
42 Sims-Williams, *The Book of Llandaf*, p. 13.
43 Insley, 'Imitation and independence', pp. 114–15; see also Ben Guy's chapter in the current volume ('The Development of Old Welsh Boundary Clauses').
44 Insley, 'Imitation and independence', Appendix 1, pp. 119–20.
45 Chad 3 and Chad 6, in Jenkins's and Owen's scheme: 'The Welsh Marginalia in the Lichfield Gospels Part I', pp. 52–5.
46 Insley, 'Imitation and independence', pp. 114–15.
47 Guy, 'Development of Old Welsh Boundary Clauses'.
48 Jon Coe, 'Dating the Boundary Clauses in the Book of Llandaf', *CMCS*, 48 (2004), 1–45 (pp. 36–43).
49 Guy, 'Development of Old Welsh Boundary Clauses', pp. 126–7.
50 See above, pp. 97–8; Davies, 'Latin charter-tradition'.
51 *AWR*, no. 480 (pp. 680–1); Pryce, 'Church of Trefeglwys'.
52 Pryce, 'Church of Trefeglwys', 48.
53 *AWR*, nos 539 (pp. 744–5), 542 (pp. 748–9), 544 (p. 750). Further proems include *AWR*, nos 544 (p. 750); 229 (pp. 378–84); 250 (pp. 411–12); 256 (pp. 419–20); Insley, 'Imitation and Independence', pp. 117–18.
54 Davies, 'Latin charter-tradition', p. 262: 'The occasional preamble and/or notification may be found'; *AWR*, p. 125 and no. 544 (p. 750).
55 See, for example: *AWR*, no. 231 (pp. 385–6).
56 Davies, 'Latin charter-tradition', pp. 266, 269–70. The charter in question is S1207 (P. H. Sawyer, *Anglo-Saxon Charters: An Annotated List and Bibliography* (London, 1968); https://esawyer.lib.cam.ac.uk (accessed 5 November 2023)), a grant by *Comes* Maenchi to St Heldenus and the community of Lanlawren. See further Charles Insley, 'Athelstan, Charters, and the English in Cornwall', in Marie Therese Flanagan and Judith A. Green (eds), *Charters and Charter Scholarship in Britain and Ireland* (Basingstoke, 2005), pp. 15–31 (p. 20); Insley, 'Boundaries of Language', pp. 357–8; Oliver J. Padel, 'Two New Pre-Conquest Charters for Cornwall', *Journal of Cornish Studies*, 6 (1978), 20–7; Padel, 'Charter of Lanlawren'.
57 See, for example: *AWR*, no. 583 (pp. 776–8).
58 Michael Powell Siddons, 'Welsh Equestrian Seals', *NLWJ*, 23 (1983–4), 292–318.
59 Lindy Brady, *Writing the Welsh Borderlands in Anglo-Saxon England* (Manchester, 2017); Max Lieberman, *The March of Wales, 1067–1300: A Borderland of Medieval Britain* (Cardiff, 2008).
60 David Crouch, 'The slow death of kingship in Glamorgan', *Morgannwg*, 29 (1985), 20–41.

61 C. P. Lewis, 'Welsh Territories and Welsh Identities in Late Anglo-Saxon England', in N. J. Higham (ed.), *Britons in Anglo-Saxon England* (Woodbridge, 2007), pp. 130–43 (pp. 136–7); Richard Morgan, 'Place-names in the Northern Marches of Wales', in O. J. Padel and D. Parsons (eds), *A Commodity of Good Names: Essays in Honour of Margaret Gelling* (Donnington, 2008), pp. 204–16.

62 David A. Carpenter, *The Minority of Henry III* (London, 1990), pp. 212, 298; *AWR*, no. 252 (pp. 412–14); G. Barraclough (ed.), *The Charters of the Anglo-Norman Earls of Chester, c.1071–1237*, The Record Society of Lancashire and Cheshire vol. 126 (Gloucester, 1988), no. 411, pp. 407–9; Rachel Swallow, 'Gateways to Power. The Castles of Ranulf III of Chester and Llywelyn the Great of Gwynedd', *Archaeological Journal*, 171 (2014), 298–311 (pp. 299–300).

63 Robert Bartlett, *The Making of Europe* (London, 1993), pp. 60–84, 269–91; see also Pryce, 'Welsh Rulers and European Change', pp. 37–51.

64 *AWR*, pp. 132–5; David Stephenson, *The Governance of Gwynedd* (Cardiff, 1984), pp. 26–39; J. Beverley Smith, *Llywelyn ap Gruffudd, Prince of Wales* (Cardiff, 1998), pp. 310–29; Charles Insley, 'From *Rex Wallie* to *Princeps Wallie*: charters and state-formation in thirteenth-century Wales', in J. R. Maddicott and D. M. Palliser (eds), *The Medieval State: Essays Presented to James Campbell* (London, 2000), pp. 179–96 (pp. 195–6).

65 Much of the most detailed discussion of the production of princely acta in Gwynedd is in *AWR*, pp. 133–41. See also Smith, *Llywelyn*, pp. 319–29; Stephenson, *Governance*, pp. 26–39 and Insley, 'From *Rex Wallie*', pp. 195–6.

66 *AWR*, p. 133.

67 *AWR*, p. 133.

68 *AWR*, no. 272 (pp. 442–3); no. 252 (pp. 412–14).

69 *AWR*, pp. 133–5.

70 R. R. Davies, *The Age of Conquest: Wales 1063–1415* (Oxford, 1991), pp. 236–55; David Stephenson, *Medieval Powys. Kingdom, Principality and Lordships, 1132–1293* (Woodbridge, 2016), pp. 97–114.

71 Davies, *Age of Conquest*, pp. 223–6; Stephenson, *Medieval Powys*, pp. 58–74.

72 Smith, *Llywelyn*, pp. 90–138.

73 *AWR*, pp. 132–5; Stephenson, *Governance*, pp. 26–8.

74 *AWR*, pp. 134–5 and nos 286 (witnessed by Einion *notario nostro*), 272 (witnessed by John, *notario nostro*), 423 (witnessed by Madog, *notario nostro*), 259 (witnessed by *cancellarius* Master Instructus, p. 424) and 292, 296, 298–9 (witnessed by *cancellarius* Master David, archdeacon of St Asaph, pp. 412–14, 460–1, 463–6).

75 Stephenson, *Governance*, pp. 28–39.

76 *AWR*, pp. 62–3; Insley, 'From *Rex Wallie*', p. 189.

77 Charles Insley, 'The Political Culture of Twelfth-century Wales', *Anglo-Norman Studies*, 30 (2007), 133–53 (pp. 145–6). See, for example: *AWR*, nos 28 (pp. 171–5) and 196 (pp. 327–9).
78 See, for example: *AWR*, nos 480, 482, 492–5, 541–2, 544 (pp. 680–3, 688–92, 746–50).
79 *AWR*, nos 200, 202, 213, 216, 218, 219, 220, 225, 226, 229, 231–5, 238–50, 252–5 (pp. 332–3, 335, 345–71, 374–7, 378–93, 394–419). *AWR*, no. 213 (pp. 344–5) is the first surviving charter of Llywelyn's as 'Prince of North Wales'.
80 For the use of 'Wallia', see Insley, 'Political Culture', 148.
81 *AWR*, no. 256 (pp. 419–21), a grant to the Hospitallers of Dolgynwal, is the earliest surviving charter to use this style, although there are doubts about its authenticity. The next surviving document to use the new style is *AWR*, no. 260 (pp. 424–8), dated May 1230.
82 *AWR*, p. 76.
83 H. D. Emmanuel (ed.), *The Latin Texts of the Welsh Laws* (Cardiff, 1967), pp. 207, 277. See also Gerald of Wales's description of the three courts: *Itinerarium Kambriae* i.10; *Descriptio Kambriae* i.4 (ed. James F. Dimock, *Giraldi Cambrensis Opera Volume 6* (London, 1868), pp. 81, 169; trans. Lewis Thorpe, *The Journey Through Wales/The Description of Wales* (London, 1978), pp. 139, 223).
84 *AWR*, p. 76 n. 601.
85 Williams, 'The succession to Gwynedd'.
86 *AWR*, no. 291 (pp. 457–60).
87 *AWR*, no. 328 (pp. 499–501).
88 *AWR*, no. 363 (pp. 536–42).
89 See above, p. 103.
90 Insley, 'Political Culture', 135; Pryce, 'Welsh Rulers and European Change', pp. 39–42, 46–50.
91 Pryce, 'Welsh Rulers and European Change', pp. 46–50.
92 See above, pp. 101–2.
93 Bartlett, *The Making of Europe*, pp. 255–60.
94 Insley, 'Imitation and Independence', p. 116.
95 Davies, *Age of Conquest*, pp. 197–201. On Llanbadarn Fawr, see Charles-Edwards, *Wales and the Britons*, pp. 648–9.
96 Davies, *Age of Conquest*, pp. 197–8.
97 Pryce, 'Welsh Rulers and European Change', p. 42.
98 Pryce, 'Anglo-Welsh Agreements'; Carr, 'Anglo-Welsh Relations', pp. 127–38.
99 Pryce, 'Owain Gwynedd'; Davies, *Age of Conquest*, pp. 49–50.
100 Smith, *Llywelyn*, pp. 167–70.

101 *AWR*, no. 361 (pp. 533–6).
102 *AWR*, no. 363 (pp. 536–42); Davies, *Age of Conquest*, pp. 313–15; Smith, *Llywelyn*, pp. 177–86.
103 *AWR*, no. 328 (pp. 499–501).
104 *AWR*, pp. 500–1; Smith, *Llywelyn*, pp. 110–14.

5

The Development of Old Welsh Boundary Clauses

Ben Guy

Introduction

During the past thirty years, Professor Pryce has done more than any other to advance our understanding of documentary culture in Wales in the twelfth and thirteenth centuries, most notably through his magnificent edition of the Welsh princely *acta*.[1] This work represents a beginning rather than an end, since it opens many new lines of enquiry. Among the numerous fascinating features of the charters in this corpus are the lengthy sequential boundary clauses, which are unusual by the standards of English royal charters in the period. These are notable not merely for their presence and length, but also because some of them include a significant number of connecting words and phrases in Welsh. Professor Pryce argues that the form of these boundary perambulations is indebted to the early medieval tradition of Welsh charter-writing exemplified in the Book of Llandaf, which contains many vernacular boundary perambulations.[2] The purpose of the present chapter is to outline the history of this tradition of early Welsh boundary clauses.

The corpus of pre-Norman Welsh charters is modest, but perhaps more substantial than sometimes assumed. The charters are preserved in four archives:

1. Seven documents of approximately ninth-century date from Llandeilo Fawr in Carmarthenshire are preserved, probably in their original form, inscribed into the 'St Chad' gospel book now in Lichfield cathedral.[3]
2. Fourteen charters of approximately eighth-century date from Llancarfan in Glamorgan are found among the various texts

appended to the Life of St Cadog of Llancarfan in a late twelfth-century manuscript.[4]
3. Around 158 charters, purporting to date from the sixth to eleventh centuries, were included in the Book of Llandaf, written around 1132. Most of these documents were edited to varying extents in the twelfth century, though it is now generally agreed that the majority of them derive from original charters of the seventh to eleventh centuries.[5]
4. Extracts from a series of charters for Clynnog Fawr in Gwynedd, purporting to date between the seventh and eleventh centuries, appear in Edward IV's confirmation charter for Clynnog Fawr, having been copied, in all likelihood, from the lost Book of St Beuno (probably another early medieval gospel book like the Lichfield gospels).[6]

Within this corpus, one finds two boundary clauses among the Llandeilo Fawr charters, two boundary clauses among the Llancarfan charters, and approximately 114 boundary clauses among the Llandaf charters (and associated texts in the same manuscript), counting once only those boundaries preserved in multiple copies.[7] Inevitably, the history of early Welsh boundary clauses rests on interpretation of the Llandaf boundaries.

The only previous attempt to study the development of early Welsh boundary clauses was published by Jon Coe in 2004.[8] Coe aimed to establish a relative chronology for the boundaries in the Book of Llandaf, ordering them according to six characteristics: two formal, three linguistic and one orthographical. While certainly being informed by Coe's study, the present discussion moves beyond his approach by setting the Book of Llandaf's boundary clauses in the context of boundary clauses more widely, and particularly by comparing them with the boundary clauses of the Llandeilo Fawr charters and those of neighbouring Anglo-Saxon England. External linguistic evidence is also brought to bear to a greater extent to aid understanding of absolute dating. Consideration of the formal characteristics of the boundaries has been separated from that of their language, since these two aspects did not develop along the same linear pathway. Other dating criteria are also considered: most important of these is the position of the boundary clause within the charter. The result of this approach is a more historically grounded appreciation of how boundary clauses developed in Wales between the seventh and twelfth centuries. When the various criteria are considered together, it is possible to distinguish those boundary clauses that are likely to be original to the charters (like the majority of witness lists) from those that were added to the charters by the compilers of the Book of Llandaf. There are also intermediate cases where boundaries were probably added to the charters between the time of the charters' creation and the time of the compilation of the Book of Llandaf.

Boundary clauses and the compilers of the Book of Llandaf

In order to understand how the compilers of the Book of Llandaf, working probably in the 1120s and early 1130s, might have approached any boundary clauses contained in the earlier documents that they had before them, it is first necessary to appreciate the nature of boundary clauses in the compilers' own time. This can be achieved by establishing a group of boundary clauses that were compiled by the compilers themselves and their contemporaries. We can be reasonably confident that the following boundary clauses were produced as part of the effort underlying the creation of the Book of Llandaf:[9] the two statements of the boundary of Llandaf's diocese, one in a papal document dated 5 April 1129 (*LL* 42, with bounds no doubt supplied by Llandaf) and the other incorporated in the Life of St Euddogwy (*LL* 134 = *Euddogwy* §6); other boundaries in the saints' Lives, such as the bounds of Llandaf itself (*LL* 69 = *Dyfrig* §1) and of Anergyng (*LL* 134 = *Euddogwy* §6); boundaries added to charters that are clearly spurious, and which are essentially hagiographical narratives appended to the saints' Lives (*LL* 123 = *Teilo* §24; *LL* 125b (× 3) = *Teilo* §27; *LL* 127a = *Teilo* §28; *LL* 141 = *Euddogwy* §14); and finally, boundaries added later by scribe B after scribe A had initially copied the charters in question (*LL* 77 [I.2] = *Dyfrig* §13; *LL* 190b [II.23]).[10] When considered as a group, these boundaries produce a remarkably consistent picture, and are linguistically consonant with another contemporary vernacular text in the Book of Llandaf, known as *Braint Teilo*.[11]

There are certain instances that reveal how the compilers treated boundary clauses that already existed in their source material. Sometimes, they recopied pre-existing boundaries in new contexts. The boundary clause of a seventh-century charter, *LL* 162b [I.13], which is plausibly one of the earliest vernacular bounds (see below), was copied out again among a series of late boundary clauses appended to a ninth-century Sequence III charter (*LL* 171b [III.5]); that the two instances of that boundary clause share an earlier common exemplar is strongly suggested by the gap that was left in the text in both cases, where that exemplar was presumably illegible. In another case, an early tenth-century charter (*LL* 237b [III.34]) contains within it a boundary clause whose form corresponds closely with that of others from that period (see below), and which seems original to the charter; the same boundary clause was also appended to an allegedly eighth-century charter concerning the same land (*LL* 167), a charter which cannot be connected with any chronological sequence and is arguably a twelfth-century forgery.[12] Again, an eighth-century charter of Sequence II (*LL* 174b [II.21]) shares a boundary clause with a Sequence III charter for Hywel ap Rhys (d. 886) (*LL* 229b [III.22]); this is very probably a pre-twelfth-century boundary clause, not least because it contains the disyllabic prepositional form *behet* (see below), but in this case it is difficult to decide which charter, if either, might originally have contained it.

The charter doublets suggest that the compilers of the Book of Llandaf not only added new boundary clauses to earlier charters, but also sometimes omitted boundary clauses that appeared in their exemplars.[13] Both processes can be seen at work in the Sequence II doublets *LL* 176a and 190b [II.22–3]: although *LL* 176a contains a boundary clause that is entirely credible in the eighth-century context of the charter, it is omitted from *LL* 190b; on the other hand, scribe B, who supplied an incorrect rubric to *LL* 190b, added a boundary at the end of that document that is clearly of late origin, and indeed it seems to pertain to the place named in the incorrect rubric rather than the place in the actual charter![14] In the Sequence I doublets *LL* 73b (= *Dyfrig* §8) and 163a [I.7–8], only the former contains a boundary clause, but it is of an early type that would be credible in a seventh-century context, and it is positioned suggestively before the witness list. It may have been omitted from *LL* 163a. Similarly, a Sequence II charter, *LL* 188b [II.26], has a boundary clause between the witness list and sanction that may well be original, but it is omitted from the doublet, *LL* 179a, which lacks a witness list and may be incomplete. On the other hand, another Sequence II charter, *LL* 180b [II.25], is appended with a boundary clause that probably dates later than the eighth century, and sure enough the doublet of this charter in the Llancarfan cartulary (*VSBG* §67) has no boundary clause. It is notable that only two of the Llancarfan charters, dating approximately to the eighth century, have a boundary clause. Similarly, it may be that a substantial proportion of the approximately contemporary Sequence II charters of the Book of Llandaf originally had no boundary clause, as discussed below.

Further doublets can reveal how the language and spelling of earlier boundary clauses could be sporadically, though certainly not consistently, modernised as they were copied into the Book of Llandaf. The Sequence III doublets *LL* 171b [III.5], part i, and *LL* 74 [III.6] (= *Dyfrig* §9) both contain the same boundary clause, which may be original to the mid-ninth-century context of 171b, yet both copies have been subjected to certain linguistic modernisations: the bilabial fricative /β/ is spelled with the standard Old Welsh <b> in 171b's *aballen* ('apple tree'), but with <u> in 74's *auallen*; 171b's *henntre* does not spell the lenition of the [t] to [d] at the beginning of the second element of the compound, but 74's *hendreb* does; on the other hand, 74's *hendreb* maintains its final fricative, unlike 171b's *henntre*.[15] Further instances of sporadic orthographical modernisation in the boundaries are revealed by the charters associated with the Lives of Dyfrig and Clydog, since independent copies of those Lives, and their charters, survive in the late twelfth-century manuscript London, British Library, Cotton Vespasian A. xiv, part i. These copies probably derive from early drafts of the Book of Llandaf.[16] In several instances, vernacular words that include the letter <i> in the Vespasian copies of boundary clauses instead use the letter <y> in the Book of Llandaf copies, probably innovatively: thus, in *LL* 73a [I.6] (= *Dyfrig* §7) the river *Gui* ('Wye') in Vespasian has become *Guy* in Llandaf.[17] This also nicely illustrates another tendency: that the names of major rivers were among the likeliest vernacular words to undergo orthographical updating when copied.[18]

The examples discussed in this section reveal two key processes. First, it is clear that much original production and collection of boundary clauses accompanied the making of the Book of Llandaf, and that the compilers associated these newly produced boundary clauses both with newly concocted charters and with charters inherited from earlier sources. Secondly, it is equally clear that those same sources themselves contained a variety of boundary clauses, which were often copied along with the charters but which could also be moved around, duplicated or omitted as suited the compilers' needs. During this process, linguistic and/or orthographic modernisation occurred sporadically, but, just as with the witness lists, this was not undertaken consistently or thoroughly.

Dating criteria

This section considers how formal and linguistic dating criteria can be used to understand the origins of the bulk of early Welsh boundary clauses surviving in the Book of Llandaf. The discussion takes its lead from Coe's 2004 article, but makes much greater use of comparative material.

Formal criteria

There are three crucial points to consider when assessing the form of boundary clauses in the Book of Llandaf. These are as follows:

1. Structure. In general, the Llandaf charters reveal a structural trend that is apparent too in the Anglo-Saxon material: the earliest boundaries consist merely of a short statement about the key boundary markers of the estate (termed here 'key-point boundaries'), while the later boundaries tend to be lengthier sequential perambulations. The chief difference between these two types, as they are understood in this study, is that 'key-point boundaries' do not describe the route that one would take to travel between the main boundary markers. Instead, key-point boundaries simply name the 'key points' (usually between two and four of them) that serve to delineate the extremities of the estate, without even necessarily indicating their interrelationship. For example, in a Sequence I charter that arguably preserves an original seventh-century boundary clause, the boundary of *Cil Hal* is described as follows (*LL* 75 [I.1] = *Dyfrig* §10): 'Finis illius: a palude magno usque ad Arganhell' ('Its boundary: from the big marsh as far as the Arianell'). Presumably these two points lay at either end of the estate, meaning that the direct route between them would go through the middle of the estate, rather than around the boundary. Within the Llandaf corpus, a recurring sub-type of the key-point boundary is the 'dimensional boundary', which specifies the relationship between two or more key points in terms of the dimensions of the estate. For example, the boundary of *Tref Ret* is described like this (*LL* 224 [III.35]): 'Finis

illius est: longitudine a Merthir Gliuis usque ad amnem Ocmur; latitudine autem a Tir i Cair usque ad uillam Oufreu' ('Its boundary is: in length, from Merthyr Glywys as far as the River Ogmore; in breadth, on the other hand, from Tir y Gaer as far as *Villa Oufreu*'). Again, this boundary clause does not perambulate the perimeter. Although key-point boundaries like these are found throughout the corpus, including among the latest charters, it became progressively more common for boundaries to be structured instead as sequential perambulations, which describe how one would proceed from point to point around the perimeter of the estate. An example of such a perambulation is Chad 6, which is quoted and translated below.

2. Language. The matrix language of the boundaries can be Latin, Welsh or a mixture of Latin and Welsh. In general, within this corpus, the higher the proportion of vernacular language in the boundary clause, the later it is likely to be.

3. Position. Boundary clauses can be (a) positioned within the text of a charter, followed by another element such as the witness list or sanction; or (b) positioned at the end of a charter, as the final element in the text. Below, it will emerge that boundary clauses positioned at the ends of charters can often be considered, on other criteria, twelfth-century additions by the compilers of the Book of Llandaf, whereas boundary clauses within charters can often be considered original to those charters.[19]

The dating implications of the formal characteristics of the Llandaf boundaries can be properly appreciated by considering them in relation to the two boundary clauses found among the Llandeilo Fawr charters, set within the wider context of the development of Anglo-Saxon boundary clauses. The more substantial of the two Llandeilo Fawr boundary clauses is 'Chad 6'. Its script is challenging to date with any precision.[20] On the one hand, the script does not exhibit any features of the 'Late Celtic' variety of Insular minuscule, as other specimens of Welsh Insular script do after *c.*850, which suggests that the date should be pushed back to the first half of the ninth century; but on the other hand, the 'square' forms of <a>, the wedges on some ascenders and the subscript letter forms all suggest that the date should be pushed forwards to the late ninth or even early tenth century.[21] The ambiguity is frustrating, but does not affect the argument below unduly. The boundary clause constitutes almost the entirety of the record. What follows is the full document insofar as it has survived:[22]

> Ostendit ista consripsio nobilitatem mainaur med diminih et mensuram eius: aper huer di cum[23] guid maun, di toldar in guo[ilaut] clun, di rit cellfin, di lihomour, di bir main[24] [...] di pul ir deruen, di cimer, di aper ferrus, di pen na[nt] ir caru, di boit bahne, di guoun hen lann, di'r hitir melin, di margles, di rit brangui, di aper istil, di licat, di pul retino[c], d[i] minid di aper he[...]

> This record shows the privilege of the estate of Myddynfych and its boundary: the mouth of the [?]*huer* to the valley of the Gwyddfan, to the holed oak in the bottom of the meadow, to the ford of the border cell, to [?]*lihomour*, to the short stone [...] to the pool of the oak, to the confluence, to the mouth of the Fferws, to the head of Nant Arw, to [?]*boit bahne*, to Henllan meadow, to the yellow cornland, to the Marlais, to the ford of the Branwy, to the mouth of the Istill, to its source, to the ferny pool, upwards to the mouth of the [...][25]

It has been demonstrated that the boundary of this *mainaur* corresponds fairly closely with the later boundary of the parish of Llandybïe, some five miles south of Llandeilo.[26] In the present context, however, the importance of this document lies with its purpose and form. We should notice that the entire purpose of the document, as it stands, it to record the boundary of the estate, which presumably belonged to the church of Llandeilo Fawr. The record does not notice any act of conveyance, nor does it even describe the estate's *nobilitas* ('privilege') as it claims at the beginning. In these respects, the record conforms to a type known also in Anglo-Saxon England, where one finds seventy such 'unattached boundary clauses': two preserved as single sheets from the eleventh century (S 1546B and S 1547), and a further sixty-eight preserved only in later cartularies and registers.[27] One must bear in mind that some of the boundary clauses now attached to charters in the Book of Llandaf may have originated in this form.

Two formal aspects of Chad 6 are significant: the boundary clause is structured as a sequential perambulation, and it is written entirely in the vernacular. Chad 6 therefore shows that vernacular sequential perambulations were being written in at least one part of Wales in the ninth or early tenth century. We can compare Chad 4, recorded in an Insular hand of the second half of the ninth century that displays Late Celtic features.[28] In Chad 4, a vernacular boundary clause is embedded within a record of conveyance. The text begins as follows:[29]

> Osdendit ista conscriptio quod dederunt ris ha hir[****] ha [**]rdid [ha] gurci [*]r[*****g******g****] cibracma, behet hirmain guidauc, ofoid celli ir lath, behet camdubr. Isem hi chet […]

> This record shows that Rhys and *Hir*[****] and [**]*rdid* and Gwrgi gave […] [the] meeting place, as far as Hirfaen Gwyddog, [?]*ofoid* grove of the rod, as far as the Camddwr. This is its render […]

In this charter, the boundary clause has been included between the dispositive clause and the statement of the estate's render. The boundary is entirely in the vernacular, but the illegibility of the beginning of the boundary, along with the obscurity of some of its words, renders it unclear whether the boundary is describing the length and breadth of the estate or a circular perambulation.

The forms of Chad 6 and Chad 4 should be understood in the context of boundary clauses in Anglo-Saxon England and beyond.[30] Like elsewhere in western Europe, England inherited a tradition of boundary clauses from late Roman private deeds. Following this model, boundary clauses in the earliest English charters, from the last third of the seventh century onwards, are short, use Latin as their matrix language, and tend to describe only the features that defined the limits of the property on the four points of the compass. The vernacular was generally used only for place-names. The form was developed further in Wessex seemingly during the reign of King Cynewulf (758–86), from whose time two lengthier perambulatory boundaries survive, written in Latin but with Old English boundary points.[31] The same may be found among two charters of Cynewulf's successor, King Beorhtric (786–802).[32] There was a further step-change in the second quarter of the ninth century, when the first contemporary Old English perambulations appear. The earliest securely attested vernacular perambulation is found in S 298 (AD 847, meaning 846), a charter of King Æthelwulf of Wessex, which survives as a contemporary single sheet. A slightly earlier vernacular boundary is found in a charter of Æthelwulf drawn up at Christ Church Canterbury and dated 838, but this survives only in later copies.[33] This charter retains the earlier compass-point structure, which remained standard practice in Kent during this period. The change to vernacular perambulations in the charters of Wessex should be considered against the background of the increasing use of the vernacular in all forms of Anglo-Saxon documentation during the first half of the ninth century, as well as in the context of Æthelwulf's apparent institution of centralised production for royal diplomas.[34] Elsewhere in England, vernacular perambulations gradually became the standard form, but Latin was not entirely replaced by the vernacular until after the end of the ninth century. In the tenth century, with the reinvigoration of centralised charter production under King Æthelstan (924–39), vernacular perambulations became the standard form in royal diplomas.

It is remarkable that vernacular boundary clauses were also being written in Wales no later than the second half of the ninth century (Chad 4), not long after the earliest English specimens were being written in Wessex; furthermore, by around the same time or shortly thereafter, such vernacular boundary clauses could adopt the form of a perambulation (Chad 6). This is strongly suggestive of shared innovation, found on both sides of the Severn estuary, quite possibly prompted by the political influence of the West Saxon dynasty of Ecgberht. This phenomenon is all the more striking when viewed from a European perspective. In Carolingian Europe, where thousands of charters survive from the eighth and ninth centuries, boundary clauses are comparatively rare. Most are Latin clauses which, like the early English ones, briefly describe the main boundary features of the cardinal points. But although some boundary perambulations occur, and although words, phrases and even sentences in Old High German are occasionally found in the boundary clauses of eastern Frankish charters, there is little to compare with the fully vernacular perambulations attested in Wessex in this period and thereafter.[35] Even in Brittany, although the ninth-century charters in the Cartulary of Redon contain some brief key-point boundaries, neighbour boundaries and also lengthier perambulations, the use of the vernacular (Old Breton) is sparing.[36] By contrast, the Llandeilo charters suggest that developments in south Wales paralleled West Saxon habits rather than those further afield.

What do we learn from this about the many boundary clauses in the Book of Llandaf? The Llandeilo boundaries show that vernacular perambulations were being written in Wales by the ninth or early tenth century, meaning that we might expect to see this reflected in the Llandaf boundaries. The comparison with Wessex also suggests that we should be inclined to view Wales's vernacular perambulations as a development from older forms that were more likely to be in Latin and structured as simple key-point boundaries. That said, we should not be tempted to assume that boundary clauses in Wales developed in a linear fashion, especially considering that the production of Welsh charters was solely in the hands of their ecclesiastical beneficiaries, so far as we know. We should expect continued formal variety within the limits of the known possibilities.

Linguistic criteria

The limited variety of language in boundary clauses inhibits the number of linguistic tests that might be applied to them, but Jon Coe identified several significant features within the corpus that are amenable to analysis. These are discussed here with closer attention paid to external evidence from the corpus of Old Welsh. It is important to note, though, that the extant remains of Old Welsh are almost entirely restricted to the period *c*.800–*c*.950; there is virtually no relevant material for comparison dating between *c*.950 and the Book of Llandaf.[37]

- The preposition(s) *behet*, *bet* ('as far as'). Outside the Book of Llandaf, the disyllabic form is attested as *biheit* in the glosses to the weights and measures tract (*s.* ix[1]); *behet* (× 2) in Chad 4 (*s.* ix[2]); both *bihit* and *bichet* in the Old Welsh computistical tract (*s.* x[1]); and *byhyt* in an undated prophetic poem in the Book of Taliesin.[38] Within the Book of Llandaf, it occurs as *behit* and *behet* (both *LL* 72b [I.5] = *Dyfrig* §6), *behet* (*LL* 121 [I.10] = *Teilo* §22), *behet* (*LL* 174b [II.21] = *LL* 229b [III.22]) and *bihet* (*LL* 204a [II.47]). By contrast, within the corpus of material clearly attributable to the twelfth century in the Book of Llandaf, as outlined above, *bet* is invariably preferred in its place. Prior to the Book of Llandaf, *bet* also occurs once in the glosses to the Juvencus manuscript, in the hand of scribe G (*s.* x[1]).[39]

The relationship between the two forms is not entirely clear. In a Welsh context, commentators have assumed that *bet* is a contracted form of *behet*.[40] However, in relation to Old Breton, where one finds what appear to be equivalent forms, Fleuriot has suggested that the disyllabic form includes the monosyllabic form as its first element, and thus that the latter is not merely a contracted form of the former.[41] Thus, in Angers, bibliothèque municipale, 477, the disyllabic forms *bichit* and *bicit* (× 2) occur among the group A glosses (*s.* ix/x) and the form *bicett* occurs among the group B glosses (*s.* x/xi), while the monosyllabic *bit* occurs four times among the group A glosses and once in the ninth-century manuscript Órleans, bibliothèque municipale, 221.[42] But, as Fleuriot has noted, it may be the case that the disyllabic Breton forms are not exactly equivalent to the Welsh forms, especially if it is right to suppose that the intermediate consonant in the Breton forms is /k/.[43] Whatever their etymological relationship, one can at least say that, in Welsh, *bet* seems to have succeeded *behet* in a *functional* sense. There is no evidence that disyllabic *behet* survived in Welsh after the first half of the tenth century. The latest charter with a boundary clause that includes *behet* is *LL* 229b [III.22], a charter of the late ninth century. After this point, boundaries invariably use *bet* where they might previously have used *behet*. Thus, considering the charters alongside the external evidence, we can at least say that the use of *behet* in a boundary probably suggests that the boundary does not post-date the first half of the tenth century.

- The definite article. As one might expect, this is very well attested in the Old Welsh corpus. In Middle and Modern Welsh, the definite article is *yr* before words beginning with a vowel, and *y* before words beginning with a consonant. In Old Welsh of the period *c.*800–950, the -*r* form (usually spelled *ir*) is invariably written, even before words beginning with a consonant. By contrast, the corpus of twelfth-century material in the Book of Llandaf contains few instances of the definite article with -*r* preceding a consonant, showing that the Middle Welsh situation then largely obtained; for instance, in *Braint Teilo* there are six definite articles before consonants with the form *y(r)*, and only one with an -*r*. As is discussed below, the boundaries themselves suggest that the -*r* of the definite article began to be dropped regularly in writing before consonants around the year 1000. This implies that most of the boundary clauses in charters dating prior to that time that contain a mixture of *r* and *r*-less forms were not concocted wholesale in the twelfth century; rather, their *r*-less forms were probably produced by the kind of haphazard linguistic updating discussed above, while their *r* forms were fortuitously left to stand.

- The preposition *di* ('to'). Although this was analysed by Coe, it has not proved to be a particularly helpful criterion for dating. By the mid-thirteenth century, the initial dental fricative /ð/- of the lenited preposition *di* or *dy* had been lost, producing Middle Welsh *i* or *y*. But in the Book of Llandaf, even among the material clearly composed in the twelfth century, it is clear that *di* still predominates, and that *d*-less forms are in the minority. A lack of vernacular manuscripts dateable to the period 1150–1250 means that the intervening position is unclear, though we might note that *di* (spelled *dy*) occurs in later copies of certain poems composed probably in the second half of the twelfth century (e.g. *Marwnad Cedifor ap Genillyn* by Llywelyn Fardd I and *Gwasgargerdd Fyrddin*), as well as in the prose texts *Culhwch ac Olwen* and *Brut y Brenhinedd* and various undated poems in the *Hengerdd* corpus.[44] In the majority of Llandaf boundaries, *di* (or *dy*) is the only form of the preposition that occurs.

There are also orthographic features that are significant for dating purposes, though unlike linguistic changes, these should not necessarily be understood as occurring within a linear sequence of change. One of these was highlighted by Coe:

- The letter <y>. This letter began to be used frequently in Welsh in the first half of the tenth century, with the Old Welsh computistical tract and the Harleian genealogies being among the more substantial witnesses to this.[45] Fortunately, the use of the letter <y> in early Welsh, including in the Book of Llandaf, has recently been the subject of a detailed study by Patrick Sims-Williams.[46] It is clear that, in the milieu of the compilers of the Book of Llandaf, there was no standard approach to this letter. Many boundary clauses in the Book of Llandaf, including some of those produced in the twelfth century, feature either no use of <y> or only occasional use, probably produced by the kind of sporadic orthographical intervention noticed above. But on other occasions, especially among the material clearly produced in the twelfth century, one finds instead indiscriminate use of <y> for various vowels. For the most part, it seems that the scribes of the Book of Llandaf copied the orthography of vernacular bounds as they found them, whether they contained <y> or not. For instance, Sims-Williams has shown that scribe B did not impose any personal preference for the use of the letter.[47] Therefore, while we might be suspicious of a boundary clause that has many instances of <y> when it is associated with a charter allegedly dating between the seventh and ninth centuries, for the most part this is not a decisive dating criterion.

The chronology of the Llandaf boundaries

The discussion below is divided between the three 'sequences' of Book of Llandaf charters, as determined by their overlapping witness lists: Sequence I belongs broadly to the seventh century, Sequence II to the eighth century and Sequence III to the period $c.850$–1100. Boundaries that were clearly added in the twelfth century are distinguished from those that are probably original, and the latter form the basis for an interpretation of the development of Welsh boundary clauses. There are also some intermediate instances that may be neither original elements of the charters that they now accompany, nor additions of the twelfth century; these may have been added to the relevant charters in the intervening period.

Sequence I

Sequence I is formed from eighteen charters (counting once the doublet comprising 73b [I.7] = *Dyfrig* §8 and 163a [I.8]). Of these, five have no boundary clause at all, as may have been the norm in this period.[48] Four others have boundary clauses that were clearly added in the twelfth century: they are all sequential vernacular perambulations that use the prepositional form *bet*, and 19/20 (95 per cent) of their definite articles before consonants lack the final *-r*.[49] Notably, all these boundary clauses are found *after* the texts of the charters, rather than within them. There are then five charters whose boundary clauses may be original. These are predominantly short, Latin key-point boundaries that describe two or more points at the extremities of the relevant estates. Moreover, in four out of five cases, the boundaries are found *within* the texts of the charters.[50] The exception, *LL* 162b [I.13], has a short, two-point vernacular clause at the end of the charter. It was mentioned above because it recurs again in *LL* 171b [III.5] among a group of boundaries that were added to that charter at a later time, and both copies of the boundary clause contain the same lacuna. If this boundary is an original part of *LL* 162b, it may be one of the earliest vernacular bounds in Welsh; at the least, it is probably an early addition.

Four boundary clauses in Sequence I remain to be discussed, and this group is the most interesting. One, a mostly Latin boundary statement incorporated into the dispositive clause of *LL* 76a [I.4] (= *Dyfrig* §11), looks potentially early despite the <y> in the apparently misunderstood vernacular phrase *ynis stratdour* (for *yn is(s)trat dour* 'in the valley of the Dore').[51] The other three are sequential perambulations with substantial vernacular elements, the first two of which occur between the statement of privileges and the witness list and the third of which is at the end of the charter.[52] The latter two, in particular, bear witness to a significant degree of code-switching between Latin and Welsh. Consider, for instance, *LL* 121:[53]

> Finis istius podi est: Clougur per uiam magnam usque ad cumulum Frut Mur. A cumulo Frut Mur recte di'r fos, usque ad petram in quattuor confinibus. O'r lech cihitan di tal ir cecyn, behet tal ir fos. O penn i fos usque ad fontem nigrum. A fonte per siluam di Clour eminus. Tal i fos cihitan Clouuric di Clour.

> The boundary of this church is: the *Clougur* along the great road as far as the barrow of the Ffrwd Mawr. From the barrow of the Ffrwd Mawr straight to the dyke, as far as the stone at the four boundaries. From the stone along to the end of the ridge, as far as the end of the dyke. From the head of the dyke as far as the black spring. From the spring through the wood to the *Clour* a short distance away. The end of the dyke along the *Clouuric* to the *Clour*.

Within the same sentences, the boundary slips effortlessly between Latin and Welsh. This is not in itself necessarily an 'early' feature: one should note that the boundary of Llandaf's diocese incorporated into the papal document of 1129 (*LL* 42) does much the same. But there are aspects of *LL* 121 that do look early. The preposition *cihitan* ('along') occurs twice, uniquely in the Book of Llandaf; this is based on the well-attested *cyhyd*, but the only comparable derivative form is Old Welsh *cihutun*, attested twice in the glosses to the early ninth-century weights and measures tract (and compare Old Breton *cohiton*, found in two boundary clauses in Redon charters, dated respectively 821 and 814–21).[54] We also find the disyllabic prepositional form *behet* here, rather than the monosyllabic form *bet* that rapidly gained ground in the tenth and eleventh centuries. Thus, even if we are reluctant to suppose that a sequential, bilingual perambulation would have been an original part of a putatively seventh-century charter, it seems unlikely that this boundary clause was added to the charter much later than the ninth century. If so, it was only lightly modernised when it was copied into the Book of Llandaf (adding <y> to *cecyn* and omitting the definite article's -*r* in *i fos* twice; cf. *ir cecyn* and *ir fos*).

Sequence II

In Sequence II there are eight charters with boundaries that were very probably added in the twelfth century.[55] In six of these charters, the boundaries appear at the end of the text, and in two they are followed by the sanction only (*LL* 156 and 157). It is probable that most of these charters originally had no boundary clause at all, although one of them, *LL* 190b, with a boundary clause added by scribe B, is a doublet of *LL* 176a [II.22], which retains a different, probably original, boundary clause (as mentioned above). They can be compared with the thirty-three charters in Sequence II that still have no boundary clause (counting once each the two pairs of doublets, *LL* 179b and 191 [II.33–4] and *LL* 175 and 186b [II.35–6]). That such a high proportion of the putatively eighth-century Sequence II charters should contain no original boundary clause is only what might be expected from the comparison with contemporary charters from Llancarfan and Anglo-Saxon England.

There are eleven charters that contain what can fairly convincingly be considered original boundary clauses.[56] These share a number of features: their matrix language is generally Latin; they are generally structured as key-point boundaries, sometimes indicating the estate's length and breadth; and in nine of the eleven, the boundaries occur *within* the charters rather than after them.[57] Where the vernacular occurs in these charters, it is convincing: thus, the definite article is only *ir* before consonants (*LL* 159b and 183a); there is no use of *bet*, whereas *bihet* occurs once (*LL* 204a); the letter <y> only occurs twice, in the names of rivers (*Guy* ['Wye'] in *LL* 183a; *Amyr* ['Gamber'] in *LL* 200); and in *LL* 202 one finds the personal names *Congint* and *Conlipan*, both with *con-* < *cuno-*, using a spelling of the vowel which was predominant only in the eighth and first half of the ninth centuries.[58]

There are several additional ambiguous categories of boundary clause in Sequence II. Three are sequential vernacular bounds positioned after their charters that have every appearance of being later additions, but which one hesitates to ascribe to the twelfth century on account of their even use of *r* and *r*-less forms of the definite article before consonants (in total, exactly seventeen instances of each form before consonants).[59] As discussed below, this may imply that the three boundaries were added to these charters before *c*.1000. There are also four that make use of the letter <y> and are again found after their charters. Two of these are sequential vernacular perambulations that are unlikely to date to the eighth century, and, unsurprisingly, one finds in them the monosyllabic prepositional form *bet* and examples of written lenition; but again, their relatively even use of *r* and *r*-less forms of the definite article before consonants makes a twelfth-century attribution questionable (in total, before consonants, nine instances with *-r* and six without *-r*).[60] Another of the boundaries with <y> (*LL* 155 [II.6] = *Euddogwy* §28) is a long Latin perambulation that might fit better into a late ninth- or early tenth-century context than an eighth-century one, as discussed below. The fourth boundary with <y> (*LL* 144 [II.1] = *Euddogwy* §16) is a short bilingual (Welsh/Latin) boundary of unusual type, which again may have been added to the charter prior to the twelfth century. A further category is represented by two charters that are adjacent to one another in the historical sequence deduced from the witness lists, though interestingly not in the paginal order of the Book of Llandaf.[61] Their boundary clauses, which occur after the charters, give the impression of having been original short Latin key-point boundaries that were later continued as vernacular perambulations. Lastly, there is one charter that contains two boundary clauses of apparently early type, but which may have been added to the charter after it was first composed (*LL* 174b [II.21]). Both are short, mainly Latin key-point boundaries, and one includes the prepositional form *behet*. But the first looks awkwardly inserted inside the dispositive clause, while the second is shared with *LL* 229b [III.22]. One suspects that 174b was altered after it was first composed, possibly because the estate that it concerns was apparently appropriated by laymen more than once in the eighth and ninth centuries.[62]

Sequence III

In Sequence III (*c.*850–1100), it becomes progressively more difficult to distinguish the boundaries that were added later, as we draw nearer to the time of the Book of Llandaf itself. Nevertheless, the *position* of the boundary clause within or after the charter remains a significant test. One can identify a cluster of five late ninth-century charters with boundaries that were clearly added later: these are all sequential vernacular perambulations positioned after the charters; they use *bet*; and, most crucially, the *r*-less form of the definite article predominates before consonants (in 31/43 instances, or 72 per cent).[63] There are also a further four boundaries that fulfil all these criteria but which show a more prominent use of the *r* form of the definite article before consonants (in total, 16 with *r* and 12 without *r*), possibly indicating that these boundaries were added before *c.*1000.[64] All of these charters may have originally lacked a boundary clause, and so can be compared with the twenty-three charters of Sequence III without boundary clauses.

With these removed from present consideration, some interesting patterns emerge across the period 850–1100. During approximately the second half of the ninth century, there are six charters with boundary clauses that can probably be considered original to the charters (counting once the doublet *LL* 171b [III.5] = *LL* 74 [III.6] (*Dyfrig* §9)); in all but one case (*LL* 199b), the boundaries are found within these charters.[65] Unlike the seemingly original boundaries of Sequence II, here we can see sequential perambulations becoming prominent (*LL* 174a, 171b [boundary 1] = 74, 171b [boundary 2], 227a), and code-switching between Latin and Welsh becoming more frequent (*LL* 170, 171b [boundary 1] = 74, 171b [boundary 2], 237a). In these respects, these boundaries can be compared with the very last apparently original boundary in Sequence II (*LL* 210a), which is similarly a sequential perambulation that code-switches between Latin and Welsh. This may have been characteristic of the period from the late eighth to the late ninth century. It is perhaps within this period that three of the ambiguous boundaries of Sequence I (*LL* 72b, 73a and 121) could most comfortably be placed.

Between the late ninth and mid-tenth centuries, a somewhat different pattern emerges. The five seemingly authentic boundaries from this period are generally longer than earlier ones, but surprisingly one finds less Welsh in them, rather than more (as might have been expected).[66] Three of them occur within their charters (*LL* 239, 237b, 224), and two after them (*LL* 233, 223). Three of them are sequential perambulations (*LL* 233, 237b, 223), while two are length-and-breadth boundaries (*LL* 239, a complex three-part boundary, and *LL* 224). These boundaries may represent the dominant type during the later years of Bishop Cyfeilliog and the episcopates of bishops Llibio and Wulffrith. Interestingly, Latin perambulations of corresponding type are found in two Cornish charters in favour of local churches from a similar period (S 450 and S 810), very unusually in an Anglo-Saxon context, where vernacular perambulations had become the norm by the tenth century; perhaps this lends support to Charles Insley's suggestion that these may have been influenced by Brittonic diplomatic practice.[67]

The two charters from the second half of the tenth century that include boundaries are almost the last that contain appreciable numbers of definite articles with -*r* before consonants (10/22 instances, or 45 per cent). One of these, dated to 955 (*LL* 218 [III.39]), has a boundary clause that occurs after the charter and is perhaps suspicious, but unfortunately other dating criteria are not so helpful in this period. The other (*LL* 244 [III.42]) has two convincing boundary clauses embedded within its dispositive clause, the first a vernacular perambulation and the second a Latin length-and-breadth boundary with Welsh place-names. After these, the majority of the charters of the eleventh-century bishops Bleddri (*c.*1000–22), Joseph (1022–45) and Herewald (1056–1104) have boundary clauses, and most of these are sequential perambulations in the vernacular, like eleventh-century Anglo-Saxon boundaries. Their linguistic profile is similar to that of the boundaries that were clearly later additions to the charters of the seventh to ninth centuries, including, interestingly, the predominance of the *r*-less form of the definite article before consonants. This is illustrated by Table 1, which tabulates the use of *r* and *r*-less forms of the definite article before consonants across the whole corpus. It can be seen that, in the eleventh century, forms of the definite article with *r* before consonants account for 0 per cent (0/11) of relevant instances in the charters of Bishop Bleddri, 24 per cent (7/29) in the charters of Bishop Joseph, and 9 per cent (3/33) in the charters of Bishop Herewald. These figures should be compared with 8 per cent (2/25) in the corpus of material probably composed in the twelfth century (see the table), and, among other groups of clearly late boundaries, 5 per cent (1/20) in the late boundaries of Sequence I, 15 per cent (6/40) in the late boundaries of Sequence II, and 28 per cent (12/43) in the late boundaries of Sequence III. However, unlike these later additions to the earlier charters, the boundary clauses of the eleventh-century charters are more often found within the charters, not after them. It seems highly likely that most of the boundary clauses associated with the eleventh-century charters in the Book of Llandaf derive from the original charters. This strongly suggests that the practice of dropping the final -*r* of the definite article before words beginning with a consonant became widespread, at least in writing in south-east Wales, around the year 1000, even if the adoption of the *r*-less form in this environment was not universal in the written language until later. This change has hitherto gone undetected because the main corpus of Old Welsh dates earlier than *c*.950. This evidence also suggests that many of the boundaries that seem to have been added to earlier charters after the time of their initial composition, but which use the *r* form of the definite article before consonants more prominently than would be expected in the eleventh and twelfth centuries, are unlikely to have been composed later than the tenth century; in these groups (grouped together as 'ambiguous' boundaries in Table 1), forms of the definite article with *r* before consonants account for 55 per cent (6/11) of relevant instances in Sequence I, 52 per cent (30/58) in Sequence II, and 57 per cent (16/28) in Sequence III. Some of these boundaries may have originally contained no *r*-less forms of the definite article at all (as one finds in Old Welsh of the period *c*.800–950), even though the *r* was omitted from some of the relevant instances when the boundaries were copied into the Book of Llandaf in the twelfth century.

Table 1: Definite articles preceding consonants in the boundaries of the Book of Llandaf

Sequence		Relevant examples	r forms before consonants		r-less forms before consonants		% r : r-less forms
			No.	/boundary	No.	/boundary	
Sequence I (s. vii)	Original boundaries	0					
	Ambiguous boundaries	3[68]	6	2	5	1.67	55:45
	Late boundaries	5[69]	1	0.2	19	3.8	5:95
Sequence II (s. viii)	Original boundaries	2[70]	3	1.5	0	0	100:0
	Ambiguous boundaries	8[71]	30	3.75	28	3.5	52:48
	Late boundaries	7[72]	6	0.86	34	4.86	15:85
Sequence III (s. ix²)	Original boundaries	2[73]	1	1	1	1	50:50
	Ambiguous boundaries	4[74]	16	4	12	3	57:43
	Late boundaries	6[75]	12	2	31	5.12	28:72
Sequence III (s. x¹)	Original boundaries	2[76]	0	0	2	1	0:100
Sequence III (s. x²)	Original boundaries	3[77]	10	3.33	12	4	45:55
Sequence III (s. xi)	Bishop Bleddri (c.1000–22)	4[78]	0	0	11	2.75	0:100
	Bishop Joseph (1022–45)	10[79]	7	0.7	22	2.2	24:76
	Bishop Herewald (1056–1104)	3[80]	3	1	30	10	9:91
Other	Material composed c.1130	6[81]	2	0.33	23	3.83	8:92
	Morgan ab Owain narrative (LL 240)	8	27	3.38	19	2.38	59:41

Unsequenced boundary clauses

Brief mention should be made of the few boundary clauses that are not found in sequenced charters, but which are not obviously products of the twelfth century. These are as follows:

- *LL* 159a = *Euddogwy* §32 for Llanerthill. This is a sequential vernacular boundary clause that looks late, although in 3/4 instances the form of the definite article before consonants is *ir*.
- *LL* 197a = *Clydog* §6. This boundary appears in a curious short charter text appended to the material associated with St Clydog. It is likely to have been inherited by Llandaf. It is mostly Latin, though includes a vernacular phrase with the prepositional form *bet*.
- *LL* 240. This is an invented narrative concerning Morgan ab Owain, king of Glywysing (d. 974), to which have been appended eight, mostly sequential vernacular boundaries. The text looks like it was created as a peg on which to hang various boundary clauses that could not be inserted elsewhere. Perhaps some of these originated as unattached boundary clauses like Chad 6. Most of them contain a significant number of definite articles with -*r* before consonants (in total, 59 per cent or 27/46 instances, similar to the 'ambiguous' categories discussed above); perhaps they really did originate in the tenth century.
- *LL* 260, in a charter of Bishop Joseph. Although the charter has no witness list, the boundary clause looks entirely credible as a product of Bishop Joseph's episcopate.

Conclusion

Despite the evident challenges that one faces when approaching the Book of Llandaf, this study has attempted to demonstrate how it can be used to tell a convincing story of the development of Welsh boundary clauses between the seventh and twelfth centuries. In the seventh and eighth centuries, boundary clauses probably appeared originally in a minority of charters, and they generally took the form of short key-point boundaries that used Latin as their matrix language. Between the late eighth and late ninth centuries, a greater degree of Latin-Welsh code-switching was introduced to the charters, and they began to take the form of sequential perambulations. In the first half of the tenth century, the boundaries became somewhat more elaborate, but tended again to be written predominantly in Latin, with less use of Welsh. By the eleventh century, however, the vernacular perambulation had certainly become the norm, even though older forms continued to be used occasionally too.

Within this context, the boundary clause with substantial vernacular elements in the Lord Rhys's charter for Strata Florida from 1184, to which Professor Pryce drew attention, can be seen as an entirely natural product of centuries of diplomatic development in south Wales. Professor Pryce's edition of the twelfth- and thirteenth-century Welsh princely charters sets a remarkably high standard for charter scholarship in Wales. It also shows how much might be gained from a comparable edition of the early Welsh charters.[82]

Notes

1 Huw Pryce, with Charles Insley, *The Acts of Welsh Rulers 1120–1283* (Cardiff, 2005).

2 *AWR*, p. 100; Huw Pryce, 'Uses of the Vernacular in the Acts of Welsh Rulers 1120–1283', in *La langue des actes: Actes du XIe Congrès international de diplomatique (Troyes, jeudi 11–Samedi 13 septembre 2003)*, at http://elec.enc.sorbonne.fr/CID2003/pryce (accessed 6 November 2023); Charles Insley, 'Imitation and independence in native Welsh administrative culture, *c.*1180–1280', in David Crook and Louise J. Wilkinson (eds), *The Growth of Royal Government under Henry III* (Woodbridge, 2015), pp. 104–21 (pp. 114–17), and see pp. 119–20 for a list of Welsh princely *acta* with boundary clauses. For the wider context of vernacular language in contemporary documents, see Thomas Brunner, 'Le passage aux langues vernaculaires dans les actes de la pratique en Occident', *Le Moyen Âge*, 115 (2009), 29–72 (p. 51 for the Welsh princely *acta*).

3 Edited in J. Gwenogvryn Evans, with John Rhys, *The Text of the Book of Llan Dâv Reproduced from the Gwysaney Manuscript* (Oxford, 1893) [hereafter *LL*], pp. xliii–xlviii. For general discussion, see Dafydd Jenkins and Morfydd E. Owen, 'The Welsh Marginalia in the Lichfield Gospels Part I', *CMCS*, 5 (1983), 37–66; Dafydd Jenkins and Morfydd E. Owen, 'The Welsh Marginalia in the Lichfield Gospels Part II: the "Surexit" Memorandum', *CMCS*, 7 (1984), 91–120.

4 A. W. Wade-Evans (ed. and trans.), *Vitae Sanctorum Britanniae et Genealogiae: The Lives and Genealogies of the Welsh Saints*, new edn by Scott Lloyd (Cardiff, 2013) [hereafter *VSBG*], pp. 124–37 (§§55–68).

5   *LL* 72–8, 121–9 and 140–275; see most recently Patrick Sims-Williams, *The Book of Llandaf as a Historical Source* (Woodbridge, 2019), with my review in *Morgannwg*, 64 (2020), 225–9. For the date of the Book of Llandaf, see John Reuben Davies, '*Liber Landavensis*: Its Date and the Identity of its Editor', *CMCS*, 35 (1998), 1–11.

6   Henry Ellis (ed.), *Registrum vulgariter nuncupatum "The Record of Caernarvon": è codice MS^{to} Harleiano 696. descriptum* (London, 1838), pp. 257–8; see Patrick Sims-Williams, 'Edward IV's confirmation charter for Clynnog Fawr', in Colin Richmond and Isobel Harvey (eds), *Recognitions: Essays Presented to Edmund Fryde* (Aberystwyth, 1996), pp. 229–41; Sims-Williams, *Book of Llandaf*, pp. 12–13.

7   The Book of Llandaf boundaries are edited and translated in Jonathan Baron Coe, 'The place-names of the Book of Llandaf' (unpublished PhD thesis, University of Wales, Aberystwyth, 2001), 957–1030.

8   Jon Coe, 'Dating the Boundary Clauses of the Book of Llandaf', *CMCS*, 48 (2004), 1–43.

9   My references to charters in the Book of Llandaf are comprised of up to three components. First, there is reference to the edition *LL*, following the usual system whereby charters are indicated by the page of the edition on which they *begin* and labelled 'a, b' etc. when multiple charters begin on the same page. Secondly, there is reference, in square brackets, to the position of a charter within Wendy Davies's three chronological sequences, as set out in her *The Llandaff Charters* (Aberystwyth, 1979); see the concordance in Sims-Williams, *Book of Llandaf*, pp. 179–81. Note, however, that Sims-Williams and myself would order Sequence I somewhat differently: Sims-Williams, *Book of Llandaf*, pp. 33–5; Ben Guy, 'The *Life* of St Dyfrig and the Lost Charters of Moccas (Mochros), Herefordshire', *CMCS*, 75 (2018), 1–37 (pp. 21–2). Thirdly, where relevant, there is reference to my editions of the Lives of Dyfrig, Teilo, Euddogwy and Clydog (hosted at *https://saints.wales/theedition* (accessed 6 November 2023)), which include texts and translations of the charters associated with those Lives.

10   For the boundaries added by B, see Daniel Huws, 'The Making of *Liber Landavensis*', *NLWJ*, 25 (1987–8), 133–60 (p. 144); repr. in his *Medieval Welsh Manuscripts* (Cardiff and Aberystwyth, 2000), pp. 123–57 (p. 142).

11   For which, see Paul Russell, '*Priuilegium Sancti Teliaui* and *Breint Teilo*', *Studia Celtica*, 50 (2016), 41–68.

12   Ben Guy, 'Rheinwg: The Lost Kingdom of South Wales', *Peritia*, 30 (2019), 97–121 (p. 115); for a different view of charter 167, see Sims-Williams, *Book of Llandaf*, pp. 66–70.

13   For the doublets, see Sims-Williams, *Book of Llandaf*, pp. 93–103; T. M. Charles-Edwards, *Wales and the Britons 350–1064* (Oxford, 2013), pp. 256–67.

14 Cf. Coe, 'Place-names of the Book of Llandaf', 561–2; Sims-Williams, *Book of Llandaf*, p. 97.
15 The question of the final fricative is complicated by a scribal error that saw the initial *b*- of the following personal name <b>*iguonui* disappear in both copies, probably due to interference with the final *b* of the preceding word: Coe, 'Place-names of the Book of Llandaf', 364–5.
16 See Guy, '*Life* of St Dyfrig', 6–7; Ben Guy, 'The Vespasian Life of St Teilo and the evolution of the *Vitae Sanctorum Wallensium*', in David N. Parsons and Paul Russell (eds), *Seintiau Cymru, Sancti Cambrenses: Astudiaethau ar Seintiau Cymru / Studies in the Saints of Wales* (Aberystwyth, 2022), pp. 1–30.
17 Other instances of <y> in Llandaf for <i> in Vespasian are found in *LL* 72b [I.5] = *Dyfrig* §6; *LL* 195 [II.41] = *Clydog* §4; *LL* 197a = *Clydog* §6.
18 Sims-Williams similarly notes the tendency for texts in the Book of Llandaf that generally prefer <i> instead of <y> nevertheless to use <y> in well-known proper names such as river names: Patrick Sims-Williams, '"Dark" and "Clear" *Y* in Medieval Welsh Orthography: Caligula Versus Teilo', *Transactions of the Philological Society*, 119 (2021), 1–39 (p. 15).
19 A similar pattern has been observed in Anglo-Saxon charters preserved in later cartularies: Michael Reed, 'Anglo-Saxon charter boundaries', in Michael Reed (ed.), *Discovering Past Landscapes* (London, 1984), pp. 261–306 (p. 271).
20 Chad 6 is the only one of the seven Chad memoranda that is not mentioned by David Dumville in *A Palaeographer's Review: The Insular System of Scripts in the Early Middle Ages*, 2 vols paginated as 1 (Suita, Osaka, 1999–2007), I, 124 and esp. nn. 28 and 30.
21 I am grateful to Helen McKee for advising me about the script of Chad 6.
22 See the edition in *LL* xlvii. I have silently expanded the abbreviations and provided modern punctuation. *LL*'s edition has been checked against images of the manuscript, the most helpful of which is the photograph of page 216 taken in 1887 and available at *https://lichfield.ou.edu/st-chad-gospels/historical-image-overlays* (accessed 6 November 2023). Letters in square brackets are those that Evans read in 1893 but which I have not been able to read with confidence.
23 Evans printed *díc guid*, but the manuscript has $\bar{c}$ for the third letter, which is the Insular abbreviation for Latin *cum*: Egerton Phillimore in Henry Owen (ed.), *The Description of Penbrokshire by George Owen of Henllys*, 4 vols (London, 1892–1936), IV, 424; for the abbreviation, see David N. Dumville, *Abbreviations Used in Insular Script before A.D. 850: Tabulation Based on the Work of W.M. Lindsay* (Cambridge, 2004), p. 1. Here it is used for the Welsh word now spelled *cwm* ('valley'), and indeed the valley is still known as *Cwm Gwyddfan*: R. J. Thomas, *Enwau Afonydd a Nentydd Cymru* (Cardiff, 1938), pp. 72–3.

24 The last full line at the end of page 216 ends with *main*. One or two words after this line, in the lower margin, have been partially cut away. Evans read ✶✶✶*erid*✶, but I cannot confirm that with confidence.

25 The translations of Chad 6, Chad 4 and *LL* 121 below are my own, but I am indebted to members of the Old Welsh Zoom group, organised by Simon Rodway, for much stimulating discussion of the Chad memoranda and some of the Llandaf boundaries. The translation is also informed by the topographical discussions noted in the following footnote.

26 Glanville R. J. Jones, 'Post-Roman Wales', in H. P. R. Finberg (ed.), *The Agrarian History of England and Wales, vol. 1, part II, A.D. 43–1042* (Cambridge, 1972), pp. 281–382 (pp. 308–11); Heather James and David Thorne, '"Mensura Med Diminih": Boundary Place-names of a Ninth-century Estate at Llandybïe, Carmarthenshire', *The Carmarthenshire Antiquary*, 56 (2020), 13–34.

27 Kathryn A. Lowe, 'The Development of the Anglo-Saxon Boundary Clause', *Nomina*, 21 (1998), 63–100 (p. 65). 'S' refers to the numbers assigned to Anglo-Saxon charters in P. H. Sawyer, *Anglo-Saxon Charters: An Annotated List and Bibliography* (London, 1968), which has been revised, updated and expanded at *https://esawyer.lib.cam.ac.uk* (accessed 6 November 2023).

28 Helen McKee, *The Cambridge Juvencus Manuscript Glossed in Latin, Old Welsh, and Old Irish* (Aberystwyth, 2000), pp. 4–5.

29 See the edition in *LL* xlv; the procedure has been the same as described above in n. 22.

30 For the development of boundary clauses in Anglo-Saxon England, see Lowe, 'Development' and, more succinctly, N. P. Brooks and S. E. Kelly (eds), *Charters of Christ Church Canterbury*, 2 vols (Oxford, 2013), I, 132–5. Although now somewhat dated, useful detail may be found in Reed, 'Anglo-Saxon charter boundaries', pp. 261–74.

31 S 262 and S 264; see the discussion in S. E. Kelly (ed.), *Charters of Bath and Wells* (Oxford, 2007), pp. 196, 198 (for no. 27 = S 262). S 264 is extant as a single sheet, possibly from the second half of the eighth century.

32 S 267 and S 268; see the discussion in S. E. Kelly (ed.), *The Charters of Abingdon Abbey*, 2 vols (Oxford, 2000–1), I, 34–6 (for no. 7 = S 268).

33 S 286, edited in Brooks and Kelly, *Charters of Christ Church Canterbury*, I, no. 68.

34 See respectively Robert Gallagher, 'The Vernacular in Anglo-Saxon Charters: Expansion and Innovation in Ninth-century England', *Historical Research*, 91 (2018), 205–35 and Simon Keynes, 'The West Saxon Charters of King Æthelwulf and his Sons', *English Historical Review*, 109 (1994), 1109–49. The two developments are considered together in Robert Gallagher, *Writing the Realm: The Written Word and the Rise of Wessex, c. 830–920* (forthcoming), ch. 2.

35 Edward Roberts, 'Boundary Clauses and the Use of the Vernacular in Eastern Frankish Charters, *c*.750–*c*.900', *Historical Research*, 91 (2018), 580–604; Edward Roberts and Francesca Tinti, 'Signalling language choice in Anglo-Saxon and Frankish charters, *c*.700–*c*.900', in Robert Gallagher, Edward Roberts and Francesca Tinti (eds), *The Languages of Early Medieval Charters: Latin, Germanic Vernaculars, and the Written Word* (Leiden, 2021), pp. 188–229 (pp. 201–2).

36 For a perambulation written substantially in the vernacular, in a charter dated 821, see Aurélien de Courson (ed.), *Cartulaire de l'abbaye de Redon en Bretagne* (Paris, 1863), p. 112, no. 146; see the sample of Redon boundaries listed in Wendy Davies, *Small Worlds: The Village Community in Early Medieval Brittany* (London, 1988), p. 34 n. 6; cf. p. 42. I owe thanks to Oliver Padel for bringing to my attention the types of boundary clause represented in the Cartulary of Redon.

37 All references to Old Welsh forms are taken from Alexander Falileyev, *Etymological Glossary of Old Welsh* (Tübingen, 2000).

38 For the latter, see Marged Haycock, *Prophecies from the Book of Taliesin* (Aberystwyth, 2013), poem 8, l. 40.

39 McKee, *Cambridge Juvencus*, pp. 23–4, 42, 358.

40 For example, J. Lloyd-Jones, *Geirfa Barddoniaeth Gynnar Gymraeg*, 2 vols (Cardiff, 1931–63), I, 54; D. Simon Evans, *A Grammar of Middle Welsh* (Dublin, 1964), p. 196. Uncertainty is expressed in *GPC*, s.v. *bed^1* (2010), *www.geiriadur.ac.uk* (accessed 6 November 2023).

41 Léon Fleuriot, *Dictionnaire des gloses en vieux Breton* (Paris, 1964), pp. 83–4.

42 Disyllabic forms: Fleuriot, *Dictionnaire*, pp. 82–3, 109; monosyllabic forms: Fleuriot, *Dictionnaire*, pp. 84–5, 164–5, 182, 288.

43 Léon Fleuriot, *Le vieux Breton: éléments d'une grammaire* (Paris, 1964), p. 291; cf. Fleuriot, *Dictionnaire*, p. 83.

44 Twelfth-century poems: Kathleen Anne Bramley and others (eds), *Gwaith Llywelyn Fardd I ac Eraill o Feirdd y Ddeuddegfed Ganrif*, CBT II (Cardiff, 1994), poem 4, l. 45 (see too poem 14, l. 5); Egerton G. B. Phillimore, 'A Fragment from Hengwrt MS. No. 202', *Y Cymmrodor*, 7 (1886), 89–154 (p. 154); J. Gwenogvryn Evans, *The Poetry in the Red Book of Hergest* (Llanbedrog, 1911), p. 5, col. 585.21–2. Prose texts: Rachel Bromwich and D. Simon Evans, *Culhwch ac Olwen* (2nd edn, Cardiff, 1997), p. 1, l. 12; Brynley F. Roberts, *Brut y Brenhinedd: Llanstephan MS. 1 Version* (Dublin, 1984), p. 16, l. 503, with note on p. 44. For examples in *Hengerdd*, see Lloyd-Jones, *Geirfa*, I, 405–6; *GPC*, s.v. *di^1*, *dy^2*, *ddi*, *ddy^1* (1960).

45 See Peter Kitson, 'Old English literacy and the provenance of Welsh *y*', in Paul Russell (ed.), *Yr Hen Iaith: Studies in Early Welsh* (Aberystwyth, 2003), pp. 49–65.

46 Sims-Williams, '"Dark" and "Clear" *Y*'.
47 Sims-Williams, '"Dark" and "Clear" *Y*', 10–11.
48 Not counting *LL* 163a, since its doublet, *LL* 73b, suggests that this charter did originally have a boundary clause.
49 *LL* 77 [I.2] = *Dyfrig* §13 (added by scribe B); *LL* 122 [I.11] = *Teilo* §23; *LL* 160 [I.16]; *LL* 165 [I.19]. The latter begins in Latin and then switches to Welsh.
50 *LL* 75 [I.1] = *Dyfrig* §10; *LL* 72a [I.3] = *Dyfrig* §5; *LL* 73b [I.7] = *Dyfrig* §8; *LL* 164 [I.18].
51 For the misunderstanding and the possible reason for the use of <y> here, see Sims-Williams, '"Dark" and "Clear" *Y*', 15–17.
52 *LL* 72b [I.5] = *Dyfrig* §6; *LL* 73a [I.6] = *Dyfrig* §7; *LL* 121 [I.10] = *Teilo* §22.
53 Text and translation adapted from *Teilo* §22.
54 Courson, *Cartulaire*, pp. 112 (no. 146) and 163 (no. 212); cf. Fleuriot, *Dictionnaire*, p. 113; Fleuriot, *Le vieux Breton*, p. 292.
55 *LL* 140 [II.2] = *Euddogwy* §13; *LL* 157 [II.11] = *Euddogwy* §30; *LL* 154 [II.13] = *Euddogwy* §27; *LL* 156 [II.18] = *Euddogwy* §29; *LL* 183b [II.20]; *LL* 190b [II.23] (added by scribe B); *LL* 195 [II.41] = *Clydog* §4; *LL* 209b [II.58].
56 *LL* 143 [II.3] = *Euddogwy* §15; *LL* 147 [II.4] = *Euddogwy* §19; *LL* 159b [II.10] = *Euddogwy* §33; *LL* 148 [II.14] = *Euddogwy* §20; *LL* 176a [II.22]; *LL* 188b [II.26]; *LL* 183a [II.37]; *LL* 202 [II.45]; *LL* 204a [II.47]; *LL* 200 [II.55]; *LL* 210a [II.63].
57 The figure 'nine' includes *LL* 147, which has two convincing boundary clauses, one within the charter and one after it, and *LL* 159b, which has two convincing boundary clauses within the charter.
58 Patrick Sims-Williams, 'The Emergence of Old Welsh, Cornish and Breton Orthography, 600–800: The Evidence of Archaic Old Welsh', *BBCS*, 38 (1991), 20–86 (p. 45).
59 *LL* 180b [II.25] (a doublet of *VSBG* §67, which has no boundary clause); *LL* 206 [II.61]; *LL* 208 [II.64].
60 *LL* 146 [II.12] = *Euddogwy* §18; *LL* 145 [II.17] = *Euddogwy* §17. For further consideration of the boundary of *LL* 146, see Andy Seaman, 'The charter material', in Alan Lane and Mark Redknap (eds), *Llangorse Crannog: The Excavation of an Early Medieval Royal Site in the Kingdom of Brycheiniog* (Oxford, 2019), pp. 414–21 (pp. 420–1); Andy Seaman, 'Llywarch Hen's Dyke: Place and Narrative in Early Medieval Wales', *Offa's Dyke Journal*, 1 (2019), 96–113; Andy Seaman, '*Finnaun y Doudec Seint*: A holy spring in early medieval Brycheiniog, Wales', in Celeste Ray (ed.), *Sacred Waters: A Cross-cultural Compendium of Hallowed Springs and Holy Wells* (London, 2020), pp. 194–210.
61 *LL* 158 [II.30] = *Euddogwy* §31; *LL* 187 [II.31].

62 For further consideration of the boundary clauses in this charter, see Ben Guy and Rory Naismith, 'Lancaut: An Early Eleventh-century Mint-place on the River Wye', *British Numismatic Journal*, 93 (2023), 95–105 (pp. 101–2).

63 *LL* 171b [III.5] (a complicated charter with multiple boundaries; boundaries 3 and 5 are implicated here); *LL* 216b [III.17]; *LL* 227b [III.19]; *LL* 228 [III.21]; *LL* 235b [III.27].

64 *LL* 171b [III.5] (see previous note; boundary 4 is implicated here); *LL* 173 [III.7]; *LL* 212 [III.9]; *LL* 225 [III.12].

65 *LL* 170 [III.1]; *LL* 174a [III.4]; *LL* 171b [III.5] (see two notes above; here boundaries 1–2 are implicated, of which the first is within the charter and the second is after it; the first boundary is reproduced in the doublet *LL* 74 [III.6] = *Dyfrig* §9); *LL* 227a [III.11]; *LL* 199b [III.16]; *LL* 237a [III.25]. A possible seventh is *LL* 229b [III.22], which shares a boundary clause with *LL* 174b [II.21], though it is unclear which charter, if either, originally contained the boundary: see above, pp. 121 and 134–5.

66 *LL* 233 [III.30]; *LL* 239 [III.33]; *LL* 237b [III.34] (boundary shared with *LL* 167; see above, p. 121); *LL* 224 [III.35]; *LL* 223 [III.36].

67 Charles Insley, 'Languages of boundaries and boundaries of language in Cornish charters', in Gallagher, Roberts and Tinti (eds), *The Languages of Early Medieval Charters*, pp. 342–77 (pp. 361–4).

68 *LL* 72b, 73a, 121.

69 *LL* 77 (×2), 122, 160, 165.

70 *LL* 159bi, 183a.

71 *LL* 144, 145, 146, 158, 180b, 187, 206, 208.

72 *LL* 140i, 154, 156, 157, 183b, 190b, 195.

73 *LL* 170, 171bii.

74 *LL* 171biv, 173, 212, 225.

75 *LL* 171biii, 171bv, 216b, 227b, 228, 235b.

76 *LL* 224, 233.

77 *LL* 218, 244i, 244ii.

78 *LL* 246, 249bii, 251i, 251ii

79 *LL* 249a, 255i, 255ii, 257i, 257ii, 259, 261, 262, 263, 264b.

80 *LL* 267, 271, 274.

81 *LL* 42, 125bi, 125biii, 127a, 134ii, 141. Note that the two boundaries in the hand of scribe B (*LL* 77 [I.2] = *Dyfrig* §13 and *LL* 190b [II.23]) have been included in the table among the 'late boundaries' of Sequences I and II respectively.

82 I would like to thank Robert Gallagher, Oliver Padel, Paul Russell, Patrick Sims-Williams and Rebecca Thomas for kindly offering feedback on drafts of this chapter. Responsibility for the final text of course remains my own.

PART II : RHAN II

HISTORY AND IDENTITY : HANES A HUNANIAETH

6

Naming and National Identity: The Monastic Orders in Late Medieval Ireland and Wales Compared

David E. Thornton

In his seminal paper entitled 'British or Welsh? National Identity in Twelfth-century Wales', Professor Huw Pryce argues that the terminological shift among Cambro-Latin writers starting *c*.1120 towards using the English-derived terms *Wallia* and *Walis* to refer to Wales and the Welsh, instead of the older words *Britannia* and *Britones*, 'did not reflect a wholesale redefinition by the Welsh of their concepts of national identity'; thus, he adds, 'notions of Wales and the Welsh as geographical and ethnic entities were already well established by 1100'.[1] The increasing use of *Wallia* and *Walis* did however provide the medieval Welsh with names by which to distinguish themselves not only from their English neighbours but also from their Brittonic ancestors. Indeed, names – whether personal, or in this case, geographical and ethnic – are one means by which, however imperfectly, one's 'identity' may be signalled to others.[2] Events of the late eleventh and early twelfth centuries, in the form of the penetration by the Anglo-Normans into parts of Wales served to muddy the onomastic and ethnic waters. Indeed, as the late Rees Davies stated, Wales was now 'divided ethnically' and the name Welsh becomes contentious.[3] The later concepts of 'the March' and 'Pura Wallia' might offer rough geographical and political means of acknowledging and reflecting this more complex situation, but they certainly did not provide a way of clarifying or redefining ethnicity in Wales. A comparable situation was to develop in Ireland, after *c*.1170, with the political conquest of significant parts of the country by Anglo-Norman lords and their king and thereafter the immigration of settlers from England and Wales. Distinctions between what were called the 'land of peace' and 'lands of war', or between the 'loyal English' and the 'Irish enemies', served to highlight both political divisions and ethnic identities, but certainly oversimplified matters considerably. The purpose of this chapter is to examine, and compare, the anthroponymic or naming patterns among monastic orders in Wales and Ireland between *c*.1200 and *c*.1540 to determine to what extent personal names reflected the ethnic identities of individual monks and regular canons, and also therefore what this may reveal about the recruitment to, and collective identities of, the relevant monasteries.

Monasteries and ethnic identity and conflict

There is plenty of evidence to demonstrate that even these – in theory – peaceful, inward-looking religious communities were not immune to the polarising and often violent political and social struggles that could rage beyond the walls of their respective cloisters. It is clear that the military conquest and political control of significant parts of Wales and Ireland by the Normans, along with the accompanying settlement in these countries of large numbers of immigrants from England (and, for Ireland, from Wales also), were events that affected and concerned not only the native Welsh and Irish laity – especially, but not exclusively, the ruling elites – but that these political and social changes played out also among the clergy, both secular and regular. For Ireland, most infamously perhaps was the so-called 'Mellifont Conspiracy' that embroiled the Cistercian abbeys during the early thirteenth century. Although recent arguments have suggested that this event was not entirely based on 'racial disharmony',[4] it seems that, after *c*.1170, there came to be in Ireland what have been called 'two virtually separate Cistercian orders': those affiliated to Mellifont – the first Cistercian abbey founded in Ireland (1142) – and those of Norman foundation, affiliated to English and Welsh abbeys.[5] By *c*.1216–17, Mellifont and many of its daughter-houses were effectively in rebellion against both the General Chapter and the Norman-founded abbeys in Ireland, and it was only through the actions of the English visitor Stephen of Lexington, abbot of Stanley, in 1228, that this 'Irish' conspiracy was eventually quashed. The problems did not stop there, however, and we find various accusations from the later thirteenth and fourteenth centuries of 'racially' motivated discrimination at Cistercian houses in Ireland. In the so-called 'Remonstrance of the Irish Princes' of 1317–18, it was claimed that the monks of both

Granard (Abbeylara) and Inch were inclined to attack and kill Irish as well as celebrate Mass, while three years later Edward II alleged that at Mellifont (again!) admission was only granted to postulants able to swear an oath that they were not English or to demonstrate that they were not related to the English.[6] Such racially motivated discrimination, by members of both 'nations' of medieval Ireland, was not restricted to the white monks, and similar claims were made for houses of other orders, on both sides of the national divide. More generally, throughout the fourteenth century, as part of a series of attempts to restrict the legal status and movement of 'mere Irish', the Parliament in Ireland passed a number of acts that sought to prohibit the admission of non-English into monasteries located within the English colony, with the threat of seizure of lands for noncompliance.[7] Interestingly enough, around 1335–7, the 'religious of Ireland' petitioned Edward III requesting that, in order to avoid discord between the English and Irish, those loyal Irish who were born and living within the king's territories should be admitted to religious orders there.[8]

For Wales, there is no event comparable to the Mellifont Conspiracy or acts of the Irish Parliament, but there is some evidence to suggest that Welsh monks and canons were not immune to such ethnic or racial disputes. Prior to the Edwardian Conquest, the close association of Welsh monasteries, and especially the Cistercian abbeys, located in *Pura Wallia*, with native Welsh rulers is well documented but is perhaps hardly surprising.[9] After the Conquest, there are a few occasional hints of ethnically or racially motivated actions by religious in Wales. For instance, in 1328, it was alleged that at Strata Marcella abbey 'unlawful assemblies to excite contentions and hatred between the English and the Welsh have been entered into', and the king duly requested of the abbot of Cîteaux that a visitation be made and that the Welsh monks of the abbey should be dispersed.[10] On a more national scale, it was the rebellion of Owain Glyndŵr, 1400–9, that seems to have divided the regular clergy (or the heads of their houses at least) along ethnic lines. As Rees Davies pointed out, from among the regular clergy, Owain drew his most 'ready and predictable' support especially from the Cistercian and Augustinian monasteries 'that were seen as essentially Welsh in orientation and sympathies'.[11] The abbots of Aberconwy, Strata Florida and Whitland, and the priors of Bardsey and Beddgelert, were duly implicated as rebels, and most notably Abbot John ap Hywel of

Llantarnam was killed in battle in 1405 on Glyndŵr's side.[12] How far these actions indicated pro-independence sympathies on the part of these superiors and their respective monasteries, or how far they were responses to 'practical politics', is a matter worth further consideration.[13]

Discussions of the ethnic or national identities of religious houses in late medieval Wales and Ireland have relied mostly, though not exclusively, upon the names of their brethren.[14] The assumption is that the forenames, surnames and occasional nicknames of the monks, regular canons and nuns can to some extent provide an indication of their bearers' ethnic backgrounds and, therefore, when taken collectively for a whole monastic community, may be one means of determining the identity and sympathies of the relevant monastery itself. Institutions are, after all, essentially no more than the sum of the individuals who live and/or work in them, and for many of the individuals who were admitted to religious houses in the late Middle Ages we often know little more about them than their names. The anthroponymic evidence used for this study is based upon the ongoing collection of prosopographical data for religious houses in Wales and in Ireland between c.1200 and 1540. For Wales, I have previously analysed the names of over 1,000 Cistercians, collected thanks largely to the tireless efforts of Revd Dr David H. Williams, to which may be added about 1,500 references to members of other religious houses in Wales.[15] The Irish database currently comprises over 10,000 entries though it is certainly incomplete as it stands. The relatively poor survival of records of ordination[16] for both Wales and Ireland means that prosopographical data is largely based upon passing notices in various other primary sources, such as charters and deeds – including for Wales those of the native rulers edited by Huw Pryce (*AWR*) – and for Irish monasteries, notices in papal registers and the *Annates*.[17] The sporadic nature of these sources and, for many of the Welsh and Irish houses examined for this chapter, the often small size of their respective monastic communities[18] means that for these monasteries we have relatively few names, especially when compared with the larger English abbeys.

The development of names in medieval Ireland and Wales

Before examining the onomastic evidence, it is necessary to consider the nature and development of both forenames and also the various types of secondary names, especially family surnames, in medieval Wales and Ireland to determine what they can, and cannot, tell us. Forenames reveal much about their bearers or, more accurately in many cases, about their bearers' parents or name-givers. In early medieval western Europe, and especially in Britain and Ireland, most individuals would have had forenames derived from words or phrases in their native, vernacular languages, though the use of Latin and 'Christian' (Classical or Hebrew) forenames was not unknown.[19] It was only during the eleventh and twelfth centuries that a relatively small corpus of Christian and Continental Germanic names began to supplement and eventually replace the local vernacular forenames in many areas. In England, this process began following the Norman Conquest and these new names soon spread into parts of Wales and Scotland, and a century or so later into Ireland.[20] This spread was partly a product of the growing cultural and political hegemony of the new 'Anglo-Norman' or Angevin realm, but was also as a direct result of the migration of settlers, initially from northern France and later from England, into these so-called 'Celtic' regions. Thus, when seeking to establish the possible ethnic or national identity of an individual in later medieval Wales or Ireland, a linguistic analysis of their forenames does not necessarily indicate their ethnicity.[21] While someone called Hywel was probably a Welshman, and Muirchertach was presumably Irish, the ethnic identities of those called *Johannes* or *Willelmus* are less readily determined from the forenames alone.[22]

In addition to the linguistic origin of a forename, other patterns of name-giving also enable us to ascertain or guess the ethnic or cultural backgrounds of their bearers. Thus, some non-local forenames gained greater currency in certain areas than in others – such as for Wales David and, before *c.*1300 at least, Adam – to the extent that they may be considered local in a cultural, if not linguistic, sense. Furthermore, I have discussed elsewhere with reference to medieval Wales the notion of 'equivalent' forenames: that is, Classical, Christian or Continental names that either were written by non-local scribes to render what were to them unfamiliar local forenames or, in some cases, even came to be given by the local population instead of the original, linguistically local name.[23] In Wales, for example, the Welsh name Hywel could be rendered using the Continental name *Hugo* (Hugh).[24] The occurrence of such equivalent names in medieval Ireland was particularly notable in English and papal documents.²⁵ In some cases, the choice of the equivalent was based simply upon its having the same initial letter or similar first syllable (thus, Conchabhar often occurs as *Cornelius*) but, sometimes, the two forenames have a broader similarity (Donnchadh as *Donatus*; Tadhg as *Thaddeus*). The common medieval Irish forenames that combine the words *Giolla* and *Maol* with a second element, often a saint's name,²⁶ could be rendered by *Gillebertus* (Gilbert) and *Malachias* (Malachy), or by means of an equivalent based on the second, hagiophoric element: thus, the many Irishmen named Patrick (*Patricius*) in papal and English royal documents were probably called Giolla Pádraig.²⁷ In some cases, the equivalent name could be used to render more than one Irish forename (*Mattheus* was used to represent both Mathghamhain and Muirgheas), and different scribes might use alternative equivalents for the same Gaelic forename (Aodh occurs as both Odo and Hugh). While a handful of these equivalents were quite frequent as forenames in medieval and early modern Europe in general (Hugh and Gilbert), the less frequent usage of most (Cornelius, Thaddeus) means we may safely assume, in these cases, that their bearers were in fact Irish.

As well as given names or forenames, one's identity (ethnic and otherwise) may be reflected in one's surname. The modern surname – in the sense of a family name usually inherited patrilineally – developed by different routes and became fixed at different times in the various parts of Britain and Ireland during the Middle Ages. In England, the surname underwent a gradual development: some Norman noble families had hereditary second names but it was only during the fourteenth century that most occupants of southern England came to have fixed hereditary surnames, and it took a little longer in the north.²⁸ In Wales, such surnames followed in the wake of the colonisation of, and migration into, parts of the country from England, both in the early twelfth century and also after *c*.1280. Many Welshmen who lived and worked within the English-controlled regions and towns found it convenient to adopt this surname system, but the majority continued to be known rather by the traditional Welsh patronymic system, whereby both men and women were designated as the son (*mab*, later *ap*) or daughter (*merch*, lenited *ferch*) of their fathers – sometimes supplemented with a descriptive nickname.²⁹ This patronymic system was widespread among the medieval Welsh and persisted in some areas even into the nineteenth century. It also explains why, when Welsh surnames did begin to develop (in the sixteenth century and later), the vast majority were patronymic in origin: Pryce and Price derive from *ap Rhys*. A few Welsh surnames proper derive from nicknames (notably Lloyd, from W. *llwyd*, grey) but hardly any are based on occupations or place-names.

The situation in late medieval Ireland was different yet again. Indeed, the Irish may well rightly claim to be among the first Europeans to have adopted a system of hereditary surnames.[30] Like the Welsh and some other early medieval peoples, the Gaels in both Ireland and Scotland had traditionally used a patronymic system of naming: individuals were generally recorded as the son (*mac*) or daughter (*ingen*) of their father, with a few men known rather as the grandson (*ua*) of their father's father. Perhaps as early as the tenth century, and definitely during the eleventh, some of these patronymics had become fixed among certain royal and aristocratic families at least, and definitely by the late Middle Ages, Irishmen both high and low were invariably known by their forename plus a hereditary patronymic surname based either on the prefix Mac- (Mc, <*mac*) or Ó/Ua- (O', <*ua*). Thus, even more so than among the Welsh much later, Gaelic surnames in the strictest sense were invariably patronymic in origin, based on one of those prefixes plus a male ancestor's forename.[31] As in Wales, the Anglo-Norman invasion of Ireland and the subsequent colonial occupation of (varying) parts of Ireland by the English royal government led to the migration into those regions of settlers from parts of England and Wales, bringing with them Norman and English surnames, as well as coining new English-style surnames in Ireland. Within these regions, the native Irish were faced with several onomastic choices. Particularly after the extent of its territory began to shrink in the wake of the Gaelic political revival, from the late thirteenth century onwards, the colonial administration in Ireland took a number of measures to control the movement and legal status of the native Irish within this territory, including regulations concerning names. The Statute of Kilkenny (1366) required Englishmen to be called by an English name, and a century later the Irish Parliament passed a law stipulating that an Irishman who lived within the English territories should 'take unto himself an English surname'.[32] In this case, whole new surnames could be adopted, or existing Gaelic patronymic surnames could be adapted by dropping the Mac/Ó- prefix.[33]

For members of the monastic orders in late medieval England, the situation was complicated by the widespread practice whereby a newly admitted monk or regular canon would cease to be known by his family surname but adopt instead what I have termed a 'monastic byname'.[34] This byname was generally a place-name, probably indicating its bearer's place of birth or recent origin, but by the end of the fifteenth century a saint's name or, very rarely, a religious virtue could be adopted instead. At most monasteries, over 80 per cent of the brethren had such a toponymic byname. Analysis of the 'surnames' of Welsh Cistercians has shown that this English system of monastic bynames was current at some abbeys, but at others it was not.[35] While the adoption of monastic bynames was perhaps more common at abbeys closer to the English border, this does not in itself prove that the relevant individual monks were themselves all English or identified as such. The practice of monastic bynaming is not attested in Ireland, except at those dependent cells manned largely by monks from a mother house in England. Even for the monasteries located in or near Dublin, where English customs and influence would be greatest, the names of the monks and canons represent a mixture of surname types (Norman, locative, occupational, descriptive, etc.). When toponyms do occur, they are generally derived from places in England or Wales and are probably, in most cases, the surnames of the bearer's settler families and not the places from which the bearers themselves had come prior to admission.

The names of regular canons in late medieval Wales and Ireland

In order to illustrate the various issues discussed briefly above, and to offer a provisional methodology for the analysis of names of medieval Welsh and Irish monks and regular canons, the remainder of this chapter will examine in more detail, and compare, the anthroponymic data from three Augustinian monasteries in Wales and three in Ireland. In each case we will briefly examine the names – forenames and 'surnames' – of the canons and priors collectively to suggest the ethnic character of the six monasteries in question. Forenames that are linguistically Welsh, or Irish, will be taken as evidence of a Welsh, or Irish, ethnic identity of their bearers, though in late medieval Ireland at least it was not unknown for a few English to bear an Irish name or nickname.[36] Linguistically non-local forenames are of course ambiguous but those that were used culturally as local names will also be counted, as will, especially for Ireland, those less common Classical or Christian names than were rendered as equivalents of local forenames. In the case of cultural and equivalent names, it should not necessarily be assumed that every single one of their bearers was *ipso facto* Welsh, or Irish, but rather that the relative frequency of these names can serve as a guide to possible ethnicity of the whole convent. For surnames, those that can be regarded as Welsh patronymics and nicknames, or Irish patronymic surnames proper, speak for themselves, though for Ireland we should not forget those Gaelicised Anglo-Irish noble families who adopted Irish versions of their surnames (such as *Mac Fheórais* used by the Berminghams). Toponymic or 'locative' surnames are more difficult to interpret, for the various reasons discussed above, but at least those derived from place-names in Wales, or Ireland, may be enumerated, even though their bearers may not necessarily have identified themselves as Welsh, or Irish. Taken together, these various name forms may therefore facilitate an understanding of the recruitment to, and the ethnic composition of, a regular community over time.

The Augustinian priory at Llanthony Prima, Monmouthshire, was founded by Hugh de Lacy, Norman lord of Ewyas, probably 1108×1118, and was located close to the English border.[37] It had a number of dependent cells, notably in Ireland (see below) and also, for a time, Llanthony Secunda at Gloucester. The two Llanthonys were officially separated in 1205, and in 1481 they were reunited but now with the former cell at Gloucester as the mother house. From *c*.1200 down to the 1530s, the names of up to 128 Augustinian canons of Llanthony Prima can be found in the extant sources.[38] Of these, twenty-two are mentioned with forenames only (mostly for the thirteenth century) and, of the remaining 106, I have been able to analyse the surnames of ninety-five canons. This analysis reveals the English character of the conventual community at Llanthony Prima.[39] None of the 128 canons had a linguistically Welsh forename, though two were called David, three Adam and three called Hugh that could be equivalent for Hywel (above). About 75 per cent bore surnames analysed derived from place-names, which suggests that they were following the 'English model' of adopting toponymic bynames on admission. Furthermore, most of the underlying place-names were from places in England, with a maximum of six derived from places in Wales, and one Irishman.[40] Of the remaining canons, nine had patronymic surnames, but none of these can necessarily be considered Welsh as such: none used the *ap* formula, and none of the underlying forenames was Welsh in origin.[41]

The distinctly English character of the community at Llanthony Prima becomes clearer if we compare the names of its canons with those from other Augustinian houses in Wales. The Priory of St John the Evangelist, Carmarthen, was established as an Augustinian house by Bernard, the Norman bishop of St David's, in or before 1127, when a short-lived Benedictine community from Battle Abbey was replaced with the canons regular.[42] The names of fifty-eight canons of Carmarthen have been identified: fifty-four occur with surnames, and forty-nine have been analysed here. Of the fifty-eight canons, at least twelve had forenames that may be considered Welsh in character.[43] Of the forty-nine surnames analysed, only about eleven (22.5 per cent) were toponymic or topographical, whereas twenty-seven appear to be patronymic in origin (55 per cent). A third of these twenty-seven patronymic surnames were Welsh *ap*-patronymics. Of the toponyms, four may be associated with Welsh places, the rest in England. In contrast, the priory at Beddgelert, Caernarvonshire, located in the Welsh heartland of Gwynedd and probably founded before 1230 by Llywelyn ab Iorwerth,[44] presents a different pattern, though it is relatively poorly documented. To date, a grand total of eighteen canons and priors can be identified, with only eight bearing a surname.[45] Admittedly, this represents a very small sample from which to generalise, but we find, of the eighteen forenames, that eight were linguistically Welsh, to which may be one David and one Adam, plus the equivalent names Hugh and Maurice. The eight surnames include four patronymics (all with *ap*), three toponyms (all of local places),[46] and one Welsh nickname/descriptive byname (Lloyd). This combination of Welsh forenames, Welsh patronymics and local place-names points to a rather different canonical population at Beddgelert than at Llanthony Prima especially.

Table 1 below attempts to summarise and compare the anthroponymic evidence outlined above for these three Augustinian monasteries by highlighting the Welsh – and possibly Welsh – naming patterns by showing: the percentage of all forenames that were linguistically or culturally Welsh, or were common equivalents of Welsh names; the percentage of the analysed 'surnames' that were Welsh (patronymics or nicknames, not toponyms); and, the percentage of the toponymic surnames derived from places in Wales. While the last criterion need not indicate that the bearers of Welsh toponyms were – or regarded themselves as – Welshmen, the distinct results for the three houses are still revealing.

Table 1: Welsh names of Augustinian canons

House	Welsh forenames (% of all canons)	Welsh surnames (% of analysed surnames)	Welsh toponyms (% of toponyms)
Llanthony Prima	6	0	8
Carmarthen	21	22	36
Beddgelert	67	62.5	100

At Llanthony Prima, there were no linguistically Welsh forenames and only a few possible culturally and equivalent Welsh forenames; nor can any of the 'surnames' be regarded as Welsh (patronymics or nicknames). Furthermore, fewer than 10 per cent of the toponymic surnames from Llanthony derive from places in Wales and all of these are recorded before Llanthony Prima became dependent on the priory at Gloucester. The evidence for Welsh names is more forthcoming for all three criteria at Carmarthen Priory, and significantly higher still for the admittedly poorly documented Beddgelert community. Taken together, these figures suggest that the monastic community at Llanthony Prima was almost exclusively English in character, with a significant non-local element, whereas at Beddgelert the convent was largely Welsh and local. At Carmarthen, the community seems to have been 'mixed' insofar as its canons included many Welshmen as well as others whose names would suggest an English identity and/or non-local origin.[47]

For Ireland, we may consider the names of the canons of another three Augustinian monasteries. The very well-documented Arrouasian canonical community at Holy Trinity (Christ Church) Cathedral Priory, Dublin, owed its origin to the introduction of the Augustinian rule by pre-Norman Archbishop Laurence O'Toole in or around 1162.[48] By the late twelfth century of course, the priory was located within the centre of English colonial rule in Ireland, which will have affected the nature of its conventual community. A total of 252 individual canons and priors have been identified to date, thanks to the survival of the priory's relatively extensive archive, including its Book of Obits.[49] Some of these canons may be duplicates because the necrology records sixty-nine canons (out of 218) who are given with their forename only. It may be suspected, though beyond proof, that most of the canons recorded without a surname date from the earlier period of the priory's history. An analysis of the names of these 252 brethren of Holy Trinity provides some interesting conclusions. As we might expect, the overall impression is of a conventual community that was largely 'English' in character, at least onomastically speaking. Thus, of the 252, the majority had forenames that conform to the late medieval Continental/Christian naming pattern discussed briefly above: over half the canons had one of just five popular 'European' forenames,[50] and a further one-third at least had other, less common such names. However, there are among the remaining brethren a small yet conspicuous number of Gaelic and Gaelic-equivalent forenames that indicate Irish identity or ancestry;[51] it is perhaps significant that most of these are recorded in the obit list without an accompanying surname, perhaps suggesting that their bearers were relatively early members of the Holy Trinity canonical convent. Turning to the surnames, 171 canons of the cathedral priory are recorded with surnames, of which 150 have been analysed so far. Most of these (eighty, or 53 per cent) are derived from place-names, with about seven more being topographical. This is a sizable number, but not as many as the 80 per cent or more at English monasteries associated with the adoption of toponymic bynames on admission. Indeed, the fact that most of these names are for places in England (and a few in Wales) suggests that these were the hereditary surnames of local families in Dublin and its environs descended from Anglo-Norman, English and Welsh settlers. A handful of the toponyms are however derived from places in Ireland, some quite a distance from Dublin,[52] and these were either hereditary locative surnames or, at a pinch, could indicate the places of origin of the individual canons. At least eleven canons had surnames derived from personal names, that is patronymic in origin, but none of these would seem to be Gaelic patronymic surnames, with the slight possible exception of William *Owen* who, however, is described in the obit list as *sacerdos noster* and may not have been a regular canon therefore. A number of the surnames were clearly of Anglo-Norman origin (Comin, Darcy, Beauchamp and Butler).

Greatconnell Priory was founded in 1202 by the Cambro-Norman justiciar Meiler FitzHenry, originally as a dependent priory of Llanthony Prima (above).[53] While its location places it in the so-called 'four obedient shires', it was within the 'outer' Pale, subject later to the Gaelicised Geraldine Earls of Kildare. In theory, Greatconnell was an 'English' monastery: thus, in 1380, it was among those monasteries required to admit only English postulants; and in 1537, Walter Wellesley, the penultimate prior and also bishop of Kildare, wrote to Thomas Cromwell complaining of the impoverishment of the priory due to the proximity of the 'wild Irish rebellers', while adding that 'no brother is elected unless he be of the English nation'.[54] An analysis of the handful of the recoverable names of priors and canons of the house indicates however that Wellesley was being somewhat liberal with the truth. Up to thirty-seven individuals may be associated with Greatconnell, of whom most (twenty-eight) are recorded with surnames. Six canons are recorded with Gaelic or Gaelic-equivalent forenames; and while many of the surnames are evidently Anglo-Norman or English in origin, such as Blake, Lawless, Punchard and Wellesley, nine were certainly Irish patronymic surnames including one prior who was called *Bayly* but also had the Irish alias *Mcnulli* (<Mac Con Uladh?).[55] Few canons of Greatconnell bore locative surnames, especially if we exclude Norman names such as *de Rocheford*, though one, *de Teaghmolyn*, was certainly of Irish origin (Timolin, Co. Kildare). By the fifteenth century at least, the canonical community at Greatconnell would seem to have been relatively ethnically mixed, as far as the names of its inmates indicate. Indeed, Bishop Wellesley himself is known to have admitted two Irishmen as recently as 1535![56]

The Arrouasian priory of St Mary, Clontuskert Omany (Cluain Tuaiscirt Ua Máine), Co. Galway, was located well within the heartland of Gaelic Ireland, in the old kingdom of Uí Mháine, Connaught.[57] It is traditionally regarded as having been founded, as well as patronised, by the local Uí Cheallaigh (O'Kelly) lords, some of whom were kings of Uí Mháine. As with Greatconnell, the evidence for members of this community is much more sparse than for Holy Trinity Cathedral Priory, and is based mostly on references in the papal registers.[58] Up to thirty-five canons and priors can be identified to date, all recorded with both forename and surname. An onomastic analysis of this sample reveals a very different pattern when compared to those for both Holy Trinity and Greatconnell. Only eleven of the canons of Clontuskert had what have been termed European Continental or Christian forenames: John and William (both three times), plus one Walter, one Nicholas and, perhaps suspiciously, three called Maurice. The remainder had forenames that were either Irish[59] or were commonly attested equivalent names.[60]

The surnames reflect a similar, and even clearer, Irish bias: almost all canons had Irish patronymic surnames, with the exception of one Anglo-Norman surname *de Burgo*. At least half of the canons were called O'Kelly, and others were apparently members of different Uí Mhaine septs.[61] Even the *de Burgo* prior of Clontuskert in 1507–9 was presumably of the Gaelicised Clanricard Burkes of Galway.

The anthroponymic evidence from these three Irish Augustinian monasteries may be summarised in tabular form thus:

Table 2: Irish names of Augustinian canons

House	Irish forenames (% of all canons)	Irish surnames (% of analysed surnames)	Irish toponyms (% of toponyms)
Holy Trinity	7	<1	10
Greatconnell	16	32	3.5
Clontuskert Omany	68	97	–

Here the contrast between the three priories is even more marked than for those in Wales. While it is perhaps not surprising that the monastic community at Holy Trinity Cathedral Priory, located as it was at the centre of English rule in Ireland, was largely English in character, whereas that at Clontuskert was essentially Gaelic, the onomastic material summarised above would suggest that matters were not always so black and white at many late medieval Irish religious houses. The occurrence of Gaelic forenames or equivalent forenames at Holy Trinity suggests that, during the late twelfth and thirteenth centuries at least, Irishmen had in fact been admitted to the priory. At Greatconnell, the rather varied pattern implies that, outside the core area of English colonial administration, and especially in areas under the control of the often rebellious and so-called 'degenerate' Anglo-Irish lords, recruitment to religious houses could in fact be more flexible and mixed.

Conclusion

In my study of the Welsh Cistercians, I attempted to compare the analyses of the names of the monks of individual abbeys with other possible indicators of political, cultural and ethnic associations.[62] In terms of patronage and benefaction, the situation among the Cistercians was not straightforward: as Huw Pryce has discussed, the native rulers certainly had a strong association with the white monks, in terms of foundation, patronage and benefaction, but they also made donations to houses of other orders, even in England.[63] For the six Augustinian houses considered here, we may note that Beddgelert and Clontuskert priories – where the onomastic evidence for Welsh and Irish identity respectively was strongest – had both been founded by native lay rulers and were located within territories (for Wales, until c.1282 at least) that were traditionally under native political control. In addition, it is perhaps not surprising that, of the three Augustinian houses in Wales, it was only the prior of Beddgelert who was outlawed for his alleged support for the rebellion of Owain Glyndŵr.[64] In contrast, it is no wonder that an early thirteenth-century Llanthony chronicler referred to the Welsh as 'savage, without any religion, vagabonds, and delighted in stealth'.[65] Another indicator, discussed with reference to the Cistercians, is their strong association with Welsh culture, and especially the production and transmission of Welsh and Welsh-language historical and literary texts, especially in the thirteenth century,[66] as well as the patronage by Cistercian abbots of Welsh *uchelwyr* (gentry, noble) poets during the fifteenth and early sixteenth centuries.[67] Of the Augustinian houses considered here, we may note that it is Carmarthen Priory, with its onomastically mixed English and Welsh canonical community, that stands out: it was there, in the mid-thirteenth century, that the early Welsh-language manuscript known as the Black Book of Carmarthen was probably produced,[68] and Morgan (alias Maurice) Winter, prior of Carmarthen c.1454–69,[69] was the subject of a praise poem or *moliant* by Lewys Glyn Cothi, in which he is referred to as a 'son to Owain ab Einion' (*mab i Owain ab Einion*).[70] In addition, however, we may note that Lewys Daron composed a request poem addressed to Dafydd Conwy, the last prior of the otherwise poorly documented Beddgelert Priory (*fl.* 1501/2–35).[71] In contrast, but not surprisingly, Llanthony Prima, with its essentially English convent, is known to have owned or produced many Latin manuscripts but none that indicates a knowledge or use of Welsh.[72] Comparable evidence from late medieval Ireland for the monastic patronage, production and transmission of vernacular Gaelic culture is largely lacking, because such work was for the most part in the hands of the so-called learned families. Thus, Fr. Canice

Mooney pointed out that the Augustinian canons were not interested in the native Irish tradition of scholarship or at least lost interest over time.[73] A few individual exceptions are known, such as the historian Adhamh Ó Cianáin, who died in 1373 as a canon of Lisgoole, Order of St Augustine, but he was himself a member of a learned family and had probably entered the monastery relatively late in life.[74]

As these various Welsh and Irish examples indicate, patterns of personal naming could differ significantly at individual monasteries, and such differences would seem indeed to reflect the ethnic or 'national' composition of the relevant religious communities. As the examples above show, however, the distribution of name and name-types was not always simple and straightforward. Thus, further detailed study of such naming patterns may serve to highlight other factors that affected naming and/or recruitment. In addition, the location of a monastery certainly determined the ethnic composition of its religious community, but other factors may also have influenced the admission to religious houses and thus the naming patterns of their convents. For example, do we see changes in names at individual houses over time, as apparently occurred at Holy Trinity Cathedral Priory?[75] How far, in Gaelic Ireland especially, did the increasing control of many monasteries by local lords and their families, such as the Uí Cheallaigh at Clontuskert Omany, and the notable decline in clerical celibacy, affect the recruitment to religious houses?[76] In addition, to what extent could monasteries that were dependent or alien priories admit local postulants and how far were such houses, like the Benedictine priories in south Wales, largely foreign-manned institutions?[77] Lastly, this article has focused on male religious communities, for which the primary sources are in general more extensive, but what can be said about the names and nationality of nuns and canonesses?[78] It is hoped that further data collection and research will serve to throw onomastic light on these and other related questions.

Notes

1 Huw Pryce, 'British or Welsh? National Identity in Twelfth-century Wales', *English Historical Review*, 116 (2001), 775–801 (p. 799).

2 For the use of ethnic names in medieval Wales, see Frederick Suppe, 'Medieval Welsh Ethnic Nicknames and Implications: for the Welsh View

of their Geopolitical Context, 1050–1400', in Christian Raffensperger (ed.), *Authorship, Worldview, and Identity in Medieval Europe* (Abingdon and New York, 2022), pp. 327–45.

3   R. R. Davies, 'The Identity of "Wales" in the Thirteenth Century', in R. R. Davies and Geraint H. Jenkins (eds), *From Medieval to Modern Wales: Historical Essays in Honour of Kenneth O. Morgan and Ralph A. Griffiths* (Cardiff, 2004), pp. 45–63 (p. 51).

4   Brendan Smith, 'The Armagh-Clogher Dispute and the "Mellifont Conspiracy": Diocesan Politics and Monastic Reform in Early Thirteenth Century Ireland', *Seanchas Ardmhacha: Journal of the Armagh Diocesan Historical Society*, 14/2 (1991), 26–38.

5   Roger Stalley, *The Cistercian Monasteries of Ireland: An Account of the History, Art, and Architecture of the White Monks in Ireland from 1142–1540* (London and New Haven, 1987), p. 16.

6   Stalley, *The Cistercian Monasteries of Ireland*, p. 22; J. A. Watt, *The Church and the Two Nations in Medieval Ireland* (Cambridge, 1970), pp. 188–9; for the Remonstrance, see Edmund Curtis and R. B. McDowell, *Irish Historical Documents, 1172–1922* (London, 1943), pp. 38–46; H. C. Maxwell Lyte, *Calendar of Close Rolls, Edward II: 1318–1323* (London, 1895), p. 404.

7   For example, Henry FitzPatrick Berry, *Statutes and Ordinances, and Acts of the Parliament of Ireland: King John to Henry V* (Dublin, 1907), pp. 272–3 (1310), 444–7 (1366), 481 (1380).

8   James F. Ferguson, 'The "Mere English" and "Mere Irish"', *Transactions of the Kilkenny Archaeological Society*, 1/3 (1851), 508–12 (p. 511).

9   J. E. Lloyd, *A History of Wales from the Earliest Times to the Edwardian Conquest*, 2 vols (3rd edn, London, 1939), II, 597; R. R. Davies, *The Age of Conquest: Wales 1063–1415* (Oxford, 1987), pp. 196–7.

10 H. C. Maxwell Lyte, *Calendar of Close Rolls, Edward III: 1333–1337* (London, 1898), p. 150; David H. Williams, *The Welsh Cistercians: Written to Commemorate the Centenary of the Death of Stephen William Williams (1837–1899) (The Father of Cistercian Archaeology in Wales)* (Leominster, 2001), p. 43.

11 R. R. Davies, *The Revolt of Owain Glyn Dŵr* (Oxford, 1995), p. 211.

12 Davies, *The Revolt of Owain Glyn Dŵr*, p. 212.

13 Williams, *The Welsh Cistercians*, pp. 52–3; but compare Karen Stöber, 'Island Monasteries in Medieval Wales', in Gabriela Signori (ed.), *Inselklöster – Klosterinseln: Topographie und Toponymie einer monastischen Formation* (Berlin, 2019), pp. 83–99 (p. 90); and Glanmor Williams, *The Welsh Church from Conquest to Reformation* (Cardiff, 1976), p. 220.

14 For example, Huw Pryce, 'The Medieval Church', in J. Beverley Smith and Llinos Beverley Smith (eds), *History of Merioneth. Volume II. The Middle Ages* (Cardiff, 2001), pp. 254–96 (p. 284).

15 David E. Thornton, 'A *Mynach* by Any Other Name …: The Anthroponymy of the Welsh Cistercians, *c*.1300–1540', *WHR*, 30 (2021), 429–68; David H. Williams, 'Fasti Cistercienses Cambrenses', *Archaeologia Cambrensis*, 163 (2014), 185–235.

16 David E. Thornton, 'How Useful are Episcopal Ordination Lists as a Source for Medieval English Monastic History?', *Journal of Ecclesiastical History*, 69/3 (2018), 493–530.

17 W. H. Bliss et al., *Calendar of Papal Registers Relating to Great Britain and Ireland*, 23 vols to date (London and Dublin, 1893–); M. A. Costello, *De Annatis Hiberniae. A Calendar of the First Fruits' Fees Levied on Papal Appointments to Benefices in Ireland A.D. 1400 to 1535 Extracted from the Vatican and other Roman Archives. Volume I: Ulster* (Dundalk, 1909), and 'Obligationes pro Annatis Diocesis Dublinensis, 1421–1520', *Archivium Hibernicum*, 2 (1913), 1–37, 39–72, and other dioceses published in later volumes of the same journal.

18 Williams, *The Welsh Church*, pp. 391–2, 561–3.

19 J. R. Davies, 'Old Testament Personal Names among the Britons: Their Occurrence and Significance before the Twelfth Century', *Viator: Medieval and Renaissance Studies*, 43/1 (2012), 175–92.

20 David A. Postles, 'The Baptismal Name in Thirteenth-century England: Processes and Patterns', *Medieval Prosopography*, 13/2 (1992), 1–52; Dave Postles, *Naming the People of England, c.1100–1350* (Newcastle, 2006), pp. 52–3, 74; Joel T. Rosenthal, 'Names and Naming Patterns in Medieval England: An Introduction', in Dave Postles and Joel T. Rosenthal (eds), *Studies on the Personal Name in Later Medieval England and Wales* (Kalamazoo, 2006), pp. 1–6 (pp. 4–5).

21 For some studies of Welsh and Irish forenames, see Melville Richards, 'Gwŷr, Gwragedd a Gwehelyth', *Transactions of the Honourable Society of the Cymmrodorion* (1965), 27–45; Peter C. Bartrum, 'Personal Names in Wales in the Fifteenth Century', *NLWJ*, 22/4 (1981–2), 462–9; Brian Ó Cuív, 'Aspects of Irish Personal Names', *Celtica*, 18 (1986), 151–84; Donnchadh Ó Corráin and Fidelma Maguire, *Gaelic Personal Names* (Dublin, 1981).

22 For convenience, we may include those Latin forenames borrowed by the Britons and Cymricised very early, thus rendering them effectively 'Welsh': for example, Ieuan from *Johannes*, Meurig from *Mauricius* and possibly Owain from *Eugenius*. See Richards, 'Gwŷr, Gwragedd a Gwehelyth', 32–3.

23 Thornton, 'A *Mynach*', 439.

24 Other equivalents include Gervase for Iorwerth, Geoffrey for Gruffuth, *Lodovicus* (Lewis) for Llywelyn, and Maurice for Morgan.

25 For a discussion of Latinised versions of Irish personal names during the twelfth century, see Marie Therese Flanagan, *The Transformation of the Irish Church in the Twelfth Century* (Woodbridge, 2010), pp. 108–11.

26 David E. Thornton, 'Names within Names: Hagiophoric and Toponymic Anthroponymy in Early Medieval Ireland', in K. S. B. Keats-Rohan and Christian Settipani (eds), *Onomastique et Parenté dans l'Occident medieval: Prosopographica et Genealogica II* (Oxford, 2000), pp. 267–82.

27 Thus, we can safely assume that the late 'Patrick Omoluger', abbot of St Mary's Clogher (Order of St Augustine), mentioned retrospectively in the Papal Registers in 1444, was the same man as *Giolla Patraicc Ua Maol Uidhir*, abbot of Clogher whose death is recorded *sub anno* 1441 in various Irish annals: Bliss et al., *Calendar of Papal Registers*, IX, 324; William B. Hennessy and B. Mac Carthy, *Annala Uladh. Annals of Ulster. Otherwise Annala Senait. Annals of Senat; A Chronicle of Irish Affairs from A.D. 431 to A.D. 1540*, 4 vols (Dublin, 1887–1901), III, 148–9.

28 R. A. McKinley, *A History of British Surnames* (London and New York, 1990), pp. 25–39; Percy H. Reaney, *The Origin of English Surnames* (London, 1987); Patrick Hanks, Richard Coates and Peter McClure, *The Oxford Dictionary of Family Names in Britain and Ireland*, 4 vols (Oxford, 2016), I, pp. xxiv–xxv.

29 T. J. Morgan and Prys Morgan, *Welsh Surnames* (Cardiff, 1985); John and Sheila Rowlands, *The Surnames of Wales. Updated & Expanded* (Llandysul, 2013); Prys Morgan, 'The Rise of Welsh Hereditary Surnames', *Nomina*, 10 (1986), 121–35; T. E. Morris, 'Welsh Surnames in the Border Counties of Wales', *Y Cymmrodor*, 43 (1932), 93–173; Sheila Rowlands, 'The Surnames of Wales', in John Rowlands and Sheila Rowlands (eds), *Welsh Family History: A Guide to Research* (Birmingham, 1998), pp. 59–75; Bruce Durie, *Welsh Genealogy* (Stroud, 2012), pp. 23–34.

30 Edward MacLysaght, *The Surnames of Ireland* (Dublin, 1985), and *Irish Families: Their Names, Arms and Origins* (Dublin, 1957); Seán de Bhulbh, *Sloinnte na h-Éireann. Irish Surnames* (Limerick, 1997), and *Sloinnte Uile Éireann: All Ireland Surnames* (Limerick, 2002).

31 Irish surnames that comprise the ancestor's status or occupation (e.g. Mac an Bháird, 'Son of the Bard') are still technically patronymic in origin, and are not occupational surnames like those that developed in England.

32 Berry, *Statutes and Ordinances*, pp. 434–5; Sparky Booker, *Cultural Exchange and Identity in Late Medieval Ireland: The English and Irish of the Four Obedient Shires* (Cambridge, 2018), p. 47.

33 Sparky Booker, 'Intermarriage in Fifteenth-century Ireland: The English and Irish in the "Four Obedient Shires"', *Proceedings of the Royal Irish Academy C*, 113 (2013), 219–50 (pp. 225–8).

34 David E. Thornton, '*Locus, Sanctus et Virtus*: Monastic Surnaming in Late Medieval and Early Tudor England Reviewed', *Journal of Medieval Monastic Studies*, 10 (2021), 211–46, and 'Northern Saints' Names as Monastic Bynames in Late Medieval and Early Tudor England', in Christiania Whitehead, Hazel

J. Hunter Blair and Denis Renevey (eds), *Late Medieval Devotion to Saints from the North of England: New Directions*, Medieval Church Studies, 48 (Turnhout, 2022), pp. 387–408.

35   Thornton, 'A *Mynach*'.
36   Booker, *Cultural Exchange and Identity*, pp. 240–5.
37   David Knowles and R. Neville Hadcock, *Medieval Religious Houses. England and Wales* (Harlow, 1971), pp. 141, 164; David H. Williams, 'Llanthony Prima Priory', *The Monmouthshire Antiquary*, 25/26 (2009–10), 13–50.
38   Williams, 'Llanthony Prima Priory', appendices 1 and 2.
39   See also F. G. Cowley, *The Monastic Order in South Wales 1066–1349* (Cardiff, 1977), pp. 43–4.
40   Abergavenny, Caerleon, Llanthony, *Ros* (twice, though possibly also from England), and *Went* (Gwent). The Irish canon of Llanthony, called Edmund *de Hibernia*, was presumably recruited via the priory's landed interests in Ireland.
41   For example, *Piers*, *Pieresone*, *Stephyns* and *Stewens*, *Symond* and *Thurgrym*. The surname *Adams* is based on a forename that may be culturally Welsh, and the name *Goderick* could be an error for Roderick (Rhydderch).
42   Knowles and Hadcock, *Medieval Religious Houses*, pp. 139, 152–3.
43   In addition to two called David and two called *Lodowicus*, we have two Griffins (Gruffudd), four or maybe five called Morgan (Maurice), one Owain and one Rhys.
44   Knowles and Hadcock, *Medieval Religious Houses*, pp. 138, 147; Alan Bott and Margaret Dunn, *A Guide to the Priory and Parish Church of St Mary Beddgelert, Gwynedd* (Godalming, 2004).
45   A number of the sixteenth-century ordinands listed by Bott and Dunn (appendix 5) as 'of the Priory' were possibly rather secular clerks ordained to the title of the priory, and have not been counted here.
46   *Conway* (Conwy), *de Evyonyd* (Eifionydd) and *de Leyn* (Llŷn). The Conway here was toponym of the last prior of Beddgelert, David Conway (*fl.* 1501/2–35). He was the son of Richard (alias Rhys) Cyffin, dean of Bangor (d. 1492), as well as brother of John (Ieuan) Conway, abbot of Bardsey (*fl.* 1507–23): 'Rhisiart Cyffin ab Ieuan Llwyd, deon Bangor, *fl.* c.1470–m. 1492', http://www.gutorglyn.net/gutorglyn/name-full/?n=nr07 (accessed 6 November 2023). However, as 'David Conwey', professed canon of St Frideswide's, Oxford, Order of St Augustine, he had been dispensed in 1499, despite a birth defect, to hold all offices within his Order: Peter D. Clarke and Patrick N. R. Zutshi, *Supplications from England and Wales in the Registers of the Apostolic Penitentiary, 1410–1503*, Canterbury & York Society, 103–5, 3 vols (Woodbridge, 2013–15), III, 108 (no. 3737). This earlier association with St Frideswide's may explain why Prior Dafydd was among those canons of Beddgelert to have a

toponymic byname. His brother Ieuan, when canon of Bardsey, had similarly been dispensed in 1485: Clarke and Zutshi, *Supplications*, II, 403 (no. 3225).

47 Compare Cowley, *The Monastic Order in South Wales*, pp. 44, 156.
48 Aubrey Gwynn and R. Neville Hadcock, *Medieval Religious Houses Ireland with An Appendix to Early Sites* (London, 1970), pp. 170–1.
49 Raymond Refaussé and Colm Lennon, *The Registers of Christ Church Cathedral, Dublin* (Dublin, 1998), pp. 37–86; Colm Lennon, 'The Book of Obits of Christ Church Cathedral, Dublin', in Raymond Gillespie and Raymond Refaussé (eds), *The Medieval Manuscripts of Christ Church Cathedral, Dublin* (Dublin, 2006), pp. 163–82.
50 John (17 per cent), William (15 per cent), Richard (8.6 per cent), Robert (7.8 per cent) and Thomas (5.7 per cent).
51 *Gyl Escoppe* (Giolla Easbuig), *Christinus* (<Giolla Críost), *Kevinus* and *Keninus* (<Giolla Caoimhghin, or Maol Caoimhghin?), and the five called Patrick (<Giolla Padraig). Equivalent names include: Bernardus (Ir. Brian?), *Edanus* (twice) for Aodh or Aodhan, *Gelalius* (*recte* Gelasius?), *Malachias* and *Marianus*. Also note *Columbinus* (Columbanus) and *Gormanus* (Ir. Gormán, or Lat. Germanus?). In addition, lay brethren called *Gyllemorus* (Giolla Muire?), *Kellagh* (Ceallach), *Gylle Granset* and *Dorotheus*.
52 For example, Ballymore, Clonard, Clontarf, Curragh, Drumsallan, Glasnevin and Slane.
53 Gwynn and Hadcock, *Medieval Religious Houses: Ireland*, p. 177.
54 J. S. Brewer and William Bullen, *Calendar of the Carew Manuscripts preserved in the Archiepiscopal Library at Lambeth*, 6 vols (London, 1867–73), I, 151.
55 *O Daly* (Ó Dalaigh), *O Doyn* (Ó Duinn), *Oheelayn* (Ó hAoileáin), *Ohengasa* or *Ennis* (Ó hAonghusa), and *O malealy* (Ó Maolalaidh?). Could the surname *Obethacan* be a misreading for *Ohethacan* (<Ó hAodhagáin)? The more ambiguous surname *More* could also be added to these (<Ó Mórdha?).
56 Namely, *Gylnawe* or *Naves O Daly* (Giolla na Naomh Ó Dalaigh) and *Hugh O Doyn* (Aodh Ó Duinn): Margaret C. Griffith, *Calendar of Inquisitions Formerly in the Office of the Chief Remembrancer of the Exchequer* (Dublin, 1991), p. 44. O'*Doyn* was still at the priory at its suppression in 1540, now known as Hugh Doyne, without the patronymic prefix, along with a possible relative Nicholas Doyne: *The Seventh Report of the Deputy Keeper of the Public Records in Ireland* (Dublin, 1875), p. 47.
57 Gwynn and Hadcock, *Medieval Religious Houses: Ireland*, p. 165; Patrick K. Egan, 'The Augustinian Priory of St. Mary Clontuskert O Many', *Journal of the Galway Archaeological and Historical Society*, 22 (1946), 1–14.
58 In addition, the Ó Ceallaigh genealogies in the Book of Uí Mhaine supply the names – and in this case the descent – of three late fourteenth-century priors: Nollaig Ó Muraíle, 'The Ó Ceallaigh Rulers of Uí Mhaine – A Genealogical

Fragment, *c*.1400: Part I', *Journal of the Galway Archaeological and Historical Society*, 60 (2008), 32–77 (pp. 62, 65).

59 Ardghal, Breasal, Cairbre, Diarmaid, Domhnall and Cinaodh, along with two Patricks.

60 Donatus, Cornelius, Malachy, Odo and Thady, to which Maurice may perhaps be added.

61 Ó Domhnalláin, Ó Fallamháin and Ó Neachtain.

62 Thornton, 'A *Mynach*', esp. 431–3.

63 Huw Pryce, 'Patrons and Patronage among the Cistercians in Wales', *Archaeologia Cambrensis*, 154 (2007), 81–95; also *AWR*, p. 55.

64 Bott and Dunn, *A Guide*, p. 22. In 1404, John Wellington, prior of Llanthony Prima, was initially accused of supporting the rebellion, but the accusation did not stick and he was acknowledged as a loyal subject by the king: A. E. Stamp (ed.), *Calendar of Close Rolls, Henry IV: Vol. II. A.D. 1402–1405* (London, 1929), p. 395; A. E. Stamp (ed.), *Calendar of Patent Rolls, Henry IV. Vol. II. A.D. 1401–1405* (London, 1905), p. 455.

65 Cowley, *The Monastic Order in South Wales*, pp. 43–4.

66 Ceridwen Lloyd-Morgan, 'Manuscripts and the Monasteries', in Janet Burton and Karen Stöber (eds), *Monastic Wales: New Approaches* (Cardiff, 2013), pp. 209–27; Daniel Huws, *Medieval Welsh Manuscripts* (Cardiff, 2000), pp. 52–3, 75–6, 189–92, 215–18, 252–4; Huw Pryce, 'Chronicling and its Contexts in Medieval Wales', in Ben Guy et al. (eds), *The Chronicles of Medieval Wales and the March: New Contexts, Studies and Texts* (Turnhout, 2020), pp. 1–32.

67 Dafydd Johnston, 'Monastic Patronage of Welsh Poetry', in Burton and Stöber (eds), *Monastic Wales*, pp. 177–90; Karen Stöber, 'The Cistercians and the Bards – Praise and Patronage in Fifteenth-century Wales', in Dylan Foster Evans, Barry J. Lewis and Ann Parry Owen (eds), *'Gwalch Cywyddau Gwŷr': Ysgrifau ar Guto'r Glyn a Chymru'r Bymthegfed Ganrif. Essays on Guto'r Glyn and Fifteenth-century Wales* (Aberystwyth, 2013), pp. 305–26.

68 Daniel Huws, *A Repertory of Welsh Manuscripts and Scribes c.800–c.1800*, 3 vols (Aberystwyth, 2022), I, 332–3; Huws, *Medieval Welsh Manuscripts*, pp. 70–2; Lloyd-Morgan, 'Manuscripts and the Monasteries', pp. 212–13.

69 David M. Smith, *The Heads of Religious Houses: England and Wales Supplement* (Cluj-Napoca, Romania, 2019), p. 171; Ralph A. Griffiths, *The Principality of Wales in the Later Middle Ages: The Structure and Personnel of Government, South Wales 1277–1536*, 2 vols (Cardiff, 1972), I, 185. Morgan was originally a secular priest, and was succeeded as prior by his son (?) Thomas ap Morris who was in turn followed by another Welshman, Gruffudd Williams: David M. Smith, *The Heads of Religious Houses: England and Wales, III: 1377–1540* (Cambridge, 2008), p. 408. It may be significant that many of the Carmarthen

canons who had Welsh forenames and/or surnames are attested during the time of these Welsh priors. For comparable comments on the role of Welsh superiors on recruitment, see Thornton, 'A *Mynach*', 459–61.

70   Dafydd Johnston (ed.), *Gwaith Lewys Glyn Cothi* (Cardiff, 1995), pp. 154–5 (no. 66), 556. Note also the eulogy by Wiliam Egwad on the court of the 'grey brothers' of Carmarthen: Catrin T. Beynon Davies, 'Cerddi'r Tai Crefydd' (unpublished MA thesis, University College of North Wales, Bangor, 1972), 41–2 (no. 16).

71   A. Cynfael Lake (ed.), *Gwaith Lewys Daron* (Cardiff, 1994); Beynon Davies, 'Cerddi'r Tai Crefydd', 238–9 (no. 116); Catrin Stevens, 'Cywydd i Ofyn March i Ddafydd Conwy, Prior Beddgelert', *Transactions of the Caernarvonshire Historical Society*, 37 (1976), 43–57. On Prior Dafydd, see above.

72   Kirsty Bennett, 'The Book Collections of Llanthony Priory from Foundation until Dissolution (*c.*1100–1538)' (unpublished PhD thesis, University of Kent, 2006), 100; Lloyd-Morgan, 'Manuscripts and the Monasteries', pp. 211–12.

73   Canice Mooney, *The Church in Gaelic Ireland: Thirteenth to Fifteenth Centuries*, History of Irish Catholicism, 2 (Dublin, 1969), p. 21.

74   Nollaig Ó Muraíle, 'The Learned Family of Ó Cianáin/Keenan', *Clogher Historical Society*, 18/3 (2005), 387–436 (p. 397).

75   Thus, see K. W. Nicholls, *Gaelic and Gaelicized Ireland in the Middle Ages* (2nd edn, Dublin, 2003), p. 122.

76   For comparable trends in celibacy in late medieval Wales, note Williams, *The Welsh Church*, pp. 401, 408.

77   Janet Burton, 'Transition and Transformation: The Benedictine Houses', in Burton and Stöber (eds), *Monastic Wales*, pp. 21–37.

78   For instance, see Dianne Hall, *Women and the Church in Medieval Ireland c.1140–1540* (Dublin, 2003), pp. 177–81.

7

Gwystlon yn *De gestis Britonum* a *Brut y Brenhinedd*

Rebecca Thomas

Ac yn gyulawn o diruawr lit y peris dallu gwystlon a uuassei yg karchar gantaw yr ys talym o amser kyn no hynny, nyt amgen deu uap Ywein Gwyned, [Katwallawn] a Chynwric, a Maredud ap yr Arglwyd Rys a rei ereill.[1]

Ac yn llawn llid enfawr, perodd ddallu'r gwystlon a fu yn y carchar ganddo am amser hir cyn hynny, sef dau fab Owain Gwynedd, Cadwallon a Cynwrig, a Maredudd ab yr Arglwydd Rhys, a rhai eraill.

Brut y Tywysogyon s.a. 1165

Yn y flwyddyn 1165, cofnoda *Brut y Tywysogyon* ymgyrch trychinebus Harri II yng Nghymru, a derfynodd gyda'r brenin yn gwylltio ac yn dallu gwystlon y Cymry. Nid yw'n glir am ba gyfnod y bu'r gwystlon yn ei feddiant. Roedd Owain Gwynedd wedi gwneud heddwch â'r brenin yn 1157, ac mae *Brut y Tywysogyon* yn cofnodi Harri'n trechu Rhys ap Gruffudd yn 1163, gan gyfeirio'n benodol at frenin Deheubarth yn rhoi gwystlon. Yn 1164, chwalwyd yr heddwch ac unodd brenhinoedd y Cymry mewn gwrthryfel.[2] Er i dywydd gwyllt mynyddoedd Berwyn ddod ag ymgyrch Harri yn eu herbyn i ben, cafodd y gwystlon eu cosbi am anufudd-dod y Cymry.

Nid pennod unigryw yn hanes perthynas y Cymry â brenin Lloegr oedd hon. Mae cofnodion *Brut y Tywysogyon* ar gyfer y ddeuddegfed ganrif a'r drydedd ar ddeg yn llawn cyfeiriadau at wystlon, fel arfer yn cael eu rhoi gan y Cymry i'r Saeson. Yn y rhan fwyaf o achosion, y weithred o roi gwystlon sydd yn cael ei chofnodi. Felly, rhoddir gwystlon i Harri I yn 1110 ac i Harri II yn 1163. Mae cofnod 1165 o ddallu gwystlon yn eithriadol yng nghyd-destun *Brut y Tywysogyon*, ond mae ffynonellau eraill yn datgelu gwystlon o Gymry a ddioddefodd mewn ffordd debyg. Yn ôl Roger o Wendover, er enghraifft, gorchmynnodd y Brenin Ioan ddienyddio'r gwystlon a gafodd gan Llywelyn ab Iorwerth yn sgil gwrthryfel y tywysog yn 1212.[3] Wedi dweud hynny, cawn hanes gwystlon mwy ffodus hefyd. Mae Hywel, mab arall i Rhys ap Gruffudd o Ddeheubarth, yn enghraifft enwog. Bu'n wystl i Harri II am sawl blwyddyn, ond cafodd ei ryddhau wedi gwella'r berthynas rhwng brenin Lloegr a Deheubarth yn 1171. Yn ddiweddarach, bu Hywel yn ymladd gyda'r brenin yn Ffrainc yn 1173 ac mae'n cael y llysenw 'Sais' yn *Brut y Tywysogyon*.[4] Nid brenin Lloegr oedd yr unig un i dderbyn gwystlon chwaith. Ceir enghreifftiau yn *Brut y Tywysogyon* o roi gwystlon ymysg y Cymry eu hunain, rhywbeth a welir yn achlysurol hefyd yn yr *acta*.[5]

Mae llond llaw o astudiaethau pwysig wedi rhoi sylw i wystlon canoloesol, gwaith Adam Kosto y pennaf yn eu plith.[6] Mae ei ddiffiniad ef o wystl yn seiliedig ar astudiaeth o ffynonellau o Ewrop ac ardal Môr y Canoldir o'r bumed ganrif hyd y bymthegfed. Mae'n cynnwys y pum agwedd canlynol:

1. Mae gwystl yn gwarantu cytundeb;
2. Nid oes modd talu pridwerth er mwyn rhyddhau gwystl;
3. Mae gwystl yn drydydd person (hynny yw, yn berson gwahanol i'r sawl sydd yn rhwym i'r cytundeb dan sylw);
4. Gall gwystl golli ei ryddid;
5. Caiff gwystl ei roi yn hytrach na'i gymryd.[7]

Gyda'i gilydd, amlinella'r agweddau hyn y gwahaniaeth rhwng gwystl a charcharor. Er bod gorgyffwrdd – mae'r ddau yn colli eu rhyddid – mae yna wahaniaethau pwysig. Yn wahanol i garcharor neu gaeth, caiff gwystl ei roi gan garfan i garfan arall am reswm penodol ac nid oes modd talu pridwerth i'w ryddhau. Yn amlwg, roedd y sefyllfa ar lawr gwlad yn fwy blêr – fel y trafodwyd eisoes, cafodd Hywel Sais ei ryddhau gan Harri II.[8] Fel rheol, fodd bynnag, roedd i wystlon statws a phwrpas gwahanol i garcharorion a chaethion.[9] Caiff hyn ei adlewyrchu yn nherminoleg y ffynonellau Lladin hefyd, sy'n gwahaniaethu rhwng *obses* ('gwystl') a *captivus* ('carcharor').[10]

Gwarantu cytundeb oedd pwrpas gwystlon. Y cyd-destun mwyaf arferol yw'r garfan a drechwyd yn filwrol yn rhoi gwystlon i'r garfan fuddugol i warantu eu hildiad. Gallai hyn gynnwys addewid o ufudd-dod, trethi neu ymrwymiad arall.[11] Gwelwn enghraifft o gytundeb o'r fath rhwng John a Llywelyn yn 1211, pan roddwyd gwystlon i'r brenin i warantu'r heddwch:

A gwedy caffel o Lywelyn diogelrwyd y vynet at y brenhin ac y dyuot, ef a aeth attaw ac a hedychawd ac ef drwy rodi gwystlon y'r brenhin o vonedhigyon y wlat ac vgein mil o warthec a deugein emys, a chenatau hefyt y'r brenhin y Beruedwlat yn dragywydawl.[12]

Ac wedi i Llywelyn gael cadarnhad ei fod yn gallu mynd a dod rhag y brenin yn ddiogel, aeth ato a gwneud heddwch ag ef trwy roi gwystlon i'r brenin o foneddigion y wlad ac ugain mil o warthag a phedwar-deg o feirch, a rhoi i'r brenin hefyd y Berfeddwlad yn eiddo dragwyddol iddo.

Tra bo cyd-destunau eraill, megis sicrhau rhyddhau unigolyn o statws uchel o'r carchar neu warantu cadoediad dros dro, dyma yw'r cyd-destun mwyaf cyffredin.[13] Yn unol â diffiniad Kosto, yn 1211 cafodd gwystlon eu rhoi gan Llywelyn (yn hytrach na'u cymryd gan John) i warantu heddwch yn sgil ei drechu.

Does dim amheuaeth bod gwystlo'n rhan allweddol o dirwedd wleidyddol Cymru yn y cyfnod hwn. Yn wir, cyfeirir yn aml at enghreifftiau Cymreig mewn trafodaethau ehangach o wystlo yn yr Oesoedd Canol, ac fe'u defnyddiwyd wrth lunio fframwaith deongliadol Kosto uchod.[14] Mae'r graddau i'r Cymry ymwneud â gwystlo yn nodedig. Mae Jenny Benham wedi awgrymu bod disgwyl i'r Cymry, ynghyd â phobloedd nad oeddent yn Gristnogion, roi gwystlon yn amlach nag eraill wrth lunio cytundebau heddwch, yn gysylltiedig, efallai, ag agweddau tuag atynt fel pobl anufudd a dueddai i dorri'r fath gytundebau.[15] Er bod y Cymry wedi cael sylw yn y cyd-destunau ehangach hyn, mae lle yn sicr ar gyfer astudiaeth fanylach o'r dystiolaeth Gymreig ei hun. Croniclau a'r *acta* sydd wedi ennyn y sylw mwyaf hyd yn hyn, wrth i haneswyr chwilio am enghreifftiau penodol o roi gwystlon. Mae gwystlon yn ymddangos mewn ystod ehangach o destunau, fodd bynnag – mewn cerddi ac mewn rhyddiaith. Nid yw'r testunau hyn o reidrwydd yn adrodd digwyddiadau hanesyddol go iawn, ond gallant daflu goleuni ar agweddau tuag at wystlo, a thrwy hynny y gweithgarwch ei hun.[16]

Bwriad y bennod hon yw cynnig trafodaeth gychwynnol o'r cwestiwn hwn trwy ganolbwyntio ar *De gestis Britonum* Sieffre o Fynwy a'r cyfieithiadau Cymraeg o'i waith, *Brut y Brenhinedd*. Ymddengys y cyfieithiadau Cymraeg am y tro cyntaf mewn llawysgrifau o'r drydedd ganrif ar ddeg, ac mae nifer o fersiynau'n goroesi sydd â pherthynas ansicr â'i gilydd.[17] Bydd y drafodaeth hon yn canolbwyntio'n bennaf ar y pedwar fersiwn sydd i'w gweld am y tro cyntaf yn y drydedd ganrif ar ddeg: Peniarth 44; Llanstephan 1; Dingestow; Peniarth 21/Peniarth 23.[18] Lle bo'n berthnasol, bydd cyfeiriadau hefyd at fersiwn Cotton Cleopatra, sy'n ymddangos yn y bedwaredd ganrif ar ddeg.[19] Mae lle i waith sylweddol ar berthynas y fersiynau hyn gyda'i gilydd, yn ogystal â'u perthynas i Ladin Sieffre.[20] Bydd y bennod hon yn tynnu sylw at rai wahaniaethau sylweddol.

Rhoi a chymryd gwystlon

Does dim patrwm amlwg i'r cyfeiriadau at wystlon a gwystlo yn *De gestis Britonum*: maent wedi eu gwasgaru trwy'r naratif. Felly, ceir cyfeiriadau at wystlon yng nghyd-destun hanes Brutus, Caesar, Arthur a Cadwallon. Does dim ychwaith unrhyw awgrym bod hyn yn arfer sydd yn datblygu dros amser – yr un yw'r gwystlon yng nghyfnod Brutus ag yng nghyfnod Cadwallon.[21] Mae'n arfer sydd yn ymestyn yn ôl i wreiddiau'r Brythoniaid, ond nid yw'n arfer sy'n unigryw iddynt. I'r gwrthwyneb, mae gwystlo yn *De gestis Britonum* yn arfer sy'n croesi ffiniau ethnig, crefyddol a gwleidyddol. Mae'r Brythoniaid, Saeson a Rhufeiniaid yn rhoi gwystlon fel ei gilydd.

Fel y trafodwyd uchod, un o brif swyddogaethau gwystlo yn yr Oesoedd Canol oedd gwarantu cytundebau. Cawn enghreifftiau niferus o wystlo at y diben hwn yn *De gestis Britonum*. Wedi eu trechu gan Arthur, mae'r Sacsoniaid yn addo talu trethi a gadael gwystlon: 'addawon nhw i dalu trethi iddo o Germania ac i adael gwystlon yno' ('promiserunt quoque se daturos ei tributum ex Germania obsidesque inde mansuros').[22] Â Sieffre ymlaen: 'cadwodd Arthur eu cyfoeth a'r gwystlon i warantu'r trethi' ('retinuit namque ipsorum opes reddendique uectigalis obsides'). Mae'r enghraifft hon yn amlygu dau o brif bwyntiau Kosto. Pwrpas y gwystlon, noda'r testun yn glir, yw gwarantu'r trethi, ac maent wedi eu rhoi gan y Sacsoniaid. Wrth reswm, mae elfen o orfodaeth: mae'r Sacsoniaid wedi eu trechi a'r unig ffordd i osgoi newyn yw trwy gytuno i delerau Arthur. Wedi dweud hynny, y rhai sydd wedi eu trechi sy'n rhoi'r gwystlon, yn hytrach na'r rhai buddugol yn eu cymryd.

Mewn enghraifft arall, mae'r weithred o roi gwystlon o dan orfodaeth yn amlycach eto. Yma, mae Cador, dug Cernyw, wedi erlid y Sacsoniaid nes lladd eu harweinydd a gorfodi'r gweddill i ildio: 'gorfododd nhw i gyd i ildio a derbyn gwystlon ganddynt' ('cunctos deditioni compulit, receptis obsidibus').[23] Ceir gorfodaeth yma (*compulit*), ond mae'r gwystlon yn cael eu derbyn (*recipere*), yn hytrach na'u cymryd, gan y buddugol o hyd. Gwelwn sefyllfa debyg rhwng Penda a Cadwallon yn y seithfed ganrif:

> Conserto deinde proelio, captus est Peanda continuo et exercitus eius peremptus. Cumque ipse alium adytum salutis non haberet, subdidit se Cadualloni deditque obsides, promittens sese cum illo Saxones inquietaturum.
>
> Wrth i'r byddinoedd gwrdd, cipiwyd Penda yn syth a dinistriwyd ei fyddin. Ni allai achub ei hun heblaw trwy ildio i Cadwallon a rhoi gwystlon, gan addo hefyd i ymladd gydag ef yn erbyn y Sacsoniaid.[24]

Yn achos Cador a Penda nid yw'r union beth y mae'r gwystlon yn ei warantu yn glir: does dim sôn am drethi yn benodol. Wedi dweud hynny, ceir sôn am addewid Penda i ymladd ar ochr Cadwallon yn erbyn y Sacsoniaid. Mae'n debyg, felly, mai teyrngarwch sydd yn cael ei warantu yn y ddau achos.

Ym mhob un o'r enghreifftiau hyn, caiff gwystlon eu rhoi yn dilyn ildiad i warantu telerau cytundeb. Ceir gwystlon mewn ambell gyd-destun arall yn *De gestis Britonum* hefyd, eto'n adlewyrchu'r arfer cyfoes. Ynghyd â gwarantu cytundebau, un o'r rhesymau mwyaf blaenllaw dros roi gwystlon oedd sicrhau rhyddhad unigolyn o garchar.[25] Yn *De gestis Britonum*, mae brenin Denmarc yn addo trethi blynyddol wedi ei warantu gan lw difrifol a gwystlon ('mandauit etiam quod pactum suum foedere iuramenti et obsidibus confirmaret') i sicrhau ei ryddhau o garchar Beli.[26] Cyffredin hefyd oedd rhoi gwystlon er mwyn gwarantu diogelwch unigolyn wrth deithio i gynhadledd heddwch.[27] Felly, yn *De gestis Britonum* gofynna Iŵl Cesar am wystlon gan y Brythoniaid er mwyn sicrhau ei ddiogelwch wrth ddod i Brydain.[28]

Yn unol â fframwaith Kosto, *obsides* a ddefnyddir yn gyson yn *De gestis Britonum*, gan wahaniaethu rhwng gwystlon a mathau eraill o garcharorion. Yn y cyfieithiadau Cymraeg, *gwystl* a *gwystlon* a gawn. Yn aml cawn gyfeiriad at roi gwystlon ynghyd â rhywbeth arall. Mewn un achos, dilyna hyn Ladin Sieffre, sydd yn nodi bod cytundeb wedi ei selio 'gyda llw a gwystlon' (*iuramenti et obsidibus*).[29] 'Llw a gwystlon' yw cyfieithiad Peniarth 44 (t. 33), tra mae gan Llanstephan 1 'arfoll a gwystlon' (t. 45). Yn yr enghraifft hon, sef brenin Denmarc yn addo gwystlon i Beli, mae'r testunau Cymraeg yn ymhelaethu rhywfaint ar naratif Sieffre. Yn ogystal â nodi bod brenin Denmarc wedi addo'r gwystlon, cyfeiriant yn ddiweddarach at Beli'n derbyn y gwystlon. Yr ail dro, cawn 'arfoll a gwystlon' eto yn Llanstephan 1 (t. 45), tra mae Peniarth 44 (t. 33) yn cyfeirio at 'gwystlon a chedernyt'. Ymddengys y parau hyn ar achlysuron eraill hefyd. Yn *Brut Dingestow*, mae Beli a Brennius yn cael 'gwystlon a chedernyt ar gywirdeb' gan ddynion Rhufain; *obsides* yn unig sydd gan Sieffre.[30] Yn achos Llanstephan 1 (t. 198), mae Penda'n cadarnhau ei deyrngarwch i Cadwallon 'trwy arfoll a gwystlon'; eto, *obsides* yn unig sydd gan Sieffre.[31] Digwydd *arfoll* ambell dro yng ngherddi Beirdd y Tywysogion, a llond llaw o weithiau yn fersiynau amrywiol *Brut y Brenhinedd*.[32] Ceir un enghraifft yn *Historia Gruffud vab Kenan*, pan mae'r llynges o Iwerddon yn 'torri eu harfoll wrth Ruffudd'.[33] Cyfieithu'r Lladin *fracta fide Griffino data* y mae'r *Historia* yma, felly gallwn ddeall bod *arfoll* yn gyfystyr â *fides*.[34] Nid yw *cedernyd* yn digwydd mor aml, ond cawn un enghraifft yn y Mabinogion, yn dwyn yr ystyr 'llw'.[35] Yn yr achosion o roi *arfoll a gwystlon* neu *cadernid a gwystlon* yn nhestunau *Brut y Brenhinedd*, ymddengys bod y gwystlon yn cadarnhau'r *arfoll* neu'r *cadernid*. Cawn rywbeth tebyg ar un achlysur yn *De gestis Britonum* – *iuramenti et obsidibus* a ddyfynnwyd uchod – ond mae'n digwydd yn fwy aml yn yr addasiadau Cymraeg. Dyma ymhelaethu o ryw fath, felly, ar rôl y gwystlon.

Fel rheol, gosodir yr un pwyslais ar 'roi' gwystlon yn nhestunau *Brut y Brenhinedd*. Felly, yn ôl Llanstephan 1 (t. 152), nid yw dug Cernyw yn gorffwys nes ei fod wedi lladd arweinydd y Sacsoniaid 'ac eu kymhell wyntau oll y law kan rody gwystlon'. Yn achos Arthur, mae'r Sacsoniaid yn addo teyrnged flynyddol 'a chadarnhav henny kan rody gwystlon' (tt. 148–9).³⁶ Wedi dweud hynny, mae sawl enghraifft nad ydynt yn dilyn y patrwm hwn. Mewn un achos, mae Coel Hen yn darostwng i Constantius ac yn cytuno i dalu'r trethi disgwyliedig i Rufain. Mae Lladin Sieffre yn dilyn y patrwm arferol: 'cadarnhawyd yr heddwch gyda derbyn gwystlon' ('pacemque receptis obsidibus confirmauerunt').³⁷ Er nad yw'n cael ei nodi yn uniongyrchol, gallwn ddeall o'r cyd-destun mai Constantius sydd yn derbyn y gwystlon i warantu'r dreth flynyddol y mae Coel Hen wedi addo ei thalu. Mae tri o fersiynau *Brut y Brenhinedd* yn cyfeirio at wystlon yn y man hwn, ac mae pob un ohonynt yn sôn am Constantius yn 'cymryd' gwystlon. Felly, yn ôl *Brut Dingestow*: 'Constans y rodes taghneued udunt, ac y kymyrth gvystlon y gan y Brytannyeit ar hynny'.³⁸ Yma, mae ystyr 'cymryd' yn amwys: gall olygu 'cymryd' yn yr ystyr fodern, neu 'dderbyn'.³⁹ Diddorol yw nodi bod 'cymryd' hefyd yn digwydd mewn sawl enghraifft yn *Brut y Tywysogyon*. Felly, yn 1171 cymhellodd yr Arglwydd Rhys Owain Cyfeiliog i ddarostwng iddo ac 'a gymerth seith wystyl y gantaw'.⁴⁰

Mae testunau *Brut y Brenhinedd* yn fwy amwys, felly, sydd yn codi cwestiynau ynghylch pwysigrwydd y gwahaniaeth rhwng 'cymryd' a 'rhoi' gwystlon, yn enwedig gan fod gwystlon fel arfer yn cael eu rhoi o dan orfodaeth. Yn wir, nid yw Sieffre ei hun yn gwbl gyson chwaith. Pan ddaw Belinus a Brennus i Rufain, er enghraifft, mae llywodraethwyr y ddinas yn addo trethi blynyddol iddynt er mwyn sicrhau'r heddwch. Mae Belinus a Brennus yn cytuno ac yn cymryd (*sumere*) gwystlon: 'sumptis igitur obsidibus, ueniam donauerunt reges cohortesque suas in Germaniam duxerunt' ('wedi cymryd gwystlon, cytunodd y brenhinoedd i'w cais ac arwain eu milwyr yn erbyn yr Almaen').⁴¹ Mae'r enghraifft hon yn arbennig o ddiddorol gan fod Sieffre yn llithro rhwng berfau. Felly, wedi i lywodraethwyr Rhufain dorri eu llw, â Belinus a Brennus ymlaen i fygwth 'y gwystlon roedden nhw wedi eu rhoi' (*obsides quos dederant*).⁴² Er mai 'rhoi' neu 'derbyn' gwystlon y gwna'r rhan fwyaf yn *De gestis Britonum*, dengys yr enghraifft hon bod modd llithro'n hawdd rhwng 'rhoi' a 'chymryd'. Mewn cyd-destun lle caiff y rhan fwyaf o wystlon eu rhoi dan orfodaeth, mater o bwyslais yn unig yw'r gwahaniaeth. Nid yw'r ffin rhwng y ddau mor gadarn, efallai, ag y mae fframwaith Kosto yn ei awgrymu.⁴³

Ceir un cyfeiriad arall yn fersiwn Cotton Cleopatra *Brut y Brenhinedd* sydd yn dangos hyblygrwydd wrth ymdrin â gwystlon. Ynghylch dug Cernyw yn erlid y Sacsoniaid: 'ac yno y llas Keldric ev tywyssawc; ac a dienghis or llu heb llad yno; agymellwyt yn geith tragywydawl' ('ac yna y lladdodd Celdric eu tywysog, a fe gymerwyd y rhai o'r fyddin na chafodd eu lladd yn gaethion tragwyddol').⁴⁴ *Obsides* sydd gan Sieffre yma, ond mae'r cyfieithiad yn cyfeirio at *geith tragywydawl*.⁴⁵ Yn yr achos hwn, felly, mae'r testun Cymraeg yn gweld gwystlon a charcharorion yn gyfnewidiol. Nid yw *Brut y Brenhinedd* yn unigryw yn hyn o beth chwaith. Yn achos disgrifiad *Brut y Tywysogyon* o ddigwyddiadau 1165, mae'r gwystlon a roddwyd gan y Cymry i Harri II yn cael eu cadw ganddo yn y carchar.⁴⁶ Niwlog yw'r ffin rhwng gwystl a charcharor yma hefyd.

Cyfnewid

Ym mron i bob achos, caiff gwystlon eu rhoi gan un garfan i garfan arall yn *De gestis Britonum* a *Brut y Brenhinedd*. Fodd bynnag, ceir un enghraifft ddiddorol nad yw'n dilyn y patrwm hwn. Sôn y mae Sieffre am y brwydro rhwng Cadfan, brenin y Brythoniaid, ac Æthelfrith, brenin y Saeson, yn y seithfed ganrif. Wedi ymosodiad Æthelfrith ar Fangor, caiff Cadfan ei ddyrchafu'n frenin ar y Brythoniaid, ac mae'r ddwy fyddin yn cwrdd:

> Deinde, cum cateruas suas in utraque parte statuerent, uenerunt amici eorum talique pacto pacem inter eos fecerunt ut Edelfridus trans Humbrum, Caduanus uero citra fluuium Britanniam possideret. Cum autem conuentionem suam obsidibus cum iure iurando confirmassent, orta est tanta amicitia inter illos ut omnia sua communia haberent.

> Yna, pan roedd byddinoedd y ddwy ochr wedi eu trefnu, daeth eu ffrindiau i wneud heddwch rhyngddynt, gan gytuno y byddai Æthelfrith yn rheoli Prydain i'r gogledd o'r Afon Humber a Cadfan i'r de o'r afon. Cadarnhasant y cytundeb gyda gwystlon a llwon, a datblygodd y fath gyfeillgarwch rhyngddynt nes iddynt ddal eu heiddo yn gyffredin.⁴⁷

Er nad yw'r Lladin yn nodi'n uniongyrchol pwy sydd yn rhoi gwystlon a llwon, mae'n debyg mai cyfnewid a gawn yma. Mae pwyslais ar gyfartaledd yn y rhan hon o *De gestis Britonum*: mae'r ddau frenin yn gwbl gyfartal yn eu statws a'u pŵer. Yn wir, fel y dyfynnir uchod, cymaint yw cyfeillgarwch Cadfan ac Æthelfrith fel eu bod yn rhannu eu heiddo. Mae'r cyfieithiadau Cymraeg yn ddiamwys ar y pwynt hwn. Yn *Brut Dingestow*, er enghraifft: 'a guedy cadarnhau y gytuot honno trvy aruoll a gvystlon o bob parth' ('wedi cadarnhau y cytundeb hwnnw trwy addewidion a gwystlon gan y ddwy ochr').[48] Yn achos Cadfan ac Æthelfrith, felly, cawn ddwy garfan gwbl gyfartal yn cyfnewid gwystlon er mwyn sicrhau cytundeb heddwch.

Mae enghreifftiau hanesyddol o gyfnewid o'r fath yn brin. Tra bo gwystlon yn cael eu cyfnewid yn achlysurol i gadarnhau cytundebau heddwch, doedd hyn ddim yn arferol. Noda Adam Kosto ymhellach fod y rhan fwyaf o enghreifftiau o'r fath gyfnewid yn digwydd yng nghyd-destun gwrthdaro rhwng diwylliannau, er enghraifft yn ystod y Croesgadau.[49] Roedd cyfnewid yn digwydd, felly, ond nid oedd yn arfer cyffredin. Awgryma Jenny Benham mai statws a gwerth gwystlon sydd yn egluro'r cyn lleied o enghreifftiau sydd o'u cyfnewid.[50] Roedd gwystlon fel arfer yn unigolion o statws â pherthynas agos i'r rhai oedd yn eu rhoi – byddai'n arferol i frenin roi mab yn wystl, er enghraifft.[51] Doedd hyn ddim yn ganlyniad dymunol: gallai rhoi etifedd yn nwylo gelyn arwain at ansefydlogrwydd gwleidyddol.[52] Mewn sefyllfa o gyfnewid gwystlon, felly, byddai rhaid i ddwy garfan ddewis gweithredu yn y modd hwn a wynebu'r ansefydlogrwydd posibl a ddilynai.

O ystyried bod achosion hanesyddol o gyfnewid gwystlon yn brin, ac mai dyma'r unig enghraifft yn *De gestis Britonum*, mae penderfyniad Sieffre i gyflwyno Cadfan ac Æthelfrith yn gweithredu fel hyn yn arwyddocaol. Mae'r rhan hon o *De gestis Britonum* wedi bod yn destun sylw estynedig gan ei bod yn ganolog i amlinelliad Sieffre o hanes y Brythoniaid o'r seithfed ganrif hyd y ddegfed. Ceir yma fersiwn creadigol o'u hanes: brenin Gwynedd oedd Cadfan, ac yn sicr doedd ei deyrnas ddim yn ymestyn dros Brydain gyfan i'r de o Afon Humber.[53] Mae R. William Leckie wedi dangos mai strategaeth fwriadol gan Sieffre oedd hon. Trwy honni bod Cadfan, a'i fab Cadwallon ar ei ôl, wedi teyrnasu dros dde Lloegr gyfan, aeth Sieffre ati i danseilio hanes y Saeson. Hynny yw, doedd Saeson Sieffre ddim mor bwerus yn y seithfed ganrif ag yr oeddent yn ymddangos yn ei ffynonellau – *Historia ecclesiastica* Beda, er enghraifft. Yn yr un modd, ceir bwlch yn *De gestis Britonum* yn dilyn Cadfan, Cadwallon a Cadwaladr. Neidia Sieffre o Gadwaladr yn y seithfed ganrif i'r ddegfed, gyda'r datganiad mai Æthelstan oedd y brenin cyntaf i deyrnasu dros Loegr gyfan. Dyma strategaeth fwriadol arall, sydd yn awgrymu bod goruchafiaeth wleidyddol y Saeson yn ddatblygiad weddol diweddar.[54] Mae dehongliad Leckie yn codi cwestiynau ynghylch swyddogaeth y gwystlon yn y rhan hon o *De gestis Britonum*. Fel y mae'r cytundeb yn bychanu pŵer y Saeson yn y de, mae cyflwyno Cadfan ac Æthelfrith yn frenhinoedd cyfartal hefyd yn awgrymu bod y Brythoniaid yr un mor bwerus â'r Saeson yn y gogledd. Mae'r broses o gyfnewid gwystlon yn pwysleisio hyn – yn enwedig gan nad yw cyfnewid gwystlon yn weithred arferol, yn hanesyddol nac ychwaith yn *De gestis Britonum*.

Ar yr olwg gyntaf, mae'n ymddangos bod *De gestis Britonum* yn mapio'n dda iawn ar yr hyn y mae haneswyr wedi ei gasglu ynghylch gwystlo yn fwy cyffredinol yn yr Oesoedd Canol. Mae yna ffocws ar 'roi' gwystlon yn hytrach na'u 'cymryd', ac mae'r rhoi fel arfer yn digwydd i warantu cytundeb o ryw fath. Fel rheol hefyd mae'r addasiadau Cymraeg yn cadw at hyn, er bod rhai eithriadau, a bod yna ddefnydd diddorol o derminoleg arbennig yn y testunau Cymraeg. Wedi dweud hynny, mae'r ymdriniaeth o gytundeb Cadfan ac Æthelfrith yn ein hatgoffa nad cronicl oedd *De gestis Britonum*. Roedd Sieffre'n gweu naratif arbennig, ac mae ei ymdriniaeth o wystlo yn dangos hynny.

Cawn un enghraifft arall sydd yn amlygu'r pwynt hwn. Wedi i Belinus a Brennius oresgyn Rhufain, mae llywodraethwyr y ddinas yn rhoi 34 o wystlon i warantu eu llw. Torrant eu llw ac mae'r brodyr yn dychwelyd i'r ddinas ac, wedi i'r llywodraethwyr wrthod ildio, yn crogi'r gwystlon o flaen y porth. Ceir trafodaeth pellach o'r bennod hon isod.[55] Yr hyn sydd yn ddiddorol yn y cyd-destun hwn yw sut y mae Sieffre yn ail-ddisgrifio Belinus a Brennius yn crogi'r gwystlon yn ddiweddarach yn *De gestis Britonum*. Yma, mae Arthur wedi derbyn llythyr gan yr ymerawdwr Lucius, sydd yn mynnu trethi gan Brydain. Ei ddadl yw bod hawl gan Rufain i drethi gan Brydain ers amser Iŵl Cesar. Ymateba Arthur gyda'r araith hon:

Nam si quia Iulius Caesar ceterique Romani reges Britanniam olim subiugauerunt uectigal nunc debere sibi ex illa reddi decernit, similiter ego censeo quod Roma michi tributum dare debet, quia antecessores mei eam antiquitus optinuerunt. Beli etenim, serenissimus ille rex Britonum, auxilio fratris sui usus, Brennii uidelicet ducis Allobrogum, suspensis in medio foro uiginti nobilioribus Romanis urbem ceperunt captamque multis temporibus possederunt.

Os yw ef [Lucius] wedi penderfynu ei fod i gael trethu gan Brydain oherwydd bod Iŵl Cesar a brenhinoedd eraill Rhufain wedi ein goresgyn, yr wyf i yn yr un modd yn credu bod Rhufain i dalu trethi i mi, oherwydd fe wnaeth fy rhagflaenwyr ei goresgyn ynghynt. Yn wir, fe wnaeth Beli, brenin mwyaf heddychlon Prydain, gyda chymorth ei frawd, Brennius, dug Allobroges, grogi ugain o foneddigion Rhufain yng nghanol y fforwm, cipio'r ddinas a'i dal am amser sylweddol.[56]

Nid yw Arthur yn crybwyll 'gwystlon' yma, ond yn cyfeirio at *nobilioribus Romanis*, ac 20 ohonynt yn hytrach na 34. Ymhellach, tra bo Beli a Brennius wedi crogi'r gwystlon o flaen porth y gaer yn yr adroddiad cynharach, yma honna Arthur eu bod nhw wedi eu crogi yng nghanol y fforwm. Mae'n bosibl bod y chwarae blêr hwn â hanes yn fwriadol: rhy Arthur araith angerddol am hawl Prydain i annibyniaeth rhag Rhufain ac, yn bryfoclyd, try ddadl Lucius ar ei phen gydag apêl at hanes. Posib ein bod ni i fod i sylweddoli bod araith Arthur yn gorsymleiddio'r gorffennol. Yn y gorsymleiddiad, collwn olwg ar y gwystlon. Fel cynghrair Cadfan ac Æthelfrith, gwelwn strategaethau naratifol Sieffre yn cael dylanwad ar ei ymdriniaeth o wystlon.

Tynged a statws

Nid yw'r gwystlon eu hunain yn gymeriadau blaenllaw yn *De gestis Britonum* fel arfer. Cyfeiriadau yn unig a gawn yn amlach na pheidio yng nghyd-destun trechu gelyn a chadarnhau eu teyrngarwch. Does dim sôn, fel rheol, am gefndir y gwystlon na'u tynged. Ni chawn fyth wybod eu henwau. Wedi dweud hynny, o bryd i'w gilydd cawn wybodaeth ychwanegol, a'r wybodaeth honno fel arfer yn ymwneud â statws y gwystlon a'u cysylltiad i'r person neu bobl sy'n eu rhoi. Cawn wybod, er enghraifft, fod Androgeus yn anfon 'ei fab ef a thri-deg o fechgyn bonheddig o'i deulu agos' ('filium suum et .xxx. nobiles iuuenes ex cognatione sua propinquos') at Cesar i warantu diogelwch yr ymerawdwr wrth ddod i Brydain.⁵⁷ Caiff dau bwynt pwysig eu hamlygu yma: mae'r gwystlon o statws uchel ac yn deulu agos. Mae hyn yn amlycach eto yn achos cytundeb Belinus a Brennus gyda llywodraethwyr Rhufain. Wedi i'r Rhufeiniaid dorri eu llw, ymosoda'r brodyr ar y ddinas a chodi crocbrennau o flaen y waliau, gan fygwth crogi'r gwystlon a roddwyd iddynt os nad yw'r Rhufeiniaid yn ildio. Parha Sieffre i egluro 'ond fe wnaeth y Rhufeiniaid, gan wynebu hyn yn gadarn, ac er gwaethaf eu cariad tuag at eu meibion a'u neiaint, barhau i amddiffyn eu hunain' ('verum Romani, in proposito suo perseuerantes, despecta natorum et nepotum pietate, sese defendere intendunt').⁵⁸ Mae pwysigrwydd y cysylltiad teuluol agos yn amlwg yma: y gobaith oedd y byddai gwystlon o'r fath yn atal y rhai a'u rhoddodd rhag torri eu llw. Yn yr achos hwn, wedi i'r Rhufeiniaid wrthod ildio, mae'r Brythoniaid yn cyflawni eu bygythiad: 'yn syth gyda dicter tanllyd, gorchmynnodd [y brodyr] grogi'r tri deg pedwar o wystlon mwyaf bonheddig yng ngolwg eu rhieni' ('confestim proterua ignescentes ira .xxiiii. nobilissimos obsidum in conspectu parentum suspendi praeceperunt').⁵⁹ Cawn bwyslais yma ar y ffaith bod y rhieni yn gorfod gwylio eu plant yn cael eu crogi, ond hefyd ar statws bonheddig y gwystlon.

Nid dyma oedd y canlyniad disgwyliedig na dymunol wrth roi a derbyn gwystlon. O bersbectif y sawl fyddai'n eu derbyn, doedd dim gwerth i wystl marw wrth warantu cytundeb. Mae Adam Kosto hefyd yn pwysleisio'r goblygiadau gwleidyddol: byddai lladd gwystl yn debygol o suro'r berthynas rhwng carfanau, carfanau a fyddai'n aml yn gymdogion o ryw fath. Roedd i wystlon werth gwleidyddol hir-dymor hefyd, gyda'u potensial i weithredu fel diplomyddion rhwng carfanau.⁶⁰ Er bod enghreifftiau niferus o wystlon yn cael eu lladd, yn aml trwy eu crogi fel yn *De gestis Britonum*, doedd hyn ddim yn ganlyniad anochel.⁶¹ Yn wir, digon posib bod y croniclau'n cyfeirio at wystlon yn cael eu lladd oherwydd bod hyn yn beth anarferol neu nodedig. Dyma'r argraff a gawn yn *De gestis Britonum* hefyd, lle oeda Sieffre ar y ddelwedd o'r crogi, gan bwysleisio'r nifer a grogwyd, a'r rhieni'n gwylio.

Mae testunau *Brut y Brenhinedd* yn amlygu ambell bwynt diddorol ychwanegol yma. Mae fersiwn Cotton Cleopatra yn cwtogi ar y naratif gan nodi: 'ac yna y parassant dyrchauel crogwyd wrth porth y gaer a chrogi y pedwar meib arugeint a gymeresseint yn gwistylon am eu kywirdeb ac ev teyrnget gan wyr ruvein' ('ac yna gwnaethon nhw godi crocbren wrth porth y gaer a chrogi'r dau ddeg pedwar mab roedden nhw wedi eu cymryd yn wystlon gan ddynion Rhufain ar gyfer eu ffyddlondeb a'u teyrngarwch').[62] Does dim bygythiad yma: caiff y gwystlon eu crogi'n syth. Cawn ein hatgoffa hefyd mai am eu *kywirdeb* a'u *teyrnget* y rhoddwyd y gwystlon; hynny yw, i gadarnhau eu haddewid o ufudd-dod a'u trethi. Ceir addasiad mwy diddorol eto yn *Brut Dingestow*:

> Ac yr guaradwyd y wyr Ruuein dyrchauael crogvyd rac bron y gaer, a menegi udunt y crogynt eu gvystlon yn diannot ony rodynt y dinas a dyuot yn eu hewyllis. A guedy guelet o Ueli a Bran wyr Ruuein yn ebryuygu eu gvystlon, sef a wnaethant vynteu, gan flemychu o antrugaravc yrlloned, peri crogi petwar gvystyl ar ugeint o dyledogyon Ruuein yg gvyd eu ryeni ac eu kenedyl.[63]

> Ac er cywilydd i ddynion Rhufain, codon nhw grocbren o flaen y gaer, a mynegi wrthynt y byddai eu gwystlon yn cael eu crogi yn syth os na fyddent yn rhoi'r ddinas a dod o dan eu hawdurdod. Ac wedi i Beli a Bran weld dynion Rhufain yn anghofio am eu gwystlon, dyma a wnaethon nhw: ar dân gyda llid anhrugarog, paron nhw i grogi dau ddeg pedwar o wystlon o foneddigion Rhufain o flaen eu rhieni a'u cenedl.

Dilyna'r cymal olaf *De gestis Britonum*: cawn gyfeiriad at grogi'r gwystlon o flaen eu teuluoedd ac mae'r ffocws ar eu statws o hyd. Mae'r gweddill yn dra gwahanol. Yn *Brut Dingestow*, mae Beli a Brennius yn codi'r pren crogi er 'gwaradwydd' i ddynion Rhufain. Awgryma hyn eu bod am godi cywilydd cyhoeddus arnynt am dorri eu llw o ffyddlondeb. Mae hyn yn wahanol i Sieffre, sy'n nodi mai'r pwrpas yw 'er mwyn cynyddu'r dinistr' (*ut maiorem cladem*). Caiff y newid hwn ei adlewyrchu ymhellach wrth i *Brut Dingestow* nodi bod dynion Rhufain wedi anghofio am eu gwystlon, neu wedi eu hesgeuluso ('ebryuygu eu gwystlon').[64] Noda Sieffre nad yw'r Rhufeiniaid wedi eu siglo, er gwaethaf eu teimladau tuag at eu meibion a'u neiaint ('verum Romani, in proposito suo perseuerantes, despecta natorum et nepotum pietate, sese defendere intendunt'). Yn *De gestis Britonum*, felly, mae ymdeimlad bod y Rhufeiniaid yn teimlo trueni dros y gwystlon, ond yn parhau i ymladd er gwaethaf hynny. Yn achos *Brut Dingestow*, gosodir y bai yn fwy pendant ar ysgwyddau dynion

Rhufain: nid yw'n arfer dda esgeuluso gwystlon yn y fath ffordd, ac mae torri cytundeb gan wybod mai'r gwystlon fydd yn dioddef yn weithred ddigywilydd. Diddorol yw gweld bod Peniarth 44 a Llanstephan 1 hefyd yn cyfeirio at ryw fath o esgeulustod. Noda Peniarth 44 (t. 38) fod dynion Rhufain yn 'dylyssỽ eỽ meybyon ac eỽ hwyryon ac eỽ neyeynt en ew gwystleyryaeth wy'; hynny yw, yn 'gadael' neu'n 'ymwrthod â nhw' yn eu gwystloniaeth. Yn ôl Llanstephan 1 (t. 50), mae dynion Rhufain yn 'tremygỽ eỽ meybon ac eỽ hwyryon'; hynny yw, eu 'diystyru' neu eu 'sarhau'. Mae pob un o'r tri cyfieithiad yn mynd ymhellach na Sieffre wrth gondemnio ymdriniaeth dynion Rhufain o'r bobl a roddwyd yn wystlon.[65]

Coda hyn gwestiynau diddorol ynghylch agweddau tuag at wystlo yng Nghymru'r drydedd ganrif ar ddeg. Fel y nodwyd eisoes, yn anaml iawn y câi gwystlon eu lladd. Wedi dweud hynny, daw un o'r enghreifftiau enwocaf yng nghyd-destun gwrthryfel Llywelyn ab Iorwerth yn erbyn y Brenin John yn 1212. Roedd Llywelyn wedi rhoi gwystlon 'o vonedhigyon y wlat' i John flwyddyn yn gynharach, ac yn ôl Roger o Wendover, fe'u lladdwyd yn sgil y gwrthryfel.[66] Mae ymateb *Brut y Tywysogyon*, sydd yn adrodd rhoi'r gwystlon yn 1211, yn amwys. Er nad yw'n adrodd, fel y gwna Roger o Wendover, gorchymyn dienyddio'r gwystlon gan y Brenin John, mae disgrifiad y cronicl o ddigwyddiadau'r flwyddyn 1212 yn cynnwys y canlynol:

> Y vlwydyn hono y croges Robert Vepwnt yn Amwythic Rys ap Maelgwn, a oed yg gwystyl y gan y brenhin, heb y vot yn seith mlwyd etto.[67]

> Y flwyddyn honno crogodd Robert Vieuxpont, yn Amwythig, Rhys ap Maelgwn, a oedd yn wystl i'r brenin a ddim eto'n saith mlwydd oed.

Diddorol yw'r pwyslais yma ar ieuenctid y gwystl dan sylw, pwyslais sydd yn taro nodyn tebyg i ystyriaeth Sieffre a *Brut y Brenhinedd* o statws gwystlon Rhufain fel meibion, wyron a neiaint. Does dim bai uniongyrchol yn cael ei roi ar y naill ochr na'r llall yma. Caiff Robert Vieuxpont ei enwi fel yr un sydd yn gyfrifol, ond dilyna'r hanes ddisgrifiad o wrthryfel Llywelyn yn erbyn y brenin, gan gynnwys ymosod ar gastell Mathrafal, a adeiladwyd gan Robert Vieuxpont.

Mae'r cyfeiriad at Rhys ap Maelgwn 'a oed yg gwystyl y gan y brenhin' hefyd yn sicrhau cysylltiad clir gyda chytundeb heddwch y flwyddyn flaenorol. Mae barn *Brut y Tywysogyon* ar y mater yn amwys, felly, ond mae posibilrwydd yn sicr bod enghreifftiau o'r fath wedi effeithio ar yr agweddau tuag at wystlo a'r rhai sydd yn torri cytundebau sydd i'w gweld yn *Brut y Brenhinedd*.[68]

Iaith a diwylliant

Yn yr enghreifftiau a drafodwyd hyd yn hyn, mae gwystlon wedi ymddangos yn yr un cyd-destun ym mhob achos, sef wrth warantu cytundeb neu wrth gosbi'r rhai sydd wedi torri cytundeb. Mae un enghraifft sydd yn dra gwahanol, ac yn cynnig mewnwelediad i'r ffordd y câi gwystlon eu trin, ynghyd ag agweddau tuag at eu rôl ddiwylliannol. Digwydd hyn yng nghyd-destun ymosodiad Claudius ar Brydain. Nid yw'r frwydr yn ffafrio'r Rhufeiniaid ac maent ar ddychwelyd i'w llongau, nes i ddyn o'r enw Hamo achub y dydd:

> Iam Claudius naues petebat, iam Romani paene dissipabantur, cum uersutus Hamo, proiectis illis quibus indutus fuerat, arma Britannica cepit et quasi Britannus contra suos pugnabat. Deinde hortabatur Britones ad insequendum, festinatum triumphum promittens; didicerat enim linguam eorum et mores, quia inter Britannicos obsides Romae nutritus fuerat.

> Roedd Claudius yn barod yn anelu am ei gychod, roedd y Rhufeiniad yn barod bron wedi eu gwasgaru, pan wnaeth y dyn clyfar Hamo dynnu ei arfau a chymryd arfau'r Brythoniaid ac ymladd yn erbyn ei bobl ei hun fel Brython. Yna anogodd y Brythoniaid i'w ddilyn, gan addo buddugoliaeth gyflym; roedd wedi dysgu eu hiaith a'u harferion, oherwydd iddo gael ei fagu ymysg y gwystlon Brythonaidd yn Rhufain.[69]

Yr awgrym a geir yma yw bod carfan o wystlon yn Rhufain – cymuned ar wahân i bob pwrpas. Fodd bynnag, dengys profiad Hamo bod cysylltiadau yn bodoli rhwng y Rhufeiniaid a'r Brythoniaid, a bod y cysylltiadau hyn yn gallu arwain at drosglwyddo iaith a diwylliant rhwng y carfanau.

Mae sylw wedi ei roi i rôl gwystlon wrth hwyluso cyfnewid
diwylliannol – a'u defnydd bwriadol at y diben hwn. Cyfeiria Kosto at
strategaeth Siarlymaen, er enghraifft, o anfon gwystlon at ganolfannau
eglwysig megis mynachdai. Mae'n bosib mai'r pwrpas oedd troi'r
gwystlon yn Gristnogion cyn eu dychwelyd i'w mamwledydd
anghristnogol.[70] Nid Siarlymaen oedd y cyntaf i ddilyn y strategaeth
hon chwaith: cyfeiria Kosto at arfer debyg er diben lledu diwylliant
yr ymerodraeth Rufeinig.[71] Yng nghyd-destun Cymru, byddai modd
ystyried unigolion megis Hywel Sais. Yn ôl testun sydd yn dilyn *Cronicon
de Wallia* yn llawysgrif Llyfrgell Cadeirlan Caerwysg 3514, rhoddwyd y
llysenw 'Sais' i Hywel gan ei fod wedi treulio cymaint o amser fel gwystl
yn Lloegr nes iddo anghofio ei iaith ei hun a dechrau siarad fel Sais.[72]
Yn yr achosion hyn, y gwystlon sydd yn mabwysiadu diwylliant y rhai
sydd yn eu dal. Yn *De gestis Britonum*, fodd bynnag, llifa'r dylanwad i'r
cyfeiriad arall: y gwystlon sydd yn pasio eu hiaith a'u diwylliant i'r rhai
sydd yn eu dal. Er gwaetha ymdriniaeth anarferol Sieffre â'r berthynas,
mae dealltwriaeth amlwg yma o rôl gwystlon fel cyfrwng i gyfnewid
diwylliant. Mae rhan helaeth o'r drafodaeth hon wedi canolbwyntio ar
bwysigrwydd gwystlon i wleidyddiaeth ganoloesol – mewn trafodaethau
rhwng carfanau ac mewn cytundebau. Gyda'r enghraifft olaf hon
o *De gestis Britonum* cawn ein rhybuddio rhag anghofio goblygiadau
diwylliannol a chymdeithasol eu rôl.

Casgliadau

I raddau, mae ymdriniaeth Sieffre o wystlon yn cefnogi casgliadau
ehangach Adam Kosto ynghylch gwystlo yn yr Oesoedd Canol. Caiff
gwystlon eu rhoi, yn hytrach na'u cymryd, er mwyn gwarantu cytundeb
o ryw fath – teyrngarwch, fel arfer, yn sgil gorchfygiad milwrol. Maent
yn unigolion o statws uchel sydd yn perthyn yn agos i'r sawl sydd yn eu
rhoi. Ceir terminoleg cyson i'w disgrifio – *obsides* yn *De gestis Britonum*,
'gwystlon' yn *Brut y Brenhinedd* – a chânt eu trin yn gategori ar wahân i
gaethion a charcharorion. Yn achlysurol caiff gwystlon eu lladd, ond mae
Sieffre yn glir nad yw'r canlyniad hwn yn ddymunol. Â *Brut y Brenhinedd*
ymhellach wrth gondemnio'r rhai sydd yn torri cytundebau ac anghofio
am y goblygiadau ar gyfer eu gwystlon. Does dim amheuaeth bod
Sieffre'n cyflwyno gwystlo fel rhan greiddiol o wleidyddiaeth yn *De
gestis Britonum*. Yn ei ymdriniaeth â gwystlon yng nghyfnodau Brutus,

Cesar, Arthur a Cadwallon, gwelwn arferion gwleidyddol y ddeuddegfed ganrif.

Wedi dweud hynny, mae tystiolaeth *De gestis Britonum* a *Brut y Brenhinedd* hefyd yn cymhlethu'r darlun rhywfaint. Er bod gwystlon yn cael eu rhoi yn hytrach na'u cymryd yn y rhan fwyaf o achosion, mae un enghraifft sydd yn tynnu'n groes i'r patrwm hwn. Cymhlethir y sefyllfa ymhellach yn yr addasiadau Cymraeg gan fod cyfeiriadau niferus at 'gymryd' gwystlon, datganiad sydd yn amwys ei ystyr. Cawn un cyfeiriad hefyd at gymryd pobl yn 'geith tragywydawl' yn hytrach na gwystlon. Gyda'i gilydd, mae'r enghreifftiau hyn yn awgrymu nad oedd awduron canoloesol yn glynu'n llym at un diffiniad o wystlon, nac ychwaith o hyd yn gwahaniaethu rhyngddynt a chaethion neu garcharorion. Fel y trafodwyd uchod, mewn achosion o roi gwystlon byddai fel arfer elfen o orfodaeth, felly ni fyddai'n syndod gweld bod y ffin rhwng gwystlon, caethion a charcharorion yn niwlog ar adegau. Pwysicach efallai na disgrifiadau ffynonellau o 'roi' neu 'gymryd' yw cyd-destun y trosglwyddiad. Hynny yw, roedd trosglwyddo gwystlon fel arfer yn rhan o gytundeb.

Er bod ymdriniaeth Sieffre o wystlon fel arfer yn cyd-fynd â'r hyn a wyddom am yr arfer yn fwy cyffredinol, nid pwrpas *De gestis Britonum* oedd gweithredu fel drych i adlewyrchu gwleidyddiaeth a chymdeithas y ddeuddegfed ganrif. Tra bo union bwrpas y testun yn bwnc dadleuol o hyd, dengys Sieffre gryn greadigrwydd wrth lunio ei naratif o hanes y Brythoniaid. Caiff hyn ddylanwad ar ei ymdriniaeth â gwystlon, fel a welwn yn ei gyflwyniad o'r gynghrair rhwng Cadfan ac Æthelfrith ac efallai hefyd yn araith Arthur yn dwyn i gof gweithredoedd Belinus a Brennius. Mae darllen y penodau hyn gyda llygad ar yr arfer o wystlo yn yr Oesoedd Canol yn taflu goleuni pellach ar rai o strategaethau Sieffre wrth lunio *De gestis Britonum*.

...

Hostages in *De gestis Britonum* and *Brut y Brenhinedd*

Abstract

Hostageship was a key part of political relations in the Middle Ages. This chapter explores how the practice was depicted in Geoffrey of Monmouth's *De gestis Britonum* and the Welsh translations known collectively as *Brut y Brenhinedd*, which started to appear in manuscripts from the thirteenth century. The discussion is situated within the framework for understanding the practice of medieval hostageship developed by scholars such as Adam Kosto and Jenny Benham. Several key aspects of the practice as understood by these scholars are exemplified by *De gestis Britonum* and *Brut y Brenhinedd*. This includes the practice of giving (rather than taking) hostages, the distinction drawn between hostages and other groups (prisoners, for example), and the tendency for hostages to be of high status and close kin relations to those giving them. However, these texts also show a greater fluidity to the practice. In other words, these rules appear not to have been followed as rigidly as the scholarly frameworks might suggest. The chapter also considers how Geoffrey's own narrative strategies impact on his presentation of hostageship, both in his unusual account of Æthelfrith and Cadfan exchanging hostages, and in Arthur's speech about the requirement to give hostages to the Roman emperors. Finally, this chapter considers the cultural impact of hostages through examining the depiction of an individual who had learned the language and customs of the Britons after spending time among the hostages in Rome. This chapter concludes that although *De gestis Britonum* and *Brut y Brenhinedd* largely support the frameworks that have been established for understanding medieval hostageship, this evidence also complicates the picture somewhat and suggests that the practice was in fact more fluid than previously realised. Reading these texts in the context of what we know about the practice of hostageship also sheds light on the narrative strategies of the texts themselves.

Nodiadau

1 *ByT* (LlC), s.a. 1165 (gol. Thomas Jones, *Brut y Tywysogyon or The Chronicle of Princes: the Red Book of Hergest Version* (Caerdydd, 1955), t. 146).
2 *ByT* (LlC), s.a. 1157, 1163, 1164 (gol. Jones, tt. 136–7, 142–7).
3 Henry G. Hewlett (gol.), *Rogeri de Wendover Liber qui dicitur Flores Historiarum ab anno domini MCLIV. Annoque Henrici Anglorum Regis Secundi Primo: The Flowers of History by Roger de Wendover*, 3 cyf. (London, 1886–9), II, 61. Gw. hefyd y cyfeiriad at ladd y gwystl Rhys ap Maelgwn (plentyn nad oedd eto'n saith oed) yn Amwythig yn yr un flwyddyn: *ByT* (LlC), s.a. 1212 (gol. Jones, t. 194).

4 *ByT* (LlC), s.a. 1171, 1173 (gol. Jones, tt. 156, 162). Am gyfeiriadau at 'Hywel Sais' gw. *ByT* (LlC), s.a. 1193, 1194, 1204 (gol. Jones, tt. 174, 186). Am drafodaeth o arwyddocâd y llysenw gw. Frederick Suppe, 'Medieval Welsh Ethnic Nicknames and Implications: for the Welsh view of their Geopolitical Context, 1050–1400', yn Christian Raffensperger (gol.), *Authorship, Worldview, and Identity in Medieval Europe* (London, 2022), tt. 325–45 (t. 329).

5 Gw. Owain Cyfeiliog yn rhoi gwystlon i Rhys ap Gruffudd yn 1171: *ByT* (LlC), s.a. 1171 (gol. Jones, t. 152). Gw. hefyd y cytundeb rhwng Maredudd ap Rhys a Llywelyn ap Gruffudd, lle y cytuna Maredudd i ddarparu gwystlon: *AWR*, tt. 519–21 (rhif 347).

6 Adam Kosto, *Hostages in the Middle Ages* (Oxford, 2012). Gw. hefyd Jenny Benham, *Peacemaking in the Middle Ages: Principles and Practice* (Manchester, 2011); Matthew Bennett a Katherine Weikert (goln), *Medieval Hostageship c.700–c.1500: hostage, captive, prisoner of war, guarantee, peacemaker* (London, 2016); Ryan Lavelle, 'The Use and Abuses of Hostages in later Anglo-Saxon England', *Early Medieval Europe*, 14 (2006), 269–96; Alice Hicklin, 'Aitire, 人質, тали, όμηρος, رهن, obses: Hostages, Political Instability, and the Writing of History *c*.900–*c*.1050 CE', *medieval worlds*, 10 (2019), 151–76.

7 Kosto, *Hostages in the Middle Ages*, t. 9.

8 Ond pwysig nodi mai datblygiad ym mherthynas Rhys ap Gruffudd a Harri oedd hynny, yn hytrach na thalu pridwerth. Am drafodaeth pellach gw. Huw Pryce, 'Rhys ap Gruffudd (1131/2–1197)', *ODNB*, https://doi.org/10.1093/ref:odnb/23464.

9 Noda Kosta hefyd bod gwystl yn ôl y diffiniad hwn yn wahanol i'r mechnïwr, sydd yn gwarantu cytundeb ond nad yw'n colli ei ryddid: *Hostages in the Middle Ages*, t. 11.

10 Kosto, *Hostages in the Middle Ages*, tt. 11–12.

11 Kosto, *Hostages in the Middle Ages*, tt. 25–6. Bydd yr achlysuron prin o ddwy garfan yn cyfnewid gwystlon yn cael eu trafod isod, gw. tt. 179–81.

12 *ByT* (LlC), s.a. 1211 (gol. Jones, t. 192).

13 Ceir trafodaeth o amrywiol gyd-destunau yn Kosto, *Hostages in the Middle Ages*, tt. 24–34.

14 Gw. er enghraifft, Benham, *Peacemaking in the Middle Ages*, tt. 159–60, 163–4; Kosto, *Hostages in the Middle Ages*, tt. 35, 45–6.

15 Benham, *Peacemaking*, tt. 160–1.

16 Cymh. Matthew Bennett, 'Warrior Narratives and Hostageship Ethos: Old French Literature and "Reality" in the Twelfth Century', yn Bennett a Weikert (goln), *Medieval Hostageship*, tt. 79–91; Hicklin, 'Aitire'.

17 Ceir ambell awgrym bod rhai beirdd yn gyfarwydd â rhyw fersiwn o ddiwedd y ddeuddegfed ganrif ymlaen, gw. Patrick Sims-Williams, *Rhai Addasiadau Cymraeg Canol o Sieffre o Fynwy* (Aberystwyth, 2011), tt. 5–6.

18 Defnyddir golygiad Henry Lewis o fersiwn Dingestow: *Brut Dingestow* (Caerdydd, 1942). Ar gyfer Peniarth 44, Llanstephan 1, defnyddir G. R. Isaac et al. (goln), *Rhyddiaith Gymraeg o Lawysgrifau'r 13eg Ganrif Fersiwn 2* (Aberystwyth, 2013), https://pure.aber.ac.uk/ws/portalfiles/portal/30954693/Rhyddiaith_y_13g_V2.pdf (cyrchwyd 31 Hydref 2023). Bydd cyfeiriadau at dudalennau'r llawysgrif fel y'u nodir yn y golygiad hwn. Daw testun fersiwn Peniarth 21/Peniarth 23 o Diana Luft, Peter Wynn Thomas a D. Mark Smith (goln), *Rhyddiaith Gymraeg 1300–1425* (Caerdydd, 2007–13), http://www.rhyddiaithganoloesol.caerdydd.ac.uk/cy/ (cyrchwyd 31 Hydref 2023).

19 John Jay Parry (gol. a chyf.), *Brut y Brenhinedd: Cotton Cleopatra Version* (Cambridge, MA, 1937).

20 Gw. y drafodaeth sydyn o'r fersiynau, y berthynas rhyngddynt, a'r dulliau cyfieithu amrywiol yn Nia Wyn Jones [cyhoeddwyd fel O. W. Jones], 'The Most Excellent Princes: Geoffrey of Monmouth and Medieval Welsh Historical Writing', yn Georgia Henley a Joshua Byron Smith (goln), *A Companion to Geoffrey of Monmouth* (Leiden, 2020), tt. 257–90 (tt. 274–5).

21 Noder bod yr ymdriniaeth hwn o wystlon yn cyd-fynd gydag ymdriniaeth cylchol Sieffre o hanes yn *De gestis Britonum* yn fwy cyffredinol. Am drafodaeth gw. Robert Hanning, *The Vision of History in Early Britain: from Gildas to Geoffrey of Monmouth* (New York, 1966), tt. 121–72.

22 *DGB*, ix.145 (gol. a chyf. Saesneg, Reeve a Wright, tt. 196–7).

23 *DGB*, ix.149 (gol. Reeve a Wright, tt. 200–1).

24 *DGB*, xi.197 (gol. Reeve a Wright, tt. 270–1).

25 Benham, *Peacemaking*, tt. 156–7.

26 *DGB*, iii.38 (gol. Reeve a Wright, tt. 50–1).

27 Kosto, *Hostages in the Middle Ages*, tt. 31, 59–61.

28 *DGB*, iv.62 (gol. Reeve a Wright, tt. 76–7).

29 *DGB*, iii.38 (gol. Reeve a Wright, t. 51).

30 *Brut Dingestow*, iii.9 (gol. Lewis, t. 37). Cymh. *DGB*, iii.43 (gol. Reeve a Wright, t. 57).

31 *DGB*, xi.197 (gol. Reeve a Wright, t. 271).

32 GPC, d.g. *arfoll* 1 (2006), https://www.geiriadur.ac.uk/gpc/gpc.html (cyrchwyd 19 Mehefin 2024).

33 D. Simon Evans (gol.), *Historia Gruffud vab Kenan* (Caerdydd, 1977), 24.8.

34 Paul Russell (gol. a chyf.), *Vita Griffini filii Conani: the Medieval Latin Life of Gruffudd ap Cynan* (Cardiff, 2005), tt. 80–1 (pennod 28).

35 GPC, d.g. *cadernid* 2.

36 Gw. hefyd fersiwn Cotton Cleopatra (gol. Parry, t. 158); *Brut Dingestow*, ix.3 (gol. Lewis, t. 147).

37 *DGB*, v.78 (gol. Reeve a Wright, t. 96).

38 *Brut Dingestow*, v.6 (gol. Lewis, t. 69). Gw. hefyd Llanstephan 1, t. 94; Peniarth 44, t. 69.
39 *GPC*, d.g. *cymryd* 1 a; b.
40 *ByT* (LlCH), s.a. 1171 (gol. Jones, t. 152). Gw, hefyd s.a. 1241 (gol. Jones, t. 236).
41 *DGB*, iii.43 (gol. Reeve a Wright, 56–7).
42 *DGB*, iii.3 (gol. Reeve a Wright, tt. 58–9).
43 Mae gwaith diweddar hefyd wedi pwysleisio pa mor gyfnewidiol oedd statws gwystl yn yr Oesoedd Canol, rhywbeth a welir yn sicr yn achos Hywel Sais: Matthew Bennett a Katherine Weikert, 'The State of Play: Medieval Hostageship and Modern Scholarship', yn Weikert a Bennett (goln), *Medieval Hostageship*, tt. 1–14 (t. 3).
44 Fersiwn Cotton Cleopatra (gol. Parry, t. 160); myfi piau'r atalnodi.
45 *DGB*, ix.148 (gol. Reeve a Wright, tt. 200–1).
46 *ByT* (LlC), s.a. 1165 (gol. Jones, t. 146).
47 *DGB*, xi.190 (gol. Reeve a Wright, tt. 260–1).
48 *Brut Dingestow*, xii.1 (gol. Lewis, t. 192). Gw. hefyd Peniarth 44, t. 72; Peniarth 23, t. 123.
49 Kosto, *Hostages in the Middle Ages*, tt. 46–7.
50 Benham, *Peacemaking*, tt. 163–5.
51 Gw. ymhellach isod, tt. 182–6.
52 Cyfeiria Benham at Llywelyn yn rhoi ei unig fab, Gruffudd, i'r Brenin John yn 1211 ac yn addo y byddai ei deyrnas yn trosglwyddo i frenin Lloegr pe na bai'n cael mab gan ei wraig, Siwan, fel enghraifft o'r garfan gryfaf yn sicrhau ansefydlogrwydd trwy fynnu gwystlon: *Peacemaking*, t. 163.
53 David E. Thornton, 'Cadfan ab Iago (*fl. c.*616–*c.*625)', *ODNB*, https://doi.org/10.1093/ref:odnb/4314.
54 R. William Leckie Jr, *The Passage of Dominion: Geoffrey of Monmouth and the Periodization of Insular History in the Twelfth Century* (Toronto, 1982), tt. 66–72. Gw. hefyd Rebecca Thomas, 'Geoffrey of Monmouth and the English Past', yn Smith a Henley (goln), *A Companion to Geoffrey of Monmouth*, tt. 105–28.
55 *DGB*, iii.43 (gol. Reeve a Wright, t. 59). Gw. isod tt. 183–5.
56 *DGB*, ix.159 (gol. Reeve a Wright, tt. 217–19).
57 *DGB*, iv.62 (gol. Reeve a Wright, t. 77).
58 *DGB*, iii.43 (gol. Reeve a Wright, t. 59).
59 *DGB*, iii.43 (gol. Reeve a Wright, t. 59).
60 Kosto, *Hostages in the Middle Ages*, tt. 45–6. Gw. enghraifft Hywel Sais uchod.
61 Gw. er enghraifft *ByT* (LlCH), s.a. 1165 (gol. Jones, t. 146); Hewlett, gol., *Rogeri de Wendover*, ii, 61. Gw. atodiad pennod X, Kosto, *Hostages in the Middle Ages*, am restr o enghreifftiau o wystlon yn cael eu lladd, gan gynnwys trwy grogi.

62 Fersiwn Cotton Cleopatra (gol. Parry, t. 52).
63 *Brut Dingestow*, iii.9 (gol. Lewis, t. 38).
64 Gw. rhestr o ystyron ac enghreifftiau yn *GPC*, d.g. *ebrfygaf*.
65 Cymh. trafodaeth Alice Hicklin o'r patrwm mewn testunau o'r oesoedd canol cynnar, sydd yn tueddu i osod bai ar y rhai hynny sy'n derbyn y gwystlon os cânt eu niweidio. Yn y testunau hyn, y Llychlynwyr sydd yn gyfrifol fel arfer: 'Aitire', 163–5.
66 *ByT* (LlC), s.a. 1211 (gol. Jones, t. 192); Hewlett (gol.), *Rogeri de Wendover*, II, 61.
67 *ByT* (LlC), s.a. 1212 (gol. Jones, t. 194). Gw. hefyd *ByT* (P20), s.a. 1212 (gol. Jones, t. 158; cyf. Jones, t. 86).
68 Byddai modd ystyried digwyddiadau'r flwyddyn 1165 yn y cyd-destun hwn hefyd (gw. uchod t. 172). Er mwyn datblygu'r ddadl hon ymhellach, mae galw am astudiaeth lawnach o'r enghreifftiau o wystlo ac ymatebion i dorri cytundebau yn y tystiolaeth o Gymru, sydd tu hwnt i allu'r bennod hon.
69 *DGB*, iv.66 (gol. Reeve a Wright, t. 83).
70 Kosto, *Hostages in the Middle Ages*, tt. 67–70; Adam J. Kosto, 'Hostages in the Carolingian World (714–840)', *Early Medieval Europe*, 11 (2002), 123–47 (tt. 144–5).
71 Kosto, *Hostages in the Middle Ages*, tt. 67–70.
72 Am y testun gw. Thomas Jones, '"Cronica de Wallia" and other documents from Exeter Cathedral Library MS. 2514', *BBCS*, 12 (1946), 27–44 (t. 41). Am drafodaeth gw. Frederick Suppe, 'Who was Rhys Sais? Some Comments on Anglo-Welsh Relations before 1066', *The Haskins Society Journal*, 7 (1995), 63–73 (tt. 67–8); Suppe, 'Medieval Welsh Ethnic Nicknames and Implications', t. 329.

8

The Context of *Laudabiliter* in the Works of Gerald of Wales[1]

Thomas M. Charles-Edwards

Laudabiliter is the name given to what purports to be a privilege from Pope Adrian IV giving his blessing to Henry II's plan to invade Ireland.[2] Its authenticity is much debated. This chapter will not address that question or add to the debate. Nor will it discuss the context in which it was issued.[3] Instead, since Gerald of Wales is, for us, both the original source for the text and included it in three of his works, the issue addressed here is the changing context that Gerald created for *Laudabiliter* within the three works. The first occurrence is in his *Expugnatio Hibernica*, of which the first version was completed before July 1189.[4] Another is in the *De principis instructione*, on which Gerald was working at intervals from *c*.1190 until 1216 or 1217.[5] A third is in Gerald's autobiographical work, which he called *De gestis Giraldi* but has been known since the late seventeenth century as *De rebus a se gestis*, completed fairly late in his lifetime (he is likely to have died in 1223).[6] The contexts of *Laudabiliter* in the three works are different and appear to reveal shifts in what Gerald thought of the English conquest of Ireland as he grew older.

A further distinction between the three texts of *Laudabiliter* is the stage of Gerald's career to which they belong and the fortunes of the Angevin kings at the time. Gerald began work on the *Topographia Hiberniae* and the *Expugnatio* during his first stay in Ireland, February 1183 to early in 1184. This was in the interval between a period when he was administering the diocese of St Davids, while the bishop, Peter de Leia, was living in England, and a later period when Gerald took service as a royal clerk – service which continued from 1184 until at least 1191. It was during his time as a royal clerk that he wrote the first versions of both *Expugnatio Hibernica* and *De principis instructione*, as well as the *Topographia Hibernie* and the *Itinerarium Kambrie*. The *Expugnatio* was thus completed as a royal clerk. The first version of *De principis instructione* was completed about the time when Gerald, disappointed at the absence of any promotion, left royal service, though he continued to receive an annual sum from the Exchequer for some years after that date.[7] The final version was produced when Prince Louis, son and heir of Philip Augustus, was in England, leading a rebellion against King John, and probably, as Robert Bartlett argues, before the death of King John in October 1216.[8] Gerald had high hopes that Louis would replace John on the throne of England. The surviving version of *De gestis* was completed in the minority of Henry III, after Prince Louis had left England.

In the *Expugnatio*, Book I ends at chapter 45 with the victory of Henry II over the serious rebellion of 1173 led by his sons and supported by Queen Eleanor, by Louis VII of France and by William the Lion, king of Scots. It was a victory, according to Gerald, that followed Henry's pilgrimage to Canterbury to do penance for the killing of Thomas Becket, a victory that found its best expression in the king's mercy towards the rebels, and thus a victory over Henry's own anger and resentment.[9] Yet, chapter 44 was headed 'The first conflict of the sons against the father' and looked forward to the mention in ii. 31 of 'The second desertion' by the young King Henry and Geoffrey, count of Brittany.[10] The *Expugnatio* was presented to Henry II shortly before his death but then dedicated to Richard, count of Poitou, in the interval between Henry's death, after he had been defeated by Richard, and Richard's own coronation as king of England.[11] The reason Gerald gave for the more succinct narrative of Book II was the burden of his work helping to prepare for a crusade, namely, the one in view after Henry II and Philip Augustus had taken the cross together at Gisors early in 1188.[12]

Book II of the *Expugnatio* begins with arrangements in Ireland as a consequence of the threat and then the outbreak of civil war in 1173, picking up the narrative from i. 44. These new arrangements entailed concessions on the part of Henry II and a drawing together between Richard fitz Gilbert, earl of Striguil and lord of Leinster, and the Children of Nest (descendants of Nest daughter of Rhys ap Tewdwr). Henry II's settlement when he left Ireland in April 1172 had included two main elements: while, in Leinster, Richard was allowed to keep the interior of the province, whereas the king retained all the former Viking seaport towns from Dublin in the north to Waterford just across the border into Munster; and, secondly, Hugh de Lacy was granted Meath, not yet conquered, as a counterweight to Richard fitz Gilbert in Leinster. In the summer of 1173, however, after Richard fitz Gilbert had obeyed the summons to join the defence of Normandy, he was granted Wicklow, one of the seaport towns. The *Song of Dermot and the Earl* supplies the detail that Richard fitz Gilbert had been entrusted with the defence of Gisors, a crucial castle and town on the border of Normandy.[13] Gerald passed over the sending of William fitz Audelin to Ireland to fill the gap occasioned by the summoning of troops from Ireland to fight the rebels in England and both rebels and French in Normandy. Gerald's Book II therefore began with Richard fitz Gilbert back in authority in Ireland and faced with 'almost all the princes of that country in open revolt against the king and himself', with his money at an end, and his unpaid soldiers threatening desertion.[14] At this point, Richard fitz Gilbert summoned Raymond le Gros back from Carew in Pembrokeshire and promised him the hand of his sister, Basilia. This was only the first of the marriages binding the settlers together, which take up chapters 1–4. Among these was the union between Richard's daughter, Aline, and William, eldest son of Maurice fitz Gerald. Maurice himself had also been summoned back from Wales and given by Richard fitz Gilbert both Wicklow and the central portion of Uí Fháeláin, including Naas, close to Kildare, the caput of Richard's lordship. The pressure of the great rebellion of 1173 thus necessitated a drawing together of Henry II and Richard fitz Gilbert, previously on poor terms, and of Richard fitz Gilbert and the Children of Nest. This territorial settlement of the mid-1170s is the one detailed in the *Song*, not the earlier ones in the lifetime of Diarmait Mac Murchada and during Henry II's stay in Ireland.[15]

After that group of chapters (ii. 1–4) comes a chapter on the privileges obtained from the Roman curia, including *Laudabiliter*. This in turn is followed by a chapter on 'the five-fold right' of the king of the English to rule over Ireland, of which the last was 'the authority of the supreme pontiffs who have responsibility for all islands'.[16] This final source of entitlement, derived from the Donation of Constantine, is the one mentioned by John of Salisbury in his *Metalogicon* when he recounted his close friendship with Pope Adrian IV and his consequent success in obtaining a privilege approving Henry II's proposal to invade and conquer Ireland.[17]

Three themes are recurrent in Gerald's three writings that include *Laudabiliter*. The first is the wheel of fortune, the way Henry gained a position of eminence among contemporary rulers, only for him in his last years to experience 'Fortune's finely calculated malice':[18] namely, discord in his own family and humiliation at the hands of his successor, Richard, in alliance with Philip Augustus. This classical theme takes a Christian form in the long-enduring patience of God towards someone he has favoured with extraordinary gifts, waiting for repentance, but that patience at last exhausted.[19] The second theme is the crusade: an element in the agreement at Avranches in May 1172, embodying the terms on which Henry was freed from the interdict laid upon him after the killing of Thomas Becket, was the king's promise to go on crusade within three years.[20] Admittedly, the outbreak of hostilities between Henry and his sons, aided by Louis VII, made a prompt fulfilment of his promise impossible;[21] but the issue came to a head again when Heraclius, patriarch of Jerusalem, came to England early in 1185 to offer Henry the keys of Jerusalem and the kingship of the Holy Land. Instead of aiding the Christians of Palestine against the Muslims, Henry chose to send his youngest son, John, against the Christian Irish.[22] The final theme was the failure of the English in Ireland to promote the Irish Church. On the English in Ireland, Gerald wrote: 'Not only have we not thought it worthy of a gift from our prince, and of the honour which it should have by right, but we are actually trying to curtail or abrogate its ancient rights and privileges, having stripped it of its lands and possessions immediately on our arrival'.[23] Gerald's own kinsmen, Raymond and Meilyr, were not spared from criticism for their failure to grant to the Church 'a portion of their new and bloodstained acquisition of land, secured at the cost of great bloodshed and the slaughter of a Christian people'.[24] As for John's expedition to Ireland in 1185, Gerald drives home this message with an account of a vision.[25] Although the settlers as a whole were accused, a particular guilt attached to Henry II, for, in *Laudabiliter*, Adrian IV's approval of Henry's intention to conquer Ireland was secured on the basis that he would, among other things, 'preserve the rights of the churches of that land intact and unimpaired'.[26]

In the *Expugnatio*, Gerald touched on these three themes at different places, though mainly in Book II, written in the leisure moments while working as a royal servant on the preparations for the crusade. In *De principis instructione*, the reversal of fortune is coupled with the crusade in the chapters following the text of *Laudabiliter*. Ireland is there of significance, first, because it was almost the final extension of the lands subject to Henry and thus, in territorial terms, the height of the wheel of his fortune. *Laudabiliter* was followed by the Council of Cashel and then a chapter taken from the *Topographia Hiberniae* on the exceptional qualities of Henry II.[27] After that, Gerald turned to the Holy Land and the need for a crusade, which allowed him to make here the criticism made in the *Expugnatio*, that Henry sent his son John against Irish Christians rather than against the Muslim threat to the Holy Land.[28] Then came a trio of chapters on Henry II, more critical than the earlier chapter that came from the *Topographia*, but the main criticism is kept until the third of the trio, entitled 'If the eventual outcome of events had been happy, then his history would have been admirable'.[29]

If, in the *Expugnatio*, criticism of the English treatment of the Irish Church is dispersed and, in *De principis instructione*, Ireland is only a subordinate aspect of the themes of rise and fall and the crusade, in *De gestis*, the theme of the English failure to protect and endow the Church is concentrated into one sequence of four chapters, allowing *Laudabiliter* to emerge much more clearly as a basis for questioning the justification for the attempted conquest.[30] An example of rearranging chronology to emphasise an argument is provided by comparing the *De gestis* with the *Expugnatio*'s account of the principal events of 1185, in which the arrival of the Patriarch Heraclius and the sending of John to Ireland, occur relatively late in Book II, separated by many chapters from *Laudabiliter*; but, in *De gestis*, the same events are recalled in a chapter prefixed to the chapter containing *Laudabiliter*, even though *Laudabiliter* was obtained thirty years earlier, shortly after Henry became king. Furthermore, the connection between the chapter on Heraclius's offer to Henry II and *Laudabiliter* is rendered unmistakeable by the second half of the chapter on Heraclius: if the failure to respond to Heraclius marked the point at which the wheel of fortune began to descend for Henry II, it was also the first of three reasons why the expedition of Henry's youngest son, John, to Ireland was a failure, the third reason being the failure to support and endow the Irish Church. After the chapter devoted to *Laudabiliter*, the reader is taken back to 1185, to a vision of a church marked out by John with a large nave for the laity and a diminutive chancel for the clergy, a vision that Gerald had when working for John in Ireland.[31] The vision was recounted in the *Expugnatio*, but its message is far more pointed because it was now placed immediately after *Laudabiliter*.

The final chapter of the sequence of four declares that John offered Gerald two bishoprics in Ireland, but that Gerald refused them both. The reason given by Gerald was his belief that, as a bishop, he would not be given the support of the lay authority that would be necessary if he were to make a success of his office. If John, as lord of Ireland,

> had turned his mind to exalting and elevating the Irish church, then he would perhaps take up the honour offered him, in order to be able to cooperate and help him in this. But since he did not expect this to happen, he preferred not holding office to being uselessly in power; and he had no wish at all to be in charge where he could not be of any use.[32]

The chronology of Gerald's treatment of *Laudabiliter* and the English in Ireland indicates that he became increasingly critical. The sequence given at the beginning of this chapter had the *Expugnatio* completed in time to be presented to Henry II shortly before his death in 1189 and then provided with a new dedication to Richard I. A lost first version of *De principis instructione* was completed in 1191, when only Book I was published, while Books II and III, perhaps only existing in outline, were kept secret until they were finally revealed in a revised form in 1216 or 1217.[33] Gerald worked on the existing text of *De gestis* along with *Libellus inuectionum* and *De iure et statu Meneuensis ecclesie*, but they are likely to have been completed after the revised *De principis instructione*. The way *Laudabiliter* is given a position in the narrative confirms that *De gestis* was Gerald's final understanding of the implications of the document. In the *Expugnatio* it was revealed to a synod in Waterford attached to another document, *Quoniam ea*, purporting to be a privilege obtained from Pope Alexander III, when Henry II was preoccupied by the rebellion of his three eldest sons in alliance with Louis VII. Henry had collected the evidence of the Council of Cashel, assembled in 1171 or 1172, for major failings in the Irish Church and despatched them to the Pope. *Quoniam ea* was presented as Alexander's response. Since Henry was under an interdict following the killing of Becket and the agreement made at Avranches in May 1172, including his being freed from interdict, was not ratified in Rome until the following September, no such document as *Quoniam ea* could have been supposed to have been sent until that September.[34] Gerald claimed that both documents, *Quoniam ea* and

Laudabiliter, were taken to Ireland by William fitz Audelin and Nicholas, prior of Wallingford, and given a formal reading in a synod of bishops summoned for this purpose at Waterford.[35] Orpen gave good reason to think that this was in March or April 1173. Whatever may be the genuineness of the two documents (and *Quoniam ea*, at least, is generally considered a forgery), their contents were known to some Irish bishops a decade before Gerald's first visit to the country.

In the revised *De principis instructione*, the chapter on the two papal privileges concerning Ireland is largely copied from the *Expugnatio*, but with an important qualification so far as *Quoniam ea* is concerned: 'The content of the second privilege is as follows, just as it was sought, as some assert or feign, although others deny that it was ever sought'.[36] Finally, in *De gestis*, *Quoniam ea* was simply omitted.

Examination of the contexts of *Laudabiliter* in the three works shows that Gerald's view of the English settlement in Ireland was more complex than is often thought. He has been regarded as an apologist for the English settlement.[37] That is evidently an exaggeration at best. The *Expugnatio* has also been regarded as an encomium of the Children of Nest.[38] That, again, is just one element in the work, for his cousins, Raymond and Meilyr, were not spared from criticism for their behaviour towards the Irish Church. Gerald regarded Henry II as a ruler of immense gifts, vast energy and, for much of his reign, blessed with good fortune, yet, in the end, a grievous disappointment, because he had refused the offer made by the Patriarch of Jerusalem, Heraclius.[39] Similarly, it appears that Gerald was increasingly pessimistic that the moral justification for the attempted conquest could be maintained. When confronted by the events of the conquest itself, the justification already contained in *Laudabiliter* was transformed into a thorough-going critique.

Notes

1 Gerald of Wales has been one of Huw Pryce's principal scholarly concerns and it is both appropriate and a pleasure to contribute a chapter on Gerald to a volume in his honour.

2 *Pontificia Hibernica*, ed. M. P. Sheehy, 2 vols (Dublin, 1962), I, 15–16, no. 4.

3 For that, see Marie Therese Flanagan, *Irish Society, Anglo-Norman Settlers, Angevin Kingship* (Oxford, 1989), pp. 38–54.

4 *Expugnatio Hibernica: The Conquest of Ireland*, ii. 5, ed. A. B. Scott and F. X. Martin (Dublin, 1978) [hereafter *Exp. Hib.*], pp. 144–6. (In this edition,

Scott was responsible for the edited text and the translation, Martin for the historical notes.) For the date, see the introduction, p. xvi, and Gerald of Wales, *Instruction for a Ruler (De Principis Instructione)*, ii. 19, ed. and trans. Robert Bartlett, Oxford Medieval Texts (Oxford, 2018) [hereafter *De prin.*], p. 542 n. 300.

5   *De prin.*, ii. 19. Bartlett shows that the first version of this work was completed in 1191. A copy of this version is known to have existed in the house of the Augustinian canons in Leicester, but the only surviving copy is of a revision of 1216–17: see Bartlett's introduction, pp. xiii–xix.

6   Gerald of Wales, *On the Deeds of Gerald (De gestis Giraldi)*, ii. 11, ed. Jacob Currie with Thomas Charles-Edwards and Paul Russell, Oxford Medieval Texts (Oxford, 2024), 116–19. In the Introduction, xlii–xlvi, Jacob Currie shows that the work was framed by Gerald as an episcopal biography, rather than an autobiography, even though Gerald never became a bishop.

7   *De prin.*, pp. xv–xvi.

8   *De prin.*, pp. xvii–xviii.

9   *Exp. Hib.*, i. 45, ed. Scott and Martin, p. 122.

10 *Exp. Hib.*, i. 44 ('Prima filiorum in patrem dissencio') and ii. 31 ('Secunda discessio regis Henrici tercii et comitis Gaufridi'), ed. Scott and Martin, pp. 120, 224.

11 *Exp. Hib.*, dedication to Richard, ed. Scott and Martin, pp. 22, 285 n. 2.

12 Cf. *De prin.*, iii. 5, ed. Bartlett, p. 586.

13 *The Song of Dermot and the Earl*, ed. and trans. G. H. Orpen (Oxford, 1892), l. 2887 = *The Deeds of the Normans in Ireland: La geste des Engleis en Yrlande*, ed. and trans. E. Mullally (Dublin, 2002), l. 2885.

14 *Exp. Hib.*, ii. 1 ('omnes fere terre illius principes regi sibique rebelles invenit').

15 *Exp. Hib.*, i. 44, *Song*, ll. 3092–5, *Deeds*, ll. 3090–3. For Naas, as well as central Uí Fháeláin, see *Song*, ll. 3088–91, *Deeds*, ll. 3084–9.

16 *Exp. Hib.*, ii. 6 ('De quinquepartito iure'; 'summorum pontificum, qui insulas omnes speciali quodam iure respiciunt').

17 John of Salisbury, *Metalogicon*, iv. 42, ed. J. B. Hall with the help of K. S. M. Keats-Rohan, Corpus Christianorum Continuatio Mediaevalis, 98 (Turnhout, 1991), p. 183; trans. J. B. Hall, Corpus Christianorum in Translation, 12 (Turnhout, 2013), p. 342.

18 *Exp. Hib.*, i. 46, ed. Scott and Martin, p. 133 ('exquisita quadam fortune malicia').

19 *Exp. Hib.*, ii. 32, ed. Scott and Martin, pp. 225–7. On the theme of rise and fall, see Bartlett's introduction to *De prin.*, pp. xxxii–xxxiii.

20 *De prin.*, ii. 6, trans. Bartlett, p. 467.

21 On Henry's promise to found three monasteries instead of fulfilling the promise made at Avranches, see Gerald's dismissive account, *De prin.*, ii. 7.

22 *Exp. Hib.*, ii. 36, ed. Scott and Martin, p. 237.
23 *Exp. Hib.*, ed. Scott and Martin, p. 243 ('non tantum principali largicione debitoque honore non iudicavimus. quinimmo terris statim sublatis et possessionibus, pristinas eidem dignitates et antiqua privilegia vel mutilare contendimus vel abrogare').
24 *Exp. Hib.*, ii. 9., ed. Scott and Martin, p. 157 ('tam nove tamque cruente conquisicionis plurima quippe sanguinis effusione Christianeque gentis interempcione fedate, partem placabilem Deoque placentem').
25 *Exp. Hib.*, ii. 36, ed. Scott and Martin, p. 243.
26 *Exp. Hib.*, ii. 5, ed. Scott and Martin, p. 145.
27 *De prin.*, ii. 19–21, ed. Bartlett, pp. 509–19.
28 *De prin.*, ii. 22–8, 30–1, ed. Bartlett, pp. 519–41, 547–59.
29 *De prin.*, ii. 31, ed. Bartlett, pp. 437, 555 ('Quod, si finis euentuum felix fuisset, historia quoque commendabilis esset').
30 *De gestis*, ii. 10–13. After these four, Gerald continues to tell his readers about his stay in Ireland in 1185–6, devoting a chapter, ii. 14, to his sermon at a council of the province of Dublin, but this is much less relevant to *Laudabiliter*.
31 *De gestis*, ii. 12.
32 *De gestis*, ii. 13, p. 123 (Currie's translation of 'si animum ipsius ad hoc datum uideret, ut ecclesiam Hibernicam extollere uellet et sublimare, se forsan, ut ad hoc cooperari et quo adiuuare posset, oblatum honorem suscepturum. Sed, quoniam hoc non attendit, maluit esse priuatus quam inutiliter in potestate constitutus nec aliquatenus ibi preesse uoluit ubi prodesse non potuit.').
33 *De prin.*, ed. Bartlett, pp. xiv–xv, xvii–xviii, and trans., p. 433.
34 For the complexities of the triangular relationship between the papacy, the Irish episcopate and Henry II at this period, see Marie Therese Flanagan, 'Henry II, the Council of Cashel and the Irish Bishops', *Peritia*, 10 (1996), 184–211.
35 G. H. Orpen, *Ireland under the Normans, 1169–1333*, 4 vols (Oxford, 1911, 1920; repr. as a single vol., Dublin, 2005), Note on the 'Date of the publication of the papal privileges', I, 312–16, repr. pp. 116–18.
36 *De prin.*, trans. Bartlett, p. 513 ('Secundi uero priuilegii tenor hic, sicut a quibusdam impetratum asseritur aut confingetur, ab aliis autem unquam impetratum fuisse negatur').
37 See, for example, Diarmuid Scully, 'The portrayal of Ireland in Bernard's Life of Malachy', in Damian Bracken and Dagmar Ó Riain-Raedel (eds), *Ireland and Europe in the Twelfth Century* (Dublin, 2006), pp. 239–56 (p. 249).
38 See, for example, F. X. Martin, in *Exp. Hib.*, p. 269.
39 The contrast is clear from *De prin.*, ii. 21, taken from *Topographia Hibernica*, iii. 46–8, ed. J. F. Dimock (London, 1867), pp. 189–91, and *De prin.*, ii. 29, taken from *Exp. Hib.*, i. 46, and *De prin.*, ii. 30 and the beginning of 31, from *Exp. Hib.*, 31.

9

The Medieval Bishops of Bangor and the Writing of Welsh History

Shaun McGuinness

From the late eleventh century onwards, we have increasingly detailed accounts of the lives and episcopates of the bishops of Bangor, and in addition to the production of theological, liturgical and instructional works, as well as day-to-day *acta*, it is clear that a number of the medieval incumbents were interested in recording history – whether by writing it themselves, commissioning scribes or influencing contemporary chroniclers and authors.[1]

Reflecting their importance in the recording of medieval Welsh history, the monastic houses of Wales, especially those of the Cistercians, have received significant scholarly attention.[2] However, there has been no detailed study focusing on the contribution in this regard of the bishops of the four dioceses of medieval Wales. Indeed, attention has been drawn to the comparative lack of scholarly endeavour afforded to medieval bishops in general.[3] That is not to say that scholars of medieval Wales have overlooked episcopal influence, but that, for the most part, bishops have not been the main focus of studies, often only being considered when their actions or inactions help elucidate a study of, for example, one or more Welsh princes.[4] The aim of this chapter is to examine to what extent the bishops of one diocese helped record the political and ecclesiastical milieu in which they found themselves, and why they did so.

Six bishops, together with one passed over bishop-elect, will be considered in chronological order, beginning with Hervey, who ensured that the details of his violent expulsion from Bangor at the end of the eleventh century were recorded, seemingly as a way of exonerating himself for his prolonged absence from his diocese. Hervey's account finds a degree of corroboration in the turbulent episcopate of one of his twelfth-century successors, Meurig (who informed the archbishop of Canterbury of the reasons for his expulsion, no doubt for much the same reason). David the Scot, Hervey's immediate successor, recorded history for a different purpose, and at the behest of another and, as we shall see, his writings could have secured his promotion to the bishopric. At the turn of the twelfth century, Rotoland, who as bishop-elect spent a great deal of time with Gerald of Wales, may well have informed the writings of that most prolific of medieval authors. The extent to which the bishops of Bangor influenced the works of contemporary chroniclers and writers will become more apparent when the contributions of Robert of Shrewsbury, Cadwgan of Llandyfái and especially Richard in the thirteenth century are considered. The chapter will conclude with Anian, whose testimony, at the start of the fourteenth century, of a miraculous event in one of the walled towns built by Edward I adds to our knowledge of the new order that had by then replaced native Welsh rule.

Hervey (1092–1109)

In 1092, following a period of successful Norman advances into Gwynedd Uwch Conwy, the Breton, Hervey, was intruded into the bishopric of Bangor.[5] He was the first Norman nominee to be imposed on the Welsh.[6] Unelected and unwanted he was soon expelled, being driven from his see as early as 1094.[7] In the words of Sir J. E. Lloyd, 'bishop and flock never arrived at an understanding', the former adopting harsh measures, the latter retaliating.[8] In Pope Paschal II's opinion, Hervey had been promoted among barbarous people in a barbarous and stupid way (*inter barbaros barbarice et stolide promotus est*).[9] However, William of Malmesbury accused Hervey of having abandoned Bangor using the excuse that he did not get on with his Welsh neighbours, in the hope of making a richer living elsewhere.[10] The Benedictine monk and historian repeated the charge referring to Hervey's lack of livelihood when in Bangor.[11] William was not the Breton's only detractor, and attention has been drawn to Hervey's poor relationship with Anselm, appointed archbishop of Canterbury the year after Hervey's consecration.[12] In 1106, King Henry I suggested that Hervey be translated to Lisieux, but Anselm's reluctance to facilitate such a translation was clear.[13] However, Hervey did at last secure a richer living, for having been appointed at the king's direction administrator of Ely Abbey, with Henry's backing he went to Rome, and after impressing Paschal II returned with papal letters authorising the creation of the new bishopric of Ely and his translation.[14]

Hervey became Ely's first bishop in 1109.[15] It was there that the circumstances of his expulsion from Bangor were recorded in detail. The cartulary-chronicle of Ely, the *Liber Eliensis*, parts of which are known to have been commissioned by Hervey, tells the story of how when he was in Bangor he struggled to cope with the 'wickedness' (*perversitas*) of a savage people (*gens effera*), and treated them with extreme rigour, and frequently repeated anathema.[16] They had no reverence for him, and he had to wield a sharp sword twice to subdue them. He employed a large force of his kinsmen and other men to curb them, but to no avail. His brother was killed, and most of his kin killed or severely wounded. As he thought the locals wished to do the same to him, and lacking sufficient defenders, he chose to flee to England and the protection of the king.[17]

Hervey's enthronement at Ely took place six months after Anselm's death, and the archbishop's companion and biographer, Eadmer, wrote of Hervey's translation: 'this preferment sought by much asking, by much promising of many kinds and by performing many services, he finally succeeded in obtaining as soon as ever Anselm, that most active father, was dead'.[18] In the face of these criticisms from certain of his ecclesiastical contemporaries, it is not hard to conjecture that the account of the bishop's treatment at the hands of the Bangor populace contained in the *Liber Eliensis* was Hervey's way of giving his side of the story, and ensuring that his reasons for securing a new prelacy in a new bishopric were recorded for posterity.

Interestingly, corroboration of Hervey's version of events, albeit some fifty years or so later, is possibly to be found in the account of one of his successors, the Welshman Meurig (consecrated in 1140).[19] As Hervey had sought refuge with the king of England, Meurig sought refuge with the archbishop of Canterbury. The wrongs perpetrated by Bangor flock and diocesan clergy alike in the mid-twelfth century were relayed by Meurig to Archbishop Theobald who in turn appealed to the pope on his suffragan's behalf.[20] Theobald did not hold back in his forthright condemnation and the tone of the accusations made is reminiscent of the allegations levelled by Hervey. The archbishop accused the populace of debasing the church of Bangor by their 'wickedness' (*malicia*).[21] As Hervey had done, Meurig resorted to excommunication and not just of the laity – Theobald lamented, 'as are the people, so is the priest' (*ut populus sic et sacerdos*), but the archbishop reserved the greatest condemnation for Owain Gwynedd (d. 1170), 'the prince of these barbarians' (*istorum barbarorum princeps*), who, according to Theobald, had despoiled the bishop of his possessions, driven him from his see and forced Meurig into exile with the archbishop.[22]

Hervey and Meurig were not the only bishops of Bangor who complained about their flock to absolve themselves from responsibility for their absences. In the thirteenth century, another Welshman, Richard (or Rhirid), who as we shall see also spent long periods in exile, begged Pope Clement IV to be allowed to resign.[23] Making accusations reminiscent of those made by both Hervey and Meurig, his supplication stated that he felt himself unable any longer to undertake the pastoral care of the church of Bangor as, inter alia, the 'wickedness of the people' (*malicia plebis*) oppressed him, for he was disturbed by many seditions and insolences.[24]

David the Scot (1120–*c*.1139)

David the Scot, Hervey's immediate albeit long-awaited successor, who was consecrated in 1120, recorded history for a different reason to that of his Breton predecessor.[25] He had been a master at the cathedral school of Würzburg, and as James Conway Davies noted, after attracting the attention of the German king, Henry V (d. 1125), by his worthy manner and the breadth of his knowledge was appointed Henry's chaplain.[26] Such were David's scholarly credentials he was requested by Henry V to write an account of the latter's expedition of 1110/1, when the German king went to Rome to browbeat Paschal II and be crowned emperor. David produced three books as part of the publicity and propaganda campaign which the emperor was preparing against the papacy and in defence of lay investiture.[27] The work was written in an easy style, to make a popular appeal to the lay reader.[28] Unfortunately all three books are now lost but they are mentioned and utilised by David's contemporaries Ekkehard of Aura, Orderic Vitalis and William of Malmesbury – William confirming that the writer was the future bishop of Bangor.[29] Orderic was impressed by David's stylish narrative.[30] However, William stated that the story was told 'with more prejudice in favour of the king than is proper for an historian'.[31] He did step back a little from his condemnation of David when he wrote that one should be lenient with him, on the ground 'he was writing panegyric, not history'.[32] This did not stop the Malmesbury historian copying, word for word, the privileges and consecration rites agreed between the emperor and Paschal II, which David had recorded.[33]

J. E. Lloyd observed that it was not hard to see why King Henry I of England had agreed to David's election as bishop of Bangor, he having written such a favourable account of the emperor's expedition to Rome and thus in support of lay investiture, a cause close to the English king's heart.[34] From a Welsh perspective, Gruffudd ap Cynan (king of Gwynedd, d. 1137) knew that David would be an acceptable choice to the king of England, and C. P. Lewis has argued that as David was scholarly, widely travelled and well connected, his appointment was a statement that Gruffudd 'aspired to make Gwynedd a European principality'.[35] If so, David's position as master at the cathedral school of Würzburg and his close relationship with the emperor were arguably more important to this scheme, but the three books he produced as the emperor's literary apologist would have brought him to prominence and to the notice of King Henry I, who, in practice, had the ultimate say in his promotion.[36] Whereas Hervey had history recorded to absolve himself from his prolonged absence from Bangor, David the Scot, it seems, was promoted to the bishopric (thus ending a lengthy *sede vacante*) because he wrote history, a history that appealed to the person who had the ultimate say in his promotion.

Rotoland (*fl. c*.1191–*c*.1204)

Arguably, one of the most interesting aspects of the contribution of the medieval bishops of Bangor to the recording of history is the extent to which they informed the writings of contemporary chroniclers and authors, and this will become more apparent when we consider the thirteenth-century bishops. However, there was also a bishop-elect who, because he spent so much time in the company of Gerald of Wales, could well have made an invaluable contribution to our knowledge of the events of the last decade of the twelfth century and the first few years of the thirteenth. The bishop-elect was Rotoland, the sub-prior of the Cistercian house of Aberconwy, whom Gerald tells us was twice elected as bishop of Bangor and twice rejected by Canterbury in favour of two Englishmen, first Alan (intruded in 1195), and then Robert (intruded in 1197).[37]

Rotoland and Gerald met when the latter was archdeacon of Brecon, and they came to know each other very well indeed, Gerald describing the bishop-elect as his fellow countryman, comrade and friend, and for a time they lodged together.[38] In fact, Rotoland (who appealed to the papacy to have his election confirmed) was present during Gerald's visits to Rome in 1199–1200, 1201 and 1203, receiving the archdeacon's support every time, and in turn speaking on Gerald's behalf on at least one occasion.[39] In 1201 they returned to England together, and on Gerald's last visit to the papal court he met Rotoland in Paris (late 1202), and they travelled together to Cîteaux and then on to Rome, where in 1203, Gerald spoke on the sub-prior's behalf, and Pope Innocent III was finally persuaded to issue a commission to investigate Rotoland's claim.[40] Further, in the summer of 1202, at Aberconwy, Rotoland had handed over money to Gerald which had been collected to support the campaign for metropolitan status for St Davids, and in December 1201, Gerald stated that he had effected a reconciliation between Rotoland and Llywelyn ab Iorwerth (prince of north Wales, d. 1240).[41]

Not only were the two men frequently in each other's company, they also shared a common bond: they were both bishops-elect (Gerald having been elected bishop of St Davids by the canons there in June 1199) who had been rejected by the archbishop of Canterbury, for in Rotoland's case being Welsh and in Gerald's case being too closely associated with the Welsh.[42] It is not hard to imagine Gerald's writings being informed and influenced by the company of his fellow bishop-elect, not only in north Wales and during each one of Gerald's visits to Rome but also when they lodged together and on their long journeys to and from the papal court. As we shall see, Rotoland certainly informed Gerald of at least one event, and he could have been Gerald's primary source for the two Bangor elections in the last decade of the twelfth century. If he was not the main source, he would surely have been able to add detail. According to Gerald, the chapter of Bangor had, by a unanimous vote, elected a 'good man' (*bonus vir*), whom the archbishop of Canterbury refused to confirm, and consecrate, because he was Welsh.[43] Instead, Archbishop Hubert Walter thrust into his place without any election at all the English Hospitaller Alan, who found no peace in Bangor and fled to exile and banishment in England, dying in the year of his consecration.[44] As soon as the Bangor chapter heard that Alan was dead, with one voice, they once again elected this good man; however, once again the archbishop refused to confirm Rotoland's election, and had a certain Englishman called Robert consecrated in his stead, but he too, like his predecessor, Gerald wrote, is now a 'wandering exile, a bishop without a city, who runs to and fro, begging at every abbey in England, and going mitre-horned hunts for vicar-ships of vacant sees'.[45] Further, Alan and Robert were no doubt at the forefront of Gerald's mind when he wrote that English bishops who were intruded into Welsh bishoprics were ignorant of the customs and language of the Welsh, and were unable to preach or hear confessions without an interpreter.[46] As far as these accusations applied to the English bishops of Bangor, Rotoland may once again have been the source, or have been able to confirm what Gerald had heard from others.

We can be certain that Rotoland did inform Gerald of at least one event. In 1203, after leaving with the commission granted by Innocent III, Rotoland entered a wood alone and had the misfortune to be robbed, the thieves taking all his money, letters and goods. He returned to the court and to the archdeacon's lodgings, and there recounted the events to Gerald, his good friend and comrade (*socio et amico bono*).[47] Other matters that Rotoland might also have informed Gerald about are the details of his appeals to the papacy, the proctor(s) employed by Hubert Walter to oppose him, the indulgence granted to him by the pope and his expulsion from the Cistercian order, all of which are recorded by Gerald.[48]

In his protracted attempt to have his election recognised, Rotoland would have had much to gain from a favourable account written by Gerald. Indeed, Gerald, who was at pains to point out that Rotoland's elections were canonical (in contrast to the uncanonical nature of the intrusion of Alan and Robert), contended that not only was the sub-prior unanimously elected twice by the cathedral chapter, he also had the unanimous support of the native people, the clergy and his prince.[49] Furthermore, the sub-prior of Aberconwy would undoubtedly have had much to impart that Gerald would have wanted to hear and record – indeed Gerald himself explicitly recognised the value of Rotoland's companionship, in one respect at least, when he stated that here was a Welshman who might help him in the suit concerning the standing of the church of St David.[50] For Rotoland the benefits of informing Gerald of the details of his election and rejection were clear, here was an ally from his own land who could support him in his appeal for papal justice, and record all that had been said and done.

Robert of Shrewsbury (1197–1212)

It is possible that Robert of Shrewsbury informed the Cottonian chronicle's (C-text of the *Annales Cambriae*) account of the events of 1211. However, it is far from certain, and is mentioned here, together with a possible motive, for the sake of completeness.

Intruded in 1197, Robert was a capable royal servant in various capacities.[51] He found himself in exile, by the latest the autumn of the following year, for in September 1198 he was with King Richard I in Normandy.[52] After Richard's death, he was entrusted by King John (1199) with collecting money to finance the business of the king's nephew, King Otto (IV), and ever the royal servant, by 1200, he was back in England where he travelled extensively with John and his court.[53] In 1201, Robert was present when an agreement between Llywelyn ab Iorwerth and the king's representatives was formalised.[54] It is likely that Robert was able to return to his bishopric from *c*.1204.[55]

Robert had been a loyal and trusted servant for many years, first to King Richard and then to King John. However, in the summer of 1211 this changed. In August of that year, John successfully invaded Gwynedd Uwch Conwy, and three native chronicles record that Robert was captured by the king's men. According to *Brut y Tywysogyon* (Red Book of Hergest), after crossing the river Conwy towards Eryri, the king 'incited some of his host to burn Bangor. And there Rhobert, bishop of Bangor, was seized in his church, but he was afterwards ransomed for two hundred falcons'.[56] A second Welsh chronicle, *O Oes Gwrtheyrn*, compiled in Gwynedd, gives a more precise location for John's whereabouts, namely Aber (Abergwyngregyn) and adds that it was his Brabançon mercenaries whom the king ordered to burn Bangor.[57] The Cottonian chronicle has important details lacking in the abovementioned sources, namely that John ordered Robert to be seized because the bishop had refused to come to him (*quia ad eum uenire noluit*).[58] As Abergwyngregyn is a mere six miles or so from Robert's cathedral this could well explain John's anger at being snubbed. Furthermore, the Cottonian chronicle tells us that when Robert was taken, he was in front of the altar wearing his episcopal vestments (*episcopum ... in ecclesia bangorensi ante altare episcopalibus indutum*).[59] These details found their way to St Davids where the Cottonian chronicle was written in the second half of the thirteenth century, although it had been maintained there for many years.⁶⁰ Robert's savage treatment at the hands of King John's men in August 1211 might well have been too much for him, for he died the following year.⁶¹ Perhaps Robert ensured that before he died his refusal to acquiesce to the demands of a monarch, who had been excommunicated in 1209, was recorded by a scribe based in Wales so that his legacy was not that of the consummate royal servant but rather defender of the Church and his Welsh diocese at that.

Cadwgan of Llandyfái (1215–c.1236)

Cadwgan of Llandyfái, the former Cistercian monk and abbot of Whitland, was consecrated in 1215.⁶² He is known to have written theological and instructional works. He may also have influenced the Breviate chronicle (B-text of the *Annales Cambriae*), and been responsible for the transmission of Welsh laws to Gwynedd. He too was well known to Gerald. We are told that his father was Irish but was a fervent and effective preacher in Welsh, and that Cadwgan (whom Gerald seemed reluctant to mention by name) had inherited his father's gift of eloquence.⁶³ However, his sermons were plagiarised – he had committed them, word for word, to memory.⁶⁴ It should be noted that Gerald had a longstanding dislike of Cadwgan, and one event in particular might explain Gerald's animosity. In 1202, when Cadwgan was a monk at Strata Florida, he persuaded the then abbot that it was against their 'Book of Uses' to allow Gerald to pawn his library to the house, and thus the archdeacon of Brecon was forced to sell his books.⁶⁵

Another thirteenth-century source, *Cronicon de Wallia*, described Cadwgan as *vir mire facundie et sapientie* (a man of wonderful eloquence and wisdom).⁶⁶ Whilst *Cronicon de Wallia* is probably a product of Whitland Abbey, and as such could be expected to be biased towards one of its own abbots, it is noteworthy that both it and Gerald describe Cadwgan as eloquent.⁶⁷ Further praise is to be found in the Peniarth MS 20 version of *Brut y Tywysogyon* which described Cadwgan as 'a man of great accomplishments and learning' (*gwr mawr ygeluydodeu ay ysgolhectot*).⁶⁸

These 'accomplishments and learning' may, in part, refer to the written works for which Cadwgan was responsible. His extant works are preserved in two thirteenth-century manuscripts and are thought to have been produced while he was bishop of Bangor and before he retired to Abbey Dore.⁶⁹ First, there is a treatise on confession, preserved in Dulwich College, London, MS 22 (L.8), which appears to have been written for the education of the Bangor diocesan clergy.[70] The second manuscript is Hereford Cathedral Archive 0.VI.8.; Cadwgan's works in this manuscript comprise a *tractatus* on a verse of Psalm 79, a series of prayers and meditations under the rubric *Orationes Domini Caducani episcopi Bangorensis*, and further meditations and prayers as well as litanies.[71] It has been said that he possessed a solid theological training, and that his preserved works combine a European scholastic tradition with a Welsh cultural tradition.[72] However, this reputation has recently been challenged by David Runciman who, noting that Cadwgan was expert at acquiring and copying texts, opines that his works in the Hereford manuscript were in fact the bishop's notes which Cadwgan may have been intending to collate into a compilation of texts for the clergy of his diocese, but which were in the end probably compiled by a monk at Abbey Dore who arranged the notes in such a way as to suggest he did not understand what he was working with.[73]

Other works have also been attributed to Cadwgan. In the sixteenth century, John Leland listed Cadwgan amongst those buried at Abbey Dore, noting 'scripsit librum omeliarum quem ego vidi. Scripsit etiam librum cui titulus, Speculum Christianorum' ('he wrote a book of homilies which I have seen. He also wrote a book entitled *Speculum Christianorum*').[74] The homilies could possibly be part of what is now Hereford Cathedral Archive 0.VI.8. *Speculum Christianorum* may survive in Balliol College MS 239, fos 27–77v, as '*Speculum Christiani*', although C. H. Talbot doubted it was Cadwgan's work.[75]

As regards the transmission of Welsh laws, Daniel Huws has suggested that Cadwgan was a possible channel for the passage into the Gwynedd legal circles of Llywelyn ab Iorwerth of the now lost Whitland Abbey *Llyfr y Tŷ Gwyn* ('The Book of the White House').[76] The mid-thirteenth-century Latin Redaction B of the Welsh laws (BL MS Cotton Vespasian E. xi), which displays a greater familiarity with Latin learning than the other Welsh lawbooks, and which Huw Pryce has noted bears the clearest evidence for any Latin lawbook of redaction in an ecclesiastical centre, was perhaps derived from *Llyfr y Tŷ Gwyn*.[77] Huws believes Vespasian E. xi is most likely to have originated in Bangor or the Cistercian house of Aberconwy.[78]

David Stephenson has suggested that it is probable that the entries for the years *c*.1211/12–19 in the Breviate chronicle were compiled at

Whitland, and that it is possible they were constructed under the influence of Cadwgan.[79] Indeed the arrival of Cadwgan as the new abbot at the mother-house of all the Cistercian abbeys of *Pura Wallia* may have been the impetus to construct a chronicle.[80] The entries include a rare report of events in south-east Wales, not far from another Cistercian house, Llantarnam Abbey, which may have been relayed by Cadwgan's half-brother who was a monk there.[81] There are also biblical references, together with a reference to the prophecies of Merlin, suggesting the writer was learned and had access to a library.[82] Of course, if Stephenson is correct, the library to which Cadwgan had access may have been supplemented by Gerald's books, acquired by the Cistercians in 1202. Indeed, scholars have made the point that the last annal shared by both the Breviate and Cottonian chronicles is 1202, after which the Cottonian chronicle remained at St Davids, and the Breviate chronicle appears to have been kept at one or more Welsh Cistercian houses, including Whitland.[83] Gerald as an archdeacon, author and scholar might have had a copy of the St Davids annals amongst the books he lost to the monks at Strata Florida in 1202, which would explain why a copy came into the hands of the Cistercians.[84]

Further, as Stephenson notes, the Breviate entries for the second decade of the thirteenth century show a particular interest in emphasising Llywelyn ab Iorwerth's increasing power and authority.[85] Although it is not clear exactly when Cadwgan became abbot at Whitland, it appears he was in post by 1212 at the latest, the very year that Robert of Shrewsbury died, and the bishopric became vacant.[86] Interestingly, Gerald stated that Cadwgan had gone to great lengths to obtain the support of Llywelyn whilst the latter was on campaign in Cardigan in 1212; knowing that the see of Bangor was vacant, he invited the prince to Whitland, entertained him lavishly and claimed to be his cousin. It was due to the prince's support that Cadwgan was elected.[87] Perhaps Cadwgan took the opportunity to ensure that Llywelyn's increasing power and authority were emphasised in the annals then being compiled at Whitland. After he became bishop, in 1215, Cadwgan repaid Llywelyn's support by acting on behalf of the prince on several occasions, and perhaps, if Stephenson is right about the provenance of the Breviate chronicle up to 1219, Cadwgan continued to exert some influence over his former house in the years after his consecration.[88]

The evidence that Cadwgan was a learned, accomplished man, who was eloquent and had access to a well-stocked library, do make it more likely that he was the driving force behind the Breviate chronicle entries for the second decade of the thirteenth century, and that he was responsible for the transmission of the now lost Whitland Abbey *Llyfr y Tŷ Gwyn* to Gwynedd. Further, his copying and acquisitional skills, and Gerald's statement about his ability to reproduce material word for word, suggest that the monk turned abbot turned bishop turned monk did more to add to and preserve written works than any other medieval bishop of Bangor.

Richard (1237–67)

After Cadwgan had retired to Abbey Dore, his successor, *magister* Richard, was destined to inform the writings of one of the greatest authors of the age, Matthew Paris. Within a few years of his consecration, the former archdeacon of Bangor was embroiled in an event which would set the tone for his episcopate. According to *Brut y Tywysogyon*, in 1239 Dafydd ap Llywelyn seized Gruffudd (his half-brother) and imprisoned him.[89] However, Matthew Paris, the monk and historian of St Albans, gave a slightly different account, stating that this did not happen until after the death of their father Llywelyn ab Iorwerth.[90] Llywelyn died on 11 April 1240, whereupon Paris tells us war ensued between the brothers until around Michaelmas 1240 when Dafydd lured Gruffudd to a peace council, under the safe conduct of the bishop of Bangor and other great men. Dafydd ordered Gruffudd to be taken and, despite the protests of the bishop and others, imprisoned.[91] Richard, incensed, excommunicated Dafydd and fled to England, where he begged Henry III to intervene. According to Paris, the bishop laid a grave complaint before the king concerning the treacherous actions of Dafydd; and, reminding Henry that Dafydd was his nephew, urged the king to have Gruffudd set free lest so villainous a transgression reach the Roman curia to his dishonour.[92] Henry, we are told, advised and ordered Dafydd to release Gruffudd so as to restore his good name and obtain absolution from the sentence of excommunication, but Dafydd refused.[93] Richard, therefore, laid a second complaint before the king.[94] Paris also recorded that when Gruffudd heard that Dafydd would not release him, he secretly sent word to Henry offering to hold his territory from the king for 200 marks a year.[95]

Gwyn A. Williams cautiously argued that Paris's dating was to be preferred to that of the Welsh chroniclers, *inter alia*, because Richard not only visited St Albans but resided there for a time.[96] Interestingly, verification from a source other than Matthew Paris has recently come to light confirming that Richard was in England at the end of 1240, for on 13 December that year he was at St Paul's in London.[97] A month or so earlier, on 5 November, he had been present at the dedication of Rochester cathedral.[98]

Other scholars have also concluded that Richard probably passed details of political developments in Gwynedd to Matthew Paris.[99] In 1241, a royal campaign was launched forcing Dafydd to surrender at Gwerneigron, near St Asaph. There on 29 August, he entered into a peace agreement with Henry III which was copied on the patent roll.[100] However, a text was also preserved in Cambridge, Corpus Christi College, MS. 16, which is the autograph manuscript of Matthew Paris's *Chronica Majora*, and whilst very closely related to the patent roll text, it records two further clauses (on folios 172v–173r), namely [xv] and [xvi] omitted in the roll.[101] The former clause stated that if Dafydd or his heirs attempted to contravene the king's peace their entire inheritance would be forfeit, whilst the latter included a statement by Dafydd that he had arranged for the bishops of Bangor and St Asaph (Hywel II) to give charters to the king in which they agreed to carry out all sentences of excommunication or interdict.[102] As Huw Pryce suggests, Paris's source for the text was probably Richard.[103] The St Albans' monk composed the annals in his *Chronica Majora* for the period 1236–50 between 1245 and early 1251, and he could easily have drawn on information supplied by Richard for his account of events in 1241, and indeed 1240.[104]

On 30 and 31 August 1241, at Rhuddlan, a revised text of the Gwerneigron agreement was ratified by Henry, and Dafydd issued two notifications.[105] Both *Brut y Tywysogyon* and Matthew Paris state that the king then summoned Dafydd to a council in London.[106] On *c.*24 October, at Westminster, the peace agreement reached (or, rather, imposed on Dafydd) at Rhuddlan was renewed with added concessions from Dafydd.[107] Neither Richard nor Hywel II sealed this latest agreement; however, the agreement stated that Dafydd acted with the will and consent of the bishops of St Asaph and Bangor, and as protection without term had been granted at Westminster for Richard on 20 October, one must assume that he was present.[108] On 24 October, again at Westminster, Dafydd issued a notification that should he die without a legitimate heir, he granted all the land of the principality of north Wales to the king and his heirs.[109] Richard certainly knew of this notification because he referred to it in a letter to Henry in 1246.[110]

The peace agreement required Dafydd to hand over Gruffudd, who was then incarcerated in the Tower of London.[111] He was there by September 1241; it was John of Lexinton who escorted him and Matthew Paris knew of this fact.[112] According to Paris, Richard went to the king and tried to have Gruffudd set free, but he laboured in vain.[113] Judging from the grant of protection issued to Richard on 20 October and the wording of the agreement on *c*.24 of the same month, as well as the fact that Richard knew of the escheat agreed by Dafydd on 24 October, it was probably about this time that Richard approached the king, relaying his intervention to Matthew Paris when he was in St Albans.

In 1244 the king and his magnates renewed their attacks on Dafydd, for, according to Paris, they were angered by a letter in which the abbots of Aberconwy and Cymer had summoned Henry to appear before them.[114] The abbots were acting on a papal mandate which was pursuant to Dafydd's petition that Henry had come against him in a hostile manner (in 1241) and forced terms upon him.[115] As J. Beverley Smith noted, within a year of the initial overtures to Rome, 'the pope concurred with the view, expressed by Matthew Paris, that every Christian knew perfectly well that the prince of Wales was no more than a minor vassal of the king of England'.[116] This sentiment may not have been that far removed from Richard's own opinion if the wording of his letter to Henry III of 20 April 1246, promising to use the whole of his power to bring Henry's enemies back to the king's fealty, is taken at face value.[117] Dafydd having died suddenly in February 1246, and his half-brother Gruffudd having pre-deceased him, Gruffudd's son Llywelyn decided to continue the war, joined by his older brother Owain.[118] Matthew Paris stated that when he heard of his uncle's death, Owain fled like a hare to Wales.[119] Within two months Richard was at Windsor where, in his letter of 20 April, he implicitly made reference to clause [xv] recorded in the autograph manuscript of Paris's *Chronica Majora* when he testified that Dafydd had bound himself to Henry that if he should ever go against the peace made between them that he, Dafydd, and his heirs should lose the right which they had in Wales or elsewhere within the kingdom of England for ever.[120]

By 1248, Richard was at St Albans. According to Matthew Paris, the impoverished bishop of Bangor came to the abbey so that he and his clerks might stay with the abbot until his bishopric, which had been ruined by war, had been restored.[121] When he returned to Gwynedd is not clear but on 11 July 1252 he was at Aberdaron.[122] In the same year, Paris recorded that Alan de la Zouche, the new justice of Chester and the Four Cantrefs, on his way to London, came to St Albans and reported on the submission of the Welsh.[123] Furthermore, the bishop of Bangor, on coming to St Albans, gave the same account.[124] One might expect de la Zouche, newly appointed and ambitious as he was, to make such a claim, but to what specific or general submission Richard was referring is unclear.

Richard's pattern of residence in St Albans with visits to Wales continued for the next five or six years. In 1254, on Maundy Thursday, Richard prepared the chrism in the church of St Albans, and in the same year, the abbot (John of Hertford) had the bishop dedicate the church of Hexton in Hertfordshire.[125] *Brut y Tywysogyon* records that in 1255 the great bell at Strata Florida was raised, and consecrated by the bishop of Bangor, and so Richard was back in Wales at this point.[126]

In 1256, Richard spent Christmas at court. He was granted simple protection for so long as he was faithful to the king and Edward his son.[127] In November of that year, Llywelyn had crossed the River Conwy, and taken control of Perfeddwlad.[128] According to the Welsh chronicles, in early December, he turned south-west and entered Meirionnydd, and then advanced into Deheubarth.[129] Matthew Paris, however, has Llywelyn attacking Powys Fadog to the south-east immediately after annexing Perfeddwlad, and Richard may have been his source.[130] Lloyd wondered if Paris had made a mistake as there is no record of this in the Welsh chronicles; however, the local leader Gruffudd ap Madog, who was forced to flee according to Paris, was compensated with land in England and Llywelyn was able to advance as far as Kinnerley in Shropshire, suggesting he did make inroads into Powys Fadog as Paris claimed.[131] There are other details that may have been supplied by Richard, including the English's oppressive administration, and that the Welsh formed a confederacy to defend their land, swearing on the gospels in the process.[132] Richard may also have informed Paris of the Welsh sending their wives, children and flocks into Eryri, rendering fords impassable and destroying bridges when Henry III advanced to Deganwy the following year; as well as the Welsh counter measure to the threat of an attack from Ireland of sending armed and provisioned galleys to do battle.[133]

We can be certain that Richard reported at least three events to Matthew Paris, for not only did he report that his bishopric had been destroyed by war in 1248, and bring news of the submission of the Welsh in 1252, it was he who informed the St Albans' historian that on 26 December 1256 the crown of Germany had been offered to Henry III's brother, the earl of Cornwall.[134] The earl was advised by Henry and others to accept the crown, which he did, turning to the bishops, including Richard, to make his acceptance speech.[135] A week later, Richard was back in St Albans, where on 2 January 1257, after the discovery of the body of St Alban, he dedicated a new altar and granted two indulgences.[136]

As Richard not only visited St Albans but resided there intermittently over a period of nine or ten years, it is not unreasonable to assume that the bishop of Bangor fed Paris's 'voracious appetite for information'.[137] Further, Richard, who may have known that Paris was compiling a contemporary history and was held in high esteem as a historical writer (by Henry III amongst others), could have chosen St Albans as his refuge for that reason.[138] In that way he could have the story of his turbulent episcopate recorded, just as Hervey had done with the Ely scribe, and Rotoland had informed Gerald of his woes. By choosing St Albans, Richard would have ensured that the reasons for his recurring exile were recorded.

Anian (1267–1305/6)

Richard's successor was Master Anian, the former archdeacon of Anglesey, who also sought refuge for a time in St Albans; however, by then there was no Matthew Paris (d. 1259) to record his story.[139] He has been associated with the Bangor Pontifical, a complete liturgical book (thought to be of East Anglian provenance) which has recorded on a flyleaf two indulgences he granted whilst in Suffolk.[140] He is less well known for a written testimony of a miracle which occurred in Conwy, one of the new walled towns built by Edward I following his conquest of Wales. The testimony, of September 1303, recorded that a boy who had fallen some twenty-eight feet from a bridge at the castle, lain overnight on a bank above the river, and then been pronounced dead, was miraculously resuscitated when the name of the late Thomas de Cantilupe, bishop of Hereford (d. 1282), was invoked.[141] The revived boy, Roger, who was the son of a cook to William de Cicon constable of the castle, was taken to the church, where Anian and the abbot of Maenan, Dafydd, were celebrating a memorial mass in front of a congregation of distinguished officials, for the knight, diplomat and royal servant John of St John (one of Cantilupe's nephews).[142] In life, Cantilupe had trusted Anian to oversee duties in his Hereford diocese; in death it transpired that he could trust Anian to promote his canonisation, and the bishop of Bangor subsequently petitioned Pope Clement V for an inquiry to be set in motion in respect of his erstwhile colleague.[143] However, for us, the record of the events of September 1303, some twenty years after the demise of the princes of Gwynedd, gives us a glimpse of the post-conquest order, and it is noteworthy that the mass for a household knight known for his military prowess, who had been a close associate of Edward I, was not held in the bishop of Bangor's own cathedral. Rather, the venue chosen was the former abbey church of Aberconwy, by then surrounded by the town walls of Conwy, and protected by the imposing castle. It is also apparent that apart from Anian and Dafydd, the witnesses who appended their seals to the testimony were not Welsh but overwhelming English and included not only Simon of Watford, the local vicar, and Roger of Bridgnorth, one of the priests of the church, but also men described as either knights or clerks of the council and household of Edward, prince of Wales (Edward of Caernarfon, the future King Edward II); men such as William of Sutton, the justiciar of north Wales, John of Havering, a former justiciar, and the Burgundian knight William de Cicon who was also the mayor of Conwy, as well as Hugh of Leominster, the former clerk of works at two of Edward I's other castles/towns in north Wales, namely Caernarfon and Harlech.[144]

Conclusion

The medieval bishops of Bangor not only wrote history: they commissioned, influenced and inspired others to do so. Whilst David wrote history at the behest of another, Hervey commissioned scribes to write his story. Hervey's narrative in *Liber Eliensis* was a way to record his version of the events that led to his swift exile from Bangor in the face of criticism from certain of his ecclesiastical contemporaries for having abandoned his Welsh flock. The allegations made by two of his successors, Meurig and Richard, both Welshmen, lend credence to

Hervey's accusations. David wrote history (or 'panegyric' as William of Malmesbury would have it) for a different reason, but by doing so was accepted by Henry I as Gruffudd ap Cynan's bishop-elect, bringing a lengthy *sede vacante* to an end. On the European stage his works were an invaluable primary source, copied and/or utilised by at least four twelfth-century writers.

Rotoland informed Gerald of Wales of at least one event, and Richard informed Matthew Paris of at least three events. Further, given that Rotoland spent much time in Gerald's company, and that Richard lived at St Albans on and off for some nine or ten years, it is likely that both were valuable sources of information about Wales and Welsh affairs for those most prolific of medieval authors. Twice elected, twice rejected, Rotoland, in his protracted attempt to have his election recognised by the pope, would have had much to gain from Gerald's advocacy and writings reminding Innocent III, inter alia, that unlike those intruded in his place, Rotoland was canonically elected, could give sermons and hear confessions in Welsh, and had the unanimous support of the native people, clergy and his prince. Rotoland may have sought Gerald out for this very purpose. Indeed, Richard, who is first recorded as residing at St Albans the year after Henry III had commissioned work from Matthew Paris, may well have chosen St Albans as his refuge in order to influence the writer. In that way he might ensure that the reasons for his exile were recorded, just as Hervey had done with the Ely scribe.

As Gerald and Matthew Paris were indebted to Rotoland and Richard, so too, it seems, were Welsh chroniclers to Cadwgan. The former abbot of Whitland, who produced theological as well as practical works for his diocesan clergy, seems to have been responsible for ensuring that the increasing power and authority of Llywelyn ab Iorwerth were recorded by native chroniclers, perhaps as part of his charm offensive to secure the prince's backing. In the mid-thirteenth century, Richard, through his association with Matthew Paris, ensured that not only were the reasons for his exile from his impoverished and war-torn bishopric recorded but also the deeds of the princes of Gwynedd – both their failings and successes. The treachery of Dafydd ap Llywelyn in incarcerating his half-brother Gruffudd, the details of Dafydd's submission to Henry III, as well as the bishop's three attempts to have Gruffudd released from captivity were relayed to the St Albans' historian, as it seems was the political and military rise of Gruffudd's son,

Llywelyn. Anian's joint testimony of a miraculous event at the beginning of the fourteenth century, which furthered the calls for the canonisation of his erstwhile colleague, Thomas de Cantilupe, incidentally detailed those who were part of the new Edwardian order that had by then replaced native Welsh rule. For a variety of reasons, and by a variety of means, the medieval bishops of Bangor recorded the events of their day, and in so doing have enriched our understanding of medieval Wales.

Notes

1   This chapter is taken from the research conducted for my doctoral thesis: 'The Bishops of Bangor and their *Acta*, 1092–1306' (unpublished PhD thesis, Bangor University, 2021). Professor Huw Pryce was my principal supervisor. The thesis contains a first edition of Bangor Episcopal *Acta* 1092–1306, which has been published by the Canterbury and York Society: *Bangor Episcopal Acta, 1092–1306* (Woodbridge, 2025).

2   So too the church of St David. Studies include those undertaken by Thomas Jones, *ByT* (RB), pp. xi–lxii; *ByT* (P20), pp. xi–lxxv; Kathleen Hughes, *The Welsh Latin Chronicles: 'Annales Cambriae' and Related Texts* (London, 1974); Caroline Brett, 'The Prefaces of Two Late Thirteenth-century Welsh Latin Chronicles', *BBCS*, 35 (1988), 63–73; Nia Wyn Jones [published as O. W. Jones], 'Historical Writing in Medieval Wales' (unpublished PhD thesis, Bangor University, 2013).

3   Mary Frances Giandrea, 'Review: *Cathedrals, Communities and Conflict in the Anglo-Norman World*, ed. P. Dalton, C. Insley and L. J. Wilkinson', *English Historical Review*, 128 (2013), 1191–3 (p. 1193).

4   See, for example, J. Beverley Smith, *Llywelyn ap Gruffudd, Prince of Wales* (Cardiff, 1998), p. 35 n. 118, and *AWR*, p. 469. The exception is James Conway Davies's *Episcopal Acts and Cognate Documents relating to Welsh Dioceses 1066–1272*, 2 vols (Cardiff, 1946–8) [hereafter *EpiscActs*], still the most complete study of medieval Welsh bishops despite the third volume, intended to cover Bangor and St Asaph, not having been published; the introduction to the same discusses the written works of two bishops of Bangor: II, 550–1 and 557.

5   *Hugh the Chanter: the History of the Church of York, 1066–1127*, ed. and trans. Charles Johnson, rev. M. Brett, C. N. L. Brooke and M. Winterbottom (Oxford, 1990), pp. 12–13; *The Ecclesiastical History of Orderic Vitalis*, ed. and trans. Marjorie Chibnall, 6 vols (Oxford, 1969–80) [hereafter *Orderic*], VI, 186–7; M. J. Pearson (ed.), *Fasti Ecclesiae Anglicanae, 1066–1300: Volume IX, the Welsh Cathedrals* (London, 2003) [hereafter *Fasti IX*], p. 1.

6 R. R. Davies, *The Age of Conquest: Wales 1063–1415* (Oxford, 2000), pp. 179, 189.
7 *EpiscActs*, I, 95. Cf. Dorothy M. Owen, 'Hervey (*d*. 1131)', *ODNB*, https://doi.org/10.1093/ref:odnb/13107; *AWR*, pp. 22, 321; N. Karn (ed.), *English Episcopal Acta 31, Ely 1109–1197* (Oxford, 2005), p. lxxi.
8 J. E. Lloyd, *A History of Wales from the Earliest Times to the Edwardian Conquest*, 2 vols (3rd edn, London, 1939), II, 448–9.
9 *Eadmeri Historia Novorum in Anglia*, ed. M. Rule (London, 1884) [hereafter *Eadmeri Historia*], p. 139; *The Letters of St Anselm of Canterbury*, ed. and trans. W. Fröhlich, 3 vols (Kalamazoo, 1990–4) [hereafter *Letters of St Anselm*], II, no. 282. Lloyd, *History of Wales*, II, 448.
10 *William of Malmesbury, Gesta Pontificum Anglorum, The History of the English Bishops*, ed. and trans. Michael Winterbottom, 2 vols (Oxford, 2009) [hereafter *GPA*], I, 493.
11 *William of Malmesbury, Gesta Regum Anglorum, The History of the English Kings*, ed. and trans. R. A. B. Mynors, R. M. Thomson and M. Winterbottom, 2 vols (Oxford, 2006) [hereafter *GRA*], I, 797.
12 Charles Warren Hollister, *Henry I*, ed. Amanda Clark Frost (London, 2001), p. 223; *EpiscActs*, I, 96.
13 *Letters of St Anselm*, III, no. 404; *Orderic*, V, 322, no. 4. *EpiscActs*, I, 96.
14 *Letters of St Anselm*, III, nos 457–60; *Liber Eliensis, A History of the Isle of Ely*, ed. J. Fairweather (Woodbridge, 2005), pp. 297, 298–302; Owen, 'Hervey'; *English Episcopal Acta 31*, ed. Karn, p. lxxi.
15 *Fasti Ecclesiae Anglicanae, 1066–1300, II, Monastic Cathedrals (Northern and Southern Provinces)*, ed. D. E. Greenway (London, 1971), p. 45.
16 Elisabeth M. C. van Houts, 'Historical Writing', in C. Harper-Bill and E. M. C. van Houts (eds), *A Companion to the Anglo-Norman World* (Woodbridge, 2003), pp. 103–22 (pp. 110, 116); *Liber Eliensis*, ed. Fairweather, pp. xiii–xxiii, 297; *Liber Eliensis*, ed. E. O. Blake (London, 1962), pp. xxxiv, 245.
17 *Liber Eliensis*, ed. Fairweather, p. 297.
18 'Quod quidem ut adipisci mereretur, multa prece, multis multarum rerum promissionibus, multorum quoque officiorum exhibitionibus, vix post obitum strenuissimi patris Anselmi obtinere potis fuit.': *Eadmeri Historia*, p. 211; translation in G. Bosanquet (ed. and trans.), *Eadmer's History of Recent Events in England, Historia Novorum in Anglia* (London, 1964), p. 226.
19 For Meurig's consecration, see *Fasti IX*, p. 2.
20 *The Letters of John of Salisbury. Volume 1: the Early Letters (1153–1161)*, ed. W. J. Millor and H. E. Butler, rev. C. N. L. Brooke (Oxford, 1986) [hereafter *Letters of John of Salisbury*], no. 87; Huw Pryce, 'Owain Gwynedd (*d*. 1170)', *ODNB*, https://doi.org/10.1093/ref:odnb/20979.

21 *Letters of John of Salisbury*, no. 87.
22 *Letters of John of Salisbury*, no. 87. The latter accusation certainly rings true, for Gerald of Wales recorded a letter he said had been written by Owain and his brother complaining that Meurig was uninvited and unwanted (*AWR*, no. 192). Further, Meurig had criticised Owain for having married his cousin; *Letters of John of Salisbury*, no. 87. Paschal II, in three of his letters written in support of Hervey, had also described the Welsh of Bangor as barbarians (*Eadmeri Historia*, p. 139; *Letters of St Anselm*, III, nos 457, 459) and Huw Pryce has recently commented on this trend: *Writing Welsh History: from the Early Middle Ages to the Twenty-first Century* (Oxford, 2022), p. 36 and n. 5.
23 The exile, during native Welsh rule, of several bishops of Bangor is examined in S. McGuinness, 'The Medieval Bishops of Bangor, 1092–1283: Intrusion, Exile and Diplomacy', in E. A. Gatti and A. M. Silvestri (eds), *Episcopal Power and Patronage in Medieval Europe, 998–1503* (forthcoming).
24 McGuinness, *Bangor Episcopal Acta*, no. 55.
25 For his consecration, see *Fasti IX*, p. 2.
26 *EpiscActs*, II, 550; Martin Brett, 'David (d. 1137×9)', *ODNB*, https://doi.org/10.1093/ref:odnb/7207; *Fasti IX*, p. 1.
27 C. P. Lewis, 'Gruffudd ap Cynan and the Normans', in Kari L. Maund (ed.), *Gruffudd ap Cynan: A Collaborative Biography* (Woodbridge, 1996), pp. 61–78 (p. 75); *EpiscActs*, II, 550; Brett, 'David'.
28 D. G. Waitz (ed.), 'Ekkehardi Uraugiensis Chronicon', in G. H. Pertz (ed.), *Monumenta Germaniae Historica, Scriptores VI* (Hannover, 1844), pp. 1–267 (p. 243). *EpiscActs*, II, 550–1; Brett, 'David'.
29 Waitz (ed.), 'Ekkehardi Uraugiensis Chronicon', p. 243; *Orderic*, I, 61, and V, 198–9 n. 3; *GRA*, I, 770–1, and used by the Kaiserchronik completed shortly after David's death, and by Johannes Aventinus c.1519–21: Brett, 'David'; *EpiscActs*, II, 551. 'David Scottus Bancornensis episcopus': *GRA*, I, 764–5.
30 *Orderic*, V, 198–9.
31 'magis in regis gratiam quam historicum deceret acclinis': *GRA*, I, 764–5.
32 'quia non historiam sed panagericum scripsit': *GRA*, I, 764–5.
33 *GRA*, I, 770–1.
34 Lloyd, *History of Wales*, II, 455. See also K. Leyser, 'England and the Empire in the Early Twelfth Century', *TRHS*, 5th series, 10 (1960), 61–84 (pp. 78–9).
35 Lewis, 'Gruffudd', pp. 75–6.
36 Eadmer, the Canterbury monk and historian, confirmed that David was consecrated with Henry I's consent: *Eadmeri Historia*, p. 259.
37 'Rawatlan(us)': *AWR*, no. 216. 'Giraldus Cambrensis, *De Invectionibus*', ed. W. S. Davies, *Y Cymmrodor*, 30 (1920), 1–248 [hereafter *De Invectionibus*] (pp. 95–6); *Giraldi Cambrensis Opera Volume 3*, ed. J. S. Brewer, p. 193; *The*

Autobiography of Giraldus Cambrensis, ed. and trans. H. E. Butler (London, 1937), pp. 208, 213. *EpiscActs*, II, 435; Rhys Williams Hays, 'Rotoland, subprior of Aberconway, and the Controversy over the See of Bangor 1199–1204', *Journal of the Historical Society of the Church in Wales*, 18 (1963), 9–19 (pp. 9–10).

38   *Giraldi Cambrensis Opera Volume 3*, ed. Brewer, pp. 240–1, 287–8; *Autobiography of Giraldus Cambrensis*, ed. and trans. Butler, pp. 266–7, 309.

39   *De Invectionibus*, pp. 50, 87, 94–6; *Giraldi Cambrensis Opera Volume 3*, ed. Brewer, pp. 193, 287; *Autobiography of Giraldus Cambrensis*, ed. and trans. Butler, pp. 173, 208, 211–13, 266–7, 277–8.

40   *Giraldi Cambrensis Opera Volume 3*, ed. Brewer, pp. 195, 240–1, 287; *De Invectionibus*, p. 116; *Autobiography of Giraldus Cambrensis*, ed. and trans. Butler, pp. 5, 220, 265–7, 271, 308; *Patrologiae Cursus Completus. Series Latina*, ed. J. P. Migne, 221 vols (1841–55), http://patristica.net/latina/ (accessed 30 November 2023), CCXV, cc. 81–2; *Calendar of Entries in the Papal Registers relating to Great Britain and Ireland. Papal letters: Vol 1, 1198–1304*, ed. and trans. W. H. Bliss (London, 1893) [hereafter *CalPapReg.*], p. 14. Rhys Williams Hays, *The History of the Abbey of Aberconway, 1186–1537* (Cardiff, 1963), pp. 28–9; *AWR*, p. 347.

41   *Giraldi Cambrensis Opera Volume 1*, ed. Brewer, p. 10; *Giraldi Cambrensis Opera Volume 3*, ed. Brewer, p. 226; *Autobiography of Giraldus Cambrensis*, ed. and trans. Butler, pp. 225 n. 1 and 251. Hays, *History of the Abbey*, p. 27; *AWR*, p. 347.

42   *De Invectionibus*, p. 95; *Autobiography of Giraldus Cambrensis*, ed. and trans. Butler, p. 213; Robert Bartlett, 'Gerald of Wales [Giraldus Cambrensis, Gerald de Barry] (*c*.1146–1220×23)', *ODNB*, https://doi.org/10.1093/ref:odnb/10769.

43   *De Invectionibus*, p. 95; *Autobiography of Giraldus Cambrensis*, ed. and trans. Butler, p. 213.

44   *De Invectionibus*, p. 95; *Autobiography of Giraldus Cambrensis*, ed. and trans. Butler, p. 213.

45   'vagus et profugus, puta nullius civitatis episcopus, per abbatias Anglie mendicando, discurrens, et cornutus incidens sedium vacantium vicarias': *Autobiography of Giraldus Cambrensis*, ed. and trans. Butler, p. 213 and n. 1; *De Invectionibus*, pp. 95–6.

46   These accusations were contained in a letter from Llywelyn ab Iorwerth, and other Welsh princes, to Innocent III, the letter only being extant in Gerald's 'De iure et statu Menevensis ecclesiae': *AWR*, no. 220. The consensus is that Gerald drafted the letter, see *AWR*, pp. 370–1.

47   *Giraldi Cambrensis Opera Volume 3*, ed. Brewer, pp. 287–8; *Autobiography of Giraldus Cambrensis*, ed. and trans. Butler, p. 309.

48 *Giraldi Cambrensis Opera Volume 1*, ed. Brewer, p. 14; *Giraldi Cambrensis Opera Volume 3*, ed. Brewer, pp. 193, 241; *De Invectionibus*, pp. 95–6, 116; *Autobiography of Giraldus Cambrensis*, ed. and trans. Butler, pp. 208–9, 211, 213, 266, 271; *AWR*, p. 347.

49 *De Invectionibus*, pp. 95–6, 116; *Giraldi Cambrensis Opera Volume 3*, ed. Brewer, p. 193; *Autobiography of Giraldus Cambrensis*, ed. and trans. Butler, pp. 208, 213, 271.

50 *Giraldi Cambrensis Opera Volume 3*, ed. Brewer, p. 193; *Autobiography of Giraldus Cambrensis*, ed. and trans. Butler, pp. 208–9.

51 R. W. Eyton, *Antiquities of Shropshire*, 12 vols (London, 1854–60), VI, 368; VIII, 106–7; X, 358–9; M. J. Angold et al., 'Colleges of Secular Canons: Shrewsbury', in A. T. Gaydon and R. B. Pugh (eds), *A History of the County of Shopshire* (London, 1973), pp. 114–23 (pp. 121–2 and nn. 196 and 222); *Pleas before the King and his Justices, 1198–1212*, ed. Doris M. Stenton, 4 vols (London, 1952–67), III, pp. lxxvii and xciii; *Historia et Cartularium Monasterii Sancti Petri Gloucestriæ*, ed. W. H. Hart, 3 vols (London, 1863–7), II, 7–8.

52 *The Cartae Antiquae, Rolls 1–10*, ed. L. Landon (London, 1939) [hereafter *CartAnt*], pp. 44–8; *Calendar of the Charter Rolls preserved in the Public Record Office*, 6 vols (London, 1903–27), *1226–1257*, I, 323–4 [hereafter *CChR*]; *CChR, 1341–1417*, V, 194–5; *Calendar of Documents Preserved in France Illustrative of the History of Great Britain and Ireland: Volume 1, A.D. 918–1206*, ed. J. H. Round (London, 1899), p. 91.

53 *Rotuli Chartarum, in Turri Londinensi asservati, vol 1, part 1*, ed. T. D. Hardy (London, 1837), 31a, 44b, 80a, 84a–b; *The Charters of the Abbey of Ystrad Marchell*, ed. G. C. G. Thomas (Aberystwyth, 1997), no. 25; *CartAnt*, p. 79.

54 *AWR*, no. 221.

55 Rotoland had been expelled from the Cistercian Order in 1202 (*Giraldi Cambrensis Opera Volume 3*, ed. Brewer, p. 241; *De Invectionibus*, p. 116; *Autobiography of Giraldus Cambrensis*, ed. and trans. Butler, pp. 266, 271); the commission from the pope of 1203 seemingly came to nothing (*EpiscActs*, II, 436); on 16 March 1204, Robert, amongst others, was tasked by John to ensure safe conduct for Llywelyn coming to the king (*Rotuli Litterarum Patentium, in Turri Londinensi asservati, vol. I, part I*, ed. T. D. Hardy (London, 1835), 39a.); and in the spring of 1205, Llywelyn was married to Joan, John's daughter (*AWR*, p. 26). Certainly, by then, one must assume the prince would have wanted to be seen to be embracing the English establishment's choice of bishop.

56 'Ac anoc rei o'e lu a oruc y losgi Bangor. Ac yno y delit Rotbert escob Bangor, yn y eglwys, ac y gwerthwyt wedy hyny yr deu cant hebawc': *ByT* (RB), s.a. 1211 (ed. and trans. Jones, pp. 190–1).

57 Nia Wyn Jones [published as O. W. Jones], 'O Oes Gwrtheyrn: A Medieval Welsh Chronicle', in Ben Guy et al. (eds), *The Chronicles of Medieval Wales and the March: New Contexts, Studies, and Texts* (Turnhout, 2020), pp. 169–230 (pp. 169, 215, 221, 227).

58 Henry Gough-Cooper (ed.), 'Annales Cambriae. The C-text, with the intercalated annalistic notices. From British Library MS Cotton Domitian A.1, folios 138r–155r' (2015), *http://croniclau.bangor.ac.uk/editions.php.en* (accessed 4 December 2023), p. 45 [c531.1].

59 Gough-Cooper (ed.), 'Annales Cambriae. The C-text', p. 45 [c531.1].

60 Hughes, *Welsh Latin Chronicles*, pp. 242–6; Brett, 'Prefaces', 63.

61 *ByT* (RB), s.a. 1212 (ed. and trans. Jones, pp. 194–5).

62 *Fasti IX*, p. 3.

63 *Giraldi Cambrensis Opera Volume 4*, ed. Brewer, pp. 163–5; Frederick George Cowley, *The Monastic Order in South Wales, 1066–1349* (Cardiff, 1977), pp. 48, 122–3; Joseph Goering and Huw Pryce, 'The *De Modo Confitendi* of Cadwgan, Bishop of Bangor', *Mediaeval Studies*, 62 (2000), 1–27 (p. 2); David Walker, 'Cadwgan [Cadwgan of Llandefai] (*d*. 1241)', *ODNB*, *https://doi.org/10.1093/ref:odnb/4320*. J. E. Lloyd stated that the unnamed bishop was, beyond doubt, Cadwgan: Lloyd, *History of Wales*, II, 688 n. 201.

64 *Giraldi Cambrensis Opera Volume 4*, ed. Brewer, p. 165. Cowley, *Monastic Order*, pp. 122–3; Goering and Pryce, '*De Modo Confitendi*', 2.

65 *Giraldi Cambrensis Opera Volume 4*, ed. Brewer, pp. 153–5; *Autobiography of Giraldus Cambrensis*, ed. and trans. Butler, pp. 250–1; Julian Harrison, 'A Note on Gerald of Wales and *Annales Cambriae*', *WHR*, 17 (1994–5), 252–5 (pp. 252–3).

66 Henry Gough-Cooper, 'Annales Cambriae. The E text, from Exeter Cathedral Library MS 3514, pp. 507–19' (2016), *http://croniclau.bangor.ac.uk/documents/AC_E_First_Edition%20%20.pdf* (accessed 20 June 2024), p. 12 [e25.4]; T. Jones (ed.), '"Cronica de Wallia" and Other Documents from Exeter Cathedral Library MS. 3514', *BBCS*, 12 (1946), 27–44 (p. 35).

67 Provenance of *Cronicon de Wallia*: Hughes, *Welsh Latin Chronicles*, p. 250 and n. 1; J. Beverley Smith, 'The "Cronica de Wallia" and the Dynasty of Dinefwr', *BBCS*, 20 (1962–4), 261–82 (pp. 279–80).

68 *ByT* (P20), s.a. 1236 (ed. Jones, p. 196; trans. Jones, p. 104).

69 Goering and Pryce, '*De Modo Confitendi*', 8; Richard Sharpe, *A Handlist of the Latin Writers of Great Britain and Ireland before 1540, with additions and corrections* (Turnhout, 2001), no. 176.

70 Printed in Goering and Pryce, '*De Modo Confitendi*', 16–27.

71 Cadwgan's works in the Hereford manuscript are printed in C. H. Talbot, 'Cadogan of Bangor', *Cîteaux in de Nederlanden*, 9 (1958), 18–40 (pp. 26–40). Goering and Pryce, '*De Modo Confitendi*', 8–11. Sharpe, *Handlist*, no. 176.

72 Goering and Pryce, '*De Modo Confitendi*', 8–11; Walker, 'Cadwgan'. See also Talbot, 'Cadogan', 24; D. H. Williams, 'The Abbey of Dore', in R. Shoesmith and R. Richardson (eds), *A Definitive History of Dore Abbey* (Little Logaston, 1997), pp. 15–36, 210 (pp. 24, 210).

73 David Runciman, 'Pastoral care according to the bishops of England and Wales (*c*.1170–1228)' (unpublished PhD thesis, University of Cambridge, 2019), 108–13.

74 Lucy Toulmin Smith (ed.), *The Itinerary of John Leland in or about the years 1535–1543: Parts IX, X and XI* (London, 1910), p. 178.

75 Talbot, 'Cadogan', 24–5. See also R. A. B. Mynors, *Catalogue of the Manuscripts of Balliol College, Oxford* (Oxford, 1963), pp. 259–60; Reginald Lane Poole and Mary Bateson (eds), *John Bale's Index of British and Other Writers* (Oxford, 1902), p. 480; *EpiscActs*, II, 557; J. Tonkin, 'After the Dissolution', in Ron Shoesmith and Ruth Richardson (eds), *A Definitive History of Dore Abbey* (Little Logaston, 1997), pp. 153–4.

76 Daniel Huws, 'Descriptions of the Welsh Manuscripts', in T. M. Charles-Edwards, Morfydd E. Owen and Paul Russell (eds), *The Welsh King and His Court* (Cardiff, 2000), pp. 415–24 (p. 418).

77 Huws, 'Descriptions', p. 418; Huw Pryce, *Native Law and the Church in Medieval Wales* (Oxford, 1993), pp. 23–5; Daniel Huws, *A Repertory of Welsh Manuscripts and Scribes c.800–c.1800*, 3 vols (Aberystwyth, 2022), I, 665.

78 Huws, 'Descriptions', p. 418.

79 David Stephenson, 'In Search of a Welsh Chronicler: The *Annales Cambriae* B-text for 1204–30', *CMCS*, 72 (2016), 73–85 (pp. 81, 83).

80 Stephenson, 'In Search of a Welsh Chronicler', 81, 83.

81 Stephenson, 'In Search of a Welsh Chronicler', 81; *Giraldi Cambrensis Opera Volume 4*, ed. Brewer, p. 163; Cowley, *Monastic Order*, p. 48; Goering and Pryce, '*De Modo Confitendi*', 2.

82 Stephenson, 'In Search of a Welsh Chronicler', 79 and n. 33.

83 Hughes, *Welsh Latin Chronicles*, p. 256; Brett, 'Prefaces', 63; Harrison, 'A Note on Gerald', 254–5.

84 Harrison, 'A Note on Gerald', 254.

85 Stephenson, 'In Search of a Welsh Chronicler', 81, 83.

86 *Giraldi Cambrensis Opera Volume 4*, ed. Brewer, pp. 162–3. Goering and Pryce, '*De Modo Confitendi*', 2 n. 6. Cf. Cowley, *Monastic Order*, p. 122; Walker, 'Cadwgan'; *EpiscActs*, II, 554–6.

87 *Giraldi Cambrensis Opera Volume 4*, ed. Brewer, pp. 162–3; Cowley, *Monastic Order*, p. 122; Goering and Pryce, '*De Modo Confitendi*', 3 and n. 8, 4 and n. 16; Lloyd, *History of Wales*, II, 688 n. 201.

88 In 1226, for example, Cadwgan was part of Llywelyn's drive to ensure that Dafydd was accepted as his rightful heir by the pope, the king of England and the Welsh themselves: Vatican City, Archivio Segreto, Reg. Vat. 13., f. 122v. no. 253; P. Pressutti (ed.), *Regesta Honorii Papae III, Iussu et Munificentia Leonis XIII Pontificis Maximi ex Vaticanis Archetypis Aliisque Fontibus*, 2 vols (Rome, 1888–95), II, no. 5907; *CalPapReg*, I, 109; McGuinness, *Bangor Episcopal Acta*, no. 31; Huw Pryce, 'Negotiating Anglo-Welsh Relations: Llywelyn the Great and Henry III', in I. W. Rowlands and B. K. U. Weiler (eds), *England and Europe in the Reign of Henry III (1216–1272)* (London, 2002), pp. 13–29 (pp. 19, 22 and nn. 47, 76).

89 *ByT* (RB), s.a. 1239 (ed. and trans. Jones, pp. 235–7); also, Gough-Cooper, 'Annales Cambriae. The E text', p. 17 [e37.2]; Jones (ed.), 'Cronica de Wallia', 38.

90 *Matthaei Parisiensis, Monachi Sancti Albani, Chronica Majora*, ed. H. R. Luard, 7 vols (London, 1872–80) [hereafter *Chronica Majora*], IV, 8, 47–8.

91 *Chronica Majora*, IV, 8, 47–8, 148 (trans. J. A. Giles, *Matthew Paris's English History, from the year 1235 to 1273*, 3 vols (London, 1852–4), I, 290); G. A. Williams, 'The Succession to Gwynedd, 1238–47', *BBCS*, 20 (1962–4), 393–413 (p. 404).

92 McGuinness, *Bangor Episcopal Acta*, no. 38; *Chronica Majora*, IV, 148–9 (trans. Giles, I, 371); *Flores Historiarum*, ed. H. R. Luard, 3 vols (London, 1890), II, 236.

93 *Chronica Majora*, IV, 148–9 (trans. Giles, I, 371); *Flores*, ed. Luard, II, 236; Williams, 'Succession', 404.

94 McGuinness, *Bangor Episcopal Acta*, no. 39; *Flores*, ed. Luard, II, 239.

95 *Chronica Majora*, IV, 149 (trans. Giles, I, 371). In May 1241, Gruffudd's wife, Senana, tried to persuade Henry to secure her husband's release (*Curia Regis Rolls* (London, 1923–), XVI, no. 1595; *AWR*, p. 454). On 12 August 1241, she agreed with Henry to pay 600 marks for the release of Gruffudd and her son, Owain, and a further 300 marks per annum (*AWR*, no. 284). This may be the matter to which Paris was referring but the details recorded by the St Albans' historian, together with their position in his *Chronica Majora* (immediately after Henry, responding to Richard's initial complaint, had advised and ordered Dafydd to release Gruffudd), seem to suggest that Gruffudd had made an earlier offer to Henry; if so, Paris may have obtained this information from Richard.

96 Williams, 'Succession', 403–8. Cf. Lloyd, *History of Wales*, II, 694 n. 2.

97 Lawrin Armstrong, 'A Misdated St Paul's Fabric Indulgence', *Notes and Queries*, 59/4 (2012), 483–7 (pp. 486–7), and see McGuinness, *Bangor Episcopal Acta*, no. 40.

98 *Flores*, ed. Luard, II, 243.

99 Pryce, *Writing Welsh History*, p. 36; *AWR*, p. 469; Smith, *Llywelyn*, p. 35 n. 118; David Carpenter, 'Dafydd ap Llywelyn's Submission to King Henry III in October 1241: A New Perspective', *WHR*, 23 (2007), 1–12 (p. 4).
100 TNA C 66/49, Patent Rolls, 25 Henry III, m. 2d (*Calendar of the Patent Rolls preserved in the Public Record Office (1232–1313)*, 9 vols (London, 1893–1913) [hereafter *CPR*], *1232–47*, p. 264), printed in *AWR*, no. 300, where it is denoted as 'B'. J. Beverley Smith, 'Dafydd ap Llywelyn (*c.*1215–1246)', *ODNB*, https://doi.org/10.1093/ref:odnb/7323; *AWR*, p. 29.
101 Denoted as 'C' in *AWR*, no. 300. The manuscript contains the text of *Chronica Majora* to 1253: Richard Vaughan, *Matthew Paris* (Cambridge, 1958), p. 21.
102 *AWR*, no. 300.
103 *AWR*, p. 469.
104 *AWR*, p. 469.
105 *AWR*, nos 301–3 and p. 469; *CPR*, *1232–1247*, p. 264.
106 *ByT* (RB), s.a. 1241 (ed. and trans. Jones, pp. 236–7); *Chronica Majora*, iv, 150. Also *AWR*, p. 477.
107 *AWR*, no. 304.
108 *CPR*, *1232–1247*, p. 261.
109 *AWR*, no. 305.
110 McGuinness, *Bangor Episcopal Acta*, no. 43.
111 *AWR*, no. 300.
112 *Calendar of the Close Rolls preserved in the Public Record Office* (London, 1900–), *1237–1242*, p. 328; *Chronica Majora*, IV, 150 (trans. Giles, I, 372); T. F. Tout revised by A. D. Carr, 'Gruffudd ap Llywelyn (*d.* 1244)', *ODNB*, https://doi.org/10.1093/ref:odnb/11696; Smith, *Llywelyn*, p. 35 n. 122.
113 F. Madden (ed.), *Matthaei Parisiensis, monachi Sancti Albani, Historia Anglorum, sive, ut vulgo dicitur, Historia Minor. Item, ejusdem Abbreviatio Chronicorum Angliae*, 3 vols (London, 1866) [hereafter *Historia Anglorum*], II, 453. On Henry's motives, see Carpenter, 'Submission', 7–8.
114 *Chronica Majora*, IV, 399–400 (trans. Giles, II, 38–9); *AWR*, no. 306.
115 *AWR*, no. 306. Benedict G. E. Wiedemann, '"Fooling the Court of the Lord Pope": Dafydd ap Llywelyn's Petition to the Curia in 1244', *WHR*, 28 (2016), 209–32 (pp. 209–32); Bryn Jones, 'Welsh Contacts with the Papacy before the Edwardian Conquest, *c.*1283' (unpublished PhD thesis, University of St Andrews, 2019), 87–8.
116 Smith, *Llywelyn*, p. 53, and n. 58, referring to *Chronica Majora*, IV, 324 (*vassalulum*).
117 McGuinness, *Bangor Episcopal Acta*, no. 43. J. Beverley Smith has suggested that Richard issued the letter at Henry's insistence (Smith, *Llywelyn*, p. 57; see also Carpenter, 'Submission', 11). However, Richard's secular loyalties may have lain with the king for some time (David Stephenson, *The Governance of*

Gwynedd (Cardiff, 1984), p. 232), and, further, he had in his episcopal capacity not only given a charter to the king promising to enforce the provisions of the agreement reached at Gwerneigron on 29 August 1241 (*AWR*, no. 300), he had sealed both of Dafydd's notifications of 31 August 1241 (*AWR*, nos 302 and 303), and given his consent to the agreement of *c.*24 October 1241 at Westminster (*AWR*, no. 304); as such he may have seen it as his duty to ensure that both the letter and spirit of those documents were recognised and enforced.

118 Williams, 'Succession', 410; *AWR*, p. 30.
119 *Chronica Majora*, IV, 518, a fact confirmed by *Annales Cestrienses* (Richard Copley Christie (ed. and trans.), *Annales Cestrienses or Chronicle of the Abbey of S. Werburg at Chester* (London, 1887), p. 66). See also Smith, *Llywelyn*, p. 49 and n. 47.
120 It was also a reference to one of Dafydd's notifications of 31 August 1241 which Richard had sealed: *AWR*, no. 303; *CPR, 1232–1247*, p. 264. Richard also made it clear that Dafydd, of his own free will, had appointed Henry heir of all his lordship in Wales if he died without an heir of his body (McGuinness, *Bangor Episcopal Acta*, no. 43), a reference to Dafydd's notification of 24 October 1241: *AWR*, no. 305.
121 *Chronica Majora*, V, 2.
122 *AWR*, no. 440; *Registrum Vulgariter Nuncupatum, 'The Record of Caernarvon', E Codice MSt° Harleiano 696 Descriptum*, ed. H. Ellis (London, 1838), p. 252.
123 *Chronica Majora*, V, 288; T. F. Tout, rev. R. R. Davies, 'Zouche [Zouch], Alan de la (*d.* 1270)', *ODNB*, https://doi.org/10.1093/ref:odnb/30300.
124 'Episcopus insuper Bangorensis ad Sanctum Albanum veniens, itidem enarravit.': *Chronica Majora*, V, 288 (trans. Giles, II, 486).
125 *Chronica Majora*, V, 432; *Flores*, ed. Luard, II, 396; *Gesta Abbatum Monasterii Sancti Albani a Thoma Walsingham*, ed. H. T. Riley (London, 1867), I, 321.
126 *ByT* (RB), s.a. 1255 (ed. and trans. Jones, pp. 246–7).
127 *CPR, 1247–1258*, p. 534.
128 *ByT* (RB), s.a. 1256 (ed. and trans. Jones, pp. 246–7); Smith, *Llywelyn*, pp. 84–5, and n. 186.
129 *ByT* (RB), s.a. 1256 (ed. and trans. Jones, pp. 246–7); Smith, *Llywelyn*, p. 91.
130 *Chronica Majora*, V, 597 and 613.
131 Lloyd, *History of Wales*, II, 719 n. 19; Smith, *Llywelyn*, 94 and n. 14.
132 *Chronica Majora*, V, 592–3, 596–7 and 613 (trans. Giles, III, 200, 204, 217).
133 *Chronica Majora*, V, 633 and 639 (trans. Giles, III, 233, 238).
134 *Chronica Majora*, V, 601–3; Nicholas Vincent, 'Richard, first earl of Cornwall and king of Germany (1209–1272)', *ODNB*, https://doi.org/10.1093/ref:odnb/23501.

135 '... Et addidit, versa facie ad episcopos, quorum unus Bangorensis Ricardus, qui haec huius paginae scriptori assertive enarravit, extiterat, ...': *Chronica Majora*, V, 602 (trans. Giles, III, 207–9); Williams, 'Succession', 406.

136 McGuinness, *Bangor Episcopal Acta*, nos. 47 and 48; *Chronica Majora*, V, 608–9; *Chronica Majora*, VI, 495 n. 1; Huw Pryce, 'Esgobaeth Bangor yn Oes y Tywysogion', in W. P. Griffith (ed.), *'Ysbryd Deallturus ac Enaid Anfarwol': Ysgrifau ar Hanes Crefydd yng Ngwynedd* (Bangor, 1999), pp. 37–57 (p. 49).

137 Quote from Simon Lloyd and Rebecca Reader, 'Paris, Matthew (*c*.1200–1259)', *ODNB*, https://doi.org/10.1093/ref:odnb/21268.

138 It is noteworthy that Richard's first stay at St Albans was in 1248, the year after Henry III had asked Matthew Paris to write a full account of the ceremony of the Holy Blood: David Carpenter, *Henry III, The Rise to Power and Personal Rule, 1207–1258* (London, 2021), p. 478.

139 1277: J. G. Edwards (ed.), *Calendar of Ancient Correspondence Concerning Wales* (Cardiff, 1935), p. 66.

140 Bangor University Archives and Special Collections, The Bangor Pontifical, f. 166; F. Roth (ed.), *The English Austin Friars, 1249–1538*, 2 vols (New York, 1961), II, 33–4, 36. East Anglican provenance: Sally Harper, 'The Bangor Pontifical', *Hanes Cerddoriaeth Cymru/Welsh Music History*, 2 (1997), 65–99 (pp. 73–6). Harper believes that the pontifical is more likely to be that of Anian II (1309–28), see pp. 65, 74. Anian I or Anian II may also be associated with a book of Aesopic fables preserved in the British Library: 'Avianus, Bishop of Bangor': BL Add MS 33781. Cf. H. L. D. Ward, *Catalogue of Romances in the Department of Manuscripts in the British Museum*, 3 vols (London, 1883–1910), II, 272–5, 335–42.

141 McGuinness, *Bangor Episcopal Acta*, no. 92; Susan J. Ridyard and Jeremy A. Ashbee, 'The Resuscitation of Roger of Conwy: a Cantilupe Miracle and the Society of Edwardian North Wales', in C. A. M. Clarke (ed.), *Power, Identity and Miracles on a Medieval Frontier* (Abingdon, 2017), pp. 61–76. Thank you to Dr Ian Bass for bringing the testimony to my attention.

142 McGuinness, *Bangor Episcopal Acta*, no. 92; Bass, 'Communities', 260–4 and n. 81; Malcolm Vale, 'St John, Sir John de (*d*. 1302)', *ODNB*, https://doi.org/10.1093/ref:odnb/24499.

143 1305. McGuinness, *Bangor Episcopal Acta*, no. 102. When Bishop Cantilupe went into exile in Normandy, 1280–1, he entrusted Anian with carrying out duties in his Hereford diocese: W. W. Capes and R. G. Griffiths (eds), *The Register of Thomas De Cantilupe, Bishop of Hereford A.D. 1275–1282* (Hereford, 1906), p. 253.

144 McGuinness, *Bangor Episcopal Acta*, no. 92; Ridyard and Ashbee, 'Resuscitation', pp. 61–76; Bass, 'Communities', 260–4; Malcolm Vale, 'St John, Sir John de (*d*. 1302)', *ODNB*, https://doi.org/10.1093/ref:odnb/24499.

10

'Pinnacles of Preaching' and Men of 'Bold Learning'?: Protestant Reforms, the History of Wales, and the Elizabethan Bishops of Bangor – A Case Study of Nicholas Robinson (c.1530–1585)

Katharine Olson

A host of expectations linked to behaviour, responsibilities, virtues and office defined the bishop's role in sixteenth-century Britain and Europe. A main scriptural basis for the role of bishop remained, as it had been, St Paul's first letter to Timothy (1 Timothy, Chapter 3, verses 1–7), with its emphasis on men who were neither pugnacious, greedy, nor too fond of drink, but instead blameless, gentle, discrete, diligent, sober and kept good hospitality.[1] A wider trend is also apparent in England and Europe from the fifteenth century into the sixteenth, which saw 'the academically-trained prelate' as 'an increasingly familiar figure', and those of higher rank 'heavily engaged in the promotion of learning throughout this period', including through the foundation of public libraries.[2] Likewise, a growing emphasis on the apostolic ideal of episcopal residence and bishops playing an active role in pastoral care in one's diocese is evident, especially from the mid-1530s.[3] Subsequent generations of Reformation bishops in the sixteenth century 'emphasized the importance of the pastoral duties of the prelate, his obligation to be a careful preacher and educator and his responsibility to provide a reformed and well-trained body of clerics'. Indeed, the largely resident bishops of the reign of Elizabeth were 'regular preachers' and met with 'more success' than those Reformation bishops who came before them in terms of realising a pastoral ministry.[4]

Expectations for reforming bishops in Elizabethan Wales included, as John Gwynfor Jones has demonstrated: 'propagating the Word of

God, revealing their profound learning ... and their fervent belief in God's grace'.[5] Likewise, in contrast to late medieval and many (though not all) early Reformation bishops of Welsh dioceses, in Elizabethan Wales, some thirteen (perhaps twelve) of the sixteen Elizabethan bishops holding sees were themselves Welsh or had Welsh connections.[6] Two Elizabethan examples from different dioceses, St Asaph and St Davids, shed light on the ways in which they sought to realise these developing expectations of the role of the bishop in his diocese. A Caernarvonshire man, the Oxbridge-educated bishop of St Asaph and administrator, Thomas Davies (c.1511–73; bishop, 1561–73), for example, hoped to create a 'learned ministry' in the diocese and his various presentations to livings were largely 'resident, hospitable, and scholarly Welsh clergy'. In 1561, he also ordered the reading of the gospel, epistles, and catechism in both English and Welsh on Sundays. He was likewise a bardic patron, worked to reorganise the diocese, and lobbied Parliament together with Humphrey Llwyd and Richard Davies for Welsh translations of the Bible and Book of Common Prayer into Welsh. He also endeavoured to endow a scholarship at Queen's College, Cambridge. The poet Siôn Tudur praised Davies as a 'Solomon of upright [just] language' (*Salmon iaith gyfion*) who had 'illuminated ... God's word to the world' (*Goleuaist ... air Duw i'r byd*).[7] Likewise, another Caernarvonshire man, the Oxford-educated scholar, translator and bishop of St Davids, Richard Davies (c.1505–81; bishop 1560–81), also endeavoured to address similar issues of pluralism, non-residency and other shortcomings of the clergy (for example, education, preaching and language), and staunchly supported Protestant reforms, including the eradication of 'superstition and idolatry' and related practices amongst the laity like 'pilgrimages to wells and blind chapels'. Learned in Hebrew, Latin, Greek, and literate in French and German, he helped to secure the 1563 Act of Parliament (5 Eliz. c.28) for the Welsh translation of the Bible and Book of Common Prayer, working with William Salesbury and Thomas Huet on the translation of the 1567 Welsh New Testament, and writing the preface to this (*Epistol at y Cembru*, with contributions from William Salesbury), setting out his vision of early British church history. Davies was himself a patron of the poets, and upon his death in 1581, his life and contributions were celebrated by poets and other contemporaries. Siôn Tudur commended him as 'a good Welshman' (*da Gymro*) and for his preaching of 'God's word' (*Gair duw*) and singled him out as a 'key [to] golden learning' (*agoriad dysg aur*), esteemed for his Welsh translations.[8]

The importance of episcopal ideals of residency, playing an active reforming role in the diocese, establishing a learned ministry, preaching, bardic patronage, learning and scholarship in Welsh (and other languages), amongst others, were significant to expectations for the role of Protestant bishops in Elizabethan Wales in life, and also emphasised in death by the poets in their elegies, sung and circulated in manuscript form. Indeed, as Jones has perceptively noticed, the later years of the sixteenth century witnessed 'an increase in Protestant propaganda in the contents of formal eulogies to bishops and other churchmen'.[9] However, despite attempts to implement Protestant reforms and the growing availability of relevant texts in Welsh, the Reformation bishops of Wales continued to face substantial challenges which meant that they were unable to fully realise their ambitions during the reign of Elizabeth.

This chapter explores the developing role, expectations and challenges of bishops in the diocese of Bangor, including their active involvement in Protestant reforms, antiquarian and historical pursuits during the latter half of the sixteenth century. It focuses on a case study of the scholarly, historical and religious contributions of the Elizabethan bishop of Bangor, Nicholas Robinson (1566–85), particularly his underexplored endeavour to write a history of Wales in National Library of Wales (NLW), Peniarth MS 383.[10] Robinson's episcopate and those of his successors reflect changing expectations for bishops in Reformation Wales in the latter half of the sixteenth century and beyond. Glanmor Williams has argued that the Elizabethan bishops of Bangor, Rowland Meyrick (1560–5), Nicholas Robinson (1566–85), Hugh Bellot (1586–95), Richard Vaughan (1596–8) and Henry Rowlands (1598–1616), were 'on the whole, a notable succession of good men', who were 'without exception, men of learning, local connections, and in marked contrast to their medieval predecessors, resident pastors'.[11] Indeed, by the second half of the sixteenth century, Bangor's bishops were almost entirely Welsh and Welsh-speaking, actively involved in their pastoral role, and often scholars in their own right. This chapter therefore focuses on a case study of one bishop's efforts, albeit imperfect, to realise the host of developing expectations for Welsh bishops during the reign of Elizabeth, from residency to preaching, effective administration, establishing a learned ministry, and combatting recusancy and 'popish' customs. In connection with these, it likewise demonstrates the nature and range of Robinson's engagement with scholarly and antiquarian pursuits and circles, and in particular his interests relating to the Welsh language, the history of Wales, and local history.

Background: the diocese of Bangor

Bangor diocese, consisting of Anglesey, Caernarfonshire, the hundred of Creuddyn, and parts of Merioneth, Denbighshire and Montgomeryshire, yielded one of the lowest incomes in England and Wales.[12] A visitation of the diocese, ordered by Archbishop Warham in 1504 upon the death of Bishop Thomas Pigot (also abbot of Chertsey), reveals that holding several rectories for extra income was standard practice, and given the poverty of the diocese, one that remained common amongst the cathedral clergy; monasteries also generally appropriated parishes. The report also reflects the widespread practice of concubinage; with forty-three clergy reported to have been married in defiance of canon law.[13] Prior to the Henrician Reformation, at most one-fifth of churches in the diocese had vicars, and clerks earning £5 p.a. or less were more common; only approximately one-quarter of livings were valued at more than £15 a year. The *Valor Ecclesiasticus* of 1535 valued it at £131 a year, making it the poorest bishopric in England and Wales.[14] The diocese was said to be worth £148 6s. 8d by an Edwardian reckoning (before 1550) of the yearly value of spiritual promotions in England; only the see of Llandaf was worth less (£144 4s. 1d).[15] Subsequent bishops not infrequently complained about its poverty. Richard Vaughan remarked in 1595/6 on the 'poor estate of the bishopric', which yielded him less than £50 yearly during first fruits. In 1598, Henry Rowlands noted that there was only a 'bare £100 a year for the bishop to live upon' remained to the bishop, with £30 a year during first fruits.[16]

In contrast, from 1417 to 1541, all bishops of Bangor were 'Englishmen, almost entirely absentees and holding important appointments in England'.[17] Most were in religious orders, and relied on income from appointments in England, where they lived. For example, the last pre-Reformation bishop of Bangor (1509–33), the Cistercian Thomas Skevington, likely a native of Leicestershire, was abbot of Beaulieu (Hampshire) by 1508 (which he continued to hold *in commendam* after his elevation to the see of Bangor in 1509), spending his time largely at Beaulieu abbey, as a non-resident bishop. Arthur Bulkeley (*c*.1495–1552/3; bishop of Bangor, 1541–52/3) provides the first Reformation example of a bishop of Bangor with Welsh connections who was resident and active in his diocese, involved in pastoral care and interested in scholarly pursuits. Bulkeley was elected bishop of Bangor on 18 November 1541, with royal assent following on 8 December.[18] He played an active role in the religious life of his diocese, including conducting the earliest Reformation visitation of a Welsh bishopric for which articles of injunction are extent.[19]

As William Hudon has reminded us: 'all religious reform – especially the episcopal – is fundamentally a local story'.[20] For the bishops of Bangor, the challenges faced by reforming bishops included the poverty of the diocese, the lack of educated Welsh-speaking clergy, and particularly those who could preach, were persistent problems in the diocese of Bangor and elsewhere in Wales. In 1561, Bangor diocese had only two men licensed to preach (not necessarily in the Welsh tongue): the dean of Bangor (a bachelor of divinity), and the vicar of Llangurig.[21] For 1561, the diocese of St Asaph had five, like Llandaf in the south. St Davids diocese had just ten by 1570, and fourteen by 1583. It was only in the 1590s that numbers crept upwards: eighteen of 155 in Llandaf, forty-three of 154 in Bangor, and fifty-four of 144 in St Asaph.[22] Indeed, the problem of providing the predominately illiterate laity with competent Welsh-speaking clergy remained paramount to the success of Protestantism in Wales, and a major challenge for the Welsh bishops of the sixteenth century and beyond. Archbishop Matthew Parker's comment to Sir William Cecil in February 1565 that he understood the diocese to be 'much out of order … having no preaching there', was very much in keeping with contemporary concerns over the progress of Protestant reforms in the Elizabethan church in Wales generally, and particularly those related to the challenges faced by bishops in the diocese of Bangor, as we shall see.[23]

Nicholas Robinson (1566–85)

We turn now to an examination of the second Elizabethan bishop of Bangor,[24] Nicholas Robinson (*c*.1530–85), who provides a fascinating case study of the nature of the religious and scholarly contributions made by contemporary bishops in Elizabethan Wales. His father's family, not dissimilar to Bulkeley's, originally came from Cheshire, and had settled in the Conwy area in north Wales, where his father, John Robinson (*fl. c.*1510–60), a bailiff and burgess, was one of the leading men of the town; the family's influence in local government and administration as well as the Caernarfonshire Court of Quarter Sessions is reflected in contemporary records.[25] His mother, Elin, likewise had English ancestry: her father, William Brickdale, was a Wirral man. However, both Robinson's parents also boasted significant links to prominent north Wales gentry families. Robinson's paternal great-grandfather was married to a sister of Owen Tudor of the Tudors of Penmynydd (Anglesey), while his maternal grandmother, Marsli, descended from a leading Flintshire gentry family, the Conways of Bodrhyddan. Robinson, a younger son, married the granddaughter of Sir William Gruffydd of Penrhyn, another leading gentry family in north-west Wales.[26] A Queens' College, Cambridge man, by 1548 he had obtained a BA and became a fellow of the college (1548–63). He emerged from his studies with an MA (1551), becoming a proctor of the college in 1556–7.[27] At the same time (1556–7), Robinson was ordained acolyte, deacon and priest by the bishop of Bangor, William Glyn.[28] Subsequently licenced as a preacher in the province of Canterbury and made chaplain to Archbishop Matthew Parker (1559), he received a BTh (1560) and a DTh (1566). He held two benefices in London as well as Northop (Flintshire), and by 1562 had also been made archdeacon of Merioneth. He signed the Thirty-Nine Articles (1563) and sat on the Commission of the Apparel of the Clergy (1564), and wrote an account of the queen's visit to the universities of Cambridge (1564) and Oxford (1566).[29]

Robinson apparently made a name for himself as a preacher of note early on. Having just received his BTh, in December 1561, he preached a sermon at St Paul's Cross in London; indeed, he appears to have been the only bishop of Bangor to have preached there during the reign of Elizabeth.[30] He was subsequently appointed one of the Queen's Lenten preachers in 1565. Robinson may have been the 'Mr. Robinson' who preached at court as one of the queen's Lenten preachers on 27 March 1565/6 in Greenwich, given his position as chaplain in Parker's household and Cambridge connections, as McCullough has noted (though John Robinson, MA, president of St John's College, Cambridge is an additional possibility).[31] His preaching drew praise from contemporaries, including the bishop of London, Edmund Grindal, as well as Sir John Wynn of

Gwydir. Wynn had heard Robinson preach at St Paul's in London on a single occasion, but frequently in the country, and characterised him as 'an excellent scholar' and 'a very wise man' who preached particularly well when he did so 'without meditation' (improvised).[32]

One of his sermons, which was apparently delivered in 1564 at St Paul's Cross in London and praised by the bishop of London (Grindal) has survived.[33] It is found in Cambridge, Corpus Christi College, MS 104 (pp. 319–34), Parker's compilation of theological tracts, sermons and gospel commentaries, etc. by Thomas Cranmer, Hugh Latimer, Martin Bucer and others.[34] Having compared it with other extant examples of his handwriting, I have identified the sermon itself as being in Robinson's own hand. This sermon, concerned with the character of 'obstinate Cain', including the killing of Abel (Genesis 4:3 and 4:8 are the text of sermon), and ultimately 'owre true reformation and repentance'.[35] He draws on a variety of examples from scripture, the early church fathers and classical sources, including Ezechias, Achab, Roboam, David, E'say (Isaiah) the prophet, Abraham, SS Paul, Luke, Mark, Peter, and John Chrysostom, the *Life of Constantine* by Eusebius of Caesarea, and the Greek philosopher Diogenes. Robinson's comments included condemnation of 'the superstitions Dames in tymes past, who through ignorance and blyndness loved well holly water'.[36] He concludes by expressing the wish that 'we maye in tyme of grace here in this world not only abstayne from old but also doe well, and so accomplishe the godly life of a good Christiane man and through Jesus Christe owre savioure'.[37] An excerpt from this, found on pp. 324–5 of the manuscript, was included by the English clergyman and historian John Strype (1643–1737) in his biography of Archbishop Matthew Parker (1504–75), *The Life and Acts of Matthew Parker*, which was first published in 1711. Strype says he discovered it among Parker's papers, and that 'it was known to be this man's, by what the archbishop in his own hand noted upon it, viz. *Concio N. Robynson*: it was preached near this time before great audience either at Court or St. Paul's Cross, by the Archbishop's order ... [as he] perceived his great ability in preaching'.[38]

When Rowland Meyrick died in 1566, Robinson, 'whom the country doth much desire', was ultimately elected in mid-September 1566, though he was not Parker's initial choice for bishop.[39] He was quickly confirmed (5 October) and consecrated by Archbishop Matthew Parker (20 October, Lambeth), with restitution of temporalities on

26 November.⁴⁰ Robinson was a pluralist and retained his various livings in England and the archdeaconry of Merioneth (which he had held since 1562) *in commendam*, later (1573) becoming archdeacon of Anglesey instead (1573–85).⁴¹

Robinson was a resident bishop who appears to have prioritised the improvement of the spiritual life of both the clergy and the laity in the diocese. This included working to increase the number of educated clergy who could preach. He was also much involved in efforts to reform the 'superstitious' religious practices of his flock and contend with the threat of recusancy. In October 1567 Robinson wrote to Cecil soberly of the poor state of religious life in his new diocese. From his experience amongst the people so far, he noted, 'ignorance contineweth many in the dregges of superstition'. He reported that this widespread 'ignorance' and 'superstition' amongst the laity included 'Images and aulters standing in churches undefaced, lewde and undecent vigils and watches observed, much pilgramege-goyng, many candels sett up to the honour of sainctes, some reliquies yet caried about, and all the Cuntreis full of bedes and knottes'. The continuation of these traditional practices and the lack of success in terms of Protestant reforms was 'chefely' due to the 'blyndnes of the clergie' and their 'greediness of getting in so bare a cuntrey' in terms of the meager salaries offered in the diocese, which did not support the robust cure of souls. Further, most of the priests were too old to be 'put to schole' and therefore were unable to teach God's word to the people, from whom the gospel also remained closed up 'from them in an unknowen [English] tounge'.⁴²

He took a stance against recusancy in the diocese, including traditional funeral practices, which he characterised as 'born out of ignorance' like the 'folishe custome there used' in Beaumaris (Anglesey) in 1570, when he wrote to Sir William Cecil about a corpse which had been buried there with candles and singing of psalms.⁴³ In May 1576, Robinson along with Thomas Yale, LLD was appointed to lead a visitation of Bangor diocese.⁴⁴ A year later, in November 1577, he replied to the enquiries of John Whitgift, bishop of Worcester and the president of the court of the Marches of Wales, about the state of the diocese. There was in the entire diocese, he wrote, a single recusant, 'one olde prieste called Humfrey Barker' in the town of Conwy, 'who beyng a verey poore man' had no goods that were known, and issues with non-attendance at church in the 'farthest partes' of Caernarfonshire in the hundreds of Llŷn and Eifionydd had been dealt with by him personally.[45] Robinson in fact investigated recusant activity on the Llŷn peninsula in March 1578, when he was appointed along with Dr Ellis Price to question those local gentry and others with links to the recusant Hugh Owen (Plas-Du, Caernarfonshire) who had fled the realm on suspicion of treason.[46]

Robinson's efforts to address recusancy in his diocese were however not regarded as sufficient by some. In the early 1580s, Robinson faced allegations of papist sympathies questioning his loyalty to the Protestant cause; they did not however result in any official action taken against him. On 28 May 1582, he wrote letters from Bangor to the earl of Leicester and Elizabeth's chief secretary, Sir Francis Walsingham. Both letters mount a staunch defence of the accusations made against him by 'malicious accusers' and outline his contributions to the religious life of the diocese. In the first, he speaks of how his sincerity in preaching Christ's gospel was known at court and both in Cambridge and London in the years before becoming bishop.[47] As bishop, he continued to preach, publicly interpreting 'some part of holly scripture' every Sunday and at assemblies, twice a week during Lent and at the Assizes. And yet, he wrote to Walsingham, 'leaned or zelouse' men had found fault with his doctrine to date. Indeed, he noted, he had been singled out as a persecutor of recusants and was 'in danger of life' due to his zeal in 'suppressing pilgrimage, night watches att tombes, prayng to Images and such like errours of papistrie: I am dayly threatened for searching out such offendours and using law against them'. Robinson claimed that he was feared by them as for a 'long tyme I laied wait for their massing priestes, and make Inquisition twise every yere for them and their hearers in every parishe'. Yet he had apparently discovered only six recusants in the diocese: one man and five women. He begged Walsingham's assistance 'in defence of myne Innocencie against the selander [slander] of papistrie' by his adversaries, adding: 'I am in conscience and before the eies of god most free from all papistrie'.[48]

His pleas appear to have been heeded, as he was appointed along with Dr William Meyrick, the vicar in spiritualities, to conduct another visitation of the diocese. This noted two recusants and four preachers in the entire diocese (three of the preachers held MAs, though one was 'now absent'), and no other public preachers, besides 'theym of the chapter and parsons in their owne cures'. This was 'by reason that there are few devynes skill full in the Wellshe tonge, nether eny speciall stipends or salaries founded or ordeyned in this dio*cese* for prechers'. Cure of souls was also variable due to the paltry stipends offered in the diocese. Robinson explained that the diocese had no churches without a curate 'utterly', but that the churches 'are very evill servid by reson the stipend is very small, and not able to maynten curate continually'.[49] As Robinson conceded, however, the implementation of Protestant reforms in the diocese was unfinished; it had been piecemeal due to the many practical difficulties which he faced as bishop, from the lack of preachers to the cure of souls to the poverty of the diocese.

As bishop, Robinson was also actively involved in his role as a justice of the peace, addressing a range of issues arising related to ecclesiastical authority and other matters. He is recorded as acting as Justice of the Peace frequently, including for the north Wales circuit, for Anglesey (1573–4, 1575, 1577, 1578, 1579, 1584), Caernarvon (1573–4, 1575, 1577, 1578–9, 1579, 1581, 1584) and Merioneth (1574, 1575, 1577, 1578, 1579, 1584). He also acted for the Chester circuit (for Denbigh, Flint, Mongomery), in the Carmarthen circuit (for Carmarthen, Cardigan and Pembroke), for the Brecon circuit (for Brecon, Glamorgan and Radnor) and for Monmouth.[50]

Writing a history of Wales:
Robinson and NLW Peniarth MS 383

Robinson made scholarly contributions relating to Welsh history and was a 'serious historian', as Daniel Huws has argued: select aspects of its contents are considered below. In particular, his largely unexplored manuscript, NLW Peniarth MS 383, shows considerable interest in collecting material related to the history of Wales and may be seen as reflecting 'the extent of his ambition'.[51] It was a compilation largely in Robinson's italic hand, with sections (pp. 125–238 and pp. 238–75) the work of two different amanuenses, in addition to a brief transcript of four leaves in the hand of Robert Vaughan (pp. 276a–h); as Huws suggests, this may well have been a later insertion. A 'galloping hand' of the latter half of the seventeenth century (1661) also made a number of historical additions from p. 338.[52] It is written largely in Latin, but contains Welsh place- and personal names as well as words and phrases in Welsh, and occasional English.

Robinson draws upon a variety of sources for Peniarth 383. These include a range of medieval and sixteenth-century English, Latin and Welsh sources. Those which he explicitly names include Gerald of Wales, *Descriptio Cambriae* and *Itinerarium Cambriae*, Roger of Wendover's *Flores Historium*, the *Chronica Majora* of Matthew Paris (a continuation of Wendover), John Bale, Richard Grafton, John Stowe, John Foxe's *Acts and Monuments* (four editions were published 1563–83) and Bede's *Historia ecclesiastica*. He also draws upon the *brutiau*, Geoffrey of Monmouth and the '*Historie Walliae*'. This may be David Powel's *Historie of Cambria* (1584), which was based on Humphrey Llwyd's unpublished 1559 manuscript of *Cronica Walliae* and a variety of another sources, as Pryce has demonstrated, or a draft of this. He also may well have had access to a manuscript copy of Llwyd's work which was in circulation; five manuscript copies have survived of this.[53] In addition, Robinson draws on Thomas Walsingham: he likely used the *Historia brevis Thomae Walsingham, ab Edwardo Primo, ad Henricum Quintum*, edited by Matthew Parker.[54] He also cites the *Perambulation of Kent*, even mentioning the specific folio number which he consulted.[55]

Rather than being just a compilation of historical texts or a 'skeleton history of Wales', it is both. The first 275 pages include excerpts or transcripts from a number of historical texts relating to medieval Welsh and English history, notably the *Descriptio Cambriae* and *Itinerarium Cambriae* of Gerald of Wales, Henry of Huntingdon's *Historia Anglorum*, and other historical and genealogical materials relating to Henry II (r. 1154–89) and King David I of Scotland (r. 1124–53), for example.[56] The first part of the book begins, for example, in the year 1188 with an account of Gerald's journey around Wales with Archbishop Baldwin to preach the cross for the Third Crusade, and travels through (variously) Hay, Brycheiniog, Ewias, Llanthony, Abergavenny, Caerleon, Cardiff, Llandaf, Kidwelly, Carmarthen, Haverford, Pembroke (Book I of Gerald's *Itinerarium Cambriae*, pp. 1–20). The subsequent section, based on the second book of the *Itinerarium Cambriae* (pp. 21–32), provides occasional explanations of place-names and demonstrates a particular interest in Anglesey.

Doubtless the most interesting part of this manuscript is the latter part, from p. 277, which was principally written by Robinson himself. Robinson's vision of the past in this part of Peniarth 383 begins with the classical past and continues up to 1457, with a particular focus on

Wales. Taken as a whole, it represents what Huws has called Robinson's 'chronological framework for a synthesis of the history of Wales'. This includes classical descriptions of Roman Britain and its history, an account (from p. 287) of the Roman Empire in Britain.[57] This section was based on the writings of various classical and medieval authors, including Suetonius, Bede, Ambrose, Sulpicius Severus, and others.[58] It covers the reigns of various Roman emperors, including Nero, Caligula, Hadrian, Constantine and Theodosius. Helena, mother of Constantine (d. 330), to whom the finding of the True Cross was attributed in medieval Welsh poetry and prose, is also mentioned.[59] Robinson's subsequent content includes individuals (some pseudo-historical) such as Maximus, Vortigern, Arthur, Constantius, Cadfan, and the sixth-century king of Gwynedd, Maelgwn Gwynedd, along with religious figures such as SS Gwenfrewi, Patrick, Dubricius (Dyfrig) and David, to the princes of Gwynedd, Powys and Deheubarth, and includes Owain Glyndŵr, for example. In this approach, like Humphrey Llwyd, he sought to dismiss and 'disprove the aspersions Polydore [the Italian writer Polydore Vergil] had cast "on the glory of the British name" by citing an array of ancient authors and invoking the deeds of British rulers from King Arthur to Llywelyn the Great [and beyond]'.[60]

Robinson organised his history (especially from p. 277 on) chronologically for the most part, and its content has a strong political focus both in terms of content and appearance, and presents a synthesis of British history, with a particular focus on Wales. There is a firm emphasis on the early British kings, like Vortimer, Arthur, Cadfan, Maelgwn Gwynedd and others, the developing history of the princes of Wales, including the princes of Powys and Deheubarth, but particularly the house of Gwynedd and its fortunes. Indeed, the chiefly political nature of the narrative is reinforced visually through its structure. To the left of the text, Robinson included a variety of columns to divide his history. The first was the year. Secondly came the English king (this varied according to period: from the mid-ninth century, kings of England are noted). After 878, the kings of England were followed by a third column noting the princes of Aberffraw (the seat of the house of Gwynedd). A fourth column shows the princes of Mathafarn (seat of the house of Powys), and a fifth column shows the princes of Dinefwr (seat of the house of Deheubarth). This tripartite division into medieval Welsh territorial units which Robinson utilises echoes that used by Humphrey

Llwyd in his 1559 *Cronica Wallia*, as does his division of the text by the names of individual Welsh and English rulers and by date (which Pryce also finds for Llwyd, and argues is 'possibly influenced by the division of English history into reigns' by sixteenth-century English historians). This strongly suggests that Robinson may have been familiar with a manuscript version of Llwyd's work (other similarities also exist, but are beyond the scope of this chapter), and (as previously demonstrated) was well acquainted with medieval and sixteenth-century English histories. Indeed, Pryce has perceptively noted how the tripartite division used by Llwyd emphasises 'the conceptualization of Wales as a historical creation, rather than simply a geographical expression'.[61] The divisions used by Robinson were not static but reflected and responded to contemporary political developments in medieval Wales as well. At the end of the twelfth century, for example, due to events relating to the houses of Powys and Deheubarth (for example, the internecine conflict after the death of the Lord Rhys in 1197), both houses disappear from the table, and only the kings of England and the princes of Aberffraw are shown, along with a date column on the far left of the page.

Robinson also demonstrates an interest in bringing together important dates in the ecclesiastical history of Wales, and in crafting a history of the different Welsh dioceses. He regularly notes the death dates of abbots and bishops across Wales (though especially the north), and sometimes notes new abbots and bishops. There are also occasional references to the construction of churches (for example, the building of Llanegwystl, or Valle Crucis, in 1200).[62] In particular, he includes (pp. 339–40) brief chronologies of important dates in the histories of the dioceses of St Davids, Llandaf, Bangor and St Asaph. For St Davids, these include 542 (St David as archbishop of St Davids; here, he appears to accept Gerald's claim about the status of St Davids within Wales). This was followed by archbishops like Samson, up to 'Sylvester Giraldus' and his battle for St Davids at the beginning of the twelfth century (1102), and a variety of late medieval bishops. These included the theologian and Carmelite friar Stephen Patrington (d. 1417; bishop of St Davids, 1415–17) and William Lyndwood (*c*.1375–1446; bishop from 1442–6, though Robinson incorrectly dates this to 1422), who was a Lincolnshire-born ecclesiastical lawyer and judge but chiefly known for his contributions to canon law in his *Provinciale*, which provided an edition, along with commentary and glosses, of legislation relating to the province of

Canterbury. He also mentions the theologian and Carmelite friar John Milverton (d. 1487), alleged in some sources to have been elected as bishop.[63] For the diocese of Llandaf, he singles out 520 as the year in which St Dubricius (St Dyfrig, fl. *c*.475–*c*.525) became the first bishop of Llandaf, and mentions other sixth-century bishops, SS Teilo and Oudoceus (Euddogwy). Edmund Bromfield (d. 1393) is noted as bishop of Llandaf in 1391; he was consecrated bishop in January 1390 and died in June 1393. Further, he incorrectly notes the Carmelite friar Thomas Peverell (d. 1419; bishop of Llandaf, 1398–1407; fled in 1402 due to the Glyndŵr revolt) as the bishop of Llandaf in 1418.[64] For the bishops of St Asaph, Robinson mentions the sixth-century saint Asaph (St Asaf, Asa), patron saint of St Asaph followed by the influential historian, author of *Historia regum Brittaniae*, and cleric 'Galfridus Arturus' (Geoffrey of Monmouth, d. 1154/5, bishop of St Asaph, 1151–4/5) as being bishop of the diocese in 1152. He also singles out the theologian and preacher John Low (*c*.1385–1467; bishop of St Asaph, 1433–44) and his successor, the Welsh-born bishop and author Reginald Pecock (*c*.1392–*c*.1459; bishop of St Asaph, 1444–50 – Robinson's dates are again slightly off).[65] Throughout his history, Robinson also notes the deaths of the bishops of St Davids, Llandaf and St Asaph with regularity, and not infrequently the appointment of their successors, as well as (more occasionally) of abbots in monasteries in these dioceses, and shows a particular interest in the Cistercian abbey of Ystrad Fflur (Strata Florida), in Cardiganshire, in line with the *brutiau*, including royal burials there.

As bishop of Bangor, however, it is unsurprising that Robinson demonstrates an abiding interest in the diocese of Bangor and its bishops. His references to the bishops of Bangor also shed further light on his use of medieval and early modern sources, and particularly his reliance on the writings of the English historian, Protestant reformer and polemicist John Bale (1495–1563). Robinson recorded St Deiniol (d. 584) as the first bishop of Bangor in the year 550, though little of his history is known. As Thomas Charles-Edwards has noted, the first record of Deiniol is the Irish martyrology of Tallaght, dating to the early ninth century, and he was also included in the *Annales Cambriae*.[66] As bishop of Bangor, Robinson would also doubtless have been aware of Deiniol's feast day (11 September). Robinson also incorrectly mentions Elfodd (Elbodus, Elfoddw, Elfoddwg) as bishop of Bangor in 603 (he was supposed to have died in 809; the use of this date was likely to associate him with St Augustine, who visited England in 597), as discussed below. Reputed to have been a reforming bishop, he was credited in the *Annales Cambriae* with changing the date of Easter and may have been associated with Abergele, where in the township of Hendegyda, there was a 'Ffynnon Efo'. Bartum also argues that the presence of similarly named contemporary bishops in the lists of bishops of Llandaf and St Davids 'suggests the presence, or at least the influence, of Elfodd in those two divisions of the South'.[67] Similar to *Brut y Tywysogyon*, he describes Elfodd as 'archbishop' (*archepiscopus*) of Venedotia, or 'archbishop of Gwynedd'; the Peniarth MS 20 version of the *Brut* mentions the death of 'Elbodi[us] archesgob Gwynedd'.[68] The antiquary, mapmaker and historian Humphrey Llwyd (*c*.1527–68) in his *Cronica Walliae* (completed 1559) calls Elfodd 'a man both godly and learned' and notes that at his death in 809 he was 'Archebishop of Northwales'.[69] David Powel's 1584 *A Historie of Cambria now called Wales ...*, an expanded version of Llwyd, uses almost verbatim wording: Elfodd was 'a man both godlie and learned' and calls him 'Archbishop of North Wales', adding 'before whose death, the sunne was sore eclipsed'.[70] Robinson's main source, however, appears to be the revised edition of the *Scriptorum illustrium maioris Brytannie ... summarium* ('Of Great Britain's Illustrious Writers ... A Summary', by John Bale (1495–1563), which first published in 1548–9). Printed in 1557–9, this revised and expanded edition was titled *Scriptorum illustrium maioris Brytanniae ... Catalogus*, and it was this which appears to have been used by Robinson. In this, the section on p. 67 regarding Elfodd contains specific details distinct from other sources used by Robinson but shared with Robinson's text, including the reference to Elbodus as 'Archespiscopus Venedotarum' ('archbishop of the Venedotes', or Gwynedd) and the detail that it was due to the clergy of Augustine that Elfodd was made archbishop. Here Robinson follows Bale's phrasing very closely.[71] Indeed, as we shall see, Bale was likely one of the main sources for Robinson's understanding of the history of the medieval church. The inclusion of Elfodd in Robinson's chronology and his alleged connection to the clergy of the 'villainous St Augustine of Canterbury' are significant too in terms of early British church history; Joseph of Arimathea was believed to have first converted the ancient Britons to Christianity. St Augustine and his followers were thought to have been responsible (notably by Bale and later Richard Davies who with William Salesbury's contributions wrote the preface to the 1567 Welsh New Testament,

Epistol at y Cembru) for the introduction into Wales of 'superstitious Roman beliefs and practices'. This 'new Christianity' which did not follow the teachings of Christ and the apostles, was – in the words of Bale – tantamount to giving the 'Antichrist a seat here in England'.[72]

Robinson's particular interests in terms of the history of the Welsh church appear to have centred around the early medieval past – early bishops and founding saints of note for the dioceses of Wales – but he also records select high and late medieval bishops of Wales who were distinguished by their preaching, education, respected as theologians, or were known for their writings. Robinson's list of notable Bangor bishops, for example, also included a number of other medieval bishops, many of them featured in Bale's 1557–9 catalogue of writers. One of these was the Cistercian monk and author Cadwgan (of Llandyfai, d. 1241) in the thirteenth century, memorably blamed by Gerald of Wales for the loss of his books and mentioned in the *brutiau* and other sources. Cadwgan was known for his learning, and a variety of works, including a book called *Speculum Christianorum*, collections of homilies and prayers, and more were attributed to him. Robinson does not record these in this list (though mentions his writings elsewhere), noting just that he was bishop of Bangor in 1225 (he was bishop of Bangor 1215–*c*.1236); this is the year in which Cadwgan died, according to Bale.[73] He singled out the fourteenth-century bishop of Bangor, Thomas Ringstead (d. 1366; bishop, 1357–66), a Dominican, as a 'theologian, and a distinguished orator [preacher]', and noted further that Ringstead had given 'certain sermons before King Edward III'. He does not mention the many theological writings attributed to Ringstead, but notes (incorrectly, as does Bale) that he died in 1370 and was buried in 'his church' ('sua ecclesia'; presumably Bangor Cathedral is meant here, though he appears to have been buried either at Huntingdon or at Blackfriars, in London).[74]

Robinson also names several other medieval bishops of Bangor from the thirteenth to fifteenth centuries. These include John Swaffham (d. 1398; bishop, 1376–98; Swaffham is noticed as a theologian and for his Cambridge education, said to have succeeded as bishop in 1392 (a date which is included in Bale's narrative), and Robinson mentions his writings elsewhere.[75] Robinson also lists John Stanbury (d. 1474; bishop, 1448–53); Hervey (d. 1131; bishop, 1092–1109); Gruffudd Yonge (*c*.1370–1437 or after, provided the bishopric of Bangor by the anti-pope at Avignon, Benedict XIII, in 1407), and John Cliderow

(d. 1435; bishop (ordained), 1425–35). He was unsure who was bishop of Bangor while Llywelyn ap Gruffudd (d. 1282) was prince of Wales ('princeps Walliae') and left a blank space for the name of the individual (Anian, d. 1305×1307).[76]

Robinson also shows interest in Welsh culture, genealogy and the descent of the Welsh princes. He mentions, for example, the 1176 celebration of the eisteddfod at the court of the Lord Rhys (d. 1197) of Deheubarth in Cardigan Castle (Robinson records it as being in 1177). Unlike the fairly brief descriptions given in Llwyd and Powel of this (which note that the Welsh poets are 'intituled by the name of *Bardh*, in Latine *Bardus*'), Robinson provides more details, including both Latin and Welsh equivalents to describe the harpists (*telynorion*), *crwth* players (*cryddorion*) and pipers (*pibyddion*), suggesting perhaps that he based his description on a version of *Brut y Tywysogion*.[77] In so doing, he highlights the cultural sophistication and complexity of medieval Wales, its language and its poetry. He also includes limited genealogical information, listing the children (and sometimes the different mothers too, as in the case of Owain Gwynedd's children) of select Welsh princes, especially for the house of Gwynedd, but also for Powys and Deheubarth, with the deaths of key princes like Owain Gwynedd, the Lord Rhys, Llywelyn Fawr and others.[78]

Peniarth 383 likewise demonstrates that like many of his contemporaries, Robinson had a particular interest in local history, especially with respect to Anglesey. In his marginal notations accompanying the second book of the *Itinerarium Cambriae* (pp. 21–32), Robinson writes, for example, about the reputedly miraculous stone that was apparently shaped like a human thigh on Anglesey mentioned by Gerald (though Gerald does not specifically name it or share its precise location). It would always return the next night to its original location, and was allegedly put to the test by Hugh, the earl of Chester, while he occupied Anglesey.[79] This stone, which Robinson frowned upon, was subsequently referred to as *Maen Morddwyd*, and was mentioned in a note in the 1585 printed edition of Gerald's *Itinerarium* edited and annotated by David Powel as 'Lapis Maen Mordhwyd'. Powel wrote that William Salesbury (1520–84) had testified to the presence of the stone in the year 1554, when it was in the cemetery wall of the churchyard at St Nidan's church; the medieval church of Llanidan, which suffered partial demolition in the nineteenth century, was dedicated to St Nidan, or Nidan ap Gwyfyw, the patron saint of the parish.[80] Robinson notes that the thigh-stone was found in the wall in 1554 and also mentions its transport some twenty years later in 1574 in a marginal note which he signed as 'N B' (as Nicholas, bishop of Bangor). This suggests that he had read Powel's note about William Salesbury in Powel's edition (or perhaps a draft of it). Robinson died on 13 February 1585, and Powel's annotated edition of the abridged 1534 edition of the two works of Gerald of Wales concerning Wales, together with Geoffrey of Monmouth's *Historia Regum Britanniae* by Pontico Virunio (1467?–1520), was published in 1585.[81] One other possibility is that Robinson had access at some point to NLW MS 3024C (Mostyn 83), the copy of Gerald's *Descriptio* and *Itinerarium Cambriae* to which William Salesbury had made annotations on most pages, including one concerning the stone on fo. 55v.[82] This copy was ultimately given by Bishop Richard Davies to William Cecil in 1564; Davies mentioned this book in a letter to Archbishop Matthew Parker in 1566.[83] Given Robinson's scholarly interests and the nature of his religious and scholarly connections in north Wales and beyond, including with Parker and other contemporaries with interests in the history of Wales and Welsh translations, this is also possible.

While beyond the scope of this chapter, further evidence exists of Robinson's interest in the local history of his diocese in the pedigrees of Anglesey families, including the Bulkeleys, which he added to NLW Peniarth MS 155, Gruffudd Hiraethog's *Lloegr Drigiant*; Huws has dated this to before 1561.[84]

Robinson's other historical and antiquarian interests and contributions

Robinson was erroneously thought to have translated the Welsh life of the medieval king of Gwynedd, Gruffudd ap Cynan (d. 1137) into Latin for Maurice Wynn of Gwydir (c.1520–80); this translation was later included in the *Book of Sir John Wyn of Gwydir*. However, this attribution to Robinson, found in several extant manuscripts of the Latin life, is incorrect, as Paul Russell has shown. He argues that the Latin translation of the Welsh life known as *Historia Gruffud vab Kenan* was the work of Edward Thelwall (d. 1610), the eldest son of Simon Thelwall (1526–86) and the fourth husband of the famed Katheryn of Berain, 1534/5–91), rather than Nicholas Robinson. Russell persuasively demonstrates that the earliest manuscript version of the Latin life (in NLW, Peniarth MS 434, pp. 1–54, which he dates to 1575×1585), which is an archetype of subsequent versions, was in Edward Thelwall's hand, and contained glosses and annotations by him. The later attributions to Robinson of some of the surviving manuscript versions of the Latin life appear to have been made while they were in the possession of the Wynns of Gwydir, and, as Russell suggests, 'it is possible that there was a deliberate attempt on their part to write Thelwall out of the story', perhaps on the basis of 'personal dislike' which had formed on the part of Sir John Wynn of Gwydir.[85]

Robinson's correspondence with Archbishop Matthew Parker sheds more light on his own antiquarian and historical interests. Parker himself was an avid antiquarian, and was particularly interested in Anglo-Saxon church history, but had more general interests in British history; these were also part of his wider aim to demonstrate that Protestantism was merely a return to the purity and uniformity of the ancient church in Britain.[86] Robinson apologised in a letter to Parker written on 7 October 1567 that a young man whom 'I mente shuld have written Edmers historie [Eadmer of Canterbury's *Historia nouorum in Anglia*] not well acquainted with this cuntrey hath not had his health so that he might accomplish my promise to your grace', but was 'bolde to send' on 'something which he hath done', with the rest promised for that winter.[87] Further, he wrote,

> There is not in this cuntrey any monumentes of antiquitie lefte, but certaine fabulose histories and that lately written, as that rude lawes of one Howell Daa, and the life of a troublesome prince or tow, which were subdued sence the Conquest: yet the people here will talke of many thinges, which appeere in no where.[88]

This correspondence also reveals more about his own efforts to find sources for writing a history of Wales, and lending of books to others with antiquarian interests. 'Mr. Darell', he told Parker, 'had an aunceant booke out of my howse here, which I would be glad your grace could get of him, or if he have pledged it here I wold gladly quite it out and send it your grace, whatsoever the charge there of shalbe'.[89] He likewise lamented his problems acquiring historical sources relating to the history of Wales: 'I am promised dayly from other parties of Wales the sight of some welshe histories, but as yet I see nothing, nether can heare certainly of any doynges of the olde Brittans, so that I suspecte that there remayneth nothing in writing'.[90]

There is also a possibility that Robinson's contributions to the 1588 Welsh Bible have been understated. Marginal additions to an edition of the 1567 Welsh New Testament have recently been identified by the excellent work of Gruffudd Antur as being in Robinson's hand, suggesting that Robinson himself may perhaps have offered assistance to the efforts of William Morgan (1545–1604) to produce the 1588 Welsh Bible.[91] Specifically, these additions are found in the introductory material to the New Testament known as *Epistol at y Cembru* ('A Letter to the Welsh People'). As Lloyd Bowen has argued, this was 'perhaps the most powerful and effective amalgamation of Welsh historical polemic and reformist argument', and a mix of 'abstruse historical research and theological argument ... [and] redolent of the Galfridian tradition so beloved of the Welsh', as well as the scholarship of early reforming Protestants.[92] It was written by Richard Davies, the bishop of St Davids, with the contributions too of William Salesbury, and was essentially a Protestant rewriting of the history of the early church in Britain; in it the ancient Britons (*hen Frytaniaid*) followed the godly, 'pure' faith of Joseph of Arimathea, 'Christ's disciple', before the coming of St Augustine of Canterbury (597) at the behest of Pope Gregory the Great to England. The Romish Christianity of the 'Saxons' was by contrast an 'impure' Christianity, of 'crosses and images', the supremacy of the pope in Rome, cries for intercession and prayers to the 'dead saints', 'mute ceremonies' and more.[93] Additions to the *Epistol* have been found by Antur in nine of sixty-two extant copies of the 1567 New Testament, all in different hands.[94] These relate to the role of Davies's colleague (*cydymaith*) William Salesbury in the text of the *Epistol*, and the extent to which he himself made additions to it or otherwise changed the text; at issue were the title of this epistle by Davies as well as a significant number (twenty-two) of its opening lines and several (four) passages.[95] Of the nine surviving copies of the 1567 Welsh New Testament with relatively early annotations, one copy has been identified by Antur as having annotations in Robinson's own hand. This is a copy (C) currently in private ownership in Cemaes, Anglesey. It contains a bookplate indicating that it previously was part of the collection of Thomas Edward Watson of St. Mary's Lodge, Newport.[96]

Antur argues that the surviving copies with early annotations to the *Epistol* may indeed have been personal copies which belonged to those Welsh scholars who provided support (whether practical in terms of lending books, etc. or more direct contributions) to Morgan's efforts as he strove to complete the 1588 Bible.[97] These men included Gabriel Goodman, David Powel, Edmwnd Prys, Richard Vaughan and the bishops of Bangor and St Asaph, who are not explicitly named. Morgan commended the two bishops for their practical support of his endeavour, through 'lending books to me that I asked for' as well as their seeing fit to 'examine, evaluate, and approve' his work.[98] It has been generally assumed that the unnamed bishops meant were William Hughes (St Asaph, 1573–1600) and Hugh Bellot (Bangor, 1585–95); both men were at Cambridge with Morgan, as was Gabriel Goodman. Richard Vaughan and Edmwnd Prys were likewise Cambridge men and were Morgan's contemporaries at St John's College there.[99] The assumption that Morgan's work on the Bible began in 1578 or perhaps 1579 (after a chance meeting with John Whitgift) has been important in this supposition, as has Robinson's 1585 death; he did not live to see the Welsh Bible published.

Yet has Robinson's contribution to the 1588 Welsh Bible perhaps been understated? Issac Thomas suggested that Morgan's work translating the Bible into Welsh did not begin until substantially later – after the death of Richard Davies in November 1581. It is in the early 1580s, then, that he came to submit his early translation work to the bishops of St Asaph and Bangor (then William Hughes and Nicholas Robinson) for approval, and only then, probably in 1583–5, was he given early encouragement by Whitgift.[100] John Gwynfor Jones also recognised the possibility, in the context of Robinson's scholarship and antiquarian interests, that he 'may well have been' the bishop of Bangor who assisted William Morgan and was named in his dedication of the 1588 Welsh Bible.[101] In connection with this, I find Antur's recent suggestion that the bishop to whom William Morgan refers to as offering practical support for his 1588 Welsh translation of the Bible may have been Robinson, rather than Hugh Bellot, who succeeded him in 1585 as bishop of Bangor, to be an interesting and quite plausible suggestion.[102]

Robinson's death and legacy

Robinson died on 13 February 1585. He was buried inside Bangor Cathedral, with his grave marked by a memorial brass, now lost. A new memorial brass for Robinson dating to 1843 is now located to the left of the memorial chapel entrance in the cathedral. His will, made on 6 April 1584, sheds some further light on Robinson's family, antiquarian interests and priorities. He made generous bequests to the church, including £10 to the dean and the chapter of Bangor towards 'the Reparation of the ffabrick of the Cathedral Churche of Bangor ... yf neede soe require', or else the same amount 'towarde the buying of a bell' for the cathedral. He also gave £5 to the church of Conway and 20s. apiece to his churches of Amlwch and Llangristiolus (Anglesey). It reflects substantial lands in north Wales, including lands held in fee simple and the leases of rectories and parsonages in Denbighshire, Caernarfonshire and Anglesey; they were divided between his wife, Jane Robinson (Brereton), and his four sons. His daughter, Margaret, received a half portion of moiety of his 'debtes, plate, and howsholdstuffe whatsoever to me belonginge (except bookes)' for her preferment in marriage. He also noted that if the child his wife was carrying (Robinson's son, Hugh) lived, it would have profits from a lease (Trawscoed, Merioneth) as well as 'one halfe of all my bookes' as its portion. Indeed, the references in his will to his books and their value, taken together with his frequent lending of books to those who shared his antiquarian interests suggests that he had a not insubstantial private library. His chief family-related concern in his will appears to have been for the upbringing of his children. He instructed his wife to 'see them brought upp honestly'. He appointed a different overseer for each of his children. His 'welbeloved' brother-in-law, Sir Randall Brereton, was responsible for the tuition and oversight of his eldest son, William Robinson, while Mr Thomas Bennett (a kinsman), Roland Mostyn and Doctor William Merrick, chancellor of the diocese, were to be responsible for his other sons during their minority. He exhorted them 'to see them brought up in the feare of god and vertue as my trust in in them'.[103] His will therefore underscores his antiquarian interests, contributions to Bangor Cathedral and religious life of the diocese, and interest in the religious education of his children.

Robinson is principally remembered for his scholarship, preaching and attempts to improve the spiritual life of his diocese. Archbishop Parker praised him during his life for his scholarship and learning, as 'a prudent man ... as learned in the humanities and theology as he was eloquent in Latin and his native tongue'.[104] The poets also emphasised his learning, preaching, scholarship, language and charity in their elegies to him, remembering him with terms similar to those found in elegies to other Elizabethan Protestant bishops, like Thomas Davies and William Hughes of St Asaph, and Richard Davies of St Davids. Upon his death, the poet Siôn Phylip wrote an elegy for Robinson, 'Mawrnad Arglwydd Nicholas Escob Bangor', which survives in at least eleven manuscripts.[105] The version in NLW, Llanstephan MS 30 (*c*.1615×1620), a collection of fifteenth- and sixteenth-century *awdlau* and *cywyddau*, which, as Daniel Huws has shown was written by an amanuensis of John Davies Mallwyd (X5) with short sections by John Davies himself,[106] contains a version of the *marwnad* on pp. 300–4. In this, he sang that the death of Robinson amounted to the 'loss of [the] pinnacle ... of preaching', and that the 'comely church' which had benefitted from his 'charity' and 'faith' had 'lost its head'. Robinson was a 'great lord for truth' amongst other prelates, and his death meant the 'death of learning and dying of scholarship'. He was compared to SS Gregory and Paul and praised as a 'beloved bishop of Bangor of bold learning for a short while / He was cherished for his success'. Such a bishop was never anticipated, 'with his dulcet language', ability in English and Welsh, and his 'saintly judgement'. He gave 'good grace to men' and was like a 'brother [to] Moses'. The poet Morus Dwyfech (Morus ap Dafydd ap Ifan ab Einion, *fl. c*.1523–90), who sang to a number of north Wales gentry families including those of Clenennau, Plas-Du, Glynllifon, Gwydir and Cefnamlwch, also wrote a series of four *englynion* to Robinson, which survive in BL Add. MS 14892 (*c*.1644, William Bodwrda), as well as two later collections of poetry, BL Add. MS 14990 and 14994 (both *c*.1800).[107] Robinson's reputation for scholarship, skill in language and his Welshness likewise seem to have been singled out in later assessments. The English clergyman and biographer of Parker, John Strype, noted in the early eighteenth century of Robinson that he was a 'Welshman', and 'eloquent in the English and Latin tongues, well furnished with human learning and divinity'.[108]

Robinson's successors, 1585–1603

Robinson's immediate successors, Hugh Bellot (1586–95), Richard Vaughan (1596–8) and Henry Rowlands (1598–1616), were all reforming Protestants, and resident bishops who shared Welsh birth or connections who were also known as scholars. Bellot (1542–96), the son of Thomas

Bellot of Great Moreton, Cheshire, and Burton, Denbighshire, had links to many important figures in the Elizabethan church in Wales, including Edmwnd Prys, the translator of the psalms, William Morgan, Gabriel Goodman (dean of Westminster) and Richard Vaughan (his successor) – they were contemporaries of his at Cambridge and friends. He held livings in Caerwys (Flintshire) and Gresford (Denbighshire) before being elected bishop of Bangor in early December 1585 after Robinson's death; he was consecrated some two months later. Under him, by 1592, some forty-three out of 154 clergy in the diocese were recorded as preachers; he was also known for his strong stance against recusancy in the diocese and was the 'man of Bangor' involved in the proceedings against William Davies.[109] He too was a scholar; it is not entirely clear whether Bellot or Robinson was meant by William Morgan in the dedication to his 1588 Welsh Bible as the bishop of Bangor who provided support, as discussed above. Glanmor Williams believed it to have been Bellot but noted that 'justifiable doubt has been expressed about how much Welsh he knew'.[110] Bellot was translated to Chester in 1595. Bellot's immediate successor, Richard Vaughan (c.1553–1607) was born on the Llŷn peninsula (Caernarfonshire), the son of Thomas ap Robert Vaughan (Fychan). Also Cambridge-educated (BA, 1574 and MA, 1577), he was a licenced preacher and had significant connections through his kinsman, John Aylmer, who was to become bishop of London. He rose quickly, holding livings in England. At likely only 42 years old, he was elected bishop of Bangor in late 1595 and consecrated in early 1596, proposed by Lord Burghley (William Cecil) and his son, Robert Cecil. Vaughan was bishop of Bangor for little more than a year and appears to have left little mark on the religious life of the diocese, though resident. He was quickly translated to the better endowed diocese of Chester (1597–1604) and then London (1604–7). He also was a scholar, and one of the six especially singled out by William Morgan in his dedication of the 1588 Welsh Bible as having given him special aid, then provost of St John's Hospital, Lutterworth.[111] He was followed by Henry Rowlands, also a native of the Llŷn peninsula. Oxford-educated, he received a MA, BTh and DTh between 1577 and 1605. Having held livings in Oxfordshire and north Wales he also became the dean of Bangor and archdeacon of Anglesey amongst other preferments. Rowlands is particularly associated with charity, education, building works and bardic patronage. During his episcopate, he bought three new bells for the cathedral church and was responsible for the repair of the transept and nave roofs there. In his extremely lengthy will, he endowed almshouses in Bangor for men to be chosen from different areas of the diocese as well as providing money for poor local scholars from the diocese to become fellows at Jesus College, Oxford. He was also a scholar with a notable library, much of which, like Arthur Bulkeley, he left to the cathedral library. Sir John Wynn of Gwydir remembered him as a 'provident governor of his church and diocese', and he was also a noted patron of the poets, and praised by Elis ap Siôn ap Morus, Syr Huw Roberts and Huw Llŷn, amongst others.[112]

Conclusion

Diocesan poverty, unlearned clergy, residency, religious instruction, preaching, low literacy rates and language all remained long-term problems in the diocese of Bangor and Wales more generally into the later years of the sixteenth century and beyond. In answer to these and other challenges, with the sixteenth-century bishops of Bangor, beginning with Arthur Bulkeley in 1542, a notable shift is apparent to bishops who were Welsh or had Welsh connections. This shift is evident elsewhere in Wales as well. In Elizabethan Wales, some thirteen (perhaps twelve) of the sixteen bishops holding sees were themselves Welsh or had Welsh connections. Reforming Elizabethan bishops – men like Nicholas Robinson and Richard Davies – played an active role in their dioceses and demonstrated an understanding of the many practical challenges which the implementation of Protestant reforms faced. They sought to prioritise the apostolic ideal of residency, the cure of souls, the religious education of the laity, the establishment of a learned ministry, address recusancy and promote preaching. But the reality was that despite their efforts to play an active religious role in their respective dioceses, many challenges remained, and they did not fully realise their religious aspirations during the reign of Elizabeth.

Nevertheless, as learned scholars, theologians and administrators, many of these men also sought to make serious contributions to scholarship and related cultural and historical pursuits. These included their efforts to locate, read, preserve and transcribe 'ancient books' or literary and historical manuscripts in Welsh and/or relating to the Welsh past, an active interest in the ancient and medieval past (especially the history of Wales), as well as ongoing bardic patronage, for example.¹¹³ Their active engagement in wider scholarly circles, and related correspondence and collaboration with other clerics and scholars in England and Wales, was also an important facet of this. Indeed, many of Robinson's contemporaries, including men like Richard Davies (*c*.1505–81) and William Salesbury (*c*.1520–*c*.1580), shared his historical and antiquarian interests.¹¹⁴ Archbishop Parker corresponded with Robinson's fellow bishops, Richard Davies (St Davids), and John Scory (Hereford) in the 1560s, for example.¹¹⁵ Davies in particular was a frequent correspondent of Parker's, updating him on his progress with Welsh translations of the Bible, but also sharing his research into the history of Wales, particularly regarding Sulien (*c*.1012–91), bishop of St Davids (1073–8, 1080–5), and Rhigyfarch (1056/7–99), his son, 'most excel*lent* in all good learning', as well as chronicle-writing. He wrote to Parker in February 1567 of how 'Rycymarch' was so commended in the 'Welche storyes' that he was reputed to be 'the wisest that ev*er* was' in Britain and the 'wisest of eny that shal*l* come'. Davies sent Parker further information regarding the history of Wales, especially 'Sulgenus' Rhigyfarch, and the history of the bishops of St Davids, including a Latin translation of passages from the *Brut y Tywysogyon*.¹¹⁶ This was part of a wider trend towards local and county history writing. Indeed, from the latter half of the sixteenth century, as Pryce argues, we witness the emergence of 'new kinds of Welsh writing', which 'focused on particular localities and were less constrained ... by assumptions about the content and chronological parameters of Welsh history derived from medieval chronicles'.¹¹⁷ This emphasis on local and county history and genealogies also demonstrates an English influence, and embraces wider trends in the development of local history writing seen in works produced for and by the Elizabethan and Stuart gentry of England.¹¹⁸

The historical interests of Nicholas Robinson of Bangor, including his underexplored collection of materials relating to the history of Wales and endeavours to write a history of Wales (both in Peniarth 383), provide an excellent example of the nature of these pursuits. They also shed light on the attempts of Welsh Protestants in Elizabethan Wales to understand and present a framework for and synthesis of the history of Wales from the classical past to the early British church, the medieval princes of Wales and beyond; Robinson's time frame continues up to 1457 and is followed by substantial space for additions. For Robinson, Wales also formed 'an integral part of Britain', and he presented the history of Wales and its princes alongside that of England, and in political terms, as a 'historical creation', as Pryce has argued for Llwyd.[119]

Robinson was praised when he died in 1585 for his learning, scholarship and eloquence in English, Latin and Welsh. The poets lamented 'the death of learning and the dying of scholarship' with his decease and Siôn Phylip mourned Robinson's passing with striking imagery of finality: the 'breaking' of the branch which had 'held up the sermon', and the 'decapitating' of the 'charity and the faith' of the Church.[120] Certainly, the stylised praise found in the elegies of contemporary poets like Siôn Phylip for Robinson was similar to elegies and eulogies for other bishops in Elizabethan Wales and may be seen as 'Protestant propaganda', in the words of John Gwynfor Jones.[121] Yet such compositions nevertheless shed light on popular mentalities, expectations and understandings of the ideal Protestant bishop in the mid-1580s in Wales. As such, they indicate the growing importance of learning, scholarship, proficiency in Welsh and other languages (Latin, Greek, Hebrew, etc.), ability to translate, preaching, Welshness, and living a godly life to the praise of contemporary Protestant bishops (e.g. the poet William Llŷn's praise of Richard Davies of St Davids and William Hughes of St Asaph).[122] This is reflected to a lesser extent, too, in a later sixteenth-century revision of the bardic grammars by the poet Simwnt Fychan. His *Pum Llyfr Kerddwriaeth* ('Five Books of Verse Craft'), in Jesus College, Oxford MS 115 (before 1578), copied and revised earlier bardic grammars; these contained explicit guidance for how various individuals, including prelates (bishops and archbishops), should be praised. His revision of the section on prelates, influenced like the rest of the *Pum Llyfr* by the Renaissance and 'bardic humanism', shows substantial continuities with previous medieval versions of the bardic grammars, but particularly emphasises the godliness of the prelate's life. While in earlier versions, prelates are praised for their 'wisdom' and 'prudence', Simwnt Fychan writes that 'piety' and 'pure life' were to be praised for prelates.[123]

Robinson therefore provides an interesting example of the nature of religious and cultural expectations linked to the Reformation bishops of Wales and their ongoing development during the reign of Elizabeth. Cambridge-educated, Welsh, resident, a renowned preacher and an active administrator, he endeavoured to create a learned ministry and provide for the cure of souls, engaging in efforts to eradicate recusancy and 'idolatry', although he did not fully realise these religious ambitions for the diocese of Bangor. At the same time, Robinson valued and sought to collect sources relating to the classical and medieval past, wrote a history of Wales (Peniarth 383), and was involved with wider scholarly circles in England and Wales (possibly even with the 1588 Bible), demonstrating an abiding personal interest in scholarly pursuits relating to the history of Wales, its religion and its culture. While his contributions to these are doubtless less significant than those of some of his contemporaries, Robinson's episcopate and scholarly and historical contributions nonetheless serve to illuminate important aspects of the developing and multifaceted roles of Welsh bishops in the later years of the sixteenth century.

Notes

1. *The Byble in Englyshe that is to saye, the content of all the holye scrypture, bothe of the olde and newe Testament* ... (London, 1540) [RSTC 2nd edn/2069], p. lxxxii.
2. Martin Heale, 'Introduction', in Martin Heale (ed.), *The Prelate in England and Europe, 1300–1560* (Woodbridge, 2014), pp. 1–13 (p. 8). Cf. also chapters by James Clarke, Wendy Scase and Felicity Heal, pp. 101–26, 127–41, 142–69.
3. For more on this, see Steven Thompson, 'The pastoral work of the English and Welsh bishops, 1500–1558' (unpublished DPhil thesis, Oxford University, 1984), 4–5, 8–9.
4. Felicity Heal, *Of Prelates and Princes: A Study in the Economic and Social Position of the Tudor Episcopate* (Cambridge, 1980), pp. 237–8.
5. J. Gwynfor Jones, *Aspects of Religious Life in Wales, c.1536–1660* (Aberystwyth, 2003), p. 176.
6. Glanmor Williams, *Wales and the Reformation* (Cardiff, 1999), p. 459.
7. J. Gwynfor Jones, 'Davies, Thomas (*c.*1511–1573)', *ODNB*, https://doi.org/10.1093/ref:odnb/7264; Jones, *Aspects of Religious Life*, pp. 176–8.
8. Glanmor Williams, 'Davies, Richard (*c.*1505–1581)', *ODNB*, https://doi.org/10.1093/ref:odnb/7255; R. Stephens, 'Gwaith Wiliam Llŷn', 3 vols (unpublished PhD thesis, University of Wales, 1983), I, 6–10 (II), 37–8 (IX).
9. Jones, *Aspects of Religious Life in Wales*, p. 174.
10. For the purposes of this chapter, I follow Jan Broadway's discussion of the historical interests of the Tudor and Stuart gentry in understanding the term 'antiquary' and their related interests to encompass the 'medieval as well as the classical past'; and as someone who 'within the context of the development of early modern historiography ... studied the past on a thematic rather than

a chronological basis ... The emphasis in antiquarian works was on the use of primary source materials'. Similarly, 'local histories' are taken to mean 'all antiquarian works written within a local rather than a national context'. Jan Broadway, *'No historie so meete': Gentry Culture and the Development of Local History in Elizabethan and Early Stuart England* (Manchester, 2006), pp. 4–5.

11 Glanmor Williams, *Welsh Reformation Essays* (Cardiff, 1967), pp. 59–60.
12 Heal, *Of Prelates and Princes*, p. 197.
13 Arthur Ivor Pryce, *The Diocese of Bangor in the Sixteenth Century* (Bangor, 1923), p. xiii.
14 Williams, *Welsh Reformation Essays*, pp. 35–6.
15 TNA, SP 10/15, f. 162; A. H. Dodd, *A History of Caernarvonshire, 1284–1900* (Caernarvon, 1968), p. 39.
16 *Calendar of MSS of the Most Hon. the Marquis of Salisbury, Preserved at Hatfield House* ... 24 vols (London, 1883–1976), VI (London, 1895), 44, VIII (London, 1899), 470.
17 Pryce, *The Diocese of Bangor*, p. x. Thomas Pygot (Pigot), abbot of Chertsey (d. 1504), elevated to the bishopric of Bangor in 1500 has been named as a native of Denbighshire; this must be treated with caution. Wood described Pygot in 1691 as 'a Denbighshire man born, as it seems'. It was apparently on this basis that Willis named him as a Denbighshire native. There were Denbighshire Pigots from at least the fourteenth century, and Pigots in Cambridgeshire, Buckinghamshire and Shropshire. The election of a Denbighshire man would have been unusual. While occasional elections of Welsh bishops to Welsh sees occurred in the reign of Henry VII (for example, Cistercians Dafydd ap Ieuan ab Iorwerth and Dafydd ap Owain to St Asaph), they were exceptional, and the Welsh genealogies do not appear to bear out this suggestion. Cf. Barrie Dobson, 'English and Welsh monastic bishops: The final century, 1433–1533', in Benjamin Thompson (ed.), *Monasteries and Society in Medieval Britain* (Stamford, 1999), pp. 348–65; C. W. Boase and Andrew Clark (eds), *Register of the University of Oxford*, 2 vols (Oxford, 1885), I, 33; A. B. Emden, *A biographical register of the University of Oxford, to A.D. 1500*, 3 vols (Oxford, 1957–9), III, 1529; Oxford University Reg. Aa, f. 116; *Calendar of Patent Rolls (CPR), A.D. 1476–1485* (London, 1901), pp. 166, 170; *Records of Convocation VI: Canterbury 1444–1509*, ed. Gerald Bray (Woodbridge, 2005), pp. 215, 277, 386; *CPR, A.D. 1485–94* (London, 1914), p. 252; *Calendar of Entries in the Papal Registers Relating to Great Britain and Ireland, Papal Letters, vol. XVII, Part I, Alexander VI (1492–1503)* (Dublin, 1994), pp. 383–5; Lambeth Palace Library, Reg. Warham II, f. 214r; Francis Godwin, *De Praesulibus Angliae Commentarius* ... (London, 1616) [RSTC 11941], p. 649; Anthony Wood, *Athenae Oxonienses*, 2 vols (London, 1691), I, 553; Browne Willis, *A survey of the cathedral church of Bangor....* (London,

1721), p. 95; Cf. *Survey of the Honour of Denbigh, 1334*, ed. Paul Vinogradoff and Frank Morgan (London, 1914), pp. 21, 29, 30, 38, 42, 56, 90, 133, 204; P. C. Bartum, *Welsh Genealogies, A.D. 1400–1500* (Aberystwyth, 1983), pp. ix, 1449, 1570, 1450–1; BL, Harleian, MS 1970, f. 59; National Library of Wales [NLW], Peniarth MS 128, f. 151; BL, Harleian, MS 1971, f. 153; NLW, SA/R1, f. 71v.

18 *L & P, Vol. XVI (1540–1)*, ed. J. Gairdner and R. H. Brodie (London, 1898), no. 1391 (6, 7); Thomas Rymer (ed.), *Foedera, Conventiones, Literæ, et cujuscunque generis Acta Publica Inter Reges Angliae* …, 10 vols (3rd edn, The Hague, 1739–45), VI, parts i and ii (1741), 76–7; John Strype, *Memorials of … Thomas Cranmer*, 2 vols (new edn, Oxford, 1840), I, 136.

19 Bulkeley's contributions to Bangor diocese, his injunctions and their significance will be explored in more detail in my forthcoming article.

20 William V. Hudon, 'Forward: The Local Nature of Episcopal Reform in the Age of the Council of Trent', in Jennifer DeSilva (ed.), *Episcopal Reform and Politics in Early Modern Europe* (Kirksville, MO, 2012), pp. ix–xiv (p. xiii).

21 Browne Willis, *A Survey of the Cathedral Church of Bangor and Edifices belonging to it* … (London, 1721), p. 269.

22 Williams, *Wales and the Reformation*, p. 391.

23 *Correspondence of Matthew Parker, D.D., Archbishop of Canterbury*, ed. John Bruce and Thomas Perowne (Cambridge, 1853), p. 259; John Strype, *The Life and Acts of Matthew Parker: The first Archbishop of Canterbury, in the reign of Queen Elizabeth*, 4 vols (Oxford, 1821), I, 404.

24 While of interest, the career and contributions of the first Elizabethan bishop of Bangor, Rowland Meyrick (1559–66) are not considered here, as they are beyond the scope of this chapter.

25 W. Ogwen Williams (ed.), *Calendar of the Caernarvonshire Quarter Sessions Records: Volume I, 1541–1558* (London and Bradford, 1956), pp. 19, 98, 99, 115, 122, 171, 184.

26 J. Gwynfor Jones, 'Robinson, Nicholas', *ODNB*, https://doi.org/10.1093/ref:odnb/23860; Albert Owen Evans, 'Nicholas Robinson (1530?–1585)', *Y Cymmrodor*, 39 (1928), 149–99. The biographical information discussed here is substantially based on Jones.

27 John Venn and J. A. Venn, *Alumni Cantabrigienses … Part I: From the Earliest Times to 1751*, 4 vols (Cambridge, 1924), III, 472.

28 Jones, 'Robinson, Nicholas'; Browne Willis, *A Survey of the Cathedral Church of Bangor and Edifices belonging to it…* (London, 1721), p. 107; Pryce, *Diocese of Bangor*, p. 50.

29 Evans, 'Nicholas Robinson', 165–6; John Nichols, *Progresses and Public Processions of Queen Elizabeth*, 3 vols (London, 1823), I, especially pp. xvi, 149–89. Robinson was said to have been the author of a Latin account of

Elizabeth's 1564 visit to Cambridge University and an English account of her 1566 visit to Oxford University. See Nichols, *Progresses and Public Processions*, I, 229–47, for an account largely in Latin; British Library, Harleian MS 7033, f. 131, in the hand of the Cambridge antiquary Thomas Baker (1656–1750).

30 Millar MacLure, *The Paul's Cross Sermons* (Toronto, 1958), pp. 186, 203, 226, 242; C. H. Cooper and Thompson Cooper, *Athenae Cantabrigienses; volume 1: 1500–1585* (London, 1858), p. 504; Evans, 'Nicholas Robinson', 161. John Salcot (Capon) had preached there while bishop of Bangor on 19 March 1536. In addition, Richard Vaughan, the former bishop of Bangor, preached at St Paul's Cross on 5 August 1605, when he was bishop of London, and Lewis Bayly, then bishop of Bangor, preached there on 24 March 1621. Cf. Torrance Kirby and P. G. Stanwood, *Paul's Cross and the Culture of Persuasion in England, 1520–1640* (Leiden, 2014).

31 John Strype, *Life and Acts of Matthew Parker*, III, Appendix XLIV, p. 135; Peter Eugene McCullough, 'The sermon at the court of Elizabeth I, 1558–1603' (unpublished PhD thesis, Princeton University, 1992), 150–1, 155; Peter E. McCullough, *Sermons at Court: Politics and religion in Elizabethan and Jacobean preaching* (Cambridge, 1998). As McCullough notes, this represents a scheduled rather than actual list of sermons, as substitutions and rearrangements of sermon dates occurred frequently.

32 Jones, 'Robinson, Nicholas'; Evans, 'Nicholas Robinson', 162.

33 Strype, *Life and Acts of Matthew Parker*, I, 464–5; Evans, 'Nicholas Robinson', 163.

34 The main text of the sermon is found on pp. 321–34; p. 319 contains the attribution to Robinson.

35 Cambridge, Corpus Christi College, MS 104, pp. 321–2.

36 Cambridge, Corpus Christi College, MS 104, p. 331.

37 Cambridge, Corpus Christi College, MS 104, p. 334.

38 Cambridge, Corpus Christi College, MS 104, p. 334.

39 *Correspondence of Matthew Parker, D.D., Archbishop of Canterbury*, p. 261; Strype, *Life and Acts of Matthew Parker*, I, 406. Robinson seems to have been a compromise candidate, whom Parker agreed to at Sir William Cecil's recommendation; he notes in a letter to Cecil on 26 February 1565, 'I shall allow your judgement toward Mr Robinson'. The two other main candidates for the bishopric were Dr Ellis Price and Thomas Huet, the Precentor of St Davids. Parker's decision was influenced by discussions with 'some wise men partly of the same country; who, in respect of good to be done there in that diocese, they wish no Welshman in Bangor', and further that the 'country was much afraid either of Ellis or Hewitt [Huet], who were, he said, very stout men: that is, who would not be opposed, but vigorously pursue their purposes'. The combined opposition meant that Parker could not

proceed for political reasons, and Robinson was then chosen as an alternative, though he, too, was a Welshman, albeit with strong connections to Parker and Cambridge; he seemingly was regarded as less apt to pursue his own agenda. Cf. Evans, 'Nicholas Robinson', 168; Jones, 'Robinson, Nicholas'.

40 John Le Neve, *Fasti Ecclesiae Anglicanae, or a Calendar of the Principal Ecclesiastical Dignitaries of England and Wales and of the Chief Officers of the Universities of Oxford and Cambridge*, corrected and contributed to by T. Duffus Hardy, 3 vols (Oxford, 1854), I, 107.

41 Jones, 'Robinson, Nicholas'; Venn and Venn, *Alumni Cantabrigienses … Part I*, III, 472.

42 7 October 1567. TNA, SP 12/44/27, f. 62; David Mathew, 'Some Elizabethan Documents', *BBCS*, 6 (1933), 77–8.

43 TNA SP12/69/14, 53, quoted in Peter Marshall, *Beliefs and the Dead in Reformation England* (Oxford, 2002), p. 128.

44 Evans, 'Nicholas Robinson', 178.

45 3 November 1577. TNA, SP 12/118/8, f. 18.

46 The account made by Robinson and Price of their actions and findings to the council is dated 24 March 1578. TNA, SP 12/123, f. 16.

47 28 May 1582, Nicholas Robinson to the earl of Leicester. TNA, SP 12/153/66, f. 130.

48 28 May 1582, Nicholas Robinson to Sir Francis Walsingham. TNA, SP 12/153/67, f. 131.

49 Evans, 'Nicholas Robinson', 182; TNA, SP 12/165/3.

50 John Gwynfor Jones, *Law, Order, and Government in Caernarfonshire, 1558–1640* (Cardiff, 1996), p. 91; J. R. S. Phillips (ed.), *The Justices of the Peace in Wales and Monmouthshire, 1541–1689* (Cardiff, 1975), pp. 2–3, 19–20, 38–9, 55–6, 95–7, 127–30, 157–9, 186–8, 205–7, 254–7, 288–9, 316–19, 346–7.

51 Daniel Huws, *A Repertory of Welsh Manuscripts and Scribes, c.800–c.1800*, 3 vols (Aberystwyth, 2022), II, 154.

52 Huws, *Repertory*, I, 459–60. The 1661 additions are on pp. 338, 453, 498, 531–3, 573–5, 586–92, as Huws notes.

53 Huw Pryce, *Writing Welsh History: from the Early Middle Ages to the Twenty-first Century* (Oxford, 2022), p. 141; Humphrey Llwyd, *Cronica Walliae*, ed. Ieuan M. Williams and J. Beverley Smith (Cardiff, 2002), pp. 4–12, for details concerning the five surviving manuscripts.

54 *Historia brevis Thomae Walsingham, ab Edwardo Primo, ad Henricum Quintum*, ed. Matthew Parker (London: Henry Bynneman, 1574).

55 NLW, Peniarth MS 383, p. 502.

56 Huws, *Repertory*, I, 459–60.

57 NLW, Peniarth MS 383, p. 287.

58 For example, NLW, Peniarth MS 383, p. 345.

59 NLW, Peniarth MS 383, p. 345.
60 Pryce, *Writing Welsh History*, p. 107.
61 Pryce, *Writing Welsh History*, pp. 134, 136.
62 NLW, Peniarth MS 383, p. 445.
63 NLW, Peniarth MS 383, p. 339; Jeremy Catto, 'Patrington, Stephen (d. 1417)', *ODNB* (2008 version), https://doi.org/10.1093/ref:odnb/21569; R. H. Helmholz, 'Lyndwood, William (c.1375–1446)', *ODNB*, https://doi.org/10.1093/ref:odnb/17264; Richard Copsey, 'Milverton, John (d. 1487)', *ODNB*, https://doi.org/10.1093/ref:odnb/18805.
64 Antonia Gransden, 'Bramfield [Bromfield], Edmund (d. 1393)', *ODNB*, https://doi.org/10.1093/ref:odnb/3505; R. G. Davies, 'Peverel [Peverell], Thomas (d. 1419)', *ODNB*, https://doi.org/10.1093/ref:odnb/22075.
65 J. C. Crick, 'Monmouth, Geoffrey of [Galfridus Arturus], d. 1154/5', *ODNB*, https://doi.org/10.1093/ref:odnb/10530; Virginia Davis, 'Lowe, John (c.1385–1467)', *ODNB*, https://doi.org/10.1093/ref:odnb/17083; Wendy Scase, 'Pecock, Reginald (b. c.1392, d. in or after 1459)', *ODNB*, https://doi.org/10.1093/ref:odnb/21749.
66 T. M. Charles-Edwards, 'Deiniol [St Deiniol, Daniel]', *ODNB*, https://doi.org/10.1093/ref:odnb/7110.
67 Peter C. Bartum, *A Welsh Classical Dictionary* (Aberystwyth, 1993), p. 239.
68 *Brut y Tywysogyon: Peniarth MS 20*, ed. Thomas Jones (Cardiff, 1941), p. 3.
69 Humphrey Llwyd, *Cronica Walliae*, pp. 85–6.
70 David Powel, *A Historie of Cambria, now called Wales* ... (London, 1584), NLW, Shelf no. 2620a (WS 1584), D.i r–D.iii v.
71 NLW, Peniarth MS 383, p. 340.
72 Williams, 'Davies, Richard (c.1505–1581)'; Williams, *Reformation Views of Church History*, esp. pp. 33–45 (at p. 39); Pryce, *Writing Welsh History*, p. 116.
73 NLW, Peniarth MS 383, p. 340. Robinson does however mention the *Speculum Christianorum* subsequently, in his further discussion of Cadwgan on p. 456. John Bale, *Scriptorum illustriu[um] maioris Brytannie quam nunc Angliam & Scotiam uocant catalogus* ... (Basel, 1557–9) [STC (2nd edn)/1296 variant], pp. 67, 272 (including a list of works attributed to Cadwgan); David Walker, 'Cadwgan [Cadwgan of Llandefai] (d. 1241)', *ODNB* (2006 version), https://doi.org/10.1093/ref:odnb/4320; *Giraldi Cambrensis Opera, Volume 6*, ed. J. S. Brewer (London, 1873). For discussion of Cadwgan, see Shaun McGuinness's chapter in this volume, pp. 211–14.
74 Robinson writes that Ringstead was a 'theologus, et orator insignis ob quasdam conciones coram Rege Edwardo 3°...' NLW, Peniarth MS 383, p. 340. Bale writes similarly that Ringstead was: 'theologius ... ob conciones quasdam coram rege Edvuardo factas, Bangorenis episcopus constituebatur'.

Bale, *Scriptorum illustriu[um] maioris Brytannie* … (1557–9), p. 477 (including a list of works attributed to Ringstead); Glanmor Williams, 'Ringstead, Thomas (d. 1366)', *ODNB*, https://doi.org/10.1093/ref:odnb/23658.

75 NLW, Peniarth MS 383, p. 340. Bale, *Scriptorum illustriu[um] maioris Brytannie* … (1557–9), p. 514 (including a list of works attributed to Swaffham).

76 NLW, Peniarth MS 383, p. 340. On the career of Anian, see Huw Pryce, 'Anian [Einion] (d. 1305×1307)', *ODNB*, https://doi.org/10.1093/ref:odnb/48535. See also Shaun McGuinness's chapter in this volume, pp. 218–19.

77 Powel, *Historie of Cambria* (1584), p. 237; NLW, Peniarth MS 383, p. 437. While it is beyond the scope of this chapter to discuss this in depth, there are some similarities between Robinson's description and those found in different versions of the *Brut y Tywysogion*, for example: ByT [P20], ed. Jones, pp. 127–8 [1176]; *Brut y Tywysogion, or the Chronicle of the Princes: Red Book of Hergest Version*, ed. and trans., Thomas Jones (Cardiff, 1955), p. 167 [1176].

78 See, for example, NLW, Peniarth MS 383, pp. 434, 438, 443, 462.

79 NLW, Peniarth MS 383, p. 27; 'Est igitur hic lapis humano femori fere conformis, cui insita virtus hoc habet...': *Giraldi Cambrensis Opera, Volume 6*, ed. James F. Dimock (London, 1868), p. 128.

80 A holy well, 'Ffynnon Idan', was found near the church and the saint reputedly lived at 'Cadair Idan'; Nidan's feast was celebrated on 30 September. Henry Rowlands, himself a vicar of Llanidan, noted that this stone had disappeared by the early eighteenth century. Thomas Jones, 'Gerald the Welshman's "Itinerary though Wales" and "Description of Wales"', *NLWJ*, 6/2 (1949), 117–48 (p. 137). *Maen Morddwydd* however should not be confused with a 'curious stone reliquary' containing pieces of bone (reputed to be those of St Nidan) discovered *c.*1700 under the church altar, contained in a small reliquary chest made of sandstone, which was subsequently moved to the new church of Llanidan. Bartum, *Welsh Classical Dictionary*, p. 505; S. Baring-Gould and John Fisher (eds), *The Lives of the British Saints*, 4 vols (London, 1907–13), IV (1913), 14–16; Angharad Llwyd, *A History of the Island of Mona, or Anglesey* (Ruthin, 1833), pp. 286–92. Today, Ffynnon Idan is described as 'a stone-lined spring; overgrown, traditionally held to be Ffynon Nidan, no trace of any structure round the spring … it fed a pod or a pool associated with St Nidan's church'; https://coflein.gov.uk/en/site/32166 (accessed 15 December 2024).

81 Pryce, *Writing Welsh History*, p. 109; 'Gulielmus Salisburius, vir in Cambriae antiquitatibus egregiè versatus, & de patria sua optimè meritus, testatur hunc lapidem de quo hic mētio fit suo tēpore viz. 1554. in muro coemiterij ecclesiae D. Aedani, in Môna insula adhuc extare': *Pontici Virunnii viri doctissimi Britannicae historiae libri sex magna et fide et diligentia conscripti: ad Britannici codicis fidem correcti, & ab infinitis mendis liberate* …, ed. David Powel (London,

1585), [STC (2nd edn)/20109], pp. 194, 200. For more about the stone, see, for example, Jones, 'Gerald the Welshman's "Itinerary though Wales" and "Description of Wales"', 137.

82 NLW, MS 3024C, f. 55v. On this manuscript and annotations by Salesbury, Davies, Powel and others, see Huws, *Repertory*, II, 183–4.

83 Robin Flower, 'Richard Davies, William Cecil, and Giraldus Cambrensis', *NLWJ*, 3/1–2 (1943), 11–14 (p. 11).

84 Huws, *Repertory*, II, 401.

85 As Russell argues, there were close links through marriage between the Thelwalls, Salusburys of Llewenni and Rug, and Wynns of Gwydir: Paul Russell (ed. and trans.), *Vita Griffini Filii Conani: The Medieval Latin Life of Gruffudd ap Cynan* (Cardiff, 2004), pp. 4–15; Huws, *Repertory*, II, 154.

86 On early Protestant views of church history, see, for example, Pryce, *Writing Welsh History*, pp. 91–120; Lloyd Bowen, 'The Battle of Britain: History and Reformation in Early Modern Wales', in T. Ó hAnnracháin and R. Armstrong (eds), *Christianities in the Early Modern Celtic World* (Basingstoke, 2014), pp. 135–50; Glanmor Williams, 'Some Protestant Views of the Early British Church', in Glanmor Williams, *Welsh Reformation Essays* (Cardiff, 1967), pp. 207–19.

87 Cambridge, Corpus Christi College, MS 114B, f. 503. This is a reference to Eadmer of Canterbury OSB (*c.*1060–after 1124), *Historia nouorum in Anglia (Eadmeri Historia Novorum)*, a chronicle concerned with English history from *c.*1066–*c.*1122. Another manuscript, Cambridge, Corpus Christi College, MS 341, contains a sixteenth-century copy of this, which appears to be a transcript of Cambridge, Corpus Christi College, MS 452 (after 1122–*c.*1150). It has been suggested (in the 1884 Rolls Series edition of the text by Rule) that it was perhaps during the period in which Dr Henry Johns possessed it that this was probably copied from Cambridge, Corpus Christi College, MS 452. For more on this, see the Parker Library Catalogue, *https://parker.stanford.edu/parker/catalog/xp845rf0297* (accessed 15 December 2024).

88 Cambridge, Corpus Christi College, MS 114B, f. 503.

89 Cambridge, Corpus Christi College, MS 114B, f. 501.

90 Cambridge, Corpus Christi College, MS 114B, f. 501.

91 Gruffudd Antur, 'Beirdd a Gwŷr Llên: rhai rhwydweithiau llawysgrifol yng Nghymru, *c.*1450–*c.*1800' (unpublished PhD thesis, Bangor University, 2023), 78–90, especially 89 for Antur's suggestion regarding Robinson's possible contributions.

92 Bowen, 'The Battle of Britain', p. 140.

93 Richard Davies, 'Testament Newydd 1567', in Garfield H. Hughes (ed.), *Rhagymadroddion 1547–1659* (Cardiff, 1976), pp. 17–43 (especially pp. 17–22).

For more on early Protestant views history, cf. Pryce, *Writing Welsh History*, pp. 91–120; Antur, 'Beirdd a Gwŷr Llên', 80.

94 Antur, 'Beirdd a Gwŷr Llên', 81.
95 Antur, 'Beirdd a Gwŷr Llên', 78–90; D. Myrddin Lloyd, 'William Salesbury and "Epistol E.M. at y Cembru"', *NLWJ*, 2 (1941–2), 14–16.
96 Antur, 'Beirdd a Gwŷr Llên', 78–90; Lloyd, 'William Salesbury', 14–16. This was Sir Thomas Edward Watson, Baronet (1851–1921), a leading figure in local business, government, and civic affairs, known for his collection of manuscripts and early printed books.
97 Antur, 'Beirdd a Gwŷr Llên', 89.
98 Ceri Lewis (ed. and trans.), *Rhagymadroddion a Chyflwyniadau Lladin, 1551–1632* (Cardiff, 1980), p. 70.
99 Glanmor Williams, *The Welsh and Their Religion* (Cardiff, 1991), pp. 173–229; Williams *Wales and the Reformation*, pp. 338–60 (pp. 343–4); Evans, 'Nicholas Robinson', 156.
100 Issac Thomas, *William Morgan a'i Feibl: William Morgan and His Bible* (Cardiff, 1988), pp. 42–6; Williams, *Wales and the Reformation*, pp. 346–7.
101 Jones, 'Robinson, Nicholas'.
102 Antur, 'Beirdd a Gwŷr Llên', 89.
103 TNA, PROB 11/68/120.
104 Williams, *Wales and the Reformation*, p. 459.
105 These include BL, Add. MSS 31097 and 14966; NLW, Brogyntyn MS 2; NLW, Cwrtmawr MSS 10, 19, 27, 454, and NLW, Llanstephan MS 30. The text of the Llanstephan MS 30 version is printed in Evans, 'Nicholas Robinson', 195–8.
106 Huws, *Repertory*, I, 67.
107 On these MSS, cf. Huws, *Repertory*, I, 611, 634.
108 John Strype, *Life and Acts of Matthew Parker*, I, 464.
109 Glanmor Williams, 'Bellot, Hugh', *ODNB*, https://doi.org/10.1093/ref:ondb/2060; D. Aneurin Thomas (ed.), *The Welsh Elizabethan Catholic Martyrs* (Cardiff, 1971), p. 299.
110 Williams, 'Bellot'.
111 Brett Usher, 'Vaughan, Richard', *ODNB*, https://doi.org/10.1093/ref:ondb/28139; Davies, *Rhagymadroddion a Chyflwyniadau Lladin*, p. 70.
112 J. Gwynfor Jones, 'Rowlands, Henry', *ODNB*, http://doi.org/10.1093/ref:ondb/24215; Pryce, *Diocese of Bangor*, pp. xxxii–xxxv, 67–75; Willis, *Survey of Bangor*, pp. 24–5, 109–10, 127, 152; TNA, PROB 11/128/256.
113 Williams, *Wales and the Reformation*, p. 459.
114 Pryce, *Writing Welsh History*, p. 114.
115 Salesbury wrote to Parker regarding his search for old manuscripts as well as other topics, like clerical marriage, while Scory's interest was in Anglo-Saxon

manuscripts found in the cathedral church of Hereford. See, for example, Cambridge, Corpus Christi College, MS 114A, ff. 447–52, 491–2, 495–6. On Matthew Parker and his circle, see, for example, May McKisack, *Medieval History in the Tudor Age* (Oxford, 1971), ch. 2.

116 Cambridge, Corpus Christi College, MS 114A, ff. 392c–392d, 392g–392k, 489–90; *ByT* (P20), trans. Thomas Jones (Cardiff, 1952), p. 18. On Sulien, cf. J. E. Lloyd, rev. Nancy Edwards, 'Sulien [Sulgen, Sulgenus]', *ODNB*, https://doi.org/10.1093/ref:odnb/26768. For the Latin translation by Davies of passages from the *Brut y Tywysogyon*, cf. Glanmor Williams, 'Bishop Sulien, Richard Davies, and Archbishop Parker', *NLWJ*, 5 (1948), 215–19.

117 Pryce, *Writing Welsh History*, p. 121.

118 On this, see Jan Broadway, *'No historie so meete'*, esp. pp. 14–56; Jan Broadway, 'Symbolic and Self-consciously Antiquarian: The Elizabethan and Early Stuart Gentry's Use of the Past', *Huntingdon Library Quarterly*, 76/4 (2013), 541–58.

119 Pryce, *Writing Welsh History*, p. 131.

120 Evans, 'Nicholas Robinson', 195–8. Cf. BL, Add. MSS 31097 and 14966; NLW, Brogyntyn MS 2; NLW, Cwrtmawr MSS 10, 19, 27, 454.

121 Jones, *Aspects of Religious Life in Wales*, p. 174.

122 *Barddoniaeth Wiliam Llŷn*, ed. J. C. Morrice (Bangor, 1908), nos LXIX, LXXIV.

123 Huws, *Repertory*, I, 738; Oxford, Jesus College MS. 15, p. 182; Michaela Jacques, *Grammar and Poetry in Late Medieval and Early Modern Wales: The Transmission and Reception of the Welsh Bardic Grammars* (Cardiff, 2024), pp. 185, 215–16, 257.

PART III : RHAN III
MEMORY AND NATION : COF CENEDL

11

Antiquarianism, Ancestry and 'Ancient Britons': Welsh Historical Consciousness, Cultural Patronage and the Identity of the Gentry, c.1800–1920

Shaun Evans

Over the last decade Huw Pryce has pioneered research into perceptions of the past and uses of history in nineteenth-century Wales. Grounded in his 2011 Kelleher Lecture on 'Culture, identity and the medieval revival in Victorian Wales', it is an interest that has blossomed into a complete assessment of history writing in Welsh culture and scholarship.[1] This chapter picks up core strands of Pryce's contribution, particularly the role of historical consciousness and antiquarian activity in shaping nineteenth-century identities and the active use, manipulation and presentation of the Welsh past to fit contemporary needs and agenda. This piece is especially interested in Wales's landowning class (broadly defined to include those groups variously referred to as the gentry, squirearchy, aristocracy and nobility). It assesses the nature and extent of their engagement with Welsh antiquarianism and what this activity suggests about their cultural outlook and attachment to Wales.[2] The principal contention is that the Welsh landowning class of the nineteenth century were deeply involved in the cultivation of a Welsh antiquarian culture which fully embraced the gentry, their family histories, genealogies, ancestral residences, landed patrimonies, historical collections and invented traditions as core elements of Wales's past and present.

Landowners who engaged in this culture usually did so out of genuine interest, though it also held significant potential as a form of social, cultural and political capital.[3] Antiquarianism was not inert. Aristocracies across Europe had long engaged in the construction of useable pasts which could be employed, subtly or aggressively, to meet social and political objectives.[4] Rosemary Sweet has noted that 'the activities and writings of eighteenth-century antiquaries reveals a constant interaction between past and present, in which antiquarian knowledge informed the culture and identities of the modern world'.[5] It is here argued that the gentry's engagement with and promotion of Welsh antiquarianism formed an important part in the performance and presentation of their status and authority within Welsh society, conjoining with their broader societal roles as landowners, politicians, officeholders, agriculturalists, industrialists and cultural patrons.

For this community, antiquarianism was an important form and expression of Welsh identity, often closely aligned to a sense of 'ancestral patriotism'. As discussed below, the cultivation of this patriotism undermines simplistic yet deeply pervasive historiographical interpretations of an 'anglicised' gentry having lost all sense of cultural attachment to Wales. This class continued to preserve and promote Wales as a distinctive cultural entity. To be sure, across the later nineteenth century this form of Welshness collided with and was eventually superseded by the Welshness constructed by a triumphant radical nonconformity, positioning an imagined *gwerin* as the true custodians of Welsh cultural tradition.[6] The visions of Welsh history and national awakening promoted by Henry Richard, Thomas Rees, O. M. Edwards and others fractured the picture of Wales cultivated through the gentry's antiquarianism.[7] The subsequent historiography of Wales produced across the twentieth century tended to position landowners in direct opposition to Welsh identity and culture.[8]

The gentry and Welsh culture before 1800

According to Prys Morgan's influential interpretation, the late seventeenth and early eighteenth centuries witnessed a fundamental collapse of traditional Welsh culture, establishing conditions for pronounced cultural revival and reinvention from the later eighteenth century.[9] This patriotic endeavour to reimagine and reassert Wales included deep engagement with the past, creating a Welsh antiquarian culture which was intricately tied to objectives of national renewal. As Jane Williams (Ysgafell, 1806–85) asserted: 'The Welshman's love of antiquities is therefore a part of his patriotism'.[10] The gentry's role in these processes has conventionally been understood as follows: from the later medieval period, alongside their positions of social and political authority, a new gentry (*uchelwyr* or *boneddigion*) elite self-consciously embraced a role of Welsh cultural leadership. This centred on bardic patronage, an intense pride in Welsh ancestry and the cultivation of a manuscript tradition which preserved the core texts of Welsh nationhood. Immersion within these environments helped to create and preserve a distinctive form of Welsh gentility (*uchelwriaeth*). Over the sixteenth and seventeenth centuries – and especially following the political unification of Wales with England – the gentry are held to have rescinded their support and patronage of Welsh culture, instead becoming entirely 'anglicised' in outlook and identity. In the words of Glanmor Williams, 'the Welsh awareness would in future have to learn to live without the participation of the gentry'.[11] Historians of early modern Welsh gentry culture increasingly view 'anglicisation' as an unsuitable framework for assessing the gentry's relationship with Wales and Welsh identity, not least because of the importance they continued to attach to their 'Ancient British' ancestry and the nature of their antiquarian and scholarly interests.[12] However, in his study of historical writing in eighteenth-century Wales, Geraint H. Jenkins concludes that 'Welsh landowners provided scant encouragement for historians ... the fact that they had lost their native language and sense of Welshness meant they were either unable or unwilling to bolster the historical heritage of Wales'.[13] Furthermore, Philip Jenkins has pointed to the 1730s as a period of fundamental change in Welsh landed society; the disappearance of established *uchelwyr* families and their replacement by a 'new' landed elite coinciding with a sharp decline in traditional Welsh cultural practice and patronage, antiquarian activity and ancestral consciousness.[14] The role of landowners in the cultural and historical revival which followed from the later eighteenth century has never been fully researched; though one or two are occasionally conjoined to the ranks of *yr hen bersoniaid llengar* ('old literary clerics') who are credited with driving the cultural and intellectual renaissance, often in direct opposition to the purifying ethos of an advancing methodism. An assumption that the landowning families had become fully 'anglicised', detached and alienated from all things Welsh, has masked the reality of their continuing engagement with ancestry and antiquarianism as expressions of Welsh patriotism.

It is possible to present an alternative picture of the gentry's engagement with the processes of Welsh cultural revival up to *c*.1800. Alongside their continuing engagement with the manuscript tradition, Welsh landowners had been key supporters of published works about the history, language, literature and topography of Wales since the advent of print; a trend which endured across the eighteenth century and beyond.[15] Eiluned Rees and Bethan Jenkins have convincingly argued that subscribing to and purchasing these books constituted a new method for the gentry to demonstrate patronage of Welsh culture and literature following the demise of the bardic tradition.[16] By *c*.1800, works such as David Powel's *The Historie of Cambria* (1584; reprinted as the *History of Wales* in 1697, 1702, 1774), John Davies's *Antiquae Linguae Britannicae* (1621), Edward Lhuyd's *Archaeologia Britannica* (1707), Willis's surveys of Welsh cathedrals (1716–21), William Wotton and Moses Williams's *Cyfreithjeu Hywel Dda ac Eraill* (1730), the various parts and editions of Thomas Pennant's immensely influential *Tour in Wales* (1778–83, 1784) and Philip Yorke's *Royal Tribes of Wales* (1799) had become mainstays in eighteenth-century Welsh country house libraries, alongside English-Welsh dictionaries, Welsh Bibles and other religious works in Welsh.[17] William Owen's *Dictionary of the Welsh Language* (1803), for example, was advertised as 'a very valuable acquisition to the Celtic Library by the Antiquary, the Scholar, the Gentleman and the Critic', with the subscription list including dozens of Welsh landowners.[18] The works of Thomas Pennant (1726–98) of Downing and Philip Yorke (1749–1804) of Erddig, published in English, both demonstrated and perpetuated a keen interest in Welsh antiquarianism amongst the squirearchy of north Wales, playing a significant role in asserting the place of the gentry – their genealogies, family histories, country houses and landed patrimonies – as integral features of Wales's past and present.[19] Richard Fenton (1747–1821), who eventually settled at Plas Glynamel, played a similar role in Pembrokeshire. In the sphere of literature, Evan Evans (Ieuan Fardd, 1731–88) dedicated his *Specimens of the Poetry of the Antient Welsh Bards* (1764) to Sir Roger Mostyn in recognition of his ancestors' record of bardic patronage; the Glamorganshire lyric poet Dafydd Nicolas (d. 1774) found a home with the Williams family of Aberpergwm from the middle of the century; the important anthology of medieval Welsh poetry published in *Gorchestion Beirdd Cymru* (1773) by the minor Merionethshire gentleman Rhys Jones (1713–1801) of

Blaenau was dedicated to William Vaughan (d. 1775) of Cors-y-gedol and received subscriptions from dozens of landowners; and the editors of the landmark *Myvyrian Archaiology of Wales* (1801–7) praised Paul Panton (1758–1822) of Plas Gwyn and Thomas Johnes (1748–1816) of Hafod for their 'patriotism' and 'liberality' in lending their manuscripts towards the completion of the work, acknowledging that:

> There still happily remains a great number of ancient manuscripts in the Welsh tongue; some of them brought together into the valuable depositories of public-spirited gentlemen, who are liberally solicitous of preserving such treasures for posterity …[20]

In the field of Welsh music too, numerous landowners subscribed to seminal publications such as John Parry's *Antient British Music* (1742) and *British Harmony* (1781), and Edward Jones's *Musical and Poetical Relicks of the Welsh Bards* (1784, 1794); which, combined with the patronage and performance exuded from houses such as Glanbrân and Wynnstay, helped to re-establish the harp as a defining fixture in Welsh culture.[21] The gentry also associated themselves with new societies which were established to rejuvenate Welsh culture. As a successor to the earlier Society of Ancient Britons, the London-based Cymmrodorion Society (1751–87) adopted core antiquarian subject interests which impinged heavily on the manuscripts of Welsh history, genealogy and poetry preserved in country house collections.[22] William Vaughan of Cors-y-gedol and Sir Watkin Williams-Wynn (1749–89) served as successive chief presidents. There were also new opportunities for the gentry to parade their Welshness within Wales, with many participating in the formal renewal of the eisteddfod movement from 1789 as patrons and focuses for literary competitions.[23]

The above picture of the gentry's cultural and antiquarian engagements across the late eighteenth century suggests that the traditional narrative prioritising breaks with the past perhaps needs to be balanced against a greater consideration of continuities. Such cumulative examples pose a challenge to the established interpretation of irrevocable landowner 'anglicisation' and cultural alienation but need to be properly contextualised. First, the Welsh gentry's intellectual, cultural and antiquarian horizons extended far beyond Wales, including a continuing fascination with classical texts and a significant interest in English and

European history. Welsh gentlemen were admitted as Fellows to the London Society of Antiquaries and subscribed to English antiquarian periodicals such as *The Gentleman's Magazine* and *The Annual Register*. Into the nineteenth century, Thomas Johnes's edition of Froissart's *Chronicles*, Sir Stephen Glynne's (1807–74) studies of church architecture and the wide-ranging writings of Sir George Cornewall Lewis (1806–63) point to the range and diversity of the gentry's antiquarian tastes, which were often shaped by broader international cultural and intellectual trends.[24] Similarly, the gentry's Welsh cultural patriotism was usually inseparable from a firm sense of belonging to a British polity and associated attachment to its monarchical, political, ecclesiastical and colonial institutions. Expressions of identity such as 'Cambro-British' and the 'Ancient Briton', which allowed for a combination of Welsh, British and English loyalties, long remained relevant to the gentry in Wales, influencing their antiquarian outlook. Furthermore, although more research is required to understand the precise chronology of the gentry's Welsh-language proficiencies, by *c.*1800 it appears likely that most could not read the Welsh-language books in their possession, nor actively lead the Welsh-language elements of antiquarian scholarship. Although the Welsh antiquarian culture cultivated by the gentry across the nineteenth century engaged closely with the Welsh language and literature, it was predominately articulated through English. This was undoubtedly accentuated by an influx of 'new' landed families, often originating outside Wales, who had acquired Welsh estates through marriage, inheritance or the profits of industrial or colonial wealth. However, as demonstrated by Lady Charlotte Guest (1812–95), most vividly in the patriotic dedication of her translation of *The Mabinogion* (1838) to her two sons, aristocrats newly established in Wales could at times provide the keenest sustenance to its literature, language and history. Sir William Paxton's (1744–1824) declaration to Col. David Williams of Henllys that 'you have made such a Welshman of me, that I am interested in everything to do with the Principality', similarly shows that newly established landowners could become vested in Welsh cultural and intellectual milieus: Scottish-born Paxton had purchased the Middleton Hall estate in Carmarthenshire through a fortune made in the service of the East India Company.[25] Nevertheless, evidence of landowner encouragement of Welsh scholarship and culture need to be balanced against regular complaints of insufficient patronage, the neglect and inaccessibility of Welsh manuscripts in their possession and downright disinterest in the promotion of Welsh literature.[26]

These contexts and contradictions framed the character of the Welsh antiquarianism developed by the gentry across the nineteenth century.

The Cambrian societies and Welsh cultural patronage

The preservation and publication of Welsh manuscripts emerged as a core objective in the cultural and intellectual life of Wales across the late eighteenth and nineteenth centuries.[27] This not only developed into a central driver of Welsh antiquarian activity but was positioned as an underpinning for patriotic endeavours to revive and nurture the literature and language of Wales in the present. This combination placed a sharp focus on the gentry's attitude towards their manuscripts and their role in supporting Wales's cultural and intellectual enrichment. Between 1818 and 1821, four provincial Cambrian societies were established across Wales 'for the preservation of the Remains of Ancient British Literature and the encouragement of the poetry and music of Wales'.[28] Initially conceived by Bishop Thomas Burgess (1756–1857) and Revd John Jenkins (Ifor Ceri, 1770–1829), the societies were immediately characterised by the active support and patronage they received from the nobility, gentry and Anglican clergy of Wales, symbolised by the vesting of their presidencies in heads of the houses of Dinefwr, Tredegar, Plas Newydd and Wynnstay – with Sir Watkin Williams-Wynn also presiding over the resurrected Cymmrodorion Society in London.

These societies were integral to the revival of the eisteddfod movement following a stagnation of the meetings held under the auspices of the Gwyneddigion Society since 1789.[29] The series of grand 'provincial' eisteddfodau organised from 1819 transitioned into national meetings following 'Eisteddfod Fawr Llangollen' in 1858. The events provided a prominent public theatre for the performance, negotiation and contestation of Welsh culture and identity. The gentry were fully incorporated into the patriotic image of Wales presented at eisteddfodau, epitomised by conscious efforts to reignite the traditional *uchelwyr* role of Welsh cultural patronage. For example, the prize-winning *englynion* at the 1822 Brecon eisteddfod were composed on the subject of 'the munificent patronage afforded to the bards by Ivor Hael and his descendants of the House of Tredegar, addressed to Sir Charles

Morgan, President of the Eisteddfod'.[30] This revival of bardic culture appears to have inspired a revitalisation of neo-traditional praise-poetry (*canu mawl*) as an accompaniment to the major dynastic milestones in aristocratic lifecycles, evinced by the dozens of *awdlau*, *cywyddau*, *cerddi* and *englynion* composed in commemoration of Sir Robert Williames Vaughan's coming of age in 1824.[31] At the same time, the harp was elevated to position of prominence in the cultural life of some Welsh country houses.[32] Aristocrats were frequently invited to preside over eisteddfod proceedings; attended en masse; featured as focuses for bardic compositions; provided prizes and premiums for competitions; and occasionally even inaugurated into the Gorsedd y Beirdd. They were also absorbed into the visual spectacle of Welshness presented at eisteddfodau. The 1850 Rhuddlan eisteddfod included 'pictorial representations of the armorial bearings of the great families of the counties of Denbigh and Flint', and portraits of Lords Mostyn and Penrhyn, and Sir Watkin Williams-Wynn adorned the platform at the 1872 Porthmadog National Eisteddfod.[33] At the Royal Denbigh Eisteddfod of 1828 much was made of the ancestral connection between the president, Sir Edward Mostyn (1785–1841) of Talacre and the central roles played by his ancestors at the seminal Caerwys eisteddfodau of 1523 and 1567.[34] The official report of the congress also delighted in the number of 'distinguished gentry' who served as vice-presidents, patrons and members of the organising committee, with the list of donations towards the event reading like a roll-call of north Wales estate owners.

The links between patronage and patriotism were normally couched in highly ancestral terms, though more recent recruits to Welsh landed society also adopted and augmented this cultural inheritance. This is exemplified by Augusta Hall, Lady Llanover (1802–96), who combined an astounding interest in Welsh music, language, literature, genealogy, costume and folk traditions with active patronage, coordinated through the vibrant Cymdeithas Cymreigyddion y Fenni (1833–54), their eisteddfodau and the cultural life of Llanover Hall.[35] The competitions at the 1840 meeting of the Abergavenny Cymreigyddion Society included additional prizes from Charlotte Guest for a history of the harp in Gwent and Morgannwg; J. H. Vivian of Singleton for a history of settlements in Gower and Pembrokeshire; Mrs Morgan of Ruperra for performances on the harp; and Thomas Wakeman of The Graig for genealogical accounts of medieval rulers of Gwent, Seisyll ap Dyfnwal and Caradog Freichfras.[36] It was John Etherington-Welch Rolls (1807–70) of The Hendre who presided on this occasion. The gentry not only provided significant financial input for eisteddfodau but served to infuse the movement with social esteem. This allowed eisteddfodic activities, centred on Welsh poetry, music, history and language, to be presented as respectable elements of a 'high' Welsh culture, worthy of cultivation and preservation, occasionally subject to royal patronage and fully compatible with the hegemony of the British state. The speeches and addresses delivered by landowners on these occasions, usually though not exclusively in English, merit detailed analysis. Their willingness to perform the role of patronage in such a public arena, coupled with the patriotic assertions they often articulated to the assembled crowd, suggests that Welshness retained a potency for Wales's landowning elite throughout the nineteenth century.

The first Cambrian Society, for Dyfed, was primarily established as an initiative for the preservation of ancient British literature, under the premise that 'The valuable remains of our ancient national literature have suffered ... irreparable losses by fires and neglect, to the great discredit of a literacy age and nation'.[37] The objective, endorsed by Wales's leading landowners, was to catalogue, transcribe and publish Welsh manuscripts and create a prospectus for a new *History of Wales*. The 'Catalogues of Welsh Manuscripts' presented at the 1824 Welshpool eisteddfod by Aneurin Owen and Angharad Llwyd emphasised that the country houses of Wales remained primary repositories of the nation's literary heritage.[38] The Cambrian societies provided the gentry with an institutional framework for responding to repeated allegations of manuscript neglect and disinterest. This aspect was eventually absorbed into the objectives of the Welsh Manuscripts Society, established in 1837 to publish the most important manuscripts of prose and poetry, with English translations. Like its precursor, it received significant support from landowners who subscribed to its published works including *Liber Landavensis* (1840), *Heraldic Visitations of Wales* (1846), *Iolo Manuscripts* (1848) and *Lives of the Cambro British Saints* (1856) – amongst the many Welsh books that were printed in Llandovery by William Rees (1808–73) of Tonn. Despite limited published outputs and major setbacks, notably the destruction of the Wynnstay library by fire in 1858, the various schemes engendered a renewed appreciation for Welsh manuscripts amongst Welsh landed society, exemplified by W. W. E. Wynne (1802–80) of Peniarth in his custodianship of the Hengwrt collection. Landowners were receptive to the seminal research on Welsh manuscripts conducted by J. Gwenogvryn Evans (1852–1930) on behalf of the Historical Manuscripts Commission towards the end of the century and numerous Welsh landowners associated themselves with the early development of the National Library, a new national repository for safeguarding the literary heritage of Wales.

Welsh histories and the country house library

Books were the principal manifestation of the gentry's engagement with Welsh antiquarianism. By *c.*1800 the wide-ranging library had been long established as a fundamental feature of the Welsh country house.[39] These libraries incorporated vast assortments of literature, knowledge and ideas, both new and old, on a multitude of subjects, in multiple languages and derived from a trade in books which was international in character. More research is required to fully understand the nature of Welsh country house libraries, not assisted by their mass dispersal and dislocation across the twentieth century.[40] However, Welsh-language books, and more prominently, books about Wales published in English or Latin, nearly always featured as a distinctive component within these cosmopolitan accumulations, marking them out from their counterparts elsewhere in Britain and Europe. John Lloyd Wynne's (1776–1822) library at Coed Coch, Denbighshire, featured dozens of older and more recent Welsh books; across the nineteenth century the Stanleys added antiquarian texts about Wales to their bookshelves at Penrhos, Anglesey; Lady Llanover confidently asserted that the Dolaucothi library in Carmarthenshire contained all of the 'learned workes' published in Welsh; William Llewellyn (d. 1865) assembled a library of 2,000 books at Glanwern House, Pontypool, including a number of 'ancient and modern Welsh histories, tours and other works relating to Wales'; Nicholas Bennett's (1823–99) library at Glanyrafon, Montgomeryshire, was famed for its Welsh volumes of history and music; and Robert Williams Llewellyn (1848–1910) kept a 'Welsh Library' at Cwrt Colman.[41] The Llanidloes printer John Pryse (1826–83) delighted that 'in no country will there be found a peasantry who are more addicted to reading than those which inhabit the mountains and valleys of Cambria', yet subscription lists also show that landowners continued to play an integral part in funding the publication of many books about Welsh history, culture, literature and language across the nineteenth century.[42] The tradition of dedicating books to landowners also continued: Peter Roberts's *Chronicle of the Kings of Britain* (1811) and Hugh Hughes's *Beauties of Cambria* (1819) to Sir Watkin Williams-Wynn; a new edition of Robert Vaughan's *British Antiquities Revived* (1834) to Sir Robert Williames Vaughan; the third edition of John Walter's *English and Welsh Dictionary* (1828) to the future Lord Dinorben; Joseph Bray's *Essay on the means of promoting the literature of Wales* (1839) to Edward Lloyd-Mostyn; William Cathrall's *History of North Wales* (1828) to William Henry Paget; and Stephen W. Williams's study of *Strata Florida* (1889) to Alice, countess of Lisburne, for example. Many of these dedications highlighted the ancestral virtues of the dedicatee, perpetuating the idea of the 'Antient Briton' and promoting the patronage of Welsh literature, culture and history as praiseworthy elements of Welsh gentility. Book-plates and ownership inscriptions preserved within nineteenth-century books also evince the gentry's attachment to Welsh antiquarianism. Sizeable collections of books about Wales, regularly augmented with fine bindings, were assembled at houses such as Kinmel, Mostyn, Coedrhiglan, Penrhyn, Penty Park, St Hilary, Foelas, Galltfaenan, Danyrallt, Rhagatt and Cefn Mabli.[43] These served as physical markers of Welsh identity within the country house setting, but more often than not were also read and used by their owners. Within his commonplace book, for example, David Lloyd (1748–1822) of Alltyrodyn included notes and extracts from the *Cambrian Register*, William Wynne's edition of Powel's *History of Wales* (1774), English-Welsh dictionaries, Iolo Morganwg's *Poems, Lyric and Pastoral* (1794), Richard Fenton's *Pembrokeshire* (1810, 1811), Samuel Rusk Meyrick's *County of Cardigan* (1808) and various Welsh *Tours*.[44] Similarly, Evelyn Lewes of Tyglyn Aeron recalled pouring over the pages of the *Iolo Manuscripts* (1848) at her aunt's house of Plas Gogerddan.[45] Landowners also appear to have been keen consumers of the lineage of English-language periodicals designed to promote Welsh antiquities: the *Cambrian Register* (1795–1818), *Cambro-Briton* (1819–22), *Cambrian Quarterly* (1829–33), *Transactions of the Cymmrodorion* (1822, 1828–43), *Archaeologia Cambrensis* (1846–) and *Bye-Gones* (1871–1939). These journals reveal the heterogenous nature of Welsh antiquarianism, blending chronography, historical biography, genealogy, Welsh medieval law, parochial history, architecture, topography, heraldry, poetry, music, language and archaeology with an overriding endeavour to investigate and give publicity to a 'hidden repository' of Wales's textual and material 'monuments'.

One of the most significant movements to emerge as part of this antiquarian culture was the entwined development of county, local and genealogical history writing.[46] In 1806, Richard Colt Hoare (1758–1838) detected a 'new spirit of topographical enquiry' in Wales, welcoming the fact that 'native Cambrians have at last directed their attention and researches towards the history and antiquities of their own country'.[47] He was reflecting on the pervading legacy of Pennant's works and the recent emergence of Welsh county histories. Having governed and administered the Welsh shires for centuries, it is unsurprising that the gentry cultivated the county as an important focus in the construction of their identities.[48] Earlier works in manuscript by gentlemen-scholars such as George Owen of Henllys ('Description of Pembrokeshire'), Rice Merrick of Cottrell ('Morganiae Archaiographia') and Robert Vaughan of Hengwrt ('Survey of Merioneth'), followed in print by Henry Rowlands's incredibly popular *Mona Antiqua Restaurata* (1723, 1766, 1775), provided precedents for this type of work in Wales.[49] Though the Welsh county histories which emerged across the nineteenth century shared many characteristics with the well-established genre in England, they were unashamedly presented as contributions towards a distinctly Welsh historiographical endeavour. It was the owners of Tredegar and Pant-y-Goitre who initially proposed the scheme for what became David Williams's *History of Monmouthshire* (1796).[50] 'In the present disposition for local History' asserted the author, 'it is not wonderful [that] the gentlemen of the county should wish to have those views of its principal scenes, accompanied by a History of its material events'. The 'books relating to British antiquities' and notes on 'the origin and connections of families and the descent of property' supplied by Philip Griffin (d. 1802) of Hadnock provided valuable source material for the *History*. The preface to William Coxe's *Historical Tour in Monmouthshire* (1801) also lists the landowners 'who favoured me with a kind and hospitable reception and promoted my researches'.[51] These Monmouthshire works were soon succeeded by similar surveys of Brecknockshire (1805–9), Cardiganshire (1808), Pembrokeshire (1810, 1811), Anglesey (1833) and Radnorshire (1859). The 1818 prospectus for Jonathan Williams's *History of Radnorshire* (1859), compiled between 1800 and 1820, was targeted at the county's gentry and clergy in the hope that they would subscribe towards its publication and 'allow free access to those stores of original authorities which they may possess'.[52] James Davies (1777–1856) of Moorcourt, Kington – a subscriber to several Welsh books – 'promoted it ... to the utmost of his power'.[53] Regular complaints from authors about local disinterest and difficulties in obtaining information were nearly always balanced with notes of thanks to individual landowners. Sir Samuel Rush Meyrick (1783–1848) expressed his obligation to David Lloyd of Alltyrodyn 'for the use of his valuable MSS. and his ready communications whenever requested', and Theophilus Jones (1758–1812) paid tribute to the duke of Beaufort and Sir Charles Morgan for their encouragement of his scheme.[54] The subscription lists appended to both works suggest that most country house libraries in Brecknockshire and Cardiganshire were furnished with copies of their new county history. It can be argued that these seminal works of Welsh historiography were in large part designed as enrichments to the intellectual culture of the Welsh county house. This is certainly how Edwin Poole (1851–95) attempted to justify his new 'Popular County History' of Brecknockshire later in the century:

> It was the prevailing fashion in the beginning of this century to issue large folio County Histories, sumptuously got up no doubt, but the very expense debarred the average man from participating in the luxury; and the original Lists of Subscribers to some of these expensive tomes prove that they were published for the few ...
>
> ... during my journeys up and down the county I met with scores of intelligent and well-read people who were lamenting they could never get hold of a copy of Jones's *Brecknockshire* ... I soon ascertained that if the clergyman and the squire in each parish possessed a copy ... they were so well preserved that the general public would never be able to command even a sight of the work.[55]

The county histories incorporated a diversity of antiquarian information but, presented in the English language, they tended to emphasise a Welsh past in which the ancestors and predecessors of Wales's landed proprietors played central parts. To assemble these works authors sought out the local knowledge, manuscripts and antiquities residing with landowners, producing a content which presented country houses, estate landscapes, church memorials, pedigrees, coats of arms, descents of property and lists of officeholders as core components of the county character. The county histories that were reissued or rewritten in the early twentieth century retained this affinity to the landed interest: the 'Glanusk Edition' of Jones's *Brecknockshire* (1909–30) incorporated additions and updates from Lord Glanusk (1840–1906), and Sir Joseph Bradney (1859–1933) of Tal-y-Coed produced a monumental *History of Monmouthshire* (1904–33).

County identities were further augmented through the establishment of historical societies. Andrew Green's study of the formation of the Caerleon Antiquarian Association (1847–) demonstrates how landowners shaped the character and activities of the association, to an extent that antiquarianism became a fixture in gentry's social calendar.[56] Similarly, the Powysland Club was established in 1868 with the earl of Powis, Lord Sudeley and Sir Watkin Williams-Wynn serving as its first president and vice-presidents, and Morris Charles Jones (1819–93), a solicitor who acquired Gungrog Hall, providing the driving inspiration. The proposal for its formation included a request that 'the county gentry and landed proprietors give copies of their pedigrees, armorial bearings and ancient deeds and MSS with accounts of their residences' for publication in *Montgomeryshire Collections*.[57] Neil Evans has suggested that engagement with these activities provided an opportunity for the gentry to express their local roots and Welshness in response to the pressures they faced from the advance of Welsh radical nonconformism.[58] The membership lists of these societies feature dozens of landowners; an affiliation that was mirrored in the establishment of other county history societies in the early twentieth century.

Paul O'Leary has pointed to the diversity of local history writing in nineteenth-century Wales.[59] Like the county histories discussed above, these works contributed to understandings of national history, whilst testifying to the continuing significance of identities rooted in more local frameworks such as the town or parish. Pennant's *History of the Parishes of Whiteford and Holywell* (1796) provided an early exemplar, in which the historical exploits and influences of his own ancestors at Downing and Bychton, and those of his still more eminent neighbours at Mostyn were presented as essential for understanding the character and significance of place. This factor permeated much of the local history writing produced in Wales across the nineteenth century, with the landed family, estate and country house highlighted as cornerstones of local identity. John Williams's *Ancient & Modern Denbigh* (1856), for example, had multiple chapters dedicated to the 'Ancient families of Denbigh'; the historical and contemporary influence of Dinefwr and Gelli Aur loomed large in *Llandilo: Past and Present* (1868); and John Roland Phillips had a section on 'Mansions' and 'Old Families' within his *History of Cilgerran* (1867). In the preface to his *History of West Gower* (1877), J. D. Davies acknowledged that his ability 'to peruse the splendid collection of ancient documents preserved at Penrice Castle' had provided an important underpinning for his endeavour, further offering his thanks to:

> Mrs Wood of Stouthall who placed many of her coloured sketches at my disposal; to Miss Talbot for drawings of many of the curiosities preserved at Penrice Castle; [and] to Mrs. Traherne of Coedriglan for much valuable information and for the drawing of the singular bone ornament found in Paviland Cave … in 1831.[60]

Some landowners were inspired to write the history of their own domains: Lord Hanmer's *Memorial of the Parish and Family of Hanmer* (1877), T. H. G. Puleston's *History of Worthenbury* (1895) and P. B. Davies-Cooke's *History of Mold Parish Church* (1905) are three examples from Flintshire. All demonstrate a deep connection to place through the combined influence of lineage, landownership and local leadership. However, as evinced by Lewis Weston Dillwyn's *Contributions towards a History of Swansea* (1840) and G. T. Clark's *The Land of Morgan* (1883), newer members of the Welsh squirearchy also engaged in the promotion of local history. This fits with Philip Jenkins's summation that 'new' landowning families in Wales had a political requirement to emphasise a 'semblance of local roots' as part of the legitimisation of their position within society and as natural successors to earlier ruling elites.[61]

Genealogical writing and gentry histories

Reflecting on his research visits to Welsh country houses across the late nineteenth century, J. Gwenogvryn Evans observed that 'a considerable section of this community takes a most astonishing interest in this subject of pedigrees'.[62] Francis Jones has argued that genealogy was an integral part of Welsh history, literature and culture.⁶³ There was a long tradition of genealogical writing in Welsh gentry culture, which from the medieval period centred on the compilation of manuscript pedigree books and later, the commissioning of heraldic pedigree rolls.⁶⁴ The manuscript tradition continued into the nineteenth century: in 1865 William Bulkeley Hughes (1797–1882) of Plas Coch commissioned a sumptuous pedigree book detailing his descent from Llywarch ap Bran and Wales's medieval kings.⁶⁵ Genealogy also exerted a significant influence on the visual appearance of the Welsh country house and parish church, with landowners continuing to parade their Welsh ancestry through omnipresent displays of heraldry. Although the landowners of Wales delighted in their inclusion in British compilations such Burke's *Peerage and Baronetage*, *Landed Gentry* and *General Armory*, they also continued to nurture a distinctively Welsh genealogical culture (and despite the condescension this continued to evoke from some English quarters).

This ancestral patriotism extended beyond family pride, incorporating heraldic displays of constructs such as the Royal and Noble Tribes of Wales, which across the nineteenth century were elevated to the status of Welsh national insignia. Virtually the whole infrastructure of Welsh antiquarianism accommodated for this continuing ancestral obsession. John Jones's *History of Wales* (1824) had an entire chapter dedicated to the subject.⁶⁶ Presented as a 'History of the Ancient Britons', it asserted that 'the pedigrees of the Welsh are subjects of national interest and family importance':

> As families descended from royal, noble, or illustrious ancestors, they are sensible of their honourable rank in society, and of the propriety of supporting the pristine dignity of their respective houses … In descendants of great men the stimulus [for imitation] must have greater force, as the individual is under a sense of duty in supporting the honour and glory of his ancestors.⁶⁷

In this respect ancestry not only served to entrench the gentry within Welsh history but remained relevant to the contemporary practice and presentation of their status and authority. Ancestry was a source of significant patriotic effusion and regularly employed in the exercise of power within Welsh society. It was habitually evoked on those occasions when landowners were positioned in face-to-face scenarios with those communities over whom they sought to exert influence and continued to feature in parliamentary election campaigns deep into the nineteenth century.[68] A stream of Welsh genealogical works appeared across the nineteenth century – including as products of Sir Thomas Phillipps's (1792–1872) Middle Hill Press – augmenting the ancestral consciousness which had been reinforced through the works of Pennant, Yorke and the new county histories.[69] *Gwaith Lewis Glyn Cothi* (1837), a publication of the Cymmrodorion Society, was packed with genealogical references, linking the gentry of fifteenth-century Wales to the tradition of bardic patronage. The year 1846 saw the eagerly anticipated publication of Meyrick's two-volume edition of Lewys Dwnn's *Heraldic Visitations of Wales* for the Welsh Manuscripts Society. This was substantially improved by the explanatory footnotes provided by W. W. E. Wynne, who was a principal cultivator of Welsh genealogical writing across the nineteenth century. The most acclaimed publication in this genre was Thomas Nicholas's *Annals and Antiquities of the Counties and County Families of Wales* (1872), packaged as 'a complete account of the great families of the Principality, combining as far as possible ancient with modern times'. Other works arranged the genealogical material on a regional basis, including the monumental *Limbus Patrum Morganiae et Glamorganiae* (1886) compiled by G. T. Clark (1809–98) of Talygarn in collaboration with Robert Jones (1811–89) of Fonmon; the six-volume compilation known as *Powys Fadog* (1881–7), collated by J. Y. W. Lloyd (1816–87) of Clochfaen and Plas Madoc; and John E. Griffith's *Pedigrees of Caernarvonshire and Anglesey Families* (1914). These works shine a spotlight on the volatility within Welsh landed society, highlighting a multitude of extinct families and frequent changes in proprietorship. But irrespective of these realities the overriding function of these works was to demonstrate continuity, parading landowning families and their country houses en bloc as innate fixtures of Wales's past and present.

The late nineteenth century also witnessed a surge in the publication of individual Welsh family pedigrees. Print runs were generally modest and occasionally restricted to private circulation, though this constituted a new departure for a product which had traditionally been fixed to manuscript, roll and church monument. An early exception was John Thomas's 'Genealogical Account of the Families of Penrhyn and Cochwillan' appended to William Williams's *Observations on the*

Snowdon Mountains (1802). Wynne published his own Peniarth family pedigree in 1872, followed by similar works on Clenennau (1876) and Ynysmaengwyn (1900). In south Wales, John Rowland (1824–91) produced comparable works on Dolaucothi (1877) and Cefn Mabli (1881), and following Wynne's example, the families of Gwysaney, Harpton, Eriviat and Tal-y-Coed published their own pedigrees.[70] The pre-eminent example of Welsh family history writing was Sir John Wynn's *History of the Gwydir family*, compiled in manuscript in the early seventeenth century. First published in 1770, with revised editions in 1827, 1878 and 1927, it was esteemed as an important Welsh history text and provided an inspiration for later compilations. Published family pedigrees were occasionally expanded to take narrative forms, with an assortment of gentry family histories produced or commissioned by landowners across the late nineteenth and early twentieth centuries.[71] It is tempting to characterise many of the later works as memorials to the fading prominence of a once-great landed elite.

Another branch of genealogical writing promoted across the period were chronological lists of county officeholders and members of parliament, dominated by the gentry and their residences. Rowlands's *Mona Antiqua Restaurata* had included 'catalogues' of the county's sheriffs and parliamentary representatives (which nineteenth-century owners of the book regularly kept up to date with annotations). Revd John Montgomery Traherne's *List of the knights of the shire for the county of Glamorgan* (1822) is typical of this type of work.[72] The most ambitious was probably Edward Breese's *Kalendars of Gwynedd* (1873) – a record of officeholding in Anglesey, Caernarfonshire and Merionethshire, again augmented by Wynne and dedicated to Lord Mostyn as lord lieutenant of Merioneth. Individual entries in these compilations were often expanded to incorporate biographical and genealogical notes. As with publications such as Edward Parry's *Royal progresses and visits to Wales* (1850, 1851) and the facsimile edition of Thomas Dineley's *Progress of the Duke of Beaufort through Wales* (1864, 1888) they emphasised the role of the gentry in connecting the history of Wales and its localities to the institutions of the British state. William Retlaw Williams's *Parliamentary History of the Principality of Wales* (1895) can be viewed as the crowning manifestation of this genre, published at a time when the landowning families saturating its pages had lost their grip on the parliamentary representation of Welsh constituencies.

In the period before the establishment of county record offices and the National Library, country houses were important storehouses of historical records. The endeavour to publish the texts of medieval Welsh literature preserved within country houses proceeded alongside initiatives to publish the administrative, legal and personal records created by landed families and estates.[73] This antiquarian activity was occasionally undertaken for practical reasons. The squire of Bronwydd, Sir Thomas Davies Lloyd (1820–77), produced *Baronia de Kemeys* (1862) as a compilation of deeds and documents which supported his efforts to assert rights as self-proclaimed lord marcher of the barony of Cemais, and John Lloyd (1833–1915) of Dinas published various *Historical Memoranda* pertaining to mineral rights and ancient customs in Breconshire and its Great Forest (1903–5).[74] Other works served as aids to further research: Traherne's *Stradling Correspondence* (1840); Clark's *Cartae et Alia Munimenta Quae ad Dominium de Glamorgancia Pertinent* (1885–1910); Morris Charles Jones's *Old Herbert papers at Powis Castle* (1886); Walter de Gray Birch's *Catalogue of the Penrice and Margam Abbey manuscripts* (1893) which underpinned his *History of Margam Abbey* (1897); Joseph Bradney's *The Diary of Walter Powell* (1907); and W. M. Myddelton's *Chirk Castle Accounts* (1910–31), for example. Research of family and estate archives fuelled new contributions to the history of Wales: historical biographies such as Traherne's *Historical Notices of Sir Matthew Cradock* (1840) and seminal studies like John Roland Phillips's *Memoirs of the Civil War in Wales and the Marches* (1874).

The Cambrian Archaeological Association

The establishment of the Cambrian Archaeological Association in 1846 was an important milestone in the intellectual and cultural history of Wales. Landowners from across Wales joined with a raft of Welsh clerics to issue an enthusiastic response to Harry Longueville Jones's (1806–70) 'manifesto' for the establishment of the association.[75] His proposals for a *mansionarium* and *chartularum* as part of a wide-ranging investigation of national antiquities encouraged a natural affinity between landowners and the objectives of the association. For half a century its presidency was dominated by leading landowners; others served on the central committee, acted as local secretaries or involved themselves in the local committees responsible for organising and hosting annual meetings across

Wales.[76] The various activities of the association – visits and excursions, discussions, exhibitions and lectures, dinners and receptions – were integrated into the social life of Wales's landowning class. Evelyn Lewes's recollections of being *Out with the Cambrians* (1934) provide important insights into how gentlewomen engaged with this culture, whilst also demonstrating how the country houses of Wales provided an essential part of the framework of Welsh antiquarianism. The architecture, family portraits, manuscripts, heraldry, antiquarian curiosities and archaeological finds displayed at country houses and estates provided a regular focus for the association's excursions, with members occasionally lending such items for public exhibitions.[77] Many country house libraries in Wales carved out a space for runs of *Archaeologia Cambrensis*: by the time of his death in 1903, C. A. Wynne-Finch had 156 volumes of the journal on his shelves at Foelas.[78] The association played an essential role in cultivating a deeper understanding of the Welsh past in all its dimensions and provided an important outlet for the antiquarian interests and insights of the gentry. The obituary for Revd John Montgomery Traherne (1788–1860) of Coedrhiglan noted that:

> He was one of the earliest members of our Association; contributed to our transactions; attended most of our meetings; took an active personal interest in our proceedings and persuaded more members to join our ranks than almost any other amongst us. His knowledge of Archaeology in general, but especially of Welsh records and remains of all kinds, was most extensive and accurate.[79]

Twenty years later similar attributes were highlighted in the obituary to W. W. E. Wynne of Peniarth:

> By his death, Welsh archaeology and genealogy have lost one of their best exponents. For the last generation no single person has done so much to elucidate the antiquities and family histories of Wales.[80]

The significant contributions made towards the various dimensions of Welsh antiquarian study by Traherne and Wynne, Octavius Morgan of The Friars, W. O. Stanley of Penrhos, Sir Stephen Glynne of Hawarden,

H. H. Knight of Tythegston, G. T. Clark of Tal-y-Garn, Thomas Wakeman of The Graig and G. G. Francis of Swansea are well known.[81] Jane Aaron has also analysed how women engaged with and contributed towards this culture – Eliza Constance Campbell (1796–1864), a daughter of Richard Pryce of Gunley, Maria Jane Williams (c.1795–1873) of Aberpergwm and Mary Isabella Jones-Parry (d. 1899) of Aberdunant are amongst the Welsh gentlewomen antiquaries not referenced elsewhere in this contribution.[82] Lady Enid Quin (d. 1891) of Dunraven was characterised in her obituary as having 'closely identified herself with the interesting annals of Cambria [having] entered with ardour upon the study of the Welsh language and history of Glamorganshire'.[83] The transactions of the Cambrian Archaeological Association evince widespread landowner engagement with Welsh antiquarianism. Joseph Ablett (1773–1848) who purchased Llanbedr Hall, Denbighshire, in 1804 was remembered as 'one of the earliest and warmest friends of *Archaeologia Cambrensis*', who showed a 'constant interest' in the success of the association.[84] Howel Gwyn (d. 1888) of Dyffryn, Neath, was thanked for the 'great interest' he took in the 'proceedings and welfare of the Association'.[85] Ancestry acted as an important driver of this antiquarian engagement: Gwyn was commemorated as 'a thorough Welshman [who] could trace his descent from Trahearn ap Einion of Talgarth who lived in the twelfth century'. Thomas Jones (1819–94) of Llanerchrugog's connection to the association was articulated in similar terms: he was 'passionately devoted to genealogy ... descended from the First Royal Tribe, into whose history and descent he entered with all the ardour of a Welshman'.[86] This culture persevered into the early twentieth century with the final generation of landowners to hold positions of status and authority within Welsh society. Hugh Robert Hughes (1827–1911) of Kinmel was recognised as 'a student deeply versed in Welsh genealogy'; W. Gwynne-Hughes of Glancothi was characterised as an 'ardent devotee' of archaeology and genealogy; and C. S. Mainwaring (1845–1920) of Galltfaenan was recognised for his 'extensive knowledge of Welsh Archaeology generally' and for his special interest in the 'history of old families and old houses'.[87]

Conclusion

In 1926, Herbert M. Vaughan (1870–1948) regretted the 'indifference or ignorance displayed by many of the gentry towards the history, literature, archaeology, legends, music and folklore of their native land'.[88] His observation cautions against pushing the arguments made across this chapter too far. Yet the squire of Llangoedmor was himself a product of the antiquarian culture which had been fostered across the nineteenth century. The interlinked strands of this chapter combine to demonstrate that Wales's landowning class engaged with and shaped an antiquarian culture which had distinctively Welsh dimensions. This incorporated history with literature, language, music and topography; aligned with, absorbed and augmented the gentry's continuing obsession with ancestry; and encouraged the preservation of cultural patronage as a core aspect of Welsh gentility. This antiquarianism appears to have permeated throughout Welsh landed society, incorporating gentlewomen and gentlemen, new and more established aristocratic entities. The meshing of antiquarian interest, ancestral pride and cultural patronage provided the ingredients of a 'high' Welsh culture which landowners employed in the preservation of their status and exercise of authority in Welsh society. It encouraged some interaction with the Welsh language, notably through eisteddfodic activities and in efforts to publish and translate earlier Welsh texts, though it was predominately an antiquarian culture articulated through the English language. Importantly, it was entirely compatible with the British and English attachments professed by the landed elite. This antiquarianism nevertheless played an important role in shaping a Welsh consciousness amongst the gentry who were often enthusiastic in their assertions of Welsh identity. Many keenly participated in the dramatic re-enactments of Welsh history performed as part of the National Pageant of Wales in 1909.[89] As Martin Johnes has pointed out, prior to the creation of national institutions and devolved structures of statehood, Wales owed much of its existence to the fact that culture and history were employed to assert Welsh identity, express national consciousness and present Wales as a distinctive entity within the United Kingdom.[90] Through their ancestral and cultural patriotism, landowners of the nineteenth century played a part in preserving Welsh nationhood. Interpretations of an 'anglicised' gentry detached from and disinterested in all things Welsh appear to be misplaced. This supplements Bethan Jenkins's assertion that historians should look beyond language for markers of difference between a politically unified England and Wales, and supports Paul O'Leary's conclusion that Welsh patriotism took multiple and contested forms across the nineteenth century.[91] The patriotic vision of Wales and Welsh history promoted so successfully through the organs of radical nonconformity from the second half of the nineteenth century should not detract from the concurrent existence of an earlier and alternative patriotic version of Wales and the Welsh past cultivated by and fully embracing of the gentry.

Notes

1. Huw Pryce, 'Culture, Identity and the Medieval Revival in Victorian Wales', *Proceedings of the Harvard Celtic Colloquium*, 31 (2011), 1–40; Huw Pryce, *J. E. Lloyd and the Creation of Welsh History: Renewing a Nation's Past* (Cardiff, 2011); Huw Pryce and Neil Evans (eds), *Writing a Small Nation's Past: Wales in Comparative Perspective, 1850–1950* (Farnham, 2013); Huw Pryce and Gwilym Owen, 'Medieval Welsh Law and the Mid-Victorian Foreshore', *Journal of Legal History*, 35/2 (2014), 172–99; Huw Pryce, *Writing Welsh History: From the Early Middle Ages to the Twenty-first Century* (Oxford, 2022).
2. Huw Pryce encouraged the author's initial exploration of these themes in Shaun Evans, 'Inventing the Bosworth tradition: Richard ap Hywel, the "King's Hole" and the Mostyn family image in the nineteenth century', *WHR*, 29/2 (2018), 218–53.
3. Philip Jenkins, 'The creation of an "Ancient Gentry": Glamorgan, 1760–1840', *WHR*, 12/1 (1984), 29–49; Matthew Cragoe, *An Anglican Aristocracy: The moral economy of the landed estate in Carmarthenshire 1832–95* (Oxford, 1996), pp. 104–9, 367.
4. Gabriele Clemens, 'Ancestors, castles, tradition: the German and Italian nobility and the discovery of the Middle Ages in the nineteenth century', *Journal of Modern Italian Studies*, 8/1 (2003), 1–15; Jan Broadway, *'No historie so meete': Gentry culture and the development of local history in Elizabethan and early Stuart England* (Manchester, 2006).
5. Rosemary Sweet, *Antiquaries: The Discovery of the Past in Eighteenth-century Britain* (London, 2004), p. xiv.
6. For useful discussions on the concept, see Frank Price Jones, 'The Gwerin of Wales', in Geraint Jenkins (ed.), *Studies in Folk Life: Essays in Honour of Iorwerth C. Peate* (London, 1969), pp. 1–13; Prys Morgan, 'The Gwerin of Wales – Myth and Reality', in Ian Hume and W. T. R. Pryce (eds), *The Welsh and their Country* (Llandysul, 1986), pp. 134–52.
7. Prys Morgan, 'A Nation of Nonconformists: Thomas Rees and Nonconformist History', in Evans and Pryce (eds), *A Small Nation's Past*, pp. 97–110.

8   For prominent examples, see O. M. Edwards, *Wales* (London, 1901), pp. 308–9, 337; David Williams, *A History of Modern Wales* (London, 1950), p. 269; A. O. H. Jarman, 'Wales a part of England, 1485–1800', in D. Myrddin Lloyd (ed.), *The Historical Basis of Welsh Nationalism* (Cardiff, 1950), pp. 78–98; Gwynfor Evans, *Land of my Fathers* (Swansea, 1978), pp. 304–9, 316–20; Geraint H. Jenkins, *The Foundations of Modern Wales: Wales, 1642–1780* (Oxford, 1987), pp. 386, 399–400, 417–18; Kenneth O. Morgan, *Wales in British Politics, 1868–1922* (Cardiff, 1991), pp. 5–10; Glanmor Williams, *Renewal and Reformation: Wales, c.1415–1642* (Oxford, 1993), pp. 461–6.

9   Prys Morgan, 'From a Death to a View: The Hunt for the Welsh Past in the Romantic Period', in Eric Hobsbawm and Terence Ranger (eds), *The Invention of Tradition* (Cambridge, 1983), pp. 43–100.

10 Jane Williams, *The Literary Remains of the Rev. Thomas Price*, 2 vols (Llandovery, 1854), I, p. x.

11 Williams, *Renewal and Reformation*, pp. 461–6.

12 For examples see Sarah Ward Clavier, *Royalism, Religion and Revolution: Wales, 1640–1688* (Woodbridge, 2021), pp. 25–96; Sadie Jarrett, *Gentility in Early Modern Wales: The Salesbury Family 1450–1720* (Cardiff, 2024), pp. 151–96.

13 Geraint H. Jenkins, 'Historical Writing in the Eighteenth Century', in Branwen Jarvis (ed.), *A Guide to Welsh Literature c.1700–1800* (Cardiff, 2000), pp. 23–44 (p. 25).

14 Philip Jenkins, 'From Edward Lhuyd to Iolo Morganwyg: The death and rebirth of Glamorgan antiquarianism', *Morgannwg*, 23 (1979), 29–47.

15 Eiluned Rees, 'Pre-1820 Welsh subscription lists', *Journal of the Welsh Bibliographical Society*, 11/1–2 (1973–4), 85–119.

16 Eiluned Rees, 'An introductory survey of 18th century Welsh libraries', *Journal of the Welsh Bibliographical Society*, 10/4 (1971), 197–258 (p. 214); Bethan Jenkins, *Between Wales and England: Anglophone Welsh Writing of the Eighteenth Century* (Cardiff, 2017), pp. 143, 151.

17 For sample eighteenth-century library catalogues, see National Library of Wales [NLW], Peniarth Estate, PB3; NLW MS 9077C; Bangor University Archives and Special Collections [BUASC], Penrhos VII, 266. See also Kathryn Hurlock, 'Reading Medieval Wales: David Powel's *Historie of Cambria* (1584) and its Readers', in Rosamund Oates and Jessica G. Purdy (eds), *Communities of Print: Books and their Readers in Early Modern Europe* (Leiden, 2022), pp. 178–93.

18 *The Cambrian*, 5 March 1804, 3.

19 Shaun Evans, '"An antient seat of a gentleman of Wales": The place of the *plas* in Thomas Pennant's *Tour in Wales* (1778–83)', in Terence Dooley and Christopher Ridgway (eds), *The Country House and its Visitors* (Dublin, 2023), pp. 196–219; Eric Griffiths, *Philip Yorke I: Squire of Erthig* (Wrexham, 1995), pp. 141–65.

20 'Welsh archaiology: the general advertisement', in Owen Jones et al., *The Myvyrian Archaiology of Wales*, 3 vols (London, 1801 and 1807), I, p. v.
21 Morgan, 'Hunt for the Welsh past', pp. 74–8; Helen Barlow, 'The Celtic Revival', in Trevor Herbert, Martin V. Clarke and Helen Barlow (eds), *A History of Welsh Music* (Cambridge, 2022), pp. 171–94.
22 R. T. Jenkins and Helen Ramage, *A History of the Honourable Society of Cymmrodorion* (London, 1951); Glenda Carr, 'The London-Welsh', in Philip Henry Jones and Eiluned Rees (eds), *A Nation and its Books: A History of the Book in Wales* (Aberystwyth, 1998), pp. 147–56.
23 Cathryn Charnell-White, *Welsh Poetry of the French Revolution, 1789–1805* (Cardiff, 2012), pp. 32–42.
24 Mark Girouard, *The Return to Camelot: Chivalry and the English Gentleman* (New Haven, 1981).
25 NLW Misc. Records 546. I am grateful to Sara Fox and Dr Lowri Ann Rees for this reference.
26 Jenkins, *Between England and Wales*, pp. 139–72.
27 Brynley F. Roberts, 'Scholarly Publishing 1820–1922', in Jones and Rees (eds), *A Nation and its Books*, pp. 221–35.
28 *The Cambrian*, 19 December 1818, 4; W. J. Rees, 'Welsh Literary Societies', *The Cambro-Briton*, 3 (1822), 224–33.
29 William Cathrall, *The History of North Wales*, 2 vols (Manchester, 1828), I, 289–305; Hywel Teifi Edwards, *Yr Eisteddfod* (Llandysul, 1976), pp. 34–78.
30 *The Cambrian*, 12 October 1822, 3.
31 *Gorawen Meirion* (Bala, 1825).
32 Osian Ellis, *The Story of the Harp in Wales* (Cardiff, 1991), pp. 65–73.
33 *Carnarvon & Denbigh Herald*, 28 September 1850, Supplement, 1–4; *The Cambrian News*, 30 August 1872, 4.
34 Thomas Griffith, *The Gwyneddion; Or an account of the Royal Denbigh Eisteddfod* (Chester, 1830), pp. 1–6, 171–4.
35 Marion Löffler, 'Hall, Augusta, Lady Llanover (1802–1896)', *Dictionary of Welsh Biography*, https://biography.wales/article/s10-HALL-AUG-1802 (accessed 6 November 2023) and further references noted therein.
36 *The Cambrian*, 11 April 1840, 2.
37 *The Gentleman's Magazine*, 89 (January 1819), 3–4.
38 Angharad Llwyd, 'Catalogue of Welsh Manuscripts', *Transactions of the Cymmrodorion*, 2 (1828), 36–58; Aneurin Owen, 'Catalogue of Welsh Manuscripts', *Transactions of the Cymmrodorion*, 2/4 (1843), 400–18.
39 Thomas Lloyd, 'Country-house libraries of the eighteenth and nineteenth centuries', in Jones and Rees (eds), *A Nation and its Books*, pp. 135–46.
40 Shaun Evans, 'Book cultures, gentry identities and the Welsh country house library: problems and possibilities for future research', *WHR*, 31/1 (2022), 17–54.

41 NLW MSS. 6619B, 23281B, 23282C; BUASC, Penrhos VII, 266; NLW, Dolaucothi estate, L6607; *Monmouthshire Merlin*, 25 February 1865, 4; *Montgomery County Times*, 19 August 1899, 8.
42 'The Publisher to the Reader', in William Rowlands, *Cambrian Bibliography*, ed. D. Silvan Evans (Llanidloes, 1869), pp. vii–viii.
43 The best guide is Herbert M. Vaughan, *The Welsh book-plates in the collection of Sir Evan Davies Jones* (London, 1920).
44 NLW MS 14990F.
45 Evelyn Lewes, *Out with the Cambrians* (London, 1934), p. 199.
46 Pryce, *Writing Welsh History*, pp. 215–25.
47 Richard Colt Hoare, 'Editor's Preface', *The Itinerary of Archbishop Baldwin through Wales*, 2 vols (London, 1806), I, pp. v–vi.
48 Lloyd Bowen, 'Fashioning communities: the county in early modern Wales', in Jacqueline Eales and Andrew Hopper (eds), *The County Community in Seventeenth-century England and Wales* (Hatfield, 2012), pp. 77–99.
49 Pryce, *Writing Welsh History*, pp. 148–54, 193–6.
50 David Williams, *The History of Monmouthshire* (London, 1796), pp. i–xi.
51 William Coxe, *An Historical Tour in Monmouthshire* (London, 1801), p. ii.
52 Jonathan Williams, *The History of Radnorshire* (Tenby, 1859), pp. 1–10.
53 R. C. B. Oliver, 'James Davies of Moorcourt, Esquire, 1777–1856', *Radnorshire Society Transactions*, 58 (1988), 47.
54 Theophilus Jones, *A History of the County of Brecknock*, 2 vols (Brecknock, 1805), I, pp. vi–vii; Samuel Rush Meyrick, *The History and Antiquities of the County of Cardigan* (London, 1808), pp. xvii–xviii.
55 Edwin Poole, *The Illustrated History and Biography of Brecknockshire* (Brecknock, 1886), pp. x–xi.
56 Andrew Green, 'The Monmouthshire and Caerleon Antiquarian Association', *gwallter* (13 October 2018), *https://gwallter.com/archaeology/the-monmouthshire-and-caerleon-antiquarian-association.html* (accessed 6 November 2023).
57 'Original proposal for the formation of the Club', *Montgomeryshire Collections*, 1 (1868), pp. i–iv; Andrew Green, 'The Powysland Club: its origin and early development', *gwallter* (13 May 2018), *https://gwallter.com/archaeology/the-powysland-club-its-origin-and-early-development.html* (accessed 6 November 2023).
58 Neil Evans, 'Remaking Nations and their Histories: The social, political and intellectual world of the early Powysland Club', *Montgomeryshire Collections*, 109 (2021), 45–86 (p. 161).
59 Paul O'Leary, 'Town and Nation: Writing Urban Histories in nineteenth- and early twentieth-century Wales', in Evans and Pryce (eds), *A Small Nation's Past*, pp. 209–22.
60 J. D. Davies, *A History of West Gower, Part 1* (Swansea, 1877), preface [p. i].
61 Jenkins, 'The creation of an "Ancient Gentry"', 29–49.

62 J. Gwenogvryn Evans, *Report on Manuscripts in the Welsh Language*, 2 vols (London, 1898), I, pt 2, p. vi.
63 Francis Jones, 'An approach to Welsh genealogy', *Transactions of the Honourable Society of Cymmrodorion* (1948), 303–446.
64 Michael Siddons, *Welsh Pedigree Rolls* (Aberystwyth, 1996); Ben Guy, *Medieval Welsh Genealogy* (Woodbridge, 2020).
65 Uncatalogued MS, Brynddu Hall, Anglesey.
66 John Jones, *The History of Wales* (London, 1824), pp. 266–303.
67 Jones, *History of Wales*, p. viii.
68 R. D. Rees, 'Electioneering ideals current in South Wales, 1790–1830', *WHR*, 2 (1964), 233–50. For examples see *North Wales Chronicle*, 17 October 1868, 8; 20 November 1880, 3.
69 Examples include Thomas Phillipps, *Glamorgan Pedigrees* (Worcester, 1845); Thomas Phillipps, *Pedigrees of Caermarthenshire, Cardiganshire and Pembrokeshire* (Worcester, 1859); William Edmunds, *Some old families in the neighbourhood of Lampeter* (Tenby, 1860); Thomas Nicholas, *The History and Antiquities of Glamorganshire and its Families* (London, 1874); William Valentine Lloyd, *Pedigrees of Montgomeryshire Families* (London, 1888); Henry Owen, *Old Pembrokeshire Families* (London, 1902).
70 W. Bryan Cooke, *The seize quartiers of the family of Bryan Cooke* (London, 1857); George Cornewall Lewis, *Pedigree of the family of Lewis of Harpton* (London, 1862); W. Wynne Ffoulkes, *Pedigree of the family of Ffoulkes of Eriviat* (London, 1874); Joseph Bradney, *Genealogical memoranda relating to the families of Hopkins of Llanfihangel Ystern Llewern …* (London, 1889).
71 Examples include *A Memoir of Chirk Castle and the Myddelton Family* (Chester, 1859); J. Askew Roberts, *Wynnstay and the Wynns* (Oswestry, 1876); John Lord Hanmer, *A Memorial of the Parish and Family of Hanmer in Flintshire* (London, 1887); W. P. Williams, *A Monograph of the Windsor Family* (Cardiff, 1879); Rachel J. Lowe, *Farm and its inhabitants with some account of the Lloyds of Dolobran* (London, 1883); J. Roland Phillips, *Memoirs of the Ancient Family of Owen of Orielton* (London, 1886); R. J. Lloyd Price, *The History of Rulace, or Rhiwlas* (1899); W. M. Myddelton, *Pedigree of the Family of Myddelton of Gwaynynog …* (1910); Margaret Mahler, *A History of Chirk Castle and Chirkland* (1912); T. A. Glenn and Ll. N. V. Lloyd-Mostyn, *The Mostyns of Mostyn* (London, 1925); Earl of Dunraven, *Dunraven Castle, Glamorgan: Some Notes of its History and Associations* (London 1926); T. A. Glenn, *The Family of Griffith of Garn* (London, 1934).
72 Other examples include John Hughes, *A History of the Parliamentary Representation of the County of Cardigan* (Aberystwyth, 1849); Joseph Joseph, 'Sheriffs of Brecknockshire and Monmouthshire', *The Cambrian Journal* (1868), 258–90; William V. Lloyd, *The Sheriffs of Montgomeryshire* (London,

1878); J. Roland Phillips, *A List of the Sheriffs of Cardiganshire* (Carmarthen, 1868); Henry Taylor, *Historic Notices of the Borough and County Town of Flint* (London, 1883), pp. 45–66; James Allen, *Notes on the Sheriffs of Pembrokeshire, 1541–1899* (Tenby, 1900); James Buckley, *Genealogies of the Carmarthenshire Sheriffs, 1539–1913*, 2 vols (Carmarthen, 1910–13).

73 Michael Riordan, 'Materials for History? Publishing records as a historical practice in eighteenth- and nineteenth-century England', *History of Humanities*, 2/1 (2017), 51–77.

74 Pryce, 'Medieval Revival in Victorian Wales', 11–12.

75 H. Longueville Jones, 'On the Study and Preservation of National Antiquities', *Archaeologia Cambrensis* [*AC*], 1/1 (January 1846), 3–16; 'The Proposed Cambrian Archaeological Association', *AC*, 1/4 (1846), 460–5.

76 Donald Moore, 'Cambrian Meetings 1847–1997', *AC*, 147 (1998), 3–55.

77 For example see Ian Kennedy, 'The Wrexham Art Treasures exhibition of 1876', *The British Art Journal*, 19/3 (2018/19), 80–6.

78 NLW, Voelas and Cefnamwlch estate, KB/15.

79 *AC*, 3rd series, 22 (April 1860), 140.

80 *AC*, 4th series, 11/43 (November 1880), 229–33.

81 A. Geoffrey Veysey, 'Sir Stephen Glynne', *Flintshire Historical Society Journal*, 30 (1982), 151–70; Christopher Smith, 'William Owen Stanley of Penrhos', *AC*, 133 (1984), 83–90; Sandra Thomas, *George Grant Francis of Swansea: Antiquary, Philanthropist and Civic Dignitary* (West Glamorgan Archives, 1993); Brian Ll. James (ed.), *G. T. Clark: Scholar Ironmaster in the Victorian Age* (Cardiff, 1998).

82 Jane Aaron, *Nineteenth-century Women's Writing in Wales: Nation, Gender and Identity* (Cardiff, 2010), pp. 47–73. See also Gwyneth Tyson Roberts, *Jane Williams, Ysgafell* (Cardiff, 2020).

83 *The Western Mail*, 3 July 1891, 5.

84 *AC*, 3/10 (April 1848), 171.

85 *AC*, 5th series, 5/17 (January 1888), 57.

86 *AC*, 5th series, 12 (1895), 224–27.

87 *AC*, 6th series, 12 (1912), 151–2; 6th series, 20 (1920), 196, 289–90.

88 Herbert Vaughan, *The South Wales Squires* (London, 1926), p. 204.

89 Hywel Teifi Edwards, *The National Pageant of Wales* (Llandysul, 2009).

90 Martin Johnes, 'History and the Making and Remaking of Wales', *History*, 5/343 (2015), 667–8.

91 Jenkins, *Between England and Wales*, p. 2; Paul O'Leary, 'The languages of patriotism in Wales, 1840–1880', in Geraint H. Jenkins (ed.), *The Welsh Language and its Social Domains, 1801–1911* (Cardiff, 2000), pp. 533–60.

12

'Th'enlighten'd crowd with grateful raptures glow': History, Setting Norms and Victorian Modernity in Eisteddfod Competitions, 1815–1855

Marion Löffler

When infant Science first began
To shed its influence on man,
And on the Fathers of our Isle
With look benignant deign'd to smile:

The Seer, whom Nature's open page
And meditation rendered sage,
Beneath the oak's wide-spreading shade,
Instruction to the crowd convey'd.

Th'enlighten'd crowd with grateful raptures glow,
And crown his head with sacred *Mistletoe*,
With mistletoe the leaves of oak they bind,
And hail him Druid, friend of humankind![1]

This 'druidic song' from Edward Jones's *Bardic Museum*, its 'words modern, altho' in imitation of the antient', was performed at the opening of the 1822 Cymmrodorion eisteddfod in London.[2] Casting the druid as nature's teacher who forged links between science, education and popular enlightenment, it is emblematic of the apparently paradox marriage of the Celtic, the historic and the modern in the Welsh cultural discourse of the first half of the nineteenth century. The concept of the druids as 'Fathers of the Isle', increasingly associated with a proto-Protestant Christianity and an imperial Enlightenment, suited late Georgian and Victorian eisteddfod patrons, organisers and competitors, all of whom had to negotiate conflicting demands. Wishing to imbue Wales with a venerable past to confirm its nationhood, they also needed to demonstrate the politically and socially non-threatening and 'useful' character of eisteddfodau whilst proving to themselves and the world that their nation was as modern as it was respectable.[3]

To this end, gentry, *hen bersoniaid llengar* and the middle classes steered cultural institutions into the safe haven of acceptable rational entertainment, just as they whitewashed the Welsh radicals of 'generation 1789' into harmless schoolmasters, translators and heirs to bardic traditions.[4] In this endeavour, historical competition subjects became convenient ideological vehicles, because they were less likely to touch on politically and religiously contentious issues than contemporary topics.[5] They satisfied a public discourse which produced title pages like that of *Seren Gomer*: the periodical title printed large in Iolo Morganwg's invented runic *coelbren y beirdd*, yet subtitle and druidic motto – 'Cyfrwng Gwybodaeth Cyffredinol i'r Cymry' (Medium of General Knowledge for the Welsh) and 'Clust y Doethion a gais Wybodaeth' (The Ear of the Wise gains Knowledge) – endorsing classic Enlightenment values (Figure 1).[6]

The eisteddfod competitions contributing to this discourse fit into the contemporary European penchant for academic prize contests.[7] Established nations like France, those aspiring to nationhood like Serbia, bemoaning a loss of statehood like Poland, or attempting to invent a nation like Belgium, perceived competitions as a means to advance progress while reinforcing or creating national identities. Given the near-absence of institutions of higher education in Wales, eisteddfod competitions were particularly important as significant facilitators of education, the transfer of knowledge and the development of research methodologies. Eisteddfod prizes provided financial and social patronage, while the prestige bestowed on winners smoothed the way to publication and national or even international fame.

The apex of these developments, the published works of Welsh historians and scholars and the later Royal National Eisteddfod of Wales, has been researched by scholars, such as Hywel Teifi Edwards, Neil Evans, Paul O'Leary and Huw Pryce, on whose shoulders this contribution rests. This article turns to earlier and perhaps less obvious

Figure 1: Title page of *Seren Gomer* (1823)

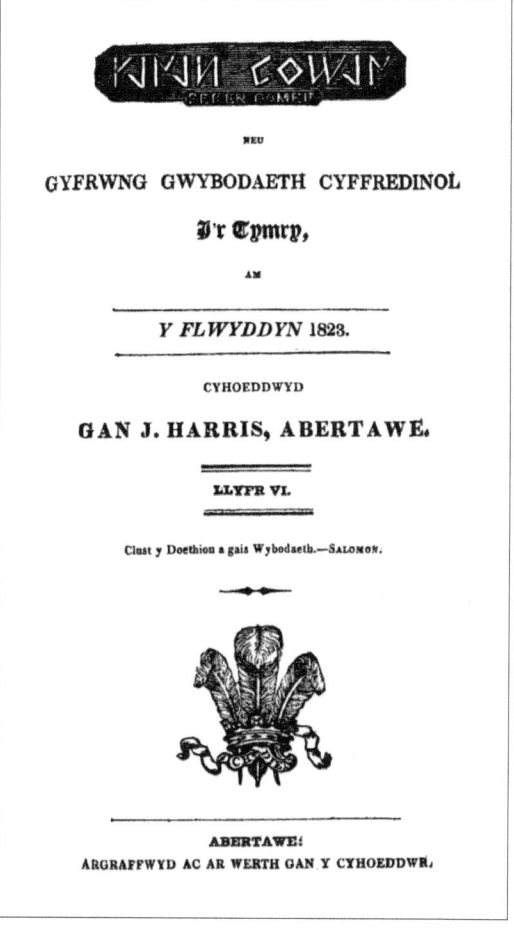

aspects of a movement which framed the future national festival as a form of rational entertainment aimed at improving morals and imparting useful knowledge whilst avoiding political content that could be interpreted as subversive. As early as 1822 eisteddfod advertisements associated the Celtic and the medieval with Empire, Enlightenment and 'Use'.[8] The *cywydd* competition on mythical 'Hu Gadarn' described him as the imperial 'planter of the first colony in this island', the essay on the Welsh language focused 'on its particular Use, with reference to the Poems of the Welsh Bards, in elucidating Historical Occurrences', while those on 'Wales from the Conquest in 1284 to the Union in 1535' and a

'Translation of the Law Triads' would further critical engagement with political and legal history.[9]

The past as an instrument of social engineering

References to the normative educational moral and utilitarian value of eisteddfodau and their competitions abound in advertisements, reports and justifications. Words like 'trefnus' (organised) and 'parchus' (respectable) litter descriptions of local events, their participants never guilty of 'glythineb na meddwdod' (gluttony or drunkenness).[10] The *Glamorgan Gazette and Merthyr Guardian* thanked the Merthyr Tydfil Cymmrodorion Society for the 'respectable' subjects of their 1824 event. Though consisting 'of mere workmen, yet their orderly conduct, their steady endeavours to investigate Welsh literature and their indefeisable [*sic*] attachment to their native Cymru' had entitled them to the respect of their countrymen.[11] As early as 1823, the Flintshire eisteddfod awarded £3 for the best essay 'in English on the utility of holding eisteddfods'.[12] Outstanding Welsh prize essays and poems led to follow-up competitions on translating them into English to showcase Welsh cultural achievements, but also to demonstrate that Welsh eisteddfodau did not stand in the way of a 'modern' bilingualism. Criticisms forced regular justifications. In 1843, the organisers of a Llanrwst Christmas eisteddfod defended their competitions against those who considered learning in general as leading to 'gyfeddach a segurdod' (dissipation and laziness) and an engagement with the poetic arts:

> o nemmawr bwys, am nad ydyw yn dysgu trafnidiaeth nac amaethyddiaeth na mwnyddiaeth; ond o'r ochr arall eu bod yn hytrach yn niweidiol trwy ddyfetha yr amser a ellid dreulio yn y pethau dan sylw. Fel gwrthateb i hyn dywedaf fo'r awenyddiaeth yn dysgu ac yn arwain at y pethau uchod, ac yn gwneuthur dyn yn fwy cymwys i'r ddyledswyddau ydynt gysylltiedig âg ef ... y mae barddoniaeth yn arwain yr amaethydd i fod yn fwy amaethyddol – yn arwain y celfyddydwr i fod yn fwy celfyddol – ac yn arwain y masnachwr i fod yn fwy masnachol.[13]

> of no importance, since they do not teach commerce nor agriculture or mining, but on the contrary are damaging, by

wasting time that could be spent on the subjects mentioned. As a refutation of this I say that poetry teaches and leads to the above things, and makes man more qualified for his duties ... poetry makes the agriculturist more agricultural – leads to the artist being more artistic – and leads to the merchant being more mercantile.

Refuting similar accusations of uselessness, Thomas Jenkins stressed in his 1838 Abergavenny essay on the history of the town and monastery of Neath 'that History writing is beneficial and profitable; to enlighten, civilise and moralise the country' ('fod Hanesyddiaeth yn llesiol a byddiol; er goleuo, gwareiddio, a moesoli'r wlad').[14] In 1853, at the last Abergavenny Cymreigyddion Society eisteddfod, Sir Benjamin Hall judged that their early hopes of being 'both national and useful' without giving 'offence to any one' had been fulfilled, since their competitions did not 'interfere in political questions nor touch upon religious topics'.[15] Chancellor Williams backed this up, assuring those who had accused the festivals of 'cultivating the Welsh language' that they promoted English, 'for what Welshman who writes for any of the prizes ... does not increase his knowledge of English?'[16] By 1855, the organisers of the Cwmafan Sïon chapel Christmas eisteddfod noted with satisfaction that:

y bydd yr holl gyfansoddwyr yn ennillwyr mawrion oherwydd eu llafur, er nad all pob un gael wobr yma am ei ysgrif. Diau genyf i bob un gael budd i'w feddwl ei hun wrth ysgrifennu ei gyfansoddiad, y bydd pob un yn well aelod cymdeithas, ac yn fwy gwasanaethgar i'w gyd-ddynion, gan ei fod wedi casglu chwaneg o wybodaeth, a hyny wedi gwneuthur argraph da ar ei deimladau.[17]

all contestants will be great winners because of their labour, though not everybody can obtain a prize for his essay. I have no doubt that the mind of each benefits from having written their composition, that each is a better member of society, and more serviceable to his fellow-men, since he has gathered more knowledge, which has made a positive impression on his feelings.

Eisteddfod competitions, then, were part of instituting an apolitical non-threatening, yet national, framework for Welsh cultural engagement to provide moral guidance and improvement for 'those whose lot in life obliged them to labour with their hands for their bread'.[18] In this, the period of a topic counted for its normative value, which was expressed most clearly by prize 'premiums' that measured usefulness in pounds and shillings. The proud 1853 account of 'the benefits diffused throughout the Principality, during the last twenty years, by means of the Eisteddfodau of the Abergavenny Cymreigyddion' concluded with a table of 'the sums of money expended in the reward of native literary merit, and of native artistic and manufacturing skill'. In total, the prizes awarded 'in Medal and Money' between 1834 and 1853 amounted to £2,374.17.0 (about £385,000 in 2024), and thirty-seven harps.[19] Eisteddfodau thus certainly benefited 'poor talented candidates' financially, serving as a 'people's university' that enabled amateur artist and scholarly activity through financial and social support.[20]

Yet, a closer investigation of the weighting of prize moneys reveals the instrumentality of sponsorship in setting norms, as well as the dominance of the written word and of non-contemporary subjects. Of the eleven competitions advertised by the London Cymmrodorion for 1822, the highest premiums of £10 each went to the *cywydd* on Celtic colonist Huw Gadarn and the essay on the 'Welsh Language, and on its particular Use ... in elucidating Historical Occurrences'.[21] The second-highest premium of seven guineas advertised for the 1824 Powys eisteddfod went to an ode on the conquest of Anglesey by Suetonius Paulinus and its effects.[22] The thirty-four prize competitions of the grand Gwent and Dyfed Royal Eisteddfod and Musical Festival held at Cardiff in 1834 reveal a similar distribution.[23] Premiums, medals and miniature 'silver harps' for shorter poems, singers and harpists did not surpass the value of £5 5s. and occasional 'travel costs', yet for longer prize poems and essays, premiums mostly exceeded £10. In this, historical subjects dominated. Only the two modern essays on 'The mineral basin of Glamorgan and the adjoining district and the national benefits arising therefrom' and 'The advantages arising from the preservation of the national language and costumes of Wales' were valued at just over £10. All essays on (pseudo-)historical subjects on the other hand – including the 'authenticity and antiquity of the bardic alphabet', 'primitive Christians by whom Welsh churches were founded', 'the early agriculture and horticulture in Wales' and a 'historical account of the Castles of Glamorgan and Monmouth' – attracted premiums of £10 to £13, and even runners-up earned up to £5. The highest premium went to competition '1. The Chair Medal worth £5, with a premium of £15' (over £3,250 in 2024), for an ode on the Welsh druids.[24] Won by Taliesin ab Iolo's 'Derwyddon', even its translation as 'The British Druids' by Henry Austin Bruce was worth a premium of £10.[25] An essay on the earliest druidic remains in Glamorgan took pride of place at £5 5s. at the 1838 Swansea eisteddfod, and the 1850 Rhuddlan eisteddfod competition on 'a summary in either language of the history of Wales from the beginnings to the present time' (second only to *englynion* on the Prince of Wales) earned the winner £20 and a trophy.[26]

A breakdown of surviving prize premiums for the Abergavenny eisteddfodau further reveals the enormous sums spent on historical subjects of the right kind, but also the social stratification indicated by the financial rewards. In 1853, for instance, singing competitions were only sponsored to a combined amount of about £14, prizes awarded for woollen craftsmanship amounted to circa £44, and the prize money for all harp competitions together came to about £78. The premiums for the two main historical essays alone, awarded to Thomas Stephens of Merthyr Tydfil for his 'Origin and Progress of the Trial by Jury in the Principality of Wales' and 'Analysis of the Remains of the Welsh poets from the earliest period down to the present time', stood at £70 and £30, respectively. Only the twenty guineas (just over £20) for the best essay on 'the proper names of places in South Wales, Gwent and Morgannwg' (also won by Stephens) came close.[27] Patrons tended to allocate the highest premiums to written contributions in the form of long poems and essays on Celtic and historical topics – alongside eulogies on royalty, aristocracy and local gentry. Beyond financial incentivisation, normative values may also be gauged by the frequency of competitions, the content of entries and by adjudications. Considering all of these, pole position went to the 'Druid, friend of Humankind'.

Druids: from educators to proto-capitalists

The Celtic medievalism which the Gorsedd of the Bards of the Isle of Britain has added to the performative aspect of eisteddfodau since Iolo

Morganwg succeeded in associating his invention with the historically attested institution in 1819 has attracted much attention.[28] Less well researched is the continued utilisation of druidism as a vehicle of demonstrating Wales's pioneering involvement in early knowledge production and dissemination, and the evolution of the concept into that of a primeval law-giver establishing order in the British Isles and Europe, and a proto-capitalist advancing 'manufacture' and commerce. Just as investigations of the Arthurian myth served to indicate Welsh significance for medieval literatures,[29] competitions on druidism aimed to substantiate claims of a fundamental Welsh role in establishing early European civilisation generally. In this, nineteenth-century poets and scholars built on the late eighteenth-century re-casting of Welsh druids cited at the beginning of this chapter.[30] As Thomas Price (Carnhuanawc) stressed in 1823, it was druids who 'disseminated that part of the light of knowledge which the ancient *world* knew; and after a long time, it was they who gave *Gods* to *Greece*, and the system of her *laws* to *Rome* herself' ('a daenodd y rhan hynny o oleuni wybodaeth, a feddai'r *byd* gynt; ac ymhen hir amser, mae nhwy a roddodd *Dduwiau* i dir *Groeg*, a chynllun ei *chyfreithiau* i Rufain ei hun').[31] Eisteddfod competitions from the 1820s to the end of our period developed this theme further. Taliesin ab Iolo's prize-winning 1834 ode 'Y Derwyddon' was dripping with Enlightenment tropes,[32] its author considering himself a 'researcher' who hammered home historical fact in poetic form.[33] From Plennydd, Alawn and Gwron – who invented writing by carving 'on retentive wood their varied lore' – to Cattwg, Aneirin and Taliesin, druids took care to 'instruct the youthful' and 'improve the sage' by dispelling 'clouds of darkness'. Nature was conquered by their burning desire for knowledge and instruction as:

> Gwyddon Ganhebon took his modest stand;
> Nor winter's cold, nor summer's burning heat
> His ardent search for wisdom could defeat;
> Nor wain the search, for on his fluent tongue
> Admiring crowds in listening wonder hung;
> On the rude stone, in just proportion trac'd,
> Whate'er fair Science taught he freely plac'd,
> Then from the hallow'd seat, in lucid train
> Dispens'd the knowledge he had toil'd to gain.[34]

This English translation, submitted to a further competition by twenty-year-old Lincoln's Inn student and future Liberal MP Henry Austin Bruce, featured an academic apparatus so extensive that it filled most of some printed pages. His classical education, academic skill and in-depth knowledge of druidism were combined, mainly to inform the public that Roman accusations of human sacrifice were false, and to provide detailed evidence of druidic ingenuity.[35] The trend of endowing prize poems and essays on the druids with extended footnotes continued in subsequent eisteddfodau. Even poetry appears composed and at times adjudicated with an eye to scholarly merit only. T. E. Watkins's *pryddest* poem on 'Castell Trefynwy', submitted to the Abergavenny eisteddfod of 1838, which celebrated Hu Gadarn, 'an excellent agriculturalist ... who first went to it to educate the Ancestors of the Britons and the way to enlighten them, And designed infrastructure and the run of the law' ('amaethydd rhagorol ... a wnaeth lywiad i gyntaf addysgu Hynafiaid y Brython a modd i'w diwallu, A lluniaw trefnidiaeth a gweini cyfiawnder'), consisted of six pages of poetry and eight pages of colour-coded 'Nodion Eglurhad' (Explanatory Notes).[36] The 1842 Abergavenny competition 'Awdl ar Derwyddiaeth' (Ode on Druidism) elicited from 'Ymgeisydd' (Competitor) twenty-four stanzas, yet most of the seven pages he submitted were filled with footnotes marked by large asterisks.[37] Over 50 per cent of the forty pages of the ode on 'Denystr y Derwyddon ym Môn' (The Destruction of the Druids on Anglesey) by renowned scholar and poet 'Ioan Tegid' (John Jones) for the 1850 Abergavenny eisteddfod was taken up by 'sylwnodau' (a new term for 'endnotes') designed to highlight that it was the war waged by the Roman armies which forced Anglesey's druids to sacrifice their archdruid 'yn erbyn eu harfer' (against their custom).[38] The ode on the same subject submitted in 1853 by 'Meudwy Mynwy a Môn' (An Anglesey and Monmouth Hermit) was criticised as 'too artistic and imaginative for history' by the adjudicator.[39]

An exception to the footnote-mania was Taliesin ab Iolo's winning entry to the 1838 Abergavenny essay contest on the bardic script *coelbren y beirdd*, of which even the published version was curiously bereft of any academic apparatus, yet perhaps deliberately so.[40] A very easy read, it widely publicised the 'fact' that Welsh druids were the inventors of the art of writing, the ultimate instrument of progressing to higher stages of civilisation. Ab Iolo's ample illustrations on construction and use of the *peithynen*, the wooden frame used for practising writing, were clearer than the self-assembly instructions provided by a well-known twentieth-century Swedish furniture company. They enabled subsequent contests on constructing bardic frames that drew in those whose forte lay in carpentry rather than poetry.[41] The artefacts thus built and commissioned delivered the ultimate material proof of the druidic invention of writing. A *peithynen* apparently made by central cultural figure, Anglican priest and historian Thomas Price (Carnhuanawc) – the earliest in the National Library of Wales collection – was significant enough to feature on postcard 138 of a series the library commissioned from Oxford University Press in the interwar years (Figure 2).[42]

Figure 2: The bardic frame made by Thomas Price 'Carnhuanawc'. Private collection M. Löffler

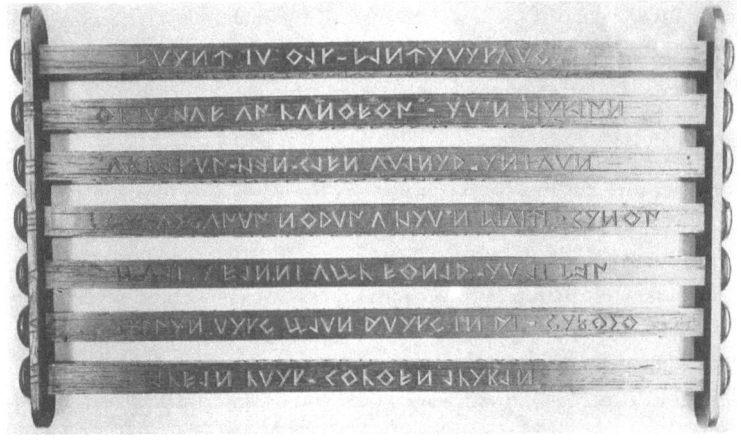

The (almost inevitable) follow-up competition to translate this Welsh essay into English, won by a 'Ieuan Grug' who naturally equipped it with ample footnotes,[43] also inspired a very heavily annotated and footnoted eighty-five page academic translation by David Howell with additions by young historian Thomas Stephens.[44] Paradoxically, researching the *coelbren* in order to provide the footnotes for the translation may have activated Stephens's doubts of its antiquity, which led to him publicly branding it a fifteenth-century forgery in his adjudication of the 1855 eisteddfod competition on 'Coelbren y Beirdd' held by the Gwir Iforiaid of Merthyr Tydfil.[45]

Stephens may have doubted the antiquity of *coelbren y beirdd*, but the druids as proponents of the earliest European civilisation long remained beyond suspicion for him as for most eisteddfod competitors. Into the 1850s eisteddfod poetry and prose consistently contributed to a discourse dominated by 'facts' on the pioneering civilisational achievements of this priestly cast. The ode submitted by 'Alawn' in 1842 presented druidic learning as the cradle of Christianity:

> Rhai can[n]oedd a miloedd maith Gwir yw hyn o Gywrein-waith
> Darlithiau, mewn deddfau da: At rhinvedd tiriona.
> Hyd oesoedd Crêd y Iesu, Derwyddiaeth yn faeth a fu,
> Yr egwyddor dymhor da; O faich oed, i fuchedda.[46]

> Some several hundreds and thousands, Truth of Masterpieces
> Lectures, in good deeds: For the virtue of humanising.
> Until the ages of the Creed of Jesus, Druidism was the nourishment,
> Of the principles of a good life; The responsibility of the ages, to live virtuously.

The winning entry by 'Emrys' listed among the arts and sciences furthered by druids 'fferylliaeth a mwnyddiaeth' (pharmacy and mining), 'llywod-ddysg' (politics), 'peirianwaith wibrennau' (astronomy) and 'amaethyddiaeth' (agriculture).[47] Philosophy, literature, history, theology, music 'a phob hynod wybodaeth' (every notable science) were noted in one of the 1853 odes on the 'Destruction of the Anglesey Druids in the year 60 by the Roman Army under Suetonius Paulinus'.[48]

Essays tended to cast druids as laying the foundations of a Christian imperialism even more conspicuously. Angharad Llwyd's *History of the Island of Mona*, victorious at the 1832 Beaumaris eisteddfod, judged druidic 'doctrine highly serviceable to facilitate the adoption' of Christianity, and filled five pages with citations on the width of druidical learning and the working of their legal system, before defending the Gaulish 'punishment of criminals by fire' with reference to the prevalence of such practices in modern colonial societies, and concluding that Roman testimony was unreliable, since these 'savages' had borrowed 'what refinement or science they had' from the Greeks.[49] How else could one explain Tacitus's boast of having slain '"unarmed victims" ... imploring the protection of their God against these lawless invaders of their rights and liberties'.[50] John Roberts's published English translation of his winning entry to the 1838 Swansea Cymreigyddion competition on druidical remains in Glamorgan cited stone circles as proof 'that the Ancient Britons were possessed of science, and great skill in using mechanical powers', and explained place-names beginning in 'Llan' as evidence of druidic assembly sites 'for the purposes of instruction', seamlessly 'converted into churches, and used for divine worship' at the coming of Christianity.[51] Citing 'the excellent treatise of Mr. Taliesin Williams', *coelbren y beirdd* was, naturally, interpreted as evidence of 'art and science handed down to us from the sages of antiquity'.[52] It was only under Roman influence that the Welsh 'fell into the same pit of guilt and depravity as the Roman, Grecians, Saxons, and other nations of the world'.[53] These competitions, and the resulting poetry and prose, built on a discourse that had long reversed classic models to brand the Romans as barbarians waging war on the higher civilisation built by druids. The short story fragment 'Y Derwydd' (The Druid) of 1805, for instance, described how angelic young druid Modred saved a severely injured Roman officer, betrayed by his own and left to die on a battlefield. Even though the Romans had tainted the druidic altar 'â gwaed ei Duwiol of[f]eiriaid a'r llwyni cysegredig ... â thrythyllwch cadgwn creulawn anniwair' ('with the blood of its Godly priests and the holy groves ... with the debauchery of cruel lascivious war-dogs'), Modred heals him in the cave that is his and his fellow Britons' refuge, because Britons 'byth yn ymhyvrydu yng ngwaed eu cyd-greaduriaid' ('never rejoice in the blood of their fellow-creatures').[54]

In this vein, the 1841 Swansea Derwyddon Society's competition on druids and human sacrifice produced a dialogue between 'macwy a Hynafieithydd' ('a youth and an Antiquary') by 'Rhydderch Gwynedd', in which a kind yet 'reverend Teacher' ('hybarch athro') enlightens a pupil upset by a public meeting discussing the fake news that the druids had practised human sacrifice.[55] Apart from condemning political meetings, the teacher advises that 'na bu ein hen dadau dysgedig erioed yn euog or fath gyflafan' ('our learned forefathers were never guilty of such a massacre'). The youth's question on the origin of such rumours elicits an essay-length reply which drew, like many others, on Greek and Roman authors, on the tenth volume of the journal of the Asiatic Society, *Asiatic Researches*, and on the indigenous bardic 'Trioedd Beirdd Ynys Prydain' to prove that, whilst such practices had been common in

Ethiopia and Phoenicia, and still were in colonial un-Christian China and India, the Welsh had never practised them.[56] On the contrary, Welsh legal traditions had risen 'uwch pob Cenedl ym moreu y byd' ('above every Nation at the dawn of the world'). The British druids' business acumen, supplying as they did, the Continent with hundreds of shiploads of metallic goods annually – from brass and iron pots to gold, silver and lead – was further proof of a stage of civilisation far above that of their continental neighbours. The conclusion – judging on a solid legal system and a thriving export economy – was that 'nyd mai barbariaid tywyll anwybodus ydoedd cynfrodorion yr ynys hon' ('the natives of this island were not dark, ignorant barbarians'). The pagan Romans, enemies of 'moesoldeb, Crefydd a chenedl y Cymry!!!' ('the morals, Religion and nation of the Welsh!!!'), had slandered the inhabitants of the British Isles.[57]

This was also the first eisteddfod competition on druidism at which historian and reformer Thomas Stephens of Merthyr Tydfil, then barely twenty years old, competed. His forty-nine-page essay submitted as 'Senex' approached the subject from a similar angle. He discounted Caesar's account of continental druidic sacrifices in wicker cages as war propaganda penned by a military leader intent on placating his troops and gaining imperial power, while Tacitus's narrative on the conquest of druidic Anglesey struck him as fiction, 'the very fabulous air' reminiscent of Homer taking 'the liberty to add some of his own notions'.[58] His exposition on the influence of druidic learning on morality compared their 'civilised society' favourably to 'the desert wilds of ~~India~~ Africa', even his self-corrections indicating the imperial mindset of this Victorian self-made man.[59] Citing English colonial travel writing, the morality of a nineteenth-century African leader of a 'mild and gentle' tribe of agriculturists and cattle breeders was likened to the ancient druidic civilisation that had laid the foundations for European supremacy:

> What a pleasing ~~character~~ portrait have we of the chief of a tribe: – 'His countenance as heavily marked with the habit of reflection vigorous in his mental and amicable in his personal qualities. Gaika was at once the friend and ruler of a happy people who universal pronounced his name with transport and blessed his seat with felicity.' Barrows Travels in Southern Africa. Might not this ~~Chief~~ savage be held up as a lesson to European

monarchs as an instance of the effects of true morality a portrait of a state to which the Druids might have and did attain by the ease of the great knowledge they possessed for wherever true knowledge exists it becomes at once an object of admiration and conduces to the happiness of its possessor and his companions as Virgil informs us.[60]

Stephens was only emulating his mentors and teachers, literary parsons like Gwallter Mechain (Walter Davies) and Carnhuanawc. As early as 1797, Gwallter Mechain had compared the 'grave and austere Gauls' favourably with the 'feeble mind of the Esquimaux Indians' and Asian 'animal machines'.[61] Carnhuanawc's 1845 essay (worth £87) 'On the Comparative Merits of the Remains of Ancient Literature in the Welsh, Irish, and Gaelic Languages', especially in elucidating 'Mental Cultivation', commented at length on the lack of complex literature in 'primitive' cultures like the 'savages of the South Seas'. He attested, too, that the 'style and spirit of the didactic Druidical compositions' evidenced 'a great, well-organized, widely extended and long-established system of moral instruction' by teachers, who knew 'the form and magnitude of the earth' and 'reasoned deeply about the nature of things'.[62] Carnhuanawc's 'Historical Account of the Statuta Walliae, or the Statutes of Rhuddlan, by which Wales was Annexed to England' for the 1848 Abergavenny eisteddfod, similarly compared 'the condition of India at the present day' to 'that of Britain under the Romans'.[63] It is no coincidence that the extensive *Literary Remains* which contained the essays, edited by another next generation admirer, historian Jane Williams, was subtitled *Essays on the Geographical Progress of Empire and Civilization*.

The concept of the druid as enlightened imperialist perhaps found a first climax in John Jones's 1850 essay 'On the State of Agriculture and the Process of Art & Manufactures in Britain during the period & under the influence of the Druidical System', published in full in the new *Archaeologia Cambrensis*.[64] Jones's opening highlighted that:

> A passive state of subserviency to a system of religious belief, formed on the works of divine Providence and the immutable laws of nature, in the absence of revealed Truths, would supply the groundwork for a state of society most favourable to the growth and cultivation of industrious habits and peaceful pursuits.[65]

Arguing that those Celtic tribes without a 'Druidical system of discipline to control and direct their natural propensities ... paid no further attention to agricultural and commercial occupations', Jones outlined that druid-led Gaul, on the other hand, had prospered, and that the combination of druidic leadership with the 'invigorating climate of Britain' had laid the early foundations for British imperial success.[66] The climate had aided 'the exercise of industry and settled habits ... affording the strongest inducement for the adoption of mechanical agents in economizing labour'.[67] The druidic 'Priesthood' had ensured that 'tillage was an object of national care & encouragement', that 'Commerce and handicraft' were furthered, and that 'all classes of society [were] encouraged in the order of subordination & mutual dependence'.[68] Flax and hemp were thus first cultivated in Britain (not Egypt) for 'the manufacture of linen and woolen [sic] fabrics' needed for sails and, of course, druidic robes.[69] Adam Smith's assertion in *The Wealth of Nations* (1776) that Britain had 'neither wind nor water mills' before the sixteenth century was disproved; the water-driven 'ancient British mill' had disappeared, because Roman education focused on 'the luxuries and refinement of society' rather than 'scientific knowledge', and the Anglo-Saxons had simply not been civilised enough to recognise its potential.[70] Thus was publicly settled any 'doubt entertained by Aristotle, whether to ascribe the origin and progress of the useful arts and sciences to the sages of western Europe, or to the light of oriental philosophy'.[71]

Scholarship and Victorian norms

Attention has long been paid to the fact that for nineteenth-century Welshmen, adherence to their own culture did not preclude loyalty to 'Queen and country', and eisteddfod competitions between the Napoleonic and the Crimean wars contributed to this discourse of dual patriotism well beyond extolling druidism.[72] The winning entry to the 1819 Carmarthen eisteddfod competition on the *Language and Learning of Britain, under the Roman Government*, in an almost Hegelian approach to the dialectics of historical processes, affirmed the benefits of subsequent invasions and subjugations of Wales:

> An enquiry into the origin and revolution of nations ... necessarily leads us to investigate the nature and extent of

those causes, which act upon the mass of population, and tend to produce those revolutions, from which various systems of political Societies arise. It includes also an examination into the agency of particular habits, manners, and customs, in maintaining the order and consistencies of aggregate bodies of men, and of the various passions and infirmities, incidental to Humanity, which conduce either to the dissolution of the old, or the formation of new Societies ... There is a climax in the scale of civilization, at which a nation may continue stationary for ages, till interrupted by the inroads of a more powerful Invader, or induced to adopt new maxims of internal policy or ambition, or new habits of luxury or economy.[73]

Four years later, Carnhuanawc, the Anglican 'literary parson' that he was, credited Asser as former bishop of St David's with laying the foundations of 'Rhyddid gwladol a chrefyddol' (civic and religious liberty) by advising and supporting King Alfred, who first united England and Wales.[74] The essay on *Historical Accounts of the Flintshire Castles* submitted by 'Gwladgarwr' (Patriot) to the 1828 Rhuddlan eisteddfod struck the same vein in highlighting 'that the Romans, on their arrival, did not find our ancient British ancestors such hordes of ignorant savages (as some historians would have us believe)'; yet it also took the reader through a lengthy inventory of internecine medieval strife that only ended with:

> gratitude 'that we were *conquered to our gain and undone to our advantage*'. When English generosity appeared, Welsh loyalty increased ... Instead of precarious liberty, they now began to enjoy a solid and permanent freedom, secured by equal and fixed laws and established under one august monarch.[75]

Wales's happy subalternity in this union was further demonstrated by a lengthy roll call of Welshmen who had contributed to Empire – from Iolo Morganwg's invented law-giver Dyfnwal Moelmud to early modern entrepreneur and MP Sir Hugh Myddelton, and Tudor-descended King George IV. The apotheosis of this line of illustrious Welsh imperialists was orientalist William Jones, 'who left his own country for the benefit of millions of his fellow creatures in a distant climate'.[76] Carnhuanawc's last eisteddfod essay demonstrates how even a few framing passages could move the political message of a scholarly work in an acceptably unionist direction. His exposition of the evidence collected by Edward I's 'royal Commission' with a reproduction of the 1284 'Statuta Walliae, or the Statutes of Rhuddlan, by which Wales was Annexed to England', interpreted the passing of the 'Statute' as the result of an unplanned chain of events, whereby Welsh efforts to 'reform' the vestiges of Dyfnwal Moelmud's laws as well as Edward's plans for 'reform' were 'unexpectedly deranged, for Llywelyn and his countrymen, unable to endure any longer the oppressions enacted by Edward's subjects' – though not by the king himself – waged 'open war'. The resulting deaths of native princes David and Llywelyn meant that 'Edward assumed the government of the country'.[77]

Whether poems and essays were researched and written to extol the pioneering efforts of proto-capitalist druids, praise the advantages of being a conquered member of the world's largest Empire or provide role models for the Victorian man, whether they dealt in invented fare or historical fact, they all strove to develop Welsh knowledge of classical and modern literature, the intellectual facilities and moral capacities of their authors, as well as the use of academic apparatus and appropriate terminologies for all manner of fields, laying the foundations for the paradigmatic swing from romantic to scientific modes of exploring the Welsh past observed from the 1860s.[78] Many early competitions, such as the 1822 task on the 'Translation of the Law Triads' or the 'Catalogue of English MSS, relating to Wales now extant in the province of Powys' advertised for the 1824 Welshpool eisteddfod, enabled the gathering and accessibility of sources;[79] other topics involved coining new terminologies. The winning entry on 'Darluniad o Gastell Caerdydd fel yr oedd yr adeiladaeth yn sefyll yn y flwyddyn 1578' (A Depiction of Cardiff Castle as the edifice stood in the year 1578) of the 1834 Cardiff eisteddfod minted and publicised architectural terms for historic monuments, drawing on the early modern translation tradition of accompanying new Welsh vocabulary by English equivalents. 'Neuadd y Sir (Shire Hall)', 'mûr-ganllawiau (battlements)', '(y)stafell yr Oged (portcullis chamber)' and 'ffenestr ebach (bay window)' appear to have been used for the first time in this sense by the author.[80] As has been demonstrated, book-length historical essays submitted to the Abergavenny eisteddfodau helped transfer new theoretical approaches and methods to Wales.[81] The winning 1838 'Essay on the Influence of

Welsh Tradition upon European Literature', for instance, expounded the changes exerted by oral transmission of events by 'elders', when:

> the propensity of age to exaggerate the occurrences of youth, the love of the marvellous generated and fostered by ignorance, the difficulty of detecting error, and the inaccuracy inseparable from oral communication, will first distort the original story; At length some bolder and more original genius, first daring to invent, will launch forth upon the trackless waters of fiction … he will exaggerate the incidents and the characters with which he is already familiar, but soon success will give him confidence, and, relying solely upon his own resources, he will draw fresh and inexhaustible treasures from the boundless realm of imagination. Under such circumstances we must naturally expect to encounter no inconsiderable difficulties in any attempts to distinguish reality from invention … the mines from which the ore itself has been drawn; or the degree in which it has been affected by the various substances with which it may have been brought into contact.[82]

The essay also defined for the Welsh researcher key terms, such as 'romance', utilising authors like Sir Walter Scott and new reference works, such as *Encyclopaedia Britannica*, while comparing and contrasting secondary sources from Warton's *History of English Poetry* to Dunlop's *History of Fiction*.[83] The over eighty-page-long 1837 essay on 'Hanes yr Arglwyddi Cyffiniol' (The History of the Marcher Lords) by 'Cattwg' impresses with length, detail and the attempt at establishing a periodisation for the Welsh Middle Ages.[84]

Peeling back another layer, unpublished submissions also reveal unintended information, such as the ingenious ways with which names were concealed (or not) by flapped-over page corners and more-or-less artful squiggles, and of adjudicators' feelings. Archdeacon John Williams elegiacally began his adjudication of Carnhuanawc's essay on the 'Statute of Rhuddlan' with the remark that the sealed envelope had 'contained the impression of the Dying Gladiator. It was his last'.[85] Most importantly, adjudicators' glosses and authors' self-corrections reveal the imposition of norms and their effect. Carnhuanawc's work as prose adjudicator from the first 1834 Abergavenny eisteddfod until his death in 1848 highlights how adjudications regulated scholarly and social norms just as much as did prize premiums. Using red ink, he crossed out passages, marked mistakes by 'x', added comments like 'Yn mherthynasol' (Irrelevant), bemoaned a lack of or incorrect Latin citations, or just noted that an essay was 'too short' (rhy fyr).[86] An author who had translated 'gair am air' (word for word) from a standard work without acknowledgement was accused of plagiarism and the essay dismissed.[87] A very tidily footnoted long essay on 'Hanes a Gweithredoedd gorchestol Owain Glyndwr' (The History and Excellent Actions of Owain Glyndŵr) was deemed too narrative, a mere 'historical synopsis' ('yn dalfyriad hanes'), and not too well written.[88] Carnhuanawc's judgement on the 1835 essay 'Hanes Bywyd Llywelyn Tywysawg Diweddar Cymru' (The Life of Llywelyn Late Prince of Wales) reminds us that historical subjects were acceptable only as long as they adhered to the accepted political framework and were 'objective':

> Y mae gormod o sylwadau anmherthysnasol yn y traethawd hwn – y mae llawer o hono yn fwy tebyg i araeth ac y mae yr awdwr yn crybwyll gormod am ei deimladau priodol ei hun – nid ydynt y fath sylwadau yn taflu un fath o oleuni ar yr hanes ond yn hytrach llanw fyny yn ddiachos.[89]

> There are too many irrelevant comments in this essay – much of it more resembles a speech and the author discusses his own private feelings too much – these kinds of comments do not throw any light on the history but rather fill up unnecessarily.

Carnhuanawc's disciple Thomas Stephens was spared excoriation in the margins of his 1844 essay 'on the evils arising from the destruction of salmon when full of spawn', which argued the traditional (or 'natural') right of the Welsh to fish their rivers for the salmon that was too expensive to buy, but scolded him directly in a letter for his 'acerbity of expression' and 'attack upon the Magistracy'. The combination of radical language and content made it impossible for Carnhuanawc to award the prize 'to a composition which evidenced the existence of abilities of the highest order'.[90] He very clearly preferred the young author's prize-winning contributions on the distant past to reading his reformist effusions on the present.

Stephens himself – perhaps the most successful, certainly the most argumentative eisteddfod competitor of his age – was no stranger to publicly reminding his peers that even competitions on historical topics needed to adhere to Victorian social norms. Part of his bitter criticism of the 1842 Abergavenny eisteddfod was his condemnation of a competition on 'vaunting braggart' Caradoc Freichfras as a 'detestable mockery!'[91] He questioned the 'utility' of this 'nonsensical subject', because this forefather of the Llanofer family satisfied neither medievalist ideas of chivalry nor Victorian norms of the self-made men into which Stephens hoped to improve the working classes around him.[92] Referencing sobriety for good measure, Caradog was dismissed as 'the greatest drunkard at the fabled Round Table of Arthur's, [whose] … butchering and dissipated propensities evidently debar him from having any species of claim upon the notice of the present age'.[93] A 'History of the Social, Moral, and Political Condition of the Welsh people during the wars of York and Lancaster', on the other hand, would be 'well worthy of attention' in his opinion.[94] Carnhuanawc, though, had no qualms adjudicating the essay, judging 'Ieuan ab Gruffydd o Lanofor' worthy of the prize, and for once writing 'Buddugoliaethus. Carnhuanawc' (Victorious. Carnhuanawc) in large letters on the title page.[95] Honouring the local gentry and keeping Unitarian firebrands in check sometimes trumped setting social norms for the working classes. Stephens's own adjudications were no less schoolmasterly than those of his revered teacher. The eight contributions sent into an 1855 essay competition on 'Dyfodiad y Kymmry i Ynys Prydain' (The Coming of the Welsh to the Island of Britain) held by the Merthyr Tydfil Gwir Iforiaid moved him to a learned refutation of all speculations as to the origins of the Welsh.[96] The essays were unceremoniously grouped into 'gwael' (bad), 'gwell' (better) and 'gorau' (best). The prize was awarded to 'Cleryn' with the note 'a mawr lles a wnawd iddo' ('and may it be very profitable for him').[97]

This article has focused on eisteddfod competitions on historical topics, the uses of Druidism, and the distribution of prize monies as instruments of establishing as well as revealing cultural and societal norms. These parameters were of course also enforced by moving eisteddfodau into temperance and working men's halls as well as by founding appropriately supervised libraries that were free from 'any active expression of radicalism'.[98] The numerous competitions and toasts on the royal family and local gentry,[99] essays and poems on the advantages of sending children to state schools, or the moral superiority of the Welsh working classes, and even a 'fug-hanes (novel)' writing competition extolling abstinence, were part of this discourse of loyalty, godliness and teetotalism.[100] Yet, such contemporary topics remained potentially contentious. Competitions like the 1840 'Civic and Religious Discord the Ruin of the Welsh Nation' were criticised as more fitting for a 'tract circulating society', and not looking 'at our outward bound transports, at our prisons, scaffolds, and the state of feeling among all classes of society'. The critic would have preferred as an 'excellent subject ... the Distinguished of the Northwalians since the Accession of the Tudors to the Throne of Great Britain'.[101] The past, or rather a combination of it with a safe present were judged to guarantee maximum 'impact' in the process of modernising Welsh culture while affirming an ancient Welsh nationhood within the framework of kingdom and Empire. The combination of competitions announced for the 1855 Cwmafan Christmas eisteddfod is indicative of this trend.[102] The three essay subjects were announced as 'Y modd mwyaf effeithiol i weithiwr a'i deulu fyw yn dda a thalu ei ffordd' (The most effective way for a worker and his family to live well and pay their way), 'Drygau Rhyfel' (The Evils of War) and 'Oliver Cromwell'. The contemporary subjects reacted to as much as attempting to remedy recent aberrations, such as the industrial unrest in south Wales and the Siege of Sevastopol that ended the bloody Crimean War. Both the content of and the adjudicator's comments on the winning entry on Oliver Cromwell demonstrate the wider remit of historical topics. Competitor 'Omicron' had succeeded because he provided 'rhybuddion dwysion i bobl ieuainc i ochelyd cyfeillion llygredig' ('dire warnings for young people to avoid corrupted company'), the like of which had almost brought this great man to fall, while focusing on the positives in Cromwell's personality as a role model, 'pwyllog ond penderfynol' ('considered yet determined') as he was.[103] Like other nineteenth-century writers, 'Omicron' claimed Cromwell for Wales and its working population, a simply clad man of humble origins, 'ei ddeall yn dreiddgar – ei gof yn dda – ei dymer yn serchog a'i feddwl yn gyflym' ('his mind piercing – his memory good – his temperament pleasant and his thinking quick').[104] Raised up by God, he was chosen to establish a new kind of Christian justice in Europe. Welsh and British patriotism were one, as the country Great Britain and the nation of Wales together were:

yn ddyledus iddo am bob gwreichionyn o ryddid sydd yn ffurf-
lywodraeth ein gwlad, yn ogystal ag eangder ein trafnidiaeth
tramor, a'n hanturiaethau celfyddydol, yr hyn a wna enw
Cromwell yn addurn i'n gwlad, ac yn ymffrost i'n cenedl.[105]

indebted to him for every spark of liberty in the constitution of
our country as well as the amplitude of our foreign commerce,
and our technical exploits, they make Cromwell an adornment
of our country and an object of pride for our nation.

Like the ancient druids, the Welsh medieval authors who had endowed European culture with chivalric motifs, and early modern Sir Hugh Myddelton, Cromwell the Welshman had contributed to the greater good, paving the way for an Empire Enlightenment of which Wales was an integral part. It is through such competition topics, the lavish prize moneys associated with them, and the adjudications designating winners whose work would be made available to the public, that the eisteddfod movement which emerged between the end of the Napoleonic Wars and the Crimean War set the norms for the High Victorian national eisteddfodau initiated by the grand 1858 Llangollen Eisteddfod and confirmed by the foundation of the National Eisteddfod Association in the wake of the Aberdare eisteddfod of 1861.[106] At Aberdare, Thomas Stephens, now an established figure, assured the chairman of the day C. Bailey, MP, that the eisteddfod was 'a symbol of nationality without disloyalty', and no 'hindrance to the cultivation of … the various forms of intellectual development presented in our own day'.[107] Alaw Goch (David Williams), whose celebrated efforts saved the festival following the destruction of the pavilion by high winds, publicly hoped that 'our friends will see, not only that no evil can come from the Eisteddfod, but that is has a great tendency to do good to the nation at large'.[108] It was not until the reforms of the 1930s and the introduction of the 'Welsh Only' rule in 1937 that the norms which played to the 'nation at large' would be superseded.

Notes

1   'A Druidical Song, and Chorus – Mr. Tinney, &c. &c. &c. Arranged by Mr. E. Jones (Vide the Relics of the Bards, Vol. 2, p 77)', in *Eisteddvod, or Congress of*

Welsh Bards, and Minstrels, Held in the Freemasons Tavern, London, on Wednesday May 22, 1822 under the Auspices of the Cymmrodorion or Royal Metropolitan Institution. Patron, the King; President, Sir W. W. Wynn, Bart. M. P. (London, 1822), pp. 6–7. All texts are reproduced using the original orthography and grammar.

2 Edward Jones, *The Bardic Museum of Primitive British Literature; and Other Admirable Rarities Forming the Second Volume of the Musical, Poetical and Historical Relicks of the Welsh Bards and Druids* (London, 1802), p. 77.

3 Even considering only eisteddfodau held by Cymreigyddion societies in Wales, and by Gwyneddigion, Cymmrodorion and others abroad makes it impossible to pay attention to all competitions between 1815 and the 'national' Eisteddfod of Llangollen, 1858. The focus is therefore on a selection of case studies. See also Dot Jones, *Statistical Evidence Relating to the Welsh Language 1801–1911. Tystiolaeth Ystadegol yn Ymwneud â'r Iaith Gymraeg 1801–1911* (Cardiff, 1998), pp. 484–5.

4 Marion Löffler, '"Generation 1789": Welsh Dissenters and radicals lost in translation', in Matthew Roberts (ed.), *Memory and Modern British Politics: Commemoration, Tradition, Legacy* (London, 2024), pp. 35–65; Huw Pryce, *Writing Welsh History: From the Middle Ages to the Twenty-first Century* (Oxford, 2022), pp. 242–3.

5 All 'pseudo-historical' topics are here understood as 'historical'. The utilisation of (near) contemporary and biblical subjects cannot be explored in this chapter.

6 *Seren Gomer*, V (1823), title page. For a short characterisation of this periodical, see Pryce, *Writing Welsh History*, p. 241.

7 Monika Baár, 'Wishful Thinking: Academic Competitions in National History', in Ilaria Porciani and Jo Tollebeek (eds), *Setting the Standards. Institutions, Networks and Communities of National Historiography*, Writing the Nation Series, 2 (Basingstoke, 2012), pp. 165–82.

8 *Eisteddvod, or Congress of Welsh Bards … 1822*, p. 7.

9 *Eisteddvod, or Congress of Welsh Bards … 1822*, p. 16; See also A. C. Rejhon, 'Hu Gadarn: Folklore and Fabrication', in Patrick K. Ford (ed.), *Celtic Folklore and Christianity: Studies in Memory of William W. Heist* (Santa Barbara, Ca., 1983), pp. 201–12.

10 'Cymreigyddion Dolgellau', *Seren Gomer*, 5/82 (1822), 219.

11 *Glamorgan Gazette and Merthyr Guardian*, 11 December 1824.

12 *The Cambrian*, 1 November 1823 (to a John Humffreys Parry of London).

13 *Cyfansoddiadau a Anfonwyd i Eisteddfod Llanrwst, Nadolig 1843* (Llanrwst, 1843), pp. 3–4.

14 National Library of Wales Manuscript [NLW MS] 13,960E, f. 283, 'Traethawd o Hanes Tref a Monachlog Castell Nedd a Chastell Aberafon yn Morganwg'.

15 'General Literature. Abergavenny Eisteddfod', in *Cambrian Journal*, 1 (Alban Eilir 1854), 44. For a typical speech accusing eisteddfodau of furthering dangerous 'national' tendencies, see *Monmouthshire Merlin*, 18 October 1845.
16 'General Literature. Abergavenny Eisteddfod', 52.
17 *Cyfansoddiadau Buddugol Eisteddfod Sïon, Cwmafan a Gynhaliwyd Dydd Nadolig, 1855, yng nghyd a'r Feirniadaeth arnynt* (Abertawy, 1856), p. 3.
18 John Rolls Esq. (Hendre), President of the Seventh Abergavenny Society Eisteddfod on 14 October 1840, in *The Cambrian*, 17 October 1840.
19 Monetary equivalences have been calculated on the basis of 'purchasing power'; NLW, MS 966C, *Report of the Abergavenny Eisteddfod, Being the Twentieth Anniversary of the Abergavenny Cymreigyddion, Held on the 12th and 13th Days of October, 1853* (Carnarvon, 1853), p. 22. Apart from the numerous articles by Maxwell Fraser, the considerable literature on the Abergavenny Cymreigyddion eisteddfodau includes Mair Elfet Thomas, *Afiaith yng Ngwent* (Caerdydd, 1978); Mair Elfet Thomas, *The Welsh Spirit of Gwent* (Cardiff, 1988); David Thorne, 'Cymreigyddion y Fenni a dechreuadau ieitheg cymharol yng Nghymru', *NLWJ*, 27/1 (1991), 97–107; Marion Löffler, 'Olion Llenyddol Ymwelwyr â Llanofer', *Llên Cymru*, 41/11 (2018), 53–88.
20 *The Cambrian*, 17 October 1840.
21 *The Cambrian*, 8 December 1821; *Eisteddvod, or Congress of Welsh Bards ... 1822*, p. 16.
22 *Seren Gomer*, 6/98 (Tachwedd 1823), 347. The highest premium went to an ode on the destruction of Jerusalem.
23 'Subjects Proposed for Prize Poems, Essays, &c. To be Awarded during the Eisteddfod', in *A Collection of English Poems and Odes, which obtained Medals and other Prizes at the Gwent and Dyfed Royal Eisteddfod, Held at Cardiff, on the 20th, 21st, and 22nd of August, 1834* (London, 1834), pp. 35–9.
24 'Subjects Proposed for Prize Poems, Essays, &c. To be Awarded during the Eisteddfod', p. 35.
25 *Gwent and Dyfed Royal Eisteddfod 1834. The Prize Translation of the Welsh Ode on the British Druids, by Mr. Taliesin Williams. By Henry A. Bruce, Esq. A Premium of £10* (London, 1835), p. 1.
26 *Seren Gomer*, 32/273 (Mehefin 1838), 184; *Yr Amserau*, 2 Hydref 1850; *Carnarvon and Denbigh Herald*, 28 September 1850.
27 'General Literature. Abergavenny Eisteddfod', 53–6.
28 Among the many treatments are Geraint and Zonia Bowen, *Hanes Gorsedd y Beirdd* (Swansea, 1991); Hywel Teifi Edwards, *Codi'r Hen Wlad yn ei Hôl, 1850–1914* (Llandysul, 1989); Hywel Teifi Edwards, *The Eisteddfod* (Cardiff, 1990); Hywel Teifi Edwards, 'Eisteddfod "Genedlaethol" Caernarfon, 1877: Prifwyl y Pafiliwn', *Trafodion Cymdeithas Hanes Sir Gaernarfon*, 67 (2006), 58–87; Owen Martell, 'Mae'r pasiant trosodd ym Mro Morgannwg (am

flwyddyn arall, beth bynnag): Iolo Morganwg, yr Orsedd a'r Eisteddfod Genedlaethol', *Tu Chwith*, 10 (1998), 76–97; Peter Lord, *Y Chwaer Dduwies: Celf, Crefft a'r Eisteddfod* (Llandysul, 1992); Dillwyn Miles, *The Secret of the Bards of the Isle of Britain* (Llandybïe, 1992); Marion Löffler, *The Literary and Historical Legacy of Iolo Morganwg* (Cardiff, 2007), pp. 41–77.

29 Huw Pryce, 'Medieval Welsh History in the Victorian Age', *CMCS*, 71 (summer 2016), 1–28 (p. 9). For a combination of both, see *The Cambrian*, 17 October 1840.

30 See Geraint H. Jenkins, *Bard of Liberty: The Political Radicalism of Iolo Morganwg* (Cardiff, 2012), pp. 91–4, 145–6.

31 *Eos Dyfed, Sef Rhai o Gyfansoddiadau a anfonwyd i Eisteddfod Caerfyrddin Medi 24, 25, 1823. At y rhai y 'chwanegwyd Hanes yr Eisteddfod* (Caerfyrddin, 1824), p. 95.

32 'Subjects Proposed for Prize Poems, Essays, &c. To be Awarded during the Eisteddfod', p. 35; see also *The Cambrian*, 14 December 1833.

33 Brynley F. Roberts, '"The Age of Restitution": Taliesin ab Iolo and the Reception of Iolo Morganwg', in Geraint H. Jenkins (ed.), *A Rattleskull Genius. The Many Faces of Iolo Morganwg* (Cardiff, 2005), pp. 461–79 (pp. 473–4).

34 *Gwent and Dyfed Royal Eisteddfod 1834*, pp. 2, 7, 11, 12.

35 *Gwent and Dyfed Royal Eisteddfod 1834*, pp. 2, 11–13, 18–21.

36 NLW, MS 13,969E, ff. 288–95, 'Pryddest dan yr Enw Castell Trefynwy' by 'Ab Gruffydd ab Arthur'.

37 NLW, MS 13,961E, ff. 157–87, 'Awdl ar Dderwyddiaeth' by 'Ymgeisydd'. His competitors 'Derwyddfardd, 'Derwydd Du' and 'Alawn' submitted similar work.

38 Cardiff, Central Library, MS 2.1030, 'Denystr y Derwyddon ym Môn' by John Jones (Ioan Tegid); 'Denystr y Derwyddon ym Môn yn y flwyddyn lxi o oedran Crist gan filwyr Rhufain o dan Paulinus Suetonius rhaglaw yr Amherawdwr Nero ym Mhrydain', copied by Henry Roberts, Curad Llangyndeyrn, co. Carm.

39 NLW, MS 13,962E, ff. 309–20, 'Awdl Dinystr Derwyddon Môn yn y flwyddyn 60 gan y Fyddin Rufeinig dan y Tywysog Suetonius Paulinus'; 'General Literature. Abergavenny Eisteddfod', 53.

40 NLW, MS 13,9560E, 'Hendra ac Awdurdodiad Coelbren y Beirdd'; *Traethawd ar Hynafiaeth ac Awdurdodaeth Coelbren y Beirdd, Yr Hwnn a Ennillodd Ariandlws a Gwobr Eisteddfod y Fenni, 1838. Gan Taliesin Williams [ab Iolo]* (Llanymddyfri, 1840).

41 Löffler, *Literary and Historical Legacy*, pp. 96–8, fig. 9.

42 NLW, Rolls, 1222–2017, 107, 'A Peithynen or Bardic Frame made by Thomas Price "Carnhuanawc"'. For an image of a later *peithynen*, see Löffler, *Literary and Historical Legacy*, fig. 9.

43 NLW, MS 13,960E.
44 NLW, Cwrtmawr MS 320C, 'Coelbren y Beirdd. A Translation of *Coelbren y Beirdd* (Llandovery, 1840) made by David Howell, "Llawdden", in 1853 at the instance of Thomas Stephens, with notes by T. Stephens', *http://hdl.handle.net/10107/5724611* (accessed 6 November 2023).
45 Thos. Stephens, 'Eisteddfod Iforawl Merthyr, 1855. Y Feirniadaeth', *Seren Gomer*, 38/482 (Tachwedd 1855), 499. See also Thomas Stephens, 'An Essay on the Bardic Alphabet called "Coelbren y Beirdd"', *Archaeologia Cambrensis*, 4th Series, 3/11 (1872), 181–210.
46 NLW, MS 13,961E, f. 163.
47 Gwilym Hiraethog (ed.), *Ceinion Emrys. Sef Gweithiau Barddonol y Diweddar Barch. W. Ambrose (Emrys) Porthmadog* (Dolgellau, 1876), pp. 93–9.
48 NLW, MS 13,962E, f. 307. The prize was awarded to Richard Parry (Gwalchmai), according to 'General Literature. Abergavenny Eisteddfod', 53.
49 Angharad Llwyd, *History of the Island of Mona, or Anglesey, including an Account of its natural Productions, Druidical Antiquities, Eminent Men ... being the Prize Essay to which was adjudged the first Premium at the Royal Beaumaris Eisteddfod which was held in the Month of August, 1832* (Rhuthin, 1833), pp. 32, 33–8. The passage on druidic remains stretches to p. 49.
50 Llwyd, *History of the Island of Mona*, p. 48.
51 J. Roberts, *Druidical Remains and Antiquities of the Ancient Britons, Principally in Glamorgan; Containing a General Account of the Same, in England, Wales, Scotland, France, &c.; with Notes and Illustrations on the Learning and Superstitions of the Druids – The Downfall of Druidism as a Religious System – and the Introduction of Christianity into Britain* (Swansea, 1842), pp. 25, 31.
52 Roberts, *Druidical Remains*, pp. 39, 47.
53 Roberts, *Druidical Remains*, p. 22.
54 Anon., 'Y Derwydd', *Greal*, III (Alban Arthan 1805), 129–32.
55 NLW, MS 3289C, 'Traethawd ar yr holiad a oedd y Derwyddon yn aberthu dynion a'i nad oeddynt; Testun Derwyddon Abertawy, a'r gymydogaeth, erbyn eu cylchwyl flynyddol sef ymddiddan rhwng macwy a Hynafiaethydd gan "Rhydderch Gwynedd" (Richard Jones), Ionawr 7fed 1841', f. 1.
56 *Asiatic Researches*, 10 (1811), 203; 'Trioedd Ynys Prydain', *Cambro-Briton*, 1 (1858).
57 NLW, MS 3289C, f. 3.
58 NLW, MS 912D (T. Stephens MS9), 'No 24 On the question whether the Druids sacrificed human beings written for the Cymreigyddion meeting to be held in the town of Swansea in June 1841' by 'Senex', ff. 21–2. See also NLW, MS 909C (T. Stephens MS 6), 'Druids: An English Essay comprising an account of Druids, Druidic customs Druidic Symbols and Alphabet by Plennydd (Thomas Stephens)'.

59 NLW, MS 912D (T. Stephens MS9), f. 26.
60 John Barrow, *An Account of Travels into the Interior of Southern Africa in the Years 1797 and 1798 including … Sketches of the physical and moral Characters of the various Tribes of inhabitants surrounding the Settlement of the Cape of Good Hope*, 2 vols (London, 1801 and 1806), I, 198–9, 202. Barrow's description was part of the British colonial contestation of South Africa. Gaïka is the European rendering of Ngqika, the much-described head of the Xhosa, described as 'Kaffers' or 'Kaffir' in nineteenth-century colonial literature.
61 [Gwallter Mechain], 'Essay on the Influence of Climate upon National Manners', in *Gwaith Parch. Walter Davies (Gwallter Mechain) dan Olygiad y Parch. D. Silvan Evans, B. D. Cyfrol III* (Caerfyrddin, 1866), pp. 179, 180, 186. This essay may not have been published until 1866, but Stephens's close relationship with Gwallter Mechain raises the distinct possibility of his reading it in manuscript. See their long letters in Adam Coward (ed.), *The Correspondence of Thomas Stephens. Revolutionising Welsh Scholarship in the Mid-nineteenth Century through Knowledge Exchange* (Aberystwyth, 2020), pp. 10–17, 21–2, 24–5, 26–8.
62 'On the Comparative Merits of the Remains of Ancient Literature in the Welsh, Irish, and Gaelic Languages, and their Value in Elucidating the Ancient History and the Mental Cultivation of the Inhabitants of Britain, Ireland, and Gaul', in *The Literary Remains of the Reverend Thomas Price, Carnhuanawc, Vicar of Cwm Dû and Rural Dean, Author of Hanes Cymru, Essays on the Geographical Progress of Empire and Civilization, etc. etc.*, 2 vols (Llandovery, 1854), I, 218, 223.
63 'An Historical Account of the Statuta Walliae, or the Statutes of Rhuddlan, by which Wales was Annexed to England by Rhynyr Ynad', in *The Literary Remains*, I, 348.
64 NLW, MS 17176E, 'On the State of Agriculture and the Process of Art & Manufactures in Britain during the period & under the influence of the Druidical System' by 'JJ'; John Jones, 'On the State of Agriculture and the Process of Art & Manufactures in Britain during the period & under the influence of the Druidical System', *Archaeologia Cambrensis Supplement 1850* (1850), 87–110.
65 NLW, MS 17176E, f. 1.
66 NLW, MS 17176E, f. 2.
67 NLW, MS 17176E, ff. 4, 6.
68 NLW, MS 17176E, ff. 9–10, 5.
69 NLW, MS 17176E, f. 4.
70 NLW, MS 17176E, ff. 7–10.
71 Jones, 'On the State of Agriculture', 110.
72 Paul O'Leary, 'The Languages of Patriotism in Wales 1840–1880', in Geraint H. Jenkins (ed.), *The Welsh Language and Social Domains 1801–1911* (Cardiff,

2000), pp. 533–60; Hywel Teifi Edwards and E. G. Millward, *Jiwbili y Fam Wen Fawr: Fictoria, 1887–1897* (Llandysul, 2002); Marion Löffler, '"Hen Wlad Fy Nhadau" a "The Land of My Fathers": Diwylliant Darostyngol yng Ngwasanaeth yr Ymerodraeth Brydeinig', *Llafur*, 13 (2022), 67–81.

73   Revd John Jones, 'An Essay on the Language and Learning of Britain, under the Roman Government, with a Particular Reference to the Testimony of Martial, (Dicitur et Nostros Cantare Britannia versus) and of Juvenal, and to the Influence of Agricola's Schools', in *Two Essays on the Subjects Proposed by the Cambrian Society in Dyfed, which gained the Respective Prizes, at the Eisteddfod held at Caermarthen, in July 1819: to which is added an account of the Proceedings at the Eisteddfod* (Caermarthen, 1822), pp. 59–60.

74   *Eos Dyfed: Sef Rhai o Gyfansoddiadau a anfonwyd i Eisteddfod Caerfyrddin*, p. 95.

75   Edward Parry, 'Essay containing an Historical Account of the Flintshire Castles; by Mr. Edward Parry, Chester', in *The Gwyneddon; or An Account of the Royal Eisteddfod, Held in September, 1828: Together with the Prize Essays and Poems on the Subjects Proposed for Adjudication at that Meeting* (Chester, 1830), p. 49. One hopes that the citation is not from the 1725 novel *Fantomina* by Eliza Haywood.

76   Parry, 'Essay containing an Historical Account', pp. 50–1.

77   'An Historical Account of the Statuta Walliae, or the Statutes of Rhuddlan, by which Wales was Annexed to England by Rhynyr Ynad', pp. 370–1.

78   Neil Evans, 'Finding a New Story: The Search for a Usable Past in Wales, 1869–1930', *Transactions of the Honourable Society of Cymmrodorion*, new ser., 10 (2004), 144–62; see also Neil Evans and Huw Pryce (eds), *Writing a Small Nation's Past Wales in Comparative Perspective, 1850–1950* (Farnham, 2013).

79   *The Cambrian*, 18 September 1824. It was awarded to Aneurin Owen Pugh.

80   'Darluniad o Gastell Caerdydd fel yr oedd yr adeiladaeth yn sefyll yn y flwyddyn 1578, a gafwyd yn Llyfrgell Rhydychain', in *Gwent and Dyfed Royal Eisteddfod 1834* (Llundain, 1835), pp. 84–5; *GPC*, s.v. 'og¹', 'ffenestr, sub. ffenestr grom (1858)', 'ebach', *https://www.geiriadur.ac.uk/gpc/gpc.html* (accessed 20 June 2024).

81   Thorne, 'Cymreigyddion y Fenni a dechreuadau ieitheg gymharol yng Nghymru'.

82   *An Essay on the Influence of Welsh Tradition upon European Literature; which Obtained the Prize Proposed by the Abergavenny Cymreigyddion Society, October, 1838* (Not Published. London, Printed by Ibotson and Palmer, Savoy Street), p. 2. See also Thomas, *Afiaith yng Ngwent*, pp. 85–91.

83   *An Essay on the Influence*, pp. 5, 10.

84   NLW, MS 13960E, ff. 176–215, 'Traethawd Hanesyddawl ar Arglwyddi y Cyffindiroedd'.

85   *The Literary Remains of the Reverend Thomas Price, Carnhuanawc*, I, 345.

86 NLW, MS 13959E, ff. 117–21, 'Hanes Bywyd Llywelyn Tywysawg Diweddar Cymru' by 'Gruffudd ab yr Ynad Coch' (1835); NLW, MS 13959E, f. 147, 'Traethawd ar Hanes Gwent o Ymadawiad y Rhuveiniaid hyd enedigaeth yr enwog Llywelyn ab Gruffudd, Tywysog diweddar Cymmry' (1835); NLW, MS 13961E, f. 78, 'Traethawd ar yr effaith Moesawl a Chynneddfawl, a gafwyd ar Drigolion Cymru, trwy Ddynoethiad o'i dirfawr Gyfoethau Diledawl' (1838).
87 NLW, MS 13959E, f. 38/1, 'Traethawd ar Hanes Dyvodiad y Grefydd Gristionogol i Brydain, ac oddiar ei ddyvodiad gyntaf hyd y chweched ganrif' (1834).
88 NLW, MS 13959E, f. 155/28, 'Hanes a Gweithredoedd gorchestol Owain Glyndwr' by 'Hanesydd Ieuanc' (1835).
89 NLW, MS 13959E, f. 121, 'Hanes Bywyd Llywelyn Tywysawg Diweddar Cymru' by 'Gruffudd ab yr Ynad Coch'.
90 NLW, MS 916E, ff. 38, 45, 92, cited in Adam Coward, 'English Anglers, Welsh Salmon and Social Justice: The Politics of Conservation in Mid-nineteenth century Wales', *WHR*, 27/4 (2015), 730–54 (pp. 747–8).
91 *The Cambrian*, 12 November 1842, cited in Marion Löffler and Gethin Rhys, 'Thomas Stephens and the Abergavenny Cymreigyddion: Letters from the *Cambrian* 1842–3', *NLWJ*, 34/4 (2009), 399–451 (p. 409).
92 *The Cambrian*, 12 November 1842.
93 *The Cambrian*, 12 November 1842.
94 *The Cambrian*, 12 November 1842.
95 NLW, MS 13961E, ff. 247–57, 'Hanes Tylwyth y Prichardiaid, Eppil Caradawc Freichfrâs; Rhai o'r sawl a gladdwyd yn Llanofor, yn 1622' by 'Olrheiniwr' (1842).
96 Stephens, 'Eisteddfod Iforawl Merthyr, 1855', 499–500.
97 Stephens, 'Eisteddfod Iforawl Merthyr, 1855', 500.
98 Charles Wilkins, 'Men I have known: Thomas Stephens', *Cymru Fu* (8 November 1889), 72.
99 See, for instance, 'Awdl oreu ar Raglywiaeth ein grasusaf Frenin Sior IV', *Seren Gomer*, 5/76 (1822), 25; 'Royal Eisteddfod Beaumaris', *North Wales Chronicle*, 4 September 1832.
100 'Traethawd ar Cymdeithasau Cymhedroldeb fel y moddion mwyaf effeithiol i ddiddymu meddwdod', *Seren Gomer*, 21/279 (Rhagfyr 1838), 373–5; 'Anerchiad i'r Dosbarthiadau Gweithiol, ar y lles a ddeillia iddeu plant oddiwrth ddyfal ofaliad am eu haddysgiad crefyddol a moesol', *Seren Gomer*, 24/312 (Medi 1841), 280–1; *Cyfansoddiadau Arobryn Ail Eisteddfod Cymrodorion Dirwestol Merthyr Tydfil* (Merthyr Tydfil, 1850), pp. 4–5; *Cardiff and Merthyr Guardian*, 29 December 1854; *Yr Amserau*, 1 Ebrill 1857.

101 'A Critical review of the Gordovigion Eisteddfod', *The Cambrian*, 8 August 1840.
102 *Cyfansoddiadau Buddugol Eisteddfod Sïon, Cwmafan a Gynhaliwyd Dydd Nadolig, 1855*, pp. 3, 7, 10.
103 *Cyfansoddiadau Buddugol Eisteddfod Sïon*, p. 10.
104 *Cyfansoddiadau Buddugol Eisteddfod Sïon*, p. 43.
105 *Cyfansoddiadau Buddugol Eisteddfod Sïon*, p. 47.
106 Hywel Teifi Edwards, *Gŵyl Gwalia. Yr Eisteddfod Genedlaethol yn Oes Aur Victoria 1858/1868* (Llandysul, 1980), pp. 9–18.
107 *The Aberdare Times*, 24 August 1861.
108 Hywel Teifi Edwards, 'Aberdâr a'r "Genedlaethol" (1861–1885–1956)', in Hywel Teifi Edwards (ed.), *Cwm Cynon. Cyfres y Cymoedd* (Llandysul,1997), p. 138.

13

'Ireland Raids Wales': Pageants and the Performance of History in the 1920s

Paul O'Leary

While the study of Welsh history was professionalised in universities in the early twentieth century, the separation between academic history and 'popular' ways of understanding the past was not always complete. As Huw Pryce demonstrated in his acclaimed study of Sir J. E. Lloyd, academic historians could be drawn into preparations for historical pageants, contributing their knowledge and expertise in ways that made the dramatisation of history for a lay public both entertaining and, potentially, an educational experience.[1] The organisation and presentation of the historical pageants held at Harlech castle in the 1920s – the subject of this chapter – provide a case study of how porous the boundary between professional history and a popular historical culture could be. It also shows how popular conceptions of history navigated an uncertain path between scholarship and the requirements of drama, in the process revealing a great deal about the assumptions of those who wrote and produced popular historical events and the legacies they left behind them. Historical pageants pose questions for the historian who seeks to understand how they represented the past and sought to ensure historical 'authenticity'.

The organised historical pageant movement in Britain began in the first decade of the twentieth century as a way of visualising the past through large costumed public spectacles under the direction of pageant masters, a new enthusiasm that was viewed by the press as a contagion and dubbed 'pageantitis'.[2] A significant feature of the pre-war years in Wales was, as Huw Pryce observed, 'the public validation of Welsh history through performance and display'.[3] Pageants were protean in character and were revived after the war in different circumstances, and often for new purposes, at a time when the performance of historical events that centred on military conflict took on a new complexion, compelling organisers to deal with the themes of war and peace in ways that took into account recent experiences and contemporary sensibilities. Furthermore, the 1920s was a decade when other changes affected the cultural matrix within which historical pageants were performed, not least the shift in patterns of consumption of the mass media and the placing of the systematic study of the history of Wales on a new footing through organisations such as the Board of Celtic Studies of the University of Wales.

By examining the pageants held at Harlech Castle in 1920, 1922 and 1927, this chapter raises questions about the representation of the past in visual form and the challenges of achieving historical 'authenticity' in such productions. In addition, these events shed light on the mobilisation of the cultural capital of middle-class networks (locally, regionally and nationally), as well as illuminating hybrid expressions of national identity. The pageants were written and performed in a decade of social and political transformation, when post-war Wales not only had to adjust to peace, but also saw the enfranchisement of some women in parliamentary elections and the rise of the Labour Party, together with the disestablishment of the Established Church and the precipitous decline of the great landed estates. Representing history to a popular audience in this context was not a neutral pursuit.

The purpose of the Harlech pageants was to raise money for a village hall to commemorate the dead of the First World War. These events have been situated in the context of post-war 'peace pageants', but this was not the only significant aspect of them.[4] The performances also embodied a particular interpretation of the history of Wales that reflected the preoccupations of the organisers and local elites, as well as those of the writers who contributed to individual episodes. An added dimension is that Ireland is a clearly discernible presence in the pageants. These themes raise questions about the authorship, form, content and reception of the pageants.

In August 1922, the Dolgellau-based newspaper *Y Dydd* ('The Day') published an article under the title *Hanes Cenedl* ('History of a Nation') in which it suggested that 'the pageant is an excellent medium for teaching history', explaining that historical pageants also engendered friendly patriotism and nurtured literary, singing and acting talents:

Famous historical figures are the material for a pageant and it is best if there is an old castle or abbey or monastery nearby the place where the acting happens. When it is decided to hold a pageant, everyone goes to it to research history books. *Brut y Tywysogion* [the chronicle of the princes], the *Mabinogion*, Dafydd ap Gwilym and the early poets [*Gogynfeirdd*] are read; the organist of the chapel or church brings old music and folk songs to light, the poets set the history of the locality to song or in *cynghanedd* [strict metre poetry], and in the end there is a clearer picture of our country in olden times than can be obtained by reading many volumes.[5]

Described here is the type of self-sustaining Welsh-language culture of the local eisteddfod and chapel vestry, with its traditions of bardic and musical creativity, that was such a strong feature of places like Merioneth either side of the First World War. This culture sustained choral traditions and singing festivals as well as literary competitions. In some respects, it chimed with the ideal of the 'Parkerian' pageant (named after Louis Napoleon Parker) that came into existence in England from 1906, with Parker insisting that his pageants be based on voluntary labour.[6] However, the Harlech pageants found it necessary to pay not only the pageant master and musicians but also some costumiers, typists, a designer and their expenses. It also had to pay the Board of Works for use of the castle and remunerate the board for the drop in visitor income while the pageants were held.

Harlech, on the north-west coast of Wales, is a small medieval castle town that was chartered in 1284; its imposing castle is one of the key structures of the Edwardian conquest of Wales, along with those at Caernarfon, Beaumaris and Conwy. The fact that it seesawed between English and Welsh control underlines its contentious history, one that was recognised but largely neutralised in the pageants. In the late eighteenth century, the castle's precipitous drop on its seaward side and its equally dramatic silhouetting against the mountains of Eryri on the landward side made it an attraction for the Romantic tourist. By the nineteenth and early twentieth centuries, the arrival of the railway, combined with the energies of local entrepreneurs and – crucially – the creation of golf links created a resort that attracted a wealthy and aristocratic elite.[7] The town attracted well-off middle-class retirees and summer visitors from the rest of the United Kingdom, some of whom were able to draw on extensive cultural networks that helped inform and shape the historical pageants. They built on a local musical culture that had developed in the coastal town in the decades before the First World War. A successful choral festival, held in the castle, was suspended in the 1880s and revived with great success in 1910, continuing until 1914 before being suspended again for the duration of the war.[8] The initial intention had been to hold a Shakespeare festival to raise money for a hall, drawing on the expertise of actor and director Patrick Kirwan, an idea that was squashed by an influential aristocratic patron, Lord Howard de Walden of Chirk Castle, who insisted on the event being rooted in the history of both Harlech and Wales.[9]

The pageants were held over three days in August. Introducing one of these days in 1922, David Lloyd George, who had a track record of encouraging the visualisation of historical characters through drama, emphasised the educational significance of pageants.[10] Five years later, his son, William, went a step further by claiming that pageants were more effective than cinema in portraying the past. Pathé News produced a short moving sequence from the 1922 pageant that focused on Margaret and Megan Lloyd George, while a sequence from the 1927 pageant was filmed for the *Empire News Bulletin* – presumably the 'cinematograph films' that were shown in 'cinemas throughout Wales'.[11] These were silent movies, with synchronised sound in moving films only becoming common in 1927. Sound – both spoken and musical – was central to the pageant spectacle and silent movies could be seen as an inferior medium for representing the past to a wider audience. By the end of the 1920s, however, questions relating to cinema had begun to dominate discussions. The poet and archdruid Elfed (Howell Elvet Lewis) remarked that the pageant of 1927 should have been filmed and shown in cinemas, especially given the scenic surroundings of Harlech Castle, and he hoped the next one (which did not happen) would be. If the Americans had these surroundings, he suggested, they would show it from New York to San Francisco.[12] It is possible he had in mind D. W. Griffith's hugely successful film 'Birth of a Nation' (1915), a deeply problematic production because of its racial portrayal of American history. What is clear, however, is that during the 1920s the promoters and audiences of the pageant had experience of different types of dramatic production, both theatrical and cinematic, and that these affected their perceptions of the events.[13] Even the academic historian R. T. Jenkins was prompted to think about the writing of history after watching a cinematic cartoon of Felix the Cat in the 1920s.[14]

Unlike the National Pageant at Cardiff in 1909, several writers collaborated on the Harlech events.[15] They can be divided into two groups: the first had London-Irish and London-Welsh connections (some of whom had been involved with Celtic revival movements before the war) and the second was mainly based at the University of Wales.

The key figure in the first group was Alfred Perceval Graves (1846–1931), an Irish Anglican who entered the civil service as a clerk in 1869 and was father of the poet Robert Graves. He became an inspector of schools in 1874, overlapping with Matthew Arnold in that position and ending his career in London. He was one of the middle-class functionaries that made the state apparatus work on a day-to-day basis. Graves also took a leading part in the revival of Irish letters, demonstrating the dual identity that allowed figures from each of the nations of the United Kingdom to inhabit and express a hybrid identity.[16] His relationship with Irish nationalists was fraught, however, resigning his membership of the Gaelic League because of its involvement in politics; he was criticised by the league's London organiser, P. S. O'Hegarty, for 'reek[ing] with a most offensive brand of loyalty ... not alone to England's dominant position in Ireland but a personal and fulsome loyalty to the King as well'.[17] His monarchism was evident in obtaining royal patronage for the Harlech pageants and trying (unsuccessfully) to secure a royal visit to them, although he had some consolation in being able to present a bound copy of the pageant book to the prince of Wales in November 1923.[18] The author of many songs and ballads, he was president of the Irish Literary Society for several years. He had been inducted into the Gorsedd of Bards of the National Eisteddfod of Wales in 1898 and published *Welsh Poetry Old and New: In English Verse* in 1912. When he retired to Harlech in 1919, he became the prime mover in organising the pageants.

Graves's main co-author in the pageant was Ernest Rhys (1859–1946), a poet and familiar figure in London literary circles, who was editor of the Everyman Library from 1906. His hybrid identity was expressed in his poem 'An Autobiography', with its opening line 'Wales England wed, so I was bred'. It continues: "Twas merry London gave me breath ... But Ireland taught me love was best: / And Irish eyes, and

London cries, and streams of Wales may tell the rest'.[19] Both Rhys and Graves knew the poet W. B. Yeats personally, with Rhys becoming a close friend of his. Graves and Rhys shared an interest in the pan-Celtic movement before the First World War when they were involved with different literary revival movements, Irish in one case and Welsh in the other.[20] The London connection also explains the involvement of Patrick Joseph Kirwan, who occupied the crucial position of pageant master in 1920 and 1922, as well as acting in some scenes himself. Born in Ireland, he was a director of drama in England and produced parts of Shakespeare plays in the reconstructed Globe Theatre at Earl's Court in 1912 (where he provided 'a spectacular, "environmental" entertainment'), and had been put in charge of the Shakespeare festival at Stratford-upon-Avon in 1914. By the 1920s, he was writing about the history and contemporary position of English drama; after Harlech, he would move on to mastermind pageants in England.[21]

The second group of writers included J. E. Lloyd (1861–1947), professor of Welsh history at the University College of North Wales (hereafter U.C.N.W., now Bangor University), and Arthur S. Turberville (1888–1945), then a lecturer at U.C.N.W. and later professor of modern history at Leeds University.[22] Lloyd had been critical of some aspects of the Cardiff pageant of 1909, which he thought to have played fast and loose with historical knowledge, and he possibly considered contributing to the Harlech pageant as a way of ensuring historical accuracy.[23] Graves invited J. E. Lloyd to perform in the planned pageant of 1929, possibly inspired by the famous English social historian G. M. Trevelyan playing Geoffrey Chaucer in the Berkhamsted pageant five years earlier; Lloyd declined the offer.[24] The literary scholar and poet Sir John Morris-Jones (1864–1929), also based at U.C.N.W., wrote an episode dealing with the strange vision of the eighteenth-century High Anglican poet Ellis Wynne.[25] To this group can be added Sir Henry Walford Davies (1869–1941) of the University College of Wales, Aberystwyth, who supervised musical arrangements in 1920, although much of that work was delegated. Once again, these figures did not conform to the image created by *Y Dydd* ('The Day') of an event in which local poets composed the words and local organists produced the music.

The identity of some of these writers was complex. Both Graves and Kirwan were Irish, one Protestant and the other Catholic (Kirwan was an active supporter of the Catholic Stage Guild), while Rhys was married to an Irishwoman. Irish characters were included in several of the pageant episodes, and Graves favoured the use of Irish tunes to accompany several performances. Even some of the Welsh contributors had strong Irish connections of one sort or another. Moreover, the contribution of David Lloyd George to the pageant of 1922, following his role in the partition of Ireland seven months earlier, added a political dimension to the spectacle. Although the pageants focused on the history of Wales, the comments of an Irish day president in 1927 allowed newspapers to claim it was a case of 'Ireland Raids Wales'.[26] By that date, the key personnel had changed. Robert Morris Davis of the British Drama League became pageant master, bringing his experience of the Bombay pageant, while the composer Josef Holbrooke was in charge of the music and Joyce Peters was mistress of the dances; she introduced Welsh steps and figures to old Welsh dance tunes that had recently been discovered in collections at the National Library of Wales.[27]

The relationship between the pageants and historical scholarship was uneasy. On the face of it, great effort was made to ensure historical accuracy. Both the National Library and the National Museum of Wales were consulted, as well as libraries in aristocratic hands. Advice about historical scholarship was sought from academic historians such as J. E. Lloyd, who also contributed an episode on Owain Glyndŵr's parliament at Harlech Castle in 1405.[28] While preparing the first version of the pageant in February 1920, Ernest Rhys stated that he had all the Cymmrodorion *Transactions* for reference and he promised to look up E. A. Lewis's *Medieval Boroughs of Snowdonia* (1912); however, despite this commitment to consult academic scholarship, he added: 'we must not lose the human interest in too much care about the history' and they should include 'a leavening of fun'.[29] He suggested that they should 'get our large effects right, & let pedantry go, eh?'[30] Shortly after this, he had a 'practical talk' with Kirwan that changed some of his views about the form of the pageant. Kirwan thought there was 'too much processional & pedestrian business' in most pageants and 'not enough dramatic relief'. Rhys repeated his view that there should be more comedy, which he thought would add to 'the reality'.[31] The use of processions in pageants was one way of involving large numbers of people but, as Graves pointed out, the narrow streets of Harlech militated against incorporating such a feature there.[32]

There was also discussion about whether the content of the pageant should reflect the town and castle alone or if it should have a wider remit.[33] A public meeting in Harlech at Easter 1920 sowed the seeds of an event that would draw on participants from across the county; Kirwan had wanted an even wider geographical net.[34] By embracing the county of Merioneth as a whole, the organisers were able to draw on the contributions of amateur dramatic groups in surrounding towns, reflecting the post-war enthusiasm for amateur drama following the establishment of the British Drama League in 1919, including in Wales.

In contrast to the main voluntary culture of Merioneth, the pageants were in English in a county where the language of everyday life for the overwhelming majority was Welsh – 86 per cent according to the census of 1921, and more than one-third of those were monoglots.[35] Ernest Rhys suggested a Welsh-language pageant, then reduced his aspiration to two, or simply one, scene in Welsh. At one point he suggested that 'Welsh folk' would find the proposed scenes 'too anglified, possibly'.[36] In the event, the 1920 pageant included one short episode in Welsh, translated by the poet Eifion Wyn (Eliseus Williams).

This raises questions about the 'assumptions [authors] share with their audiences'. The years either side of the First World War produced enthusiasm for, and criticism of, the thriving and increasingly professionalised Welsh-speaking drama.[37] Against that background, pageants could be seen as frivolous and unwelcome interlopers in a dramatic landscape with largely conservative tastes, and in a swingeing critique of 1911, the literary scholar W. J. Gruffydd contrasted the vacuousness of the so-called 'national' pageant of Wales at Cardiff in 1909 with his ideal of a truly national theatre, also condemning the authors for being outsiders.[38] Comparable arguments about a clash between the imported practices and assumptions of the popular English stage to Welsh-language theatre were made by Saunders Lewis in 1919, when local drama groups had become very popular.[39] The eisteddfod, both local and national, provided an avenue for such productions, but although the Harlech pageants depended on drama groups from across the county and beyond, the pageants remained English in speech. This undoubtedly reflects the backgrounds of the organisers, who were incomers or outsiders, and there is here an echo of Graves's original plans for a Shakespeare festival that would have been directed at such an audience. It is also significant that the pageants were held during the summer, when the local population was augmented by tourists and those who owned or rented summer homes.

There was a discussion about the form the pageants should take. Rhys favoured 'short, sonorous speeches, & drama conveyed by action rather than dialogue'. However, the intervention of Kirwan, an experienced dramatist, changed this. Rhys thought that 'stagey dialogue sounds forced to a modern audience that likes direct speech & clear emphasis', but dialogue was the main form used.[40] In June 1920, Rhys and Kirwan showed the preliminary text to an unnamed 'sympathetic critic, who had written plays & was also of some Celtic savvy', who suggested shortening the scene on Owain Glyndŵr and thought the siege scene lacked dramatic moments; Rhys responded: 'I daresay the Pageant-Master could work up some siege sensations?'[41] Music was a key feature of the pageants, with compositions by Hubert Davies in 1920. In 1922, this was nominally under the supervision of the conductor Walford Davies, but the extensive correspondence between Graves and Charles H. Clements of Aberystwyth demonstrates the extent to which the latter researched and scored the music, fitted it to the text and sourced musicians and instruments. He had particular problems with arrangements for the 'Irish airs' requested by Graves.[42]

Correspondence between the organisers of the 1920 pageant makes clear that the production was a negotiation between attempts to achieve authenticity and historical accuracy on the one hand, and the production of an impressive spectacle on the other. The last could trump the other two, and it is unclear how far the text for individual episodes that was supplied by the two historians, Lloyd and Turberville, was adjusted and re-written for dramatic effect. This boundary was blurred by the fact that the pageant included mythical, literary and symbolical episodes as well as those relating to verifiable historical events connected with the castle. According to Ernest Rhys in the handbook for the 1920 pageant, 'the wonderful thing about Harlech Castle is that it is the whole history of Wales written in grey cipher on its stones'.[43] Decoding that cipher, he implied, was a straightforward act, with the solidity of the imposing structure creating an impression of historical legibility. The pageant was held in the courtyard of the castle, which acted as both an open-air theatre and a material reminder of the history being performed, but the implication of Rhys's statement – that history could be read from the edifice – is belied by the protracted discussions over the content and form of the pageant and his fear that the performances were too 'anglified'. A castle could be 'read' in different ways.

The version of history presented in the Harlech pageants was a combination of the content of episodes and their framing by the introductory remarks of day presidents. It also reflected the cultural background of some of the key writers. When Pathé News filmed parts of the 1922 festival, it was billed as a Welsh National Pageant, and this framing was evident in the types of historical and mythical episodes that were performed. The format these writers produced changed during the 1920s, with half the episodes in 1920 based on mythology and the other half on history. In 1922, there were nine episodes – two based on mythology, another on a literary work and the remainder on history, beginning with the drowning of the mythical *Cantre'r Gwaelod* ('The Lowland Hundred') and ending with the successful annexation of Wales to England, although also including an out-of-sequence detour into the Cromwellian siege of Harlech castle.

The pageant was held in the courtyard of the castle, and the physical surroundings were both a theatre and a tangible reminder of the history being performed, with trumpeters announcing events from the ramparts. In many ways, the castle itself can be considered a member of the cast. The programme for the 1922 pageant ('Under Royal Patronage'), comprised the following episodes:[44]

I. The Great Sea Flood, by Patrick J. Kirwan. Chief characters: Prince Elphin, Lady Angharad, Teitherin and Seithenin. Acted by Mrs David Roberts and the Barmouth Company.

II. The Wooing of Branwen, by Alfred Perceval Graves. Chief characters: King Brân of Britain, the Queen Mother, Matholwch, King of Ireland and the Princess Branwen. Acted chiefly by Mr and Mrs Graves's Harlech Company.

III. The Preaching of the Crusades, by Professor Arthur S. Turberville. Chief characters: Archbishop Baldwin, Gerald Barry (Geraldus [Giraldus] Cambrensis), Archdeacon of St David's, and Prince Meredyth [Maredudd]. Acted by an Ardudwy Company.

IV. Owain Glyndŵr at Harlech, by Professor J. E. Lloyd. Chief characters: Owain and Lady Glyndŵr, Edmund Mortimer and Lady Mortimer, Chancellor Young and Bishop of Bangor. Acted by a Cricieth Company.

V. Queen Margaret's Visit to Harlech Castle, by Alfred Perceval Graves. Chief characters: Queen Margaret, Edward Prince of Wales, Jasper Tudor, Dafydd ab Einion, Lord Northwold and Lloyd of Cwmbychan. Acted by a Harlech company.

VI. Archdeacon as Prys Psalmodist, by Patrick J. Kirwan. Chief characters: Archdeacon and his lay clerk. Acted by descendants of Archdeacon Prys.

VII. The End of the Royalist Defence of Harlech, by Alfred Perceval Graves. Chief characters: Colonel Owen and Sir Arthur Blayney, Captain Edwards and Mari of the Morfa. Acted by a Porthmadog company.

VIII. The Sleeping Bard (*Y Bardd Cwsg*), by Sir John Morris-Jones. Chief characters: the first sleeping bard, Ellis Wynne, the second sleeping bard, Merlin and Taliesin. Acted by Sir John Morris Jones as the Sleeping Bard and a Penrhyndeudraeth company.

IX. The Coming of Peace, by Alfred Perceval Graves and Patrick J. Kirwan. Chief characters: King Edward I, King Henry VII, Peace and the Mother of Wales. Acted by a Bronwen party.[45]

Taken together, the episodes are a combination of the mythical and literary with historical events. On the one hand, some contributors drew on local traditions and medieval tales (such as the Mabinogion) that related to the castle, whereas two professional historians brought their scholarship to bear on specific historical events and personalities. The result is a patchwork of approaches to the past, drawing on popular understandings of history as well as historical research, that finds its unifying focus in the castle. This fits a pattern described by Peter Burke as creating historical narratives through performance by 'practising bricolage, assembling fragments of the past into new patterns'.[46] The 'bricolage' at Harlech in the 1920s presented a distinctive interpretation of Welsh history.

The episodes were knit together during the dress rehearsal a week before the production.[47] The opening mythological scene was matched by the penultimate scene that dealt with the vision of an eighteenth-century High Churchman who had been born near Harlech, Elis Wynne's *Gweledigaetheu y Bardd Cwsc* ('Visions of the Sleeping Bard') of 1703. In between, the national history carries a strong sense of the role of monarchy and aristocracy as historical agents, as well as the centrality of Anglicanism to the history of Wales, themes that were not entirely consonant with the sense of the Welsh as a Liberal, Nonconformist people that had developed in the nineteenth and early twentieth centuries. The organisers tried to balance this by involving representatives of different political and religious traditions among the actors and day presidents, although in 1920 and 1922 in particular these figures were mainly chosen from local elites.

In 1920, Margaret Lloyd George, the prime minister's wife and a public figure in her own right through work in organisations like the North Wales Heroes Memorial Fund that was set up to create war memorials, said that the pageants recalled 'the glorious story of their country's picturesque and heroic past' and they were being held in memory of those 'who had done so much for Wales and the Empire'.[48] The connection between past and present was explicit in her address. The Great War was overtly present in the final episode, the Coming of Peace ('a symbolical masque'[49]), in which figures representing Wales and Britannia appeared hand-in-hand accompanied by 'wounded men in khaki, attended by Red Cross nurses'. This, it was said, 'illustrated the gallant new order that succeeded the heroic old', and it was claimed that this episode would make the most direct appeal to Welsh patriotism.[50] It is this evocation of the First World War that has been emphasised by historians who have commented on the Harlech pageants.[51]

Two of the day presidents in 1922 represented starkly contrasting aspects of public life, in both political and religious terms. The disestablishment of the Church of England in Wales in 1919, which had created a new Anglican province with its own archbishop after a long and often bitter campaign, had echoes in the 1922 pageant. As one of the day presidents, A. G. Edwards, the recently appointed first Archbishop of Wales, responded warmly to the scene that 'faithfully describes how Archbishop Baldwin and Giraldus Cambrensis preached the Crusade in the neighbourhood'. He identified with Giraldus, who he considered to be 'the most interesting character in the whole history of Wales', noting that he was 'partly Norman and partly Welsh'. Edwards had supported an earlier publication by A. P. Graves, and his appearance at the pageant was the continuation of an association between two Anglicans, one Irish and one Welsh, who straddled cultural fault lines in their respective cultures.[52] By contrast, David Lloyd George, who presided on a different day, was a Liberal Nonconformist who had been one of the architects of Church disestablishment. He saw the history of Glyndŵr as one of the 'romances' of Wales. Comparing Owain to Bonnie Prince Charlie, he saw the two as having similar relationships to their respective countries: what Prince Charlie was to the Highlands of Scotland, Glyndŵr was to the Highlands of Wales, 'a constant source of guessing and perplexity'. This prompted Lloyd George to indulge in some counterfactual speculation about the course of British history:

> What would have happened in these islands if the Severn had not been in flood, and Glyndwr had joined Hotspur and Mortimer? The same question was put supposing Prince Charlie had advanced from Derby, which would always be a question that would agitate curious minds. The whole history, not merely of Wales, but probably of England, would have changed.[53]

These were the words of a statesman who had spent the preceding years as prime minister helping to re-draw the boundaries of Europe according to the principle of national self-determination and who had been an uncompromising negotiator with Irish republicans in the discussions culminating in the Anglo-Irish Treaty of 1921. His thoughts on British history were more than abstract musings and were undoubtedly sparked by the challenges of his own statecraft. In the emphases on different aspects of history by these public figures, therefore, we get a glimpse of the different, and potentially discordant, ways in which spectators might have received and interpreted the history being performed.

The most obvious route to achieving 'authenticity' in performances was through the creation of elaborate costumes to underline the 'otherness' of the past. There were 200 actors to dress in 1920 and 300 in 1922. An unsuccessful attempt was made to secure costumes that had been used in the National Pageant at Cardiff in 1909, and most of the Harlech costumes appear to have been made by local sewing groups under Kirwan's direction, using Dion Clayton Calthrop's book of 1906, *English Costume* ('among many others').[54] The costumes required for the episode on Glyndŵr's parliament of 1405, played by Cricieth actors, were designed by Herbert Norris, a specialist in the field of historical costumes from London, augmented by suits of armour loaned by Lord Howard de Walden, who insisted on being recompensed if they were damaged.[55] Black and white film and photographs[56] of the time do not reveal the colour that struck observers. In 1922, Margaret Lloyd George was 'resplendent in a dress of silver and blue', while her daughter Megan wore 'a striking creation of gold and red'. The dull colour of the coats of mail worn by Glyndŵr and Mortimer were contrasted with the colourful costumes of the women.[57] The few surviving costumes confirm an impression of colour.[58] Colin Gresham, who took part in the pageant as a young boy, recalled Owain's armour differently to the press report: he described it as 'a magnificent suit of golden plate armour with a surcoat over it displaying his [Owain's] four lions rampant'.[59]

A contrast between past and present was evident to one commentator in the difference between the costumed actors thronging the town's streets and 'the moderns', that is, spectators, waiting to enter the castle.[60] Even so, by breaking down the barrier between everyday spaces and the performance space in the castle, the boundary between past and present was breached. Colin Gresham recalled seeing the bizarre spectacle of one actor wearing a suit of plate armour while driving his open-top sports car, and photographs in the press and commemorative albums included one of an actor in full costume with a cigarette holder in his mouth and another pouring tea from a thermos flask.[61] Using elaborate costumes to emphasise the otherness of the past achieved only so much. The presentism of the pageants was evident in the way some members of local elites were cast as actors. Lord and Lady Howard de Walden performed in 1920, for example, while members of the Lloyd George family took part in 1922. The local council and the mayor also appeared as their predecessors in one episode. Historical time was collapsed into the present by including modern elites and descendants of figures from the past at a time when aristocratic influence was in retreat and the social and economic position of the great estates was being undermined.[62] A new voice was heard in 1927, when Professor Robert Richards, the son of a slate quarryman and under-secretary of state for India in the first Labour government, performed an opening ceremony.[63]

Spectators reacted more favourably to some episodes than to others.[64] In the episode on the flooding of *Cantre'r Gwaelod* ('The Lowland Hundred'), the sound of the sea against the walls of the castle was produced by gravel tipped in a large garden sieve. The breaking of the sea wall was marked by men, women and children running from the stage through the audience, followed by the 'sea waves' that engulfed everyone, sweeping out of the castle courtyard and leaving an empty stage. The 'waves' were children in blue acting the part of 'Foam Maidens'. A commentator in 1920 judged this to have been 'depicted with satisfying realism', while another in 1922 found the episode simply 'weird'.[65] Possibly the scene acted as an uncomfortable reminder of the 'deluge' of the First World War, a metaphor for the overwhelming character of that conflict first used by Lloyd George in December 1915 ('it is the deluge, it is a convulsion of Nature').[66] The imagery of an inundation was also present in the final episode, 'The Coming of Peace', but in this case it was the less threatening 'rising tide' of 'Brotherhood'.[67]

The Glyndŵr episode was a highlight of the pageant. In 1922, Patrick Kirwan played Owain, but the attraction was Margaret Lloyd George, as Lady Glyndŵr, and her children – Megan as Owain's daughter and Major Gwilym as Edmund Mortimer.[68] The women were being presented as the heirs to Glyndŵr, a kind of Welsh 'first family'. They had no words to say and simply appeared in a tableau, as if their mere presence was sufficient to confer reflected prestige on proceedings. At a time when women over thirty had recently received the vote, the appearance of women from the prime minister's family meant that they, as well as female characters in other episodes, can be seen as symbols of women's agency in the past.[69] In 1914, Lloyd George had mobilised the history of Glyndŵr to encourage Welsh support for the war, so much so (as Huw Pryce has shown) that one Welsh-American in 1914 claimed: 'Glyndwr is David Lloyd George'.[70] Had the prime minister appeared in the pageant as Owain alongside his family, however, there is a danger the episode would have collapsed under the weight of its own inflated symbolism.

For the author of this episode, the historian J. E. Lloyd, Glyndŵr was a national hero. This interpretation affirmed a view of the medieval prince that had emerged during the nineteenth century and was cemented by commemorations of the prince's 500th anniversary in 1915, when he was represented as both a national and a military hero. The Board of Education official celebrations of St David's Day also gave him a prominent position. The fact that he had fought against the English Crown did not trouble contemporaries, and his portrayal as a patriotic hero was consistent with the Liberal conception of empire, not in opposition to it. As Huw Pryce has written: 'the Glyndŵr who survived in the memory is a multi-faceted figure that every age will interpret in the light of its own circumstances'. He argues convincingly that Glyndŵr and his memory represent a *lieu de mémoire* ('realm of memory'), as popularised by the French historian Pierre Nora.[71]

The hybrid nature of expressions of national identity in the pageants is illustrated by a composition by Graves, 'The Song of the Heather', which was sung during the episode on Glyndŵr. It is unlikely that J. E. Lloyd decided to conclude the scene with this song, especially as Owain is made to say, anachronistically, that it was 'a song to unite the Sons of the Celt under the heather plume that flourished on all our unvanquished heights'.[72] The lyrics reflected the song's origins as Graves's anthem of the Celtic League, a group of cultural patriots from the Celtic nations who met periodically to celebrate their languages and cultures, and it was translated into Welsh by T. Gwynn Jones. The song began life in the 1890s as a celebration of the six nations of the Celtic world, turning into a hymn to the integration of the British Isles in one national community.[73] It acknowledged that history had sometimes not run smoothly, and that Hugh O'Neill, Robert the Bruce and Llewelyn the Last 'drew steel / For Erin's and Alba's and Cambria's weal', but the present was a different matter. The last stanza ran:

> This flower of the free is the heather, the heather;
> It springs where the sea and the land meet together;
> Four nations are we, yet beneath its bright feather
> To-day we are one wheresoever we be.[74]

By 1922, it was difficult to talk of the four nations of the British Isles as being united. Between 1919 and 1921, Ireland had experienced a bitter war of independence, during which Lloyd George had sent the hated Black and Tans to that country where they carried out atrocities. The prime minister and his cabinet secretary, Thomas Jones (also present at the pageant) had been key figures in the negotiations leading to the Anglo-Irish Treaty that confirmed the partition of Ireland into two jurisdictions with their own parliaments. Whatever else they were in 1922, the four nations were not 'one'.

As an Irish Protestant, Graves was keenly aware of events on the other side of the Irish Sea. He had included the song in the pageant of 1920, when Ireland was in turmoil but still united and some people continued to hope for a peaceful resolution of the Irish Question. The lyrics make more sense in the context of 1920 than in the changed circumstances of 1922: in the summer of 1920, for example, adverts placed by the Fellowship of Reconciliation in the local press urged peaceful arbitration instead of the armed conflict that was then happening.[75] There was, therefore, a fluidity to the expression of national identity in the pageant that reflected changing political circumstances as well as the personal backgrounds of writers such as Graves and Rhys. Graves returned to the theme of the place of Wales in the UK in 1927 when he wrote that the final episode:

> recapitulates the history of the castle from the days of Edward I to the present time, through periods of storm and stress to that of perfect amity between the allegorical figures of Britannia and Wales, and closes with a song of praise of Wales. Then the characters of all the episodes enter and fill the central stage behind the figure of Peace. All will then sing the Welsh National Anthem, '*Hen Wlad fy Nhadau*' … following it with 'God Save the King'.[76]

This is the voice of a southern Irish Protestant, viewing events in Ireland from a home in Harlech that he named 'Erinfa', or 'Erin's Place'. On one level, the script of the pageant was about how the different nations of the United Kingdom had overcome their historical differences, whereas contemporary developments raised questions about the finality of that process. Coincidentally, Lloyd George's attendance at Harlech occurred against the background of the killing of the Irish leader Michael Collins by anti-treaty forces in west Cork in August 1922. Collins had been incarcerated at Frongoch (the 'University of Revolution') in Merioneth, some 47 kilometres from Harlech, following the Easter Rising of 1916. The shadow of Ireland was never far away from the pageants.[77]

How do we situate the Harlech historical pageants in the lineage examined so expertly by Huw Pryce in his study of historical writing and interpretation from the early Middle Ages to the twenty-first century?[78] First, the pageants had an educational legacy. Teachers in Merioneth and Caernarfonshire circulated pageant books left over from the pageant of 1920 among 'their elder scholars', while other material was used in reading books for elementary schools.[79] The existence of substantial handbooks and programmes, as well as commemorative photo albums, meant that those who attended performances had a tangible memento that could be re-used and re-cycled. The second consideration is more difficult to answer. The relationship between the pageants and attempts to represent historical truth poses challenges for the historian who is wedded to the presentation of research through the written word alone, although the contributions by professional historians like Lloyd and Turberville suggest they were not troubled by working with a dramatic medium. Like cinema, pageants promised the immediacy of sight and sound (through dialogue, costume, music and the castle) to provide a view onto the past. Drama necessitated the invention of dialogue. It also focused on individuals and, in the case of Harlech, these were mostly members of various elites; the absence of the processional element used in some other pageants excluded the majority of people from collective historical agency, as did the use of the English language in a mostly Welsh-speaking area. The narrative of the past, weaving together myth and verifiable historical events and characters, was not entirely seamless. Glyndŵr was, after all, a rebel prince. The contradiction between a celebration of an Anglican elite and the reality of a Liberal Nonconformist political culture inevitably raised questions about what view of the past was being presented for consumption. Conflicting political voices also contextualised performances for those who attended.

The Harlech events exhibited some features that could be found in historical pageants performed elsewhere in the 1920s, such as the use of an historic monument, the employment of a pageant master, a mainly top-down view of the past that focused on ancient or mythological events and the medieval and early modern periods, together with an emphasis on peace and the mobilisation of local elites in support of the performances. However, there was no uniform approach to this protean genre of public performance, as shown by the inclusion of figures that represented modernity in the pageants of 1927 at Conwy Castle (the civil engineer Thomas Telford) and Montgomeryshire (the industrialist and utopian socialist Robert Owen).[80] At the end of the 1930s, Communist-inspired pageants in south Wales demonstrated how people's history could be accommodated to this form of historical visualisation.[81] Among the distinctive features of the Harlech pageants was the way in which the intellectual resources of the University of Wales were mobilised in tandem with middle-class networks extending from London to this coastal resort to create an event that was unusual in its sophistication for such a small place. It was a combination of London Welsh connections and the proximity of Lloyd George's constituency home that secured his attendance and his family's involvement. No other pageant could equal the coup of involving a prime minister and international statesman, and it was this that attracted much newspaper coverage and the attention of filmed news bulletins.

If the Harlech pageants aimed for an authentic representation of the past, it was symbolical rather than literal in character for the most part; it was an approach that was comfortable with the interweaving of historical events and mythology, as well as the presentation of discordant musical traditions. This speaks to an older part of the tradition of history writing essayed by Huw Pryce, and one that preceded the professionalisation of the study of the past. However, there is a very modern challenge here too. Some commentators in the 1920s referred to the potential uses of cinema in relation to pageants, and perhaps we should look towards the epistemological challenges of film as a way of representing the past for evaluating the historical truth conveyed by pageants.[82]

Notes

1 Huw Pryce, *J. E. Lloyd and the Creation of Welsh History* (Cardiff, 2011), pp. 65, 199 n. 15.

2 See Angela Bartie et al. (eds), *Restaging the Past: Historical Pageants, Culture and Society in Modern Britain* (London, 2020).

3 Huw Pryce, *Writing Welsh History: From the Early Middle Ages to the Twenty-first Century* (Oxford, 2022), p. 304.

4 Angela Bartie et al., '"And those who live, how shall I tell their fame?" Historical pageants, collective remembrance and the First World War, 1919–39', *Historical Research*, 90/249 (2017), 636–61 (p. 653).

5 *Y Dydd*, 18 August 1922. On education: Angela Bartie et al., '"History taught in the pageant way": education and historical performance in twentieth-century Britain', *History of Education*, 48 (2019), 156–79.

6 Robert Withington, *English Pageantry: An Historical Outline*, 2 vols (Cambridge, 1918–20), II, 198.

7 John Hirst, 'Resort development on the Cambrian coast' (unpublished PhD thesis, Aberystwyth University, 2017), 79–100.

8 *Weekly Mail*, 6 August 1910; *Cambrian News and Merionethshire Standard*, 10 July 1914.

9 Hazel Walford Davies, '"The country of my heart": Lord Howard de Walden and Wales', *Transactions of the Honourable Society of Cymmrodorion*, new series, 20 (2014), 18–34 (pp. 28–9).

10   *Baner ac Amserau Cymru*, 25 March 1903.
11   *Empire News Bulletin*, 18 Aug 1927, No. 136, NoS ID 048326, Story no. 3/10; *The Times*, 19 August 1927.
12   *South Wales News*, 18 August 1927.
13   Peter Miskell, *A Social History of the Cinema in Wales, 1918–1951: Pulpits, Coal Pits and Fleapits* (Cardiff, 2006).
14   T. Robin Chapman, 'Yr apêl at Felix: agweddau ar hanesyddiaeth R. T. Jenkins (1881–1969)', *WHR*, 30/4 (2021), 609–35.
15   Hywel Teifi Edwards, *The National Pageant of Wales* (Llandysul, 2009); Anwen Jones, 'Celfyddydau Perfformiadol Cymru: Hanes Newydd, Hanesyddiaeth Newydd – Hywel Teifi Edwards a Phasiant Cenedlaethol Cymru, 1909', in Anwen Jones (ed.), *Perfformio'r Genedl: Ar Drywydd Hywel Teifi Edwards* (Cardiff, 2017), pp. 164–95.
16   Fran Brearton, *The Great War in Irish Poetry: W. B. Yeats to Michael Longley* (Oxford, 2003), pp. 101–4; Jean Moorcroft Wilson, *From Great War Poet to Good-bye to All That (1895–1929)* (London, 2018), ch. 1.
17   Richard Kirkland, *Irish London: A Cultural History, 1850–1916* (London, 2021), p. 16; Mary MacDiarmada, *Art O'Brien and Irish Nationalism in London, 1900–25* (Dublin, 2020), p. 63.
18   *The Times*, 1 November 1923.
19   Ernest Rhys, *A London Rose & Other Rhymes* (London, 1894), p. 113; R. F. Foster, *W. B. Yeats: A Life, 1: The Apprentice Mage, 1865–1914* (Oxford, 1998), pp. 63, 76, 107, 161.
20   Tomos Owen, 'London-Welsh writing, 1890–1915: Ernest Rhys, Arthur Machen, W. H. Davies, and Caradoc Evans' (unpublished PhD thesis, Cardiff University, 2011), 63; Daniel Williams, 'Pan-Celticism and the Limits of Post-colonialism: W. B. Yeats, Ernest Rhys and William Sharp in the 1890s', in Tony Brown and Russell Stephens (eds), *Nations and Relations: Writing Across the British Isles* (Cardiff, 2000), pp. 1–29.
21   Obituary, *The Times*, 15 February 1929; Marion F. O'Connor, 'Theatre of the Empire: "Shakespeare's England" at Earl's Court, 1912', in Jean E. Howard and Marion F. O'Connor (eds), *Shakespeare Reproduced: The Text in History and Ideology* (Abingdon, 2005), pp. 86–98 (p. 96 n).
22   Pryce, *Lloyd*, pp. 68, 69.
23   Jones, 'Celfyddydau Perfformiadol Cymru', p. 185.
24   'Introduction', Bartie et al. (eds), *Restaging the Past*, p. 3.
25   I. Williams, 'Jones, Sir John Morris (1864–1929)', rev. D. Ben Rees, *ODNB*, https://doi.org/10.1093/ref:odnb/35120.
26   *Western Mail*, 20 August 1927; *South Wales News*, 20 August 1927; *Manchester Guardian*, 20 August 1927.

27 Alfred Perceval Graves, 'The Coming Harlech Pageant', *The Bookman* (August 1927), 266.
28 National Library of Wales [NLW] 3264D, J. E. Lloyd to Alfred Perceval Graves [hereafter APG], 16 March 1920.
29 NLW 3264D, Rhys to APG, 17 February 1920.
30 NLW 3264D, Rhys to APG, 2 March 1920.
31 NLW 3264D, Rhys to APG, 5 March 1920.
32 A. P. Graves, 'Harlech of the Sieges', *The Spectator*, 22 July 1927.
33 On town and castle histories, see Paul O'Leary, 'Town and Nation: Writing Urban Histories in Nineteenth- and Early Twentieth-century Wales', in Neil Evans and Huw Pryce (eds), *Writing a Small Nation's Past: Wales in Comparative Perspective, 1850–1950* (London, 2016), pp. 209–22.
34 NLW 3264D, Kirwan to APG, 'St. George's Day, 1920' and 30 April 1920; Rhys to APG, 22 April 1920.
35 J. W. Aitchison and Harold Carter, 'The Welsh Language, 1921–1991: A Geolinguistic Perspective', in Geraint H. Jenkins and Mari A. Williams (eds), *Let's Do Our Best for the Ancient Tongue: The Welsh Language in the Twentieth Century* (Cardiff, 2000), pp. 29–107 (p. 34).
36 NLW 3264D, Rhys to APG, 9 March 1920.
37 Ioan Williams, 'Towards National Identities: Welsh Theatres', in Baz Kershaw (ed.), *The Cambridge History of British Theatre, Volume 3: Since 1895* (Cambridge, 2004), pp. 242–72 (pp. 245–52 on 'The Drama Movement', quote at p. 244).
38 W. J. Gruffudd, 'Drama i Gymru', *Y Beirniad*, 1 (1911), 49–54 (p. 53). I am grateful to Rebecca Thomas for this reference.
39 J. S[aunders]. Lewis, 'The present state of Welsh drama', *Welsh Outlook*, 6/12 (December 1919), 302–4.
40 NLW 3264D, Rhys to APG, 9 March 1920, 9 April 1920.
41 NLW 3264D, Rhys to APG, 7 June 1920.
42 NLW 3264D, esp. Charles H. Clements to APG, 23 March 1920.
43 *The Harlech Historical Pageant* (Aberystwyth, 1920), p. 3; *Welsh Outlook* (July 1922), 155.
44 Advertisement in *Y Rhedegydd*, 10 August 1922.
45 Alfred Perceval Graves and Ernest Rhys, *The Pageant of Harlech Castle, August 21st–26th, 1922: Book of Words* (Newtown, 1922).
46 Peter Burke, 'Co-memorations: Performing the Past', in Karin Tilmans, Frank van Vree and Jay Winter (eds), *Performing the Past: Memory, History, and Identity in Modern Europe* (Amsterdam, 2010), pp. 105–18 (p. 106).
47 Colin Gresham, 'The Harlech Pageant, 1922', *Merioneth Historical and Record Society*, 9 (1981), 97–105.

48 Angela Gaffney, *Aftermath: Remembering the Great War in Wales* (Cardiff, 1998), pp. 48, 50–1, 126; *Morning Post*, 24 August 1920.
49 *Daily Telegraph*, 25 August 1920.
50 *Morning Post*, 24 August 1920; *Liverpool Daily Courier*, 23 August 1920.
51 Bartie et al., '"And those who live, how shall I tell their fame?"'
52 *North Wales Observer*, 24 August 1922; *The Times*, 22 August 1922; A. P. Graves, *Welsh Poetry Old and New: In English Verse* (London, 1912), pp. vii–viii. Also Huw Pryce, 'Gerald of Wales and the Welsh Past', in Georgia Henley and Joseph McMullen (eds), *Gerald of Wales: New Perspectives on a Medieval Writer and Critic* (Cardiff, 2018), pp. 19–46.
53 *North Wales Observer*, 31 August 1922.
54 NLW 3264D, Kirwan to APG, 15 March 1920.
55 Gresham, 'The Harlech Pageant, 1922', 97–105; Herbert Norris, *Costume and Fashion: The Evolution of European Dress through the Earlier Ages* (London, 1924).
56 For example, National Museum of Wales, The National Pageant, Harlech Castle, Merionethshire, 21–6 August 1922, https://museum.wales/historic-photography/?search=pageant (accessed 7 November 2023).
57 *North Wales Observer*, 24 August 1922; *The Times*, 22 August 1922; Walford Davies, '"The country of my heart"', 28–9.
58 National Museum of Wales, Dress worn by lady in waiting at Harlech Pageant, 1922, designed by Herbert Norris, https://museum.wales/collections/online/object/6fe14fb7-4093-3748-a433-b7be4bbb9457/Dress/ (accessed 7 November 2023).
59 Gresham, 'The Harlech Pageant, 1922', 101.
60 *Liverpool Daily Courier*, 23 August 1920.
61 Gresham, 'The Harlech Pageant, 1922', 97–105.
62 John Davies, 'The end of the great estates and the rise of freehold farming in Wales', *WHR*, 7/2 (1974), 186–212.
63 *The Times*, 22 August 1927.
64 *North Wales Observer*, 24 August 1922.
65 *Liverpool Daily Courier*, 23 August 1920; *North Wales Observer*, 24 August 1922.
66 Adam Tooze, *The Deluge: The Great War and the Remaking of Global Order, 1916–1931* (London, 2014), electronic edition, no pagination.
67 Graves and Rhys, *Book of Words*, p. 79.
68 Gresham, 'The Harlech Pageant, 1922', 97–105.
69 Zoë Thomas, 'Historical Pageants, Citizenship and the Performance of Women's History before Second-wave Feminism', in Bartie et al. (eds), *Restaging the Past*, pp. 108–31.
70 Huw Pryce, 'Cofio Glyndŵr', *Trafodion Anrhydeddus Gymdeithas y Cymmrodorion*, 22 (2016), 43–60 (p. 60).

71 Pryce, 'Cofio Glyndŵr', 59.
72 Graves and Rhys, *Book of Words*, p. 32.
73 A. P. Graves, *To Return to All That* (London, 1930), pp. 282–3; translation in NLW 3264D. NLW, E. T. John Papers, 4829, APG to Prof. Ivor Williams, 18 June 1927.
74 *Song Book of Choruses sung at the Harlech Historical Pageant, August 21st to 26th 1922* (Barmouth, 1922), p. 8.
75 For example, *Y Cymro*, 4 August 1920.
76 Graves, 'The Coming Harlech Pageant', 266.
77 *North Wales Observer*, 31 August 1922.
78 Pryce, *Writing Welsh History*.
79 Graves, 'Welsh Pageants and Pageants', *Welsh Outlook*, 14/8 (August 1927), 219–20; NLW, E. Morgan Humphreys Papers, A/1366-8, H. Ellis Hughes to E. Morgan Humphreys, [?] September 1927.
80 Angela Bartie et al., 'The Conway Pageant: Pageant Plays', The Redress of the Past, *http://www.historicalpageants.ac.uk/pageants/1039/* (accessed 7 November 2023); *Book of Ye Pageante: the Pageant of Montgomeryshire* (Welshpool, 1927).
81 Daryl Leeworthy, '"A Chorus of Greek Poignancy": Communism, Class and Pageantry in Interwar South Wales', in Bartie et al. (eds), *Restaging the Past*, pp. 180–200.
82 For example, Marcia Landy (ed.), *The Historical Film: History and Memory in Media* (London, 2001).

14

Tattooing Owain Glyndŵr? The Body, Memory and Interpretations of Welsh History

Mari Elin Wiliam,
with the assistance of Owen Hurcum[1]

Introduction

Historically in British (and Welsh) society tattoos have been synonymous with a range of occupations and classes: criminality, prostitution, military service, biker gangs, aristocracy (apparently Edward VII and George V had been tattooed) and, increasingly from the 1990s, celebrity.[2] Jane Caplan, an Oxford historian specialising in identification and the individual, stipulates that 'marking signs of identity directly on the body had become associated with marginality and dishonourable status in medieval and early modern Europe'.[3] Body modification in many western societies, voluntary or otherwise, has never quite shed this subcultural current of deviancy, with tattoos often interpreted as a means of 'othering' the recipient, to exhibit them as socially undesirable, different, unique or as affiliated to a distinct group (regimental and gang tattoos are a classic example of this).[4] However, for Matt Lodder, one of the foremost British academic historians of tattooing, the tattoo is not necessarily a sinister symbol of difference, but instead is a vital insight into individual identity and societal belonging.[5] As he argues, 'tattoos are intangible cultural heritage. They offer deeper insights into the people who made them, the people who bore them and the cultural contexts in which they were produced'.[6] This conceptualisation of tattoos as 'intangible cultural heritage' percolates throughout this chapter – reinforcing sociological analyses of them as a means of 'marking culture' – with Welsh-inspired designs suggesting the potency of the past in the formation of contemporary, everyday notions of Welshness.[7]

Historical studies on eugenics, physical culture and nationalism show the connection between the individual human body and nationhood,[8] and the exploration of tattoos (along with clothing, jewellery and other bodily modifications) is another means of researching the body as a canvas for national identity.[9] Whilst scholarship on tattoos is burgeoning from ethnographic and sociological angles, historians of tattooing in modern Britain so far have tended to focus more on issues such as maritime tattoos, criminality and the art of tattooing.[10] So, the close association forged between a tattooed person and their sense of nationhood is mostly on the sidelines of historiography, and has certainly not been addressed in a Welsh context.

Whilst there is an illustrious corpus of work on art history and nationhood in Wales,[11] and a rich seam examining physical sport and identity,[12] the bond between body art and attachment to nationhood has been mostly left to the occasional light-hearted news item and social media posts.[13] This may well be because of lingering sentiments about the subaltern nature of tattoos, or an idea that they are merely an aesthetic decoration, but regardless of why, they are very much placed in the lower leagues of the primary source hierarchy. However, this chapter will argue that this is a misplaced neglect since tattoos can give remarkable insight into *Alltagsgeschichte* (the history of everyday life) and the relationship between the 'ordinary' body and feelings of patriotism.[14] Indeed, although Welshness and nationalism are totems in the political historiography of the modern era, the scholarship inevitably unveils elite perspectives since it is based on party archives, policy processes and leadership.[15] It is challenging to examine the penetration of nationhood into 'normal' life, although oral history projects such as *Media and the Memory in Wales 1950–2000* demonstrate the potential of interviewing everyday people about their recollections of watershed events, such as Tryweryn.[16] Historians can also learn from ethnographic approaches to everyday Welshness, with the recent work of Daniel Evans on Porthcawl highlighting the 'persistence of hierarchical nationhood' blighting individuals from 'British Wales', many of whom associated strongly with Wales but never felt 'properly national' since they did not live in the mythologised *Y Fro Gymraeg*.[17]

As Huw Pryce has argued in his groundbreaking, cross-period scholarship on Welsh historical writing, the production of history has often been shaped not by the past per se, but by the desire of authors to fulfil present-day needs and values, particularly to construct a sense of Welsh nationhood.[18] Arguably, tattoos which involve traces of the past are deployed in a partially similar vein: they reflect the individual's preferred perspective on history and perpetuate heroic myths useful to the tattooed person's sense of nationhood. In this regard, they provide insights into both the reinvention of national memory and the power of popular history.[19] In Wales, where the marginalisation of Welsh history in schools has been subject to heated debate, historical tattoos ('accurate' or not) reflect a desire to connect with the past, often against the odds.[20]

Exploring tattoos can feel tantalisingly uncomfortable. First, they are not in the historian's traditional toolkit and, secondly (for this research at least), they involve interpreting very recent, twenty-first-century material as historical primary sources.[21] After celebrity professional sportsmen such as the American basketball player Dennis Rodman started displaying elaborate and extensive body art from the early 1990s, tattoos have become increasingly socially desirable and prevalent.[22] This ubiquity, combined with the growth of social media platforms to display body art, makes viewing tattoos far more accessible than in the past, enabling research into the etching of historical nationhood onto the contemporary human body. As media historian Nick Hall has argued, 'Online video sharing and social media have brought to the surface, and to some degree democratized, a shared impulse to record and re-enact history before it fades from living memory'.[23]

The social media research undertaken here focused mainly on Instagram since the platform specialises in the sharing of images. Additional material was garnered from two other leading platforms, Twitter (now X) and Facebook. As Stecko-Żukowska argues in a sociological study into the use of Instagram by tattoo artists in Poland, the app has created new 'structures of power' in the industry, transforming the tattoo scene as artists deploy their own 'vernacular, grassroots ways to tame the medium'.[24] So, initial searches were conducted using hashtags such as #welshtattoo #cymrutattoo which helped to identify tattooists who advertised some of their designs as Welsh. This also helped to pinpoint the types of historical Welsh tattoos that people tend to favour. Searches were then conducted for specific categories such as #owainglyndwr and #welshpinup which unveiled several designs which were not necessarily hashtagged as #welshtattoo. Articles about newsworthy tattoos from platforms such as *Wales Online* and *BBC News* were consulted and helped guide the Instagram search.

The ethics of social media research is a prominent issue amongst academics in sociological, communication and psychological fields, with an argument that traditional boundaries involving consent, anonymity and copyright are increasingly blurred, and should be subject to a common-sense 'ethical pluralism' dependent on context.[25] Although historians are yet to fully engage in this discussion, in the present study content from social media is only integrated if the accounts are openly accessible and searchable, without privacy constraints. Since the majority of tattooists deploy sites such as Instagram to curate their art and to advertise their designs, they do not insist on followers making requests for access or 'friend' status since they are public channels. Anonymity is also not pressing due to this: indeed, insisting on it could be problematic since tattooists need to be credited with the copyright of their images and designs. Where personal social media accounts have been consulted, these are only utilised if, again, they are publicly accessible and that the individual has over 1,500 followers. This number suggests that they have a well-developed social media profile and are comfortable with sustaining a public image.[26] One oral history interview has been conducted with a tattooed individual, and although anonymity was offered, they preferred for their name to be used.

The social media sources discussed in this article have been analysed in a threefold manner: the tattoo design, the deployment of hashtags and post comments. This combination of image and succinct text provides a visual primary source akin to historical postcards, with both also sharing a sense of immediacy that provides a vibrant insight into everyday identities.[27] Although it can be challenging to conclusively discern class, gender and even tattoo placement from some of the images, the tattoo motifs are usually revealing, and, where relevant, comparisons are made with nationalist-oriented clothing slogans and branding.

The first section of the chapter explores the reworking of the 'heroic', medieval Welsh past in tattoos, examining the vogue for Owain Glyndŵr designs along with the conflicting messages conveyed by having certain Welsh castles etched on the skin. The second section focuses on the reimagining of the contemporary past by concentrating on *Yma o Hyd*, football-inspired inscriptions and Welsh national costume tattoos (often known as 'Welsh pin-up girl' designs). Ultimately this chapter will argue that the decorated human body is an overlooked but vital segment of Welsh historical memory, acting as a conduit between national and gender identities in the past and present, and showing the potency of idealised cultural heritage in everyday life.

Needling the heroic (and conflicted) past: Owain Glyndŵr

Leaning on Pierre Nora's work on the construction of national memory in France, Huw Pryce has described Owain Glyndŵr and his uprising in the early fifteenth century as a leading *lieu de mémoire* ('realm of memory') in Wales.[28] Glyndŵr has been moulded into a national hero since he was discovered by antiquarians in the eighteenth century, and whilst he has been the foundation for some of the classic and pioneering works in Welsh history, he has also imbued the popular historical memory, as most notably demonstrated in Elissa Henken's explorations in Glyndŵr folklore during the 1980s and 1990s.[29] He has become a grassroots icon, traversing the boundaries between academic and public spheres as a populist symbol of nationalist resistance and Welsh national distinctiveness. For example, in the 2004 Culturenet Cymru public vote on '100 Welsh heroes', Glyndŵr was only just pushed into second place by a far more recent 'hero', Aneurin Bevan (and he beat Bevan in a 2002 BBC poll to reveal the '100 Greatest Britons', becoming the highest-ranking Welshman).[30]

Since Glyndŵr is a strong feature of the patriotic consciousness in Wales, unsurprisingly his portrayal as a heroic, warrior figure has permeated Welsh tattoo culture. Four tattoo designs depicting a version of 'Glyndŵr' are analysed here as they provide comparable images of how he is embodied in twenty-first-century imaginations. All the designs take inspiration from Glyndŵr as military leader, reflecting the iconic First World War image of him by the Swansea illustrator Arthur Cadwgan Michael. This depicts Glyndŵr, sword in hand, leading his army from the front, magnificently erect on a grey steed and glancing sideways as if in anticipation of an imminent charge.[31] This is an image rich in traditional notions of masculinity: the 'great man', head and shoulders above his loyal followers, in action on the battlefield with all the threat of violence, bloodshed and death inherent in such a vision. It is also echoed in the bronze statue of Owain Glyndŵr on horseback which was unveiled in Corwen in 2007 to commemorate him as a local hero, and to replace a previous statue that conveyed a rather too benign and timid Glyndŵr.[32]

By the 2000s, 'metrosexual' celebrity footballers such as David Beckham were adorning themselves in highly conspicuous tattoos, and Glyndŵr became associated with this trend in 2008 when the Wales men's football captain, Craig Bellamy, revealed that he had a Owain Glyndŵr design woven into an intricate tattoo sleeve on his arm.[33] He noted that it was a depiction of the pivotal Battle of Bryn Glas (1402), which he had developed in tandem with his tattooist. Elements of the design had been inspired by the style of the Glyndŵr statue in the Marble Hall 'Heroes of Wales' display in Cardiff, where he was included as an example of 'Statemanship and Martial Prowess'.[34] Bellamy professed his admiration for Glyndŵr as 'the biggest Welsh hero we have ever had and I am massive on him'.[35] He explained to the media that his decision to get the tattoo was based on his fondness for reading about Welsh history, stipulating 'I think each and every one of us needs to know more about the proud history in Wales, to be honest'.[36] Bellamy was brought up in Cardiff and is mainly non-Welsh-speaking, spending most of his professional career in England, so his quest to associate his body with the Welsh past shows the power of Glyndŵr as a modern icon traversing established hierarchies of Welshness. Additionally, in his familiarity both with a crucial battle in the Glyndŵr uprising and the pantheon of Welsh heroes, Bellamy had clearly invested time familiarising himself with the subject, so the tattoo was more than an arbitrary, hazy vision of a 'hero'. Indeed, by having it placed on his forearm, a location visible both to himself and to others, the footballer was making Glyndŵr a prominent part of his self-identity.[37]

Bellamy's revelation about the tattoo occurred in the media round prior to a decisive World Cup qualifier against Germany, arguably in the hope that the Welsh team would evoke the spirit of Glyndŵr in the match (they lost). The tabloid press certainly adopted this message, with a *Daily Mirror* headline claiming: 'Fighter Bellamy: I'll Lead a Revolt'.[38] The report described Glyndŵr as a 'Freedom Fighter' and 'the father of Welsh nationalism', suggesting that in having an 'image of the warrior on his right arm', Bellamy was a custodian of his legacy as he prepared to 'lead his nation into battle with Germany'. Whilst this war-like rhetoric was a gift in a tabloid era renowned for German-baiting 'banter', it also reveals how Glyndŵr could be reimagined into a twenty-first-century hero 'battling' the Germans simply because the Wales captain had him tattooed on a limb.[39] This demonstrated that Glyndŵr as an emblem of historical national resistance was a deeply embedded idea which could be amalgamated into Welsh sporting identity. By discussing his Owain Glyndŵr tattoo prior to an important national football match, Bellamy was also hoping to resurrect the romantic past of a small nation confronting a dominant external threat, which was a common motivational thread in the Welsh sporting arena.[40] But, more crucially, he showed how an aspect of Welsh history was so important to him on a personal level that he wanted it permanently etched on his skin.

Bellamy was not the only one feeling the draw of Owain Glyndŵr. Paul Worley from Flintshire gained publicity in 2009 when his full-back tattoo with Glyndŵr as centrepiece was headlined in the north Wales newspaper, *The Daily Post*, as 'Patriotic Welshman has giant tattoo of Owain Glyndŵr'.[41] This tattoo includes both 'obvious' representations of Wales, such as daffodils, alongside more closed signifiers, namely that the figure is actually Glyndŵr. Whilst the etching of the warrior bears some resemblance to the Corwen statue, it could easily be of any medieval figure in a suit of armour, and rather obscure to people with a tenuous grasp of Welsh heritage. Worley explained that he was motivated to get the design because he was a 'proud Welshman' and Glyndŵr had been his hero since childhood due to him being a 'freedom fighter' for an independent Wales. He felt it was 'a great way to show my patriotism'. To reinforce this, the Glyndŵr silhouette in his back piece is surrounded by stereotypical motifs of Welshness, such as a giant dragon, along with a flourish of a Celtic knot design and the words in Welsh 'Rhyddid i'm gwlad' ('freedom for my country'). In his application of 'heroic' language to explain the tattoo Worley reflects much of Bellamy's rationale; however, he also utilises the memory of Glyndŵr to represent a claim for a separatist Wales, and in that sense his tattoo is more blatantly political.

Mildly paradoxically, the tattoo also includes a depiction of Rhuddlan Castle, the fortress on the river Clwyd in north-east Wales completed as part of Edward I's conquest of Wales in 1282. The town itself became synonymous with a watershed moment in Welsh history as the site of the 1284 Statute of Rhuddlan, which was Edward I's blueprint for ruling his lands in Wales.[42] Although Glyndŵr's forces tried to take the castle during their uprising, this failed, so the key question is why it forms such a visible part of a design that advocates for Welsh freedom and separatism. Considering that the Edwardian Conquest of Wales has become a popular part of a nationalist narrative of oppression – with commemorations at Cilmeri of the 'tragic' Welsh past at the hands of the 'English' – it is unlikely that the tattoo is celebrating this history.[43] Instead, due to the prevalence of other national stereotypes in the piece, it may simply be outlining another common representation of Wales, one of it as a land of castles. As Euryn Roberts has highlighted in his work on Cestyll '83 – a festival led by the Wales Tourist Board to promote the castles of Wales – they were contested heritage sites that could be claimed in a multitude of ways. Whilst for many Welsh nationalists Cestyll '83 was seen 'as a celebration of the 1282–3 conquest writ large', for the tourism industry it was an opportunity to showcase an 'important symbol of distinctiveness' to attract American dollars.[44]

Figure 1: Tattoo of Conwy Castle on Glennydd, c.@Elliw Williams

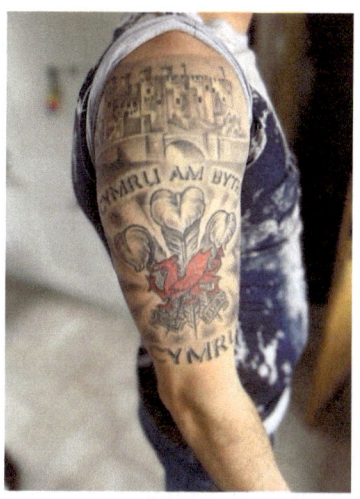

Glennydd (pictured in Figure 1) explained that he has a tattoo of the Edwardian Conwy Castle because of fond childhood memories of visiting it with his grandparents, and felt that this was a natural addition to a Welsh tattoo sleeve because he is a 'proud Welshman'.[45] Therefore, in Worley's tattoo, Rhuddlan Castle is probably not a symbol of Welsh subjugation, but has been unconsciously reclaimed as architecture that is synonymous with the cultural heritage of the Welsh landscape in northeast Wales, where Worley resided. This reinforces the archaeologist Barbara Bender's observation that 'the landscape is never inert, people … re-work it, appropriate and contest it'.[46]

Edwardian castles are popular tropes in Welsh tattoos, appearing also in a tattoo etched in 2014 in D&S Dark Arts in Maesteg, southeast Wales, and advertised on the parlour's Instagram account with the hashtags #owainglyndwr #welshtattoo #welshsleeve.[47] In this instance, Conwy Castle forms the backdrop to Glyndŵr. This could potentially of course be because Glyndŵr's forces had some military successes there in c.1401/2, and so the castle is included as a symbol of resistance. However, detailing this historical nuance seems unlikely, so again the castle is probably included as a distinctive Welsh landmark to fulfil the promise of a #welshtattoo building up to a #welshsleeve. The text which underlines the tattoo is 'Gorau Chwarae Cyd Chwarae' ('the best form of play is playing together'), the motto of the Wales Football Association, and it is adorned with the classic motifs of daffodils and a Celtic cross. Overall, this suggests that the inclusion of Conwy Castle is once more not in jubilation of the Edwardian Conquest, but as a decorative feature which rapidly augments the sleeve to 'Welsh'.

Additionally, even though #owainglyndwr is the first descriptor for the tattoo, the individual depicted seems to be more akin to the bronze statue on a plinth of Llywelyn Fawr in Conwy, which was completed in 1898.[48] The crown on the head, the Victorian-style moustache and the sideways glance all seem redolent of Conwy's version of Llywelyn, dovetailing with the inked inclusion of Conwy Castle. However, in the tattoo (in contrast to the statue) the figure poses with the coat of arms of Glyndŵr. Although the coat of arms associated with Llywelyn Fawr and Llywelyn ap Gruffudd was also red and gold with four lions, their lions were passant whereas Glyndŵr's are rampant.[49] This is a tattoo of Llywelyn Fawr holding the crest of Owain Glyndŵr in a tattoo that aims to convey Glyndŵr. Claiming that a tattoo is of Glyndŵr, even though it has Llywelyn associations, makes sense from a heroic perspective: whilst the former was grappling to free Wales from its subjugation, the latter's crest was a reminder of its loss and conquest.

To add to the visual kaleidoscope, in Figure 2 is another tattoo with #owainglyndwr, this time conveying him in a debonair manner, with flowing hair and a handlebar moustache, evoking visions of English Civil War cavaliers, Victorian-era soldiers and matinee idols.

Figure 2: Owain Glyndŵr traditional tattoo, design by @chrisbarrett_tattoo on @wrexhamink Instagram page, post 1 July 2016

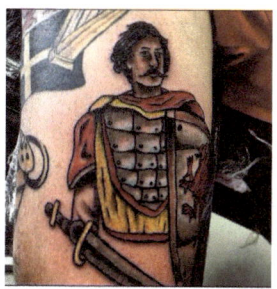

The dominant trope here is romantic-militarism, with the shield, suit of armour and sword all seeming moderately benign. Some depictions of Llywelyn ap Gruffudd, especially in children's books, portray him in a very similar style, leading to the conclusion that many 'Owain Glyndŵr' tattoos conflate different native Welsh 'heroes'.[50] In part this could be down to a lack of grounding in Welsh history, but also, of course, part of the mystique of medieval leaders is that their appearance is often nebulous and subject to guesswork.[51] In truth, the statues of Llywelyn Fawr in Conwy and Owain Glyndŵr in Corwen are merely artists' impressions to complement a public space, and in a similar manner, a tattooist also possesses a creative licence to etch the Welsh past in their own way.

Owain Glyndŵr has also become an attractive feature on Welsh-branded clothing, with the fashion company Cowbois selling designs with slogans, for example, 'REBEL Owain Glyndŵr', glamourising him on colourful t-shirts and hoodies for adults and children.[52] Whilst this is a mainstream way of shaping the popular memory about Glyndŵr, his name can also be embroidered for more militant purposes. During the mid-1980s the quasi-paramilitary Parti Lliw Meibion Glyndŵr (The Sons of Glyndŵr Colour Party) appeared in parades at patriotic commemorations clad in military uniforms, dark sunglasses and berets.[53] The Parti Lliw evoked the arson campaign against holiday homes that had emerged in late 1979 in parts of Wales, which became associated with the elusive group Meibion Glyndŵr. Letters purportedly from them claiming responsibility for burnings or letter-bombs were signed by 'Rhys Gethin', one of the leaders of the Glyndŵr revolt, lacing that part of late medieval Welsh history with the militant nationalist resistance effort in the 1980s.[54] The Parti Lliw marched in shirts embossed with a crest that blended their name with a white eagle (of Snowdon), seemingly echoing the vibes of the Free Wales Army (FWA), an uniformed group that coveted attention in the 1960s by engaging in public spectacles and making wild (and mostly unsubstantiated) claims that they possessed nuclear bombs and kamikaze dogs.[55] By exhibiting clothing that placed Glyndŵr's name alongside the symbol of the FWA, the Parti Lliw were meshing two mythologised nationalist symbols of resistance from the Welsh past. Even though Glyndŵr's uprising and the displays of the FWA were centuries apart, for the Parti Lliw (and more recent incarnations such as the group Balchder Cymru) they were heroic signifiers of the battle for the freedom of Wales, and their choice of uniform shaped them as the 'inheritors' of this tradition.

So, whilst Owain Glyndŵr's incursions onto the nationalist body have manifested in a range of ways, as these examples show, a common thread is an admiration for his qualities as a military leader, freedom fighter and as an icon of resistance. These mirror a desire to link the past with the present and future: having a tattoo of Owain Glyndŵr shows an aspiration to honour the distinctive Welsh past, with the future aim of resurrecting such a spirit of resistance to 'free' Wales from its shackles. In the present, everyday life the tattooed individual claims the traits with which they associate Glyndŵr: power, a warrior-essence and the potential to be a Welsh hero themselves. A dermatological study into male footballers argued that many possessed extensive and bold tattoos as a means of 'enhancing dominance', and the vogue for combining Glyndŵr with visions of colossal Welsh castles supports this claim.[56] In a sense, for the tattooed individual, the precise origin story of their selected castle does not matter so much, it is about the symbolism offered by these dominant features in the Welsh landscape: it is a macho Welshness based on a conflicted history. As Pryce and others have shown, the afterlife of Glyndŵr is very malleable, and arguably his appropriation on the body imbibes a masculine cultural heritage alongside a reverence for a popularly mythologised Welsh past.

Inking the contemporary Welsh past

Whilst there is certainly a vogue in Welsh tattooing circles for echoes of the medieval, heroic and pugilistic past, symbols of more recent history are also popular motifs to express national sentiments. Examples can be discovered of tattoos related to the coal mining industry, with one particularly elaborate design produced at Miss Rie's Tattoo Studio in Newport in 2021 showcasing an upper-arm tattoo of a pithead along with an etching of the local Chartist leader, Zephaniah Williams.[57] This design conveys a nostalgia for the industrial past and the spirit of radicalism associated with south Wales. Tattoos commemorating the flooding of the Tryweryn valley in 1965 can also be found, although considering the rash of interest and replication of the original *Cofiwch Dryweryn* Llanrhystud graffiti since 2019, this is more muted than expected. Searches on Instagram, X and Facebook for 'Tryweryn tattoo' (along with Welsh-language versions) evinced very few results, highlighting an interesting chasm between the intense absorption of the *Cofiwch Dryweryn* slogan into the public space and patriotic mindset in Wales, but limited interest in having it permanently carved onto the body.[58] By contrast, this section will predominantly focus on two popular modern tropes in 'Welsh tattoo' searches: the spate of patriotic tattoos inspired by the Welsh men's football team qualifying for three major championships since 2016 and interpretations of the 'traditional' Welsh lady. Research of both these case studies raise points related to Welshness, cultural invention and gender.

Yma o Hyd

The tattooed emblem most often associated with sport in Wales is the crest of the Welsh Rugby Union, which consists of the heraldry of the prince of Wales: a plume of three feathers, a crown and the German inscription *Ich Dien* (I serve). Whilst an example of this type of tattoo can be seen in Figure 1 (and would be an interesting research avenue in its own right), the focus in this segment will instead be on football-inspired insignia, as a flurry of tattoos have appeared in response to the vitality around the national football team since the tenure of Gary Speed as manager in 2010/11. With Wales qualifying for the men's European championships in 2016 and 2020, and making a World Cup appearance in 2022, football, and its icons such as Gareth Bale, have captured the national imagination in an unprecedented manner.[59] The Football Association of Wales's utilisation of Welsh-language folk singer Dafydd Iwan's early 1980s nationalist anthem *Yma o Hyd* ('We're Still Here') as part of this success has made the song an attractive text for body modification.

Historically, football as a national game in Wales was overshadowed by the more successful international rugby team, and it has also struggled to be seen as 'Welsh' since fan loyalties often traversed into the English top-tier or community level.[60] Wales's only previous men's World Cup appearance in 1958 was greeted tepidly in the Welsh media, but '1958' became mythologised as the team continuously failed to qualify for other major championships, and when a new Wales football merchandise company was established in 2010 it was called Spirit of '58.[61] The slogan 'Spirit of '58' is embroidered and inscribed onto clothing, jewellery and even golf balls, nostalgically reminding the wearers of Welsh footballing history, and connecting a past glory to contemporary culture.

The FAW has also had a historical turn, selecting the protest song, *Yma o Hyd*, as its official theme song for the 2022 World Cup. It was conceived in the tumult of the early 1980s, a despairing time for many Welsh nationalists due to the failure of the 1979 devolution referendum vote and the advent of Thatcherism.[62] The lyrics applaud Wales's survival against the odds from Roman times onwards, and the FAW used it as accompaniment to a video that interspersed clips of present-day players with past painful failures, and flashed to iconic images in the 'oppressed' history of modern Wales such as Tryweryn, Welsh Language Society protests, the Miners' Strike and the 'yes' vote for devolution in 1997.[63] This was the FAW channelling a nationalist interpretation of the Welsh past and blending it with the spirit of Welsh football.[64] This was designed to paint an image of a small country overcoming historical obstacles and mustering this energy of resistance on the modern-day football field (reflecting some of Craig Bellamy's Owain Glyndŵr rhetoric back in 2008).

It is unsurprising perhaps that this surge in *Yma o Hyd* popularity led to a spate of tattoos, and due to the World Cup being a prominent event in the news cycle there is far more accessible information on these types of tattoos than on many others discussed in this chapter. In November 2022, *BBC Wales* ran a piece on the trend for *Yma o Hyd* tattoos, quoting Huw Roberts – who had a black and white tattoo of the Welsh football crest with 'Yma o Hyd' imprinted boldly at the top – as saying 'it's going to be there forever just like the Welsh language and culture'.[65] Clearly the appeal of the tattoo was to have a perpetual reminder of Welshness expressed through the prism of football. Lisa Williams from Flintshire had 'Yma o Hyd' etched on her forearm, along with a duo of daffodils, stating that she also liked the permanence of it, which contrasted with the more ephemeral quality of bucket hats and Wales shirts.[66] In a fiery Twitter post Williams explained that *Yma o Hyd* meant that the Welsh were still around despite 'the English castles, the Welsh Not, Tryweryn … I support independence. I am not an extremist, I am Welsh'.[67] This post had tagged both #Annibyniaeth (Independence) and @IndyWalesFans, firmly slotting it as a design with separatist implications. This showcases the meaningfulness of this tattoo for Williams: it is not merely a cluster of flowers and a trendy inscription, but one that represents the depth of national sentiment, with the skin carved in echoes of the oppressed history of Wales. *Yma o Hyd* is not necessarily deployed in a footballing context in this regard (even though the tattoo may have been inspired by football), but in a political, 'Yes Cymru' sense, one that is close to the original sentiments of the song.

The Abolish Westminster Twitter account in June 2022 shared two other images of *Yma o Hyd*-inspired tattoos alongside Williams's, stipulating 'These are amazing'.[68] A heart design was tattooed for the Welsh performer and singer Bronwen Lewis. It adopts from the Traditional Americana tattoo style with an excerpt from *Yma o Hyd*'s chorus wrapped around a heart. Lewis shared the design on Twitter by noting 'Cymru am byth' ('Wales forever'), receiving a flurry of replies from women who had similar designs or others who coveted one.[69] These tattoos are feminine in design, with naturalistic fonts, flower motifs and are relatively petite in size. This reflects ethnographic studies into tattoos and gender, which tend to observe that women's tattoos are smaller and more discreet compared to the extensive sleeves favoured by men.[70] However, most of the *Yma o Hyd* designs also seemed to be placed on the forearm or calf, a place where the design would be visible to the tattooed person and to others, signifying that this was an expression of national identity that individuals wanted to display publicly. These designs contradict the usual assumption of nationalist and footballing tattoos being bold and masculine, showing the presence of femininity in modern constructions of Welsh nationhood.[71]

Welsh ladies

In the twentieth century the image of the 'Welsh lady' in what was deemed to be the national costume of Wales became a pervasive stereotype and a bastion of Welsh tourism and its souvenir industry.[72] As Christine Stevens argues, this style of dress was based on rural and peasant workwear seen in Wales during the eighteenth and nineteenth centuries, but it was popularised and homogenised into a 'national costume' by Lady Augusta Hall (Lady Llanofer), who felt it was a way of strengthening the cohesion of Welsh national identity and of supporting the Welsh woollen industry against the evils of the cotton incursion.[73] Regardless of authenticity, the national costume has become associated with the air of an 'invented tradition', and although on the one hand it can be viewed as a sign of Wales's unique nationhood, it also retains an air of artificiality.[74] For Frank Price-Jones, a prominent Welsh-language columnist and commentator writing in 1958, the national dress was a *hylltod* (ugliness) forced on the Welsh people by Hall and imitated by only the most tasteless of Welsh people.[75] Critics such as Price-Jones felt that the national costume, alongside tokenistic celebrations such as St David's Day, were sugary and sentimental expressions of Welshness, masking the true crisis of Welsh governance and language.

However, for many people in their everyday lives, both in Wales and beyond, the silhouette of the Welsh lady was an instantaneous and welcome flagging of Welsh nationhood, making it an enticing subject for artists, including tattooists.[76] In the same way that Glyndŵr is a pliable image, the Welsh lady is as well, and from the range of Welsh national costume tattoos surveyed it is evident that the fashion has evolved dramatically from the idealised versions upheld by Lady Llanofer. Whereas the 'traditional' national costume involved ensconcing almost the entire body with heavily layered woollen garments, many of the tattoos take a more minimalist approach. In fact, the most prevalent hashtag attached to Welsh national costume tattoos was #PinupGirl.

This is epitomised in Figure 3, where the tattoo produced in Wrexham integrates the key requirements of a pin-up girl, a style that developed during the Second World War and had become a staple for tattoo artists on their flash sheets by the 1950s.[77]

Figure 3: Welsh pin-up girl, @chrisbarret_tattooer working from Wrexham Ink, Instagram, 1 June 2016

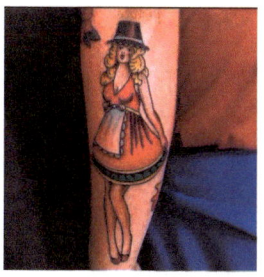

Pin-ups are at the core of the Old School or Traditional Americana style of tattooing, which is seen in these designs with the bold colour infills and lines. There is first an alluring pout, with the red lipstick immediately sexualising the image. As Lisa Eldridge illuminates in her history of make-up, red lips can be a sign of arousal, health and vitality, and women have spent centuries experimenting with different forms of rouge on their lips and cheekbones.[78] Secondly, there is the hourglass figure, bringing an immediate 1950s vibe to the design. Thirdly, the 'Welsh dress' finishes above the knee, with ample attention given to delineating the bosom with a cleavage enhancing cut, making it reminiscent of one of the classic pin-up girls, Marilyn Monroe. In the tattoo there is a hint of the skirt fluttering upwards: a reminder of one of the iconic images of Monroe with her dress being provocatively blasted by a wind machine.[79]

However, whilst the design holds much that would be familiar in the American pin-up girl trajectory, it is also arrestingly Welsh. The black hat gives it immediate recognition as a Welsh symbol, and the model also wears a short apron or pinny, which echoes elements of the national costume. The dress itself is red with a green border encircling its hem, combining the two colours most associated with the Welsh national flag. The use of a tall hat and the colour red is reiterated in Figure 4, which also adopts the flavour of the pin-up girl but in a more overtly sexualised manner, since this 'Welsh lady' is also clad in suspenders, making it reminiscent of the bawdy British seaside postcard.[80] It was described by the tattooist as a '[s]exy St David's pinup', bonding two Welsh cultural icons.

Figure 4: 'Sexy St David's Pinup', @butterstattoouk
Instagram page, 17 February 2023

Whilst these tattoos express a feminine Welshness, the culture of pin-up girls is a controversial one from a feminist perspective and, during the 1970s, it became conflated with opposition to beauty pageants and pornography as displays that objectified and exploited women. However, even though criticisms of 'raunch eroticism' and 'porn wars' have resurged in the twenty-first century, this is a conflicting issue for feminists, as there is an argument that the alluring feminine is a powerful entity, and that women should be free from the moral judgements of all (including feminists themselves).[81] Therefore, a tattoo depicting a Welsh pin-up girl can be both a patriotic symbol of Welsh distinctiveness and simultaneously reflective of patriarchy and misogyny. There is evidence from social media that males and females opt for Welsh pin-up tattoos, and a tattooist from Cardiff with she/her pronouns has a flash sheet of Welsh designs containing feisty and sensual Welsh ladies.[82] This flash sheet has #welshindependence attached to it, suggestive of the fact that people searching Instagram for posts related to Welsh separatism would also be interested in getting one of these tattoos.

The gender fluidity of the Welsh national costume is reflected in the tattoo in Figure 5, entitled 'Bearded Welsh Lady'. This time the image is not so sexualised nor as reflective of the pin-up girl tradition (beyond the overtly blushed cheeks), but it does illuminate how the Welsh national costume can be reinvented for different epochs.

Whilst the original 'invention' of a national costume for Wales in the nineteenth century was to satisfy cravings for Welsh nationhood, arguably a Welsh lady with a beard is a modernising development that

Figure 5: Bearded Welsh lady, Frontier Tattoo Parlour Cardiff, tattooist @christcollinstattoo, 29 June 2022

situates this tradition in a twenty-first-century context, where trans and non-binary rights are topical and urgent issues.[83]

These tattoos are founded on cross-cultural encounters between American popular culture and a Welsh invented tradition, and both tattooist and recipients clearly embrace this hybridity. They show the strong affiliation between gender and national identity, with the 'Welsh lady' simultaneously representing a pious, religious, pastoral Welshness and a more raunchy, Americanised influence, at odds with the matronly impression of the Welsh 'Mam'.[84] Ultimately, this demonstrates that for individuals who have a Welsh lady inked on their skin the national costume is both a fluid concept and an icon of cultural heritage.

Yma o Hyd tattoos echo how Welsh football's conjuring of the past can redefine places of memory, with a song initially planned as a Welsh linguistic nationalist riposte to Thatcher in the 1980s moving from being a limited totem for *Y Fro Gymraeg* to framing an inclusive everyday Welshness that people enthusiastically chisel onto their skin. In a similar manner, Welsh pin-up girl tattoos demonstrate how the national costume can be reinterpreted and sexualised whilst still retaining its stereotypical Welshness. In both case studies, we see the (mostly) recent Welsh past being resurrected and reworked to suit contemporary cultural and gendered contexts.

Conclusion

According to Matt Lodder:

> Tattooing is old and new at the same time. The designs on any tattooed body are always of a particular moment, and each tattoo tells us something particular about its moment of

creation. But fundamentally, tattooing has not changed much in thousands of years.[85]

The same approach can be applied to Welshness: whilst it is a heterogeneous concept, which is constantly remade and manipulated according to values, desires and temporality, at its core is a longing for the past and a yearning for the 'authentic' essentialist identity.[86] Combining body art with nationhood unveils how individuals covet and reinterpret their cultural heritage, offering insights into the shaping of popular historical memory about the Welsh past.

There are three key findings from this research. First, it suggests the richness in looking beyond the traditional hierarchies of Welsh identity and towards the presence of patriotism and nationhood in everyday life. Examples of Welsh tattoos were unearthed across Wales, with many produced in places such as Wrexham, on the border with England and traditionally lumped into 'British' Wales. This complicates assumptions about hierarchies of Welshness, reinforcing the sociological literature on the topic.[87] Most of the tattoos and clothing considered here have been adorned by 'ordinary' people, who feel so attached to their Welshness that they want it as a perpetual reminder on their skin. As Karl Broome conveyed in an ethnographic study of a kitchen tattooist in south-east London, 'for the people involved … being tattooed is a profoundly "meaningful" socio-sensual experience'.[88] Although focus has been placed on some prominent individuals, such as the former Wales football captain Craig Bellamy, this is not a discussion of Welsh cultural elites. Whilst applying 'class' descriptors has been avoided (partially due to lack of information), the tattoos certainly provide a non-elite perspective on identity and its flagging in daily life.

Secondly, inspired by Huw Pryce's scholarship, the chapter argues that the reimagining of Welsh history in body art shows the potency of the Welsh past in twenty-first-century society. Whilst some of the designs heralding the 'heroic' past contain potential contradictions, and even inaccuracies, they provide an insight into the construction of popular historical memory. For example, the inclusion of Edwardian castles alongside Owain Glyndŵr (or Glyndŵr-Llywelyn hybrids) may be paradoxical in some nationalist interpretations of Welsh history, but it is also suggestive of the 'ownership' of the castles being claimed as part of the distinctively Welsh landscape. *Yma o Hyd* has also reflected societal change in clambering from being a niche Welsh-language anthem in the 1980s to becoming a mainstream trope and tattoo design in twenty-first-century Welshness. Similarly, the development of Lady Llanofer's national costume into 'Welsh pin-up girl' tattoos may feel like heresy to traditionalists, but in a sense it is the reinvention of an already invented tradition, with the modernisation sustaining the Welsh lady as an icon of Welshness.

Thirdly, this research suggests the confluence of gender, body art and Welsh nationhood, reinforcing Jill A. Fisher's observation that tattoos mark the 'complex relationship between the physical and social body'.[89] Body adornment can be a crucial element of self-identification, meaning a tattoo of Owain Glyndŵr conveys not only a sense of patriotism, but also represents traits such as masculinity, strength or pugilism that may be coveted by the tattooed individual. Glyndŵr, in particular, is an appealing design for men, which was reflected in the sartorial identity of quasi-paramilitary nationalists such as the Parti Lliw who were intent on cultivating a macho sense of nationhood. Although both pin-up girl designs and football tattoos are also traditionally considered masculine-oriented, the appeal of these tattoos in Welsh identity are far more gender fluid than anticipated.

Moreover, this chapter demonstrates how much research scope there is in examining Welsh tattoos and clothing – indeed the body more broadly – as part of historical memory. As with any primary source there are methodological complexities with using artwork and social media posts, and probably the greatest challenge here was the sparsity of information on some of the designs, although analysing the motifs and hashtags themselves were fruitful. To resolve this, future avenues could include a substantial oral history project with tattooists and tattooed individuals, potentially leading to a national database of body art and a study of tattoo parlour culture in Wales.[90] Another pathway would be to consider the choice of language in tattoos, which could yield intriguing findings about linguistic cultural inheritance in Wales. Finally, even though this chapter has concentrated on distinctively Welsh iconography, looking at contested identities in other tattoo genres, such as the prince of Wales feathers and military designs, may highlight interesting points revolving around Britishness and Welshness.

Although by the end of the twentieth century tattoos had gained more cultural acceptability in British society, they also could be associated with impromptu and impetuous decisions – getting a Las Vegas tattoo in a 24-hour parlour or a drunken stag night tattoo in Ibiza, for example. However, what is indisputable is that many of the designs studied here are intricate and would take planning and several sittings to complete, showing the seriousness invested in the tattoos and, by extension, the individual's cultural heritage. Some of the tattoos may be historically foggy, but as Estyn, the school inspectorate for Wales, reported in 2021:

> In a majority of schools, pupils have little knowledge of the historical events that have shaped their local area and can name few significant Welsh people from history ... As a result, they do not develop a progressive and coherent conceptual understanding of the history of Wales.[91]

Indeed, although inconsistency in historical knowledge may be evident, what the tattoos do show is a reverence for the Welsh past. Perhaps it is a mythologised, exaggerated and reimagined past but, nonetheless, it shows that Welsh history is an indelible legacy in everyday patriotism, and that a study of an Owain Glyndŵr tattoo is as meritorious as perusing a political archive.

Notes

1. *Diolch yn fawr* to Owen Hurcum who completed a Bangor University-funded feasibility study into 'Tattoos and Identity in Wales' in July 2020. Their report inspired this chapter.
2. 'The name for Britain comes from our ancient love of tattoos', *BBC Future*, 10 November 2016, https://www.bbc.com/future/article/20161110-the-name-for-britain-comes-from-our-ancient-love-of-tattoos (accessed 11 October 2023); Robert Shoemaker and Zoe Alker, 'How Tattoos became fashionable in Victorian England', *The Conversation*, 12 December 2019, https://theconversation.com/how-tattoos-became-fashionable-in-victorian-england-122487 (accessed 11 October 2023).
3. Jane Caplan, 'Signature and Sign', Museum of London lecture, 30 June 2014, https://brewminate.com/speaking-scars-tattoos-in-the-19th-century/ (accessed 11 October 2023). See also by Caplan, *Written on the Body: The Tattoo in European and American History* (Princeton, 2000).
4. Clinton R. Sanders, 'Marks of Mischief: Becoming and Being Tattooed', *Journal of Contemporary Ethnography*, 16 (1988), 395–432.

5   Matt Lodder, *Painted People: Humanity in 21 Tattoos* (London, 2022).

6   Lodder, *Painted People*, p. 3.

7   Jill A. Fisher, 'Tattooing the Body, Marking Culture', *Body and Society*, 8/4 (2002), 91–107 (p. 104).

8   See, for example, Ina Zweiniger-Bargielowska, *Managing the Body: Beauty, Health and Fitness in Britain 1880–1939* (Oxford, 2011); Andres Reggiani and Pablo Scharagrodsky, 'Building a Disciplined and Efficient Body: Nationalism, Eugenics and Physical Culture in Interwar Argentina', *History of Sport*, 39/15 (2022), 1591–1610; Cynthia Miller-Idriss, 'Soldier, sailor, rebel, rule-breaker: masculinity and the body in the German far right', *Gender and Education*, 29/2 (2017), 199–215.

9   Mie Hiramoto, 'Inked Nostalgia: displaying identity through tattoos as Hawaii local practice', *Journal of Multilingual and Multicultural Development*, 36/2 (2015), 107–23.

10   Matt Lodder, '"Things of the sea": iconographic continuities between tattooing and handicraft in Georgian-era maritime culture', *Sculpture Journal*, 24/2 (2015), 195–210; Zoe Alker and Robert Shoemaker, 'Convicts and the Cultural Significance of Tattooing in Nineteenth-century Britain', *Journal of British Studies*, 61/4 (2022), 835–62.

11   Peter Lord's numerous publications are pivotal, such as *Imaging the Nation* (Cardiff, 2000).

12   See works by Martin Johnes, such as 'Eighty minute patriots? National identity and sport in modern Wales', *International Journal of the History of Sport*, 17 (2000), 93–110; 'We hate England! We hate England? National identity and anti-Englishness in Welsh soccer fan culture', *Cycnos*, 25 (2008), 143–57.

13   'Watch Wales' tattoo superfan get inked AGAIN to mark side's latest Euro 2016 win', *North Wales Live*, 27 June 2016, *https://www.dailypost.co.uk/news/north-wales-news/watch-wales-tattoo-superfan-inked-11533216* (accessed 11 October 2023).

14   For more on the origins of this German approach to history from below see Alf Ludtke (ed.), *The History of Everyday Life: Reconstructing Historical Experiences and Ways of Life* (Princeton, 1995).

15   The scholarship on Welsh devolution is extensive: John Gilbert Evans, *Devolution in Wales: Claims and Responses 1937–1979* (Cardiff, 2006); Richard Wyn Jones and Roger Scully, *Wales says Yes* (Cardiff, 2012).

16   *Media and the Memory in Wales*, People's Collection Wales, *https://www.peoplescollection.wales/users/8777* (accessed 11 October 2023). Richard King's *Brittle with Relics* (London, 2022) is also based on oral history, mainly with leading cultural activists.

17   Daniel Evans, 'Welshness in "British Wales": negotiating national identity at the margins', *Nations and Nationalism*, 25/1 (2019), 176–90.

18 Huw Pryce, *Writing Welsh History: From the Early Middle Ages to the Twenty-first Century* (Oxford, 2022) and *J. E. Lloyd and the Creation of Welsh History* (Cardiff, 2011).
19 Laura Carter, *Histories of Everyday Life: The Making of Popular Social History in Britain, c.1918–1979* (Oxford, 2021); Jeffrey K. Olick, Vered Vinitzky-Seroussi and Daniel Levy (eds), *The Collective Memory Reader* (Oxford, 2011).
20 Jeremy Miles, 'Welsh History in the Curriculum for Wales', Welsh Government Written Statement, 15 November 2022, *https://www.gov.wales/written-statement-welsh-history-curriculum-wales* (accessed 11 October 2023); Heledd Fychan, 'We're Proud to Be Yma o Hyd – now it's time to learn what it means', *Nation.Cymru*, 20 November 2022, *https://nation.cymru/opinion/were-proud-to-be-yma-o-hyd-now-its-time-to-learn-what-that-means/* (accessed 11 October 2023).
21 Theoretical approaches for using visual sources in history (not necessarily art history) do not tend to address body art. See, for example, Peter Burke, *Eyewitnessing: The Uses of Images as Historical Evidence* (Cornell, 2008).
22 Lodder, *Painted People*, p. 275.
23 Nick Hall, 'Bringing the Living Back to Life: What happens when we reenact the recent past?', in Nick Hall and John Ellis (eds), *Hands on Media History: A New Methodology in the Humanities and Social Sciences* (Abingdon, 2020), pp. 26–42 (p. 40).
24 Agnieszka Stecko-Żukowska, 'The Poachers of Instagram – Tattoo Artists in Poland and their Tactics in Social Media', *Studia Humanistyczne AGH*, 21/2 (2022), 41–58.
25 Kelsey Beninger, 'Social Media Users' Views on the Ethics of Social Media Research', in Luke Sloan and Anabel Quan-Haase (eds), *The SAGE Handbook of Social Media Research Methods* (London, 2016), pp. 57–72 (p. 58).
26 Nano-influencers can begin to monetise their accounts from 1,000 followers upwards, suggesting that accounts in this realm and above are aiming for public profile and reach, see Feed Pixel, *https://feedpixel.com/instagram-money-calculator/* (accessed 11 October 2023). Permission has been granted for all images reproduced.
27 Esther Milne, *Letters, Postcards, E-mail: Technologies of Presence* (Abingdon, 2010), esp. pp. 109–27.
28 Huw Pryce, 'Cofio Glyndŵr', *Trafodion Anrhydeddus Gymdeithas y Cymmrodorion*, 22 (2016), 43–60.
29 J. E. Lloyd, *Owen Glendower* (Oxford, 1931) and R. R. Davies, *The Revolt of Owain Glyndŵr* (Oxford, 1995); Elissa Henken, *National Redeemer: Owain Glyndŵr in Welsh Tradition* (Cardiff, 1996).
30 Culturenet Cymru, '100 Welsh Heroes' (2004), *https://web.archive.org/web/20140413214449/http:/www.100welshheroes.com/en/homepage* (accessed

11 October 2023); BBC, 'The Top 100 Great Britons' (2002), *https://web.archive.org/web/20030401083737/http://www.bbc.co.uk/history/programmes/greatbritons/list.shtml* (accessed 11 October 2023).

31 See the image on *https://en.wikipedia.org/wiki/File:Glendower_by_A.C.Michael.jpg* (accessed 11 October 2023).

32 For comparative images of the statues see Llangollen Museum, *http://www.llangollenmuseum.org.uk/MythsAndLegends/OwainGlyndwr/Statue.htm* (accessed 11 October 2023).

33 David Coad, 'Euro 2004 and Football Fashion', *Journal of Sport and Social Issues*, 29/1 (2005), 124–6 (p. 126). See image of the tattoo at *https://bodyartguru.com/craig-bellamy-tattoos/* (accessed 11 October 2023).

34 Angela Gaffney, '"A National Valhalla for Wales": D. A. Thomas and the Welsh Historical Sculpture Scheme, 1910–1916', *Transactions of the Honourable Society of Cymmrodorion* (1998/9), 132–44 (p. 135).

35 'Fighter Bellamy: I'll Lead a Revolt', *The Mirror*, 15 October 2008, *https://www.thefreelibrary.com/Football%3a+FIGHTER+BELLAMY%3a+I%27LL+LEAD+A+REVOLT%3b+GERMANY+v+WALES%2c...-a0186927342* (accessed 11 October 2023).

36 'Bellamy armed for Battle', *The Western Mail*, 15 October 2008, *https://www.walesonline.co.uk/sport/football/football-news/bellamy-armed-for-the-battle-2146233* (accessed 11 October 2023).

37 *The Mirror*, 15 October 2008.

38 *The Mirror*, 15 October 2008.

39 Christopher Young, 'Two World Wars and One World Cup: Humour, Trauma and the Asymmetric Relationship in Anglo-German Football', *Sport in History*, 27 (2007), 1–23.

40 The oppressed Welsh past probably was most famously (or infamously) captured in a 1977 pre-match talk by the Wales men's rugby captain, Phil Bennett, when he made a trawl through historical exploitations of Wales by their opponents England. 'Look at what these bastards have done to Wales', was his opening gambit, claiming the English had taken Welsh coal, water, houses and given nothing in return. Although a mythology has grown around this speech, Bennett confirmed it had happened, see *https://www.youtube.com/watch?v=FgSpinRxevc* (accessed 11 October 2023).

41 'Look: Patriotic Welshman has a giant tattoo of Owain Glyndŵr', *Daily Post/North Wales Live*, 27 July 2009, *https://www.dailypost.co.uk/whats-on/whats-on-news/gallery/glyndwr-tattoo-7289904* (accessed 11 October 2023).

42 R. R. Davies, *The Age of Conquest: Wales 1063–1415* (Oxford, 2000).

43 Plaid Cymru president Jill Evans was criticised in 2012 for being 'baptised' at a well near Cilmeri as part of a commemorative event, see Meibion Cymru, 'The Well', *https://www.youtube.com/watch?v=gjJ6di8t-1w&t=190s* (accessed

11 October 2023). For a discussion on how Cilmeri has saturated Welsh historical consciousness see J. Beverley Smith, *Llywelyn ap Gruffudd: Prince of Wales* (2nd edn, Cardiff, 2014), esp. pp. 590–605.

44   Euryn Rhys Roberts, 'Medieval Past, Modern Concerns: The Wales 1983 Festival of Castles', Research Seminar Paper, Bangor University, p. 2.

45   Mari Wiliam interview with Glennydd, 10 January 2023.

46   Barbara Bender (ed.), *Landscape: Politics and Perspectives* (Oxford, 1993), p. 3.

47   Welsh Sleeve by @ds_darkarts, https://www.instagram.com/p/v_aqI4CVfD/?igsh=MTFrcWluNzFycjl1dQ==, Instagram post 29 November 2014 (accessed 24 July 2024).

48   VADS, Statue of Prince Llywelyn ap Iorwerth with Fountain, Conwy, https://www.vads.ac.uk/digital/collection/PMSA/id/563/rec/2 (accessed 11 October 2023).

49   Diolch yn fawr to Dr Nia Jones for her guidance.

50   See, for example, 'Pwerbwynt Llywelyn ein Llyw Olaf Blwyddyn 1 a 2', Cwricwlwm i Gymru – Adnoddau Cymraeg, *Twinkl*, https://www.twinkl.co.uk/resource/perbwynt-llywelyn-ein-llyw-olaf-cc1-cc2-wl-hu-141 (accessed 11 October 2023).

51   Peter Lord, *Medieval Vision* (Cardiff, 2003).

52   For the designs, see https://cowbois.com/oedolion-2.html (accessed 12 October 2023).

53   See the image of Siôn Aubrey Roberts, the only person convicted for the arson campaign, in his Parti Lliw uniform in 'The story of Meibion Glyndwr: the politics, the cause and the unsolved crimes told by the people behind the nationalist movement', *WalesOnline*, 12 December 2021, https://www.walesonline.co.uk/news/wales-news/story-meibion-glyndwr-politics-cause-22251120 (accessed 12 October 2023).

54   Alwyn Gruffydd, *Mae Rhywun yn Gwybod* (Llanrwst, 2004).

55   Mari Elin Wiliam and Gary Robinson, '"White Eagle Rising": The visual and material culture of 1960s Welsh nationalism', 2018 NAASWCH conference, Bangor University. For a comprehensive overview of militant nationalism see Wyn Thomas, *Hands off Wales: Nationhood and Militancy* (Llandysul, 2013).

56   Simon M. Mueller et al., 'Role of tattoos in football: Behavioural Patterns and success – analysis of the FIFA World Cup 2018', *Clinics in Dermatology*, 38 (2020), 788–92 (p. 791).

57   @missreastattoostudio, https://www.instagram.com/p/CQNhlo5haLt/?igshid=YmMyMTA2M2Y%3D, Instagram post, 17 June 2021 (accessed 12 October 2023).

58   For more on the resurgence in Tryweryn graffiti in the twenty-first century see Mari Emlyn, *Cofiwch Dryweryn: Cymru'n Deffro/Wales Awakening*

(Talybont, 2019); a Tryweryn tattoo from 2019 can be seen on *https://www.bbc.co.uk/news/uk-wales-48108677* (accessed 12 October 2023).

59 'Incredible Mural created in Caernarfon ahead of Wales' World Cup Campaign', *North Wales Chronicle*, 8 November 2022, *https://www.northwaleschronicle.co.uk/news/23108528.incredible-mural-created-caernarfon-ahead-wales-world-cup-campaign/* (accessed 12 October 2023).
60 Phil Stead, *Red Dragons: The Story of Welsh Football* (3rd edn, Talybont, 2022).
61 See *https://spiritof58wales.bigcartel.com/* (accessed 12 October 2023).
62 E. Wyn James, 'Painting the World Green: Dafydd Iwan and the Welsh Protest Ballad', *Folk Music Journal*, 8/5 (2005), 594–618.
63 FA Wales, 'Yma o Hyd (Official Cymru World Cup 2022 Song)', *You Tube*, 7 November 2022, *https://www.youtube.com/watch?v=43Fag8ZQcz4* (accessed 12 October 2023).
64 Ifan Morgan Jones, 'Why the FAW's epic Yma o Hyd video is a brave (and controversial) take on what it means to be Welsh', *Nation.Cymru*, 7 November 2022, *https://nation.cymru/opinion/why-the-faws-epic-yma-o-hyd-video-is-a-brave-and-controversial-take-on-what-it-means-to-be-welsh/* (accessed 12 October 2023).
65 BBC Wales, 'Yma o Hyd: Welsh World Cup anthem seeing rise in tattoos', 29 November 2022, *https://www.bbc.co.uk/news/uk-wales-63769606* (accessed 12 October 2023).
66 BBC Wales, 'Yma o Hyd: Welsh World Cup anthem seeing rise in tattoos'.
67 @lLisa_Peggy, *https://twitter.com/lLisa_Peggy/status/1555090853470867456*, Twitter post, 4 August 2022 (accessed 12 October 2023).
68 @AbolishWestmin, *https://twitter.com/AbolishWestmin/status/1540081125632221184?cxt=HHwWgIC9qfjnu98qAAAA*, Twitter post, 23 June 2022 (accessed 12 October 2023).
69 @BronwenLewis_, *https://twitter.com/BronwenLewis_/status/1540066961866067968*, Twitter post, 23 June 2022 (accessed 12 October 2023).
70 Joel Watson, '"Why did You Put That There?" Gender, Materialism and Tattoo Consumption', *Advances in Consumer Research*, 25 (1998), 453–60.
71 Rosalind Gill, Karen Henwood and Carl McLean, 'Body projects and the regulation of normative masculinity', *Body and Society*, 11/1 (2005), 37–62.
72 Mari Elin Wiliam, 'Shifting sands: postcards and the visual identity of north Wales seaside resorts during the twentieth-century', 2016 NAASWCH Conference, Harvard University.
73 Christine Stevens, 'Welsh Peasant Dress – Workwear or National Costume?', *Textile History*, 33/1 (2002), 63–78.
74 See the work of Prys Morgan, including 'From a Death to a View: The Hunt for the Welsh Past in the Romantic Period', in E. Hobsbawm and T. O. Ranger (eds), *The Invention of Tradition* (Cambridge, 1983), pp. 43–100.
75 'Daniel', *Baner ac Amserau Cymru*, 6 March 1958.

76 Curnow Vosper's *Salem* (1908) is probably one of the most renowned depictions of the Welsh national costume.
77 See examples of this in Michael McCabe, *New York City Tattoo: The Oral History of an Urban Art* (San Francisco, 1997 and 2013), for example p. 90, 'Bill Jones flash from Coney Island'.
78 Lisa Eldridge, *Face Paint: The Story of Makeup* (London, 2015).
79 Yohana Desta, 'The Untold Story Behind an Iconic Marilyn Monroe Moment', *Vanity Fair*, 13 January 2017.
80 Postal Museum, 'Saucy Seaside Postcards and Censorship', 21 August 2021, *https://www.postalmuseum.org/blog/saucy-seaside-postcards-and-censorship/* (accessed 12 October 2023).
81 Pamela Church Gibson, 'Pornostyle: sexualised dress and the fracturing of feminism', *Fashion Theory*, 18/2 (2014), 189–206 (p. 202).
82 @chrisbarrett_tattooer, Wrexham, *https://www.instagram.com/p/Ck_gbj_Ihir/?igshid=YmMyMTA2M2Y%3D*, Instagram post, 22 November 2022 (accessed 12 October 2023); Welsh flash sheet by @brokenpoke, Cardiff, *https://www.instagram.com/p/CUhl0ZBAXrI/*, Instagram post, 21 September 2021 (accessed 12 October 2023).
83 Jhaiho, '8 Trans Tattoos that reflect who you are, and who you are becoming', *Medium*, 20 November 2018, *https://medium.com/@jhaiho17/8-trans-tattoos-that-reflect-who-you-are-and-who-you-are-becoming-fe95de8f22d6* (accessed 12 October 2023).
84 Angela V. John, *Our Mothers' Land: Chapters in Welsh Women's History 1830–1939* (Cardiff, 1991). An interesting comparable trajectory for a Welsh 'heroine' is discussed in Susan M. Johns, *Gender, nation and conquest in the high Middle Ages: Nest of Deheubarth* (Manchester, 2016).
85 Lodder, *Painted People*, p. 283.
86 Wil Griffith, 'Saving the Soul of the Nation: Essentialist Nationalism and Interwar Rural Wales', *Rural History*, 21/2 (2010), 177–94.
87 Evans, 'Welshness in British Wales'; Robin Mann and Steve Fenton, *Nation, class and resentment: The politics of national identity in England, Scotland and Wales* (London, 2017).
88 Karl Broome, 'Tattooing starts at home: tattooing, affectivity, and sociality', *Fashion Theory*, 10/3 (2006), 333–50 (p. 347).
89 Fisher, 'Marking Culture', 104.
90 See, for example, Digital Panopticon, 'Tracing London Convicts in Britain & Australia, 1780–1925', which includes a searchable tattoo database, *https://www.digitalpanopticon.org/* (accessed 12 October 2023).
91 Estyn, *The Teaching of Welsh History including Black, Asian and Minority Ethnic History, Identity and Culture* (October 2021), *https://www.estyn.gov.wales/book/print/pdf/20673* (accessed 12 October 2023), p. 13.

15

'Time Present and Time Past': Narrating Nation and Society in Welsh Historical Writing, 1970–2010[1]

Neil Evans

In his 2019 O'Donnell lecture, Huw Pryce asked: 'Why write the history of Wales?' After a typically masterly survey of around 1,500 years of Welsh historiography, he concluded that there was no simple answer to the question and that many different approaches and arguments had been used. But he pointed out that the writing of history often revealed as much about the time of composition as about the past. Most, if not all, of his subjects were engaged with a conception of the Welsh nation and sometimes of nationalism. The simple answer to his question is that choosing Wales as a historical subject in itself is an engagement with the nation and a means of legitimating it.[2] John Davies confronts the issue directly: 'the writing of the history of any country is to some extent a metaphysical act, but the fact that there exists the will to undertake the task indicates that it is a substantive act also'.[3] I take this to mean that a nation is, in some respects, an intangible idea and is often seen as a thing of the spirit or an essence and, to a nationalist, the supreme object of loyalty. Even to be part of an imagined community, the least primordial or metaphysical approach to the nation, means seeing something in common with the members of the nation who will be mostly unknown to us and of varied and possibly disparate social classes, and living in different parts of the country which is geographically and economically varied. Martin Daunton poses the issue with his customary clarity and incisiveness:

> it may well be that Welsh historians will benefit more from a comparison between parts of Wales and analogous areas in the rest of Britain than they will from a romantic pursuit of Welsh

identity. Wales as a nation is one organising principle, but so is Wales as a collection of disparate regions.[4]

A. H. Dodd said much the same from an opposite viewpoint over a decade before. For him, nationalism gave Welsh history unity and made it a distinct discipline. Without this rationale, it was 'a mere geographical region'.[5]

From the late Middle Ages until the early twentieth century, writers of the history of Wales struggled to engage with the near past and the present. The distinctive history of Wales seemed to end in 1282 or 1536 – a glorious past which had then merged into a larger entity. For many, there was no longer a distinct Welsh History.[6] J. E. Lloyd, as Huw Pryce has shown, thought that the early years of the history were the most important and could sustain it into the future.[7] But when Lloyd did engage with the recent past he was at best ambivalent about it. Industrialisation meant: 'in large measure … the submergence of what was characteristically Welsh under a tide of foreign influence – the extension of England into what was once Wales'.[8] His words are almost identical with those of Saunders Lewis in his broadly contemporaneous poem 'Y Dilyw' (The Deluge).[9] For Lloyd, this process had led to the fragmentation of whatever unity Wales had once possessed, the loss of the Welsh language from large parts of the country and the break-up of Liberal political dominance because of the twin forces of industrial politics and an infant nationalist party. All was far from lost as there were now national institutions, a cultural revival, scholarly standards for the language and the language had defied the predictions of the 1860s that it faced imminent extinction. Welsh communities outside Wales were also real achievements. He ended with the words of 'Hen Wlad fy Nhadau': 'O bydded yr hên iaith barhau' ('Long may the old language endure').[10] Owen M. Edwards perhaps embraced the present more enthusiastically with his novel division of Welsh history into two great ages: 'the age of the princes' and the 'age of the people'. But he was sparing in his direct engagement with modern history and it was a common feeling that Wales had been sundered and large areas effectively annexed to England.[11]

Writing the history of modern Wales was an endeavour of the later twentieth century. My concern in this chapter will be to examine how the more detailed exploration of modern history was influenced by views of the Welsh nation and its social structure and how they varied in the work of four major historians: A. H. Dodd, Glanmor Williams, Gwyn A. Williams and John Davies. I have restricted this to works which cover the whole chronological span of the history of Wales and excluded living writers. Such questions were posed over two decades ago by Michael Roberts. He observed that in the 1960s Welsh historians had created a 'modernist' history of Wales. He did not define what he meant by that, but it clearly means a perspective which fully values the industrial period and sees that as the culmination of Welsh history. However, developments since then had led to queries about this perspective. Historians and other academics had come to see Wales as fundamentally divided, of only qualified modernity as an 'internal colony' or of constrained and limited industrialisation. It was an invented nation and constantly redefined. The grand narrative of heavy industry and mining was challenged by de-industrialisation and it was also hard to sustain 'any simple notion of Welsh history as the cultural core of a nation state in waiting'.[12] Like Huw Pryce, he was observing that historical writing is always shaped by the present and, I add to this, concerns about the future.

The title of this chapter comes from T. S. Eliot:

> Time present and time past
> Are both perhaps present in time future[13]

I hope to illuminate different ways in which a national history might be written and to argue that the history of a nation must always be in some sense a total history, at least in the claim that all members share characteristics. There will always be an overall conception of the nature of society involved and how that society changes or endures. It has been argued that: 'we cannot think about society without in some way or other implying a theory of history'.[14] I argue that the converse also applies – to write the history of a nation we have to imply a theory of society or at the very least a view of its structure. Sociology and history both emerged in something like their modern form as responses to the great changes of the nineteenth century, though the one focused on economic and social transformation and the other on nations and the state. The term 'total history' is forever associated with the *Annales* school. I am not seeking to measure these historians by the *Annales* gold standard: there is no such thing and it would be foolish to think that their approaches, diverse as they were and are, have somehow resolved all the problems of writing history.[15] Nor am I trying to measure one Welsh scholar against another or far less score points off them with a more recent perspective. Rather, what I am trying to do is to tease out some of their assumptions and analyses in order that we might think more coherently and systematically about the nature of Wales and its society.

Life in Wales

A. H. Dodd published his *Life in Wales* in 1972 in a Batsford series otherwise known as Life in England. Eleven years before, he had published another volume in the series, *Life in Elizabethan England*. The series was aimed at a non-academic audience and the books are very short but profusely illustrated. The volumes in the series often seem to exemplify G. M. Trevelyan's notorious view of social history as the 'history of a people with the politics left out'.[16] Dodd's own Elizabethan volume does rather take that line in that it is topically arranged with no strong narrative and provides a wide range of colourful anecdotes. His book on Wales, by contrast, does not adopt this form but is more in accord with the way in which Trevelyan had seen his social history as filling a gap between the existing political history and the more recently emerging economic history: 'the social scene grows out of economic conditions, to much the same extent that political events in their turn grow out of social conditions. Without social history, economic history is barren and political history is unintelligible'.[17] Dodd took on all those dimensions and wove them together to make the cloth of the nation. He was eighty years old when the book appeared and it was his last book as well as one of his last publications. In 1977, after his death in 1975, it was reissued in paperback as *A Short History of Wales* and detached from the series. We may see it as the culmination of his work, which had spanned fifty years, and this becomes clearer if we link it with some essays and articles that he had previously published.

He starts his book forthrightly with a declaration:

> For countless ages the land between Offa's frontier and the sea had been swept by successive waves of prospectors and settlers, each following lines determined by the physical lay-out of the country, and all combining to produce the Welsh people.

Westward lay a long and exposed coast line with projecting arms in Llŷn and Pembrokeshire and frequent indentations which invited the invader from Ireland or Spain or Brittany; eastward the main river valleys as well as the southern coastal plain, lay open to incursions from the English lowlands. Broken though the country is, geography has given it a certain natural unity and a natural frontier — the palaeozoic outcrops underlying Offa's engineering feat. Within these bounds successive cultures have been absorbed and adapted until there emerged a heritage stubbornly cherished in the teeth even of military conquest.[18]

Geography was a potential container but it was human action that placed a nation within it. He took the story back to the earliest archaeological evidence available to him but Wales as a nation has a distinct point of arrival: 'by the middle of the ninth century, Cymru had become a distinct country and a distinct people'.[19] This unity was cultural and linguistic rather than political, though there was some political consolidation and the ninth-century scholar Nennius, author of *Historia Brittonum*, illustrated that there was some pride in their history. Dodd's framework throughout is the changing nature of relationships with England and divisions and alliances within Wales; he sometimes speaks of 'pressures' on Wales and there are clearly those exercised by the English state. There is much on the development of religion, literary culture and education over the centuries. A comment on late medieval Wales could be a summary of much of the book: there was a 'persistent and distinctive thread of Welsh life'.[20]

But he never loses sight of everyday life and of social class. He is always concerned to tell us about the nature of housing in so far as it could be known. He argues Gerald of Wales's strictures on it was probably a description of temporary *hafodtai* rather than permanent proper buildings. Homes of the *uchelwyr* were likely to be rectangular and those of bondsmen circular. There was some rebuilding of habitations in the later Middle Ages but it almost certainly did not extend to the homes of the poorest.[21] A thread of concern for the poorest runs through the book. In the earlier Middle Ages bondsmen outnumbered the rest of the population and were probably the descendants of earlier conquered populations. The growth of population in the high Middle Ages meant the expansion of the *gwelyau* and a growth of the free population. Bondsmen were now about one-third of a larger population. The Black Death shrank them to some 10 per cent of the population. Under the Tudors their fate was uncertain but Henry VIII freed his own bondsmen – provided they paid him for the privilege. Bond hamlets became consolidated into compact farms. In the enclosure movement of the Napoleonic era the big owners were the main beneficiaries and the small freeholder less so. Cottagers and squatters were the hardest hit.[22] His focus was on the nation but he never lost sight of the social divisions within it.

These concerns were of long standing for Dodd. The longest, final chapter in *The Industrial Revolution in North Wales* (1933) is that on 'The Labouring Poor'. When he was president of the Cambrian Archaeological Association, he chose as his topic 'Jack and his House' and invoked archaeology (a method rather than a period he presciently averred) as one means of exploring it. But his concern extended into the modern period when the rehousing of the working class came into its own.[23] He could describe class divisions in vivid analogies:

> Eighteenth-century politics in Wales, as in most of England, amounted to little more than a gentlemanly game of cricket, with exclusive family groups at the wicket, their dependants in the outfield, and glittering trophies for the champions.[24]

The rest of the population were mere spectators or locked out of the ground one presumes. Tudor Wales was a society divided between old and new as starkly the divisions between the Celts and the Romans. It is hard not to think of the fashionable modernisation theories of the 1950s and 1960s, which posited a dual economy and society with the traditional, underdeveloped third world starkly separated from an implanted, often American, modern sector.[25] In the eighteenth century, Wales developed its own educational and religious movements which 'responded to emotional tides over much of western Europe; but the economic development which followed owed their impetus mainly to fashions originating in England, and transplanted into Wales either by force of example or direct "colonization"'.[26]

None of this makes Dodd into a Marxist or far less a postcolonial theorist. His book on Elizabethan England very much includes Wales as somewhere now fully integrated into the realm (and to its benefit) though it is sometimes compared and contrasted with the north of England as areas apart from the core England of the south-east and midlands. The index has some twenty-eight references to Wales in a book of 166 pages of text. Five years before the publication of this book, he had sensitively explored the nature of the frontier in a wide-ranging article. He dealt with conquest, politics and warfare, culture and religious ideas before coming finally to economic connections as if in a conscious rejection of the schema of vulgar Marxism.[27]

Yet he seemed to think that political alignments would quickly conform to economic realities and found it necessary to ponder when they did not.

> The prolongation into the industrial age of a radicalism based on the preoccupations of rural Nonconformity – the fight against privilege, attachment to the soil and to a language and traditions beginning to lose ground in the towns – is not easy to explain.[28]

His explanation is that the Welsh-language press, educators, preachers and lecturers had a wide circulation, and English-language newspapers had a limited circulation. Political education came from such sources – from the traditional intellectuals of the bourgeoisie rather than the organic ones of the proletariat a follower of Gramsci might argue. English-language publications challenged this position and industrialisation itself was a threat. By the contemporary period, industrial Wales had settled down to 'bread and butter politics' while Plaid Cymru appealed only to rural Wales.[29] He describes early nineteenth-century Swansea as a 'havoc' and is glad that only Parys Mountain rivalled it in north Wales. Rhosllannerchrugog was mercifully, like Merthyr, merely an overgrown village. However, immigrants were mainly from the surrounding areas and Montgomeryshire was never 'swamped' by its towns; the quarrying areas remained essentially rural. This is not as explicit as Lloyd's condemnation of the new industrial areas but it has distinct echoes of it.

The catastrophe that hit Wales originated in Sarajevo rather than across the border:

> The outbreak of war in 1914 brought that creative period to an end, shattered many illusions, and opened a new chapter in

Welsh history, whose trend, even after half a century, is still not easy to discern.[30]

In context, the creative period is not simply the late Victorian and Edwardian era but that which stretched back to the Methodist revival, education improvement and industrial expansion. Twentieth-century Wales is then disposed of in the briefest of postscripts. General social trends like the decline of the gentry, church-going and the rise of a cosmopolitan popular culture had been blunted a little by the improved legal status of the Welsh language and broadcasting but there was, for him, no confidence in the future. 'How far this historic character of life in Wales will be able to hold its own against these currently only the future can show'.[31] Welshness had run like a thread through a hierarchical society and had been developed and enlarged constantly, but had clearly given it some coherence. That was no longer secure in the future.

Fire on Cambria's altar: religion, language and nationality

Glanmor Williams never wrote a general history of Wales. He considered that different periods required different abilities and referred to the enterprise of a single volume history by one historian as 'doing a John Davies'.[32] However, apart from establishing a framework for Welsh history which gave proper recognition to modern history, he also edited the Oxford/University of Wales Press six-volume history of Wales and saw four volumes appear in his lifetime. Another has subsequently been published. More significantly for my purpose here, he wrote essays which covered all periods of Welsh history apart from the twentieth century. In 1979, he collected many of these under the title *Religion, Language and Nationality in Wales* and wrote a long introductory essay with the same title which was cross-referenced to the other essays. Effectively this amounts to a general history. Twelve years later, he published another collection of essays – *The Welsh and their Religion* – with an even longer introductory essay: 'Fire on Cambria's Altar'. These two essays combined probably have as many words in them – and they overlap with each other only minimally – as Dodd's *Life in Wales*. Williams's essays provide a means of examining his overall view of Welsh nationality, society and its prospects.

The central thread in these essays is religion. His belief in Protestant Nonconformity was a central element in his life and while he developed wider and alternative perspectives on the Reformation it was essentially that standpoint which informed his analysis.[33] In the first essay, it is approached as intellectual history, focusing on key texts and individuals, whereas the second tends towards *mentalité* with a concern for wider cultural attitudes – and uses the English word mentality at one point. The French word is, of course, central to the *Annales* school. Though Lucien Febvre is cited in the bibliography of his *The Welsh Church from Conquest to Reformation*, and he later affirmed the value of engagement with French and German historiography on the Reformation, it is more likely that his engagement with Welsh literature and his sense of place had more to do with his approach than any slavish following of European trends. In all his work, when he mentions an abbey or monastery, we are in no doubt that he knows it on the ground from its remains as well as from the historical record. When he gained a Leverhulme Fellowship to advance his research in 1957–8, some of it was to finance visits to relevant sites.[34]

Gildas provides him with the first view of how the Welsh saw themselves and it is a religious view. In the later essay, Christianity is present in Wales before a sense of Welshness had emerged. So religion is foundational and it remains a running thread – more of a highway really – throughout the centuries until the twentieth.[35] The Welsh conception of history is seen as being like the Hebrew – a chosen people which has fallen from Grace. But there were other and sometimes contradictory foci of loyalty and identity to narrower units and institutions and to the lineages of kings and later princes. As well as being Welsh, people could also see themselves as being Britons – descendants of Trojans – or people of a *gwlad* or region. Saxon perfidy was added to divine retribution as a cause of Welsh downfall. A sense of history ran through this and prophecy of a return to former glories connected it with the future. Underpinning this was the free population who are seen as the basis of this identity; unlike Dodd the unfree are present only as an implicit 'other'. There were many external pressures from across the border and circumstances changed quite dramatically at times, especially with the coming of the Normans and then with the era of Renaissance and Reformation, which were not confined to the intellectual spheres but involved changes in secular power and economic growth.

Industrialisation might have been thought to be another sea change, but it appears rather unannounced though with a pervasive impact.

Throughout it all, there was a growth in religious institutions and their influence on the survival and extension of an identity. In fundamentals, all was secure until the breakdown of isolation in language and culture in the twentieth century. Until then there had been: 'the transmission of a way of life, largely intact, from one generation to another'.[36] While there were many responses to this, they were far from entirely successful and Wales in the 1970s was seen as two cultures mutually almost incomprehensible to each other, and he thought it threatened to be as divisive as religion had been in the sixteenth century. However, both had claims to Welshness. Industrial society was Welsh and Glanmor Williams could never agree with Saunders Lewis, or indeed, J. E. Lloyd, that it was a place which had once been Wales. He pleaded for mutual understanding between them. Language was not the only component of national identity and it was only comparatively recently that it had come to be seen as such.[37] The Welsh were: 'too small a people to indulge in the masochistic luxury of self-inflicted wounds'.[38]

While there was a strong sense of a tradition and continuity coming to an end, much of his exposition had been about adaptation and renewal. He stressed the flexibility and adaptability of the old prophetic tradition, yet focused above all on the translation of the Bible, which he referred to as having saved the Welsh.[39] However, clearly it had not really been saved apart from the sense in which William Salesbury had wanted to save it – that is, from being simply the language of the farmyard. It was remade. Religion was linked with the patriotic and literary inheritance and in no other Celtic part of the British Isles was there: 'the same conscious and energetic *response* to the challenges of the new age and the printed book'.[40] There is both a sense of change running through the essays and the occasional surfacing of some sort of essence of Welshness – perhaps the metaphysical quality to which John Davies refers. The changes of the Reformation era, including the revival of the idea of a Celtic church, wedded religion to 'some basic and *primordial* instincts in the Welsh attitude towards language, religion and patriotism'.[41] In the later essay: 'from the outset the Christian religion seemed to be part of the essence of Welshness'.[42]

In the later essay there is a conscious engagement with continuity and turning points.[43] The age of the saints was 'the bed-rock of a specifically Welsh Christian tradition to which all subsequent religious achievement was referred and by which it was measured'.[44] However, if religion is seen as being at the core of Welsh identity it is clearly not the same thing for all Welsh people. In the medieval period, for most people attendance must have been sporadic because of the distances it was necessary to travel in order to go to church. Care was taken over recording the landmarks of life – birth, marriage and death – though there was a 'collective Christianity' rooted in trust in the saints, the ritual of the clergy to prevent evil and ensure salvation. Cistercians rather than Dominicans predominated, and the church embraced Welsh literature and history. The vision and idealism of the church was confined to a small group and especially the higher clergy. As for the people: 'their religion was performed and to a large extent believed, for them by others'.[45] When the church recovered from the challenges of the fourteenth and fifteenth centuries – Black Death, taxation to pay for the French Wars and Glyndŵr – it was at the expense of the people it served. Yet perhaps Glanmor Williams's disenchantment is greatest in the Victorian era, normally seen as the high-tide of Welsh religiosity. R. Tudur Jones claimed: 'Wales, in 1890, was a Christian country'.[46] Williams probes beneath the surface using the 'exquisitely sensitive' writings of Daniel Owen (a fine description of his own writing too) to show a society in which religion had complete domination but was used by those seeking acceptance and respectability for selfish ends.[47] Some of Owen's characters are so roguish that they tax and strain his sense of humour and tolerance of human foibles.[48]

The twentieth century then provides a tragic coda. The decline is uninterrupted and diametrically opposed to the previous history. This is a general process in Europe but the Welsh-language dimension makes it peculiar to Wales. The fragility of the structure that Daniel Owen had hinted at was fully exposed. Society was no longer held together by church and God. It is interesting to note in passing that he thought the chapels the central binding force of his boyhood in Dowlais.[49] All the social and cultural trends of the modern world now militated against religion – what Max Weber called the 'disenchantment of the world'.[50] But he did not follow the path to Evangelical revivalism which beckoned to many Welsh literary scholars. He perceived no latter-day Elijah on the mountain top. The fire which had burned brightly on the altar was now a smoky and fitful flame. For someone who had put religion at the centre of Welshness, it was a sad but realistic admission.[51]

When was Wales?

Gwyn A. Williams was a multitalented person. To find the depths of his genius it is necessary to penetrate through the surface layers. He was, first of all, for many people a highly engaging lecturer with a dramatic and breath-taking delivery. When he was a lecturer in Aberystwyth and relatively unknown and unpublished, he had a following of postgraduate students who were not historians yet went from lecture to lecture. He needed large lecture rooms, far bigger than the enrolments in his classes required. In York at least one major historian was turned away from sociology by his lectures.[52] From the late 1970s this talent was transferred to television and most famously in the series *The Dragon has Two Tongues*, where he engaged in weekly combat with Wynford Vaughan Thomas with the debate polarised between Wynford's insistence on continuity and Gwyn A. Williams's on 'ruptures' in the experience of the Welsh. The third element was, of course, his writing, with a stream of books, articles and essays over a period of around forty years. All of these share a unique prose style and this is probably the aspect of his work – and his persona – of which most people are aware. He could vividly evoke landscapes populated by communities and their interactions, with cultural resonances and myths permeating them and individuals evoked as breathing human beings. His metaphors and images were arresting, surprising and sometimes oxymoronic. It was impossible not to sit up and take notice, and to be stimulated. He was funny: ironic, witty and irreverent. The Normans were 'high-born bandits'. Examples could be multiplied: Wales before the late eighteenth century is 'Oxfam territory' and Herefordshire is depicted as a 'lowland Snowdonia with a West Country accent'.

But he was also a Marxist who took theory seriously and who was a pioneer in Britain of the study of Gramsci. This was rooted in wide reading in Marxist theory in general and it informed his historical analysis throughout. In the bubbling energy of his prose, its vitality and imagination, narrative and theory are mixed. This is especially true in his general analysis of Wales most famously presented in his BBC radio lecture of 1979 and the book of the TV series, both of which were called *When was Wales?*. The lecture asserted powerfully that nations are manufactured rather than grow 'naturally' and took on a nostalgic but strangely comfortable view of Wales. He distinguished between the Welsh people and the Welsh nation, with the latter being a succession of conceptions very different from each other. Wales had been defined by England by the ninth century and with each transformation the Welsh nation adapted to a new British reality. The tone of the lecture was apocalyptic. The events of 1979 – the overwhelming vote against devolved powers, the substantial Conservative vote in the 1979 Westminster elections and the European elections threatened to expunge the Welsh nation. If we wanted it, we needed to go out and remake it – a task made even harder by its incompatibility with the current, emerging global form of the capitalist system. It was a clear challenge to established Wales. On the recording of the lecture, you can almost hear the intake of breath when he advocated the Europe of a clutch of Marxists and Gramsci, in particular, and said: 'the Europe of Saunders Lewis's *Brad* is our enemy'. In the TV series, Wynford Vaughan Thomas seems to personify that comfortably established Wales.

His major book spells out the approach and the theory in an introductory chapter. Essentially, he combines two approaches. One is Marxism, but the Marx of *The Eighteenth Brumaire of Louis Bonaparte* and its famous epigram: men make their own history but not in circumstances of their own choosing.[53] The second is the idea of geographical determinism which was well established in Welsh historiography, but which Gwyn A. Williams interprets not as absolute determinism but as its variant, possibilism. A determinist sees a river as an obstacle. A possibilist sees it as a potential means of transport. This almost certainly came from the *Annales* school and the suspicion is given weight by his stress on demography as the differentiating factor between pre-industrial and industrial Wales. Of course, this also owed much to the work of the Welsh demographer and economist Brinley Thomas, but its more general application has an *Annales* air about it. The second generation of *Annales* scholars made demographic matters into key drivers of historical development and as an alternative to Marxist views.[54]

People make their own history against the circumstances in which they find themselves – both those created by prior and new historical circumstances and by geography. Agency is critical but cannot operate in a vacuum. If Dodd sees the land of Wales as something like an accommodating mould for the nation, Gwyn A. Williams sees it as a perilous rock on to which we cling. Wales has a rocky face; Merioneth is 'rock-ribbed'. A succession of challenges comes from across the border:

Anglo-Saxons who define Wales; Normans who make it adapt in a European context; the new British state of the eighteenth century, which leads to a transformation of the economy, education and religion; the Industrial Revolution which produces a working-class as well as middle-class Nonconformist nation.

Wales is made by the Welsh people in circumstances chosen by others. Within, it has its own social struggles. The feudal state-makers of Gwynedd need to increase the number of bondsmen in order to enhance their power. Their subservient lords need more freemen in order to build up their power. From the Middle Ages to the modern period, a frontier is drawn across Wales which is as significant and shares its boundaries with Emrys Bowen's inner and outer Wales, but which is seen as an area of creative interaction and not as a threat from which the fortress of inner Wales needs protection.[55] It is akin to the idea of borderlands which has done so much to shape American ideas of the interactions between Indigenous peoples and multiple colonisers in earlier history.[56] The 1970s crisis of Wales is underpinned by a broad process of divergence throughout the twentieth century.

This polarity – structure and agency – can be related to the apocalyptic aspects of Gwyn A. Williams's analysis. Gramcsi famously borrowed a motto from Romain Roland: 'pessimism of the intellect, optimism of the will'.[57] The survival of Wales has been a minor miracle – optimism and agency – triumphing over pessimism, power and structure. The challenge for the future is a massive one and it needs another miracle.

There is a pattern in all this which is dialectical. Thesis: each new regime across the border; antithesis: the responses in Wales; and synthesis: a new outcome. He rejects any spirit or essence of Wales, such as the racial characteristics of Celts which infused analysis from at least Tom Ellis to Emrys Bowen, and dismissed Hegel, the inventor of the dialectic as 'mysticism and infantilism'.[58] Not much room for metaphysics here, then. But an iteration of Wales is always present in every period: no manifestation of Wales is ever more Welsh than any other. What is ever present is a sense of the past that is different from England's. This explains Williams's sense of duty as a people's remembrancer. Wales has lost its sense of history and succumbed to myths. Hegel may have been more use to him than Williams's dismissal suggests. In his dialectic, something of the old always survives and the word 'Geist' usually translated as 'spirit' also means 'mind' in German. To understand the end point of history as spirit might be to see it as mystical. Understanding it as mind puts a rather different complexion on it but Hegel saw history as moving *inexorably* towards Geist. For Williams, there is no clear destination for Wales: everything depends upon our actions to make the best of our situation. It is illuminating to consider Williams's analysis of Spanish history as a dialectical process of reason and unreason but one which was never resolved: it was stuck in an 'impossible revolution' with no synthesis.[59] Hegel's work allowed for this and the tripartite thesis/antithesis/synthesis is a textbook simplification rather than a rigid formula.[60] In Williams's written texts there is no use of the word 'rupture', a term that has a particular meaning in the work of the sociologist Stuart Hall.[61] The drama of a TV argument was not the same as the exposition of position on the page. But it is interesting to speculate on how that idea might have played out comparatively and in debate with professional Welsh historians rather than a distinguished journalist and broadcaster but distinctly amateur historian.

Hanes Cymru

If A. H. Dodd and Glanmor Williams were ambivalent about the twentieth century and Gwyn A. Williams thought it offered the Welsh equivalent of the old Marxist options of 'socialism or barbarism', John Davies embraced the present and the future with an almost irenic confidence. The period 1914 to 2007 takes up 217 pages out of 711 in the revised and extended version – or 31 per cent of the text and twice the percentage in *When was Wales?*. This is far from an afterthought or postscript. No other period in Welsh history was given such intense analysis and discussion. But it is the conclusion which is most striking: 'the first edition of this book ended with the suggestion that the fullness of the Welsh nation is yet to be. It is a privilege to live to see that that prophecy is not without foundation'.[62]

How did he come to such a conclusion? In 1979 he was so despondent at the result of the referendum that he considered leaving Wales altogether.[63] His book was published in 1990 and in English in 1993 before the 1997 referendum and before the renewed movement for devolution had gathered much pace, though he found John Osmond's commitment to the cause inspirational. But the book had in the main been written by 1986. The language is telling: it is a 'prophecy' and we are back in metaphysical territory. But what had affected that? I can only suggest that it was the act of writing *Hanes Cymru* – truly a glory of the Welsh intellect – which had consumed him in the intervening years. His view of the past promised much for the future.

Unlike Gwyn A. Williams's book, it is a history of Wales and not a history of the Welsh so it takes us back as far as geology, science and archaeology will allow us. All the most important technical and human developments were made long before the Welsh appeared on the scene, so the nation is located against humanity in general. Geography and geology give a country its personality so are important factors in its identity. One of the themes of the book is the diversity of Wales and its communities but combined with a sense that they are all Welsh and equally so. He explored Wales from an early age and had an encyclopaedic knowledge of its communities and landscapes.[64] *Hanes Cymru* is structured around maps which were his conceptions and not simply the illustrative insertions of his publisher. Each chapter has title from places symbolic of the period and these are well scattered across the face of Wales. Throughout the book a wider context is not simply invoked but is ever present and active. The people of Wales are always actively involved in the process of history. He rejects diffusionist ideas in archaeology by which innovations were transmitted from centres to peripheries as relics of nineteenth-century imperialism. The anti-imperialism continues in his rejection of the influence of the Roman period. Wales was conceived on its death bed. The point applied more widely throughout the book in the sense that the Welsh nation is seen as an active and distinct agent in history.

The period 800–1282 is where he really gets into his stride and reveals much of his conception of Wales. It is half a millennium of ferment and promise. He constantly uses the perspective of the whole of the history of Wales to make sweeping and insightful judgement about distinctive phases of development. The theme here is the trend to state-building. This is European in scope but Wales is a full participant in it. There is a conscious movement towards a Welsh state and the reduction in the number of rival kingdoms and principalities shows the trend. Hywel Dda was probably codifying the Welsh laws as part of a nation and state-building enterprise. Most historians are more qualified in their views of all of this and see it as tenuous, unconscious and doomed to failure. Wendy Davies's powerful account of early medieval Wales might be termed a 'minimalist' account of state-building. She rejected any trend towards it and stressed the weaknesses. John Davies's account is the polar opposite. We might term it 'maximalist'.[65] There is little doubt that Gwynedd is at the centre of the process in his view. The attitudes of rival rulers and lesser lords are dismissed (following Keith Williams-Jones) as 'Petainistic'.[66] It was not doomed to failure. Llywelyn ap Gruffydd (d. 1282) needed time which he was not given but had he had it, fourteenth-century England would not have had the will to destroy his state.

Wales was an active participant in the world of its time. The roots of English involvement in Ireland were planted in Wales; the conquest of Wales aided the development of international finance capital and forced the king into raising the necessary funds through consent.[67] Owain Glyndŵr was not doomed to failure by circumstances and he had a better chance of success than Robert the Bruce. Nor was the 1979 referendum doomed to failure: might it have been won by being held the previous year before the 'winter of discontent' and with firm and vigorous support from government ministers? The 'union' of 1536 was a consolidation rather than a revolution and had the useful side-effect of making everyone living in Wales, Welsh. This might be seen as the basis of a claim to civic nationalism but he later argues that there was no legal or constitutional basis for this and he asks the key probing question of civic nationalism: what is it that distinguishes Welsh civic nationalism from other forms of it? This is a problem detected in all accounts of it: there is always a hidden cultural dimension. But the creation of the Welsh Office confirmed the territorial integrity of Wales.

The Industrial Revolution is a 'gear change' and seen as being dominated by demographic factors. The modern section of the book is structured by a command of the increasingly abundant government statistics which are used to paint sometimes surprising images of the country and the relationships between its communities; they are not simply decorative.[68] His mother's early instruction in mathematics is constantly put to good use.[69] Again, Wales is vital in the world: unlike textile industries, heavy industry and coal as a fuel were the fundamental changes of the era.

A central feature is his catholic approach; citations range across the political and cultural spectrum from Peter Stead to Tecwyn Lloyd. His facility in explaining theological issues led me to question my assumption of John Davies's atheism but he amply confirms the assumption in his autobiography. Nothing Welsh seems alien to him.[70] And while all the historians examined here make comparisons and invoke the wider context of Britain and Europe, none do it as consistently and insistently as Davies.

Conclusion

Some of the variations in the outlooks of these four great historians can be explained by personal biography. A. H. Dodd was born at the very end of 1891 and lived through the final days of the Victorian and Edwardian eras. In the summer of 1914, he had just graduated from Oxford and was about to join a group promoting women's suffrage in the West Country. He was contemplating research on the era of Richard II. He volunteered for the RAMC, worked as a stretcher bearer and had experiences that would give him nightmares for the rest of his life. It was the war which turned him towards modern history, though he did argue that the era of Richard II was the foundation for that.[71]

Glanmor Williams was born in 1920 into a depressed Dowlais, the most dismal aspects he seems to have been sheltered from by being an only child and by his intellectual ability. He went to university when he was seventeen and was rejected for military service so did not encounter the horrors of the twentieth century directly as Dodd had done. But he was in many respects always 'bachgen bach o Dowlais [a little boy from Dowlais]', more fully engaged with an industrial civilisation than was Dodd, even though it never became the focus of his own research. He embraced its historical significance and did much to promote its study. He recognised fully that a non-Welsh-speaking Welsh identity existed and had to be taken seriously.

Gwyn A. Williams was born in Dowlais five years later and in the relatively more privileged position of being the son of two schoolteachers. Politics intervened more obviously than in Glanmor Williams's case as he became a member of the Young Communist League and would remain a Marxist for the rest of his life – despite his membership of Plaid Cymru in his later years. As a 19-year-old, he landed in Normandy, had life-changing experiences in the next year before returning to go to university – in Aberystwyth as Glanmor Williams had done. By then he was twenty-two.[72]

John Davies was born in the Rhondda in 1938 but quickly moved to Cardiganshire to the village of Bwlchllan near Llangeitho which would give him a name and an identity in later life. His experience of the war was that of a child and he came of age as post-war prosperity began to emerge. He was curiously unmarked by youth culture, team sports and singing, but otherwise a child of the 1950s rather than the 1960s.[73]

All apart from Dodd experienced 1979 as a trauma. Dodd was dead before it happened and had expressed the opinion that the creation of national institutions was more significant than any political achievement, so perhaps it would not have been a major disappointment for him. Only Glanmor Williams and John Davies lived to see 1997 and the creation of the Senedd, but for neither did it seem to lead to a serious revision of their views.

Conceptions of society were important to all, though perhaps not the determining factor for any of them. The nation is the central conception for all of them. But the meaning of the nation varies. None completely invokes a primordial conception of it, though possibly it underlies John Davies's view. Gwyn A. Williams occupies the opposite pole as the most fully developed constructivist view. Glanmor Williams invokes both at different points. Dodd died before such modern views emerged; however, he saw no raison d'être for Welsh history without a sense of nationalism.

How did the nation interact with social analysis and particularly with class? For all, power in all its dimension is dominated by the relationship of Welsh ruling groups to the English British state and the alliances or divisions that arise from this. Dodd most consistently invokes the poorest in society but his narrative is far from being driven by them. It is emphatically not a 'history from below'. He sees seventeenth-century Wales as inherently hierarchical.[74] Gwyn A. Williams expresses sympathy and identifies with the working population and with women, but his narrative is driven by the relationship with England. Glanmor Williams, in his wider work, did occasionally write about the poor but his work on nationality stressed the role of the free population and then of the middle classes. He saw the gentry as having a central role in Welsh history. When he came to give a presidential address to the Cambrian Archaeological Society he chose a bishop's palace as his favourite structure in Wales, unlike Dodd's focus on the housing of the ordinary people.[75]

What gave impetus to social changes? A. H. Dodd's approach was multifaceted as we have seen and accorded no priority to economic change – though he expressed surprise when social and cultural trends diverged from economic change. Glanmor Williams explained the changes in the Reformation era in terms of a new monarchical state and its relations with the church as well as the values of the Renaissance and printing. Economic change and population growth, as for Dodd, came last in his schema 'but certainly not least in importance'.[76] John Davies saw demography as the key to modern Welsh history but as something which was neither caused by economic trends or caused them, though there were subtle relations between them. He is at pains to emphasise that population growth affected all of Europe and not simply industrial nations. Numbers made a difference as they meant concentration which affected social, cultural and political life.[77] Gwyn A. Williams, as we have seen, assigned a particular importance to demography.

All my subjects employed comparisons. Dodd made a systematic comparison of Wales and Brittany; none of the others were as focused.[78] Perhaps John Davies used them most continuously, finding Wales to be less feeble and undeveloped when held up against other small nations, particularly in Eastern Europe.[79] Beyond this, he raised a fundamental issue about comparison. Asked for his opinion on Gwyn A. Williams's view of Welsh history as one of constant ruptures, he asked the question: compared with what? Not with sixteenth-century Mexico or modern Poland, he averred. It challenged Gwyn A. Williams's view in an important way. What was his standard? Clearly it referred to a particular view of the Welsh past, but was it also a comparison with England seen as rather caricatured, Whiggish view of continuity and evolution? These are questions that could lead to significant advances in the understanding of Wales if they were to be answered effectively.[80]

Huw Pryce has pointed out that Wales was unusual, if not unique, in nineteenth-century Europe in failing to develop a people's history, with a stress on the common people or ancient institutions.[81] Instead it embraced a narrative of princes in a sort of pale imitation of English kings and queens. Perhaps the challenge for the future is to try to write a history from below, a people's history which gives full weight to the ordinary people from Dodd's unfree population through to the common people who populate Gwyn A. Williams's archivally based research in the eighteenth and early nineteenth century. Such an approach dominates modern Welsh history or at least large tracts of it. Medieval history seems still to have princes at the centre.[82] Archaeology offers a different route into medieval history less focused on the occupants of the *llys*.[83]

It has been said that no narrative history of a country is ever entirely superseded. By addressing such works by major historians we can draw out approaches and understandings beyond the surface details of the texts. In political theory and sociology, texts are studied closely over generations for their continuing insights. Perhaps we need to recognise that the frameworks and insights of great historians offer the same possibilities to our discipline.

Notes

1 I am grateful to David Sullivan for discussing Hegel with me and to Alun Gwynedd Jones for a helpful observation. Paul O'Leary and I have discussed Gwyn A. Williams for many years, much to my benefit. Beca Brychan kindly discussed her father with me and consulted Anna Brychan and Janet Davies in the process.

2 Huw Pryce, 'Why Write the History of Wales – Then and Now?', O Donnell Lecture, Bangor University, 25 May 2019; see also Huw Pryce, *Writing Welsh History: From the Early Middle Ages to the Twenty-first Century* (Oxford, 2022), pp. 1–2, 383.

3 John Davies, *The History of Wales* [*Hanes Cymru*, 1990; *History of Wales*, 1993] (rev. edn, London, 2007), p. 486.

4 M. J. Daunton, 'Review of Kenneth O. Morgan, *Rebirth of a Nation: Wales 1880–1980*', *English Historical Review*, XCVII (1982), 160–1 (p. 161).

5 A. H. Dodd, 'Nationalism in Wales: A Historical Assessment', *Transactions of the Honorable Society of Cymmrodorion* (1970), 33–49 (p. 34).

6 Neil Evans, '"When Men and Mountains Meet": Historians' Interpretations of the History of Wales, 1890–1970', *WHR*, 22 (2004), 222–51; Neil Evans, 'Finding a New Story: The Search for a Usable Past in Wales, 1869–1930', *Transactions of the Honourable Society of Cymmrodorion* (2004), 138–56; Neil Evans, 'Remaking Nations and their History: The Social, Political and Intellectual World of the Early Powysland Club', *Montgomeryshire Collections*, 109 (2021), 45–86.

7 Huw Pryce, *J. E. Lloyd and the Creation of Welsh History* (Cardiff, 2011), pp. 90–3.

8 J. E. Lloyd, *A History of Wales* (London, 1930), p. 60.

9 'The Deluge 1939', trans. Gwyn Thomas, in Alun R. Jones and Gwyn Thomas (eds), *Presenting Saunders Lewis* (Cardiff, 1973), pp. 177–9 (esp. p. 177).

10 Lloyd, *History*, pp. 70–8.
11 W. T. R. Pryce, 'Region or National Territory? Regionalism and the Idea of the Country of Wales *c*.1927–1998', *WHR*, 23 (2006), 99–152.
12 Michael Roberts, 'Introduction', in Michael Roberts and Simone Clarke (eds), *Women and Gender in Early Modern Wales* (Cardiff, 2000), pp. 4–5 (quotation at p. 5).
13 T. S. Eliot, 'Burnt Norton', in *Four Quartets*, available at *http://www.davidgorman.com/4quartets/1-norton.htm* (accessed 7 November 2023).
14 Ian Craib, *Classical Social Theory: An Introduction to the Thought of Marx, Weber, Durkheim and Simmel* (Oxford, 1997), p. 185.
15 Peter Burke, *The French Historical Revolution: The* Annales *School, 1929–89* (Cambridge, 1990).
16 G. M. Trevelyan, *Illustrated English Social History Vol 1* (London, 1942), p. xi.
17 Trevelyan, *English Social History*, p. 11.
18 A. H. Dodd, *A Short History of Wales* (London, 1977), p. 1.
19 Dodd, *Short History*, p. 19.
20 Dodd, *Short History*, p. 38
21 Dodd, *Short History*, p. 50
22 Dodd, *Short History*, pp. 21, 25, 43, 47, 50, 57, 75.
23 A. H. Dodd, 'Jack and his House', *Archaeologia Cambrensis*, LIX (1960), 1–12.
24 Dodd, *Short History*, p. 138.
25 W. Arthur Lewis, a key proponent of the dual economy thesis, was an external examiner in Bangor in the period. I have no evidence that Dodd met him or was influenced by him and the idea was commonly expressed.
26 Dodd, *Short History*, p. 103.
27 A. H. Dodd, 'Borderers and Highlanders', *History*, 41 (1956), 53–66.
28 Dodd, *Short History*, p. 156.
29 Dodd, *Short History*, p. 164.
30 Dodd, *Short History*, p. 159.
31 Dodd, *Short History*, p. 165.
32 Neil Evans, interview with Glanmor Williams, 28 June 2001.
33 Katharine Olson and Huw Pryce, 'A Reluctant Medievalist?', pp. 30–57 (esp. pp. 36–40); and Geraint H. Jenkins, 'Language, Religion and Nationality', pp. 142–62, both in Geraint H. Jenkins and Gareth Elwyn Jones (eds), *Degrees of Influence: A Memorial Volume for Glanmor Williams* (Cardiff, 2008).
34 Glanmor Williams, *The Welsh Church: From Conquest to Reformation* (Cardiff, 1962; rev edn, 1976) p. 577; Glanmor Williams, *A Life* (Cardiff, 2002), pp. 87, 104.
35 Glanmor Williams, 'Religion, Language and Nationality in Wales', in his *Religion, Language and Nationality in Wales: Historical Essays* (Cardiff, 1979);

Glanmor Williams, 'Fire on Cambria's Altar', in his *The Welsh and their Religion* (Cardiff, 1991).

36 Williams, *Religion, Language*, p. 29.
37 Williams, *Religion, Language*, pp. 32–3, 145–6.
38 Williams, *Religion, Language*, p. 33.
39 Williams, *Religion, Language*, pp. 71–3, 134.
40 Williams, *Religion, Language*, p. 134; italics are my own.
41 Williams, *Religion, Language*, p. 18; italics are my own.
42 Williams, 'Cambria's Altar', p. 14.
43 Williams, 'Cambria's Altar', p. 1.
44 Williams, 'Cambria's Altar', p. 4.
45 Williams, 'Cambria's Altar', p. 23.
46 R. Tudur Jones, *Faith and the Crisis of a Nation: Wales 1890–1914* (Cardiff, 2004), p. 1.
47 Williams, 'Cambria's Altar', p. 64.
48 Williams, 'Cambria's Altar', pp. 64–8.
49 Williams, *A Life*, pp. 10–11.
50 The phrase derives from Schiller but the idea was widely used in German romanticism culminating in Nietzsche. Jeffrey E. Green, 'Two Meanings of Disenchantment', *Philosophy and Theology*, 17/1–2 (2005), 51–84 (pp. 52–4).
51 Cf. Jones *Faith and Crisis*, p. 419. But note Glanmor Williams's thought that Christianity might be revived through happenings outside the West. Jenkins, 'Language, Religion', p. 148.
52 Information from the late Martin Eckley; conversation with Deian Hopkin, Cardiff, 28 October 2022; conversation with John Brueilly, Mulheim, May 2002.
53 Karl Marx, 'The Eighteenth Brumaire of Louis Bonaparte', extract in Lewis S. Feuer (ed.), *Marx and Engels: Basic Writings on Politics and Philosophy* (London and Glasgow, 1969), p. 360. Translations of this vary and I have used a commonly shortened version.
54 Gwyn A. Williams, *When was Wales: A History of the Welsh* (London, 1985). The lecture 'When was Wales?' is reprinted in his collection of essays, *The Welsh in their History* (London, 1982). Later references to that edition. Burke, *French Historical Revolution*, ch. 2 and esp. pp. 56–64.
55 See discussion in Evans, 'When Men and Mountains Meet', 245–6, 250.
56 Pekka Hämäläinen and Samuel Truett, 'On Borderlands', *Journal of American History*, 98/2 (2011), 338–61.
57 F. Antonini, 'Pessimism of the Intellect, Optimism of the Will: Gramsci's Political Thought in the Last Miscellaneous Notebooks', *Rethinking Marxism*, 31/1 (2019), 42–57; Williams, *When was Wales?*, p. 200.

58 Williams, 'When was Wales?', pp. 190, 191–4; Williams, *When was Wales?*, pp. 2, 5, 62, 141–3.
59 Gwyn A. Williams, *Goya and the Impossible Revolution* (London, 1976), esp. pp. 6, 139, 162–7, 176–8.
60 Peter Singer, *Hegel: A Very Short Introduction* (Oxford, 2001) is a helpful and clear exposition of Hegel's views.
61 Stuart Hall, *The Fateful Triangle; Race, Ethnicity, Nation* (Cambridge, MA, 2017), pp. 9, 18, 21, 91.
62 Davies, *A History of Wales*, p. 711.
63 John Davies, *A Life in History* (Talybont, 2015), pp. 112–13.
64 Students of his in Swansea in the 1960s said he gave advice on good pubs to drink in on Sundays where the police cars could be seen coming for miles. John Davies and Marian Delyth, *Wales: The 100 Places to See before you Die* (Talybont, 2010), p. 6; Davies, *Life in History*, pp. 47–9, 65.
65 Wendy Davies, *Wales in the Early Middle Ages* (Leicester, 1982), chs 3–5.
66 For an opposite view, see David Stephenson, *Medieval Wales, c.1050–1334: Centuries of Ambiguity* (Cardiff, 2019).
67 Later on, the halt of Bonnie Prince Charlies at Derby in 1745 is seen as a product of lack of Welsh support for Jacobitism: Davies, *History of Wales*, p. 291.
68 Burke, *French Historical Revolution*, pp. 52–4.
69 Davies, *Life in History*.
70 Davies, *Life in History*, pp. 23–4, 42, 50, 61–2. Rugby, football, chapels and the singing of songs were alien to him, of course. But he discusses all of these in the book.
71 Neil Evans, 'Beyond 1282: A. H. Dodd and the Problem of Modern Welsh History', in Neil Evans and Huw Pryce (eds), *Writing a Small Nation's Past: Wales in Comparative Perspective, 1850–1950* (London, 2013), pp. 223–36.
72 Gwyn A. Williams, *Fishers of Men: Stories Towards an Autobiography* (Llandysul, 1996).
73 Davies, *Life in History*, pp. 44, 46, 60, 66.
74 A. H. Dodd, *Studies in Stuart Wales* (Cardiff, 1952; 2nd edn, 1971), ch. 1.
75 Williams, *Religion, Language*, ch. 7; Williams, 'Henry de Gower: Bishop and Builder', in his *The Welsh and their Religion*, ch. 3, p. 93.
76 Williams, *Religion, Language*, pp. 14–15 (quotation at p. 14).
77 Davies, *History of Wales*, pp. 311–14.
78 A. H. Dodd, 'Wales and Brittany', *Proceedings of the Llandudno, Colwyn Bay and District Field Club*, 22 (1949), 1–10.
79 Robin Okey, *Towards Modern Nationhood: Wales and Slovenia in Comparison. 1750–1914* (Cardiff, 2023) compellingly develops this perspective.

80 John Davies, comments in the discussion of his lecture 'Whose Memory Do We Keep?', National Library of Wales, 15 September 2006.
81 Huw Pryce, 'Medieval Welsh History in the Victorian Age', *CMCS*, 71 (2016), 1–28 (pp. 4–5).
82 Stephenson, *Medieval Wales*, is a brilliant foray into the period but does not challenge the framework. For an exception, see Matthew Frank Stephens, *The Economy of Medieval Wales, 1067–1536* (Cardiff, 2019).
83 For an exemplification of this, see Nancy Edwards, *Life in Early Medieval Wales* (Oxford, 2023).

16

Llyfryddiaeth o Weithiau Cyhoeddedig Huw Pryce ⁝ A Bibliography of the Published Works of Huw Pryce (hyd 2023 ⁝ to 2023)

Rhidian Griffiths

1983

'Hanesyddiaeth Cymru', yn Robert Rhys (gol.), *Arolwg 1982* ([Lerpwl]: Cyhoeddiadau Modern Cymreig, [1983]), 62–6.

Articles relating to the history of Wales published mainly in 1981: I. Welsh history before 1660, *WHR*, 11 (1982–3), 585–9.

Review: Brynley F. Roberts, *Gerald of Wales* (Cardiff: University of Wales Press, 1982); Robert Bartlett, *Gerald of Wales, 1146–1223* (Oxford: Oxford University Press, 1982), *WHR*, 11 (1982–3), 556–8.

Review: Wendy Davies, *Wales in the Early Middle Ages* (Leicester: Leicester University Press, 1982), *Anglesey Antiquarian Society and Field Club Transactions* (1983), 125–6.

1984

'Ail-gloriannu Gerallt Gymro', *Y Faner*, 2 Mawrth 1984, 12–13.

'Ecclesiastical sanctuary in thirteenth-century Welsh law', *Journal of Legal History*, 5/3 (1984), 1–13 (special issue on Custom, Courts and Counsel); repr. in Albert Kiralfy, Michelle Slatter and Roger Virgoe (eds), *Custom, Courts and Counsel: selected papers of the 6th British Legal History conference, Norwich 1983* (London: Frank Cass, 1985), pp. 1–13.

Articles relating to the history of Wales published mainly in 1982: I. Welsh history before 1660, *WHR*, 12 (1984–5), 295–301.

Review: D. B. Walters, *The Comparative Legal Method. Marriage, Divorce and the Spouses: Property Rights in Early Medieval European Law and in Cyfraith Hywel*, 1982; Daniel Huws, *The Medieval Codex with reference to the Welsh Law Books*, 1980; Dafydd Ifans, *William Salesbury and the Welsh Laws*, 1980; William Linnard, *Trees in the Law of Hywel*, 1979; David Stephenson, *Thirteenth Century Welsh Law Courts*, 1980 (Aberystwyth: Canolfan Uwchefrydiau Cymreig a Cheltaidd, Pamffledi Cyfraith Hywel/Pamphlets on Welsh Law), *WHR*, 12 (1984–5), 255–6.

1985

'Enghraifft o croc "crocbren" yn y *Canu i Gadfan*?' (cyfraniad i) 'Nodiadau amrywiol = Miscellaneous notes', *BBCS*, 32 (1985), 166–8.

Articles relating to the history of Wales published mainly in 1983: I. Welsh history before 1660, *WHR*, 12 (1984–5), 611–15.

Adolygiad: A. D. Carr a Dafydd Jenkins, *Trem ar Gyfraith Hywel* (Hendy Gwyn ar Daf: Cymdeithas Genedlaethol Hywel Dda, 1985); *A Look at Hywel's Law* (Hendy Gwyn ar Daf: Cymdeithas Genedlaethol Hywel Dda, 1985), *Trafodion Cymdeithas Hanes Sir Gaernarfon*, 46 (1985), 171.

Review: A. D. Carr, *Medieval Anglesey* (Llangefni: Anglesey Antiquarian Society, 1982), *Archaeologia Cambrensis*, 134 (1985), 242–4.

Review: Donald Matthew, *Atlas of Medieval Europe* (Oxford: Phaidon, 1983), *WHR*, 12 (1984–5), 432–3.

Review: David Stephenson, *The Governance of Gwynedd* (Cardiff: University of Wales Press, 1984); David Stephenson, *The Last Prince of Wales: Llywelyn and King Edward: the End of the Welsh Dream, 1282–3* (Buckingham: Barracuda Books, 1983), *CMCS*, 9 (summer 1985), 108–9.

1986

Gerallt Gymro am ei Gyfoeswyr, detholwyd gyda rhagair a nodiadau gan Huw Pryce; cyfieithwyd gan Glenda Carr, Cyfres Be' Ddywedodd…? 9 ([Bangor]: Y Colegiwm Cymraeg, 1986).

[e-argraffiad 2013 dan y teitl *Be' ddywedodd Gerallt Gymro am ei Gyfoeswyr* (Bangor: Uned Technolegau Iaith, Canolfan Bedwyr, Prifysgol Bangor gyda nawdd Y Coleg Cymraeg Cenedlaethol); cyhoeddwyd Caerfyrddin: Y Coleg Cymraeg Cenedlaethol, 2014].

'Duw yn lle mach: briduw yng Nghyfraith Hywel', in T. M. Charles-Edwards, Morfydd E. Owen and D. B. Walters (eds), *Lawyers and Laymen: Studies in the History of Law presented to Professor Dafydd Jenkins* (Cardiff: University of Wales Press, 1986), pp. 47–71.

'Early Irish canons and medieval Welsh law', *Peritia: Journal of the Medieval Academy of Ireland*, 5 (1986), 107–27.

'The prologues to the Welsh Lawbooks', *BBCS*, 33 (1986), 151–87.

Articles relating to the history of Wales published mainly in 1984: I. Welsh history before 1660, *WHR*, 13 (1986–7), 256–60.

Review: David H. Williams, *The Welsh Cistercians* (Caldey: Cyhoeddiadau Sistersaidd, 1984), *WHR*, 13 (1986–7), 108–9.

Review: Lesley M. Smith (ed.), *The Making of Britain: The Middle Ages* (London: Macmillan, 1985), *WHR*, 13 (1986–7), 222–3.

1987

'In search of a medieval society: Deheubarth in the writings of Gerald of Wales', *WHR*, 13 (1986–7), 265–81.

Articles relating to the history of Wales published mainly in 1985: I. Welsh history before 1660, *WHR*, 13 (1986–7), 527–33.

Adolygiad: Nesta Lloyd a Morfydd E. Owen (goln), *Drych yr Oesoedd Canol* (Caerdydd: Gwasg Prifysgol Cymru, 1986), *Cylchgrawn Hanes Cymru*, 13 (1986–7), 494–5.

Adolygiad: Dafydd Jenkins (trans. and ed.), *The Law of Hywel Dda: Law Texts from Medieval Wales* (Llandysul: Gomer, 1986), *Llais Llyfrau* (gwanwyn 1987), 10.

Review: Henry Mayr-Harting and R. I. Moore (eds), *Studies ... presented to R. H. C. Davis* (London and Ronceverte: Hambledon, 1985), *WHR*, 13 (1986–7), 485–7.

1988

'Cymru Gerallt', *Cof Cenedl*, III (1988), 1–30.

'Church and society in Wales, 1150–1250: an Irish perspective', in R. R. Davies (ed.), *The British Isles 1100–1500: Comparisons, Contrasts and Connections* (Edinburgh: John Donald, 1988), pp. 27–47.

'Gerald, King Arthur, and the legendary history of Britain', in Charles Kightly (ed.), *A Mirror of Medieval Wales: Gerald of Wales and his Journey of 1188* (Cardiff: Cadw, Welsh Historic Monuments, 1988), pp. 36–7.

Articles relating to the history of Wales published mainly in 1986: I. Welsh history before 1660, *WHR*, 14 (1988–9), 344–51.

Review: C. N. L. Brooke, *The Church and the Welsh Border in the Central Middle Ages* (Woodbridge: Boydell, 1986), *WHR*, 14 (1988–9), 130–1.

Review: Gerald R. Morgan, *Romans in Wales* (Cardiff: University of Wales Press, 1987); Robert M. Morris, *Gerald of Wales* (Cardiff: University of Wales Press, 1987); Robert M. Morris, *Gerald and his World* (Cardiff: University of Wales Press, 1987); John W. Roberts, *Medieval Welsh Monasteries* (Cardiff: University of Wales Press, 1987), *WHR*, 14 (1988–9), 171–2.

Review: R. R. Davies, *Conquest, Coexistence and Change: Wales 1063–1415* (Oxford: Clarendon Press, 1987), *CMCS*, 15 (summer 1988), 98–9.

Review: Art Cosgrove (ed.), *A New History of Ireland. – II: Medieval, 1169–1534* (Oxford: Clarendon, 1987), *WHR*, 14 (1988–9), 308–10.

Review: Ian F. Fletcher, *Latin Redaction A of the Law of Hywel* (Aberystwyth: Centre for Advanced Welsh and Celtic Studies, 1986), *Irish Jurist*, n.s. 21/2 (1988 for 1986), 373–5.

Short notice: Anthony Goodman and Michael Cyprien, *A Traveller's Guide to Early Medieval Britain* (London: Routledge, 1986), *WHR*, 14 (1988–9), 173.

1989

'Gerald's journey through Wales', *Journal of Welsh Ecclesiastical History*, 6 (1989), 17–34.

Articles relating to the history of Wales published mainly in 1987: I. Welsh history before 1660, *WHR*, 14 (1988–9), 670–7.

Review: Wendy Davies, *Small Worlds: The Village Community in Early Medieval Brittany* (London: Duckworth, 1988), *WHR*, 14 (1988–9), 631–2.

Review: D. Simon Evans (ed.), *The Welsh Life of St David* (Cardiff: University of Wales Press, 1988), *WHR*, 14 (1988–9), 630–1.

Review: Roger Stalley, *The Cistercian Monasteries of Ireland* (New Haven and London: Yale University Press, 1987), *History and Archaeology Review*, 4 (summer 1989), 82.

1990

'Medieval Welsh law', *Scéala Scoil an Léinn Cheiltigh /Newsletter of the School of Celtic Studies*, 4 (December 1990), 30–4.

Articles relating to the history of Wales published mainly in 1988: I. Welsh history before 1660, *WHR*, 15 (1990–1), 317–22.

Review article: 'Medieval agrarian history': H. E. Hallam (ed.), *The Agrarian History of England and Wales, vol. 2: 1042–1350* (Cambridge: Cambridge University Press, 1988), *WHR*, 15 (1990–1), 275–8.

Review: David Crouch (ed.), *Llandaff Episcopal Acta, 1140–1287* (Cardiff: South Wales Record Society, 1989), *WHR*, 15 (1990–1), 118–19.

1991

Review: Marie Therese Flanagan, *Irish Society, Anglo-Norman settlers, Angevin Kingship: Interactions in Ireland in the Late Twelfth Century* (Oxford: Clarendon Press, 1989), *History*, 76 (1991), 279–80.

Review: Paul Barbier, *The Age of Owain Gwynedd* (Felinfach: Llanerch, 1990), *Medieval History*, 1 (1991), 170.

Review: *Adomnan's Life of Columba* / edited with translation and notes by Alan Orr Anderson and by Marjorie Ogilvie Anderson (London and New York: Nelson, 1991), *Medieval History*, 1 (1991), 169–70.

Review: James P. Mackey (ed.), *An Introduction to Celtic Christianity* (Edinburgh: T. & T. Clark, 1989), *Logos*, 1 (1991), 48–9.

Review: T. M. Charles-Edwards, *The Welsh Laws* (Cardiff: University of Wales Press, 1989), *WHR*, 15 (1990–1), 451–3.

1992

'Ecclesiastical wealth in early medieval Wales', in Nancy Edwards and Alan Lane (eds), *The Early Church in Wales and the West: Recent Work in Early Christian Archaeology, History and Place-names* (Oxford: Oxbow, 1992), pp. 22–32.

'Pastoral care in early medieval Wales', in John Blair and Richard Sharpe (eds), *Pastoral Care before the Parish* (Leicester: Leicester University Press, 1992), pp. 41–62.

Adolygiad: Melville Richards (gol.), *Cyfreithiau Hywel Dda yn ôl Llawysgrif Coleg yr Iesu LVII Rhydychen* (Caerdydd: Gwasg Prifysgol Cymru, arg. diw. 1990), *Studia Celtica*, 26/27 (1991/2), 277–9.

Review: David Walker, *Medieval Wales* (Cambridge: Cambridge University Press, 1990); R. R. Davies, *Domination and Conquest: The Experience of Ireland, Scotland and Wales, 1100–1300* (Cambridge: Cambridge University Press, 1990), *History*, 77 (1992), 96–7.

Review: James Given, *State and Society in Medieval Europe: Gwynedd and Languedoc under Outside Rule* (Ithaca, NY: Cornell University Press, 1990), *WHR*, 16 (1992–3), 119–20.

1993

Native Law and the Church in Medieval Wales (Oxford: Clarendon Press, 1993).

'The church of Trefeglwys and the end of the "Celtic" charter tradition in twelfth-century Wales', *CMCS*, 25 (summer 1993), 15–54.

Review: Elissa R. Henken, *The Welsh Saints: A Study in Patterned Lives* (Woodbridge: Brewer, 1991), *Journal of Ecclesiastical History*, 44 (1993), 342–3.

1994

'A new edition of the *Historia divae Monacellae*', *Montgomeryshire Collections*, 82 (1994), 23–40.

Review: Jeanne-Marie Boivin, *L'Irlande au Moyen Âge* (Paris: Librairie Honoré Champion, 1993), *WHR*, 17 (1994–5), 260–1.

1995

'Cyfeiriad cynnar at fyfyrwyr o Gymru yn Lloegr', *Yr Aradr: Cylchgrawn Cymdeithas Dafydd ap Gwilym, Rhydychen*, 6 (Nadolig 1995), 19–21.

'Yr eglwys a'r gyfraith yng Nghymru'r Oesoedd Canol', *Cof Cenedl*, X (1995), 1–30.

(contribution to) C. J. Arnold and J. W. Huggett, 'Excavations at Mathrafal, Powys, 1989', *Montgomeryshire Collections*, 83 (1995), 59–74 (61–5).

Review (with Bruce Griffiths): T. M. Charles-Edwards, *Early Irish and Welsh Kinship* (Oxford: Clarendon Press, 1993), *Cahiers de Civilisation Médiévale*, 38 (1995), 370–1.

1996

(gol. gyda Nerys Ann Jones), *Yr Arglwydd Rhys* (Caerdydd: Gwasg Prifysgol Cymru, 1996):
    (gyda Nerys Ann Jones), 'Rhagymadrodd', tt. 1–17.
    'Yr eglwys yn oes yr Arglwydd Rhys', tt. 145–77.
    'Y canu Lladin er cof am yr Arglwydd Rhys', tt. 212–23.
(general editor) K. L. Maund, *Handlist of the Acts of Native Welsh Rulers, 1132–1283* (Cardiff: University of Wales Press, 1996):
    'Foreword', p. v.
(gyda Nerys Ann Jones) 'Bradwr ynteu arwr? Cofio Rhys ap Gruffydd', *Barn*, 402/3 (Gorffennaf/Awst 1996), 20–2.
Adolygiad (gyda Nancy Edwards): R. Gerallt Jones and Christopher J. Arnold (eds), *Enlli* (Cardiff: University of Wales Press, 1996), *Archaeology in Wales*, 36 (1996), 44 (yn Gymraeg gyda chrynodeb yn Saesneg / in Welsh with English summary).
Review: Robin Chapman Stacey, *The Road to Judgment: from Custom to Court in Medieval Ireland and Wales* (Philadelphia: University of Pennsylvania Press, 1994), *English Historical Review*, 111 (1996), 1233–4.

1997

Review: R. R. Davies, *The Revolt of Owain Glyn Dŵr* (Oxford: Oxford University Press, 1995), *English Historical Review*, 112 (1997), 142–3.
Review: Michael Richter, *Studies in Medieval Language and Culture* (Blackrock: Four Courts Press, 1995), *WHR*, 18 (1996–7), 527–9.
Review: Glanmor Williams, *Owain Glyndŵr* (2nd edn, Cardiff: University of Wales Press, 1993), *Archaeologia Cambrensis*, 144 (1995, pub. 1997), 243–4.

1998

(ed.), *Literacy in Medieval Celtic Societies* (Cambridge: Cambridge University Press, 1998):
    'Introduction', pp. 1–14.

'A cross-border career: Giraldus Cambrensis between Wales and England', in R[einhard] Schneider (ed.), *Grenzgänger* (Saarbrücken: Kommission für Saarländische Landesgeschichte und Volksforschung, 1998), pp. 45–60.

'The origins and the medieval period', in Philip Henry Jones and Eiluned Rees (eds), *A Nation and its Books* (Aberystwyth: National Library of Wales in association with Aberystwyth Centre for the Book, 1998), pp. 1–23.

'Owain Gwynedd and Louis VII: the Franco-Welsh diplomacy of the first Prince of Wales', *WHR*, 19 (1998–9), 1–28.

Review: Roger Turvey, *The Lord Rhys: Prince of Deheubarth* (Llandysul: Gomer, 1997), *WHR*, 19 (1998–9), 148–9.

Review: Graham C. G. Thomas (ed.), *The Charters of the Abbey of Ystrad Marchell* (Aberystwyth: National Library of Wales, 1997), *CMCS*, 35 (summer 1998), 79–81.

1999

'Esgobaeth Bangor yn Oes y Tywysogion', yn W. P. Griffith (gol.), *'Ysbryd Deallturus ac Enaid Anfarwol': Ysgrifau ar Hanes Crefydd yng Ngwynedd* (Bangor: Canolfan Uwchefrydiau Crefydd yng Nghymru, Prifysgol Cymru Bangor, 1999), tt. 37–57.

'Medieval experiences: Wales 1000–1415', in Gareth Elwyn Jones and Dai Smith (eds), *The People of Wales* (Llandysul: Gomer, 1999), pp. 11–47.

2000

'The context and purpose of the earliest Welsh lawbooks', *CMCS*, 39 (summer 2000), 39–63.

'The household priest (*offeiriad teulu*)', in T. M. Charles-Edwards, Morfydd E. Owen and Paul Russell (eds), *The Welsh King and his Court* (Cardiff: University of Wales Press, 2000), pp. 82–93.

'Lawbooks and literacy in medieval Wales', *Speculum*, 75 (2000), 29–67.

(with Joseph Goering), 'The *De modo confitendi* of Cadwgan, Bishop of Bangor', *Mediaeval Studies*, 62 (2000), 1–27.

Review: Brendan Smith (ed.), *Britain and Ireland, 900–1300: Insular Responses to Medieval European Change* (New York: Cambridge University Press, 1999), *International History Review*, 22 (2000), 881–3.

2001

'British or Welsh? National identity in twelfth-century Wales', *English Historical Review*, 116 (2001), 775–801.

'Frontier Wales c.1063–1282', in Prys Morgan (ed.), *The Tempus History of Wales, 25,000 B.C.–A.D. 2000* (Stroud: Tempus in association with the National Library of Wales, 2001), pp. 77–106.

'The medieval Church', in J. Beverley Smith and Llinos Beverley Smith (eds), *History of Merioneth. Volume II: The Middle Ages* (Cardiff: University of Wales Press on behalf of the Merioneth Historical and Record Society, 2001), pp. 254–96.

'Welsh custom and canon law, 1150–1300', in Kenneth Pennington, Stanley Chodorow and Keith H. Kendall (eds), *Proceedings of the Tenth International Congress of Medieval Canon Law* (Monumenta iuris canonici; 11) (Vatican City: Biblioteca Apostolica Vaticana, 2001), pp. 781–97.

Review: John Gillingham, *The English in the Twelfth Century: Imperialism, National Identity and Political Values* (Woodbridge: Boydell, 1999), *WHR*, 20 (2000–1), 770–1.

Review: D. A. Trotter (ed.), *Multilingualism in Later Medieval Britain* (Cambridge: Brewer, 2000), *CMCS*, 41 (summer 2001), 71–3.

2002

'Negotiating Anglo-Welsh relations: Llywelyn the Great and Henry III', in Björn K. U. Weiler with Ifor W. Rowlands (eds), *England and Europe in the Reign of Henry III (1216–1272)* (Aldershot; Burlington VT: Ashgate, 2002), pp. 13–29.

Adolygiad: Daniel Huws, *Medieval Welsh Manuscripts* (Cardiff: University of Wales Press, 2000), *Y Traethodydd*, 157 (2002), 123–6.

Review: David H. Williams, *The Welsh Cistercians* (Leominster: Gracewing, 2001), *Journal of Welsh Religious History*, n.s. 2 (2002), 97–9.

Review: Mark Atherton (ed.), *Celts and Christians: New Approaches to the Religious Traditions of Britain and Ireland* (Cardiff: University of Wales Press, 2002), *Archaeology in Wales*, 42 (2002), 184–5.

2003

'The Christianization of society', in Wendy Davies (ed.), *From the Vikings to the Normans* (Oxford and New York: Oxford University Press, 2003), pp. 139–67.

'Wales: religion and piety', in S. H. Rigby (ed.), *A Companion to Britain in the Later Middle Ages* (Malden, MA and Oxford: Blackwell, 2003), pp. 411–29.

'Welsh rulers and the written word, 1120–1283', in Peter Thorau, Sabine Penth und Rüdiger Fuchs (eds), *Regionen Europas – Europa der Regionen: Festschrift für Kurt-Ulrich Jäschke zum 65. Geburtstag* (Köln, Weimar und Wien: Böhlau Verlag, 2003), pp. 75–88.

Review: Robert B. Patterson, *The Scriptorium of Margam Abbey and the Scribes of Early Angevin Glamorgan: Secretarial Administration in a Welsh Marcher Barony* (Woodbridge: Boydell Press, 2001), *WHR*, 21 (2002–3), 776–8.

Review: Robert C. Palmer, *Selling the Church: The English Parish in Law, Commerce, and Religion, 1350–1550* (Chapel Hill: University of North Carolina Press, 2002), *American Historical Review*, 108 (2003), 1516–17.

Review: Roger Turvey, *The Welsh Princes: The Native Rulers of Wales 1063–1283* (Harlow: Longman, 2002), *Transactions of the Caernarfonshire Historical Society*, 64 (2003), 136–9.

Review: Ieuan M. Williams (ed.), *Humphrey Llwyd: Cronica Walliae* (Cardiff: University of Wales Press, 2002), *CMCS*, 45 (summer 2003), 92–3.

2004

'Modern nationality and the medieval past: the Wales of John Edward Lloyd', in R. R. Davies and Geraint H. Jenkins (eds), *From Medieval to Modern Wales: Historical Essays in Honour of Kenneth O. Morgan and Ralph A. Griffiths* (Cardiff: University of Wales Press, 2004), pp. 14–29.

(with Aled Jones), 'Editorial note', *WHR*, 22 (2004–5), [iii].

Contributions to H. C. G. Matthew and Brian Harrison (eds), *ODNB* (Oxford: Oxford University Press in association with the British Academy, 2004), online at *oxforddnb.com*:

'Anian [Einion] (d. 1305×7), bishop of Bangor'
'Bleddyn ap Cynfyn (d. 1075), king of Gwynedd and of Powys'

'Caradog (1060×75–1124), hermit and monk'
'Gruffudd ap Cynan (1054/5–1137), king of Gwynedd'
[T. F. Tout, revised by Huw Pryce] 'Gruffudd ap Rhys (d. 1137), ruler in south Wales'
'Madog ap Maredudd (d. 1160), king of Powys'
'Owain Gwynedd [Owain ap Gruffudd] (d. 1170), king of Gwynedd'
'Sir John Prise [Syr Siôn ap Rhys], administrator and scholar (1501/2–1555)' (with revisions online, 2005, 2007, 2008)
'Rhys ap Gruffudd (1131/2–1197), prince of Deheubarth'.

2005

(ed. with the assistance of Charles Insley), *The Acts of Welsh Rulers, 1120–1283* (Cardiff: University of Wales Press, 2005) (repr. with corrections, 2010).

'Culture, power and the charters of Welsh rulers', in Marie Therese Flanagan and Judith A. Green (eds), *Charters and Charter Scholarship in Britain and Ireland* (Basingstoke; New York: Palgrave Macmillan, 2005), pp. 184–202.

'From the Neolithic to Nonconformity: J. E. Lloyd and the history of Caernarfonshire', *Transactions of the Caernarfonshire Historical Society*, 66 (2005), 14–37.

'Frontier Wales *c.*1063–1282', in Prys Morgan (ed.), *Wales: An Illustrated History* (Stroud: Tempus, 2005), pp. 89–125.

'Uses of the vernacular in the acts of Welsh rulers 1120–1283', *La Langue des Actes. Section 2: Confins et Contacts:* Actes du XIe Congrès International de Diplomatique (2003), http://elec.enc.sorbonne.fr/CID2003/pryce (accessed 10 April 2023)

Adolygiad: Peter Lord, *Diwylliant Gweledol Cymru: Gweledigaeth yr Oesoedd Canol* (Caerdydd: Gwasg Prifysgol Cymru, 2003), *Y Traethodydd*, 160 (2005), 250–2.

Review: Robert Bartlett, *The Hanged Man: A Story of Miracle, Memory, and Colonialism in the Middle Ages* (Princeton and Oxford: Princeton University Press, 2004), *WHR*, 22 (2004–5), 786–7.

Review: Jane Cartwright (ed.), *Celtic Hagiography and Saints' Cults* (Cardiff: University of Wales Press, 2003), *Archaeologia Cambrensis*, 151 (2002, pub. 2005), 166–7.

2006

(gyda Richard Wyn Jones a Spencer Smith) *Tywysogion* (Caerdydd: Hughes a'i Fab/S4C, 2006) (seiliwyd ar y gyfres *Tywysogion*, cynhyrchiad Ffilmiau'r Bont i S4C).

Eisteddfod lecture 2003 ('"Draig Powys": Madog ap Maredudd, Mathrafal a Meifod') [crynodeb/summary], *Archaeologia Cambrensis*, 153 (2004, pub. 2006), 201–2.

'Cenedligrwydd a chymdeithas: dehongli Oes y Tywysogion' (Darlith Goffa T. Jones Pierce, 2005), *Trafodion Cymdeithas Hanes Sir Gaernarfon*, 67 (2006), 12–29.

2007

(ed. with John Watts), *Power and Identity in the Middle Ages: Essays in Memory of Rees Davies* (Oxford: Oxford University Press, 2007):
(with John Watts) 'Introduction', pp. 1–4.
'Welsh rulers and European change, *c*.1100–1282', pp. 37–51.

Hynafiaid: Hil, Cenedl a Gwreiddiau'r Cymry (Darlith Goffa Syr Thomas Parry-Williams, 2004) (Aberystwyth: Canolfan Uwchefrydiau Cymreig a Cheltaidd, 2007).

'Grym y gair ysgrifenedig: Tywysogion Cymru a'u dogfennau, 1120–1283', *Cof Cenedl*, XXII (2007), 1–31.

'The dynasty of Deheubarth and the church of St Davids', in J. Wyn Evans and Jonathan M. Wooding (eds), *St David of Wales: Cult, Church and Nation* (Woodbridge: Boydell Press, 2007), pp. 305–16.

'Patrons and patronage among the Cistercians in Wales', *Archaeologia Cambrensis*, 154 (2005, pub. 2007), 81–95.

2008

'The Normans in Welsh history' (R. Allen Brown Memorial Lecture), *Anglo-Norman Studies*, 30 (Proceedings of the Battle Conference, 2007), 1–18.

(with Katharine K. Olson), 'The reluctant medievalist?', in Geraint H. Jenkins and Gareth Elwyn Jones (eds), *Degrees of Influence: A Memorial Volume for Glanmor Williams* (Cardiff: University of Wales Press, 2008), pp. 30–57.

2009

'Conversions to Christianity', in Pauline Stafford (ed.), *A Companion to the Early Middle Ages: Britain and Ireland, c.500–c.1100* (Chichester: Wiley-Blackwell, 2009), pp. 143–59.

'Robert Rees Davies, 1938–2005', *Proceedings of the British Academy*, 161 (2009), 135–55.

Review: Roger Turvey, *Llywelyn the Great, Prince of Gwynedd* (Llandysul: Gomer, 2007), *WHR*, 24 (2008–9), 134–6.

2010

'Llywelyn the Great and Llywelyn the Last – fighters for Welsh independence', *Western Mail*, 21 September 2010, 15–17.

'National identity in medieval Wales – Welsh or British?', *Western Mail*, 22 September 2010, 19–21.

'Foreword', in Diane M. Williams and John R. Kenyon (eds), *The Impact of the Edwardian Castles in Wales: The Proceedings of a Conference held at Bangor University, 7–9 September 2007* (Oxford: Oxbow Books; Oakville, CT: David Brown Book Co., 2010), p. xi.

Contributions to Robert E. Bjork (ed.), *The Oxford Dictionary of the Middle Ages* (Oxford: Oxford University Press, 4v., 2010):
  'Annals and Chronicles: Ireland – Irish Annals', I, 73
  'Annals and Chronicles: Wales – Chronicle of the Welsh Princes', I, 73
  'Hywel Dda, Laws of', II, 831–2.

(with Aled Jones), 'Editorial note', *WHR*, 25 (2010–11), 1–2.
(with Aled Jones), 'Editorial note', *WHR*, 25 (2010–11), 157–60.
(with Aled Jones), '*Welsh History Review* makes its own mark at 50', *Western Mail Magazine*, 18 September 2010, 8, 10.

2011

J. E. Lloyd and the Creation of Welsh History: Renewing a Nation's Past (Cardiff: University of Wales Press, 2011).

'Anglo-Welsh agreements, 1201–77', in R. A. Griffiths and P. R. Schofield (eds), *Wales and the Welsh in the Middle Ages: Essays presented to J. Beverley Smith* (Cardiff: University of Wales Press, 2011), pp. 1–19.

'Gerald of Wales, Gildas, and the *Descriptio Kambriae*', in Fiona Edmonds and Paul Russell (eds), *Tome: Studies in Medieval Celtic History and Law in honour of Thomas Charles-Edwards* (Woodbridge: Boydell Press, 2011), pp. 115–24.

'Llywelyn the Great and Llywelyn the Last – for themselves or for Wales?', in H. V. Bowen (ed.), *A New History of Wales: Myths and Realities in Welsh History* (Llandysul: Gomer, 2011), pp. 28–34.

'Were we Welsh or were we British?', in H. V. Bowen (ed.), *A New History of Wales: Myths and Realities in Welsh History* (Llandysul: Gomer, 2011), pp. 35–41.

2012

'Culture, identity and the medieval revival in Victorian Wales' (J. V. Kelleher Lecture), *Proceedings of the Harvard Celtic Colloquium*, 31 (2011 [2012]), 1–40.

'John Edward Lloyd (1861–1947): hanesydd Cymru', *Y Traethodydd*, 167 (2012), 101–16.

Adolygiad: Hirokazu Tsurishima (ed.), *Nations in Medieval Britain* (Donington: Shaun Tyas, 2010), *Y Traethodydd*, 167 (2012), 117–20.

2013

(ed. with Neil Evans), *Writing a Small Nation's Past: Wales in Comparative Perspective, 1850–1950* (Farnham and Burlington, VT: Ashgate, 2013) [issued online by Routledge, 2016]:

    (with Neil Evans), 'Writing a small nation's past: states, race and historical culture', pp. 3–30.

    'J. E. Lloyd's *History of Wales* (1911): publication and reception', pp. 49–64.

'Llwybr llwyddiant: cip ar hanes Tywysogion Gwynedd a'u safleoedd', *Etifeddiaeth y Cymry*, 54 (gwanwyn 2013), 11–12.

'The story of success: a snapshot of the history of the Princes of Gwynedd and their sites', *Heritage in Wales*, 54 (spring 2013), 11–12.

Review: T. M. Charles-Edwards, *Wales and the Britons 350–1064* (Oxford: Oxford University Press, 2012), *Archaeologia Cambrensis*, 161 (2012, pub. 2013), 415–16.

2014

(with Paul O'Leary), 'Editorial note', *WHR*, 27 (2014–15), 1–3.
(with J. Gwilym Owen), 'Medieval Welsh law and the mid-Victorian foreshore', *Journal of Legal History*, 35 (2014), 172–99.
Review: Roger Turvey, *Owain Gwynedd, Prince of the Welsh* (Talybont: Y Lolfa, 2013), *WHR*, 27 (2014), 157–8.

2015

'The last Welsh prince of Wales', *BBC History Magazine* (Christmas 2015), 60–4.
Review: Seán Duffy (ed.), *Princes, Prelates and Poets in Medieval Ireland: Essays in Honour of Katharine Simms* (Dublin: Four Courts Press, 2013), *History*, 100 (2015), 112–14.

2016

'Cofio Glyndŵr', *Trafodion Anrhydeddus Gymdeithas y Cymmrodorion*, cyfres newydd, 22 (2016), 43–60.
'Giraldus and the Geraldines', in Peter Crooks and Seán Duffy (eds), *The Geraldines and Medieval Ireland: The Making of a Myth* (Dublin: Four Courts Press, 2016), pp. 53–68.
'Harry Longueville Jones, FSA, medieval Paris and the heritage measures of the July monarchy', *Antiquaries Journal*, 96 (2016), 391–414.
'Jones, Harry Longueville (1806–1870), archaeolegydd ac addysgwr', *Y Bywgraffiadur Cymreig*, *bywgraffiadur.cymru*; 'Jones, Harry Longueville (1806–1870)', archaeologist and educationalist', *Dictionary of Welsh Biography*, *biography.wales* (accessed 10 April 2023).
'Medieval Welsh history in the Victorian age', *CMCS*, 71 (summer 2016), 1–28.
Review: John Prise, *Historia Britannicae defensio: A Defence of the British History*, ed. and trans. Ceri Davies (Toronto: Pontifical Institute of Mediaeval Studies; Oxford: Bodleian Library, 2015), *WHR*, 28 (2016), 182–5.
Review: Ken Lloyd Gruffydd, ed. M. D. Matthews, *Maritime Wales in the Middle Ages: 1039–1542* (Wrexham: Bridge Books, 2016), *Cymru a'r Môr*, 37 (2016), 204–5.

2017

Review: Gruffydd Aled Williams, *Dyddiau Olaf Owain Glyndŵr* (Talybont: Y Lolfa, 2015), *CMCS*, 73 (summer 2017), 63–5.

2018

'Gerald of Wales and the Welsh past', in Georgia Henley and A. Joseph McMullen (eds), *Gerald of Wales: New Perspectives on a Medieval Writer and Critic* (Cardiff: University of Wales Press, 2018), pp. 19–45.

'Historians and the Treaty of Montgomery', *Montgomeryshire Collections*, 106 (2018), 5–18.

Review: Alice Taylor, *The Shape of the State in Medieval Scotland, 1124–1290* (Oxford: Oxford University Press, 2016), *Speculum*, 93 (2018), 274–5.

2019

(with Nia Wyn Jones [published as O. W. Jones]), 'Historical writing in medieval Wales', in Jennifer Jahner, Emily Steiner and Elizabeth M. Tyler (eds), *Medieval Historical Writing: Britain and Ireland, 500–1500* (Cambridge: Cambridge University Press, 2019), pp. 208–24.

'Tony Carr 1938–2019', *Barn*, 677 (Mehefin 2019), 43.

Review: Robin Chapman Stacey, *Law and the Imagination in Medieval Wales* (Philadelphia: University of Pennsylvania Press, 2018), *Studia Celtica*, 53 (2019), 184–5.

2020

'Chronicling and its contexts in medieval Wales', in Ben Guy et al. (eds), *The Chronicles of Medieval Wales and the March: New Contexts, Studies and Texts* (Turnhout: Brepols, 2020), pp. 1–32.

'Cofebau a hanes – cwestiynau anodd', *Barn*, 690 (Gorffennaf 2020), 4–5.

'The Irish and Welsh Middle Ages in the Victorian period', in Joanne Parker and Corinna Wagner (eds), *The Oxford Handbook of Victorian Medievalism* (Oxford: Oxford University Press, 2020), pp. 215–34.

Obituary: 'Antony David ("Tony") Carr (1938–2019)', *WHR*, 30 (2020–1), 121–5.

2021

'Gerald of Wales: medieval ethnographer of the Welsh', in W. John Morgan and Fiona Bowie (eds), *Social Anthropologies of the Welsh: Past and Present* (Canon Pyon: Sean Kingston Publishing, 2021), pp. 41–55.

Adolygiad: Hazel Walford Davies, *O. M.: Cofiant Syr Owen Morgan Edwards* (Llandysul: Gomer, 2020), *Cylchgrawn Hanes Cymru*, 30 (2020–1), 417–19.

Review: Geraint H. Jenkins, Richard Suggett and Eryn M. White (eds), *Cardiganshire County History. Vol. 2: Medieval and Early Modern Cardiganshire* (Cardiff: University of Wales Press, 2019), *WHR*, 30 (2020–1), 636–38.

2022

Writing Welsh History: From the Early Middle Ages to the Twenty-first Century (Oxford: Oxford University Press, 2022).

'Ar drywydd hanes hanes Cymru', *Barn*, 717 (Hydref 2022), 18–19.

'Hanes cenedlaethol', yn Meilyr Powel a Gethin Matthews (goln), *Llunio Hanes: Hanesyddiaeth a Chrefft yr Hanesydd* (Caerdydd: Gwasg Prifysgol Cymru ar ran y Coleg Cymraeg Cenedlaethol, 2022) (e-lyfr), tt. 45–64.

'"Hanes Prydain Fawr – hanes ein gwlad enedigiol [*sic*] ein hunain!" Gwladgarwch Prydeinig hanesyddiaeth Gymraeg y bedwaredd ganrif ar bymtheg', *Y Traethodydd*, 176 (2022), 210–26.

'Iachawdwriaeth, rhagluniaeth a hanes: Theophilus Evans a *Drych y Prif Oesoedd*', *Y Traethodydd*, 176 (2022), 16–26.

'Welsh law in Elizabethan histories of Wales', in Sara Elin Roberts, Simon Rodway and A. Falileyev (eds), *Cyfarwydd mewn Cyfraith: Studies in honour of Morfydd E. Owen* (Bangor: Cymdeithas Hanes Cyfraith Cymru / The Welsh Legal History Society [2022]), pp. 98–111.

Adolygiad: Adam M. Coward (ed.), *The Correspondence of Thomas Stephens: Revolutionising Welsh Scholarship in the Mid-nineteenth Century through Knowledge Exchange* (Aberystwyth: Celtic Studies Publications, 2020), *Llên Cymru*, 45 (2022), 245–8.

Review: Craig Owen Jones, *Princely Ambition: Ideology, Landscape and Castle-building in Gwynedd, 1194–1283* (Hatfield: University of Hertfordshire Press, 2022), *Journal of the Merioneth Historical and Record Society*, 19 (2022), 96–7.

2023

'Gorffennol heddiw', *O'r Pedwar Gwynt*, 21 (gwanwyn 2023), 7–10.

'Iachawdwriaeth, rhagluniaeth a hanes: Theophilus Evans a *Drych y Prif Oesoedd*', yn A. Cynfael Lake a D. Densil Morgan (goln), *Gofal ein Gwinllan: ysgrifau ar gyfraniad Yr Eglwys yng Nghymru i'n llên a'n hanes a'n diwylliant*. Cyfrol 1 (Talybont: Y Lolfa, 2023), tt. 105–18.

Adolygiad: David Austin, *Ystrad Fflur: Hanes a Thirwedd Mynachlog Gymreig* (Ymddiriedolaeth Ystrad Fflur, 2022), *Y Traethodydd*, 178 (2023), 58–9.

Review: Barry J. Lewis et al., *A History of Christianity in Wales* (Cardiff: University of Wales Press, 2022), *Studia Celtica*, 57 (2023), 169–71.

Review: Brynley F. Roberts, *Edward Lhwyd, c.1660–1709: Naturalist, Antiquary, Philologist* (Cardiff: University of Wales Press, 2022), *Archaeologia Cambrensis*, 172 (2023), 268–9.

Carwn ddiolch i Iwan ap Dafydd, Nancy Edwards, Angharad Elias, John Moore a Paul O'Leary am eu cymorth.

I wish to thank Iwan ap Dafydd, Nancy Edwards, Angharad Elias, John Moore and Paul O'Leary for their assistance.

MANUSCRIPTS CITED :
RHESTR O LAWYSGRIFAU

Aberystwyth, National Library of Wales, Brogyntyn MS 2
Aberystwyth, National Library of Wales, Cwrtmawr MS 10
Aberystwyth, National Library of Wales, Cwrtmawr MS 19
Aberystwyth, National Library of Wales, Cwrtmawr MS 27
Aberystwyth, National Library of Wales, Cwrtmawr MS 320
Aberystwyth, National Library of Wales, Cwrtmawr MS 454
Aberystwyth, National Library of Wales, Dolaucothi estate, L6607
Aberystwyth, National Library of Wales, E. Morgan Humphreys Papers
Aberystwyth, National Library of Wales, E. T. John Papers
Aberystwyth, National Library of Wales, Llanstephan, MS 30
Aberystwyth, National Library of Wales, MS 320C
Aberystwyth, National Library of Wales, MS 909C
Aberystwyth, National Library of Wales, MS 912D
Aberystwyth, National Library of Wales, MS 966C
Aberystwyth, National Library of Wales, MS 3024C (Mostyn 83)
Aberystwyth, National Library of Wales, MS 3264D
Aberystwyth, National Library of Wales, MS 3289C
Aberystwyth, National Library of Wales, MS 6619B
Aberystwyth, National Library of Wales, MS 9077C
Aberystwyth, National Library of Wales, MS 13959E
Aberystwyth, National Library of Wales, MS 13960E
Aberystwyth, National Library of Wales, MS 13961E
Aberystwyth, National Library of Wales, MS 14990F
Aberystwyth, National Library of Wales, MS 17176E
Aberystwyth, National Library of Wales, MS 23281B
Aberystwyth, National Library of Wales, MS 23282C
Aberystwyth, National Library of Wales, Peniarth MS 16
Aberystwyth, National Library of Wales, Peniarth MS 45
Aberystwyth, National Library of Wales, Peniarth MS 128
Aberystwyth, National Library of Wales, Peniarth MS 155
Aberystwyth, National Library of Wales, Peniarth MS 231B (*Llyfr Coch Asaph*)
Aberystwyth, National Library of Wales, Peniarth MS 383
Aberystwyth, National Library of Wales, Peniarth MS 434
Aberystwyth, National Library of Wales, Peniarth Estate, PB3

Aberystwyth, National Library of Wales, St Asaph Diocesan Records, SA/R1
Aberystwyth, National Library of Wales, Rolls, 1222–2017, 107
Aberystwyth, National Library of Wales, Voelas and Cefnamwlch Estate, KB/15
Bangor, Bangor University Archives and Special Collections, The Bangor Pontifical
Bangor, Bangor University Archives and Special Collections, Penrhos VII
Cambridge, Corpus Christi College, MS 104
Cambridge, Corpus Christi College, MS 114A
Cambridge, Corpus Christi College, 114B
Cambridge, Corpus Christi College, MS 452
Cardiff, Central Library, MS 2.1030
London, British Library, Additional MS 14966
London, British Library, Additional MS 31097
London, British Library, Additional MS 33781
London, British Library, Cotton Cleopatra D. iii
London, British Library, Cotton Julius D. x
London, British Library, Harleian MS 1970
London, British Library, Harleian MS 1971
London, British Library, Harleian MS 7033
London, British Library, Harley MS 420
London, British Library, Harley MS 3725
London, The National Archives, C 66/49 (Patent Rolls, 25 Henry III)
London, The National Archives, SP 10/15, 12/69/14, 12/118/8, 12/123, 12/153/66, 12/153/67, 12/165/3
London, The National Archives, PROB 11/68/120, 11/128/256
Oxford, Exeter College, MS 158
Brynddu Hall, Anglesey, Uncatalogued MS
Vatican City, Archivio Segreto, Reg. Vat. 13
Vatican City, Biblioteca Apostolica Vaticana, MS Vat. Lat. 4015

SELECTED BIBLIOGRAPHY : LLYFRYDDIAETH DDETHOL

Aaron, Jane, *Nineteenth-century Women's Writing in Wales: Nation, Gender and Identity* (Cardiff, 2010)

Aitchison, J. W., and Harold Carter, 'The Welsh Language, 1921–1991: A Geolinguistic Perspective', in Geraint H. Jenkins and Mari A. Williams (eds), *Let's Do Our Best for the Ancient Tongue: The Welsh Language in the Twentieth Century* (Cardiff, 2000), pp. 29–107

Alker, Zoe, and Robert Shoemaker, 'Convicts and the Cultural Significance of Tattooing in Nineteenth-century Britain', *Journal of British Studies*, 61/4 (2022), 835–62

Allen, James, *Notes on the Sheriffs of Pembrokeshire, 1541–1899* (Tenby, 1900)

Andrews, Rhian M., 'Y Bardd yn Llysgennad, Rhan 1: Llywarch Brydydd y Moch yn Neheubarth', *Dwned*, 20 (2014), 11–30

Andrews, Rhian M., 'Y Bardd yn Llysgennad, Rhan 2: Bleddyn Fardd yn Neheubarth', *Dwned*, 21 (2015), 49–68

Antur, Gruffudd, 'Beirdd a Gwŷr Llên: rhai rhwydweithiau llawysgrifol yng Nghymru, *c.*1450–*c.*1800' (unpublished PhD thesis, Bangor University, 2023)

Armstrong, Lawrin, 'A Misdated St Paul's Fabric Indulgence', *Notes and Queries*, 59/4 (2012), 483–7

Baár, Monika, 'Wishful Thinking: Academic Competitions in National History', in Ilaria Porciani and Jo Tollebeek (eds), *Setting the Standards. Institutions, Networks and Communities of National Historiography* (Basingstoke, 2012), pp. 165–82

Baring-Gould, S., and John Fisher (eds), *The Lives of the British Saints*, 4 vols (London, 1907–13)

Barlow, Helen, 'The Celtic Revival', in Trevor Herbert, Martin V. Clarke and Helen Barlow (eds), *A History of Welsh Music* (Cambridge, 2022), pp. 171–94

Barraclough, G. (ed.), *The Charters of the Anglo-Norman Earls of Chester, c.1071–1237*, The Record Society of Lancashire and Cheshire, 126 (Gloucester, 1988)

Barrow, John, *An Account of Travels into the Interior of Southern Africa in the Years 1797 and 1798 including … Sketches of the physical and moral Characters of the various Tribes of inhabitants surrounding the Settlement of the Cape of Good Hope*, 2 vols (London, 1801 and 1806)

Bartie, Angela et al., '"And those who live, how shall I tell their fame?" Historical pageants, collective remembrance and the First World War, 1919–39', *Historical Research*, 90/249 (2017), 636–61

Bartie, Angela et al., '"History taught in the pageant way": education and historical performance in twentieth-century Britain', *History of Education*, 48 (2019), 156–79

Bartie, Angela et al. (eds), *Restaging the Past: Historical Pageants, Culture and Society in Modern Britain* (London, 2020)

Bartlett, Robert, *The Making of Europe* (London, 1993)

Bartlett, Robert, 'Gerald of Wales and the *History of Llanthony Priory*', in Henley and McMullen (eds), *Gerald of Wales*, pp. 81–96

Bartlett, Robert (ed. and trans.), *Instruction for a Ruler (De Principis Instructione)*, Oxford Medieval Texts (Oxford, 2018)

Bartlett, Robert, *The History of Llanthony Priory* (Oxford, 2022)

Bartrum, P. C. (ed.), *Early Welsh Genealogical Tracts* (Cardiff, 1966)

Bartrum, Peter C., 'Personal Names in Wales in the Fifteenth Century', *NLWJ*, 22/4 (1981–2), 462–9

Bartrum, Peter C. (ed.), *Welsh Genealogies, A.D. 1400–1500* (Aberystwyth, 1983)

Bartrum, Peter C., *A Welsh Classical Dictionary* (Aberystwyth, 1993)

Bass, Ian L., 'Communities of Remembrance: Religious Orders and the Cult of Thomas de Cantilupe, Bishop of Hereford (1275–82)', *The Journal of Medieval Monastic Studies*, 7 (2018), 237–72

Bates, David, 'The earliest Norman writs', *English Historical Review*, 100 (1985), 266–84

Bender, Barbara (ed.), *Landscape: Politics and Perspectives* (Oxford, 1993)

Benham, Jenny, *Peacemaking in the Middle Ages: Principles and Practice* (Manchester, 2011)

Beninger, Kelsey, 'Social Media Users' Views on the Ethics of Social Media Research', in Luke Sloan and Anabel Quan-Haase (eds), *The SAGE Handbook of Social Media Research Methods* (London, 2016), pp. 57–72

Bennett, Kirsty, 'The Book Collections of Llanthony Priory from Foundation until Dissolution (*c.*1100–1538)' (unpublished PhD thesis, University of Kent, 2006)

Bennett, Matthew, 'Warrior Narratives and Hostageship Ethos: Old French Literature and "Reality" in the Twelfth Century', in Bennett and Weikert (eds), *Medieval Hostageship*, pp. 79–91

Bennett, Matthew, and Katherine Weikert (eds), *Medieval Hostageship c.700–c.1500: Hostage, Captive, Prisoner of War, Guarantee, Peacemaker* (London, 2016)

Berry, Henry FitzPatrick, *Statutes and Ordinances, and Acts of the Parliament of Ireland: King John to Henry V* (Dublin, 1907)

Blake, E. O. (ed.), *Liber Eliensis* (London, 1962)

Bliss, W. H. (ed. and trans.), *Calendar of Entries in the Papal Registers relating to Great Britain and Ireland. Papal letters: Vol 1, 1198–1304* (London, 1893)

Boase C. W., and Andrew Clark (eds), *Register of the University of Oxford*, 2 vols (Oxford, 1885)

Bollard, John K. (ed.), *Englynion y Beddau: the Stanzas of the Graves* (Llanrwst, 2015)

Booker, Sparky, *Cultural Exchange and Identity in Late Medieval Ireland: The English and Irish of the Four Obedient Shires* (Cambridge, 2018)

Bosanquet, G. (ed. and trans.), *Eadmer's History of Recent Events in England, Historia Novorum in Anglia* (London, 1964)

Bott, Alan, and Margaret Dunn, *A Guide to the Priory and Parish Church of St Mary Beddgelert, Gwynedd* (Godalming, 2004)

Bowen, Geraint, and Zonia Bowen, *Hanes Gorsedd y Beirdd* (Swansea, 1991)

Bowen, Lloyd, 'Fashioning communities: the county in early modern Wales', in Jacqueline Eales and Andrew Hopper (eds), *The County Community in Seventeenth-century England and Wales* (Hatfield, 2012), pp. 77–99

Bowen, Lloyd, 'The Battle of Britain: History and Reformation in Early Modern Wales', in T. Ó hAnnracháin and R. Armstrong (eds), *Christianities in the Early Modern Celtic World* (Basingstoke, 2014), pp. 135–50

Boyle, S. D., 'Excavations at Hen Waliau, Caernarfon, 1952–1985', *BBCS*, 38 (1991), 191–212

Bradney, Joseph, *Genealogical memoranda relating to the families of Hopkins of Llanfihangel Ystern Llewern …* (London, 1889)

Brady, Lindy, *Writing the Welsh Borderlands in Anglo-Saxon England* (Manchester, 2017)

Bramley, Katherine Anne and others (eds), *Gwaith Llywelyn Fardd I ac Eraill o Feirdd y Ddeuddegfed Ganrif*, CBT II (Cardiff, 1994)

Bray, Gerald (ed.), *Records of Convocation VI: Canterbury 1444–1509* (Woodbridge, 2005)

Brearton, Fran, *The Great War in Irish Poetry: W. B. Yeats to Michael Longley* (Oxford, 2003)

Brett, Caroline, 'The Prefaces of Two Late Thirteenth-century Welsh Latin Chronicles', *BBCS*, 35 (1988), 63–73

Brewer, J. S., James F. Dimock and George F. Warner (ed.), *Giraldi Cambrensis Opera*, 8 vols (London, 1861–91)

Brewer J. S., and William Bullen (eds), *Calendar of the Carew Manuscripts preserved in the Archiepiscopal Library at Lambeth*, 6 vols (London, 1867–73)

Broadway, Jan, *'No historie so meete': Gentry culture and the development of local history in Elizabethan and early Stuart England* (Manchester, 2006)

Broadway, Jan, 'Symbolic and Self-consciously Antiquarian: The Elizabethan and Early Stuart Gentry's Use of the Past', *Huntington Library Quarterly*, 76/4 (2013), 541–58

Bromwich, Rachel, 'The Tristan of the Welsh', in Rachel Bromwich, A. O. H. Jarman and Brynley F. Roberts (eds), *The Arthur of the Welsh: The Arthurian Legend in Medieval Welsh Literature* (Cardiff, 1991), pp. 209–28

Bromwich, Rachel, 'Cyfeiriadau Traddodiadol a Chwedlonol y Gogynfeirdd', in Morfydd E. Owen and Brynley F. Roberts (eds), *Beirdd a Thywysogion: Barddoniaeth Llys yng Nghymru, Iwerddon a'r Alban* (Cardiff, 1996), pp. 201–18

Bromwich, Rachel, 'The Triads of the Horses', in Sioned Davies and Nerys Ann Jones (eds), *The Horse in Celtic Culture: Medieval Welsh Perspectives* (Cardiff, 1997), pp. 102–20

Bromwich, Rachel, *Trioedd Ynys Prydein: the Triads of the Island of Britain* (4th edn, Cardiff, 2014)

Bromwich, Rachel, and D. Simon Evans (eds), *Culhwch ac Olwen: an Edition and Study of the Oldest Arthurian Tale* (Cardiff, 1992; 2nd edn, Cardiff, 1997)

Brooks, N. P., and S. E. Kelly (eds), *Charters of Christ Church Canterbury*, 2 vols (Oxford, 2013)

Broome, Karl, 'Tattooing starts at home: tattooing, affectivity, and sociality', *Fashion Theory*, 10/3 (2006), 333–50

Broun, Dauvit, *The Charters of Gaelic Scotland and Ireland in the Early Middle Ages*, Quiggin Pamphlets on the Sources of Medieval Gaelic History, 2 (Cambridge, 1995)

Broun, Dauvit, 'The Welsh identity of the kingdom of Strathclyde *c*.900–*c*.1200', *Innes Review*, 55 (2004), 111–80

Bruce, John, and Thomas Perowne (ed.), *Correspondence of Matthew Parker, D.D., Archbishop of Canterbury* (Cambridge, 1853)

Brunner, Thomas, 'Le passage aux langues vernaculaires dans les actes de la pratique en Occident', *Le Moyen Age*, 115 (2009), 29–72

Buckley, James, *Genealogies of the Carmarthenshire Sheriffs, 1539–1913*, 2 vols (Carmarthen, 1910–13)

Burke, Peter, *The French Historical Revolution: The Annales School, 1929–89* (Cambridge, 1990)

Burke, Peter, *Eyewitnessing: The Uses of Images as Historical Evidence* (Cornell, 2008)

Burke, Peter, 'Co-memorations: Performing the Past', in Karin Tilmans, Frank van Vree and Jay Winter (eds), *Performing the Past: Memory, History, and Identity in Modern Europe* (Amsterdam, 2010), pp. 105–18

Burton, Janet, 'Transition and Transformation: The Benedictine Houses', in Janet Burton and Karen Stöber (eds), *Monastic Wales: New Approaches* (Cardiff, 2013), pp. 21–37

Butler, H. E. (ed.), *The Autobiography of Gerald of Wales* (Woodbridge, 2005)
Calendar of MSS of the Most Hon. the Marquis of Salisbury, Preserved at Hatfield House ... 24 vols (London, 1883–1976)
Calendar of Patent Rolls, A.D. 1476–1485 (London, 1901)
Calendar of Patent Rolls, A.D. 1485–94 (London, 1914)
Capes, W. W., and R. G. Griffiths (eds), *The Register of Thomas De Cantilupe, Bishop of Hereford A.D. 1275–1282* (Hereford, 1906)
Caplan, Jane, *Written on the Body: The Tattoo in European and American History* (Princeton, 2000)
Carpenter, David, *The Minority of Henry III* (London, 1990)
Carpenter, David, 'Dafydd ap Llywelyn's Submission to King Henry III in October 1241: A New Perspective', *WHR*, 23 (2007), 1–12
Carr, A. D., 'Anglo-Welsh Relations, 1066–1282', in M. Jones and M. Vale (eds), *England and her Neighbours, 1066–1453: Essays in Honour of Pierre Chaplais* (London, 1989), pp. 121–38
Carr, Glenda, 'The London-Welsh', in Philip Henry Jones and Eiluned Rees (eds), *A Nation and its Books: A History of the Book in Wales* (Aberystwyth, 1998), pp. 147–56
Carter, Laura, *Histories of Everyday Life: The Making of Popular Social History in Britain, c.1918–1979* (Oxford, 2021)
Cathrall, William, *The History of North Wales*, 2 vols (Manchester, 1828)
Chapman, T. Robin, 'Yr apêl at Felix: agweddau ar hanesyddiaeth R. T. Jenkins (1881–1969)', *WHR*, 30/4 (2021), 609–35
Charles-Edwards, T. M., *Wales and the Britons, 350–1064* (Oxford, 2012)
Charnell-White, Cathryn, *Welsh Poetry of the French Revolution, 1789–1805* (Cardiff, 2012)
Chibnall, Marjorie (ed. and trans.), *The Ecclesiastical History of Orderic Vitalis*, 6 vols (Oxford, 1969–80)
Christie, Richard Copley (ed.), *Annales Cestrienses or Chronicle of the Abbey of S. Werburg at Chester* (London, 1887)
Clark, G. T. (ed.), *Cartae et Alia Munimenta quae ad Dominium de Glamorgancia Pertinet*, 6 vols (Cardiff, 1910)
Clarke, Peter D., and Patrick N. R. Zutshi, *Supplications from England and Wales in the Registers of the Apostolic Penitentiary, 1410–1503*, Canterbury & York Society 103–5, 3 vols (Woodbridge, 2013–15)
Clemens, Gabriele, 'Ancestors, castles, tradition: the German and Italian nobility and the discovery of the Middle Ages in the nineteenth century', *Journal of Modern Italian Studies*, 8/1 (2003), 1–15
Coad, David, 'Euro 2004 and Football Fashion', *Journal of Sport and Social Issues*, 29/1 (2005), 124–6

Coe, Jon, 'Dating the Boundary Clauses in the Book of Llandaf', *CMCS*, 48 (2004), 1–45

Coe, Jonathan Baron, 'The place-names of the Book of Llandaf' (unpublished PhD thesis, University of Wales, Aberystwyth, 2001)

Cooke, W. Bryan, *The seize quartiers of the family of Bryan Cooke* (London, 1857)

Costello, M. A., *De Annatis Hiberniae. A Calendar of the First Fruits' Fees Levied on Papal Appointments to Benefices in Ireland A. D. 1400 to 1535 Extracted from the Vatican and other Roman Archives. Volume I: Ulster* (Dundalk, 1909)

Costello, M. A., 'Obligationes pro Annatis Diocesis Dublinensis, 1421–1520', *Archivium Hibernicum*, 2 (1913), 1–72

Costigan (Bosco), N. G. et al. (eds), *Gwaith Dafydd Benfras ac eraill o feirdd hanner cyntaf y drydedd ganrif ar ddeg*, CBT VI (Cardiff, 1995)

Coward, Adam, 'English Anglers, Welsh Salmon and Social Justice: The Politics of Conservation in Mid-nineteenth-century Wales', *WHR*, 27/4 (2015), 730–54

Cowley, F. G., *The Monastic Order in South Wales 1066–1349* (Cardiff, 1977)

Coxe, William, *An Historical Tour in Monmouthshire* (London, 1801)

Craib, Ian, *Classical Social Theory: An Introduction to the Thought of Marx, Weber, Durkheim and Simmel* (Oxford, 1997)

Crouch, David, 'The slow death of kingship in Glamorgan', *Morgannwg*, 29 (1985), 20–41

Curtis, Edmund, and R. B. McDowell (eds), *Irish Historical Documents, 1172–1922* (London, 1943)

Daunton, M. J., 'Review of Kenneth O. Morgan, *Rebirth of a Nation: Wales 1880–1980*', *English Historical Review*, 97 (1982), 160–1

Davies, Catrin T. Beynon, 'Cerddi'r Tai Crefydd' (unpublished MA thesis, University College of North Wales, Bangor, 1972)

Davies, Hazel Walford, '"The country of my heart": Lord Howard de Walden and Wales', *Transactions of the Honourable Society of Cymmrodorion*, new series, 20 (2014), 18–34

Davies, James Conway, *Episcopal Acts and Cognate Documents Relating to Welsh Dioceses 1066–1272*, 2 vols (Cardiff, 1944–6)

Davies, John, 'The end of the great estates and the rise of freehold farming in Wales', *WHR*, 7/2 (1974), 186–212

Davies, John, *The History of Wales* [*Hanes Cymru*, 1990; *History of Wales*, 1993] (rev. edn, London, 2007)

Davies, John, *A Life in History* (Talybont, 2015)

Davies, John, and Marian Delyth, *Wales: The 100 Places to see before you Die* (Talybont, 2010)

Davies, John Reuben, '*Liber Landavensis*: Its Date and the Identity of its Editor', *CMCS*, 35 (1998), 1–11

Davies, John Reuben, *The Book of Llandaff and the Norman Church in Wales* (Woodbridge, 2002)

Davies, John Reuben, 'Old Testament Personal Names among the Britons: Their Occurrence and Significance before the Twelfth Century', *Viator: Medieval and Renaissance Studies*, 43/1 (2012), 175–92

Davies, R. R., *The Age of Conquest: Wales 1063–1415* (Oxford, 1991)

Davies, R. R., *The Revolt of Owain Glyn Dŵr* (Oxford, 1995)

Davies, R. R., *The First English Empire: Power and Identities in the British Isles 1093–1343. The Ford Lectures Delivered in the University of Oxford in Hilary Term 1998* (Oxford, 2000)

Davies, R. R., 'The Identity of "Wales" in the Thirteenth Century', in R. R. Davies and Geraint H. Jenkins (eds), *From Medieval to Modern Wales: Historical Essays in Honour of Kenneth O. Morgan and Ralph A. Griffiths* (Cardiff, 2004), pp. 45–63

Davies, W. S. (ed.), 'Giraldus Cambrensis, *De Invectionibus*', *Y Cymmrodor*, 30 (1920), 1–248

Davies, Wendy, 'St Mary's Worcester and *Liber Landavensis*', *Journal of the Society of Archivists*, 4 (1972), 459–85 (repr. in her *Welsh History in the Early Middle Ages*, no. I)

Davies, Wendy, *An Early Welsh Microcosm. Studies in the Llandaff Charters* (London, 1978)

Davies, Wendy, 'Land and Power in Early Medieval Wales', *Past and Present*, 81 (1978), 3–23

Davies, Wendy, 'Roman Settlements and Post-Roman estates in South-east Wales', in P. J. Casey (ed.), *The End of Roman Britain. Papers arising from a Conference, Durham 1978*, B.A.R. British Series 71 (Oxford, 1978), pp. 153–73

Davies, Wendy, *The Llandaff Charters* (Aberystwyth, 1979)

Davies, Wendy, 'The Latin charter-tradition in western Britain, Brittany and Ireland in the early mediaeval period', in Dorothy Whitelock, Rosamond McKitterick and David Dumville (eds), *Ireland in Early Mediaeval Europe. Studies in Memory of Kathleen Hughes* (Cambridge, 1982), pp. 258–80

Davies, Wendy, *Wales in the Early Middle Ages* (Leicester, 1982)

Davies, Wendy, *Small Worlds: The Village Community in Early Medieval Brittany* (London, 1988)

Davies, Wendy, *Welsh History in the Early Middle Ages* (Farnham, 2009)

de Bhulbh, Seán, *Sloinnte na h-Éireann. Irish Surnames* (Limerick, 1997)

de Courson, Aurélien (ed.), *Cartulaire de l'abbaye de Redon en Bretagne* (Paris, 1863)

Dobson, Barrie, 'English and Welsh monastic bishops: The final century, 1433–1533', in Benjamin Thompson (ed.), *Monasteries and Society in Medieval Britain* (Stamford, 1999), 348–65

Dodd, A. H., 'Wales and Brittany', *Proceedings of the Llandudno, Colwyn Bay and District Field Club*, 22 (1949), 1–10

Dodd, A. H., *Studies in Stuart Wales* (Cardiff, 1952; 2nd edn, 1971)

Dodd, A. H., 'Borderers and Highlanders', *History*, new series, 41 (1956), 53–66

Dodd, A. H., 'Jack and his House', *Archaeologia Cambrensis*, 59 (1960), 1–12

Dodd, A. H., *A History of Caernarvonshire, 1284–1900* (Caernarvon, 1968)

Dodd, A. H., 'Nationalism in Wales: A Historical Assessment', *Transactions of the Honorable Society of Cymmrodorion* (1970), 33–49

Dodd, A. H., *A Short History of Wales* (London, 1977)

Doyne, Nicholas, *The Seventh Report of the Deputy Keeper of the Public Records in Ireland* (Dublin, 1875)

Duggan, Anne J. (ed.), *The Correspondence of Thomas Becket, Archbishop of Canterbury, 1162–1170*, 2 vols (Oxford, 2001)

Dumville, David, *A Palaeographer's Review: The Insular System of Scripts in the Early Middle Ages*, 2 vols paginated as 1 (Suita, Osaka, 1999–2007)

Dumville, David N., *Abbreviations Used in Insular Script before A.D. 850: Tabulation Based on the Work of W. M. Lindsay* (Cambridge, 2004)

Durie, Bruce, *Welsh Genealogy* (Stroud, 2012)

Edmunds, William, *Some old families in the neighbourhood of Lampeter* (Tenby, 1860)

Edwards, Hywel Teifi, *Yr Eisteddfod* (Llandysul, 1976)

Edwards, Hywel Teifi, *Gŵyl Gwalia. Yr Eisteddfod Genedlaethol yn Oes Aur Victoria 1858/1868* (Llandysul, 1980)

Edwards, Hywel Teifi, *Codi'r Hen Wlad yn ei Hôl, 1850–1914* (Llandysul, 1989)

Edwards, Hywel Teifi, *The Eisteddfod* (Cardiff, 1990)

Edwards, Hywel Teifi (ed.), *Cwm Cynon. Cyfres y Cymoedd* (Llandysul, 1997)

Edwards, Hywel Teifi, 'Eisteddfod "Genedlaethol" Caernarfon, 1877: Prifwyl y Pafiliwn', *Trafodion Cymdeithas Hanes Sir Gaernarfon*, 67 (2006), 58–87

Edwards, Hywel Teifi, *The National Pageant of Wales* (Llandysul, 2009)

Edwards, Hywel Teifi, and E. G. Millward, *Jiwbilî y Fam Wen Fawr: Fictoria, 1887–1897* (Llandysul, 2002)

Edwards, J. G. (ed.), *Calendar of Ancient Correspondence Concerning Wales* (Cardiff, 1935)

Edwards, J. G. (ed.), *Littere Wallie preserved in Liber A in the Public Record Office* (Cardiff, 1940)

Edwards, O. M., *Wales* (London, 1901)

Egan, Patrick K., 'The Augustinian Priory of St. Mary Clontuskert O Many', *Journal of the Galway Archaeological and Historical Society*, 22 (1946), 1–14

Eldridge, Lisa, *Face Paint: The Story of Makeup* (London, 2015)

Ellis, Henry (ed.), *Registrum vulgariter nuncupatum 'The Record of Caernarvon': è codice MS^{to} Harleiano 696. descriptum* (London, 1838)

Ellis, Henry (ed.), *Register and Chronicle of Aberconway from the Harleian MS. 3725* (London, 1847)

Ellis, Osian, *The Story of the Harp in Wales* (Cardiff, 1991)

Emden, A. B., *A biographical register of the University of Oxford, to A.D. 1500*, 3 vols (Oxford, 1957–9)

Emmanuel, Hywel D. (ed.), *The Latin Texts of the Welsh Laws* (Cardiff, 1967)

Evans, Albert Owen, 'Nicholas Robinson (1530?–1585)', *Y Cymmrodor*, 39 (1928), 149–99

Evans, D. Simon, *A Grammar of Middle Welsh* (Dublin, 1964)

Evans, D. Simon (ed.), *Historia Gruffud vab Kenan* (Cardiff, 1977)

Evans, Daniel, 'Welshness in "British Wales": negotiating national identity at the margins', *Nations and Nationalism*, 25/1 (2019), 176–90

Evans, Dylan Foster (ed.), *Gwaith Rhys Goch Eryri* (Aberystwyth, 2007)

Evans, Gwynfor, *Land of my Fathers* (Swansea, 1978)

Evans, J. Gwenogvryn, with John Rhys, *The Text of the Book of Llan Dâv* (Oxford, 1893)

Evans, J. Gwenogvryn, *The Poetry in the Red Book of Hergest* (Llanbedrog, 1911)

Evans, Neil, 'Finding a New Story: The Search for a Usable Past in Wales, 1869–1930', *Transactions of the Honourable Society of Cymmrodorion*, new ser., 10 (2004), 144–62

Evans, Neil, '"When Men and Mountains Meet": Historians' Interpretations of the History of Wales, 1890–1970', *WHR*, 22 (2004), 222–51

Evans, Neil, 'Beyond 1282: A. H. Dodd and the Problem of Modern Welsh History', in Pryce and Evans (eds), *Writing a Small Nation's Past*, pp. 223–36

Evans, Neil, 'Remaking nations and their histories: the social, political and intellectual world of the early Powysland Club', *Montgomeryshire Collections*, 109 (2021), 45–86

Evans, Shaun, 'Inventing the Bosworth tradition: Richard ap Hywel, the "King's Hole" and the Mostyn family image in the nineteenth century', *WHR*, 29/2 (2018), 218–53

Evans, Shaun, 'Book cultures, gentry identities and the Welsh country house library: problems and possibilities for future research', *WHR*, 31/1 (2022), 17–54

Evans, Shaun, '"An antient seat of a gentleman of Wales": The place of the *plas* in Thomas Pennant's *Tour in Wales* (1778–83)', in Terence Dooley and Christopher Ridgway (eds), *The Country House and its Visitors* (Dublin, 2023), pp. 196–219

Eyton, R. W., *Antiquities of Shropshire*, 12 vols (London, 1854–60)

Fairweather, J. (ed.), *Liber Eliensis, A History of the Isle of Ely* (Woodbridge, 2005)

Falileyev, Alexander, *Etymological Glossary of Old Welsh* (Tübingen, 2000)

Ferguson, James F., 'The "Mere English" and "Mere Irish"', *Transactions of the Kilkenny Archaeological Society*, 1/3 (1851), 508–12

Feuer, Lewis S. (ed.), *Marx and Engels: Basic Writings on Politics and Philosophy* (London and Glasgow, 1969)

Ffoulkes, W. Wynne, *Pedigree of the family of Ffoulkes of Eriviat* (London, 1874)

Fisher, Jill A., 'Tattooing the Body, Marking Culture', *Body and Society*, 8/4 (2002), 91–107

Fitzpatrick-Matthews, Keith J., 'Genealogia Brittonum: revisiting the textual tradition of the Historia Brittonum', *Studia Celtica*, 54 (2020), 45–73

Flanagan, Marie Therese, *Irish Society, Anglo-Norman Settlers, Angevin Kingship* (Oxford, 1989)

Flanagan, Marie Therese, 'Henry II, the Council of Cashel and the Irish Bishops', *Peritia*, 10 (1996), 184–211

Flanagan, Marie Therese, *The Transformation of the Irish Church in the Twelfth Century* (Woodbridge, 2010)

Fleuriot, Léon, *Dictionnaire des gloses en vieux Breton* (Paris, 1964)

Fleuriot, Léon, *Le vieux Breton: éléments d'une grammaire* (Paris, 1964)

Flower, Robin, 'Richard Davies, William Cecil, and Giraldus Cambrensis', *NLWJ*, 3/1–2 (1943), 11–14

Foster, Joseph (ed.), *Alumni Oxonienses* (Oxford, 1891)

Foster, R. F., *W. B. Yeats: A Life, 1: The Apprentice Mage, 1865–1914* (Oxford, 1998)

Fröhlich, W. (ed. and trans.), *The Letters of St. Anselm of Canterbury*, 3 vols (Kalamazoo, 1990–4)

Gaffney, Angela, *Aftermath: Remembering the Great War in Wales* (Cardiff, 1998)

Gaffney, Angela, '"A National Valhalla for Wales": D. A. Thomas and the Welsh Historical Sculpture Scheme, 1910–1916', *Transactions of the Honourable Society of Cymmrodorion* (1998/9), 132–44

Gairdner, J., and R. H. Brodie (ed.), *L & P, Vol. XVI (1540–1)* (London, 1898)

Gairdner, J., and R. H. Brodie (ed.), *L & P, Vol. XVII (1542)* (London, 1900)

Gallagher, Robert, 'The Vernacular in Anglo-Saxon Charters: Expansion and Innovation in Ninth-century England', *Historical Research*, 91 (2018), 205–35

Gallagher, Robert, *Writing the Realm: The Written Word and the Rise of Wessex, c.830–920* (forthcoming)

Gibson, Pamela Church, 'Pornostyle: sexualised dress and the fracturing of feminism', *Fashion Theory*, 18/2 (2014), 189–206

Giles, J. A. (trans.), *Matthew Paris's English History, from the year 1235 to 1273*, 3 vols (London, 1852–4)

Gill, Rosalind, Karen Henwood and Carl McLean, 'Body Projects and the regulation of normative masculinity', *Body and Society*, 11/1 (2005), 37–62

Girouard, Mark, *The Return to Camelot: Chivalry and the English Gentleman* (New Haven, 1981)

Glenn, T. A., *The Family of Griffith of Garn* (London, 1934)

Glenn, T. A., and Ll. N. V. Lloyd-Mostyn, *The Mostyns of Mostyn* (London, 1925)

Godwin, Francis, *De Praesulibus Angliae Commentarius ...* (London, 1616)

Godwin, Francis, *The succession of the bishops of England ...* (2nd edn, London, 1625)

Goering, Joseph, and Huw Pryce, 'The *De Modo Confitendi* of Cadwgan, Bishop of Bangor', *Mediaeval Studies*, 62 (2000), 1–27

Gough-Cooper, Henry (ed.), 'Annales Cambriae. The B Text. From London, National Archives, MS E164/1, pp. 2–26' (2015), online at *http://croniclau. bangor.ac.uk/documents/AC%20B%20first%20edition.pdf* (accessed 15 August 2022)

Gough-Cooper, Henry (ed.), 'Annales Cambriae. The C-text, with the intercalated annalistic notices. From British Library MS Cotton Domitian A.1, folios 138r–155r' (2015), *http://croniclau.bangor.ac.uk/editions.php.en* (accessed 4 December 2023)

Gough-Cooper, Henry (ed.), 'Annales Cambriae. The E text, from Exeter Cathedral Library MS 3514, pp. 507–19' (2016), *http://croniclau.bangor.ac.uk/documents/AC_E_First_Edition.pdf* (accessed 20 June 2024)

Gough-Cooper, Henry, 'Meet the ancestors? Evidence for antecedent texts in the late thirteenth-century Welsh Latin chronicles', in Guy et al. (eds), *Chronicles of Medieval Wales and the March*, pp. 107–37

Gransden, Antonia, *Historical Writing in England* (London, 1984)

Graves, Alfred Perceval, *Welsh Poetry Old and New: In English Verse* (London, 1912)

Graves, Alfred Perceval, 'Harlech of the Sieges', *The Spectator* (22 July 1927)

Graves, Alfred Perceval, 'The Coming Harlech Pageant', *The Bookman* (August 1927), 266

Graves, Alfred Perceval, 'Welsh Pageants and Pageants', *Welsh Outlook*, 14/8 (August 1927), 219–20

Graves, Alfred Perceval, *To Return to All That* (London, 1930)

Graves, Alfred Perceval, and Ernest Rhys, *The Pageant of Harlech Castle, August 21st–26th, 1922: Book of Words* (Newtown, 1922)

Greenway, D. E. (ed.), *Fasti Ecclesiae Anglicanae, 1066–1300, II, Monastic Cathedrals (Northern and Southern Provinces)* (London, 1971)

Gresham, Colin, 'The Harlech Pageant, 1922', *Merioneth Historical and Record Society*, 9 (1981), 97–105

Griffith, Margaret C., *Calendar of Inquisitions Formerly in the Office of the Chief Remembrancer of the Exchequer* (Dublin, 1991)

Griffith, Thomas, *The Gwyneddion; Or an account of the Royal Denbigh Eisteddfod* (Chester, 1830)

Griffith, Wil, 'Saving the Soul of the Nation: Essentialist Nationalism and Interwar Rural Wales', *Rural History*, 21/2 (2010), 177–94

Griffiths, Eric, *Philip Yorke I: Squire of Erthig* (Wrexham, 1995)

Griffiths, Ralph A., *The Principality of Wales in the Later Middle Ages: The Structure and Personnel of Government, South Wales 1277–1536*, 2 vols (Cardiff, 1972)

Gruffudd, W. J., 'Drama i Gymru', *Y Beirniad*, 1 (1911), 49–54

Gruffudd, W. J., *Math vab Mathonwy: An Inquiry into the Origins and Development of the Fourth Branch of the Mabinogi with a Text and a Translation* (Cardiff, 1928)

Gruffudd, W. J., *Rhiannon: An Inquiry into the Origins of the First and Third Branches of the Mabinogi* (Cardiff, 1953)

Gruffydd, Alwyn, *Mae Rhywun yn Gwybod* (Llanrwst, 2004)

Guy, Ben, 'The Origins of the Compilation of Welsh Historical Texts in Harley 3859', *Studia Celtica*, 49 (2015), 21–56

Guy, Ben, 'Constantine, Helena, Maximus: on the appropriation of Roman history in medieval Wales, c.800–1250', *Journal of Medieval History*, 44 (2018), 381–405

Guy, Ben, 'The *Life* of St Dyfrig and the Lost Charters of Moccas (Mochros), Herefordshire', *CMCS*, 75 (2018), 1–37

Guy, Ben, 'Rheinwg: The Lost Kingdom of South Wales', *Peritia*, 30 (2019), 97–121

Guy, Ben, 'Geoffrey of Monmouth's Welsh Sources', in Joshua Byron Smith and Georgia Henley (eds), *A Companion to Geoffrey of Monmouth* (Leiden, 2020), pp. 31–66

Guy, Ben, *Medieval Welsh Genealogy: An Introduction and Textual Study* (Woodbridge, 2020)

Guy, Ben, 'The Vespasian Life of St Teilo and the evolution of the *Vitae Sanctorum Wallensium*', in David N. Parsons and Paul Russell (eds), *Seintiau Cymru, Sancti Cambrenses: Astudiaethau ar Seintiau Cymru / Studies in the Saints of Wales* (Aberystwyth, 2022), pp. 1–30

Guy, Ben, and Rory Naismith, 'Lancaut: An Early Eleventh-century Mint-place on the River Wye', *British Numismatic Journal*, 93 (2023), 95–105

Guy, Ben et al. (eds), *The Chronicles of Medieval Wales and the March* (Turnhout, 2020)

Gwynn, Aubrey, and R. Neville Hadcock, *Medieval Religious Houses: Ireland with An Appendix to Early Sites* (London, 1970)

Hagger, Mark, 'The earliest Norman writs revisited', *Historical Research*, 82 (2009), 181–205

Hall, Dianne, *Women and the Church in Medieval Ireland c.1140–1540* (Dublin, 2003)

Hall, J. B. (trans.), *John of Salisbury: Metalogicon*, Corpus Christianorum in Translation 12 (Turnhout, 2013)

Hall, J. B., with K. S. B. Keats-Rohan (eds), *Ioannes Saresberiensis: Metalogicon*, Corpus Christianorum Continuatio Mediaevalis 98 (Turnhout, 1991)

Hall, Nick, 'Bringing the Living Back to Life: What happens when we reenact the recent past?', in Nick Hall and John Ellis (eds), *Hands on Media History: A New Methodology in the Humanities and Social Sciences* (Abingdon, 2020), pp. 26–42

Hall, Stuart, *The Fateful Triangle; Race, Ethnicity, Nation* (Cambridge, MA, 2017)

Hallam, Elizabeth, and Charles West, *Capetian France 987–1328* (3rd edn, Abingdon, 2020)

Hämäläinen, Pekka, and Samuel Truett, 'On Borderlands', *Journal of American History*, 98/2 (2011), 338–61

Hamp, Eric P., 'On the Justification of Ordering in TYP', *Studia Celtica*, 16 (1981), 104–9

Hanks, Patrick, Richard Coates and Peter McClure, *The Oxford Dictionary of Family Names in Britain and Ireland*, 4 vols (Oxford, 2016)

Hanmer, John Lord, *A Memorial of the Parish and Family of Hanmer in Flintshire* (London, 1887)

Hanning, Robert, *The Vision of History in Early Britain: from Gildas to Geoffrey of Monmouth* (New York, 1966)

Hardy, T. D. (ed.), *Rotuli Litterarum Patentium, in Turri Londinensi asservati, vol. I, part I* (London, 1835)

Hardy, T. D. (ed.), *Rotuli Chartarum, in Turri Londinensi asservati, vol 1, part 1* (London, 1837)

Harmer, F. E., *Anglo-Saxon Writs* (Manchester, 1952)

Harper, S., 'The Bangor Pontifical', *Hanes Cerddoriaeth Cymru/Welsh Music History*, 2 (1997), 65–99

Harrison, Julian, 'A Note on Gerald of Wales and *Annales Cambriae*', *WHR*, 17 (1994–5), 252–5

Harrison, Julian, 'Cistercian Chronicling in the British Isles', in Dauvit Broun and Julian Harrison (eds), *The Chronicle of Melrose Abbey. A stratigraphic edition. Volume I: Introduction and facsimile edition* (Woodbridge, 2007), pp. 13–28

Hart, W. H. (ed.), *Historia et Cartularium Monasterii Sancti Petri Gloucestriæ*, 3 vols (London, 1863–7)

Haycock, Marged (ed.), *Prophecies from the Book of Taliesin* (Aberystwyth, 2013)

Hays, Rhys Williams, *The History of the Abbey of Aberconway, 1186–1537* (Cardiff, 1963)

Hays, Rhys Williams, 'Rotoland, subprior of Aberconway, and the Controversy over the See of Bangor 1199–1204', *Journal of the Historical Society of the Church in Wales*, 18 (1963), 9–19

Heal, Felicity, *Of Prelates and Princes: A Study of the Economic and Social Position of the Tudor Episcopate* (Cambridge, 1980)

Heale, Martin (ed.), *The Prelate in England and Europe, 1300–1560* (Woodbridge, 2014)

Henken, Elissa, *National Redeemer: Owain Glyndŵr in Welsh Tradition* (Cardiff, 1996)

Henley, Georgia, 'Gerald's Circulation and Reception in Wales: The Case of *Claddedigaeth Arthur*', in Henley and McMullen (eds), *Gerald of Wales*, pp. 223–42

Henley, Georgia, 'The Cardiff chronicle in London, British Library, MS Royal 6 B XI', in Guy et al. (eds), *Chronicles of Medieval Wales and the March*, pp. 231–87

Henley, Georgia, 'Networks of Chronicle Writing in Western Britain: The Case of Worcester and Wales', in Francesca Tinti and D. A. Woodman (eds), *Constructing History across the Norman Conquest* (Woodbridge, 2022), pp. 227–70

Henley, Georgia, *Reimagining the Past in the Borderlands of Medieval England and Wales* (Oxford, 2024)

Henley, Georgia, and A. Joseph McMullen (eds), *Gerald of Wales: New Perspectives on a Medieval Writer and Critic* (Cardiff, 2018)

Hennessy, William B., and B. Mac Carthy, *Annala Uladh. Annals of Ulster. Otherwise Annala Senait. Annals of Senate; A Chronicle of Irish Affairs from A.D. 431 to A.D. 1540*, 4 vols (Dublin, 1887–1901)

Hewlett, Henry G. (ed.), *Rogeri de Wendover Liber qui dicitur Flores Historiarum ab anno domini MCLIV. Annoque Henrici Anglorum Regis Secundi Primo: The Flowers of History by Roger de Wendover*, 3 vols (London, 1886–9)

Hicklin, Alice, 'Aitire, 人質, тали, όμηρος, رهن, obses: Hostages, Political Instability, and the Writing of History *c*.900–*c*.1050 CE', *medieval worlds*, 10 (2019), 151–76

Hiraethog, Gwilym (ed.), *Ceinion Emrys. Sef Gweithiau Barddonol y Diweddar Barch. W. Ambrose (Emrys) Porthmadog* (Dolgellau, 1876)

Hiramoto, Mie, 'Inked Nostalgia: displaying identity through tattoos as Hawaii local practice', *Journal of Multilingual and Multicultural Development*, 36/2 (2015), 107–23

Hirst, John, 'Resort development on the Cambrian coast' (unpublished PhD thesis, Aberystwyth University, 2017)

Hoare, Richard Colt (trans.), *The Itinerary of Archbishop Baldwin through Wales*, 2 vols (London, 1806)

Hollister, Charles Warren, *Henry I*, ed. Amanda Clark Frost (London, 2001)

Hughes, Garfield H. (ed.), *Rhagymadroddion 1547–1659* (Caerdydd, 1976)

Hughes, Ian (ed.), *Manawydan uab Llyr* (Cardiff, 2007)

Hughes, Ian (ed.), *Math uab Mathonwy: The Fourth Branch of the Mabinogi* (Dublin, 2013)

Hughes, John, *A History of the Parliamentary Representation of the County of Cardigan* (Aberystwyth, 1849)

Hughes, Kathleen, 'The Welsh Latin chronicles: Annales Cambriae and related texts', in Kathleen Hughes, *Celtic Britain in the Early Middle Ages: Studies in Welsh and Scottish Sources by the Late Kathleen Hughes*, ed. David Dumville (Woodbridge, 1980), pp. 67–85

Hurlock, Kathryn, 'Reading Medieval Wales: David Powel's *Historie of Cambria* (1584) and its Readers', in Rosamund Oates and Jessica G. Purdy (eds), *Communities of Print: Books and their Readers in Early Modern Europe* (Leiden, 2022), pp. 178–93

Huws, Daniel, 'The Making of *Liber Landavensis*', *NLWJ*, 25 (1987–8), 133–60

Huws, Daniel, 'Descriptions of the Welsh Manuscripts', in T. M. Charles-Edwards, Morfydd E. Owen and Paul Russell (eds), *The Welsh King and His Court* (Cardiff, 2000), pp. 415–24

Huws, Daniel, *Medieval Welsh Manuscripts* (Aberystwyth, 2000)

Huws, Daniel, *A Repertory of Welsh Manuscripts and Scribes, c.800–c.1800*, 3 vols (Aberystwyth, 2022)

Ifans, Rhiannon (ed.), *Gwaith Syr Dafydd Trefor* (Aberystwyth, 2005)

Insley, Charles, 'From *Rex Wallie* to *Princeps Wallie*: charters and state-formation in thirteenth-century Wales', in J. R. Maddicott and D. M. Palliser (eds), *The Medieval State: Essays Presented to James Campbell* (London, 2000), pp. 179–96

Insley, Charles, 'Athelstan, Charters, and the English in Cornwall', in Marie Therese Flanagan and Judith Green (eds), *Charters and Charter Scholarship in Britain and Ireland* (Basingstoke, 2005), pp. 15–31

Insley, Charles, 'The Political Culture of Twelfth-century Wales', *Anglo-Norman Studies*, 30 (2007), 133–53

Insley, Charles, 'Southumbria', in Pauline Stafford (ed.), *A Companion to the Early Middle Ages: Britain and Ireland c.500–c.1100* (London, 2009), pp. 322–40

Insley, Charles, 'Imitation and Independence in Native Welsh Administrative Culture, c.1180–1280', in David Crook and Louise J. Wilkinson (eds), *The Growth of Royal Government under Henry III* (Woodbridge, 2015), pp. 104–20

Insley, Charles, 'Languages of Boundaries and Boundaries of Language in Cornish Charters of the Tenth and Eleventh Centuries', in Robert Gallagher, Edward Roberts and Francesca Tinti (eds), *The Languages of Early Medieval Charters: Latin, Germanic Vernaculars and the Written Word* (Leiden, 2020), pp. 342–77

Isaac, G. R. et al. (ed.), *Rhyddiaith Gymraeg o Lawysgrifau'r 13eg Ganrif Fersiwn 2* (Aberystwyth, 2013), https://pure.aber.ac.uk/ws/portalfiles/portal/30954693/Rhyddiaith_y_13g_V2.pdf (accessed 24 June 2024)

James, Brian Ll. (ed.), *G. T. Clark: Scholar Ironmaster in the Victorian Age* (Cardiff, 1998)

James, E. Wyn, 'Painting the World Green: Dafydd Iwan and the Welsh Protest Ballad', *Folk Music Journal*, 8/5 (2005), 594–618

James, Heather, and David Thorne, '"Mensura Med Diminih": Boundary Place-names of a Ninth-century Estate at Llandybïe, Carmarthenshire', *The Carmarthenshire Antiquary*, 56 (2020), 13–34

Jarman, A. O. H., 'Wales a part of England, 1485–1800', in D. Myrddin Lloyd (ed.), *The Historical Basis of Welsh Nationalism* (Cardiff, 1950), pp. 78–98

Jarman, A. O. H., with E. D. Jones (ed.), *Llyfr Du Caerfyrddin* (Cardiff, 1982)

Jarrett, Sadie, *Gentility in Early Modern Wales: The Salesbury Family 1450–1720* (Cardiff, 2024)

Jenkins, Bethan, *Between Wales and England: Anglophone Welsh Writing of the Eighteenth Century* (Cardiff, 2017)

Jenkins, Dafydd, 'A Family of Medieval Welsh Lawyers', in Dafydd Jenkins (ed.), *Celtic Law Papers Introductory to Welsh Medieval Law and Government* (Brussels, 1973), pp. 121–33

Jenkins, Dafydd (ed.), *Damweiniau Colan, Llyfr y Damweiniau yn ôl Llawysgrif Peniarth 30* (Aberystwyth, 1973)

Jenkins, Dafydd, and Morfydd E. Owen, 'The Welsh Marginalia in the Lichfield Gospels Part I', *CMCS*, 5 (1983), 37–66

Jenkins, Dafydd, and Morfydd E. Owen, 'The Welsh Marginalia in the Lichfield Gospels Part II: The "Surexit" Memorandum', *CMCS*, 7 (1984), 91–120

Jenkins, Geraint H., *The Foundations of Modern Wales: Wales, 1642–1780* (Oxford, 1987)

Jenkins, Geraint H., 'Historical Writing in the Eighteenth Century', in Branwen Jarvis (ed.), *A Guide to Welsh Literature c.1700–1800* (Cardiff, 2000), pp. 23–44

Jenkins, Geraint H., 'Language, Religion and Nationality', in Geraint H. Jenkins and Gareth Elwyn Jones (eds), *Degrees of Influence: A Memorial Volume for Glanmor Williams* (Cardiff, 2008), pp. 142–62

Jenkins, Geraint H., *Bard of Liberty: The Political Radicalism of Iolo Morganwg* (Cardiff, 2012)

Jenkins, Philip, 'From Edward Lhuyd to Iolo Morganwyg: The death and rebirth of Glamorgan antiquarianism', *Morgannwg*, 23 (1979), 29–47

Jenkins, Philip, 'The creation of an "Ancient Gentry": Glamorgan, 1760–1840', *WHR*, 12/1 (1984), 29–49

Jenkins, R. T., and Helen Ramage, *A History of the Honourable Society of Cymmrodorion* (London, 1951)

Johnes, Martin, 'Eighty minute patriots? National identity and sport in modern Wales', *International Journal of the History of Sport*, 17 (2000), 93–110

Johnes, Martin, 'History and the Making and Remaking of Wales', *History*, 5/343 (2015), 667–8

Johns, C. N., 'The Celtic Monasteries of North Wales', *Trafodion Cymdeithas Hanes Sir Gaernarfon*, 21 (1960), 14–43

Johns, Susan M., *Gender, Nation and Conquest in the High Middle Ages: Nest of Deheubarth* (Manchester, 2016)

Johnson, Charles (ed. and trans.), rev. M. Brett, C. N. L. Brooke and M. Winterbottom, *Hugh the Chanter: The History of the Church of York, 1066–1127* (Oxford, 1990)

Johnston, Dafydd (ed.), *Gwaith Lewys Glyn Cothi* (Cardiff, 1995)

Johnston, Dafydd, 'Monastic Patronage of Welsh Poetry', in Janet Burton and Karen Stöber (eds), *Monastic Wales: New Approaches* (Cardiff, 2013), pp. 177–90

Jones, Anwen, 'Celfyddydau Perfformiadol Cymru: Hanes Newydd, Hanesyddiaeth Newydd – Hywel Teifi Edwards a Phasiant Cenedlaethol Cymru, 1909', in Anwen Jones (ed.), *Perfformio'r Genedl: Ar Drywydd Hywel Teifi Edwards* (Cardiff, 2017), pp. 164–95

Jones, Bryn, 'Welsh Contacts with the Papacy before the Edwardian Conquest, c.1283' (unpublished PhD thesis, University of St Andrews, 2019)

Jones, Dot, *Statistical Evidence Relating to the Welsh Language 1801–1911. Tystiolaeth Ystadegol yn Ymwneud â'r Iaith Gymraeg 1801–1911* (Cardiff, 1998)

Jones, Edward, *The Bardic Museum of Primitive British Literature; and Other Admirable Rarities Forming the Second Volume of the Musical, Poetical and Historical Relicks of the Welsh Bards and Druids* (London, 1802)

Jones, Elin M., and Nerys Ann Jones (eds), *Gwaith Llywarch ap Llywelyn, 'Prydydd y Moch'*, CBT V (Cardiff, 1991)

Jones, Francis, 'An approach to Welsh genealogy', *Transactions of the Honourable Society of Cymmrodorion* (1948), 303–446

Jones, Frank Price, 'The Gwerin of Wales', in Geraint H. Jenkins (ed.), *Studies in Folk Life: Essays in Honour of Iorwerth C. Peate* (London, 1969), pp. 1–13

Jones, Glanville R. J., 'Post-Roman Wales', in H. P. R. Finberg (ed.), *The Agrarian History of England and Wales, vol. 1, part II, A.D. 43–1042* (Cambridge, 1972), pp. 281–382

Jones, H. Longueville, 'On the Study and Preservation of National Antiquities', *Archaeologia Cambrensis*, 1/1 (1846), 3–16

Jones, John, *The History of Wales* (London, 1824)

Jones, John, 'On the State of Agriculture and the Process of Art & Manufactures in Britain during the period & under the influence of the Druidical System', *Archaeologia Cambrensis Supplement 1850* (1850), 87–110

Jones, John Gwynfor, *Law, Order, and Government in Caernarfonshire, 1558–1640* (Cardiff, 1996)

Jones, John Gwynfor, *Aspects of Religious Life in Wales, c.1536–1660* (Aberystwyth, 2003)

Jones, Revd John, 'An Essay on the Language and Learning of Britain, under the Roman Government, with a Particular Reference to the Testimony of Martial, (Dicitur et Nostros Cantare Britannia versus) and of Juvenal, and to the Influence of Agricola's Schools', in *Two Essays on the Subjects Proposed by the Cambrian Society in Dyfed, which gained the Respective Prizes, at the Eisteddfod held at Caermarthen, in July 1819: to which is added an account of the Proceedings at the Eisteddfod* (Caermarthen, 1822), pp. 59–60

Jones, Nia Wyn [published as O. W. Jones], 'Historical Writing in Medieval Wales' (unpublished PhD thesis, Bangor University, 2013)

Jones, Nia Wyn [published as O. W. Jones], 'Brut y Tywysogion: The History of the Princes, and Twelfth-century Cambro-Latin Historical Writing', *Haskins Society Journal*, 26 (2014), 209–27

Jones, Nia Wyn [published as O. W. Jones], 'The Most Excellent Princes: Geoffrey of Monmouth and Medieval Welsh Historical Writing', in Joshua Byron Smith and Georgia Henley (eds), *A Companion to Geoffrey of Monmouth* (Leiden, 2020), pp. 257–90

Jones, Nia Wyn [published as O. W. Jones], '*O Oes Gwrtheyrn*: A Medieval Welsh Chronicle', in Guy et al. (eds), *Chronicles of Medieval Wales and the March*, pp. 169–229

Jones, Owen et al., *The Myvyrian Archaiology of Wales*, 3 vols (London, 1801–7)

Jones, Philip Henry, and Eiluned Rees (eds), *A Nation and its Books: A History of the Book in Wales* (Aberystwyth, 1998)

Jones, R. Tudur, *Faith and the Crisis of a Nation: Wales 1890–1914* (Cardiff, 2004)

Jones, Richard Wyn, and Roger Scully, *Wales says Yes* (Cardiff, 2012)

Jones, Theophilus, *A History of the County of Brecknock*, 2 vols (Brecknock, 1805)

Jones, Thomas, '"Cronica de Wallia" and other documents from Exeter Cathedral Library MS 3514', *BBCS*, XII (November 1946), 27–44

Jones, Thomas, 'Gerald the Welshman's "Itinerary though Wales" and "Description of Wales"', *NLWJ*, 6/2 (1949), 117–48

Jones, Thomas (ed.), *Brut y Tywysogion: Peniarth MS. 20* (Cardiff, 1941)

Jones, Thomas (trans.), *Brut y Tywysogyon or The Chronicle of Princes, Peniarth MS. 20 Version* (Cardiff, 1952)

Jones, Thomas (ed. and trans.), *Brut y Tywysogyon or The Chronicle of Princes: The Red Book of Hergest Version* (Caerdydd, 1955)

Joseph, Joseph, 'Sheriffs of Brecknockshire and Monmouthshire', *The Cambrian Journal* (1868), 258–90

Karn, N. (ed.), *English Episcopal Acta 31, Ely 1109–1197* (Oxford, 2005)

Kelly, S. E. (ed.), *The Charters of Abingdon Abbey*, 2 vols (Oxford, 2000–1)

Kelly, S. E. (ed.), *Charters of Bath and Wells* (Oxford, 2007)

Kennedy, Ian, 'The Wrexham Art Treasures exhibition of 1876', *The British Art Journal*, 19/3 (2018/19), 80–6

Ker, Neil R., *Medieval Libraries of Great Britain: A List of Surviving Books* (2nd edn, London, 1964)

Keynes, Simon D., 'Welsh Kings at Anglo-Saxon Royal Assemblies (928–55)', *Haskins Society Journal*, 26 (2014), 69–122

Keynes, Simon D., 'The West Saxon Charters of King Æthelwulf and his Sons', *English Historical Review*, 109 (1994), 1109–49

King, Richard, *Brittle with Relics* (London, 2022)

Kirby, D. P., 'Hywel Dda: Anglophil?', *WHR*, 8 (1976), 1–13

Kirby, Torrance, and P. G. Stanwood, *Paul's Cross and the Culture of Persuasion in England, 1520–1640* (Leiden, 2014)

Kirkland, Richard, *Irish London: A Cultural History, 1850–1916* (London, 2021)

Kitson, Peter, 'Old English literacy and the provenance of Welsh *y*', in Paul Russell (ed.), *Yr Hen Iaith: Studies in Early Welsh* (Aberystwyth, 2003), pp. 49–65

Knowles, David, and R. Neville Hadcock, *Medieval Religious Houses. England and Wales* (Harlow, 1971)

Koch, John T., 'A Welsh Window on the Iron Age: Manawydan, Mandubracios', *CMCS*, 14 (1987), 17–52

Kosto, Adam J., 'Hostages in the Carolingian World (714–840)', *Early Medieval Europe*, 11 (2002), 123–47

Kosto, Adam J., *Hostages in the Middle Ages* (Oxford, 2012)

Koziol, Geoffrey, *The Politics of Memory and Identity in Carolingian Royal Diplomas* (Turnhout, 2012)

Lake, A. Cynfael (ed.), *Gwaith Lewys Daron* (Cardiff, 1994)

Landy, Marcia (ed.), *The Historical Film: History and Memory in Media* (London, 2001)

Lane, Alan, and Mark Redknap (eds), *Llangorse Crannog: The Excavation of an Early Medieval Royal Site in the Kingdom of Brycheiniog* (Oxford, 2019)

Lavelle, Ryan, 'The Use and Abuses of Hostages in later Anglo-Saxon England', *Early Medieval Europe*, 14 (2006), 269–96

Le Neve, John (ed.), *Fasti Ecclesiae Anglicanae, or a Calendar of the Principal Ecclesiastical Dignitaries of England and Wales and of the Chief Officers of the Universities of Oxford and Cambridge*, corrected and contributed to by T. Duffus Hardy, 3 vols (Oxford, 1854)

Leckie Jr, R. William, *The Passage of Dominion: Geoffrey of Monmouth and the Periodization of Insular History in the Twelfth Century* (Toronto, 1982)

Leeworthy, Daryl, '"A Chorus of Greek Poignancy": Communism, Class and Pageantry in Interwar South Wales', in Bartie et al. (eds), *Restaging the Past*, pp. 180–200

Lennon, Colm, 'The Book of Obits of Christ Church Cathedral, Dublin', in Raymond Gillespie and Raymond Refaussé (eds), *The Medieval Manuscripts of Christ Church Cathedral, Dublin* (Dublin, 2006), pp. 163–82

Lewes, Evelyn, *Out with the Cambrians* (London, 1934)

Lewis, Barry, 'Arthurian References in Medieval Welsh Poetry, *c*.1100–*c*.1540', in Ceridwen Lloyd Morgan and Erich Poppe (eds), *Arthur in the Celtic Languages* (Cardiff, 2019), pp. 187–202

Lewis, Barry, 'Approaching the Genealogies of the Welsh Saints', in David N. Parsons and Paul Russell (eds), *Seintiau Cymru, Sancti Cambrenses Astudiaethau ar Seintiau Cymru Studies in the Saints of Wales* (Aberystwyth, 2022)

Lewis, Barry (ed.), *Bonedd y Saint: An Edition and Study of the Genealogies of the Welsh Saints* (Dublin, 2023)

Lewis, C. P., 'Gruffudd ap Cynan and the Normans', in Kari L. Maund (ed.), *Gruffudd ap Cynan: A Collaborative Biography* (Woodbridge, 1996), pp. 61–78

Lewis, C. P., 'Welsh Territories and Welsh Identities in Late Anglo-Saxon England', in N. J. Higham (ed.), *Britons in Anglo-Saxon England* (Woodbridge, 2007), pp. 130–43

Lewis, Ceri (ed. and trans.), *Rhagymadroddion a Chyflwyniadau Lladin, 1551–1632* (Caerdydd, 1980)

Lewis, George Cornewall, *Pedigree of the family of Lewis of Harpton* (London, 1862)

Lewis, Henry (ed.), *Brut Dingestow* (Cardiff, 1942)

Lewis, J. S[aunders]., 'The present state of Welsh drama', *Welsh Outlook*, 6/12 (December 1919), 302–4

Leyser, K., 'England and the Empire in the Early Twelfth Century', *Transactions of the Royal Historical Society*, 5th series, 10 (1960), 61–84

Lieberman, Max, *The March of Wales, 1067–1300: A Borderland of Medieval Britain* (Cardiff, 2008)

Lloyd, D. Myrddin, 'Barddoniaeth Cynddelw Brydydd Mawr II: Canu i Owain Gwynedd', *Y Llenor*, 13 (1934), 49–59

Lloyd, D. Myrddin, 'William Salesbury and "Epistol E.M. at y Cembru"', *NLWJ*, 2 (1941–2), 14–16

Lloyd, John Edward, *A History of Wales from the Earliest Times to the Edwardian Conquest*, 2 vols (3rd edn, London, 1939)

Lloyd, Thomas, 'Country-house libraries of the eighteenth and nineteenth centuries', in Philip Henry Jones and Eiluned Rees (eds), *A Nation and its Books: A History of the Book in Wales* (Aberystwyth, 1998), pp. 135–46

Lloyd, William V., *The Sheriffs of Montgomeryshire* (London, 1878)

Lloyd, William V., *Pedigrees of Montgomeryshire Families* (London, 1888)

Lloyd-Jones, J., *Geirfa Barddoniaeth Gynnar Gymraeg*, 2 vols (Cardiff, 1931–63)

Lloyd-Morgan, Ceridwen, 'Manuscripts and the Monasteries', in Janet Burton and Karen Stöber (eds), *Monastic Wales: New Approaches* (Cardiff, 2013), pp. 209–27

Llwyd, Angharad, 'Catalogue of Welsh Manuscripts', *Transactions of the Cymmrodorion*, 2 (1828), 36–58

Llwyd, Angharad, *History of the Island of Mona, or Anglesey, including an Account of its natural Productions, Druidical Antiquities, Eminent Men ... being the Prize Essay to which was adjudged the first Premium at the Royal Beaumaris Eisteddfod which was held in the Month of August, 1832* (Rhuthin, 1833)

Lodder, Matt, '"Things of the sea": iconographic continuities between tattooing and handicraft in Georgian-era maritime culture', *Sculpture Journal*, 24/2 (2015), 195–210

Lodder, Matt, *Painted People: Humanity in 21 Tattoos* (London, 2022)

Löffler, Marion, *The Literary and Historical Legacy of Iolo Morganwg* (Cardiff, 2007)

Löffler, Marion, 'Olion Llenyddol Ymwelwyr â Llanofer', *Llên Cymru*, 41/11 (2018), 53–88

Löffler, Marion, '"Hen Wlad Fy Nhadau" a "The Land of My Fathers": Diwylliant Darostyngol yng Ngwasanaeth yr Ymerodraeth Brydeinig', *Llafur*, 13 (2022), 67–81

Löffler, Marion, '"Generation 1789": Welsh Dissenters and radicals lost in translation', in Matthew Roberts (ed.), *Memory and Modern British Politics: Commemoration, Tradition, Legacy* (London, 2024), pp. 35–65

Löffler, Marion, and Gethin Rhys, 'Thomas Stephens and the Abergavenny Cymreigyddion: Letters from the *Cambrian* 1842–3', *NLWJ*, 34/4 (2009), 399–451

Lord, Peter, *Y Chwaer Dduwies: Celf, Crefft a'r Eisteddfod* (Llandysul, 1992)

Lord, Peter, *Imaging the Nation* (Cardiff, 2000)

Lord, Peter, *Medieval Vision* (Cardiff, 2003)

Lowe, Kathryn A., 'The Development of the Anglo-Saxon Boundary Clause', *Nomina*, 21 (1998), 63–100

Lowe, Rachel J., *Farm and its inhabitants with some account of the Lloyds of Dolobran* (London, 1883)

Luard, Henry Richards (ed.), *Annales Monastici*, 5 vols (London, 1864–9)

Luard, Henry Richards (ed.), *Matthaei Parisiensis, Monachi Sancti Albani, Chronica Majora*, 7 vols (London, 1872–80)

Luard, Henry Richards (ed.), *Flores Historiarum*, 3 vols (London, 1890)

Ludtke, Alf (ed.), *The History of Everyday Life: Reconstructing Historical Experiences and Ways of Life* (Princeton, 1995)

Luft, Diana, 'The NLW Peniarth 32 Latin Chronicle', *Studia Celtica*, 44 (2010), 47–70

Luft, Diana, Peter Wynn Thomas and D. Mark Smith (eds), *Rhyddiaith Gymraeg 1300–1425* (Caerdydd, 2007–13), http://www.rhyddiaithganoloesol.caerdydd.ac.uk/cy/ (accessed 24 June 2024)

Lyte, H. C. Maxwell, *Calendar of Close Rolls, Edward II: 1318–1323* (London, 1895)

Lyte, H. C. Maxwell, *Calendar of Close Rolls, Edward III: 1333–1337* (London, 1898)

Mac Cana, Proinsais, *The Mabinogi* (2nd edn, Cardiff, 1992)

MacLure, Millar, *The Paul's Cross Sermons* (Toronto, 1958)

McCabe, Michael, *New York City Tattoo: The Oral History of an Urban Art* (San Francisco, 2013)

McCullough, Peter E., *Sermons at Court: Politics and religion in Elizabethan and Jacobean preaching* (Cambridge, 1998)

McCullough, Peter Eugene, 'The sermon at the court of Elizabeth I, 1558–1603', (unpublished PhD thesis, Princeton University, 1992)

MacDiarmada, Mary, *Art O'Brien and Irish Nationalism in London, 1900–25* (Dublin, 2020)

McKee, Helen, *The Cambridge Juvencus Manuscript Glossed in Latin, Old Welsh, and Old Irish* (Aberystwyth, 2000)

McKinley, R. A., *A History of British Surnames* (London and New York, 1990)

McKisack, May, *Medieval History in the Tudor Age* (Oxford, 1971)

MacLysaght, Edward, *Irish Families: Their Names, Arms and Origins* (Dublin, 1957)

MacLysaght, Edward, *The Surnames of Ireland* (Dublin, 1985)

Madden, F. (ed.), *Matthaei Parisiensis, monachi Sancti Albani, Historia Anglorum, sive, ut vulgo dicitur, Historia Minor. Item, ejusdem Abbreviatio Chronicorum Angliae*, 3 vols (London, 1866)

Mann, Robin, and Steve Fenton, *Nation, class and resentment: The politics of national identity in England, Scotland and Wales* (London, 2017)

Marshall, Peter, *Beliefs and the Dead in Reformation England* (Oxford, 2002)

Martell, Owen, 'Mae'r pasiant trosodd ym Mro Morgannwg (am flwyddyn arall, beth bynnag): Iolo Morganwg, yr Orsedd a'r Eisteddfod Genedlaethol', *Tu Chwith*, 10 (1998), 76–97

Maund, Kari, *A Handlist of the Acts of Welsh Rulers* (Cardiff, 1996)

Meecham-Jones, Simon, 'Style, Truth and Irony: Listening to the Voice of Gerald of Wales's Writings', in Henley and McMullen (eds), *Gerald of Wales*, pp. 127–43

Meyrick, Samuel Rush, *The History and Antiquities of the County of Cardigan* (London, 1808)

Meyrick, Samuel Rush, *Heraldic Visitations of Wales and Parts of the Marches between 1586 and 1613 … by Lewys Dwnn* (Llandovery, 1846)

Migne, J. P. (ed.), *Patrologiae Cursus Completus. Series Latina*, 221 vols (1841–55), http://patristica.net/latina/ (accessed 30 November 2023)

Miles, Dillwyn, *The Secret of the Bards of the Isle of Britain* (Llandybïe, 1992)

Miller-Idriss, Cynthia, 'Soldier, sailor, rebel, rule-breaker: masculinity and the body in the German far right', *Gender and Education*, 29/2 (2017), 199–215

Millor, W. J., and H. E. Butler, rev. C. N. L. Brooke (ed.), *The Letters of John of Salisbury. Volume 1: The Early Letters (1153–1161)* (Oxford, 1986)

Milne, Esther, *Letters, Postcards, E-mail: Technologies of Presence* (Abingdon, 2010)

Miskell, Peter, *A Social History of the Cinema in Wales, 1918–1951: Pulpits, Coal Pits and Fleapits* (Cardiff, 2006)

Molyneaux, George, *The Formation of the English Kingdom in the Tenth Century* (Oxford, 2015)

Mooney, Canice, *The Church in Gaelic Ireland: Thirteenth to Fifteenth Centuries*, History of Irish Catholicism, 2 (Dublin, 1969)

Moore, Donald, 'Cambrian Meetings 1847–1997', *Archaeologia Cambrensis*, 147 (1998), 3–55

Morgan, Kenneth O., *Wales in British Politics, 1868–1922* (Cardiff, 1991)

Morgan, Prys, 'From a Death to a View: The Hunt for the Welsh Past in the Romantic Period', in Eric Hobsbawm and Terence Ranger (eds), *The Invention of Tradition* (Cambridge, 1983), pp. 43–100

Morgan, Prys, 'The Gwerin of Wales – Myth and Reality', in Ian Hume and W. T. R. Pryce (eds), *The Welsh and their Country* (Llandysul, 1986), pp. 134–52

Morgan, Prys, 'The Rise of Welsh Hereditary Surnames', *Nomina*, 10 (1986), 121–35

Morgan, Prys, 'A Nation of Nonconformists: Thomas Rees and Nonconformist History', in Pryce and Evans (eds), *Writing a Small Nation's Past*, pp. 97–110

Morgan, Richard, 'Place-names in the Northern Marches of Wales', in Oliver J. Padel and David Parsons (eds), *A Commodity of Good Names: Essays in Honour of Margaret Gelling* (Donnington, 2008), pp. 204–16

Morgan, T. J., and Prys Morgan, *Welsh Surnames* (Cardiff, 1985)

Morrice, J. C. (ed.), *Barddoniaeth Wiliam Llŷn* (Bangor, 1908)

Morris, J. (ed.), *Nennius: British History and the Welsh Annals* (Chichester, 1980)

Morris, T. E., 'Welsh Surnames in the Border Counties of Wales', *Y Cymmrodor*, 43 (1932), 93–173

Mueller, Simon M. et al., 'Role of tattoos in football: Behavioural Patterns and success – analysis of the FIFA World Cup 2018', *Clinics in Dermatology*, 38 (2020), 788–92

Mullally, E. (ed. and trans.), *The Deeds of the Normans in Ireland: La geste des Engleis en Yrlande* (Dublin, 2002)

Mynors, R. A. B., *Catalogue of the Manuscripts of Balliol College, Oxford* (Oxford, 1963)

Mynors, R. A. B., R. M. Thomson and M. Winterbottom (ed. and trans.), *William of Malmesbury, Gesta Regum Anglorum, The History of the English Kings*, 2 vols (Oxford, 2006)

Nicholas, Thomas, *The History and Antiquities of Glamorganshire and its Families* (London, 1874)

Nicholls, K. W., *Gaelic and Gaelicized Ireland in the Middle Ages* (2nd edn, Dublin, 2003)

Nichols, John (ed.), *Progresses and Public Processions of Queen Elizabeth*, 3 vols (London, 1823)

Norris, Herbert, *Costume and Fashion: The Evolution of European Dress through the Earlier Ages* (London, 1924)

Ó Corráin, Donnchadh, and Fidelma Maguire, *Gaelic Personal Names* (Dublin, 1981)

Ó Cuív, Brian, 'Aspects of Irish Personal Names', *Celtica*, 18 (1986), 151–84

Ó Muraíle, Nollaig, 'The Learned Family of Ó Cianáin/Keenan', *Clogher Historical Society*, 18/3 (2005), 387–436

Ó Muraíle, Nollaig, 'The Ó Ceallaigh Rulers of Uí Mhaine – A Genealogical Fragment, *c*.1400: Part I', *Journal of the Galway Archaeological and Historical Society*, 60 (2008), 32–77

O'Connor, Marion F., 'Theatre of the Empire: "Shakespeare's England" at Earl's Court, 1912', in Jean E. Howard and Marion F. O'Connor (eds), *Shakespeare Reproduced: The Text in History and Ideology* (Abingdon, 2005), pp. 86–96

O'Leary, Paul, 'The languages of patriotism in Wales, 1840–1880', in Geraint H. Jenkins (ed.), *The Welsh Language and its Social Domains, 1801–1911* (Cardiff, 2000), pp. 533–60

O'Leary, Paul, 'Town and Nation: Writing Urban Histories in nineteenth- and early twentieth-century Wales', in Pryce and Evans (eds), *Writing a Small Nation's Past*, pp. 209–22

Okey, Robin, *Towards Modern Nationhood: Wales and Slovenia in Comparison. 1750–1914* (Cardiff, 2023)

Olick, Jeffrey K., Vered Vinitzky-Seroussi and Daniel Levy (eds), *The Collective Memory Reader* (Oxford, 2011)

Olson, Katharine, and Huw Pryce, 'A Reluctant Medievalist?', in Geraint H. Jenkins and Gareth Elwyn Jones (eds), *Degrees of Influence: A Memorial Volume for Glanmor Williams* (Cardiff, 2008), pp. 30–57

Oram, Richard, *Domination and Lordship: Scotland 1070–1230* (Edinburgh, 2011)

Orpen, G. H. (ed. and trans.), *The Song of Dermot and the Earl* (Oxford, 1892)

Orpen, G. H., *Ireland under the Normans, 1169–1333*, 4 vols (Oxford, 1911, 1920; repr. as a single vol. Dublin, 2005)

Owen, Aneurin, 'Catalogue of Welsh Manuscripts', *Transactions of the Cymmrodorion*, 2/4 (1843), 400–18

Owen, Henry, *Old Pembrokeshire Families* (London, 1902)

Owen, Henry (ed.), *The Description of Penbrokshire by George Owen of Henllys*, 4 vols (London, 1892–1936)

Owen, Morfydd, 'Royal Propaganda: Stories from the Law-Texts', in Morfydd Owen, Paul Russell and Thomas Charles-Edwards (eds), *The Welsh King and his Court* (Cardiff, 2000)

Owen, Tomos, 'London-Welsh writing, 1890–1915: Ernest Rhys, Arthur Machen, W. H. Davies, and Caradoc Evans' (unpublished PhD thesis, Cardiff University, 2011)

Padel, Oliver J., 'Two New Pre-Conquest Charters for Cornwall', *Journal of Cornish Studies*, 6 (1978), 20–7

Padel, Oliver J., 'The Charter of Lanlawren (Cornwall)', in Katherine O'Brien O'Keeffe and Andy Orchard (eds), *Latin Learning and English Lore: Studies in Anglo-Saxon Literature for Michael Lapidge* (Toronto, 2005), pp. 74–85

Parry, Edward, 'Essay containing an Historical Account of the Flintshire Castles; by Mr. Edward Parry, Chester', in *The Gwyneddon; or An Account of the Royal Eisteddfod, Held in September, 1828: Together with the Prize Essays and Poems on the Subjects Proposed for Adjudication at that Meeting* (Chester, 1830), p. 49

Parry, John Jay (ed.), *Brut y Brenhinedd, Cotton Cleopatra Version* (Cambridge, MA, 1937)

Patterson, R. B., *The Scriptorium of Margam Abbey and the Scribes of Early Angevin Glamorgan* (Woodbridge, 2002)

Phillimore, Egerton G. B., 'A Fragment from Hengwrt MS. No. 202', *Y Cymmrodor*, 7 (1886), 89–154

Phillipps, Thomas, *Glamorgan Pedigrees* (Worcester, 1845)

Phillipps, Thomas, *Pedigrees of Caermarthenshire, Cardiganshire and Pembrokeshire* (Worcester, 1859)

Phillips, J. R. S. (ed.), *The Justices of the Peace in Wales and Monmouthshire, 1541–1689* (Cardiff, 1975)

Phillips, J. Roland, *A List of the Sheriffs of Cardiganshire* (Carmarthen, 1868)

Phillips, J. Roland, *Memoirs of the Ancient Family of Owen of Orielton* (London, 1886)

Piette, Gwenno, *Brittany: A Concise History* (Cardiff, 2008)

Poole, Edwin, *The Illustrated History and Biography of Brecknockshire* (Brecknock, 1886)

Poole, Reginald Lane and Mary Bateson (eds), *John Bale's Index of British and Other Writers* (Oxford, 1902)

Postles, David A., 'The Baptismal Name in Thirteenth-century England: Processes and Patterns', *Medieval Prosopography*, 13/2 (1992), 1–52

Postles, David A., *Naming the People of England, c.1100–1350* (Newcastle, 2006)
Powel, David, *A Historie of Cambria, now called Wales* ... (London, 1584)
Pressutti, P. (ed.), *Regesta Honorii Papae III, Iussu et Munificentia Leonis XIII Pontificis Maximi ex Vaticanis Archetypis Aliisque Fontibus*, 2 vols (Rome, 1888–95)
Price, R. J. Lloyd, *The History of Rulace, or Rhiwlas* (1899)
Pryce, Arthur Ivor, *The Diocese of Bangor in the Sixteenth Century* (Bangor, 1923)
Pryce, Huw, 'The Church of Trefeglwys and the End of the "Celtic" Charter Tradition in Twelfth-century Wales', *CMCS*, 25 (1993), 15–54
Pryce, Huw, *Native Law and the Church in Medieval Wales* (Oxford, 1993)
Pryce, Huw, 'Owain Gwynedd and Louis VII: the Franco-Welsh Diplomacy of the First Prince of Wales', *WHR*, 19 (1998), 1–28
Pryce, Huw, 'Esgobaeth Bangor yn Oes y Tywysogion', in W. P. Griffith (ed.), '*Ysbryd Deallturus ac Enaid Anfarwol*': *Ysgrifau ar Hanes Crefydd yng Ngwynedd* (Bangor, 1999), pp. 37–57
Pryce, Huw, 'British or Welsh? National Identity in Twelfth-century Wales', *English Historical Review*, 116/468 (2001), 775–801
Pryce, Huw, 'The Medieval Church', in J. Beverley Smith and Llinos Beverley Smith (eds), *History of Merioneth. Volume II. The Middle Ages* (Cardiff, 2001), pp. 254–96
Pryce, Huw, 'Negotiating Anglo-Welsh Relations: Llywelyn the Great and Henry III', in I. W. Rowlands and B. K. U. Weiler (eds), *England and Europe in the Reign of Henry III (1216–1272)* (London, 2002), pp. 13–29
Pryce, Huw, 'Uses of the Vernacular in the Acts of Welsh Rulers 1120–1283', in *La langue des actes: Actes du XIe Congrès international de diplomatique* (Troyes, jeudi 11–Samedi 13 septembre 2003), at *http://elec.enc.sorbonne.fr/CID2003/pryce* (accessed 6 November 2023)
Pryce, Huw, 'Culture, power and the charters of Welsh rulers', in Marie Therese Flanagan and Judith Green (eds), *Charters and Charter Scholarship in Britain and Ireland* (London, 2005), pp. 184–202
Pryce, Huw, 'Patrons and Patronage among the Cistercians in Wales', *Archaeologia Cambrensis*, 154 (2007), 81–95
Pryce, Huw, 'Welsh Rulers and European Change', in Huw Pryce and John Watts (eds), *Power and Identity in the Middle Ages: Essays in Memory of Sir Rees Davies* (Oxford, 2007), pp. 37–51
Pryce, Huw, 'Anglo-Welsh Agreements, 1201–77', in R. A. Griffiths and P. R. Schofield (eds), *Wales and the Welsh in the Middle Ages: Essays Presented to J. B. Smith* (Cardiff, 2011), pp. 1–19
Pryce, Huw, 'Culture, Identity and the Medieval Revival in Victorian Wales', *Proceedings of the Harvard Celtic Colloquium*, 31 (2011), 1–40

Pryce, Huw, 'Gerald of Wales, Gildas and the *Descriptio Kambriae*', in Fiona Edmonds and Paul Russell (eds), *Tome: Studies in Medieval Celtic History and Law in Honour of Thomas Charles-Edwards* (Woodbridge, 2011), pp. 115–24

Pryce, Huw, *J. E. Lloyd and the Creation of Welsh History: Renewing a Nation's Past* (Cardiff, 2011)

Pryce, Huw, 'Cofio Glyndŵr', *Trafodion Anrhydeddus Gymdeithas y Cymmrodorion*, 22 (2016), 43–60

Pryce, Huw, 'Giraldus and the Geraldines', in Peter Crooks and Seán Duffy (eds), *The Geraldines and Medieval Ireland: The Making of a Myth* (Dublin, 2016), pp. 53–68

Pryce, Huw, 'Medieval Welsh History in the Victorian Age', *CMCS*, 71 (summer 2016), 1–28

Pryce, Huw, 'Gerald of Wales and the Welsh Past', in Henley and McMullen (eds), *Gerald of Wales*, pp. 19–45

Pryce, Huw, 'Chronicling and its contexts in medieval Wales', in Guy et al. (eds), *Chronicles of Medieval Wales and the March*, pp. 1–32

Pryce, Huw, 'Gerald of Wales: Medieval Ethnographer of the Welsh', in W. John Morgan and Fiona Bowie (eds), *Social Anthropologies of the Welsh: Past and Present* (Canon Pyon, 2021), pp. 41–55

Pryce, Huw, *Writing Welsh History: From the Early Middle Ages to the Twenty-first Century* (Oxford, 2022)

Pryce, Huw, and Gwilym Owen, 'Medieval Welsh Law and the Mid-Victorian Foreshore', *Journal of Legal History*, 35/2 (2014), 172–99

Pryce, Huw, and Neil Evans (eds), *Writing a Small Nation's Past: Wales in Comparative Perspective, 1850–1950* (Farnham, 2013)

Pryce, Huw, with Charles Insley (ed.), *The Acts of Welsh Rulers 1100–1283* (Cardiff, 2005)

Pryce, W. T. R., 'Region or National Territory? Regionalism and the Idea of the Country of Wales *c*.1927–1998', *WHR*, 23 (2006), 99–152

Reaney, Percy H., *The Origin of English Surnames* (London, 1987)

Reed, M., 'Anglo-Saxon charter boundaries', in Michael Reed (ed.), *Discovering Past Landscapes* (London, 1984), pp. 261–306

Rees, Eiluned, 'An introductory survey of 18th century Welsh libraries', *Journal of the Welsh Bibliographical Society*, 10/4 (1971), 197–258

Rees, Eiluned, 'Pre-1820 Welsh subscription lists', *Journal of the Welsh Bibliographical Society*, 11/1–2 (1973–4), 85–119

Rees, R. D., 'Electioneering ideals current in South Wales, 1790–1830', *WHR*, 2 (1964), 233–50

Rees, W. J., 'Welsh Literary Societies', *The Cambro-Briton*, 3 (1822), 224–33

Reeve, Michael D., and Neil Wright (eds), *Geoffrey of Monmouth, the History of the Kings of Britain: An Edition and Translation of De gestis Britonum (Historia Regum Britanniae)* (Woodbridge, 2007)

Refaussé, Raymond, and Colm Lennon, *The Registers of Christ Church Cathedral, Dublin* (Dublin, 1998)

Reggiani, Andrés, and Pablo Scharagrodsky, 'Building a Disciplined and Efficient Body: Nationalism, Eugenics and Physical Culture in Interwar Argentina', *History of Sport*, 39/15 (2022), 1591–1610

Rejhon, A. C., 'Hu Gadarn: Folklore and Fabrication', in Patrick K. Ford (ed.), *Celtic Folklore and Christianity: Studies in Memory of William W. Heist* (Santa Barbara, CA, 1983), pp. 201–12

Rhys, Ernest, *A London Rose & Other Rhymes* (London, 1894)

Richards, Melville (ed.), *Breudwyt Ronabwy Allan o'r Llyfr Coch o Hergest* (Cardiff, 1948)

Richards, Melville, 'Gwŷr, Gwragedd a Gwehelyth', *Transactions of the Honourable Society of the Cymmrodorion* (1965), 27–45

Ridyard, Susan J., and Jeremy A. Ashbee, 'The Resuscitation of Roger of Conwy: a Cantilupe Miracle and the Society of Edwardian North Wales', in C. A. M. Clarke (ed.), *Power, Identity and Miracles on a Medieval Frontier* (Abingdon, 2017), pp. 61–76. First published in the *Journal of Medieval History*, 41/3 (2015), 309–24

Riley, H. T. (ed.), *Gesta Abbatum Monasterii Sancti Albani a Thoma Walsingham* (London, 1867)

Riordan, Michael, 'Materials for History? Publishing records as a historical practice in eighteenth- and nineteenth-century England', *History of Humanities*, 2/1 (2017), 51–77

Roberts, Brynley F., 'The Treatment of Personal Names in the Early Welsh Versions of *Historia regum Britanniae*', *BBCS*, 25 (1972–4), 274–90

Roberts, Brynley F. (ed.), *Cyfranc Lludd a Llefelys* (Dublin, 1975)

Roberts, Brynley F., 'Fersiwn Dingestow o *Brut y Brenhinedd*', *BBCS*, 27 (1976–8), 331–61

Roberts, Brynley F. (ed.), *Brut y Brenhinedd: Llanstephan MS. 1 Version* (Dublin, 1984)

Roberts, Brynley F., 'Geoffrey of Monmouth, *Historia Regum Britanniae* and *Brut y Brenhinedd*', in Rachel Bromwich, A. O. H. Jarman and Brynley F. Roberts (eds), *The Arthur of the Welsh: The Arthurian Legend in Medieval Welsh Literature* (Cardiff, 1991), pp. 97–119

Roberts, Brynley F., 'Scholarly Publishing 1820–1922', in Philip Henry Jones and Eiluned Rees (eds), *A Nation and its Books: A History of the Book in Wales* (Aberystwyth, 1998), pp. 221–35

Roberts, Brynley F., '"The Age of Restitution": Taliesin ab Iolo and the Reception of Iolo Morganwg', in Geraint H. Jenkins (ed.), *A Rattleskull Genius: The Many Faces of Iolo Morganwg* (Cardiff, 2005), pp. 461–79

Roberts, Brynley F. (ed.), *Breudwyt Maxen Wledic* (Dublin, 2005)

Roberts, Edward, 'Boundary Clauses and the Use of the Vernacular in Eastern Frankish Charters, *c.*750–*c.*900', *Historical Research*, 91 (2018), 580–604

Roberts, Edward, and Francesca Tinti, 'Signalling language choice in Anglo-Saxon and Frankish charters, *c.*700–*c.*900', in Robert Gallagher, Edward Roberts and Francesca Tinti (eds), *The Languages of Early Medieval Charters: Latin, Germanic Vernaculars, and the Written Word* (Leiden, 2021), pp. 188–229

Roberts, Gwyneth Tyson, *Jane Williams, Ysgafell* (Cardiff, 2020)

Roberts, J., *Druidical Remains and Antiquities of the Ancient Britons, Principally in Glamorgan; Containing a General Account of the Same, in England, Wales, Scotland, France, &c.; with Notes and Illustrations on the Learning and Superstitions of the Druids – The Downfall of Druidism as a Religious System – and the Introduction of Christianity into Britain* (Swansea, 1842)

Roberts, J. Askew, *Wynnstay and the Wynns* (Oswestry, 1876)

Roberts, William, and Simone Clarke (eds), *Women and Gender in Early Modern Wales* (Cardiff, 2000)

Rosenthal, Joel T., 'Names and Naming Patterns in Medieval England: An Introduction', in Dave Postles and Joel T. Rosenthal (eds), *Studies on the Personal Name in Later Medieval England and Wales* (Kalamazoo, 2006), pp. 1–6

Roth, F. (ed.), *The English Austin Friars, 1249–1538*, 2 vols (New York, 1961)

Rowlands, John, and Sheila Rowlands, *The Surnames of Wales. Updated & Expanded* (Llandysul, 2013)

Rowlands, Sheila, 'The Surnames of Wales', in John Rowlands and Sheila Rowlands (eds), *Welsh Family History: A Guide to Research* (Birmingham, 1998), pp. 59–75

Rowlands, William, *Cambrian Bibliography*, ed. D. Silvan Evans (Llanidloes, 1869)

Rule, M. (ed.), *Eadmeri Historia Novorum in Anglia* (London, 1884)

Runciman, David, 'Pastoral care according to the bishops of England and Wales (*c.*1170–1228)' (unpublished PhD thesis, University of Cambridge, 2019)

Russell, Paul (ed. and trans.), *Vita Griffini filii Conani* (Cardiff, 2005)

Russell, Paul, '*Priuilegium Sancti Teliaui* and *Breint Teilo*', *Studia Celtica*, 50 (2016), 41–68

Rymer, Thomas (ed.), *Foedera, Conventiones, Literæ, et cujuscunque generis Acta Publica Inter Reges Angliae...*, 10 vols (3rd edn, The Hague, 1739–45)

Sanders, Clinton R., 'Marks of Mischief: Becoming and Being Tattooed', *Journal of Contemporary Ethnography*, 16 (1988), 395–432

Sawyer, P. H., *Anglo-Saxon Charters: An Annotated List and Bibliography* (London, 1968)

Seaman, Andy, 'Llywarch Hen's Dyke: Place and Narrative in Early Medieval Wales', *Offa's Dyke Journal*, 1 (2019), 96–113

Seaman, Andy, '*Finnaun y Doudec Seint*: A Holy Spring in Early Medieval Brycheiniog, Wales', in Celeste Ray (ed.), *Sacred Waters: A Cross-cultural Compendium of Hallowed Springs and Holy Wells* (London, 2020), pp. 194–210

Scott, A. B., and F. X. Martin (ed.), *Expugnatio Hibernica: The Conquest of Ireland* (Dublin, 1978)

Scully, Diarmuid, 'The portrayal of Ireland in Bernard's Life of Malachy', in Damian Bracken and Dagmar Ó Riain-Raedel (eds), *Ireland and Europe in the Twelfth Century* (Dublin, 2006), pp. 239–56

Sharpe, Richard, *A Handlist of the Latin Writers of Great Britain and Ireland before 1540, with additions and corrections* (Turnhout, 2001)

Sharpe, Richard, 'The use of writs in the Eleventh Century', *Anglo-Saxon England*, 32 (2003), 247–91

Sheehy, M. P. (ed.), *Pontificia Hibernica*, 2 vols (Dublin, 1962)

Shercliff, Rebecca, 'Arthur in *Trioedd Ynys Prydain*', in Ceridwen Lloyd Morgan and Erich Poppe (eds), *Arthur in the Celtic Languages* (Cardiff, 2019), pp. 173–86

Siddons, Michael Powell, 'Welsh Equestrian Seals', *NLWJ*, 23 (1983–4), 292–318

Siddons, Michael Powell, *Welsh Pedigree Rolls* (Aberystwyth, 1996)

Singer, Peter, *Hegel: A Very Short Introduction* (Oxford, 2001)

Sims-Williams, Patrick, 'The Emergence of Old Welsh, Cornish and Breton Orthography, 600–800: The Evidence of Archaic Old Welsh', *BBCS*, 38 (1991), 20–86

Sims-Williams, Patrick, 'Edward IV's Confirmation Charter for Clynnog Fawr', in Colin Richmond and Isobel Harvey (eds), *Recognitions: Essays Presented to Edmund Fryde* (Aberystwyth, 1996), pp. 229–42

Sims-Williams, Patrick, 'Clas Beuno and the Four Branches of the Mabinogi', in Bernhard Maier, Stefan Zimmer and Christiane Batke (eds), *150 'Jahre Mabinogion' – Deutsch-Walisische Kulturbeziehungen* (Tübingen, 2001), pp. 111–27

Sims-Williams, Patrick, *Rhai Addasiadau Cymraeg Canol o Sieffre o Fynwy* (Aberystwyth, 2011)

Sims-Williams, Patrick, *The Book of Llandaf as a Historical Source* (Woodbridge, 2019)

Sims-Williams, Patrick, '"Dark" and "Clear" *Y* in Medieval Welsh Orthography: Caligula Versus Teilo', *Transactions of the Philological Society*, 119 (2021), 1–39

Smith, Brendan, 'The Armagh-Clogher Dispute and the "Mellifont Conspiracy": Diocesan Politics and Monastic Reform in Early Thirteenth Century Ireland', *Seanchas Ardmhacha: Journal of the Armagh Diocesan Historical Society*, 14/2 (1991), 26–38

Smith, Christopher, 'William Owen Stanley of Penrhos', *Archaeologia Cambrensis*, 133 (1984), 83–90

Smith, David M., *The Heads of Religious Houses: England and Wales, III: 1377–1540* (Cambridge, 2008)

Smith, David M., *The Heads of Religious Houses: England and Wales Supplement* (Cluj-Napoca, Romania, 2019)

Smith, J. Beverley, 'The "Cronica de Wallia" and the Dynasty of Dinefwr', *BBCS*, 20 (1962–4), 261–82

Smith, J. Beverley, *Llywelyn ap Gruffudd, Prince of Wales* (Cardiff, 1998)

Smith, J. Beverley, 'Historical writing in medieval Wales: the composition of *Brenhinedd y Saesson*', *Studia Celtica*, 52 (2008), 55–86

Smith, Lucy Toulmin (ed.), *The Itinerary of John Leland in or about the years 1535–1543: Parts IX, X and XI* (London, 1910)

Spence, John, 'Genealogies of Noble Families in Anglo-Norman', in Raluca L. Radulescu and Edward Donald Kennedy (eds), *Broken Lines: Genealogical Literature in Medieval Britain and France*, Medieval Texts and Cultures of Northern Europe, 16 (Turnhout, 2008), pp. 63–78

Spence, John, *Reimagining History in Anglo-Norman Prose Chronicles* (Woodbridge and Rochester, 2013)

Stalley, Roger, *The Cistercian Monasteries of Ireland: An Account of the History, Art, and Architecture of the White Monks in Ireland from 1142–1540* (London and New Haven, 1987)

Stamp, A. E. (ed.), *Calendar of Patent Rolls, Henry IV. Vol. II. A.D. 1401–1405* (London, 1905)

Stamp, A. E. (ed.), *Calendar of Close Rolls, Henry IV: Vol. II. A.D. 1402–1405* (London, 1929)

Stead, Phil, *Red Dragons: The Story of Welsh Football* (Talybont, 2022)

Stecko-Zukowska, Agnieszka, 'The Poachers of Instagram – Tattoo Artists in Poland and their Tactics in Social Media', *Studia Humanistyczne AGH*, 21/2 (2022), 41–58

Stenton, Doris M. (ed.), *The Great Roll of the Pipe for the ninth year of the reign of King Richard the First* (London, printed for the Pipe Roll Society, 1931)

Stenton, Doris M. (ed.), *The Great Roll of the Pipe for the tenth year of the reign of King Richard the First* (London, printed for the Pipe Roll Society, 1932)

Stenton, Doris M. (ed.), *Pleas before the King and his Justices, 1198–1212*, 4 vols (London, 1952–67)

Stephens, Matthew Frank, *The Economy of Medieval Wales, 1067–1536* (Cardiff, 2019)

Stephens, R., 'Gwaith Wiliam Llŷn', 3 vols (unpublished PhD thesis, University of Wales, 1983)

Stephens, Thos, 'Eisteddfod Iforawl Merthyr, 1855. Y Feirniadaeth', *Seren Gomer*, 38/482 (Tachwedd 1855), 499

Stephens, Thos, 'An Essay on the Bardic Alphabet called "Coelbren y Beirdd"', *Archaeologia Cambrensis*, fourth series, 3/11 (1872), 181–210

Stephenson, David, *The Governance of Gwynedd* (Cardiff, 1984)

Stephenson, David, *The Aberconwy Chronicle*, Kathleen Hughes Memorial Lectures on Mediaeval Welsh History, 2 (Cambridge, 2002)

Stephenson, David, 'Gerald of Wales and Annales Cambriae', *CMCS*, 60 (2010), 23–37

Stephenson, David, 'The chronicler at Cwm-hir abbey 1257–63', in R. A. Griffiths and P. R. Schofield (eds), *Wales and the Welsh in the Middle Ages* (Cardiff, 2011), pp. 29–45

Stephenson, David, 'In search of a Welsh chronicler: the *Annales Cambriae* B-text for 1204–30', *CMCS*, 72 (2016), 73–85

Stephenson, David, *Medieval Powys: Kingdom, Principality and Lordships, 1132–1293* (Woodbridge, 2016)

Stephenson, David, *Medieval Wales, c.1050–1334: Centuries of Ambiguity* (Cardiff, 2019)

Stephenson, David, 'The Continuation of *Brut y Tywysogyon* in NLW, MS Peniarth 20 Revisited', in Guy et al. (eds), *Chronicles of Medieval Wales and the March*, pp. 155–68

Stevens, Catrin, 'Cywydd i Ofyn March i Ddafydd Conwy, Prior Beddgelert', *Transactions of the Caernarvonshire Historical Society*, 37 (1976), 43–57

Stevens, Christine, 'Welsh Peasant Dress – Workwear or National Costume?', *Textile History*, 33/1 (2002), 63–78

Stöber, Karen, 'The Cistercians and the Bards – Praise and Patronage in Fifteenth-century Wales', in Dylan Foster Evans, Barry J. Lewis and Ann Parry Owen (eds), *'Gwalch Cywyddau Gwŷr': Ysgrifau ar Guto'r Glyn a Chymru'r Bymthegfed Ganrif. Essays on Guto'r Glyn and Fifteenth-century Wales* (Aberystwyth, 2013), pp. 305–26

Stöber, Karen, 'Island Monasteries in Medieval Wales', in Gabriela Signori (ed.), *Inselklöster – Klosterinseln: Topographie und Toponymie einer monastischen Formation* (Berlin, 2019), pp. 83–99

Strype, John (ed.), *The Life and Acts of Matthew Parker: The first Archbishop of Canterbury, in the reign of Queen Elizabeth*, 4 vols (Oxford, 1821)

Strype, John (ed.), *Memorials of … Thomas Cranmer*, 2 vols (new edn, Oxford, 1840)

Suggett, Richard, 'Church-building in Late Medieval Wales', in R. A. Griffiths and P. R. Schofield (eds), *Wales and the Welsh in the Middle Ages: Essays Presented to J. Beverley Smith* (Cardiff, 2011), pp. 180–202.

Suppe, Frederick 'Who was Rhys Sais? Some Comments on Anglo-Welsh Relations before 1066', *The Haskins Society Journal*, 7 (1995), 63–73

Suppe, Frederick, 'Medieval Welsh Ethnic Nicknames and Implications: for the Welsh View of their Geopolitical Context, 1050–1400', in Christian Raffensperger (ed.), *Authorship, Worldview, and Identity in Medieval Europe* (Abingdon and New York, 2022), pp. 327–45

Swallow, Rachel, 'Gateways to Power. The Castles of Ranulf III of Chester and Llywelyn the Great of Gwynedd', *Archaeological Journal*, 171 (2014), 298–311

Sweet, Rosemary, *Antiquaries: The Discovery of the Past in Eighteenth-century Britain* (London, 2004)

Talbot, C. H., 'Cadogan of Bangor', *Cîteaux in de Nederlanden*, 9 (1958), 18–40

Taylor, Henry, *Historic Notices of the Borough and County Town of Flint* (London, 1883)

Thomas, D. Aneurin, *The Welsh Elizabethan Catholic Martyrs* (Cardiff, 1971)

Thomas, Graham C. G. (ed.), *The Charters of the Abbey of Ystrad Marchell* (Aberystwyth, 1997)

Thomas, Issac, *William Morgan a'i Feibl: William Morgan and His Bible* (Cardiff, 1988)

Thomas, Mair Elfet, *Afiaith yng Ngwent* (Caerdydd, 1978)

Thomas, Mair Elfet, *The Welsh Spirit of Gwent* (Cardiff, 1988)

Thomas, R. J., *Enwau Afonydd a Nentydd Cymru* (Cardiff, 1938)

Thomas, Rebecca, 'Geoffrey of Monmouth and the English Past', in Joshua Byron Smith and Georgia Henley (eds), *A Companion to Geoffrey of Monmouth* (Leiden, 2020), pp. 105–28

Thomas, Rebecca, *History and Identity in Early Medieval Wales* (Cambridge, 2022)

Thomas, Sandra, *George Grant Francis of Swansea: Antiquary, Philanthropist and Civic Dignitary* (West Glamorgan Archives, 1993)

Thomas, Wyn, *Hands off Wales: Nationhood and Militancy* (Llandysul, 2013)

Thomas, Zoë, 'Historical Pageants, Citizenship and the Performance of Women's History before Second-wave Feminism', in Bartie et al. (eds), *Restaging the Past*, pp. 108–31

Thorne, David, 'Cymreigyddion y Fenni a dechreuadau ieitheg cymharol yng Nghymru', *NLWJ*, 27/1 (1991), 97–107

Thornton, David E., 'Names within Names: Hagiophoric and Toponymic Anthroponymy in Early Medieval Ireland', in K. S. B. Keats-Rohan and Christian Settipani (eds), *Onomastique et Parenté dans l'Occident medieval: Prosopographica et Genealogica II* (Oxford, 2000), pp. 267–82

Thornton, David E., 'How Useful are Episcopal Ordination Lists as a Source for Medieval English Monastic History?', *Journal of Ecclesiastical History*, 69/3 (2018), 493–530

Thornton, David E., '*Locus, Sanctus et Virtus*: Monastic Surnaming in Late Medieval and Early Tudor England Reviewed', *Journal of Medieval Monastic Studies*, 10 (2021), 211–46

Thornton, David E., 'A *Mynach* by Any Other Name …: The Anthroponymy of the Welsh Cistercians, *c*.1300–1540', *WHR*, 30/4 (2021), 429–68

Thornton, David E., 'Northern Saints' Names as Monastic Bynames in Late Medieval and Early Tudor England', in Christiania Whitehead, Hazel J. Hunter Blair and Denis Renevey (eds), *Late Medieval Devotion to Saints from the North of England: New Directions*, Medieval Church Studies, 48 (Turnhout, 2022), pp. 387–408

Thorpe, Lewis (ed. and trans.), *Gerald of Wales: The Journey through Wales and the Description of Wales* (London, 1978)

Tonkin, J., 'After the Dissolution', in Ron Shoesmith and Ruth Richardson (eds), *A Definitive History of Dore Abbey* (Little Logaston, 1997), pp. 153–4

Tooze, Adam, *The Deluge: The Great War and the Remaking of Global Order, 1916–1931* (London, 2014)

Trevelyan, G. M., *Illustrated English Social History Vol 1* (London, 1942)

Tudor, Philippa, '"All youthe to learne the Creade and Tenne commaundementes": Unpublished Draft Injunctions of Henry VIII's Reign', *Historical Research*, 63/151 (1990), 212–17

Tudor, Philippa, 'Religious instruction for children and adolescents in the early English Reformation', *Journal of Ecclesiastical History*, XXXV (1984), 391–413

Tyson, Diana B., 'A Medieval Genealogy of the Lords of Brecknock', *Nottingham Medieval Studies*, 48 (2004), 1–14

van Caenegem, R. C., *Royal Writs in England from the Conquest to Glanvill: Studies in the Early History of the Common Law* (London, 1959)

van Houts, Elisabeth M. C., 'Historical Writing', in C. Harper-Bill and E. M. C. van Houts (eds), *A Companion to the Anglo-Norman World* (Woodbridge, 2003), pp. 103–22

Vaughan, Herbert, *The South Wales Squires* (London, 1926)

Vaughan, Herbert M., *The Welsh book-plates in the collection of Sir Evan Davies Jones* (London, 1920)

Vaughan, Richard, *Matthew Paris* (Cambridge, 1958)

Venn, John, and J. A. Venn (eds), *Alumni Cantabrigienses … Part I: From the Earliest Times to 1751*, 4 vols (Cambridge, 1924)

Veysey, A. Geoffrey, 'Sir Stephen Glynne', *Flintshire Historical Society Journal*, 30 (1982), 151–70

Wade-Evans, A. W. (ed. and trans.), *Vitae Sanctorum Britanniae et Genealogiae: The Lives and Genealogies of the Welsh Saints* (Cardiff, 1944; new edn by Scott Lloyd, Cardiff, 2013)

Waitz, D. G. (ed.), 'Ekkehardi Uraugiensis Chronicon', in G. H. Pertz (ed.), *Monumenta Germaniae Historica, Scriptores VI* (Hannover, 1844), pp. 1–267

Ward, H. L. D., *Catalogue of Romances in the Department of Manuscripts in the British Museum*, 3 vols (London, 1883–1910)

Ward Clavier, Sarah, *Royalism, Religion and Revolution: Wales, 1640–1688* (Woodbridge, 2021)

Watson, Joel, '"Why did You Put That There?" Gender, Materialism and Tattoo Consumption', *Advances in Consumer Research*, 25 (1998), 453–60

Watt, J. A., *The Church and the Two Nations in Medieval Ireland* (Cambridge, 1970)

Wharton, Henry (ed.), *Anglia Sacra Pars Secunda* (London, 1691)

Wiedemann, Benedict G. E., '"Fooling the Court of the Lord Pope": Dafydd ap Llywelyn's Petition to the Curia in 1244', *WHR*, 28 (2016), 209–32

Williams, D. H., 'The Abbey of Dore', in R. Shoesmith and R. Richardson (eds), *A Definitive History of Dore Abbey* (Little Logaston, 1997), pp. 15–36 and 210

Williams, Daniel, 'Pan-Celticism and the Limits of Post-colonialism: W. B. Yeats, Ernest Rhys and William Sharp in the 1890s', in Tony Brown and Russell Stephens (eds), *Nations and Relations: Writing across the British Isles* (Cardiff, 2000), pp. 1–29

Williams, David, *The History of Monmouthshire* (London, 1796)

Williams, David, *A History of Modern Wales* (London, 1950)

Williams, David H., *The Welsh Cistercians* (Caldey Island, 1984)

Williams, David H., *The Welsh Cistercians: Written to Commemorate the Centenary of the Death of Stephen William Williams (1837–1899) (The Father of Cistercian Archaeology in Wales)* (Leominster, 2001)

Williams, David H., 'Llanthony Prima Priory', *The Monmouthshire Antiquary*, 25/26 (2009–10), 13–50

Williams, David H., 'Fasti Cistercienses Cambrenses', *Archaeologia Cambrensis*, 163 (2014), 185–235

Williams, G. A., 'The Succession to Gwynedd, 1238–47', *BBCS*, 20 (1962–4), 393–413

Williams, Glanmor, 'Bishop Sulien, Richard Davies, and Archbishop Parker', *NLWJ*, 5 (1948), 215–19

Williams, Glanmor, 'Religion, Language and Nationality in Wales', in Glanmor Williams, *Religion, Language and Nationality in Wales: Historical Essays* (Cardiff, 1979)

Williams, Glanmor, 'Fire on Cambria's Altar', in Glanmor Williams, *The Welsh and their Religion* (Cardiff, 1991)

Williams, Glanmor, *The Welsh and Their Religion* (Cardiff, 1991)

Williams, Glanmor, *Renewal and Reformation: Wales, c.1415–1642* (Oxford, 1993)

Williams, Glanmor, *A Life* (Cardiff, 2002)
Williams, Gwyn A., *Goya and the Impossible Revolution* (London, 1976)
Williams, Gwyn A., *The Welsh in their History* (London, 1982)
Williams, Gwyn A., *Fishers of Men: Stories Towards an Autobiography* (Llandysul, 1996)
Williams, Hugh, *Gildas: De Excidio Britanniae*, 2 vols (London, 1899)
Williams, Ieuan M., and J. Beverley Smith (ed.), *Cronica Walliae* (Cardiff, 2002)
Williams, Ifor, 'Hen Chwedlau', *Transactions of the Honourable Society of Cymmrodorion 1946–1947* (1948), 28–58
Williams, Ifor (ed.), *Pedeir Keinc y Mabinogi allan o Lyfr Gwyn Rhydderch* (Cardiff, 1930)
Williams, Ioan, 'Towards National Identities: Welsh Theatres', in Baz Kershaw (ed.), *The Cambridge History of British Theatre, Volume 3: Since 1895* (Cambridge, 2004), pp. 242–72
Williams, J. E. Caerwyn, and P. I. Lynch (eds), *Gwaith Meilyr Brydydd a'i Ddisgynyddion*, CBT I (Cardiff, 1994)
Williams, Jane, *The Literary Remains of the Rev. Thomas Price*, 2 vols (Llandovery, 1854–5)
Williams, Jonathan, *The History of Radnorshire* (Tenby, 1859)
Williams, W. Ogwen (ed.), *Calendar of the Caernarvonshire Quarter Sessions Records: Volume I, 1541–1558* (London and Bradford, 1956)
Williams, W. P., *A Monograph of the Windsor Family* (Cardiff, 1879)
Wilkins, Charles, 'Men I have known: Thomas Stephens', *Cymru Fu* (8 November 1889), 72
Willis, Browne, *A Survey of the Cathedral Church of Bangor and Edifices belonging to it …* (London, 1721)
Wilson, Jean Moorcroft, *From Great War Poet to Good-bye to All That (1895–1929)* (London, 2018)
Winterbottom, Michael (ed. and trans.), *William of Malmesbury, Gesta Pontificum Anglorum, The History of the English Bishops*, 2 vols (Oxford, 2009)
Withington, Robert, *English Pageantry: An Historical Outline*, 2 vols (Cambridge, 1918–20)
Wood, Anthony, *Athenae Oxonienses*, 2 vols (London, 1691)
Young, Christopher, 'Two World Wars and One World Cup: Humour, Trauma and the Asymmetric Relationship in Anglo-German Football', *Sport in History*, 27 (2007), 1–23
Zweiniger-Bargielowska, Ina, *Managing the Body: Beauty, Health and Fitness in Britain 1880–1939* (Oxford, 2011)

INDEX ⋮ MYNEGAI

A

Aberconwy Abbey 14, 24, 36, 104, 207, 208, 209, 212, 219
   abbots of 47, 151, 216
   burial of Welsh princes at 48
   foundation of 48
   patronage of 48
   Register and Chronicle of the Abbey of Aberconwy 36, 46–52, 55 n. 39
Abergavenny 14, 242, 278, 303, 304, 305, 307, 312, 315, 316, 318
Æthelfrith (d. *c.*616) 179–81, 182, 188, 189
Anian (d. 1305/6), bishop 204, 218–19, 221, 231 n. 140, 231 n. 143, 248
Annales Cambriae 245, 246
   B-text (Breviate Chronicle) 14, 15, 19, 20–1, 211, 212–13, 214
   C-text (Cottonian Chronicle) 31 n. 4, 210–11, 213
Annales school 381–2, 387, 391
Annals of Chester 16–17, 26, 33 n. 17, 35 n. 42, 230 n. 119
Annals of Tewkesbury 16, 33 n. 17, 51
Annals of Worcester 51
Anselm (*c.*1033–1109), archbishop of Canterbury 204, 205
Arthur, king (legendary) 243, 318
   in *Breuddwyd Rhonabwy* 77
   in *Culhwch ac Olwen* 60, 63–4, 84 n. 48
   in *Brut y Brenhinedd* 178
   in *De gestis Britonum* 64, 88 n. 102, 175–6, 181–2, 188, 189
   in poetry 74, 76, 89 n. 114, 91 n. 121
   in *Trioedd Ynys Prydein* 59–60, 63–4, 72, 74, 76, 79, 82 n. 24, 89 n. 114, 91 n. 121
Augustinian canons, names of 156–64

B

Bale, John (1495–1563) 242, 245, 246–7
Bangor 66, 168 n. 46, 253, 334, 400 n. 25
   bishops of 3–4, 8, 203–21, 234, 235–6, 237, 245–6, 247–8, 252, 254–6, 260 n. 17, 262 n. 30, 262 n. 39, 338
      see also Anian; Bellot, Hugh; Bulkeley, Arthur; Cadwgan; David the Scot; Hervey; Richard; Robinson, Nicholas; Rotoland; Vaughan, Richard
   diocese of 234, 235–6, 239, 244, 256, 257
Bangor Pontifical 218, 231 n. 140
Bardsey (Ynys Enlli) 151, 168–9 n. 46
Beddgelert, priory 65, 66, 72, 85 n. 66, 86 n. 71, 151, 158, 163
   canons of 158, 159, 168–9 n. 46
Bede, *Historia ecclesiastica* 180, 242, 243
Bellot, Hugh (1542–96), bishop 234, 252, 254–5
Bernard (d. 1148), bishop 65, 158
Bernard de Neufmarché (d. 1121x5?) 41, 42–3, 46, 52
Bible, Welsh translation of 233, 246–7, 251–2, 255, 257, 259, 274, 388
   see also Book of Common Prayer; Davies, Richard; *Epistol at y Cembru*; Huet, Thomas; Morgan, William; Robinson, Nicholas; Salesbury, William

Book of Common Prayer, Welsh
    translation of 233
Bonedd y Saint 57, 64, 80, 84–5 n. 57
Brecon 208, 211, 241, 277
    lordship of 38, 41, 43, 44, 46
    see also Genealogy of the Lords of
        Brecknock
Breuddwyd Maxen Wledig 61, 67–8,
    71–2, 88 n. 95
Breuddwyd Rhonabwy 77
Bronllys Castle 44–5, 54 n. 26
Brut y Brenhinedd 71, 73, 130, 175
    Cotton Cleopatra version 175,
        179, 183–4
    Dingestow version 57, 81 n. 12,
        175, 177, 178, 180, 184–5
    Peniarth 44 version 175, 177, 185
    Llanstephan 1 version 175, 177,
        185
    Peniarth 21/23 version 175
    hostages in 175, 177–9, 180,
        183–6, 187–9
Brut y Tywysogyon 16, 19, 21, 22, 25,
    26–7, 210, 211, 214, 215, 217,
    246, 248, 257, 331
    deaths of abbots recorded in 23–5
    references to hostages in 172–3,
        178, 179, 185–6
    sources used in 13, 14–15, 23,
        28–30
Brutus (legendary) 175, 187
Brychan Brycheiniog 46
Bulkeley, Arthur (*c*.1495–1552/3),
    bishop 236, 237, 249, 256

C

Cadfan ab Iago, king of Gwynedd
    179–81, 182, 188, 189,
    243
Cadwaladr ap Cadwallon (Cadwaladr
    Fendigaid), king of Gwynedd
    89 n. 114, 181
Cadwallon ap Cadfan (d. 634), king of
    Gwynedd 74, 89 n. 114, 175,
    176, 177, 180, 181, 188

Cadwgan of Llandyfái (d. 1241),
    bishop 204, 211–14, 220,
    228 n. 88, 247, 264 n. 72
Caerleon 28–30, 242, 284
Caernarfon, Roman forts 88 n. 95
    see also Edward I, castles of
Cambrian Archaeological Association
    289–91, 384, 397
Caradog of Llancarfan
    Life of Gildas 60, 72
Cardiff Chronicle 17, 19, 33 n. 16
Carmarthen, Priory of St John the
    Evangelist 158, 159, 163,
    170–1 n. 69, 171 n. 70
charters 92–110, 118–40
    boundary clauses in 100–1,
        118–40
    development of 93–4, 99, 101,
        102–3, 126
    in an English context 98, 100–1,
        102, 118, 123, 124, 125, 126–7,
        133, 136, 142 n. 19
    individuals involved in production
        of 104, 106, 108
    language of 124, 126–7, 128–40
    shared use of across Wales, Brittany
        and Cornwall 97–8, 102, 136
    survival of 95–6, 98–102
    use of by Welsh rulers 95, 98, 101,
        102–7, 107–9
    use of titles in 105–7
    see also diplomas; *Liber Landavensis*
        (Book of Llandaf), charters in;
        writs
Cistercians 103, 213, 389
    chronicling by 13–14, 22–30, 203
    grants to 22–3, 34 n. 30
    in Ireland 150–1, 152
    names of 152, 156, 162
    networks for the transmission of
        information 22–30
    patronage of 163
    role in charter production 103,
        108
    sympathies of 150–2

see also Aberconwy Abbey; Hailes Abbey; Llantarnam Abbey; Margam Abbey; Mellifont Abbey; Strata Florida; Strata Marcella; Whitland
Clynnog Fawr 56, 62, 64–6, 69, 80, 99–100, 119
Coelbren y Beirdd 300, 301, 307–8, 309, 310
see also druids; Iolo Morganwg
Conwy, town of 218–19, 239
see also Edward I, castles of
County histories, development of 282–4, 287
Cronicon de Wallia 19–20, 22, 187, 211
Culhwch ac Olwen 60, 62–4, 72, 80, 84 n. 49, 84 n. 53, 130
Cwm-hir Abbey 14, 24, 34 n. 30
Cyfranc Lludd a Llefelys 71, 73
Cymer Abbey 101, 216
Cynddelw Brydydd Mawr 74, 75, 90 n. 116

D

Dafydd ap Llywelyn (*c*.1215–46) 48, 107, 214–16, 220, 228 n. 88, 228 n. 95, 229–30 n. 117, 230 n. 120
Dafydd Benfras, poet 76
Daniel ap Sulien 13
David the Scot, bishop 204, 206–7, 219, 220
Davies, John, author of *Antiquae Linguae Britannicae* 274
Davies, John, historian 5, 9, 379, 381, 386, 388, 393–6, 397–9
Davies, Richard (*c*.1505–81), bishop of St Davids 233, 246–7, 249, 251, 252, 254, 256, 257, 258
Davies, Thomas (*c*.1511–73), bishop of St Asaph 233, 254
diplomas 93, 94, 98
Dodd, A. H. 5, 9, 380, 381, 382–6, 387, 391, 393, 396–9

druids 299–300, 305, 306–13, 315, 318, 320

E

Eadmer of Canterbury, historian 205, 223 n. 36, 250, 266 n. 86
Edward I 48, 204, 217, 218, 219, 339, 345
    castles of 219, 331, 346, 358, 359, 370
    conquest of Wales 92, 95, 109, 151, 221, 315, 331, 358–61
Edward II 151, 219
Edward III 151, 247
Edward IV 119
Edward Lhuyd 274
Edwards, O. M. 272, 380
Ekkehard of Aura 206
eisteddfod 248, 331, 333, 336
    competitions 300–20
        adjudication of 316–18, 320
        prize money for 304–5, 320
        topics of 304–5, 306–13, 313–16, 319, 320
    participation of gentry in 275, 277–9, 292, 318
Eliot, T. S. 381
Elizabeth I 232, 234, 237, 240, 256, 258, 261–2 n. 29
Ely, abbey and bishopric 205, 218, 220
Englynion y Beddau 65, 86 n. 71
Epistol at y Cembru 233, 247, 251–2
    see also Davies, Richard; Salesbury, William
Epitome historiae Britanniae 48–51, 55 n. 39

G

Genealogy of the Lords of Brecknock 36, 37, 38, 41–6, 51, 52, 54 n. 26
gentry, Welsh 271–93
    anglicisation of 273, 275–6, 292–3
    interest in genealogy 285–8, 290
    language of 273, 276, 279, 292
    libraries of 274, 280–2, 290

gentry, Welsh (continued)
  role in preservation and publication of manuscripts 273, 274, 276–7, 277, 279–80, 290, 292
  see also eisteddfod, participation of gentry in
Geoffrey of Monmouth 245
  De gestis Britonum (*Historia Regum Brtianniae*), author of 48, 49, 61, 64, 70–1, 72, 73, 79, 83 n. 35, 242, 249
  hostages in 3, 8, 175–89
  treatment of early medieval history in 88 n 102, 180–1, 188
Gerald of Wales 52, 211, 213, 214, 223 n. 22, 244, 247, 338, 340, 383
  as a source for travel to and from Welsh monasteries 14, 32 n. 6
  attitude towards women 44
  attitude towards the Welsh 40
  career of 194–5, 197, 199, 208, 202 n. 32
  De gestis Giraldi, author of 194, 198–9, 201 n. 6
  De iure et statu Meneuensis ecclesie, author of 199
  De principis instructione, author of 194, 201 n. 5, 198, 199, 200
  Descriptio Kambriae, author of 36, 48, 49–51, 116 n. 83, 242, 249
  Expugnatio Hibernica, author of 53 n. 12, 194, 195–6, 197–9, 200
  History of Llanthony Priory, potential author of 36, 37, 41, 42
  Itinerarium Kambriae, author of 36, 37, 40, 42, 43–6, 53 n.11, 116 n. 83, 195, 242, 248, 249
  Libellus inuectionum, author of 199
  Speculum ecclesiae, author of 37
  relationship with Rotoland, bishop of Bangor 204, 207–9, 218, 220
  Topographia Hiberniae, author of 194, 195, 198

Gildas 60, 387
Gorsedd y Beirdd (Gorsedd of the Bards) 278, 305–6, 333
  see also druids; Eisteddfod; Iolo Morganwg
Gramsci, Antonio 385, 390, 391
Graves, Alfred Perceval (1846–1931) 333–5, 336, 337, 338, 339, 340, 344–5
Greatconnell Priory 160–1, 162
Gruffudd ap Cynan (d. 1137), king of Gwynedd 207, 220, 249
Gruffudd ap Cynan (d. 1200), prince of Gwynedd 24, 48
Gruffudd ap Llywelyn (d. 1244), 49, 76, 107, 192 n. 52, 214, 216, 220, 228 n. 95
Guest, Charlotte (1812–95) 276, 278
Gwalchmai ap Meilyr, poet 74
Gwenwynwyn 25–7, 74, 76

H
Hailes Abbey 46–7, 51, 55 n. 32, 55 n. 37
Hall, Augusta, Lady Llanover (1802–96) 278, 280, 366, 371
Harlech Castle, pageants at 329–47
  costumes used 341–2
  educational value of 345–6
  form of 337–9
  historical accuracy of 335, 337, 346, 347
  language of 336, 346
  people involved in 333–5
  response to 342–3
  role of castle in 337, 338
harp, instrument 248, 275, 278, 304, 305
Hegel, G. W. F. 313, 392–3
Hen Ogledd (Old North) 59, 60, 74
Henry I 40, 42–3, 173, 204–5, 207, 220
Henry II 3, 28–9, 30, 107, 109, 172, 173, 179, 194–200, 201 n. 21, 202 n. 34, 242

Index : Mynegai

Henry III 15, 107, 195, 214, 215, 216, 217, 218, 220, 228 n. 95, 229 n. 117, 230 n. 120, 231 n. 138
Henry of Huntingdon, *Historia Anglorum* 242
Hereford
　bishops of 37, 39, 218–19, 257
　earls of 38, 40–1
　St Peter's monastery 39
Hervey (d. 1131), bishop 203, 204–6, 218, 219–20, 223 n. 22, 247
Historia Brittonum 2, 7, 68-70, 72, 78, 79, 80, 82 n. 24, 86, n. 77, 88 n. 102, 383
Historia Gruffud vab Kenan 177, 249
Holy Trinity (Christ Church) Cathedral Priory, Dublin 159–60, 161, 162, 164
hostages (gwystlon) 3, 29, 172–89
　as distinct from prisoners 173, 179, 188
　as guarantors of agreements 173, 174, 175–6, 180, 181, 183, 186, 187
　exchange of 179–81
　given to Henry II 172–3, 179, 193 n. 68
　given to John 173, 174, 185
　killing of 172, 173, 181–2, 183–6, 189 n. 3
　role in cultural exchange 186–7
　status of 180, 182–3, 185
　see also Geoffrey of Monmouth, *De gestis Britonum*, hostages in
Huet, Thomas 233, 262 n. 39
Hugh de Lacy (d. 1186) 39–40, 53 n. 12, 196
Hugh de Lacy, Norman baron 38, 52, 53 n. 10, 157
　Cronica Walliae, author of 242, 243–4, 246, 248
Hywel II, bishop of St Asaph 215
Hywel ab Iorwerth 28–30, 25 n. 49
Hywel ap Gruffudd, prince of Gwynedd (d. 1216) 48

Hywel ap Rhys (Hywel Sais)
　death of 19–22
　hostage of Henry II 173, 187, 192 n. 43, 187, 192 n. 60
　nickname Hywel Sais 173, 187
Hywel ap Rhys (d. 886), king of Glywysing 121
Hywel Dda 394

I

Iolo Morganwg 281, 300, 305–6, 314
Iorwerth ab Owain of Caerleon 28–30
Iorwerth ap Madog, family of 65–6
Iwan, Dafydd 364
　see also Yma o Hyd

J

Joan (Siwan) 16–19, 192 n. 52, 225 n. 55
John, king 16, 20, 173, 174, 192 n. 52, 185, 195, 197, 198, 199, 210–11, 225 n. 55
John of Salisbury 196
Julius Caesar 68, 69, 70, 72–3, 175, 177, 181–2, 188, 311

K

Kirwan, Patrick Joseph 332, 334, 335, 336, 337, 338, 339, 341, 343

L

Laudabiliter 194–200
Leland, John 212
Lestrange, John 26, 27, 35 n. 42
Lewis, Saunders 336, 380, 388, 391
Lewys Glyn Cothi 163, 287
Liber Landavensis (Book of Llandaf)
　charters in 3, 7, 93, 96–7, 98, 100, 110, 119, 120–4, 128–40
Lichfield Gospels (St Chad Gospels) 96, 98, 99, 100, 101, 118, 124–8, 139
Life of Robert of Béthune 37, 38
Life of St Cadog of Llancarfan 71
　charters in 96, 98, 118–19, 121–2

Llanbadarn Fawr 13, 31 n. 2, 108
Llandaf, diocese of 48, 51, 235, 236, 244, 245, 246
    see also Liber Landavensis (Book of Llandaf)
Llantarnam Abbey 28, 30, 35 n. 49, 35 n. 52, 152, 213
Llanthony
    Llanthony Prima (Monmouthshire) 36, 37, 38, 39–40, 157, 158, 159 160, 163, 170 n. 64
    Llanthony Secunda (Gloucester) 37, 38, 39–41, 157
    see also Gerald of Wales, *History of Llanthony Priory*, potential author of
Lloyd, J. E. 2, 6, 329, 334, 335, 337, 338, 343, 344, 346, 380, 385, 388
Lloyd George, David 332, 335, 340–1, 343, 344, 345, 347
Llwyd, Angharad (1780–1866) 279, 309
Llwyd, Humphrey 1, 6, 233, 243, 246, 258
Llyfr y Tŷ Gwyn (The Book of the White House) 212, 214
Llywarch ap Llywelyn, poet 74, 76, 91 n. 121
Llywelyn ab Iorwerth (*c*.1173–1240) (Llywelyn Fawr) 48, 49, 85–6 n. 68, 158, 243, 248, 361
    acta of 96, 101, 104–5, 224 n. 46
    death of 107, 214, 248
    execution of William de Braose by 16–19, 33 n. 16
    father of 55 n. 41
    gives hostages to King John 173, 174, 185, 192 n. 52
    poetry relating to 74–5, 76, 91 n. 123
    relationship with bishops of Bangor 208, 210, 212, 213, 220, 225 n. 55, 227 n. 88
    relationship with Marcher lords 103, 104
    statue of 360
    titles of 106–7, 115 n. 79
Llywelyn ap Gruffudd (d. 1282) 49, 86 n. 71, 248, 344, 360, 361, 395
    acta of 109
    eisteddfod essays about 315, 317
    poetry to 66
    receives hostages 189 n. 5
    rise to power of 216, 217, 221
    title used by 107, 109
    Treaty of Montgomery 15, 33 n. 12, 107, 109
    truce with Henry III (1260) 15

M
Madog ap Llywelyn 14
Madog ap Maredudd (1131–61), king of Powys 101, 102, 104
Margam Abbey 34 n. 35, 96, 108, 289
Margam Annals 17–19
Marxism 384, 385, 390, 391, 393, 396
Mellifont Abbey 150–1
Methodism 273, 386
Meurig, bishop 204, 205–6, 219, 223 n. 22
Morgan, William (1545–1604) 251, 252, 255
Morris-Jones, John 334, 339
Myvyrian Archaiology of Wales 275

N
nonconformism 272, 284, 293, 340, 346, 385, 386, 392

O
O Oes Gwrtheyrn 210
Orderic Vitalis 206
Owain Cyfeiliog 25, 26, 101, 102, 178, 190 n. 5
Owain Glyndŵr 243, 245, 338, 342, 346, 389, 395
    eisteddfod essays on 317

pageants about 335, 337, 338, 341, 342, 343–4, 346
support for 151, 152, 163
see also Tattoos, of Owain Glyndŵr
Owain Gwynedd (d. 1170) 65, 74, 88 n. 108, 105, 106, 107, 109, 172, 206, 223 n. 22, 248
Owen, Daniel, novelist 389

P

pageants, historical 330–2
see also Harlech Castle, pageants at
Paris, Matthew 214–18, 220, 231 n. 138, 242
Parker, Matthew, archbishop 236, 237, 238, 242, 249, 250
Pedair Cainc y Mabinogi (Four Branches of the Mabinogi) 59, 62, 65, 66, 70, 78, 80, 177
Penda, king of Mercia 176, 177
Pennant, Thomas 274, 282, 284, 287
personal names
  as indicators of ethnic identity 153–6
  Irish 153–4, 155
  Welsh 153, 154–5
Plaid Cymru 375 n. 43, 385, 396
Pool castle 25–7
Powel, David 252
  Historie of Cambria, author of 242, 246, 248, 274, 281
  edition of *Itinerarium Cambriae* 248, 249
Price, Thomas (Carnhuanawc) 306, 308, 312, 314–15, 316–17, 318

R

referendum
  devolution (1979) 364, 391, 393, 395, 397
  devolution (1997) 364, 393, 397
Rhodri Mawr (d. 878) 48–51, 55 n. 39, 87 n. 81
Rhys, Ernest (1859–1946) 333–5, 336, 337, 345

Rhys ap Gruffudd (the Lord Rhys) 15, 19, 20, 22, 27, 29, 32 n. 10, 34 n. 28, 55 n. 39, 104, 105, 140, 172, 173, 178, 190 n. 5, 190 n. 8, 244, 248
Rhys ap Tewdwr (d. 1093) 41, 195
Rhys Gryg 76
Richard, bishop 204, 206, 214–18, 219, 220, 228 n. 95, 229–30 n. 117, 230 n. 120, 231 n. 138
Richard I 195, 197, 199, 210
Richard fitz Gilbert, earl of Striguil and lord of Leinster 195–6
Robert, bishop of Bangor 207, 209
Robert of Shrewsbury 204, 210–11, 213, 225 n. 55
Robinson, Nicholas (*c*.1530–85), bishop of Bangor 236–59
  correspondence with Matthew Parker 250–1
  death of 252–4, 258
  early career of 237–8
  election as bishop 238–9, 262 n. 39
  historian of Wales 241–9, 257–8, 259
  potential contribution to the 1588 Welsh Bible 251–2
Roger of Wendover 173, 185, 242
Rotoland, bishop 4, 8, 204, 207–9, 218, 220
Rowlands, Henry (1551–1616), bishop 234, 235, 254, 255, 265 n. 79

S

St Asaph 115 n. 74, 215, 233, 236, 244, 245, 252, 254, 258, 260 n. 17
St Davids 24, 59–60, 82 n. 26, 209, 262 n. 39, 338
  bishops of 23, 44–5, 157, 208, 233, 244, 245, 246, 257, 314
  chronicles at 14, 31 n. 4, 210, 213
  diocese of 194, 233, 236, 244
  see also Davies, Richard, bishop of St Davids
St David's Day 366

St Mary Priory, Clontuskert Omany 161–2, 163
Salesbury, William 233, 246–7, 248, 249, 251, 257, 267 n. 114, 388
Stephens, Thomas (1821–75) 305, 308, 311–12, 317, 318, 320, 325 n. 61
Strata Florida 32 n. 6, 34 n. 30, 48, 140, 151, 211, 213, 217, 245, 281
   burial at 19, 20, 21, 22
   chronicles at 14, 23, 25, 27, 30, 35 n. 50, 108
Strata Marcella 24, 25, 26–7, 34 n. 30, 96, 101–2, 108, 112 n. 16, 151
surnames, development of 154–6

T

Talley Abbey 20–2
Tattoos 352–72
   and football 357–8, 360, 362, 363–6, 369, 371
   and gender 365–6, 368, 371
   and Tryweryn 363, 365
   of castles 358–60, 362, 370
   of Owain Glyndŵr 355, 356–62, 364, 366, 370, 371, 372
   of Welsh national costume 355, 366–9, 371
Trioedd Ynys Prydein 56–81, 310
   connection with Bonedd y Saint 64, 84–5 n. 57
   connection with Clynnog Fawr 62, 64–6, 69
   connection with court poetry 58, 66, 73–7, 89–90 n. 114
   connection with *Culhwch ac Olwen* 62–4, 72
   connection with Englynion y Beddau 65
   connections with Pedair Cainc y Mabinogi 62, 65, 70
   geographical focus of 59–60, 72
   influence of *Breuddwyd Maxen Wledig* on 61, 67–8, 71–2
   influence of *Historia Brittonum* on 68–70, 72, 73, 78, 79, 82 n. 24
   references to twelfth-century figures in 58–9
   relationship with *De gestis Britonum* 61, 70, 71, 72
   Trioedd y Meirch 58
   Y Gyfres Gynnar (Early Version) 57–9
Tryweryn 353, 363, 364, 365
Theobald, archbishop of Canterbury 205–6

U

Urban, bishop of Llandaf (d. 1134) 39

V

Vaughan, Richard (*c*.1553–1607), bishop of Bangor 234, 235, 252, 254, 255, 262 n. 30
Vaughan, Robert, antiquary 241, 281, 282

W, Y

Weber, Max 389
Welsh history
   definition of 379–80
   teaching of in schools 354, 372
Welsh laws, medieval 214, 250, 281
   officials mentioned in 105
   political centres mentioned in 106
   transmission of 65–6, 211, 212
Whitland 14, 23, 34 n. 30, 151, 211, 212, 213, 214, 220
William de Braose the Younger 16–19, 22, 33 n. 16
William of Malmesbury 204, 206–7, 220
Williams, Glanmor 381, 386–9, 393, 396–9
Williams, Gwyn A. 381, 390–3, 394, 396–9
Williams, Jane (Ysgafell, 1806–85) 272, 312
writs, development of 94
Wynn, John, of Gwydir, Sir 237–8, 249, 250, 256, 288
Yma o Hyd 355, 363–5, 369, 370–1